WITHDRAWN 30|3|2?

THOMAS TALLIS SCHOOL LIBRARY

D0306981

007136

007136

ASIANS
IN THE
MILLENNIUM

Who's Who of Asian Acheivers in Britain

published by

EASTERN
Eye
FOR THE ASIAN PERSPECTIVE

and ASIAN TIMES

Compiled & Edited by John Hughes

ASIANS IN THE MILLENNIUM

First published in 1999, London, England

Published by:
Ethnic Media Group

Publisher:
Sarwar Ahmed

Compiled and Edited by:
John Hughes

Production Manager:
Nadeem Khan

Researchers:
Kiran Lyall
Fatema Sheikh
Bimla Lyall

Photo Editor:
Sohail Anjum

Software Consultant:
Faiz Parkar

© **Copyright:** Ethnic Media Group. All rights reserved. No part of this publication may be reproduced or transmitted by any means without the prior written permission of the Publishers

Printed and Bound in UK by:
Alden Press, Oxford.

British Library Cataloguing in Publication Data
A catalogue record for this book is available at the British Library and Book Data

ISBN: 0-9533744-0-8

Ethnic Media Group, 1st Floor, 148 Cambridge Heath Road, London E1 5QJ, England, Tel: 0171 702 8012, Fax: 0171 702 7937

CONTENTS

ASIANS IN THE MILLENNIUM

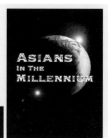

ASIANS IN THE MILLENNIUM

Marketing Manager *Mits Sahini* · Circulation Manager *Chris Piper* · Advertising Manager *Wayne Bower* ·
Corporate Advertising *Asif Yusuf*

Asians in the Millennium is published by Ethnic Media Group
148 Cambridge Heath Road, London E1 5QJ Tel: 0171 702 8012 Fax: 0171 702 7937
1999 © All Rights reserved. No part of this publication may be reproduced or stored electronically without permission of the publisher.
Printed by Alden Press, Oxford

EDITOR'S NOTE

For those who may ask why publish ASIANS IN THE MILLENNIUM - A Who's Who of Asian Achievers in Britain? the contents of this first edition speaks for itself. Asian contributions to Britain's wealth and advancement are incalculable. The immense personal contributions made during this century, including two world wars, have yet to be accurately recorded. This directory provides a glimpse into today's vast treasure trove of Asian Achievers in Britain.

ASIANS IN THE MILLENNIUM profiles over 1,000 Asians in Britain who are making a positive contribution to their communities, their families, their companies and the wider society. Entries have been through a process of nominations. The public were invited through the pages of Ethnic Media Group publications and community radio programs to nominate people who have been successful in their various fields, or who have made positive contributions to the community, or who have been achievers through hard work.

Those who were nominated were sent an official entry form to be completed and returned with a photo. We also used a telephone Hotline so that nominations could be made easier. For those well known and famous Asians who are not in this first directory I can assure readers that entry forms were sent to most of them.

While absolute attention was paid to the detail of each returned entry form we will have misread some information and been unable to decipher others. In such cases we attempted to contact the entrants with queries. We have only used submitted information and therefore any mistakes are unintentional. The unique nature of the ASIANS IN THE MILLENNIUM is that there are as many authors as there are entries.

The inclusion of Britain's Richest 200 Asians provides a comprehensive insight to the enterprise skills of Asian businesses in Britain.

I want to thank all those who took the time to make nominations and those who returned their entry forms. Immediately after the London racist bombing campaign in April 1999 I was inundated with calls from entrants requesting that I do not print telephone numbers and addresses. For any of these entries I will gladly forward any correspondence providing it is inside a stamped envelope.

My thanks must also go to the publisher Sarwar Ahmed for his belief in my project and to the entire staff at Ethnic Media Group, especially Faiz Parkar for his computer skills and Nadeem Khan for his positive input. I have listed those in the acknowledgements for special thanks. The boss and his cheerful team at the Yellow Advertiser, South Woodford were a great help in our moment of need - thanks David. My assistant Kiran Lyall has been on the project from the beginning and was an invaluable asset throughout.

John Hughes
Compiler & Editor
1 October, 1999

ACKNOWLEDGEMENTS
I would like to thank the following for their help with this book:

Zeenat Mansuri
David Wheaton
Sharon Aitkin
Hasna Begum Ali
Shurma Rahman
Ghazala Ahmed
Fiona Waye CVCP
Kelly Sims Diva Entertainments
Iqbal Nandra Radio 1
Dipen Rajyaguru 1990 Trust

Island Records
Commission for Racial Equality
Bobby Syed
Ansel Wong
Media Moguls
Terry Singh / Ash Rahman
Zulfi Asian Football League
Charlotte May BMA Public Affairs
Sophia Mirza
Mulberry School for Girls, Class 8B

Choudhury	Mohib	49
Choudhury	Purba	49
Choudhury	Sohail Moktadeir	49
Chowdhury	Ahmed Us Samad	49
Chowdhury	Ghulam Ahmed	49
Chowdhury	Golam Sobhan	50
Chowdhury	Harminder Kaur	50
Chowdhury	Morzina	50
Chowdhury	Rahima Mazeda	50
Chowdhury	Wahidus Samad	50
Chowdry	Billquees	50
Chowdry	Sabina	50
Chrysanthou	Amita Ranjana	50
Contractor	Shamsunnisa	51
Coovadia	Hajera	51
Corea	Charika Rajini	51
Corea	Ivan	51
Corea	Monica	51
Corea	Vernon	51

D

Da Goma	Ramona	53
Dabhi	Bhanumati	53
Dabhi	Rina	53
Dabydeen	David	53
Dada	Feroze Ahmad	53
Dada	Haroon A.	53
Dahele	Jashwant Singh	53
Daji	Mohammed Altaf	53
Dalal	Maneck Sohrab	54
Dang	Mohinder Singh	54
Daniel	Shirley Miriam	54
Dar	Ibrahim	54
Darbar	Mohansinh	54
Das	Bhagabat Charan	54
Das	Bimal Krishna	54
Das	Meneka	55
Das	Sankar Kumar	55
Datta	Sekharjit	55
Davda	Gira	55
Davda	Tanvi	55
Davdra	Kishor	55
De Souza	Ava	55
De Souza	Daphne	56
Dega	Raman Kumar	56
Dehlavi	Jamil	56
Deo	Surendra Inder	56
Deol	John	56
Desai	Kanoobhai	56
Desai	Madhubhai	56
Desai	Rajesh	56
Desai	Sumantrai	57
Desai	Surendra	57
Deu	Amerjit Singh	57
Devi	Nilima	57
Devsi	Bhajan Singh	57
Dey	Misri	57
Dhadyalla	Dharambir Singh	57
Dhaliwal	Navdeep	57
Dhaliwal	Spinder	58
Dhama	Satya Prakesh	58
Dhamrait	Mohan Singh	58
Dhandia	Sarup Singh	58
Dharni	Achharpaul	58
Dhatt	Mohinder Singh	58
Dheer	Ranjit	58
Dhesy	Hari Singh	58
Dhillon	Ashifa	59
Dhillon	Gurdip Singh	59
Dhillon	Sundeep	59
Dhillon	Tarsem Singh	59
Dhindsa	Bahal Singh	59
Dhindsa	Rani	59
Dhir	Anuja	59
Dholakia	Navnit	59
Dholakia	Shashikant	60
Dhorajia	Maganlal	60
Dhuga	Kalvir Singh	60
Dhupa	Venu	60

Din	Rashid Ahmed	60
Din	Rasshied Ali	60
Ditta	Ajaz Ahmed	60
Dolby	Christopher John	60
Dosanjh	Amrik Singh	61
Dosanjh	Narinder (Kriss)	61
Doshi	Kirti Kumar	61
Dotiwala	Jasmine	61
Drabu	Khalid Jeevani	61
Drabu	Khurshid	61
Duggal	Diamond	61
Duggal	Simon	61
Dutt	Kalyan Kumar	62
Dutt	Vijay	62

E

Eaoyor	Shaikh	63
Emmanuel	Heather	63

F

Faress	Souad	65
Farooq	Ghazala	65
Fernandes	Maria	65
Fernandes	Vasco	65
Fitter	Mehru	65
Flather	Baroness Shreela	65
Foolchand	Madhun Kumar	65
Freeman-Pask	Abigail	65

G

Gadhia	Sunil	67
Gadhvi	Nitu	67
Gafoor	Antony David	67
Ganatra	Nitin	67
Ganatra	Ravin J	67
Gandhi	Atul	67
Gandhi	Jagdish	67
Gazara	Don	67
Gelu	Mahomed Iqbal	67
George	John	68
Ghaffur	Tarique	68
Ghai	Usha Rani	68
Ghani	Tanveer	68
Ghatora	Harjinder Singh	68
Ghatore	Onkar Singh	68
Ghauri	Abdus Khan	68
Ghauri	Nazim Khan	69
Ghazi	Saad	69
Ghosh	Arun Chandra	69
Ghosh	Shiulie	69
Ghosh	Sushmita	69
Gidoomal	Ram	69
Gifford	Zerbanoo	69
Gill	Amit	70
Gill	Charan Singh	70
Gill	Gurbans Kaur	70
Gill	Harjit Singh	70
Gill	Reenu	70
Gill	Satnam Singh	70
Gill	Seema	70
Gill	Sheem S	70
Gill	Sucha Singh	71
Glover	Christopher	71
Gobindram	Sushma	71
Godagama	Shantha	71
Godbole	Maheshwar	71
Godbole	Shibani	71
Godbole	Vinata	71
Gohal	Jasbir (Jazz)	71
Gola	Gurdev Singh	72
Gola	Parpoor Singh	72
Gonsalves	Aileen	72
Govindji	Azmina	72

Gowda	Hanume Thimme	72
Goyal	Baldev Krishan	72
Grewal	Robinder Kaur	72
Grover	Avtar Singh	72
Grover	Charanjit Kaur	73
Gulamhusein	Mohamed Yusuf	73
Gulati	Om Prakash	73
Gulfam	M. Akhtar	73
Gupta	Bharat Kumar	73
Gupta	Chaman Lall	73
Gupta	Narendra Kumar	73
Gupta	Rama Prakash	74
Gupta	Suraj Narain	74
Gupta	Suresh Kumar	74
Gurusinghe	Nihal	74

H

Habib	Mohammad	75
Hadi	Nilima Rahman	75
Hafeez	Bashir-Ul	75
Hamal	Prem Bikram	75
Hameed	Aqueela	75
Hameed	Sheikh	75
Hanif	Tarique	75
Hannan	Janifar Jenny	75
Hansrani	Vidya Parkash	76
Haq	Robeel	76
Haqqani	Mustafa	76
Haque	M D Zainul	76
Haridas	Thekkummuri	76
Harun	Abu Bakar	76
Hashmi	Zia Akhtar	76
Hassan	Ghulam	76
Hassan	Mahmood Ul	77
Hayder	Ali Mohammed	77
Hayee	Foqia	77
Hayes	Georgie	77
Heer	Atma	77
Hirani	Arjun	77
Hiro	Dilip	77
Hoque	Anam	77
Horabin	Roshan	78
Hossain	Irina	78
Huda	Zamir-ul	78
Hulugalle	Surekha	78
Huq	Khan	78
Husain	Hasanat	78
Husain	Shehzad	78
Husain	Syed Nasir	78
Husaini	Mehdi	79
Hussain	Ahmed	79
Hussain	Akhtar	79
Hussain	Corrine	79
Hussain	Imran	79
Hussain	Mian Farrukh	79
Hussain	Nurun Nahar	79
Hussain	Shelim	79

I

Indrani	Seeta	81
Iqbal	Asif	81
Iqbal	Ifran	81
Iqbal	Imran	81
Iqbal	Nahim	81
Iqbal	Wasim	81
Iqbal	Zafar	81
Ishani	Anil	81
Ishani	Lutfali Kassam	81
Islam	Nazrul	81
Islam	Nazrul	82
Islam	Nozrul	82
Islam	Saleha	82
Islam	Sanchita	82
Islam	Shaidul	82
Ismail	Thalaath	82

J

Jabbar	Sifui	83
Jabeen	Zara	83
Jacko	Ali	83
Jafferji	Zarina	83
Jagjivan	Nathubhai	83
Jagpal	Bally	83
Jain	Jiwan Dhar	83
Jain	Kundanmal	83
Jain	Neerja	84
Jain	Ramnik	84
Jalal	Rajan	84
Jamu	Inder Singh	84
Janki	Dadi	84
Jansari	Chandrakant	84
Jariwala	Popatlal	84
Jasani	Annand	85
Jasani	Bharat	85
Jashapara	Ashok	85
Jaspal	Harinder Kaur	85
Jassar	Sham Singh	85
Javed	Asam	85
Jawanda	Avtar Singh	85
Jayachandra	Chickaballadur	86
Jeet	Surjit Singh	86
Jeevanjee	Anver	86
Jeevanjee	Sara	86
Jetha	Bebz Gulamali	86
Jeyasingh	Shobana	86
Jhalla	Sanjay Praful	86
Jhanjee	Viney	86
Jobanputra	Jay	87
Jogee	Moussa	87
Jolly	Gunita	87
Jolly	Jit Singh	87
Jolly	Sujata	87
Jolly	Super	87
Joseph	George Gherghese	87
Joy	Belal Hussain	87
Junankar	Sudhir N	88
Jung	Iftikhar Hamidullah	88
Juss	Satvinder Singh	88
Juttla	Jaswinder Singh	88

K

Kabir	Mahmuda	89
Kadri	Mushtaq Ahmad	89
Kahlon	Sody Singh	89
Kalhan	Rajesh	89
Kalipha	Stefan	89
Kallah	Ajaib Singh	89
Kalra	Surjit Singh	89
Kalsi	Prem Singh	89
Kamal	Mustafa	90
Kamlana	Sikandar Hayat	90
Kapasi	Jafferhussein Akbarali	90
Kapoor	Anish	90
Kapoor	Dinesh	90
Kapoor	Rajinder Nath	90
Kapoor	Sukhbir Singh	90
Kapur	Annup Raj	90
Kapur	Steven	91
Karapiet	Rashid	91
Kareem	Fiaz Rafiq	91
Kash	Mamta	91
Kassam	Fatima Hassanali	91
Kassam	Ismail	91
Kassam	Karim Hassanali	91
Kathrani	Ratilal K	91
Kaur	Gurdev	92
Kaur	Ranbir	92
Kaur	Rita Gulsharan	92
Kaur	Ushawant	92
Kaushal	Jagdish	92
Kazmi	Syed	92
Khabbra	Narinder	92
Khaleque	Ferdouse	92
Khalid	Ghazanfer	93
Khalsa	Bhopinder Kaur	93
Khalsa	Prithvipal Singh	93
Khalsa-Sagoo	Sarwan Singh	93
Khan	Alauddin	93

Khan	Asad Amin	93
Khan	Asifa Jahanara	93
Khan	Athair	94
Khan	B Hakim	94
Khan	Faroque	94
Khan	Forhad	94
Khan	GMMH Rahman	94
Khan	Imran	94
Khan	Imran Ahmed	94
Khan	Javed	94
Khan	Kamaluddin	95
Khan	Kamran	95
Khan	Mahmood Shafi	95
Khan	Mahtab	95
Khan	Meher	95
Khan	Mohammad	95
Khan	Mohib	95
Khan	Muhammad Munir	95
Khan	Mumtaz	96
Khan	Mutahar Hussain	96
Khan	Muzahid	96
Khan	Nadeem	96
Khan	Nas	96
Khan	Nawaz	96
Khan	Rabnawaz	96
Khan	Raja Arif	96
Khan	Seema	97
Khan	Shafi	97
Khan	Shaheen	97
Khan	Shasha	97
Khan	Sher Afzal	97
Khan	Tariq Aziz	97
Khan	Zahire	97
Khan	Zakir	98
Khan-Cheema	Akram	98
Khanchandani	Hargundas	98
Khanna	Lalit	98
Khanom	Syeda	98
Khanom	Syeda Shorifa	98
Khara	Bhupat Ray	98
Khareghat	Madanlal Thakor	99
Khayum	Abdul	99
Khehra	Charanjit Singh	99
Khosla	Anil	99
Khwaja	Ilyas	99
Kiani	Muhammad Sabir	99
Kiani	Rukhsana Jabeen	99
Kidambi	Ananta Venkatachary	99
King	Rani Anne	100
Kirk	Kaptin	100
Kirubakaran	Kumaravelu	100
Kohli	Sewa Singh	100
Kotecha	Dinesh	100
Kotecha	Jaymini	100
Kotecha	Vinodkumar Bhanulal	100
Koysor	Abdul	100
Krishnamma	Ranjit	101
Krishnatreya	Keshava Chandra	101
Kumar	Ashok	101
Kumar	Ashok	101
Kumar	Pravesh	101
Kumar	Suresh	101
Kumar	Surjit	101
Kumari-Bowles	Krishna	101

L

Lahiri	Sajal	103
Lakha	Amir	103
Lakha	Ram Prakash	103
Lakhani	Poonam	103
Lal	Archie	103
Lal	Pyare	103
Laleriya	Tarsame Singh	103
LALI		103
Lall	D B	104
Lamba	Ashok	104
Lata	Pushpa	104
Lehal	John	104
Litterwala	Jandu	104
Lotay	Rajinder Kaur	104
Ludi	Badrul	104
Luther	Tony Singh	104
Lyall	Priya	104

M

Maan	Bashir Ahmed	105
Madon	Faridoon	105
Madon-Michael	Shirin	105
Mahan	Jaishan	105
Mahil	Jesvir Kaur	105
Mahmood	Sakander	105
Mahmud	Raihan N	105
Mahtani	Deepak	105
Majid-Khan	Fazal Shariff	106
Makanji	Narendra	106
Makda	Hajra	106
Makwana	Hemraj Dahya	106
Malhotra	Kailash Chand	106
Malik	Adeeba	106
Malik	Aftab	106
Malik	Afzal	106
Malik	Hanzala	107
Malik	Krishan Narayan	107
Malik	M. Rafique	107
Malik	Nasser	107
Malik	Shahid	107
Mall	Gurcharan	107
Mallal	Raza	107
Mamujee	Abdulla	108
Manchanda	Keith	108
Manchanda	Surinder Singh	108
Mandair	Mohinder Singh	108
Manidas	Sadanandan	108
Maniyar	Ghulam Ahmed	108
Mann	Amritpal Singh	108
Mann	Mewa Singh	108
Mannan	Sabeeha	109
Markandya	Anil	109
Martins	Rabinder (Rabi)	109
Marwa	Rashpal Emil	109
Mascarenhas	Dimitri	109
Massey	Jamila	109
Massey	Reginald	109
Master	Ghanashyam	109
Matadar	Muhammed	110
Matharu	Ajmer Singh	110
Matharu	Nirminder	110
Mathur	Rakesh	110
Matin	Tanya	110
Mawji	Amin	110
Mayer	John	110
Mazumdar	Sukumar	110
MC	Panjabi	110
McNair	Bruce	111
Meah Khan	Tara	111
Mehra	Harish Kumar	111
Mehta	Atul	111
Mehta	Khushru M	111
Mehta	Sital	111
Meisuria	Sarla	111
Miah	Anawar Babul	111
Miah	Hosoun	112
Miah	Jusna Begum	112
Miah	Rajhana Begum	112
Miah	Shahid	112
Miah	Shofik	112
Miah	Shofique	112
Mian	Nighat Mehmud	112
Minhas	K B Raj Singh	112
Mirza	Jeff	112
Mirza	Nazia	113
Mirza	Shazia	113
Misra	Anjuu	113
Misra	Surendra	113
Mistry	Vasant	113
Moghal	Manzoor Elahi	113
Mohammad	Abdullah	113
Mohammad	Ash	113
Mohan	Karam Chand	114
Mohindra	Sudarshon	114
Mokis	Mansur Ahmed	114
Mondal	Bijoy Krishna	114
Mondal	Dolly	114
Moraes	Claude Ajit	114
Morbiwalla	Rashida	114
Mughal	Fiyaz	114
Mukhtar	Syeda-Masooda	115
Mullick	Biman	115
Mun	Gul Ahmed	115
Munasinghe	Sepale	115

Munisamy	Pitambarum	115
Murshid	Ghulam	115
Murshid	Kumar	115
Musafir	Sachdev	115
Musaji	Fahera Sindhu	116
Mustafa	Syed Mohammed	116
Muzaffar	Sayed Abu	116
Myrrpurey	Sarjit Singh	116

N

Nadirshaw	Zenobia	117
Nafisa	Marium	117
Nagra	Parminder K	117
Nagra	Sandeep	117
Nagra	Tommy	117
Nahar	Kewal	117
Naher	Nazmin	117
Naib	Sham Lal	117
Naik	Balwant	118
Naik	Jigar	118
Najib	Mohammad	118
Nakarja	Yogesh	118
Nanda	Ramesh	118
Nandakumara	Mattur	118
Nandanwar	Swatantra	118
Naqvi	Syed Z H Haider	118
Naru	Bhopinder Singh	119
Nasir	Bushra	119
Nasreen	Shazia	119
Nassa	Avi	119
Nath	Narinder Thakur	119
Nath	Pathikonda	119
Nathoo	Gavaral Mohamed	119
Navaz	Dil	119
Nayar	Jai K	120
Nayar	Lali	120
Naz	Farah	120
Naz	Nazrul Islam	120
Nazir-Ali	Michael	120
Nazran	Balbir Kaur	120
Nijabat	Reedah	120
Nijhawan	Krishan Kumar	121
Nirgunananthan	Dineshi	121
Nixon	Antony	121
Noor	Naranjan Singh	121
Notay	Harmesh Singh	121

O

Ohbi	Harjinder	123

P

Pabla	Parshotam Singh	125
Padake	Helen Mohan	125
Pajwani	Kishor	125
Pal	Badal	125
Pal	Julie	125
Palim	Alamail	125
Paliwal	Kanti Chandra	125
Pall	Subash Singh	125
Panchal	Dharmish	125
Pande	Shiv	126
Pandya	Nalinikant	126
Pandya	Rajendra	126
Pandya	Ram Chandra	126
Pankhania	Tara	126
Pardesi	Silinder	126
Parekh	Deepak	126
Parekh	Haresh (Harry)	126
Parekh	Kamal	127
Parekh	Meena	127
Parekh	Paksha (Rakhee)	127
Parhar	Kartar Singh	127
Parikh	Ashok	127
Parmar	Maganlal Trikam	127
Parmar	Nimita	127

Parmar	Satpal Singh	127
Parmar	Satwant	128
Parnandi	Venkata Aditya	128
Partha-Sarathi	Joniah	128
Parvez	Shazad	128
Pasha	Badrun Nesa	128
Pasha	Sahera	128
Passan	Jagdeep Singh	128
Patara	Talwinder Singh	128
Patel	Adam Hafejee	129
Patel	Anwer Ibrahim	129
Patel	Babubhai Ashabhai	129
Patel	Bhikhu C	129
Patel	Bhupendra	129
Patel	Farida	129
Patel	Indira	129
Patel	Janakbhai	129
Patel	Kamlesh	130
Patel	Lata K.D.	130
Patel	Mukhand Jayantilal	130
Patel	Mukundray (Mike)	130
Patel	Naina	130
Patel	Pravinbhai M	130
Patel	Ramesh Ashabhai M	130
Patel	Ramesh B	130
Patel	Ramesh U	131
Patel	Said	131
Patel	Vijay	131
Patel-Vekaria	Manji	131
Pathak	Madhu Lata	131
Pathak	Suresh Kumar	131
Pattwal	Rajinder Singh	131
Paul	Swraj	131
Pawar	Priya	132
Persaud	Raj	132
Phull	Sukhjit Singh	132
Pillaye	Jayshree	132
Pinto	Domingos	132
Pitrola	Bipin	132
Ponda	Bipin	132
Pooni	HS	132
Pooran Singh	Balmati	133
Popat	Ashwin Kantilal	133
Popat	Gopal Bhai	133
Popat	Vinod Bhagwanji	133
Prasad	Roopendra Kumar	133
Prashar	Usha	133
Puri	Ashok Kumar	133
Puri	Gurdeep Singh	133
Puri	Kailash	134
Puri	Om	134

Q

Qadir	Parvez	135
Qureshi	Khawar Mehmood	135
Qureshi	Murad	135
Qureshi	Shakeel Ahmed	135
Qureshi	Shamim Ahmed	135

R

Raheja	Sudesh	137
Rahman	Aliur	137
Rahman	Ashadur	137
Rahman	Ehsanur	137
Rahman	Ehtesham	137
Rahman	Ekramur	137
Rahman	Mohammad	137
Rahman	Mohibur	137
Rai	Ajit Singh	138
Rai	John Singh	138
Rai	Kuldip	138
Rai	Sudharam	138
Raindi	Prem	138
Rait	Satwant Kaur	138
Raizada	Jagdish Singh	138
Raja	Laila	138
Raja	Sushila	139
Rajyaguru	Dipen	139
Rajyaguru	Hitendra M	139
Raman	Abdool Cader	139
Ramanee	Sakuntala	139

Ramdeholl	Krishna	139
Ramnarine	Ramnarace	139
Ramraj	Bishnauth	139
Ramzan	Shahbaz	140
Rana	Diljit	140
Rana	Ranjit Singh	140
Rana	Satvinder	140
Rao	Rajesh Kanu	140
Rashid	A M Faz	140
Rashid	Bajloor	140
Ratna	Kiran	141
Rattan	Harmegh Singh	141
Raval	Hina	141
Rawat	Saffia	141
Rawtani	Sujan	141
Razao	Mohammed	141
Rehman	Abdul	141
Rehman	Sajjad	141
Rehman	Shafiq	142
Rellon	Lakhvir	142
Reza	Shahab	142
Ritu	DJ	142
Robins	Serena B	142
Rohatgi	Pradip Krishna 'Roy'	142
Rouf	Mahmoud A	142
Rouf	Mohammed Abdur	142
Roy	Nirmal	143
Roy	Sukla	143
Ruparel	Madhu	143
Ruparell	Mahendra Hirji	143
Ruparell	Shantoo	143
Russell	Bibi	143

S

Sadiq	Imtiaz	145
Sadullah	Shahed	145
Saeed	Mohammed	145
Safiruddin	Syed	145
Sagoo	Dev	145
Sahni	Gurnam Singh	145
Sahni	Trilochan Singh	145
Sahota	Gurdial Singh	145
Sahota	Krishan Kaur	146
Sajid	Dr Abduljalil	146
Sakaria	Himat	146
Salam	Abdul	146
Saleem	Sajad	146
Saleemi	Mohammad Hussain	146
Salim	Mohammad Khurram	146
Samant	Kamalnath	146
Samant	Shaila	147
Samarth	Alaknanda	147
Samra	Sukhveer	147
Samrai	Rocky	147
Sandhu	Amarjit Singh	147
Sandhu	Bhupinder	147
Sandhu	Darshan Singh	147
Sandhu	Devinder	147
Sandhu	Gurdip Singh	148
Sanga	Abtar	148
Sangha	Perminder	148
Sangha	Rakshpal Singh	148
Sangha	Sujinder Singh	148
Sanghera	Mandeep	148
Sanghrajka	Jay	148
Sanj	San-J	148
Sarcar	Maitreyee	148
Sarin	Tony	149
Saroop	Narinder	149
Sarpal	Ved Singh	149
Sarwar	Zubeda B	149
Sattar	Abdul Rahim	149
Saund	Balwinder Kaur	149
Sawhney	Nitin	149
Saxena	Sideshwar Raj	149
Sayeed	Moulana Sheikh Abu	150
Seehra	Sarup Singh	150
Sehgal	Sachin	150
Sehmi	Heronimo	150
Seth	Hari Krishan	150
Sethi	Ramesh	150
Sethi	Ritu	150
Seyan	Manoharpal Singh	150
Shah	Ansar Fatima	151
Shah	Bharat	151

Shah	Dinesh Chandra P	151
Shah	Ela Mahendra	151
Shah	Natubhai	151
Shah	Ranchhodlal Chunilal	151
Shah	Shireen	151
Shah	Suchita	152
Shaheed	Mesbah	152
Shahjahan	Khadija	152
Shahjahan	Taslima	152
Shahraz	Qaisra	152
Shahzad	Ghulam Rasul	152
Shaikh	Shuja	152
Shankar	KS Bhavani	152
Sharif	Khalid	153
Sharma	Amita	153
Sharma	Dial	153
Sharma	Jagdish Rai	153
Sharma	Lal	153
Sharma	Prem	153
Sharma	Rajesh	153
Sharma	Ravi	153
Sharma	Sanjay	154
Sharma	Shiv	154
Sharma	Suraj	154
Sharma	Swaran	154
Sharma	Vijay	154
Shastry	HVS	154
Shehzadi	Musarat	154
Sheikh	Dj	154
Sheikh	Iftikhar Hassan	155
Sheikh	Javaid	155
Sheikh	Maqsood Ellahie	155
Sheikh	Mohammad Younas	155
Sheikh	Saleem Raza	155
Sheikh	Yasmin	155
Sherwani	Kevin	155
Shin		155
Shivdasani	Sonu	156
Shourie	Jiwan Kumar	156
Shrestha	Padma Prakash	156
Shrivastav	Baluji	156
Shukla	Hari	156
Sidat	Salim	156
Siddiqui	Abdul Majeed	156
Sidhu	Ajit Singh	156
Sidhu	Amarjit	157
Sidhu	Gurcharan Singh	157
Sidhu	Kulwinder	157
Sidhu	Malini Christina	157
Sidhu	Navjot (Jo)	157
Sidhu	Pritam Singh	157
Sihota	Mohan Singh	157
Sikandar Raja	Naureen	157
Singh	Ajab Samrah	158
Singh	Ajeet	158
Singh	Amrit Kumari	158
Singh	Balbir	158
Singh	Balbir	158
Singh	Baldev	158
Singh	Daljit Kaur	158
Singh	Europe	158
Singh	Gulab	159
Singh	Gurparshad 'Ricky'	159
Singh	Harmander	159
Singh	Harmindar	159
Singh	Jagtar	159
Singh	Jaswant	159
Singh	Jugdish	159
Singh	Krishan Kumar	159
Singh	Kumar	160
Singh	Manjit	160
Singh	Mota	160
Singh	Rabindra Kumari	160
Singh	Rajendra "Reg"	160
Singh	Ranjit	160
Singh	Riti	160
Singh	Shyam Pratap	161
Singh	Terry	161
Singh	Tjinder	161
Singh	Yvonne	161
Singhania	Gomti Devi	161
Singhania	Vishwa Nath	161
Sinha	Aswinee Kumar	161
Sivanesan	Sivasakti	162
Smalley	Nina	162
Soar	Sowaran Singh	162
Sockananthan	Wimal	162
Sodha	Ansuya	162
Sohal	Paul Singh	162
Sokhal	Mohan Singh	162

Solanki	Marcus Jayant	162
Solanki	Vijay	163
Sond	Daljit Singh	163
Sondhi	Ranjit	163
Soni	Ramesh Kumar	163
Soni	Seema	163
Soni	Sushil	153
Sood	Manish	163
Sood	Manjula Paul	163
Sood	Manoj	164
Sootarsing	Gita	164
Souisi	Imane	164
Srinivasan	Nagan	164
Srivastava	Ashok Kumar	164
Stubbs	Sukhvinder Kaur	164
Sudra	Babulal V	164
Sukul	Diwakar	165
Sumana -	Siri	165
Summan	Dalvir Singh	165
Swarup	Arun Kumar	165
Syed	Bobby Ayyus	165
Syed	Shaheen	165
Syed	Sultana	165

T

Talukder	Abdul Bari	167
Tanna	Ashwin Kumar	167
Tariq	Mohammed	167
Taunque	Jagjit Singh	167
Taunque	Satinder Kaur	167
Tewari	Virendra Kumar	167
Thakar	Rashmi	167
Thaker	Subhash	167
Thakerar	Navinbhai Rugnath	168
Thakoordin	Jim	168
Thakrar	Rohan	168
Thakrar	Subhash Kanji	168
Thammaiah	Keekira	168
Theathi	Gurbax Singh	168
Thind	Gurbachan Singh	168
Tinn-Ngyutin	Natalie	168
Todiwala	Cyrus Rustom	169
Toki	Abdul Aziz	169
Trehan	Ashwini Kumar	169
Trivedi	Shanker	169
Tulsiani	Prem	169

U

Uddin	Ala	171
Uddin	Baroness	171
Uddin	Juli Begum	171
Uddin	Mohammed Foiz	171
Ullah	Ansar Ahmed	171
Uppal	Balbir Singh	171
Uppal	Paramjit	171

V

Vadgama	Pankaj	173
Vadher	Vinod Vashram	173
Vadhia	Kishor	173
Vaidyanathan	Arun	173
Vaqas	Babar	173
Vara	Shailesh	173
Varma	Indira	173
Varma	Navin	173
Varma	Thanram Rama	174
Vaz	Keith	174
Vaz	Merlyn	174
Vaz	Valerie Carol	174
Venkatesham	Guduguntla	174
Venugopal	Srirama S	174
Verma	Deepak	174
Verma	Jatinder	174
Verma	Mehar	175

Verma	Ramesh	175
Verma	Veena	175
Vibhuti	Nalini	175
Vibhuti	Ravi	175
Vijayakumar	Kalamandalam	175
Vijayaratnam	Kanapathipillai	175
Vir	Parminder	175
Virdee	Bal Singh	176
Virdee	Manjeet Singh	176
Virdi	Harvey	176
Virdi	Surjit Singh	176
Virk	Hardish	176
Virk	Jasvir	176
Virk	Lakhbir	176
Virk	Manjinder	176
Virk	Paven	177
Vyas	Bharti	177

W

Wadia	Nina	179
Waghela	Hansa	179
Walayat	Mohammad	179
Wali	Zahid	179
Wallia	Sunita	179
Wanigesekera	Allen	179
Warsi	Perween	179
Warsi	Talib	180
Weerasekera	Thushani	180
Wewage-Dep	Andrew	180
Wickramasinghe	Narin Chandra	180
Wickramsinghe	Priya	180
Wijesuriya	Kumarjit	180
Winship	Kulsum	180
Wong	Ansel	180

Y

Yacoub	Andreas	181
Yadagudde	Prakash	181
Yadav	Mamta	181
Yadav	Pradeep	181
Yahor	Mehmooda	181
Yaqoob	Mohammad	181
Yogeswaran	Manickam	181
Young	Morgan	182
Yusuf	Altaf	182

Z

Zahawi	Nadhim	183
Zaiwalla	Sarosh	183
Zaki	Antony	183
Zamal	Misbah	183
Zeria	Ishaque Hassan	183
Zumla	Alimuddin	183
Zutshi	Derek	183

ENTRY FORMAT IN ASIANS IN THE MILLENNIUM

Each entry is in a standard format for easy reading. First we use the title followed by a first name, surname and honours where applicable. This is followed by a profession/occupation, the next entry is the current position/occupation, the name of an organisation/company and/or an address where given. All other information is standard. The personal profiles are either in the first or third person as submitted. Contact telephone numbers and addresses have been left out at the request of entrants. Nominations are not attached to every entry at the request of those making nominations.

INDEX OF
LATE ENTRIES

WHO'S WHO PROJECT

Class 8B at Mulberry School for Girls undertook a unique project during the summer of 1999 - to discover how many Asian names are in the WHO'S WHO 1999 Edition (the first Who's Who was published 150 years ago and contained 500 names, the publisher's statement claims that the WHO'S WHO is the recognized source book of information on people of influence and interest in all fields), there are reportedly 30,000 entries in the 1999 edition.

The brief for the Class 8B was to search the 2,239 pages of the Who's Who and list all Asian names commonly used in the Asian Sub-continent, specifically India, Pakistan, Bangladesh and Sri Lanka. They found 124 typical Asian names of people inside and outside Britain.

Our thanks go to: Ali Farjana Begum; Ali Firuja Begum; Ali Sajia Begum; Chowdhury Rahima Khanam; Hannan Janifar Yeasmin; Hussain Nurun Nahar; Kalam Roujee Yasmin; Khaleque Shamina Begum; Khan Shuba Khatun; Miah Jusna Begum; Miah Rajhana Begum; Miah Shahana Begum; Miah Shipa Begum; Nahar Nazmin; Quadir Hafsa Khanam; Rahman Shelina Khanam; Rahman Sufiya Begum; Raja Naureen Sikandar; Shahid Suheli Begum; Uddin Julfa Begum; Uddin Nadira Begum; Uddin Rehana Begum; Uddin Sabina Begum; Ullah Salma Begum; Wadud Isma Khatun; Uddin Juli Begum. 26 pupils each took responsibility for one letter. They presented their findings in a report and each pupil received an Ethnic Media Group Certificate for Achievement.

Abbreviations

This list of abbreviations is included merely as a guide to most of those contained in this directory and it does not necessarily imply any professional or other qualifications

ABAA	British Association of Accountants & Auditors
ABIM	Association of British Insecticide Manufacturers
ACA	Associate, Institute of Chartered Accountants
ACCA	Associate, Association of Chartered Certified Accountants
ACEA	Association of Cost and Executive Accountants
ACFI	Advisory Committee on Flight Information
ACGI	Associate of the City Guilds Institute London
ACIB	Associate, Chartered Institute of Bankers
ACLS	American Council of Learned Societies
ACMA	Associate, Chartered Institute of Management Accountants
ACP	Associate, College of Preceptors (Teachers/Trainors) Association of Clinical Pathologists.
ADV ST	Advance Stoppage (MUGU)
AFA	Associate, Institute of Financial Accountants
AFBPS	Associate Fellow, British Psychological Society
AFCS	Automatic Flight Control System
AGS M&D	Associate Guildhall School of Music and Drama
AGSM	Associate Guildhall School of Music and Drama
AHCIMA	Associate of Hotel, Catering and Institutional Management Association
AIDPM	Associate of the Institute of Data Processing Management
AIEC	Associate, Institution of Civil Engineers Associate of the Institute of Sales and Marketing Management
ALA	Associate Library Association
ALAM	Associate London Academy of Music and Dramatic Art
ALCM	Associate London College of Music
ALSTD	Associate of the Imperial Society of Teachers of Dance
AMIEE	Associate Member, Institution of Electrical Engineers
ARAM	Associate Royal Academy of Music
ARCM	Associate, Royal College of Music
ARCS	Associate Royal College of Science
ASA	Associate Member Society of Actuaries
ATCL	Associate Trinity College of Music, London
ATI	Associate Textile Institute
ATII	Associate Member of Chartered Institute of Taxation
B.Com	Bachelor of Commerce
B.Ed	Bachelor of Education
B.Eng	Bachelor of Engineering
B.Mus	Bachelor of Music
B.Pharm	Bachelor of Pharmacy
BA	Bachelor of Arts
BAJ	Bachelor of Arts in Journalism
BAMS	British American Minesweeper
BBA	Bachelor of Business Administration, British Bankers Association
BD	Bachelor of Divinity
BFA	Bachelor of Fine Arts
BL	Bachelor of Law, British Library
BLitt	Bachelor of Letters
BMA	British Medical Association
BOV	Burntout Velocity
BSc	Bachelor of Science
BT	Bachelor of Teaching / British Telecommunications
BTEC	Business and Technology Education Council
BVC	Bushveldt Carabineers

C Chem	Chartered Chemist
C.Eng	Chartered Engineer
C Math	Chartered Mathematician
C Phys	Chartered Physicist
C.Text	Chartered Textile Technologist
C&G	City & Guilds
CA	Chartered Accountant
CAA	Civil Aviation Authority
CAM	Communications, Advertising and Marketing
CBiol	Chartered Biologist
CCPR	Central Council of Physical Recreation
CD	Canadian Forces Decoration, Commander, Order of Distinction, Civil Defence, Compact Disc
Cert Ed	Certificate of Education
CIBSE	Chartered Institution of Building Services Engineers
CIDESCO	International Committee for Esthetics and Cosmetolgy
CIFP	Committee for Instrumental Flight Plans
CIMA	Chartered Institute of Management Accountants
CISA	Certified Information System Auditor
CMA)	Certified Management Accountant
CMS	Church Mission, Church Missionary Society, Certificate in Management Studies
CNAA	Council for National Academic Awards
CQSW	Certificate of Qualification in Social Work
CRCCYP	Certificate in the Residential Care of Children and Young People
CRSW	Certificate in Residential Social Work
CSM	Certificate Shopping Centre Manager
CTD	Certificate of Tax Deposit/ Corporate Technology Database
D.Med	Doctor of Medicine
D.Phil	Doctor of Philosophy
DA	Diploma of Arts, Diploma of Anaethesia, Doctor of Arts
DASE	Diploma in Advanced Studies in Education
DCH	Diploma in Child Health
DD	Doctor of Divinity
DDS	Doctor of Dental Surgery
DHMSA	Diploma in the History of Medicine
DHO	Director of Home Operations
DHY	Derelet Hara Yollon
DIC	Diploma of the Imperial College
Dip Ed	Diploma in Education
Dip HE	Diploma of Higher Education
DLitt	Dotor of Literature, Doctor of Letters
DMA	Diploma in Municipal Administration
DMC	Design Module Controller
DMH	Dept of Mental Health
DMRD	Diploma in Medical Radiological Diagnosis
DMS	Director of Medical Services
DOMS	Diploma in Ophthalmic Medicine and Surgery
DPEd	Doctor of Pedagogy
DPhil	Doctor of Philosophy
DPM	Diploma in Psychological Medicine
DRCOG	Diploma of Royal College of Obstetrictians and Gynaecologists
DSc	Doctor of Science
DSSc	Doctor of Social Science
DSW	Director of Special Weapons
DTCD	Diploma in Tuberculosis and Chest Diseases
DTM&H	Diploma in Tropical Medicine and Hygiene
DTP	Driver Training Platoon
EMRT	Ethnic Minority Recruiting Team
ENB	English National Board Careers Advisory Centre

ENG	Engineer Officer
Eur-Ing	European Engineer
F InstCM	Fellow of the Institute of Commercial Management
F InstSMM	Fellow, Institute of Sales and Marketing Management
FAAI	Fellow, Institute of Administrative Accounting Data
FBCO	Fellow British College of Optometrists
FBHI	Fellow, British Horological Institute
FCA	Fellow, Institute of Chartered Accountants, Fellow, Institute of Chartered Accountants in Australia, Fellow, New Zealand Society of Accountants, Federation of Canadian Artists
FCCA	Fellow Chartered Association of Certified Accountants
FCCP	Friends Coordinating Committee on Peace
FCIB	Fellow, Corporation of Insurance Brokers, Fellow, Chartered Institute of Bankers
FCIOB	Fellow, Chartered Institute of Building
FCIS	Fellow, Institute of Chartered Secretaries and Administrators
FCIT	Fellow, Chartered Institute of Transport
FFA	Fellow, Faculty of Actuaries, Fellow, Institute of Financial Accountants
FFAEM	Fellow, Faculty of Accident and Emergency
FFARCS	Fellow, Faculty of Anaesthetists, Royal College of Surgeons of England
FFBA	Fellow. Corporation of Executives and Administrators
FFPHM	Fellow, Faculty of Public Health Medicine
FFRRCSI	Fellow, Faculty of Radiologists, Royal College of Surgeons of Ireland
FIAP	Fellow Institution of Analysts and Programmers
FIBiol	Fellow, Institute of Biology
FICA	Fellow, Commonwealth Institute of Accountants, Fellow Institute of Chartered Accountants in England and Wales
FIEE	Fellow of the Institution of Electrical Engineers
FIIA	Fellow, Institute of Industrial Administration, Fellow Institute of Internal Auditors
FIM	Fellow Institute of Materials
FIMechE	Fellow Institution of Mechanical Engineers
FMAAT	Fellow Member, Association of Accounting Technicians
FPC	Family Practitioner Committee
FRAeS	Fellow, Royal Aeronautical Society
FRAS	Fellow, Royal Astronomical Society
FRC.Path	Fellow of Royal College of Pathology
FRCO	Fellow, Royal College of Organists
FRCP	Fellow, Royal College of Physicians
FRCPCH	Fellow, Royal College of Paediatrics and Child Health
FRCPE	Fellow, Royal College of Physicians
FRCPsych	Fellow, Royal College of Psychiatrists
FRCR	Fellow, Royal College of Radiologists
FRCS	Fellow, Royal College of Surgeons of England
FRCSEd	Fellow, Royal College of Surgeons of Edinburgh
FRGS	Fellow, Royal Geographical Society
FRHS	Fellow, Royal Horticultural Society
FRICS	Fellow, Royal Institution of Chartered Surveyors
FRNS	Fellow Royal Numismatic Society
FRPharmS	Fellow, Royal Pharmaceutical Society
FRSA	Fellow Royal Society of Arts
FRSH	Fellow, Royal Society for the Promotion of Health
FRSM	Fellow, Royal Society of Medicine
GPI	Greenpeace International/Grocery Price Index
HCS	Higher Civil Service
HETC	Computer & Commercial Industries/Heavy Equipment Test Chamber

HNC	Higher National Certificate
HND	Higher National Diploma
IDTA	International Differential Treatment Association
IEEE	Institute of Electrical and Electronics Engineers
ITEC	Information Technology Electronics and Computers
IWO	Institution of Water Officers
LDSRCS	Licentiate in Dental Surgery of the Royal College of Surgeons
LJ	Lord Justice
LL.B	Bachelor of Laws
LLM	Master of Law
LMPA	Qualified Member of the Masters Photographers Association
LMSSA	Licentiate in Medicine and Surgery
LRAM	Licentiate, Royal Academy of Music
LRCP	Licentiate, Royal College of Physicians, London
LRSM	Licentiate, Royal Schools of Music
LTCL	Licentiate of Trinity College of Music
M.Com	Master of Commerce
M.Ed	Master of Education
M.Imgt	Member, Institute of Management
M. Mus	Master of Music
M.Phil	Master of Philosophy
M Soc Sc	Master of Social Sciences
MA	Master of Arts
MAAT	Member, Association of Accounting Technicians
Maj	Major General
MASC	Member, Australian Society of Calligraphers
MASCE	Member, American Society of Civil Engineers
MB	Medal of Bravery, Bachelor of Medicine
MBA	Master of Business Administration
MBBChin	Bachelor of Medicine
MBBS	Bachelor of Medicine/ Bachelor of Science/Batchelor of Surgery
MBIM	Member, British Institute of Management
MCIH	Member of Chartered Institute of Housing
MCIOB	Member, Chartered Institute of Building
MCIT	Member, Chartered Institute of Transport
MCIWEM	Member, Chartered Institution of Water and Environmental Management
MD	Doctor of Medicine, Military District
MED	Master of Education
MFA	Master of Fine Arts
MFPHM	Member, Faculty of Public Health Medicine
MIED	Member Institution of Engineering Designers
MIEE	Member Institution of Electrical Engineers
MIFM	Member Institute of Fisheries Management
MIIA	Member, Institute of Industrial Administration
MIMI	Member, Institute of the Motor Industry
MIMM	Member, Institution of Mining and Metallurgy
MInst P	Member, Institute of Physics
MIPD	Member, Institute of Personnel and Development
MIRSE	Member, Institute of Railway Signal Engineers
MIRTE	Member, Institute of Road Transport Engineers
MLitt	Master of Letters
MRCGP	Member, Royal College of General Practitioners
MRCP	Member of Royal College of Physicians, London
MRC	Member Royal College of Psychiatrists
MRPharms	Member, Royal Pharmaceutical Society
MRTPI	Member, Royal Town Planning Institute
MS	Master of Surgery, Master of Science
MSA	Master of Science, Agricuture (US), Mineralogical Society of America
MSc	Master of Science
NCA	National Certificate of Agriculture
NCDT	National Council of Drama Training

NCTJ	National Council for the Training of Journalists
NDN	National Diffusion Network
NEBSS	National Examinations Board for Supervisory Studies
ONC	Office of New Careers
OND	Ordinary National Diploma
PA	Pakistan Army, Personnal Assistant
PADI	Professional Association of Diving Instructors
PGCE	Post Graduate Certificate of Education
PhD	Doctor of Philosophy
PHEC	Human Ecology
PPA	Periodical Publishers Association
PQ	Physically Qualified/Province of Quebec
QTS	Qualification Test Specification
RADA	Royal Academy of Dramatic Arts
RAMC	Royal Army Medical Corps
RCA	Member, Royal Canadian Academy of Arts, Royal College of Art, Royal Cambrian Academy
RCOG	Royal College of Obstetricians and Gynaecologists
RCR	Royal College of Radiologists
RGN	Registered General Nurse
RIBA	Royal Institute of British Architects
RICS	Royal Institution of Chartered Surveyors
RJ	Royal Jordanian Airlines
RM	Royal Marines, Resident Magistrate, Registered Midwife
RMN	Registered Mental Nurse
RN	Royal Navy, Registered Nurse
RNT	Registered Nurse Tutor, Royal National Theatre
RSA	Royal Society of Arts
SCM	State Certified Midwife, Student Christian Movement
SFA	Securities and Future Authority
SMIEEE	Senior Member, Institute of Electrical and Electronics Engineers
SMO	Senior Medical Officer, Sovereign Military Order
SRN	State Registered Nurse
SWA	State Welfare Agency
TD	Territorial Army Efficiency Decoration
TESOL	Teaching English to Speakers of Other Languages
UPI	United Press International
USPTR	US Professional Tennis Registry
YMCA	Young Men's Christian Association

Reaching the _heart_ of multi-cultural Britain

Ethnic Media Group represents Britain's diverse Black and Asian communities. The group's four nationally circulated newspapers, New Nation, Eastern Eye, Asian Times and Caribbean Times, reach over 500,000 readers every week and are the main source of news, views and information for this prosperous and growing sector of Britain. The papers' recruitment section, Jobs Direct, has already helped thousands find employment and is packed every week with hundreds of job opportunities. 'Public Sector', a weekly pull-out section in Asian Times and Caribbean Times, is unique, being the only supplement covering news and features for Britain's ethnic minority workers in this important field. Together the papers cater for every taste, every kind of reader and reach the people who really matter. Ethnic Media Group titles provide a gateway to the British Black and Asian communities.

For more information call: 0171 702 8012

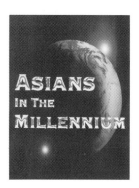

ASIANS
in the
MILLENNIUM

Who's Who Of Asian Achievers

First Edition

ETHNIC MEDIA GROUP

publishers of

 Caribbean Times  ASIAN TIMES

WHO'S WHO OF ASIAN ACHIEVERS
PAGE GUIDE

WHO'S WHO OF ASIAN ACHIEVERS

MRS NOOR AATHIKA (Social Worker)

Student, Bath Black and other Ethnic Minority Senior Citizens Project, 17 Chandler Close, Weston Bath, Bath, BA1 4EG

PLACE OF BIRTH: India, 13.2.77
MARITAL STATUS: Married
COLLEGE: Bath Spa University / College
ACADEMIC QUALIFICATIONS: BSc Hons, Social Sciences
HOBBIES AND INTERESTS: Cooking, reading, swimming, aerobics, music
PERSONAL PROFILE: I am going to be in the final year at university. I work part-time for the Bath Black and other Ethnic Minority Senior Citizen's Project. I work for elderly Asian people in Bath, encourage them to visit the project for lunch and take advantage of the services provided. I have been able to get nearly six members to the project.

MR LUCKSHAN ABEYSURIYA (Accountant)

Self Employed, LA Accounting Services, Fairholme, Eden Mount Road, Grange-Over-Sands, Cumbria, LA11 6BN

PLACE OF BIRTH: Sri Lanka, 12.5.34
MARITAL STATUS: Married
CHILDREN: 4
COLLEGE: University of Colombo and Lancaster
ACADEMIC QUALIFICATIONS: MA International Relations
PROFESSIONAL QUALIFICATIONS: Chartered Accountant (P Q)
MEMBERSHIPS: Amnesty International Board. UNA SL Chairman
HOBBIES AND INTERESTS: Cricket, walking
PERSONAL PROFILE: Lived in UK for 40 years. Very active in human rights work. Board member of AI UK. Also chair of United Nations Association SL. Working for ethnic harmony.
NOMINATED BY: Dr Khalid Sharif

MS SUDARSHAN KAUR ABROL MBE (Headteacher-Rtd)

Non-Executive Director of Women's Trust, UK Asian Women Conference National Executive, 18 Amberley Green, Great Barr, Birmingham, B43 5TJ

PLACE OF BIRTH: India, 9.9.37
MARITAL STATUS: Single (Divorced)
CHILDREN: One (Surinder)
COLLEGE: Punjab University, Birmingham University
ACADEMIC QUALIFICATIONS: BA, MA, B Ed. DCP. M Ed (Special Education)
PROFESSIONAL QUALIFICATIONS: M Ed (Special Education) Unvi of B'ham
DIRECTORSHIPS: Birmingham Womens Host. Trust
MEMBERSHIPS: NAHT, The City College
HONOURS/AWARDS: MBE (1989)
HOBBIES AND INTERESTS: Community service, support, helping the disadvantaged
PERSONAL PROFILE: Worked as a teacher and headteacher for 35 years in Britain. Trained Ofsted team inspector. Non-executive director Women's Health Trust. Director/board member of BVSC, corporation member of the City College, Birmingham. Vice-chair of Black Ethnic Minority Disability Partnership. Love to help / support the disadvantage service to the community. Love my grandson.

DR MEMIS ACAR (Mechanical Engineer)

Senior Lecturer, Loughborough University, Department of Mechanical Engineering, Loughborough, LE11 3TU

PLACE OF BIRTH: Turkey, 14.6.51
MARITAL STATUS: Married
CHILDREN: Two (Baris, Baran Galip)
COLLEGE: METU, UMIST, Loughborough
ACADEMIC QUALIFICATIONS: BS, MSc, PhD
PROFESSIONAL QUALIFICATIONS: C Eng, CText, Eur-Ing
MEMBERSHIPS: IMeche, The Textile Institute, ASME
HONOURS/AWARDS: Royal Academy of Engineering London, 'Engineering Foresight Award'.
HOBBIES AND INTERESTS: Turkish folk dancing, cooking, travelling
EMAIL: m.acar@lboro.ac.uk
WEB SITE: lboro.ac.uk/departments/mc
PERSONAL PROFILE: Born in Cappadocia, Turkey. Studied mechanical engineering at Middle East Technical University, Ankara. Won a government grant for masters and doctorate studies in the UK in the field of textile machinery. Currently senior lecturer at Loughborough University and a leading expert in textile machinery research and technological development.
NOMINATED BY: Veronica King, Loughborough University

MR JAY ACHARYA (Teacher)

Rushey Mead School, 20 Ardath Road, Leicester, LE4 6JA

PLACE OF BIRTH: Tanzania, 28.5.67
MARITAL STATUS: Single
COLLEGE: Liverpool Polytechnic
ACADEMIC QUALIFICATIONS: BSc Hons, PGCE
PROFESSIONAL QUALIFICATIONS: PGCE
HONOURS/AWARDS: Outstanding performance in GCE, A-Level sport studies
HOBBIES AND INTERESTS: Almost all sports, reading, cooking, travelling
PERSONAL PROFILE: My main interest lies in developing opportunities for young people across all areas of life-especially sport. As a teacher of PE I have coached numerous sports teams which have been very successful. The majority of team members are of Asian origin and I take great delight in eradicating the myth that Asians cannot play sport.
NOMINATED BY: T Dhillon

DR SUSHMA DILIP ACQUILLA (Doctor)

Consultant-Lecturer, County Durham Health Authority, Kilifi House, 2 Leven Close, Stokesley, Middlesbrough, TS9 5AU

PLACE OF BIRTH: India, 14.12.48
MARITAL STATUS: Married
CHILDREN: 3 (Rajeev, Avaneesh, Maneesh)
COLLEGE: Bhopal Medical College, India
ACADEMIC QUALIFICATIONS: MBBS LRCP, MRCS, DCH, FFPHM
PROFESSIONAL QUALIFICATIONS: FFPHM. Lecturer in Epidemiology. Medical consultant (PG, CEW 7 PHM)
DIRECTORSHIPS: Director of Training, Faculty of Public Health Medicine, London. Pine Care Homes, West Close
MEMBERSHIPS: BMA, Society Of Social Medicines, International Medical Commission on Bhopal
HONOURS/AWARDS: Baum Prize European Environmental Epidem.
HOBBIES AND INTERESTS: Swimming, travelling, cooking and Indian classical dance, music
EMAIL: s.d.acquilla@newcastle.ac.uk
PERSONAL PROFILE: First Indian woman to be appointed as Director Of Public Health in England and Wales and Director of Training for the Faculty of Public Health Medicine. I am a trustee of Aycliffe School for children with special needs. My big achievement is that I consider being able to help victims of the Bhopal Gas Disaster through the membership of International Commission in Bhopal. I have always believed that if you work hard then rewards (not necessarily monetary) will follow sooner or later.

MRS MUMTAZ AFZAL (Fundraiser)

Pakistan Women's Organisation,

PLACE OF BIRTH: Pakistan, 21.10.27
MARITAL STATUS: Married
CHILDREN: Three (Samina, Shahid, Yasmin)
MEMBERSHIPS: President-Pakistan Women's Organisation
HONOURS/AWARDS: 1999 Merton Council Community Award
HOBBIES AND INTERESTS: Fundraising, reading
PERSONAL PROFILE: Through my presidency of the Pakistan Women's Organisation over many years I have contributed to the Pakistan community in South London and have developed it's relationship with other sections of the community. I have also worked extensively as a charity volunteer, organising fundraising activities for local and international charities.
NOMINATED BY: M M Rana

MR NAZIR AFZAL (Lawyer)

Prosecutor, Crown Prosecution Service, 50 Ludgate Hill, London, EC4M 7EX

PLACE OF BIRTH: Birmingham, 1.10.62
MARITAL STATUS: Married
CHILDREN: 2 (Marina Afzal-Khan, Shaan M Afzal-Khan)
COLLEGE: Birmingham
ACADEMIC QUALIFICATIONS: LLB Hons
PROFESSIONAL QUALIFICATIONS: Solicitor-Advocate
HONOURS/AWARDS: Honorary Life Member, Guild of Students, University of Birmingham
HOBBIES AND INTERESTS: Writing, cinema
PERSONAL PROFILE: Solicitor by qualification, Nazir has been prosecuting in central London since 1991. He is the first prosecutor with higher courts advocacy rights. He is a qualified trainer of lawyers and responsible for external liaison. Proud of his Pathan heritage. He is highly ambitious but always a family man at heart.
NOMINATED BY: Mrs Sukhi Afzal

CLLR VICTOR AGARWAL (Risk Management)

Risk Management, Spelthorne Borough Council, Council Offices, Knowle Green, Staines, TW18 1XB

PLACE OF BIRTH: London, 11.12.73
MARITAL STATUS: Single
COLLEGE: Surrey University Roskide, University of Denmark, University of North Carolina US.
ACADEMIC QUALIFICATIONS: BSc Hons
MEMBERSHIPS: Labour Party
HONOURS/AWARDS: Outstanding Academic Achievement-NCW
HOBBIES AND INTERESTS: To serve the public, travelling, soccer
PERSONAL PROFILE: Victor Agarwal joined the Labour Party at 17, at 18 he became a school governor, at 19 he was elected chairman of governors. At 21 he fought his first election. 1997 he won a by-election and became Britain's youngest councillor. Recently he has been appointed to the board of a 2nd school. All this in Surrey hardly an ethnic minority area.
NOMINATED BY: Dudley Pitcher

MR JAWAHAR LAL AGGARWAL (Opthalmic Surgeon)

Con. Opthalmic Surgeon, Huddersfield Royal Infirmary, 7 The Ghyll, Fixby, Huddersfield, HD2 2FE

PLACE OF BIRTH: India, 10.2.39
MARITAL STATUS: Married
CHILDREN: Two (Nikita, Ajay)
COLLEGE: Medical College Amritsar
PROFESSIONAL QUALIFICATIONS: MBBS, FRCS (Eng), FRCOPATH (Lond), DORCPS (Lond)
MEMBERSHIPS: BMA, European Society of Cataract & Refractive Surgeons
HONOURS/AWARDS: 25 years service to the NHS, C award.
HOBBIES AND INTERESTS: Walking
PERSONAL PROFILE: Arrived England 26 Nov 1964. Worked in various hospitals training in ophthalmology and obtained FRCS from the Royal College of Surgeons, London 1977. Appointed Consultant Ophthalmic Surgeon with special interest in diabetic eye disease at Huddersfield Royal Infirmary in 1978. Published various papers in Ophth. I was a keen sportsman and played football for school and college teams. Present secretary of Yorkshire Indian Society, a Life Member ODA UK and Hindu Cultural Society of Bradford.

MS NEELAM AGGARWAL (Non Executive Director NHS)

Non Executive Director NHS, Hayworth House, 20 Thenford Street, Northampton, NN1 5QT

PLACE OF BIRTH: India, 5.1.59
MARITAL STATUS: Married
CHILDREN: Two (Tina, Seema)
COLLEGE: Meerut University
ACADEMIC QUALIFICATIONS: BA, (Hindi, Sanskrit and Sociology) Personnel Training on Recruitment.. RSA English
DIRECTORSHIPS: Northampton Millennium Park Trust
MEMBERSHIPS: Chair-Indian Hindu Welfare Organisation 1996-to date. Vice-Chair Dostiyo (Asian Women & Girls Org.). Governor Northampton College Board
HONOURS/AWARDS: NHS Non Executive Directorship appointment made by Health Secretary, MP Frank Dobson.
HOBBIES AND INTERESTS: Reading, walking, cooking, talking on various topics
PERSONAL PROFILE: Chair: Indian Hindu Welfare Organisation from 1996 to date. Personnel Committee NREC. Director: Northampton Millennium Park Trust. Governor: Northampton College Board. Vice-Chair: Dostiyo from 1992 to 1995. Northampton Racial Equality Council from 1995 to date. Involved in: Home Office Police Training Scheme: BBC Open University Access course; Running workshops on Hindu culture: teaching cooking; translation and interpretation. Guest speaker.
NOMINATED BY: Anu Ben Vadhana

MR RAJESH AGGARWAL (Music Promoter)

Director, Raj Music, 109 Edison Road, Stafford, ST16 3NH

PLACE OF BIRTH: Kenya, 23.2.58
MARITAL STATUS: Married
CHILDREN: Two (Sohil, Sahil)
COLLEGE: Stafford College
ACADEMIC QUALIFICATIONS: Catering, marketing and computing
PROFESSIONAL QUALIFICATIONS: City & Guilds Catering, Hygience RIPPAH
HOBBIES AND INTERESTS: God, music, humanity, human rights
PERSONAL PROFILE: Have been promoting reggae music for over 10 years. Now promoting TSAGAZA HAB and Israel movements.

MR TITU AHAD (Chef)

Assistant Chef, The Valley Indian Restaurant, The Old Station House, Station Road, Corbridge, NE45 5AY

PLACE OF BIRTH: Bangladesh, 3.10.76
MARITAL STATUS: Single
HOBBIES AND INTERESTS: Wearing and collecting baseball caps
PERSONAL PROFILE: Titu is a young assistant chef at the Valley Restaurant. He heard of the plight of acid burns victims in Bangladesh and decided to run his first half marathon, just 3 weeks later, in their aid. He completed the 13 miles, Great North Run, in under 2 hours and raised over £300.

MR DEEPAL AHANGAMA (Financial Consultant)

Manager-Consultant, Independent Financial Advice Centre Ltd, Colwell House, 39 High Street, Crawley, RH10 1BQ

PLACE OF BIRTH: Sri Lanka, 27.5.54
MARITAL STATUS: Married
CHILDREN: One (Carlene)
COLLEGE: St Thomas' College
ACADEMIC QUALIFICATIONS: GCE's
PROFESSIONAL QUALIFICATIONS: FPC 1,2 & 3
HOBBIES AND INTERESTS: Most sports, travelling, reading & voluntary work with ethnic minority groups.
PERSONAL PROFILE: An independent financial consultant managing a family owned private limited company chaired by his wife Linda. A keen spokesman he is 1st Eleven captain & chairman of Horley Cricket Club which was founded in 1792. He is the honorary treasurer for the Sri Lankan Cricket Board in the UK.

DURGA DASS AHIR JP (Community Advisor)

Councillor-JP, Telford Wrekin Council, 1 Wheatley Crescent, Hadley, Telford, TF1 4PZ

PLACE OF BIRTH: Punjab, 5.6.39
MARITAL STATUS: Married
CHILDREN: Four (Arvind, Anil, Anita, Kalpna)
COLLEGE: Punjab University, Camp College New Delhi
PROFESSIONAL QUALIFICATIONS: Volunteer advice worker, Project supervisor Asian cultural project. Justice of the Peace,
MEMBERSHIPS: Race Equality Forum of Telford and Shropshire, GMB Race Advisory Committee
HONOURS/AWARDS: Award for Excellence 1994-95, West Mercia Constabulary Special Award. Prince of Wales Royal Invitation to St James's Palace.
HOBBIES AND INTERESTS: Political lobbying, attending social functions
PERSONAL PROFILE: Joined NDMC, New Delhi, Clerical 1959-Feb 1962. COD Donnington, Telford, as checker/messenger 1962, GKN Sankey, Telford, as welder 1963, Volunteer advice worker with Asian Cultural Society and with Telford Development Corporation 1985-86. JP 1991.

MR RIAZ AHMAD JP (Accountant)

Riaz Ahmad & Co, Hilton House, 26-28 Hilton Street, Manchester, M1 2EH

PLACE OF BIRTH: Dhoria, 13.6.53
MARITAL STATUS: Married
CHILDREN: Four (Neelam, Hassan, Hussain, Abubakar)
COLLEGE: Huddersfield
PROFESSIONAL QUALIFICATIONS: FCCA
DIRECTORSHIPS: Oldham NHS Trust
MEMBERSHIPS: Oldham Council
HONOURS/AWARDS: Justice of the Peace
HOBBIES AND INTERESTS: Walking, swimming
PERSONAL PROFILE: Magistrate-Oldham, councillor-Oldham MBC, chairman-Environment Service Oldham MBC, director-Oldham NHS Trust

---

'Appointed Consultant Ophthalmic Surgeon with special interest in diabetic eye disease at Huddersfield Royal Infirmary in 1978. Published various papers in Ophth'

JAWAHAR LAL AGGARWAL

CLLR SHAMA AHMAD (Councillor)

London Borough of Newham, Newham Town Hall, East Ham, London, E6 2RP

PLACE OF BIRTH: Pakistan
MARITAL STATUS: Married
COLLEGE: CB Degree College, Pakistan
ACADEMIC QUALIFICATIONS: BA, B Ed
PROFESSIONAL QUALIFICATIONS: Headteacher
MEMBERSHIPS: Labour Party. Chair of Women's Committee, Member of Policy and Resources Committee. Police Consultative Committee
HONOURS/AWARDS: Deputy Mayor 1993/4. Mayor 1996/7
PERSONAL PROFILE: Shama is married to Mahmood Ahmad who is also a councillor in the London Borough of Newham. They became the first Muslim couple to hold elected office together in the United Kingdom. She was elected the first Asian Muslim woman councillor in Newham in 1990. She is very much part of the team that are shaping Newham's future as a place that people will want to live and work in but despite all her success she has not forgotten her roots or the fact that it is the ordinary people who matter in life.

DR SHAMIM IQBAL AHMAD (Senior Lecturer)

University Senior Lecturer, Nottingham Trent University, Department of Life Sciences, Clifton Lane, Nottingham, NG11 8NS

PLACE OF BIRTH: India, 20.12.45
MARITAL STATUS: Married
CHILDREN: Three
ACADEMIC QUALIFICATIONS: BSc, MSc, Ph D
MEMBERSHIPS: European Association Cancer Research. European Soc Photobiol, Biochemistry Society
HOBBIES AND INTERESTS: Photography, creative writing
EMAIL: shamim.ahmad@ntu.ac.uk
PERSONAL PROFILE: Obtained PhD from Leicester University. Carrying out research on cancer of skin and Fancons Anaemia. Developer of anti-fungal agent. Published over 50 papers in scientific journals. Collaborating in research with Russia, US, Holland, France, Germany, Poland and Philippines.

DR SHEIKH RAFI AHMAD (Scientist)

Head of Centre, Centre for Applied Laser Spectroscopy, Monte Rosa, 15 Vicarage Lane, Shrivenham, Swindon, SN6 8DT

PLACE OF BIRTH: Bangladesh, 4.2.44
MARITAL STATUS: Married
CHILDREN: Three (Sakhina, Emma, Tariq)
COLLEGE: Oriel / Oxford
ACADEMIC QUALIFICATIONS: MSc (Dhaka), D.Phil (Oxon)
HOBBIES AND INTERESTS: Reading, travelling, charity work
PERSONAL PROFILE: Internally recognised expertise in the application of laser spectroscopy for both basic research and industrial application. Co-ordinator of two EEC-funded research projects. The research results through various PhD student schemes under Dr Ahmad's supervision are being commercialised (3 patents pending). He has 46 publications which involved collaboration with EU countries, US, Japan and Bangladesh.
NOMINATED BY: Prof F R Hartley, Cranfield University

PROF AKBAR AHMED (Academic Fellow)

Managing Director, QPL (Quiad Project Limited), Selwyn College Cambridge, Cambridge, CB3 9DL

PLACE OF BIRTH: Allahabad, 15.1.43
MARITAL STATUS: Married
CHILDREN: 4 (Amineh, Babar, Umar, Nafees)
COLLEGE: Cambridge
ACADEMIC QUALIFICATIONS: PhD
PROFESSIONAL QUALIFICATIONS: PhD
DIRECTORSHIPS: QPL, MD
MEMBERSHIPS: Oxford and Cambridge Club
HONOURS/AWARDS: Sir Percy Sykes Medal UK, Star of Excellence Pakistan
HOBBIES AND INTERESTS: Travel
PERSONAL PROFILE: Akbar Ahmed launched what became the 'Jinnah Quartet' a decade ago: The Jinnah film (QPL); a documentary Mr Jinnah: The Making of Pakistan; an academic book Jinnah, Pakistan and Islamic Identity: The Search for Saladin, Routledge, London; and a graphic novel The Quaid: Jinnah and the Story of Pakistan, published by Oxford University Press (winner of The President's Award 1998).
NOMINATED BY: Qaisra Shahraz & Mohammed Hussain

MR ANJUM AHMED (Quantitative Analyst)

Manager, Enron Europe Ltd, 40 Grosvenor Place, London, SW1P 3ET

PLACE OF BIRTH: Pakistan, 3.2.71
MARITAL STATUS: Single
COLLEGE: Oxford University
ACADEMIC QUALIFICATIONS: BA, M Eng Hons Degree in 'Engineering & Materials'
PROFESSIONAL QUALIFICATIONS: Securities & Financial Derivatives Representative
MEMBERSHIPS: Old Emanuel Association
HONOURS/AWARDS: Ealing Amateur Playstation Champion
HOBBIES AND INTERESTS: Skiing, mountain-biking, Bruce Springsteen and value investing
EMAIL: aahmad@enron.co.uk
PERSONAL PROFILE: I remain grateful to my parents for bringing me to England as I would not have had such a brilliant education otherwise. England still represents one of the best countries in the world for equality of opportunity. If you want to make it big, you can do it here.

MISS BUSHRA AHMED (Managing Director)

Managing Director, The Legendary Joe Bloggs Inc, Co, The Legendary Building, Bury New Road, Manchester, M8 8FR

PLACE OF BIRTH: Pakistan, 2.2.61
MARITAL STATUS: Single
HOBBIES AND INTERESTS: Go-karting, restaurants, travelling, shopping
EMAIL: joe.bloggs@dial.pipex.com
PERSONAL PROFILE: I currently have two major projects on the go: My continued high profile within Joe Bloggs clothing; Plus management of Sabina, a female artiste. Music has always been a passion of mine, and I aim to achieve the level of success-if not more-that I created with Joe Bloggs.

MR FAROOQ AHMED (Youth Worker)

Chairperson-Coordinator, Khrysalis Youth Committee, South Street, Rochdale, OL16 2EP

PLACE OF BIRTH: Rochdale, 18.7.75
MARITAL STATUS: Married
COLLEGE: West Thames College
ACADEMIC QUALIFICATIONS: BTEC Fashion Design & National Diploma in Constructed Designs
HONOURS/AWARDS: Greater Manchester Young Achiever Award
PERSONAL PROFILE: Otherwise known as MC to everyone. Hectic life assisting charities and fund-raising events in our community, and giving my support to youths to fulfil their goals and ambitions. Helped young talented individuals to become national and international stars. Recently featured on television about my youth work and achievements. Musically, SIN-CHRONIC (Hip-hop band) has been widely recognised, and striving to rock the Millennium.
NOMINATED BY: Luthfa Begum

MR IQBAL AHMED (CEO-Food Processing)

Chairman & Managing Director, Seafood Marketing International Plc, Seamark House, Edge Lane, Droylesden, Manchester, M43 6BB

PLACE OF BIRTH: Bangladesh, 4.8.56
MARITAL STATUS: Married
CHILDREN: Three (Shahida, Manzur, Naheed)
COLLEGE: London
ACADEMIC QUALIFICATIONS: Diploma in Business Management
DIRECTORSHIPS: Seafood Marketing Int Plc, Seafood Marketing (Bangladesh) Ltd
MEMBERSHIPS: Founder Member of Southern Asia Advisory Group, DTI. Royal Oldham Hospital MR Scanner appeal-Life member, Bangladesh Cultural Centre
HONOURS/AWARDS: Businessman of the Year 1999 Bangladesh, British Chamber of Commerce Queen's Award for Export Acheivement-1998 (Seamark)
HOBBIES AND INTERESTS: Family life, various sports, swimming, badminton, squash, tennis, cricket
EMAIL: sales@seamark.co.uk
PERSONAL PROFILE: I came to England in 1971, joining our successful family business, Iqbal Brothers in 1976. I formed Seamark in 1991 to concentrate on seafood processing (mainly shrimps) and the export market. This very successful business received the Queens Award for Export Achievement in 1998.

MR KAZI BILAL AHMED (CLOTHING MANUFACTOR)

Managing Director, Jacob International Ltd, 13 Wicker Street, Stepney, London, E1 1QF

PLACE OF BIRTH: London, 18.11.79
MARITAL STATUS: Single
COLLEGE: Hackney College
ACADEMIC QUALIFICATIONS: O-Levels and GNVQ Certificate
HONOURS/AWARDS: One of the best leading factories in the market
HOBBIES AND INTERESTS: Listening to Hindi music, watching films, socialising with friends, family, close ones
PERSONAL PROFILE: Energetic and qualifying person. Keen, reliable, likes working in a team, can work on my own, under pressure to deadlines. As a managing director I have put a lot of effort into my company by nominating and promoting, its been named one of the leading garments factories in the market trade.

MR KHURSHID AHMED (MANAGING DIRECTOR)

Z-Tex Enterprises Ltd, 59 Lacrosse Avenue, Coppice, Oldham, OL8 4LU

PLACE OF BIRTH: Pakistan, 29.11.58
MARITAL STATUS: Married
CHILDREN: Four (Imran, Razwan, Usman, Arfan)
COLLEGE: Oldham Tech/BIHE
ACADEMIC QUALIFICATIONS: ATI (Association of Textile Institute)
PROFESSIONAL QUALIFICATIONS: ATI
HOBBIES AND INTERESTS: Politics, reading, travelling, exploring the world
PERSONAL PROFILE: I came to the UK in 1970 and completed my secondary education as well as working in a textile mill for five years. Later started own business of manufacturing household soft furnishings employing three people. Today we have grown to a limited company employing forty people with a turnover of two million pounds-hopefully increasing this to five million in the next two years.
NOMINATED BY: Mrs C M Sarcar

MR NASIR AHMED (COMMUNITY WORKER)

President, Bangladesh Islamic Centre & Mosque, 28 George Street, Lozells, Birmingham, B19 1NX

PLACE OF BIRTH: Bangladesh, 3.1.27
MARITAL STATUS: Married
CHILDREN: Six (Nurjahan, Saleh, Afia, Aleya, Amina, Nurunnehar)
COLLEGE: Mongoljonbi High School (Bangladesh)
ACADEMIC QUALIFICATIONS: GCSE's
PROFESSIONAL QUALIFICATIONS: Post Office-porter, hot stamper, restaurant proprietor
DIRECTORSHIPS: Trustee of Bangladesh Welfare Association
HOBBIES AND INTERESTS: Community work
PERSONAL PROFILE: Mr Ahmed has been working for the Bangladesh community since 1957. He was general secretary-Bangladesh Welfare 1983-1991. He is founder of Bangladesh Council 1988 and chairman 1990 -1997. He is founder of Bangladesh Multi-Purpose Centre 1997 and present trustee. He is also the founder of Bangladesh Islamic Centre in Lozells.
NOMINATED BY: Abdul Gofur

LORD NAZIR AHMED (WORKING PEER)

Lord Ahmed of Rotherham, House of Lords, 152 East Bawtry Road, Rotherham, S60 4LG

PLACE OF BIRTH: Kashmir, 24.4.57
MARITAL STATUS: Married
CHILDREN: Three (Marayam, Ahmar, Babar)
COLLEGE: Sheffield
ACADEMIC QUALIFICATIONS: BA Public Admin
DIRECTORSHIPS: Owner of Kilnhurst Business Park, Rotherham
MEMBERSHIPS: Amnesty International, TUC, USDAW, Labour Party
HOBBIES AND INTERESTS: Volleyball
PERSONAL PROFILE: Elected councillor in Rotherham 1990, appointed youngest magistrate in 1992. Founder of National Forum of British Muslim Councillors. Campaigner of Kashmiri right of self determination. Active in shop worker's union. Vice chairman of South Yorks Labour Party, appointed the first Muslim male in the House of Lords on 20th June 1998 and introduced into the House of Lords on 13th Oct 1998.

MR NAZIR AHMED (BARRISTER)

34 Midship Point, The Quarter Deck, London, E14 8SW

PLACE OF BIRTH: Bangladesh, 5.2.71
MARITAL STATUS: Married
CHILDREN: One
COLLEGE: City University, QMW, University of London
ACADEMIC QUALIFICATIONS: LLB Hons Law. Cert LC (London)
PROFESSIONAL QUALIFICATIONS: Barrister-at-Law (Lincoln's Inn)
MEMBERSHIPS: General Council of the Bar. Member of The Law Society, Life Member of the Honourable Society of Lincoln's Inn. JCWI. GMIAU.
HONOURS/AWARDS: Education Board's Scholarship in the HSC exams in Bangladesh
HOBBIES AND INTERESTS: Badminton, historical places, reading, collecting books, helping other people
PERSONAL PROFILE: Besides my studies, I have worked actively to better my community in the East End for the last nine years. To a great extent I made a difference to the lives of people around me. I have held and am still holding various positions in different types of social and community organisations. Associate member Spitalfields Community Association.

CLLR RAJIB AHMED (COUNCILLOR)

London Borough of Tower Hamlets, 21 Arabian House, Ernest Street, London, E1 4SN

PLACE OF BIRTH: Bangladesh, 7.6.62
MARITAL STATUS: Married
CHILDREN: Two (Robi, Rejwana)
DIRECTORSHIPS: Tower Hamlets Citizens Advice Bureau
MEMBERSHIPS: Amnesty International, Labour Party, Bengali Literary Society
HOBBIES AND INTERESTS: Music, drama, gardening, helping vulnerables, meeting people, politics
PERSONAL PROFILE: Long-standing community activist, singer, drama artist, write poems in Bengali, elected councillor, kind, sympathetic, polite, caring, responsible, passionate, energetic, honest, reliable, loving, community leader, achiever, human rights activist, well known within the community.

SARWAR AHMED (PUBLISHER)

Ethnic Media Group, 148 Cambridge Heath Road, London E1 5QJ

PLACE OF BIRTH: Keighly, West Yorks. 9.7.71
MARITAL STATUS: Married
CHILDREN: Two (Imaan, Indiya)
MEMBERSHIPS: Sits on the Newspaper Panel of the Competition Commission, formerly known as the Monopolies and Mergers Commission
PERSONAL PROFILE: Launched Eastern Eye newspaper with his brother Sarz in 1989. Currently publisher of Ethnic Media Group, which produces the weekly titles Eastern Eye, Asian Times, Caribbean Times and New Nation, along with the quarterly magazine Asian Wedding and the annual list of Britain's Richest Asian 200.

SARZ AHMED (PUBLISHER)

Surma Newsweekly, 40 Wessex Street, London E1OLB

PLACE OF BIRTH: Keighly, West Yorks. 9.4.69
MARITAL STATUS: Married
CHILDREN: One (Adil)
ACADEMIC QUALIFICATIONS: BA in Media
MEMBERSHIPS: Sylheti-Londoni Partnership
HOBBIES AND INTERESTS: Football, cinema
PERSONAL PROFILE: Founded Eastern Eye newspaper with his brother Sarwar in November 1989. Publishes Surma, Britain's largest selling Bengali newspaper.

Elected councillor in Rotherham 1990, appointed youngest magistrate in 1992. Founder of National Forum of British Muslim Councillors

LORD NAZIR ALI

MR SHAFI UDDIN ABUL HASNAT AHMED
(MARINE SURVEYOR-RTD)

Poet, Author, Researcher, Oaktown Publications, 100 Western Avenue, East Acton, London, W3 7TX

PLACE OF BIRTH: Bangladesh, 1.1.37
MARITAL STATUS: Married
CHILDREN: Two (Hasnat Rafi Uddin, Meraz Ali)
COLLEGE: R.N. Dockyard College, UL, O/U
ACADEMIC QUALIFICATIONS: LL.B Hons, BA Hons; Degree in Marine / Mechanical Engineering
PROFESSIONAL QUALIFICATIONS: Extra First Class DOT Certificate, Chartered Engineer (C.Eng), European Engineer (EUR Ing)
MEMBERSHIPS: Fellow of Institute of Marine Engineer's, Mathematical Association; Bengali Literary Society
HONOURS/AWARDS: Listed in Marquis' Who's Who in the World 1996; Inst of Marine Engineers, Silver Medal 1970
HOBBIES AND INTERESTS: Poetry, literature, science and mathematics, writing, research, publication
PERSONAL PROFILE: Ex-Merchant navy engineer officer. Service with UK DOT as marine and principal marine surveyor 25 years. IMO adviser to Bangladesh 1980-82. Publications; Absolute Theory of Universe; Tagore's Eleven; Fermat's Last Theorem Provided. Peterloo poetry award. Distinguished poet award. Listed in: Who's Who in the World 1996 and Who's Who in Engineering and Science 1998.

MR SHAMI AHMED (CHIEF EXECUTIVE)

Chief Executive, The Legendary Joe Bloggs Incorporated Co, The Legendary Building, Bury New Road, Manchester, M8 8FR

PLACE OF BIRTH: Pakistan, 7.7.62
MARITAL STATUS: Married
ACADEMIC QUALIFICATIONS: Honorary Fellowship at Lancashire Polytechnic, 1991
HOBBIES AND INTERESTS: Working out, eating out, cinema
EMAIL: joe.bloggs@dial.pipex.com
PERSONAL PROFILE: I started in business at the age of 14, buying for my family's wholesalers. Following that I built up the Joe Bloggs empire within 10 years and it is still growing! I am now the proud owner of a property company, plus eight other companies, including Gabicci and Elizabeth Emmanuel.
NOMINATED BY: University of Central Lancashire

CLLR SHAUKAT AHMED (LOCAL GOVT OFFICER)

Councillor, Bradford City Council, 21 The Boundary, off Allerton Road, Bradford, BD8 0BQ

PLACE OF BIRTH: Bangladesh, 5.11.55
MARITAL STATUS: Married
CHILDREN: Two (Suhail, Maeesha)
COLLEGE: Leeds University
ACADEMIC QUALIFICATIONS: BSc Hons
DIRECTORSHIPS: Moghuls of India Ltd
MEMBERSHIPS: MIEE
HOBBIES AND INTERESTS: Badminton, cards, cooking
PERSONAL PROFILE: Political activist, founder chair of Manningham Housing Association. Founder of Bangladeshi Youth Organisation. Member of Labour Party for 20 years and serving as councillor for eight years. Currently chair of Regeneration Board (M&G) work for Leeds City Council. Also involved in civil rights campaign. Hope to be a member of parliament soon.

MR SHOFI AHMED (SCIENTIST-POET)

Editor, Planet East, 15 Ronalds Road, London, N5 1XF

PLACE OF BIRTH: Bangladesh, 18.5.71
MARITAL STATUS: Married
CHILDREN: One (Zohura)
MEMBERSHIPS: International News Syndicate
HONOURS/AWARDS: 1995 Daily Telegraph, Young Science Writer
HOBBIES AND INTERESTS: Badminton
PERSONAL PROFILE: A poet and award winning scientist. His book 'Reason and the Origin' has been hailed by the Royal Society's SCAN magazine for combining the art of literature with the disipline of science. He is a winner of the Daily Telegraph's National Science Writer Competition in 1995. His wife's name is Ayesha

> ## Dedicated family man who is passionate about health and fitness and is an expert commentator on life
>
> **THUFAYEL AHMED**

SYED SHAHED AHMED (RESTAURATEUR)

Proprietor, Bengal Brasserie, 79 Springbank Road, Hither Green, London, SE13 6SS

PLACE OF BIRTH: Sylhet, 17.4.69
MARITAL STATUS: Married
CHILDREN: Two (Ejjaz, Rayma)
HONOURS/AWARDS: British Curry Award. High Commissioner's Thanks for charity work
HOBBIES AND INTERESTS: Cinema, squash
PERSONAL PROFILE: Owner of two restaurants and two houses freehold. Came to this country 1985 and worked in a restaurant for only five years to begin with, then set up my own with two other business partners. Now sole owner.

THUFAYEL AHMED (DIRECTOR)

40 Wessex Street, London E2 0LB

PLACE OF BIRTH: Keighly, West Yorks. 5.6.67
MARITAL STATUS: Married
CHILDREN: Three, Neelam, Jerin, Adam
MEMBERSHIPS: Curry-eaters guide, Newspaper Society, Editorial board Surma newspaper.
PERSONAL PROFILE: Popular columnist in Eastern Eye since November 89. Founder member of the Sylheti-Londoni Partnership. Dedicated family man who is passionate about health and fitness and is an expert commentator on life.

MRS ZAKIA MASUD AHMED (COMMUNITY DEV. WORKER)

Project Worker, Pakistan Women Association, 14 Eskdale Close, Penylon, Cardiff, CF2 5LF

PLACE OF BIRTH: Pakistan, 3.3.43
MARITAL STATUS: Married
CHILDREN: Four (Alveena, Almeera, Kashif, Almeena)
COLLEGE: Punjab University
ACADEMIC QUALIFICATIONS: Bachelor of Arts
MEMBERSHIPS: SCCD Mewn Cymru. Black volunteer sector of Wales (Network).
HOBBIES AND INTERESTS: Helping others organising social and cultural events
PERSONAL PROFILE: I have been committed to raising the profile of Asian women in Wales for past 27 years. During this time I have achieved setting up the first 'Women Only' centre in Wales catering for the need's of minority ethnic communities. Currently I am chair of Pakistan Women Association. President of Pakistan Educational and Cultural Association, chair of Asian Cultural Association.

MR KOOAVOOR RAMACHANDRA AITHAL
(ARCHITECT-ENGINEER)

Managing Director, KRA Designs Limited, 69 Mount Road, Penn, Wolverhampton, WV4 5SS

PLACE OF BIRTH: India, 13.9.37
MARITAL STATUS: Married
CHILDREN: Three (Anand, VIttal, Vinod)
COLLEGE: Mysore University, India
ACADEMIC QUALIFICATIONS: BE (Civil), GD Arch
PROFESSIONAL QUALIFICATIONS: Fellow of the Indian Institute of Architects, Graduate-The Institution of Structual Engineers
DIRECTORSHIPS: Company Director (KRA Designs)
HOBBIES AND INTERESTS: Reading, travel, crosswords
EMAIL: ram.aithal@dial.pipex.com
PERSONAL PROFILE: Educated in Mysore and Bombay. Specialist in timber engineering and housing. Member-BSI Code Committees for 10 years. Magistrate since 1980. Member-Lord Chancellor's advisory committee since 1990. Mental Health Act-manager since 1995. Lay member-Lord Chancellors interviewing panel. Advisor (design) for many Hindu and Sikh temples in the UK.

MR ALI AKBAR (ACCOUNTANT)

Manager-Treasurer, Shah Jalal Bangla School, 22 Kimberley Road, Penylan, Cardiff, CF2 5DH

PLACE OF BIRTH: Bangladesh, 26.11.62
MARITAL STATUS: Married (Jasmin)
CHILDREN: Three (Shahana, Shabana, Javed)
COLLEGE: Sheffield
ACADEMIC QUALIFICATIONS: Maths
PROFESSIONAL QUALIFICATIONS: Business
MEMBERSHIPS: Wales Educational Board. Cardiff first Race Equality. Cardiff Action, local community group.
HONOURS/AWARDS: Letter from HM Queen for work with the community.
HOBBIES AND INTERESTS: Football, travel, meeting and helping people
PERSONAL PROFILE: I am a businessman. I came to this country in 1975 with my parents. Been living in Cardiff for the past 20 years. I give my free time to our community for education, language and English.

CLLR JAMIL AKHTAR JP (JUSTICE OF THE PEACE)

Councillor (Chair of Housing), Kirklees Metropolitan Council, Crown Court Buildings, Princess Street, Huddersfield, HD1 2TT

PLACE OF BIRTH: Pakistan
MARITAL STATUS: Married
CHILDREN: Three (Naveed, Sidrah, Hasib)
MEMBERSHIPS: Labour Party, Transport & General Workers Union

PERSONAL PROFILE: Magistrate for the last 14 years and Labour councillor for 11 years. Previously chair of Highways and Transport Committee, present Chair of Housing Committee for three years and chair of Housing Task Force for Yorkshire and Humberside Regional Assembly. Member of West Yorkshire Valuation Tribunal. I was the first Black councillor elected in Kirklees.

PROF MUHAMMAD AKHTAR (UNIVERSITY PROFESSOR)

Emeritus Prof of Biochemistry, University of Southampton, Bassett Crescent East, Southampton, SO16 7PX

PLACE OF BIRTH: India, 23.2.33
MARITAL STATUS: Married
CHILDREN: Two (Marcus Imran, Daniel Azeem)
COLLEGE: University of Punjab, Pakistan, Imperial College, University of London
ACADEMIC QUALIFICATIONS: BSc, MSc (Gold Medalllist), PHd DIC
PROFESSIONAL QUALIFICATIONS: Research scientist, Senior lecturer,
DIRECTORSHIPS: Chairman, Institute of Biomolecular Sciences, Director SERC Molecular Recognition Centre
MEMBERSHIPS: Fellow Royal Society, Founding Fellow Third World Academy of Sciences
HONOURS/AWARDS: Third World Academy of Sciences Medal Lecturer. Royal Society of Chemistry Flintoff Medal
PERSONAL PROFILE: A Fellow of the Royal Society and one of the most eminent scientists in the UK. Through a symbiosis of chemical and biochemical knowledge he has contributed to diverse areas, for example; enzyme mechanisms, synthesis and biosynthesis of steroids and porphyrins, biochemistry of vision, and genetic and mechanistic aspects of the biosynthesis of antibiotics. A member of several professional bodies, he is actively involved in international scientific affairs through the Third World Academy of Sciences, of which he is a Founding Fellow.
NOMINATED BY: A J Strike, University Of Southampton

MS SHAMIN AKHTAR (ASSISTANT DIRECTOR)

Assistant Director, Lothian Equal Access Progs for Schools, 58 George Squares, Edinburgh, EH8 9JU

DATE OF BIRTH: 25.5.72
MARITAL STATUS: Single
COLLEGE: University of Abertay, Dundee
ACADEMIC QUALIFICATIONS: BSc Hons, Biotechnology
DIRECTORSHIPS: President NUS Scotland 1997-1998
MEMBERSHIPS: ACTSA (Action for Southern Africa), MSF, Labour Party
HOBBIES AND INTERESTS: Listening to music, travelling, women's Issues, anti-racism
PERSONAL PROFILE: Shamin has continually managed to achieve her goals and ambitions. She was the first Black president of NUS Scotland and now works on a pioneering access to higher education project putting her principles into action. All who know her respect her for her dedication, compassion, good humour and loyalty.
NOMINATED BY: Fraser Stewart

MS SIDDIQUA AKHTAR (ACTRESS-COMEDIENNE)

Mahoney Gretton Associates, Fulham, London

PLACE OF BIRTH: Chelsea
MARITAL STATUS: Cough, Cough !!
COLLEGE: Exeter University
ACADEMIC QUALIFICATIONS: BA Hons Eng / Drama (3 A-Levels, 11 O-Levels)
MEMBERSHIPS: Equity Member
HOBBIES AND INTERESTS: Cycling, reading, anyone on the planet funnier than Sanjeev Bhasker
PERSONAL PROFILE: Constantly mistaken for Meera Syal, I am campaigning to have free eye tests for the Asian community, yet also considering changing my name by deed poll to Mirror Syal. I would rather die than dare become a doctor (my mother's wish) but knowing my luck I would be the doctor who had to try and save my life.

MISS TASLEEM AKHTAR (STUDENT)

Liverpool John Moores University,

PLACE OF BIRTH: Yorkshire, 7.8.70
MARITAL STATUS: Single
COLLEGE: Liverpool John Moores University
ACADEMIC QUALIFICATIONS: Currently studying applied community studies BA Hons
MEMBERSHIPS: Elected-Nat. Union of Student Services Ltd. (NUS)
HOBBIES AND INTERESTS: Politics, media
PERSONAL PROFILE: Tasleem is currently in her final year studying, for the last two years, she was elected as a Sabbatical Officer. Firstly, as the equal opportunities officer and the following year as the first female and first Asian president of her university. The future - a placement at Mersey Television Co. and also an offer of an internship at MS magazine in New York, US.
NOMINATED BY: Alison Wild, Liverpool John Moores Uni

MOHD JAHANGIR ALAM (MANAGEMENT CONSULTANT)

Management Consultant, Bangladeshies for Equal Rights, 95 Waldronsmoor, Kingsheath, Birmingham, B14 6RT

PLACE OF BIRTH: Bangladesh, 1.3.49
MARITAL STATUS: Married
COLLEGE: Ruskin College, Oxford
ACADEMIC QUALIFICATIONS: BA (Hon), CQSW
PROFESSIONAL QUALIFICATIONS: Mlmgt. MICSE
DIRECTORSHIPS: Shalifidal Housing Co-operatives
MEMBERSHIPS: Association of Asian Social Workers UK, Bangladesh Council, CPAG,
HONOURS/AWARDS: Merit award by Cambridge Biographical Society
HOBBIES AND INTERESTS: Current affairs, campaigning to establish equality, swimming, badminton, wining, dining
PERSONAL PROFILE: Mr Alam is well known nationally amongst Asian communities in UK, particularly Bangladesh communities, for his tireless campaigning work on employment, training, housing and education on the basis of equality. He is the first Asian in the country to become a Labour deputy leader in 1986. He also contested the parliamentary seat of Bethnal Green in 1987, which he lost by three votes to Peter Shore to be selected . He is a founder member of many Asian organisations and leading light in Labour politics.

MR SAGHIR ALAM (COMMERCIAL LITIGATOR)

Commercial Litigation, Kashmir Educational & Cultural Development Trust, Gilharo & Co Solicitors, 31-33 Doncaster gate, Rotherham, S65 1DF

PLACE OF BIRTH: Rotherham, 9.10.69
MARITAL STATUS: Married
CHILDREN: One (Hasan Alam)
COLLEGE: Nottingham
ACADEMIC QUALIFICATIONS: Business, LLB Hons Degree
PROFESSIONAL QUALIFICATIONS: Studied legal practice course
DIRECTORSHIPS: Chief Executive, Kashmir Trust
MEMBERSHIPS: Chamber-TEC Council, Community Health Council
HONOURS/AWARDS: Youth Awards, Cutler Awards
HOBBIES AND INTERESTS: Squash, outdoor sports, reading, business
PERSONAL PROFILE: Working for a long established firm of solicitors. Specialising in commercial litigation. Chief Executive of Kashmir Trust. Chair of Business Enterprise Board. Elected member of Chamber of Commerce Training Enterprise Council. Member of local government committee and Rotherham Community Health Council making major contribution to the local community and businesses
NOMINATED BY: Arshad Ali-Chairperson Employment Committee

DR SYED ALAUDDIN (MANAGEMENT CONSULTANT)

Director, Federation of Afro-Asian Association UK (FAA), 25 Sunnybank Road, Manchester, M13 0XF

PLACE OF BIRTH: India, 18.4.33
MARITAL STATUS: Married
CHILDREN: Two (Taz Syed, Syeda Luna Tamannah)
COLLEGE: St Andrews Manchester University, Thomas Jefferson and TIU in US
PROFESSIONAL QUALIFICATIONS: MSc, MEd, LLM, PhD, ABAA, AFCS, FIMA, FBIM
DIRECTORSHIPS: FAA
PERSONAL PROFILE: President, Afro Asian Society, Manchester (1969) President, NSPCC, Longsight Area; Hon Secretary, Manchester Council for Voluntary Service; parliamentary candidate-Central Constituency, Manchester (1979) Stretford (1983). President, Federation of Afro-Asian Associations (UK); fought in the liberation movements of British India and Bangladesh.
NOMINATED BY: Dr Shafiq Rehman

MR AMIN ALI (Managing Director)

The Red Fort, 77 Dean Street, London, W1V 5HA

PLACE OF BIRTH: Bangladesh
CHILDREN: Four
DIRECTORSHIPS: Soho Spice, Raisechance Ltd, Red Fort, Introplan Ltd, Busabank Ltd
PERSONAL PROFILE: Vanguard of the movement to create up market, stylistic Indian restaurants. Pioneer of many advances in how we appreciate Indian food today. Creator of Britain's most acclaimed and high profile restaurants, including 'The Red Fort' and 'Soho Spice'. Role model to many in the Bangladeshi community as a result of his charity, political and community work (co-founder and gen secretary, Bengali Workers Action Group; Sponsor, One World Action; Campaigner for Labour Party to target ethnic vote).

MR AYUB KOROM ALI (Local Govt Officer)

Head of Community Languages, London Borough of Tower Hamlets, 60A Latimar Road, Forest Gate, London, E7 0LN

PLACE OF BIRTH: Bangladesh, 4.2.61
MARITAL STATUS: Married
CHILDREN: Two (Samin Ahbab, Tanzim Absar)
COLLEGE: Ruskin College, Oxford University, Brunel University
ACADEMIC QUALIFICATIONS: MA, CQSW
PROFESSIONAL QUALIFICATIONS: CQSW
DIRECTORSHIPS: Non Executive Director, Newham Community Health
MEMBERSHIPS: NHS Trust. Labour Party
HOBBIES AND INTERESTS: Badminton, travelling, politics
EMAIL: aybil@yahoo.com
PERSONAL PROFILE: Since leaving university I have been an active member of the Labour Party. I am currently chair of my local branch-a post I have held for the last three years. I have also led a number of voluntary organisations-mainly working for the BD community. Presently I am secretary of UK BD Education Trust and GLBA.
NOMINATED BY: Shofi Ahmed, YGF

ENAM ALI (Restaurateur)

Proprietor, Le Raj, 211 Firtree Road, Epsom Downs, KT17 3LB

PLACE OF BIRTH: Bangladesh, 1.12.61
MARITAL STATUS: Married
CHILDREN: Three (Rumana , Muhaiman, Jahid)
COLLEGE: North East, Surrey College
ACADEMIC QUALIFICATIONS: BA
PROFESSIONAL QUALIFICATIONS: Consultant and lecturer for catering industry
DIRECTORSHIPS: Director of International Affairs (British Bangladesh Chamber of Commerce)
MEMBERSHIPS: FSB
HONOURS/AWARDS: Personality of the Year 1998, Restaurant of the Year 1992
HOBBIES AND INTERESTS: Flying, cricket, current affairs, designing
WEB SITE: www.leraj.com
PERSONAL PROFILE: Founder and chairman of the Guild of Bangladesh Restaurateurs, Founder of Dine Bangladeshi Campaign-to highlight the identity of 85% of the restaurant industry for the first time as Bangladeshi. Rather than the blanket term-Indian. Pioneer of worlds first flying restaurant.

MR MASHAHID ALI (Restaurant Manager)

Manager, Anondho Dara Newport Bengali Youth Organisation, 15 Harrow Road, Newport, NP9 0BU

PLACE OF BIRTH: Bangladesh, 2.1.72
MARITAL STATUS: Married
CHILDREN: Two (Hamid, Salma)
COLLEGE: Nash Campus
ACADEMIC QUALIFICATIONS: GCSE, A-Level pass
MEMBERSHIPS: Chairman (Anondho Dhara Newport)
HOBBIES AND INTERESTS: Reading, computer, spending time with my children, community work and events
PERSONAL PROFILE: Anondho Dhara established since 1995, I am the chairman, it gives me great pleasure to represent the Bengali youth organisation. I am a family man. I like to help others by helping to organise mela, cultural shows, sports events and recently the flood appeal raising plenty of money for the victims in Bangladesh. I am also a voluntary correspondent for the local paper 'Argus'.
NOMINATED BY: Mr Mahmud Ali Shah

DR MOHAMMED ALI (Economic Dev. Specialist)

Chief Executive, QED, West Bowling Centre, Clipstone Street, Bradford, BD5 8EA

PLACE OF BIRTH: Pakistan, 15.8.56
MARITAL STATUS: Married
CHILDREN: 4 (Nazia, Saira, Asif, Nasir)
COLLEGE: Bradford
ACADEMIC QUALIFICATIONS: BSc (Hon) D BA
DIRECTORSHIPS: Pukaar Foundation, Quest Recruitment. Bradford Chamber of Commerce and Industry
MEMBERSHIPS: Institute of Directors, Institute of Management
HONOURS/AWARDS: Honorary Doctorate for work with Asian communities.
HOBBIES AND INTERESTS: Reading, current affairs, charity work
EMAIL: M.ali@qed-limited.demon.co.uk
PERSONAL PROFILE: Born in Pakistan, came to UK at the age of 13. First ten years spent getting education. Next ten working in private, public and national voluntary organisations. In 1990 set up QED, now a national leading organisation which aims to improve economic circumstances for ethnic groups mainly targeting Asian communities. In 1997 was awarded Honorary Doctorate by University of Bradford for work with Asian communities.
NOMINATED BY: Harjap Singh Pooni and Phil Ward

MR NASIM ALI (Youth Worker)

Youth Team Manager, Kings Cross & Brunswick Neighbourhood Association, Marchmont Centre, 62 Marchmont Street, London, WC1N 1AB

PLACE OF BIRTH: Bangladesh, 7.2.69
MARITAL STATUS: Single
COLLEGE: University of Kent
ACADEMIC QUALIFICATIONS: Dip He in Informal and Community Education
PROFESSIONAL QUALIFICATIONS: BA in Informal and Community Education
DIRECTORSHIPS: Kings Cross Partnership
HONOURS/AWARDS: BURA, CRE Local Authority Race Award
HOBBIES AND INTERESTS: Football, supporting the community
EMAIL: kcbna@aol.com
PERSONAL PROFILE: A very experienced youth worker who's innovative work has received various awards nationally and locally. My work has helped to unite conflict Bengali and white youths. Last year I was awarded the Camden Good Citizen award for my contribution to youth work in Camden.
NOMINATED BY: Shamsir Islam

MR ROOFUL AMIN ALI (Chartered Accountancy)

Trainee Chartered Accountant, Grant Thornton Chartered Accountants, 109 Midland Road, Welingborough, NN8 1LU

PLACE OF BIRTH: Sheffied, 30.4.73
MARITAL STATUS: Single
COLLEGE: University of Sheffield
ACADEMIC QUALIFICATIONS: BA Hons Accounting & Fin Mgmt Class:2.1. 3 A-levels. 9 GCSEs
PROFESSIONAL QUALIFICATIONS: Assoc. of Chartered Accountants
MEMBERSHIPS: Windsor Fellowship. Wellingborough Mosque Executive Cttee
HONOURS/AWARDS: Won competition for design of a one off football stripe for Adidas
HOBBIES AND INTERESTS: Art and design, football, music
PERSONAL PROFILE: A 'Creative Accountant'-Whilst training as a chartered accountant with Grant Thornton, he has conveyed a penchant for artistic flair, producing numerous pieces of artwork. He attended Sheffield University, thereby defying national statistics which portray Bangladeshis as 'low achievers'. His 'work ethic' provides inspiration to his brothers and local Islamic community.

MR SHIPU ALI (Student)

The Clubhouse, 141 Cleveland Street, London, W1P 5PH

PLACE OF BIRTH: London, 28.7.83
MARITAL STATUS: Single
COLLEGE: Holloway School
ACADEMIC QUALIFICATIONS: Doing GCSEs
PROFESSIONAL QUALIFICATIONS: FA Junior team managers course and basic first aid
HOBBIES AND INTERESTS: I like playing football, pool, snooker, reading books
PERSONAL PROFILE: I manage a local youth club football team aged between 11-14 years old. The youth club organises many activities as well as sports. I work as a volunteer on Monday and Wednesday evenings in the youth club. Our training sessions are open to any local young people.
NOMINATED BY: Ash Rahman

MR SURUZ ALI (Restaurant Manager)

Lalbagh Indian Restaurant, 31 Leopold Road, Coventry, CV1 5BL

PLACE OF BIRTH: Bangladesh, 1.1.55
MARITAL STATUS: Married
CHILDREN: Five (Dabir, Kabir, Dilwar, Anwar Hussain, Farhana Begum)
COLLEGE: Basic
ACADEMIC QUALIFICATIONS: Restaurant Manager
HOBBIES AND INTERESTS: Sports

MR SYED HASAN ALI (Manager)

Maksyed Indian Takeaway, 56 Thursby Road, Burnley, BB10 3DF

PLACE OF BIRTH: Bangladesh, 15.4.76
MARITAL STATUS: Married
CHILDREN: 1 (Syed Shaheen)
COLLEGE: Burnley College
MEMBERSHIPS: Goroforum Party
HONOURS/AWARDS: Army Youth Club
HOBBIES AND INTERESTS: Shooting, body-building
PERSONAL PROFILE: I am Asian, Sunni Muslim, Bengali, married with a child son, I have worked my way up to become a respected manager of a takeaway, I have worked so hard, I've worked with the English and the Asian community. The main thing I want to say is 'Life is short make the most of it'.
NOMINATED BY: Syed Husain Ali

MRS SAMEENA SAIF ALI-KHAN (Producer-Presenter)

Journalism, BBC, 26 Hilary Avenue, Heald Green, Stockport, SK8 3AF

PLACE OF BIRTH: Manchester, 30.12.68
MARITAL STATUS: Married
CHILDREN: One (Dhanyal Aamir)
COLLEGE: Salford University
ACADEMIC QUALIFICATIONS: BSc Physiology / Chem. MA TV Features & TV Documentary Production
HONOURS/AWARDS: Certificate of Thanks from Islamic Relief
HOBBIES AND INTERESTS: Drama, reading, fashion, music, travel
PERSONAL PROFILE: Produced / presented first youth radio programme for Asians in Manchester in 1991. Produced an hour long radio documentary for BBC to commemorate India and Pakistan Jubilee Independence called "From Curypot to Hotpot-50 years of change for Lancashire's Asians". Now produce and present the Asian Groove, youth programme with a difference! and Asian Word-a twice weekly news and current affairs programme.

MR SHAFIQ ALIM (Restaurateur)

Owner/Chef, Masaledar Restaurant, 121 Upper Tooting Road, Tooting, London, SW17

PLACE OF BIRTH: Tanzania, 21.9.66
MARITAL STATUS: Single
COLLEGE: University of London
ACADEMIC QUALIFICATIONS: Ext, Reading Law
HOBBIES AND INTERESTS: Squash, hockey, poetry
PERSONAL PROFILE: Born in 1966 in Tanzania emigrated to Bihar, India in 1974. Arrived London in 1980. He could not speak English. Through evening classes and self teaching he is presently preparing for his LLB finals, running a successful restaurant, working on two books and possible TV show.
NOMINATED BY: Ushma Vyas

MR ELMO ALLES (Ornithologist)

Ecotourist Consultant, 4 Nylands Avenue, Kew, Richmond, TW9 4HH

PLACE OF BIRTH: Sri Lanka, 7.7.36
MARITAL STATUS: Married
CHILDREN: Four (Nadhini, Pradeep, Enakshi, Anusha)
COLLEGE: City of Westminster
ACADEMIC QUALIFICATIONS: Degree
PROFESSIONAL QUALIFICATIONS: Management
DIRECTORSHIPS: Edgecourt Holdings
MEMBERSHIPS: Birdlife International, Oriental Bird Club
HOBBIES AND INTERESTS: Conservation
EMAIL: 114312.3477@compuserve.com
PERSONAL PROFILE: Voluntary forest warden RSPB. President SLNHS. Member-National Geographic Society US.

CLLR SOYFUL ALOM (Community Worker)

Director, Tower Hamlets Council, 31 Avis Square, Stepney, London, E1 0QD

PLACE OF BIRTH: Bangladesh, 20.10.60
MARITAL STATUS: Married
CHILDREN: Four (Ansar, Kamral, Tasneem, Zibrit)
COLLEGE: Guildhall University
ACADEMIC QUALIFICATIONS: BA
MEMBERSHIPS: Labour Party, Co-op and SEA

MR PRAVINBHAI N AMIN (Highway Design Manager)

Borough of Royal Kingston, Directorate of Environmental Services, Guildhall, Kingston Upon Thames, KT1 1EU

PLACE OF BIRTH: Kenya
DIRECTORSHIPS: National President of National Association of Patidar Samaj, President of Sardar Patel Memorial Society UK
MEMBERSHIPS: Advisory Council Member of Vallabh Nidhi, Wembley, Vice president of Vaso Nagrik Mandal
HONOURS/AWARDS: Mayor's award
HOBBIES AND INTERESTS: Cricket, golf
PERSONAL PROFILE: Pravinbhai N Amin was born in Kenya and graduated as a civil engineer in Kenya. He arrived in the UK in 1966 and joined John Mowlem & Co. and was involved in projects like, Blackwall Northern Approach, London Bridge, Tilbury Docks Development etc. His contribution in the development, design and implementation of Kingston Town Centre relief road won him a mayor's award.
NOMINATED BY: Kanoobhai Desai

MR TARIQ AMIN (Managing Director)

Amin Poultry Ltd, 83 Featherstall Road North, Westwood, Oldham, OL9 6QB

PLACE OF BIRTH: Pakistan, 21.1.52
MARITAL STATUS: Married
CHILDREN: Three (Adil, Tabassum, Hasin)
COLLEGE: Self taught
ACADEMIC QUALIFICATIONS: Management & Marketing Skills
DIRECTORSHIPS: Director of Oldham Chamber of Commerce
MEMBERSHIPS: Member of Oldham Partnership Board (Oldham Council)
HONOURS/AWARDS: Westwood Business Man of the Year
HOBBIES AND INTERESTS: Charitable work including the Asian scanner appeal
PERSONAL PROFILE: Founder member and chairman of the Asian Business Association in Oldham. Successful businessman. Market leader in Halal poultry in the North West. Involved in charitable work, member of the Royal Oldham Asian Scanner Appeal Committee. 1999 sees further expansion of the company moving to a purpose-built 5000sq. ft premises.
NOMINATED BY: Kaushif Asfal and Fozia Amin

Creator of Britain's most acclaimed and high profile restaurants, including 'The Red Fort' and 'Soho Spice'

AMIN ALI

Successful businessman. Market leader in Halal poultry in the North West. Involved in charitable work, member of the Royal Oldham Asian Scanner Appeal Committee

TARIQ AMIN

MR AMIT (Music Producer)

HONOURS/AWARDS: 1993 & 1995' No 1 Night club dj's (London)
HOBBIES AND INTERESTS: Music, rapping
PERSONAL PROFILE: Amit has been involved in the Asian Dj scene since 1982. Amit began dee-jaying at the age of 14. He was the youngest ever to Dj at the world renowned Hippodrome at the age of 17. While being an active member of X-Zecutive, Amit formed his Dj/rap crew 'Badd Company.' Amit split from X-Zecutive in 1996 and is now concentrating on the Dj side of things with Badd Company.

MRS YASHWANTI C AMLANI MBE
(Project Development Officer)

Project Development Officer, Asian Cultural Consultant, Flat 2, 5 Beaufort Road, Bristol, BS8 2JT

PLACE OF BIRTH: Kenya, 20.2.39
MARITAL STATUS: Married
CHILDREN: Two (Anand, Cheitanya)
COLLEGE: Pitmans College
ACADEMIC QUALIFICATIONS: Secretary Asian Consultant
MEMBERSHIPS: Hindu Temple / Patron, Mahatma Gandhi Foundation
HONOURS/AWARDS: Interfaith. MBE (1997) Mother India International Award (1992)
HOBBIES AND INTERESTS: Reading, walking, nature, badminton, meeting people
PERSONAL PROFILE: She is at present involved in Ayurvedic herbal help for cancer, developing work with the homeless, and working on educational resource book "Ramayan" for children with a different perspective all together. She is a voluntary co-ordinator and editor of community magazine "Gaurav".

MR MOHAMMED AMRAN (Commissioner CRE)

Commission For Racial Equality, Elliott House, 10-12 Allington Street, London, SW1E 5EH

PLACE OF BIRTH: Pakistan, 20.11.75
MARITAL STATUS: Single
ACADEMIC QUALIFICATIONS: BTEC First (Health & Social Care), BTEC National (Public Service)
PROFESSIONAL QUALIFICATIONS: Dip / HE, Youth and Community Worker
HOBBIES AND INTERESTS: Football and community work
PERSONAL PROFILE: I am a young person who has achieved so much at a young age. I have graduated as a youth and community worker and a commissioner of CRE. I have been involved in voluntary community work for the last five years. I have worked and helped the young and elderly, able and disabled.
NOMINATED BY: Asam Javed

MS ANITA ANAND (Journalist)

Head of Local Programming, Zee TV, Unit 7-9, Belvue Business Centre, Belvue Road, Northolt, UB5 5QQ

PLACE OF BIRTH: London, 28.4.72
MARITAL STATUS: Single
COLLEGE: Kings College London
ACADEMIC QUALIFICATIONS: BA Hons, Fellow at the RSA
HONOURS/AWARDS: English Speaking Union national champion. ESU Scholarship winner
HOBBIES AND INTERESTS: Reading, cooking, poetry, my cat!
EMAIL: anita.anand@zeetv.co.uk
PERSONAL PROFILE: Anita Anand has worked in the field of television journalism for almost eight years. She is also a regular contributor to radio and has been a columnist for India Today magazine and Asian Age newspaper. She has recently been appointed Head of Local Programming for Zee TV.

> 'Anand Associates was sponsor of Britain's Richest 200 Asians' magazine 1998, sharing the platform at the launch ceremony with Prime Minister Tony Blair'
>
> **BHUPINDER ANAND**

MR BHUPINDER SINGH ANAND (Managing Director)

Independent Financial Advisor, Anand Associates Ltd, 5 Oldbury Place, London, W1M 3AN

PLACE OF BIRTH: India, 2.10.63
MARITAL STATUS: Married
CHILDREN: Two (Anishka, Savraj)
COLLEGE: Oxford Brookes University
PROFESSIONAL QUALIFICATIONS: Associate of Chartered Insurance, Institute Advanced Financial Planning certificate
MEMBERSHIPS: Soc. of Financial Advisors. Associate of Life Insurance. Million Dollar Round Table. Govt Policy Action Team. Founding Pres Young Punjabis (YPs)
HONOURS/AWARDS: Independent Financial Advisor of the Year 1995-by Planned Savings magazine. Evening Standard 'Best IFA in the Capital 1998'
HOBBIES AND INTERESTS: Reading, writing, travel, public speaking, organising events.
PERSONAL PROFILE: Recognised as one of Britain's best financial advisers. Personal finance editor for Eastern Eye newspaper, Tandoori magazine, Zee TV and regular contributor to various mainstream media. Anand Associates was sponsor of Britain's Richest 200 Asians' magazine 1998, sharing the platform at the launch ceremony with Prime Minister Tony Blair.

KOBI ABUL BASHOR ANSARI (Poet-Writer)

33 Woolridge Way, Loddiges Road, London, E9 6PP

PLACE OF BIRTH: Bangladesh, 1.1.27
MARITAL STATUS: Married
CHILDREN: Five (Zenith Rahman, Jali Bashor, Amjad Suleman, Rahel Akhtar, Abul Hasanat)
HOBBIES AND INTERESTS: Writing, poetry, travelling
PERSONAL PROFILE: First I would like to take this opportunity to thank my son Amjad Suleman for nominating my name for such an excellent publication. I was born in Bangladesh 1927. I have been writing poetry since the age of 14. My first poem was titled 'Bashkor' meaning rising sun. I have since been writing in Bengali newspapers, published books and released musical records.
NOMINATED BY: Amjad Suleman

MINA ANWAR (Actress-Singer)

179 Lichfield Court, Sheen Road,, Richmond, TW9 1AZ

PLACE OF BIRTH: Blackburn, 20.9.69
MARITAL STATUS: Married
COLLEGE: Mountview Theatre School
ACADEMIC QUALIFICATIONS: 9 O-levels, 2 A-levels
PROFESSIONAL QUALIFICATIONS: Three Years acting diploma. A-level in contemporary dance and drama. Ten years training in singing classical jazz.
HOBBIES AND INTERESTS: Holistic medicine and astrology, history of ancient civilisations, travel.
EMAIL: minanwar@hotmail.com
PERSONAL PROFILE: Coming from a working class background, came to London to study acting and singing. I shot to fame by being the first Asian lead in a mainstream sitcom 'Thin Blue Line' then went on to make the film 'Flight' which won three awards in 1998.

MR NASEEM ANWAR (Head of EO Unit)

Head Of Equal Opportunities Unit, Liverpool John Moore's University, Roscoe Cottage, 9 Roscoe Street, Liverpool, L1 2SX

PLACE OF BIRTH: Pakistan, 19.10.58
MARITAL STATUS: Married
CHILDREN: One (Isra)
COLLEGE: University of Essex, University of Keele
ACADEMIC QUALIFICATIONS: BA Hons Sociology & Post Graduate
PROFESSIONAL QUALIFICATIONS: Post Graduate Certificate in Education
EMAIL: N.Anwar@LIVJM.AC.UK
PERSONAL PROFILE: Naseem has been committed to the issues of social justice since the mid 1970's. More recently he has been involved with ground breaking research in higher education on ethics and values and organisational transformation. Currently, he is one of the few pioneers implementing equal opportunities within the university sector. Naseem puts his achievements down to the inspiring support of his parents in Halesowen, West Midlands.
NOMINATED BY: Alison Wild, Liverpool John Moores Uni.

YASMIN ANWAR (TV EXECUTIVE)

Commissioning Editor, Channel 4 Television, 124 Horseferry Road, London, SW1P 2TX

PLACE OF BIRTH: London, 3.4.62
MARITAL STATUS: Married
COLLEGE: Wadham College, Oxford
ACADEMIC QUALIFICATIONS: BA Hons, Oxon
MEMBERSHIPS: Royal Television Society, Women in Film and Television Board Member
PERSONAL PROFILE: Previous employment includes business and international news production, television documentary research and a stint as a management trainee in local government. Libertarian by temperament.

MRS PREETI ARORA (LAWYER)

Advocate Foreign Lawyer, 45 Villiers Road, Southall, UB1 3BS

PLACE OF BIRTH: India, 31.12.60
MARITAL STATUS: Married
COLLEGE: Law Society
ACADEMIC QUALIFICATIONS: World Champion in arm wrestling and judo national champion
PROFESSIONAL QUALIFICATIONS: MA, LLB
HONOURS/AWARDS: World trophy, Miss Judo 1984 in India
HOBBIES AND INTERESTS: Sports, legal cases
PERSONAL PROFILE: I have been World Champion in Arm Wrestling twice and Inter State Judo Champion and have a Miss Judo award. I was practising in Delhi as an Advocate in high courts and supreme court for five years. I arrived in England on 10th April 1998. I am a foreign lawyer and I want to go in to space also.
NOMINATED BY: Balbir Singh Kanwal

CLLR ABDUL ASAD (COUNCILLOR-MAYOR)

Volunteer Co-ordinator, London Borough of Tower Hamlets, 9 Ames Cottage, Maroon Street, Poplar, London, E14 7QX

PLACE OF BIRTH: Bangladesh, 12.1.57
MARITAL STATUS: Married
CHILDREN: Three (Raju, Ronie, Shammy)
ACADEMIC QUALIFICATIONS: Science degree
PROFESSIONAL QUALIFICATIONS: Youth and community work
MEMBERSHIPS: Councillor (elected)
HONOURS/AWARDS: Badminton
HOBBIES AND INTERESTS: Football, badminton, reading
PERSONAL PROFILE: Councillor Asad has lived and worked in Tower Hamlets for the past 20 years. Married with three children, works as a volunteer co-ordinator for CAPA civil rights group. One of longest, serving councillors in Tower Hamlets.
NOMINATED BY: Shofi Ahmed, YGF

MR ALI ASGHAR (BUSINESSMAN)

Worcester Racial Equality Council, 1 Victoria Avenue, Worcester, WR5 1EE

PLACE OF BIRTH: Pakistan, 12.1.42
MARITAL STATUS: Married
CHILDREN: Seven (Rukhsana, Nasir, Fida, Rehana, Razwana, Shakufta, Siamah)
DIRECTORSHIPS: Member of Board of Directors / WREC
PERSONAL PROFILE: For over 30 years I have been working for the welfare of the Pakistani and other minority ethnic communities. I have helped in the development and establishment of community projects and the improvement of the communities.
NOMINATED BY: Cllr Dan Wicksteed

> 'As 16 year old boy came to this country, dreamed about buying a house in four acres of land with swimming pool, bar-room, snooker room etc. Bought dream house in May 1987 at the age of 35'
>
> **GURMEET SINGH ATHWAL**

MR KASHIF ASHRAF (PR MANAGER)

Public Relations Manager, Mobile Direct, 27 Featherstall Road North, Westwood, Oldham, OL9 6QA

PLACE OF BIRTH: Oldham, 10.2.68
MARITAL STATUS: Married
COLLEGE: UMIST
ACADEMIC QUALIFICATIONS: BSc Hons Management Sciences
PROFESSIONAL QUALIFICATIONS: Post Graduate Diploma in Careers Guidance
DIRECTORSHIPS: Governor of a primary school
MEMBERSHIPS: Governor of Oldham College
HOBBIES AND INTERESTS: Charity work. Involved in Oldham scanner appeal
PERSONAL PROFILE: Successfully opened two new businesses since 1994. Also built up a property portfolio over the last few years which includes commercial and residential property. Involved locally in charitable organisation. Also governor of a local college and primary school. Founder member of the first Asian Business Association in Oldham.

MR GURMEET SINGH ATHWAL (POSTMASTER-BUSINESSMAN)

Owner, Athwals Supermarkets, Twigmoor House, Messingham Lane, Scawby, DN20 9AZ

PLACE OF BIRTH: India, 17.7.52
MARITAL STATUS: Married
CHILDREN: Three (Kul, Hap, Raj)
PROFESSIONAL QUALIFICATIONS: I am a successful bussinessman
DIRECTORSHIPS: Owner of three supermarkets and post office
MEMBERSHIPS: Sponsors two local football teams U 11's and U 13's.
HOBBIES AND INTERESTS: Swimming, playing snooker , football
PERSONAL PROFILE: 'Dream come true'. As 16 year old boy came to this country, dreamed about buying a house in four acres of land with swimming pool, bar-room, snooker room etc. Bought dream house in May 1987 at the age of 35. God helps them who help themselves. I employ 30 full and part-time staff.

MR SURINDER AUJLA (BUSINESS DIRECTOR)

Empress Building Centre Ltd, 137 Long Lane, Finchley, London, N3 2HY

PLACE OF BIRTH: India, 15.3.55
MARITAL STATUS: Married
CHILDREN: 2 (Rupy, Jasmin)
COLLEGE: GND Uni Amritsar
ACADEMIC QUALIFICATIONS: MA Punjabi
PROFESSIONAL QUALIFICATIONS: Professional sales director
DIRECTORSHIPS: Managing Director
MEMBERSHIPS: Lions Club INT, Advisors of Punjab Mail INT
HOBBIES AND INTERESTS: Writer, tennis, squash, social work
PERSONAL PROFILE: MA Punjabi from Lylpur. Khalsa College Jullundhar, Punjab. Worked for Punjabi State UNI. Text Book Board, Chandigarh. Came to the UK 1981. Started my business of selling bathroom and heating products in 1986 and become a professional businessman.

MR BURJOR AVARI MBE (UNIVERSITY LECTURER)

Principal Lecturer, Manchester Metropolitan University, Academic Div., All Saints, Manchester, M15 6BH

PLACE OF BIRTH: India, 9.11.38
MARITAL STATUS: Married
CHILDREN: Two (Rushna, Anahita)
COLLEGE: Manchester University
ACADEMIC QUALIFICATIONS: MA (Manchester)
PROFESSIONAL QUALIFICATIONS: Dip Ed (Oxford)
HONOURS/AWARDS: MBE
HOBBIES AND INTERESTS: Reading, cooking
PERSONAL PROFILE: Burjor Avari worked in school for 22 years before becoming head of multicultural education in the Borough of Tameside. He was awarded for work in that field. He now promotes inter-cultural studies in higher education organising many lectures in various fields of ethnic studies and community life.
NOMINATED BY: Dr S M Godbole

MR NAZIR AHMED AWAN (Managing Director)

Awan Marketing International Ltd, 24-25 Great Hampton Street, Birmingham, B18 6AA

PLACE OF BIRTH: Peshawar, 28.2.53
MARITAL STATUS: Married
CHILDREN: 2 (Noor Jehan, Amer Awan)
COLLEGE: NBC
ACADEMIC QUALIFICATIONS: Mechanical Engineering
DIRECTORSHIPS: City Challenge, B A B A.
MEMBERSHIPS: Institute of Asian Business, Save the Children
HOBBIES AND INTERESTS: Cricket, swimming, badminton, keep-fit,
PERSONAL PROFILE: Running an electronics import-export business. Also a property company. Sit on boards of City Challenge, BABA, IAB and Save the Children. Have been involved in public life for last ten years. Aim to go into politics in the next five years and serve the community.

SHAMIM AZAD (Writing-Teaching)

188 Perth Road, Ilford, IG2 6DZ

PLACE OF BIRTH: Bangladesh
MARITAL STATUS: Married
CHILDREN: Two (Eeshita, Sajib)
COLLEGE: University of Dhaka, Bangladesh
ACADEMIC QUALIFICATIONS: BA Hons, MA
PROFESSIONAL QUALIFICATIONS: QTS, UK
HONOURS/AWARDS: Bichitra, Weekly News Mag, Bangladesh
HOBBIES AND INTERESTS: Visiting galleries, music (East and West)
PERSONAL PROFILE: A prolific writer who has been involved extensively with print and broadcast media in Bangladesh. Working for Bangladesh radio as well as BBC radio, England. Writing for some of the leading Bengali dailies and weeklies including Prothom Allo. Authored three volumes of poetry and two novels. Staged number of plays with Half Moon Theatre. Currently engaged in writing and translating.

MR NADEEM AZAM (Writer)

Self- employed, freelancer, CJB Books Ltd, 30 Eskdale House, Stanhope Street, Regent's Park, London, NW1 3SB

PLACE OF BIRTH: W. Yorks, 1.5.72
MARITAL STATUS: Single
COLLEGE: Bradford University
ACADEMIC QUALIFICATIONS: BA Hons Political Science
MEMBERSHIPS: National Union of Journalists. Assoc of Independent Entrepreneurs
HONOURS/AWARDS: Alan Wilson Memorial Literary Prize
HOBBIES AND INTERESTS: Reading books on religion, politics, arts, music
EMAIL: email@nazam.com
WEB SITE: www.nazam.com
PERSONAL PROFILE: Hailed by the Observer as 'an up-and-coming Muslim writer', Asam has written for several British Islamic publications including 'Impact International', 'Q-News and Islamica'. Having 'retired' from journalism, he is near to completing his second book "The Veil : Women, Islam and Modernity" for which he is seeking a publisher.
NOMINATED BY: Taranum Sultana

MR SONNY S AZHAKESAN (Producer)

Researcher/Assist Producer, Asianet Cable TV, 24A Ropery Street, Mile End, London, E3 4QF

PLACE OF BIRTH: Singapore, 16.12.63
MARITAL STATUS: Single
COLLEGE: Kingston University, Warwick University
ACADEMIC QUALIFICATIONS: BSc Hons, Chemistry (2:1), MSc in Information Technology
PROFESSIONAL QUALIFICATIONS: G R S C
MEMBERSHIPS: Peter Sellars Foundation (Ltd), Bombay Film Workshop
HONOURS/AWARDS: Arts Council of GB-Film Award (short film)
HOBBIES AND INTERESTS: Sports (weight-training), travel, cookery, wine, film-making
EMAIL: sonny52@hotmail.com
WEB SITE: www.asianet.tv.com
PERSONAL PROFILE: I am a multi-skilled TV producer, who was also a co-founder of two British Asian publications-'The Asian Post' and 'Monsoon'. I am well-educated, analytical, creative, cosmopolitan, well-travelled and have a deep commitment in raising the profile and success of British Asians particularly in the visual media-e.g. TV/Film. I see myself as entrepreneurial and a risk-taker.

MR SHERAZ AZIZ (Systems Developer)

18 Lemington Avenue, King Cross, Halifax, HX01 3XD

PLACE OF BIRTH: Halifax, 20.7.80
MARITAL STATUS: Single
ACADEMIC QUALIFICATIONS: 9 GCSE's and 3 A-Levels
DIRECTORSHIPS: Vice-chairman of the Parkinson Lane Neighbourhood Association
MEMBERSHIPS: Amnesty International
HOBBIES AND INTERESTS: Helping the local and wider community, politics
PERSONAL PROFILE: Having studied at nationally recognised grammar schools, I am a systems developer for a financial institution. I work on behalf of Amnesty International. I am the vice-chairman of the local neighbourhood association. I am a contact within the Asian community for the local media.
NOMINATED BY: Aftab Aziz

MR SYED NADIR 'DARAZ' AZIZ (Restaurateur)

Restaurateur, The Valley & The Valley Junction 397, The Old Station House, Station Road, Corbridge, NE45 5AY

PLACE OF BIRTH: Bangladesh, 9.1.56
MARITAL STATUS: Married
CHILDREN: Two (Rajni, Nabil)
DIRECTORSHIPS: The Valley Junction 397 Ltd
MEMBERSHIPS: North East Chamber Of Commerce. Restaurateur of GB Association. Ass.Gen Sec Bangladesh Caterer Assoc., Gen Sec North East BCA. Chair Bangladesh Jobo-Shonga NE
HOBBIES AND INTERESTS: Care for the Bangladesh community
PERSONAL PROFILE: Daraz owns the Valley, home of the unique "Passage to India" train service and the Valley Junction 397. Chairman, Newcastle Bangladesh Association. Raising £30,000 for the Bangladesh Community Centre. He has highlighted the plight of Bangladeshi acid burns victims. Raised the profile of the Bangladeshi community in the north east.

DR SABIHA QAMAR AZMI (Clinical Psychologist)

Royal Bolton Hospital, Azmi House, 25 Sheepfoot Lane, Prestwich, Manchester, M25 0BN

PLACE OF BIRTH: India, 16.3.72
MARITAL STATUS: Single
COLLEGE: University Of Manchester, University Of Wales
ACADEMIC QUALIFICATIONS: BSc Hons, PhD
PROFESSIONAL QUALIFICATIONS: D.Clin.Psy
MEMBERSHIPS: British Psychological Society, Division of Clinical Psychology
HONOURS/AWARDS: Research Associate, University of Manchester
HOBBIES AND INTERESTS: Reading, travelling, sports
PERSONAL PROFILE: Came to England at the age of 11. Author of three books on Asians and learning disabilities in Britain. Researched and published numerous articles on race and learning disabilities, clinical psychology and race. Founder of Aashiyana Carers Association; member of various bodies.
NOMINATED BY: Worcester Racial Equality Council

MR WAQAR AZMI (Executive Director)

Worcester Racial Equality Council, 17 Haines Avenue, Harley-Warren, Warndon Villages, Worcester, WR4 0DG

PLACE OF BIRTH: India, 22.2.70
MARITAL STATUS: Single
COLLEGE: UCL, Southampton Inst.
ACADEMIC QUALIFICATIONS: BA Hons Politics with Social Policy, Dip, PhD
DIRECTORSHIPS: Chamber of Commerce, Training and Enterprise H&W
MEMBERSHIPS: Institute of Directors
HONOURS/AWARDS: Honorary Research Fellow at University College Worcester.(UCW)
HOBBIES AND INTERESTS: Travel, reading, badminton
PERSONAL PROFILE: Came to England at the age of 13. Appointed lecturer at University of Central Lancashire at the age of 21 (1991-93); lecturer at Southampton Institute (1993-96); executive director of WREC (1996 -date); awarded Research Fellow at UCW; published work and articles on ethnic minorities; co-founded comparative ethnic studies unit and the West Midlands Racial Equality Forum; consultant and member of several bodies.
NOMINATED BY: Cllr Dan Wicksteed

September 1 1992: Outraged newsagents turn to Eastern Eye in a bid to ban *Asian Babes* magazine described by community leaders as 'an insulting and demeaning rag with a 'destructive effect on the Asian community'

JAZZY B (ARTIST)

Singer, Kiss Records

PERSONAL PROFILE: He's known as the Crown Prince of Bhangra and his following world-wide is immense. Jazzy B is most definitely folk and undoubtedly funky while maintaining his street credentials and his 'desi' panache. He has proved that it is not just his image that attracts the fans-it's also down to his musical capabilities and the exhilarating stage presence he delivers

SHAHIN BADAR (SINGER)

Prospects Associations, 28 Magpie Close, Forest Gate, London, E7 9DE

PLACE OF BIRTH: Colchester, 17.6.69
MARITAL STATUS: Single
HONOURS/AWARDS: Double Platinum Disc Award 1997, sales over 600, 000, mainstream No 1 album.
HOBBIES AND INTERESTS: Singing, socialising, keeping fit, reading
PERSONAL PROFILE: Double Platinum Disc recipient. Launched London's first Children's Hospice Week. Bhangra hit song 'Jind Meriyeh'. Judge at Miss Great Britain / Universe finals. Raised funds for Bangladesh flood appeal. Featured on Biggest Selling Dance Album 1997. No 8 hit smash Bitch Up and No 1 international hit. EMMA Award finalist 1999 for best newcomer. Music columnist for newspaper Weekly East .
NOMINATED BY: Olu Oyenigba, Prospects Associates

MR BILLY SINGH BADHAN (STUDENT)

Moseley Park Grammar School,

PLACE OF BIRTH: Wolverhampton, 14.9.83
ACADEMIC QUALIFICATIONS: Currently studying for GCSE's, Hopes to read law as future ambition
HONOURS/AWARDS: West Midlands Powerlifting Champion U21's and U23's, all acheived in the 67.5 kg
HOBBIES AND INTERESTS: Playing football, weight-training
PERSONAL PROFILE: Billy has watched his two elder brothers achieve national awards in power lifting. He has trained very hard over the years and was able to win a championship. He is also hoping to win the British Powerlifting Championships in 1999.
NOMINATED BY: Mac Singh

MR MAC SINGH BADHAN (GYM INSTRUCTOR)

Mac's Planet, Health & Fitness Centre, 9 Wellington Road, Bilston, WV14 6AA

PLACE OF BIRTH: Wolverhampton, 19.5.75
MARITAL STATUS: Married
COLLEGE: Wolverhampton University
ACADEMIC QUALIFICATIONS: BA Hons Business Administration
PROFESSIONAL QUALIFICATIONS: Fitness Instructor (BAWLA)
DIRECTORSHIPS: Mac's Planet
HONOURS/AWARDS: British Powerlifting Champion
HOBBIES AND INTERESTS: Acting, weight-training, scriptwriting, singing
PERSONAL PROFILE: I have achieved the following: Strongest 14 and 15 years-old throughout the United Kingdom 1989 and 1990. International Martial Arts Championships 1992 in Holland. British Powerlifting Champion 1995. With the above achievements I have also played a part in the film 'London' directed by Gurinder Chada. After seeing my acting talent, Vijayta Films gave me an opportunity in their next movie, directed by Sunny Deol.

MR RICKY SINGH BADHAN (STUDENT)

PLACE OF BIRTH: Wolverhampton, 18.2.78
COLLEGE: Wolverhampton University
ACADEMIC QUALIFICATIONS: BTEC Science GNVQ, studying for computer programming degree
HONOURS/AWARDS: West Midlands and British Powerlifting Champion U21's & U23's, All Midland Team Champion, Eng V Scot Champion. GB vs South Africa Champion (60 Kg Class)
HOBBIES AND INTERESTS: Buying and selling cars, collecting old collectors item vehicles, favourite hobby is weight training
PERSONAL PROFILE: Ricky has watched his elder brother achieve national awards in powerlifting. He has trained very hard and was able to accomplish his dream. He has been selected to compete in European and World Championships representing Britain.

MRS DEEDAR BAHRA (HEAD OF COMMUNITY EDUCATION)

Freelance Radio Presenter, Wesley Hall Community Project, 107 Oak FM 'Asians Connections', PO Box 107, Loughborough, LE11 5XP

PLACE OF BIRTH: Kenya
MARITAL STATUS: Married
CHILDREN: Two (Narita, Kiren)
PERSONAL PROFILE: Head of a large community project. Tremendous, contribution in the development and promotion of educational, social, cultural and recreational activities for the Asian community. Freelance radio presenter for the last 15 years-numerous awards for specialist radio programmes/compering/ and for successful management of local community radio initiatives.
NOMINATED BY: Amarjit Singh

MISS MANJINDER BAINS (STUDENT)

PLACE OF BIRTH: England, 31.1.78
MARITAL STATUS: Single
COLLEGE: Kings College London
ACADEMIC QUALIFICATIONS: 6 A*'s, 4 A's GCSE, 3 A's A-level
HONOURS/AWARDS: A-Level prize for Maths, Chemistry, Biology
HOBBIES AND INTERESTS: Dance
EMAIL: manjinder.bains@kcl.ac.uk
PERSONAL PROFILE: My academic success first received recognition when I achieved the highest GCSE results in my borough. At A-level I achieved three grade A's and am currently in my third year of dentistry at university. I hope to continue to excel in my chosen profession as I have done so in my education.
NOMINATED BY: Bimla Lyall

DR NADIA BAKHSH (DOCTOR)

Medical SHO, 14 Canterbury Avenue, Ilford, IG1 3NA

PLACE OF BIRTH: Barking, 25.10.72
MARITAL STATUS: Single
COLLEGE: The London Hospital Medical College
ACADEMIC QUALIFICATIONS: MBBS
MEMBERSHIPS: Muslim-Jews Doctor's Group
HOBBIES AND INTERESTS: Travelling, reading, music, films
PERSONAL PROFILE: As a young schoolgirl, Nadia wrote 'My Holidays in Pakistan' when she was only seven and 'Eid Mubarik' when she was ten – probably the youngest published writer in Britain. Extracts from 'Eid Mubarik' have been included in recommended textbooks on school assemblies and Islamic studies at GCSE level.
NOMINATED BY: Qadir Bakhsh

'I have achieved the following: Strongest 14 and 15 years-old throughout the United Kingdom 1989 and 1990. International Martial Arts Championships 1992 in Holland. British Powerlifting Champion 1995'

MAC SINGH BADHAN

MR QADIR BAKHSH (Consultant Publisher)

Managing Editor, Eagles Consultancy Cheetah Books, 14 Canterbury Avenue, Ilford, IG3 3NA

PLACE OF BIRTH: Pakistan, 5.1.44
MARITAL STATUS: Married
CHILDREN: Two (Nadia, Tanzila)
ACADEMIC QUALIFICATIONS: BA, MA, MSc
PROFESSIONAL QUALIFICATIONS: Cert. Community Relations
DIRECTORSHIPS: Asian Business Association
MEMBERSHIPS: British Psychologist Society
HONOURS/AWARDS: Community Awards
HOBBIES AND INTERESTS: Cooking, listening to music
EMAIL: qadir@eagle14.swinterned.co.uk
PERSONAL PROFILE: Advisor to a number of organisations and associations e.g. Ilford Islamic Centre, Barking Mosque, Eaton Road Muslim Community Centre, Muslim Burial Trust, ALERT against harassment and violence in Waltham Forest and Newham. Founded an education charity Uswa-e-Hasna Institute to publish education material for children for character building, good citizenship training and political and civic socialisation.
NOMINATED BY: Lynne Harrington

MRS RUKHSANA BAKHSH JP (Teacher)

Primary Team Leader, Barking and Dagenham Local Authority, 14 Canterbury Avenue, Ilford, IG1 3NA

PLACE OF BIRTH: Pakistan, 4.4.44
MARITAL STATUS: Married
CHILDREN: Two (Nadia, Tanzila)
COLLEGE: Peshawar University
ACADEMIC QUALIFICATIONS: MA Psychology, B.Ed
MEMBERSHIPS: Barking Standing Conf. on Religious Ed
HOBBIES AND INTERESTS: Cooking, entertaining, theatre, music, poetry, bhangra
PERSONAL PROFILE: Came to England 1970. Career: Higher executive officer in civil service and a teacher. Voluntary work: Promoting good race relations and community relations. English as a second language for Asian women. Writes and speaks on Asian communities issues and multicultural anti-racist education. Appointed Justice of the Peace in 1992. A member of Board of Trustees, the Qalb Mental Health and Day Care Centre.

DR NEELAM BAKSHI (Actress-Doctor)

Magnolia Management, 136 Hicks Avenue, Greenford, UB6 8HB

PLACE OF BIRTH: India, 13.4.66
COLLEGE: UCL, Actors Institute
ACADEMIC QUALIFICATIONS: MBBS, DREOG, MRC Psych.
PROFESSIONAL QUALIFICATIONS: Trained actress
MEMBERSHIPS: Equity
HOBBIES AND INTERESTS: Dancing, singing, skiing
PERSONAL PROFILE: Qualified as a psychiatrist with interest in psychotherapy, also trained actress with various prestigious TV, film and theatre roles.

MR SHAHAGIR FARUK BAKTH (Job Consultant)

Shahnan Employment Bureau, 33 Princelet Street, London, E1 5LP

PLACE OF BIRTH: Sunamganj, 31.8.48
MARITAL STATUS: Married
CHILDREN: Three (Shahnan, Safwana, Eva)
COLLEGE: Dhaka University
ACADEMIC QUALIFICATIONS: MSc
PROFESSIONAL QUALIFICATIONS: AMCIEH
DIRECTORSHIPS: Bangladesh British Chamber of Commerce
MEMBERSHIPS: London Historical Society
HOBBIES AND INTERESTS: Politics, reading papers, travelling, debate, astronomy
EMAIL: bakth@telegraph.co.uk
PERSONAL PROFILE: Former lecturer of physics. Chairman, Conservative Party in Tower Hamlets. Founder-chairman, Sunamganj Association known as 'Suprobash'. Steering Committee. Member of New Deal of Tower Hamlets and City Side Regeneration Company. Probably the only Bangladeshi who has very high profile connections with mainstream Conservative Party.

MR NAVNEET BALE (Hotelier)

Vice President-Finance, Taj International Hotels Ltd, St James Court Hotel, Buckingham Gate, London, SW1E 6AF

PLACE OF BIRTH: Dehradun, 9.1.56
MARITAL STATUS: Married
CHILDREN: Two (Kabir, Karan)
COLLEGE: IIM Calcutta
ACADEMIC QUALIFICATIONS: B.Tech, MBA
DIRECTORSHIPS: Taj International Hotels Ltd. Bombay Brasserie Ltd, St James Court Hotel Ltd
MEMBERSHIPS: British Assoc. of Hotel Accountants.
HOBBIES AND INTERESTS: Golf, tennis, cricket
PERSONAL PROFILE: Member of Tata Administrative Service, the premier cadre in India's Tata Group of companies. Trained in Tata Engineering and Tata Unisys before joining Taj Group.

MISS BEGUM FAUJA BALI (Student)

PLACE OF BIRTH: Bangladesh, 10.6.86
MARITAL STATUS: Single
COLLEGE: Mulberry School for Girls
HONOURS/AWARDS: Three certificates for PE and one for environmental projects
HOBBIES AND INTERESTS: Dancing, reading, listening to music
PERSONAL PROFILE: I am a 13 year old student in Mulberry School, I am in class 8B. I will be going onto Year 9 in September. I have been involved in environmental projects and was awarded a certificate. My future ambition is to work in a crèche.

MRS MRIDULA BALJEKAR (Food Writer-Broadcaster)

Freelance Food Consultant, Toit Vert, 25 Heatherley Road, Camberly, GU15 3LX

PLACE OF BIRTH: India, 1.2.52
MARITAL STATUS: Married
CHILDREN: Two (Maneesha, Sneha)
COLLEGE: Guwahati Assam
ACADEMIC QUALIFICATIONS: BA in Economics, English and Politics
MEMBERSHIPS: Guild of Food Writers
HOBBIES AND INTERESTS: Cooking, interior decorating, reading, music
PERSONAL PROFILE: I have written eight cookery books on Indian cuisine. First book sold 250,000 copies since 1990. Worked as consultant to the Tesco supermarket chain for four years. Presented 3 X13 part-Indian cookery series for Carlton TV Food Network.
NOMINATED BY: Sharon Aitkin

MS PAMELA BALLANTINE (Psychotherapist)

Senior Child Psychotherapist, Redbridge Racial Equality Council, 5 Russell Gardens, Ley Street, Ilford, IG2 7BY

PLACE OF BIRTH: India, 16.4.38
MARITAL STATUS: Single
CHILDREN: 1 (William)
COLLEGE: Bristol University, LSE
ACADEMIC QUALIFICATIONS: BA Hons, Cert of Education, Diploma in Social Admin
MEMBERSHIPS: Group Analytic Society (London)
HOBBIES AND INTERESTS: Travel
PERSONAL PROFILE: Chair six years Redbridge Racial Equality Council. Chair four years Redbridge Police Community Consultative Group. Chair Racial Incidents Panel. Adolescent group psychotherapist race relations campaigner for over 20 years.

'I have written eight cookery books on Indian cuisine. First book sold 250,000 copies since 1990. Worked as consultant to the Tesco supermarket chain for four years'

MRIDULA BALJEKAR

MR BAIDYA NATH BANDYOPADHYAY
(VOCATIONAL ADVISER-IT)

Freelance Consultant, 50 Linden Way, Southgate, London, N14 4NE

PLACE OF BIRTH: India, 19.5.41
MARITAL STATUS: Married
CHILDREN: One (Bidisha)
COLLEGE: London University
ACADEMIC QUALIFICATIONS: MSc (Salford), M.Phil (Lond.), Cert.Ed (Lond.), Grad Dip IT (CNAA)
PROFESSIONAL QUALIFICATIONS: Cert Electronic DP, Trained in Microsoft
MEMBERSHIPS: British Computer Society, Royal Society of Chemistry
HONOURS/AWARDS: Received a number of vocational training awards in IT
HOBBIES AND INTERESTS: Reading life, work of Indian Nobel Laureates
PERSONAL PROFILE: Initially I started my career as a chemist. I worked under the supervision of Nobel Laureate Sir George Porter during 1974-77 at the Royal Institution London and published, an original research paper in the Royal Society of Chemistry Journal. Last 14 years I have been working in computer applications.

DR ARUP KUMAR BANERJEE OBE (HOSPITAL CONSULTANT)

Consultant/Service Director, Bolton Hosp NHS Trust, 2 Pilling Field, Egerton, Bolton, BL7 9UG

PLACE OF BIRTH: Calcutta, 28.11.35
MARITAL STATUS: Married
CHILDREN: Three (Arpan, Anjan, Avijit)
COLLEGE: Calcutta
ACADEMIC QUALIFICATIONS: MBBS (Cal)
PROFESSIONAL QUALIFICATIONS: FRCP Lond, FRCP Edin, FRCP Glasg, FRCP Ire
DIRECTORSHIPS: Ex Medical Director, Ex Vice Chair North Western RHA
MEMBERSHIPS: Ex-President of British Geriatrics Society
HONOURS/AWARDS: OBE (Jan 1996)
HOBBIES AND INTERESTS: Travel, music, literature
PERSONAL PROFILE: Interested in medical education, research and service development. Specialist in the care of older people at an international level.

KAMAL BANGER (FREESTYLE WRESTLER)

GB Team Captain, 130 Farnham Road, Handsworth, Birmingham, B21 8EE

PLACE OF BIRTH: Birmingham, 27.10.82
MARITAL STATUS: Single
HONOURS/AWARDS: Five times British champion, numerous area titles
HOBBIES AND INTERESTS: Keeping fit, swimming, martial art movies
PERSONAL PROFILE: My father introduced me to wrestling at the age of six. I began competing and my greatest successes include becoming five times British Champion and being captain of the GB Team. Wrestling has taken me to US, France, Belgium and soon to Poland, India and Australia. I hope to fulfill my dream of becoming an Olympic champion.
NOMINATED BY: J E Ault, Midlands Region Olympic Wrestling Association

MISS RAHILA BANO (ASIAN AFFAIRS CORRESPONDENT)

BBC Radio Northwest (Lancashire & Gt Manchester, BBC NW-Asian Network, Darwen Street, Blackburn, BB2 2EA

PLACE OF BIRTH: Birmingham, 4.1.68
MARITAL STATUS: Single
MEMBERSHIPS: East Lancs Health Authority Panel. Ethnic Minority Women's Forum, Blackburn College Panel
HONOURS/AWARDS: Shortlisted EMMA Awards-TV News and CRE RIMA Awards-TV News in 1998
HOBBIES AND INTERESTS: Swimming, Asian cooking, reading, cinema, theatre
PERSONAL PROFILE: Currently responsible for producing Asian programmes for BBC Radio Lancashire and BBC GMR and inputting Asian stories into regional TV news and mainstream programmes. Originally from Birmingham she started her BBC career with BBC Radio WM; WM Heartlands and WM Asian Network; including short spell with Midlands Today, She's single and lives in the NW.
NOMINATED BY: S Taylor

MRS INDERJIT KAUR BANS (COUNSELLOR)

Group Facilitator-Counsellor, c/o Depression Alliance, 35 Westminster Bridge Road, London, SE1 7JB

PLACE OF BIRTH: New Delhi, 13.11.50
MARITAL STATUS: Married
CHILDREN: Four (Karen, Pamela, Ranjit, Amar)
HOBBIES AND INTERESTS: Yoga, meditation, reading, working with people, travelling
WEB SITE: snokes@ndc.k.web.co.uk
PERSONAL PROFILE: A qualified counsellor, coming from isolated Asian community, having fulfilled a role of wife and mother with in-depth cultural understanding. Going from strength to strength. Particular interest in empowering Asian women. Provides inspirational thought provoking seminars on mental health issues, creates an environment of mutual-trust and understanding. Also introduction to basic meditation and relaxation techniques.
NOMINATED BY: Mrs I K Bans

MR MALKIAT SINGH BANSAL (OPTICIAN)

Director, Bansal Opticians, 64 Lansdowne Road, Handsworth, Birmingham, B21 9AT

PLACE OF BIRTH: India, 16.9.26
MARITAL STATUS: Married
CHILDREN: Six
PROFESSIONAL QUALIFICATIONS: FBDO, FBHI
DIRECTORSHIPS: Two firms
MEMBERSHIPS: Rotarian, Freemason
HONOURS/AWARDS: Freeman of the City of London
HOBBIES AND INTERESTS: Sports, walking
PERSONAL PROFILE: On the community level his contributions to the Gurdwara and the Sikh Union were invaluable. He founded the '64 Secondary School. This dedication even continues today as a governor of two schools in Birmingham, president of Rosehill Residents Association and vice chairman of Traders Association, member of Police Consultation Committee, and lay visitor-West Midland Police.
NOMINATED BY: Gurmeet Singh Soor

MISS GHAZALA BASHIR (STUDENT-POET LAUREATE)

Poet Laureate,

PLACE OF BIRTH: Middlesborough, 27.1.78
COLLEGE: University of Teeside
ACADEMIC QUALIFICATIONS: BA Hons English and History
PROFESSIONAL QUALIFICATIONS: Youth Worker (Part-time)
HONOURS/AWARDS: Poet Laureateship for Middlesborough
HOBBIES AND INTERESTS: Writing, reflecting, creating
PERSONAL PROFILE: I was born and brought up in Middlesborough. I have always had an interest in writing. I started writing poetry at fifteen and have taken part in various creative activities. As Poet Laureate I have done poetry readings, read poetry on local radio and been published in local press. I should have a collection of poetry published later in the year.

DR DEV BASRA (FACIAL COSMETIC SURGEON)

Consultant, 111 Harley Street, London, W1N 1DG

PLACE OF BIRTH: India, 9.1.42
MARITAL STATUS: Married
CHILDREN: Three
ACADEMIC QUALIFICATIONS: MBBS
PROFESSIONAL QUALIFICATIONS: FRCS
MEMBERSHIPS: Royal Society of Medicine
HOBBIES AND INTERESTS: Sculptor, photography, painting, design
PERSONAL PROFILE: Surgeon various NHS hospitals 1966-1976. Private practice aesthetic plastic surgery 1977-, professional sculptor 1986 -, president Indian Association of Cosmetic Surgeons, vice-president Federation Europeene Des Societes Nationales De Chirurgie Esthetique. Book: The Ageing Skin 1986.

> Surgeon various NHS hospitals 1966-1976. Private practice aesthetic plastic surgery 1977-, professional sculptor 1986-, president Indian Association of Cosmetic Surgeons
>
> **DR DEV BASRA**

MRS KAMALJIT KAUR BASRAN (OPERATIONS DIRECTOR)

Operations Director, Authentic Indian Foods Ltd, Al Stockport Trading Estate, Yew Street, Stockport, SK4 2JZ

PLACE OF BIRTH: India, 1.1.51
MARITAL STATUS: Married
CHILDREN: Two (Parminder Singh, Manminder Singh)
COLLEGE: Sheffield University
ACADEMIC QUALIFICATIONS: BA (History)
PROFESSIONAL QUALIFICATIONS: Postgrad Teaching Diploma
DIRECTORSHIPS: Three companies
HOBBIES AND INTERESTS: Charity events, work, family, shopping
PERSONAL PROFILE: Came to England in 1960 with no English. Excellent O and A- Levels meant parents grudgingly sent her to university. Went into teaching A- Level history before having two boys and eventually starting Authentic Indian Foods with husband Lak. Complete dedication to business and family means a rewarding balanced life.

MR LAKHBIR SINGH BASRAN (MANAGING DIRECTOR)

Managing Director, Authentic Indian Foods Ltd, Unit A1, Stockport Trading Estate, Yew Street, Stockport, SK4 2JE

PLACE OF BIRTH: India, 12.10.48
MARITAL STATUS: Married
CHILDREN: Two (Parminder, Manminder)
COLLEGE: Salford University
ACADEMIC QUALIFICATIONS: BSc Mechanical Engineering
DIRECTORSHIPS: Three companies
MEMBERSHIPS: Institute of Directors
HONOURS/AWARDS: Nominated best salesman of German food products in UK 1985
HOBBIES AND INTERESTS: Charity events, veteran footballer, keen follower of Man Utd
PERSONAL PROFILE: Happy and contented, came to England in the fifties with no English. Worked hard at school to gain university place and eventual degree and worked for the T I Engineering Group. Upset family by leaving engineering. Went into sales with Mars and never looked back. Ideal for company is blue chip professionalism with good honest family values.

DR ANURADHA BASU (ACADEMIC-RESEARCHER)

University Lecturer, Unversity of Reading, Dept of Economics, Whiteknights, PO Box 218, Reading, RG6 6AA

PLACE OF BIRTH: India, 23.6.60
MARITAL STATUS: Married
CHILDREN: Two (Nikhil, Tara)
COLLEGE: Kings College, Cambridge University
ACADEMIC QUALIFICATIONS: BA, MBA, MPHI, PhD
MEMBERSHIPS: Fellow Royal Society of Arts
PERSONAL PROFILE: University academic with research interests in entrepreneurship and economic institutions. Research director of study on Asian entrepreneurs in Britain at Reading University. Author of several publications including Public Expenditure Decision. Making: The Indian Experience (Sage 1995). Educated at Delhi, Calcutta and Cambridge Universities.

CLLR DHIREN BASU (JOURNALIST)

Publisher and Editor, New World Weekly Ltd, 234 Holloway Road, London, N7 8DP

PLACE OF BIRTH: Bangladesh, 1.1.43
MARITAL STATUS: Married
CHILDREN: One (Mousumi)
COLLEGE: Dhaka University
ACADEMIC QUALIFICATIONS: BA Hons, MA, LL.B
PROFESSIONAL QUALIFICATIONS: LL.B
DIRECTORSHIPS: New World Weekly Ltd. Trustee Raj Foundation
MEMBERSHIPS: Overseas Bengali Assoc., Bengali International Diabetic Association. Fabian Society
HONOURS/AWARDS: Winner of shot put, javelin and hammer at University three years running.
HOBBIES AND INTERESTS: Fundraising for charities e.g. flood and earthquake appeals, victim support, political talks, presentations
PERSONAL PROFILE: In 1989 I founded and edited New World a multicultural newspaper. It has carried interviews with Tony Blair, Jack Straw, David Blunkett etc. I am also a dedicated councillor. Last year I was the mayor for London Borough of Haringey and am currently the chair of the Equalities Co-ordinating Committee at Haringey Council. I am the organising secretary of Overseas Bengali Association and previously chairman of an Asian organisation in North London.

MRS JHUMUR BASU (SCHOOLTEACHER-RTD.)

Housewife, Forum for Indian TV Viewers, 109 Kenton Lane, Kenton, Harrow, HA3 8UJ

PLACE OF BIRTH: Calcutta, 21.9.47
MARITAL STATUS: Married
CHILDREN: One (Niyoti)
COLLEGE: University of Bombay
ACADEMIC QUALIFICATIONS: BA (Eng Lit) BEd
PROFESSIONAL QUALIFICATIONS: M.Ed
HONOURS/AWARDS: In public speaking, acting on stage (drama) in UK
HOBBIES AND INTERESTS: Drama, music, public speaking, voluntary work in charitable institutions
PERSONAL PROFILE: Born in Calcutta, raised in Bombay. Graduate and masters in education. Teacher in Bombay and London secondary and junior schools. Interest in drama, music, public speaking and charity work.

DR VIJAY BATHLA (GENERAL PRACTITIONER)

Doctor, Handsworth Medical Centre, 143 Albert Road, Handsworth, Birmingham, B21 9LE

PLACE OF BIRTH: Ambala Cantt, 13.5.49
MARITAL STATUS: Married
CHILDREN: Two (Sonia, Sonul)
COLLEGE: Banares Hindu University
ACADEMIC QUALIFICATIONS: MBBS, MD, FRCGP
PROFESSIONAL QUALIFICATIONS: MBBS, MD, FRCGP
DIRECTORSHIPS: BMA
MEMBERSHIPS: RCGP, BMA, ODA, LMC, Birmingham MAAG
HONOURS/AWARDS: FRCP, FODA
HOBBIES AND INTERESTS: Table tennis
PERSONAL PROFILE: Principal general practitioner since 1983, Vice chairman, Birmingham Sub Faculty RCGP 1992-93. Chairman Birmingham RCGP Sub Faculty 1993-95. Member MAAG Birmingham since 1991, Sandwell BMA secretary since 1992, BMA council member since 1998. Chairman Ladywood commissioning group since 1996. Member of LMC since 1986. Secretary Overseas Doctor Association Birmingham 1986 -90. Chairman ODA 1991 to date.

MR VIBHAKER BAXI (INVESTMENT ADVISOR)

Chairman & Managing Director, Navras Records Ltd, 22 Sherwood Road, Hendon, London, NW4 1AD

PLACE OF BIRTH: India, 25.12.47
MARITAL STATUS: Married
CHILDREN: One (Mamta)
COLLEGE: University of Surrey, Manchester Business School
ACADEMIC QUALIFICATIONS: BSc Hons, Physics MBA
DIRECTORSHIPS: Navras Records Ltd (London). Navras Records (Pvt) Ltd Mumbia, India
MEMBERSHIPS: Institute of Directors
HOBBIES AND INTERESTS: Music, travel, reading , current affairs, wines
PERSONAL PROFILE: 1974-94 Treasurer, Managing Director and global money market manager respectively with Citibank, Chemical Bank and HSBC/Midland Bank. Since 1995 advise/manage investment funds for private clients / banks, notably AAA rated AMAS Hinduja Bond Fund (Geneva) and Opus Fund (Bahamas). Set up Navras Records (1992)-A quality music label specialising in live recording of classical and traditional music from Indian subcontinent, with the largest, most diversified catalogue in this genre of music outside of India.

DR RAJAN BEDI (ELECTRONICS DESIGN ENGINEER)

Senior Design Engineer, 62 Silverwood Close, Cambridge, CB1 3HA

PLACE OF BIRTH: N.Ireland, 30.6.68
MARITAL STATUS: Single
COLLEGE: University of Edinburgh
ACADEMIC QUALIFICATIONS: PhD BEng Hons BIS
PROFESSIONAL QUALIFICATIONS: MIEE
MEMBERSHIPS: Executive Committee Indian Culture Association of Cambridge
HONOURS/AWARDS: Royal Society Fellowship, Cowan House Scholarship, J S Scott Scholarships
HOBBIES AND INTERESTS: Indian/Asian history, culture and art, tabla playing, sports
EMAIL: Rajan.Bedi@arm.com
PERSONAL PROFILE: After graduating with a doctorate from the University of Edinburgh in 1994, Dr Bedi was awarded a Royal Society Fellowship to represent the UK by undertaking a period of specialist research at the prestigious 'Institut de recherches cliniques de Montreal' in Canada. Dr Bedi is currently a senior design engineer with Advanced RISC Machines Ltd. in Cambridge and has recently been approached to submit a biography to 'Marquis Who's Who in the World'.

MR RAMAN BEDI (Professor)

Dental Surgery, National Centre for Transcultural Oral Health, University of London, 256 Gray's Inn Road, London, WC1X 8LD

PLACE OF BIRTH: India, 20.5.53
MARITAL STATUS: Married
CHILDREN: Three (Daniel, Jacob, Isaac)
COLLEGE: Bristol University
ACADEMIC QUALIFICATIONS: BDS, MSc, DDS
PROFESSIONAL QUALIFICATIONS: FOSRCS
DIRECTORSHIPS: Eastman Dental Institute
MEMBERSHIPS: Royal Society of Medicine, British Dental Association
HOBBIES AND INTERESTS: Tennis, chess, football
PERSONAL PROFILE: Professor Bedi is the director of the WHO - Collaborating Centre for oral health disability and culture. He is a consultant in paediatric dentistry. He was the first South Asian dentist to hold a professorship in dentistry in England and Wales.

MR RAMESH CHANDER BEDI (Business Consultant)

Director-Direct Marketing, Sony Music Entertainment (UK) Ltd, 24 Barnway, Wembley, HA9 9NW

PLACE OF BIRTH: Delhi
MARITAL STATUS: Married
CHILDREN: Two (Anita, Rita)
ACADEMIC QUALIFICATIONS: MA
PROFESSIONAL QUALIFICATIONS: MIOH, ACMA
DIRECTORSHIPS: Sony Music (UK)
MEMBERSHIPS: ICMA
HOBBIES AND INTERESTS: Music, cultural activities
PERSONAL PROFILE: Came to the UK 30 years ago, acquired professional qualifications and experience. Held various senior commercial positions and was appointed director in 1988. Set up and launched Sony Indian Music in the UK. Take a keen interest in promoting Indian culture and music.

MRS VEENA BEDI (Teacher)

Headteacher, Hambrough Primary School, 24 Barnway, Wembley, HA9 9NW

PLACE OF BIRTH: India, 8.6.48
MARITAL STATUS: Married
CHILDREN: Two (Anita, Rita)
ACADEMIC QUALIFICATIONS: MA
PROFESSIONAL QUALIFICATIONS: B.Ed
HOBBIES AND INTERESTS: Art, organising cultural programmes
PERSONAL PROFILE: Came to the UK from India in 1970. Have spent over 26 years in the education field in the UK. Initiated and produced several educational and cultural programmes for younger people inside the school as well as outside the schools. It is my ambition to use current media technology to promote Asian culture.

MR WISHWA MITTER BEDI (Managing Director)

M/S WM Bedi Ltd, 27 St Mary's Gate, Lace Market, Nottingham, NG1 1PJ

PLACE OF BIRTH: India, 26.4.26
MARITAL STATUS: Married
CHILDREN: Three (Rajan, Meera, Sanjiv)
COLLEGE: Punjab University
ACADEMIC QUALIFICATIONS: Graduate
DIRECTORSHIPS: Managing Director
HOBBIES AND INTERESTS: Badminton, tennis, golf, bridge
PERSONAL PROFILE: After graduation lived in Simla from 1949-55 migrated to UK in 1955 and started lace business in a small way. Over a period became lace manufacturers and wholesalers in lace fabrics and fashion trimmings. We also export to a few countries around the world.

DR OSMAN BEG (Consultant Engineer)

Author, Samarkhand House, 18 Milton Grove, Whalley Range, Manchester, M16 0BP

PLACE OF BIRTH: Dewsbury, 27.9.69
MARITAL STATUS: Single
COLLEGE: Manchester University
ACADEMIC QUALIFICATIONS: B.Eng Hons, PhD (Hydrodynamics)
PROFESSIONAL QUALIFICATIONS: Associate Member Institution of Structural Engineers
DIRECTORSHIPS: Vector Dynamics Services Manchester
MEMBERSHIPS: Fellow International Geothermal Assoc, AMASME, AMSES, AMGRC, AMNFIRE, PA
HONOURS/AWARDS: Environmental Impact Abbey National Award (1981), Jack Allen Hydrodynamics Prize (1992)
HOBBIES AND INTERESTS: Cinema, Latino dance music, Iqbal's poetry
PERSONAL PROFILE: Employed at EQE International (1996-1997) involved in seismic analysis, hurricanes insurance. Director of computer modelling at Ovearup & Partners 1997-99, Manchester, involved in millennium wheel, fire dynamics, composites. Established 'Girls Science Awards' (10) at Kasenmoor School, Hollinwood 1997 Author of Infinite Regression (autobiography) Computational Thermoconvection (2000).
NOMINATED BY: Miss T Anwar Beg

MISS HENA BEGUM (Student)

Lancashire Constabulary, Parker Lane, Burnley

PLACE OF BIRTH: Burnley, 28.11.77
MARITAL STATUS: Single
COLLEGE: Stockport College
PROFESSIONAL QUALIFICATIONS: HND in Caring Services
HONOURS/AWARDS: Climbing Snowdon, competent crew, hardworking acheivement
HOBBIES AND INTERESTS: Working out in gym, tae kwondo, travel
PERSONAL PROFILE: I consider myself a hardworking, conscientious person who has adapted many experiences by working within the community. Other experiences that I have undertook is working in various establishments such as with older people, people with disabilities, children etc. in order to meet their needs. Growing up as part of Bangladeshi community I realised the fact that there needs to be a vast improvement for the Bengali and Pakistani communities.
NOMINATED BY: Reha Begum, Bangladesh Welfare Association

MISS KIBRIA BEGUM (Student)

PLACE OF BIRTH: Bangladesh, 19.5.81
COLLEGE: Mulberry School For Girls
ACADEMIC QUALIFICATIONS: 11 GCSE's, Doing 3 A-Levels
HOBBIES AND INTERESTS: Basketball, swimming
PERSONAL PROFILE: I am a student at Mulberry School For Girls where I am studying 3 A-Levels-chemistry, biology, maths. I would like to go on to do medicine in the hope of becoming a doctor and currently have two offers from King's University and Imperial. Last March I spent a week in New York courtesy of the United Nations, after being chosen to represent Mulberry School in the US.
NOMINATED BY: Sultana Rashid

MISS REHANA BEGUM (Student)

PLACE OF BIRTH: London, 12.10.85
MARITAL STATUS: Single
COLLEGE: Mulberry School for Girls
HONOURS/AWARDS: Certificates
HOBBIES AND INTERESTS: Sport, cooking, reading
PERSONAL PROFILE: I am 13 years old I go to Mulberry School for Girls. My favourite subjects are maths, English, science, PE, dance and drama. I really like going to Mulberry. I like working hard. When I leave school I want to graduate, I want to work in computing.

'Came to the UK from India in 1970. Have spent over
26 years in the education field in the UK'

VEENA BEDI

MISS SHAHIDA (SHEILA) BEGUM (STUDENT)

Sixth Former,

PLACE OF BIRTH: London, 24.1.82
COLLEGE: Mulberry School Sixth Form
ACADEMIC QUALIFICATIONS: GCSE, A*, 5 A's, 5 B's and a C
HOBBIES AND INTERESTS: Loves all kinds of sport, art and design
PERSONAL PROFILE: I am a very lively and enthusiastic person who loves playing sports and meeting different people. I was chosen as part of the Mulberry delegation to represent Britain at the United Nation's Student Conference in New York, March 1998. My life's ambition is to go into the business and IT world and be a millionaire by the time I'm 20, OK then 25!!
NOMINATED BY: Shamsun Nahar Hussain

MISS SHAZNA BEGUM (STUDENT)

Mulberry School for Girls, London

PLACE OF BIRTH: Bangladesh, 2.2.85
MARITAL STATUS: Single
COLLEGE: Mulberry School for Girls
HOBBIES AND INTERESTS: Reading books, basketball, football
PERSONAL PROFILE: I have yet to take my GCSE's, but in 1996 I took my SAT's test and made it to the national top 10% in the country. My predicted grades in all subjects were passed with 3 A*'s and 4 A's. In my spare time I like to read a wide range of books. I love playing netball and basketball. I have played for my school, Mulberry School for Girls on many occasions. I recently took part in a United Nations School Conference.

MISS SHELLY BEGUM (STUDENT)

Mulberry Sixth Form Centre, 226 Cable Street, London, E1 0BL

PLACE OF BIRTH: England, 13.7.81
MARITAL STATUS: Single
COLLEGE: Mulberry Sixth Form Centre
ACADEMIC QUALIFICATIONS: 8 GCSE's, A-C 1997
MEMBERSHIPS: Youth club
HONOURS/AWARDS: For taking part in a United Nations Conference
HOBBIES AND INTERESTS: Football, basketball, kickboxing, music
PERSONAL PROFILE: I am a very friendly and reliable person. I like socialising with people as I enjoy other people's company and helping people. I have organised an employers afternoon at my Sixth Form where I was responsible for everything, including the entertainment and catering.
NOMINATED BY: Lepa Yasmin

TAHIRA REETHA BEGUM (STUDENT)

Mulberry School for Girls, London

PLACE OF BIRTH: London, 15.9.82
MARITAL STATUS: Single
COLLEGE: Mulberry School for Girls
HOBBIES AND INTERESTS: Reading, writing, public speaking, current affairs
PERSONAL PROFILE: I am a student studying for my GCSE's. This year I won the Tower Hamlets Public Speaking competition. I was recently selected as a delegate to attend a United Nation's School Conference on Human Rights. This has given me an interest in taking part in politics and expressing my opinion on issues that affect young Asian women.
NOMINATED BY: Sultana Rashid

> 'This year I won the Tower Hamlets Public Speaking competition. I was recently selected as a delegate to attend a United Nation's School Conference on Human Rights'

TAHIRA REETHA BEGUM

MR AMIT BHADHURI (EDUCATION WELFARE OFFICER)

Doncaster Met Borough Council, The Council House, College Road, Doncaster, DN1 3AD

PLACE OF BIRTH: India, 1.12.46
MARITAL STATUS: Married
CHILDREN: Two (Gitanjali, Arjun)
COLLEGE: Calcutta University, York University
ACADEMIC QUALIFICATIONS: BA Cert in EW
PROFESSIONAL QUALIFICATIONS: Cert in Ed Welfare
HOBBIES AND INTERESTS: Anti-racist work and campaign, sports, music
PERSONAL PROFILE: Over the past 15 years I have worked tirelessly in promoting race relations, equal opportunity policy and practice, justice for all and have worked for disadvantaged minorities. At present my involvement in the above area covers-Race Relations Officer of Transport & General Worker's Union in Doncaster Council. Founder member of Doncaster Ethnic Minority Forum. Executive member of Doncaster Citizen's Advice Bureau. Member of South Yorkshire Police Ethnic Minority Panel.
NOMINATED BY: Shafiq A Khan

MS ANITA BHALLA (JOURNALIST)

BBC Midlands Today, BBC, Pebble Mill Road, Birmingham, B5 7QQ

PLACE OF BIRTH: Kenya
MARITAL STATUS: Married
CHILDREN: Two
COLLEGE: Birmingham
ACADEMIC QUALIFICATIONS: Teaching-Journalist Cert Ed Currently completing MA Media and Communications
PROFESSIONAL QUALIFICATIONS: Journalism-Teaching
DIRECTORSHIPS: Chair Midlands Arts Centre, Selly Oak College
MEMBERSHIPS: NUJ, Royal Society of Arts
HONOURS/AWARDS: 1995-CRE News Reporter of the Year and runner-up in 1996
HOBBIES AND INTERESTS: Arts, music, cinema, reading
PERSONAL PROFILE: Chair of Midlands Arts College. Director Symphony Hall-Birmingham. Trustee-Community Development Foundation. Trustee-Selly Oak College. Member-Asia Resource Centre.

CLLR BACHAN SINGH BHALLA (COUNCILLOR)

Chief Whip Labour Group, Cambridgeshire County Council, 102 Pheasant Rise, Bar Hill, Cambridge, CB3 8SB

PLACE OF BIRTH: India, 2.11.26
MARITAL STATUS: Married
CHILDREN: Three (Manjit, Jagmohan, Anita)
PROFESSIONAL QUALIFICATIONS: Inspectorate Studies Qualification
MEMBERSHIPS: British Indian Councillors Association
HOBBIES AND INTERESTS: Community, social work, sports
PERSONAL PROFILE: Elected to Cambridgeshire County Council 1993; Labour Group Chief Whip 1997- Special interests: equal opportunities policy in local government, nursery and religious education. Assistant secretary National Association of Black, Asian and Ethnic Minority Councillors 1998 -. Executive panel member Imperial War Museum, Duxford Airfield 1993-. Executive Committee Cambridge Citizens Advice Bureau 1997.

MR BIKRAM SINGH BHAMRA
(BROADCASTER-INTERPRETER-TRANSLATOR)

Freelance, 21 Littleover Avenue, Hall Green, Birmingham, B28 9HR

PLACE OF BIRTH: India, 29.11.29
MARITAL STATUS: Married
CHILDREN: Four (Kanwaljeet K, Satvinder K, Chitranjan K, Harjoat S)
COLLEGE: Randhir College, Kapurthala
PROFESSIONAL QUALIFICATIONS: DPSI
MEMBERSHIPS: MITI, APCI
HOBBIES AND INTERESTS: Classical and instrumental music, poetry
PERSONAL PROFILE: Interpreter and translator for New Scotland Yard 1970. Freelance presenter and broadcaster BBC Radio Medway 1973-1988. Also take keen interest in community and religious institutions. Undertake social work to help the Asian community; particularly older members of the community.

MR KULJIT BHAMRA (Music Producer)

Keda Records and Red Fort Studios, The Sight & Sound Centre, Priory Way, Southall, UB2 5EB

PLACE OF BIRTH: Kenya, 28.4.59
MARITAL STATUS: Divorced
CHILDREN: Three (Rupinder, Mandip, Dilraj)
COLLEGE: Middlesex University
ACADEMIC QUALIFICATIONS: BSc Civil Engineering
HONOURS/AWARDS: Best Musical Director 1986/1987. Platinium Disc 1987. Two Gold Discs 1988.1996 Movie International Appreciation Award
HOBBIES AND INTERESTS: Music, lectures, demonstration workshop
PERSONAL PROFILE: Kuljit Bhamra is a virtuoso tabla player, composer and record producer. He is one of the most influential musicians working behind the scenes in British Asian music. He has composed, produced and recorded more than 700 songs to date-many of which have been international hits on the Asian music circuit. Keda Records is synonymous with making overnight 'Bhangra' stars.

MR RANJIT SINGH BHAMRA (Artist-Consultant)

PLACE OF BIRTH: Uganda, 9.11.57
MARITAL STATUS: Single
COLLEGE: National Star Centre College for people with disabilities. University of Portsmouth
ACADEMIC QUALIFICATIONS: O-Levels, RSA Stage 1 English & Arithmetic
PROFESSIONAL QUALIFICATIONS: The International Association of Book-Keepers Limited, Amateur Radio Certificate
DIRECTORSHIPS: Mgmt Board-London & Quadrant Bexley Housing Assoc., Chair Bexley Social Services Inspection. Consultant for Global Access Consultancy
MEMBERSHIPS: Radio Society of Great Britain, Disabled Drivers Association, Disabled Photographers Association, Mouth & Foot Painting Artists Association
HOBBIES AND INTERESTS: Music-fav. Asian arts Ravi Shankar, concerts, cinema, theatre, painting, visiting galleries, history of art, photography, reading, astronomy, philosophy
PERSONAL PROFILE: As a keen amateur artist Ranjit Bhamra has had many one-man exhibitions and is a student member of the Mouth and Foot Painting Arts Association. He is a hard worker in the local community and supporter of many charitable causes. Despite his severe disability he leads a very active life.
NOMINATED BY: Malkit Sehra

MR HIRALAL BHANDERI (Photographer)

Operational LEB Director, Dimond Photo Ltd, 28 Ballards Lane, Finchley Central, London, N3 2BJ

PLACE OF BIRTH: Kenya, 9.7.56
MARITAL STATUS: Married
CHILDREN: Two (Bijal, Sunil)
ACADEMIC QUALIFICATIONS: Dip. Commercial Photography
PROFESSIONAL QUALIFICATIONS: Dip.-P.I.
DIRECTORSHIPS: Dimond Photo Ltd
MEMBERSHIPS: PMA International, Cineworld Publications Inter.
HONOURS/AWARDS: Best Photographer 1998
HOBBIES AND INTERESTS: Photography, jogging, fitness, swimming
PERSONAL PROFILE: Asian School of Photography consultant-consultant in business trouble shooting, specialising in photo business.

MR BASHESHAR NATH BHANOT (Teacher)

ESL, Mayfield High School, Mayfield College, Goodmayes, Ilford, IG3 9JY

PLACE OF BIRTH: India, 15.6.35
MARITAL STATUS: Married
CHILDREN: Four (Shashi, Ravi, Ritu, Seema)
COLLEGE: Punjab, India
ACADEMIC QUALIFICATIONS: BA & MA History
PROFESSIONAL QUALIFICATIONS: Post Graduate, Diploma in Education, Sheffield
MEMBERSHIPS: Overseas Friends of the BJP-secretary
HONOURS/AWARDS: Long service award in teaching from L B Redbridge
HOBBIES AND INTERESTS: Work for the betterment of Hindu temples and organisations
PERSONAL PROFILE: Served Kenya Government Education Department 1959-1972 Retired on pension. Teaching in LB of Redbridge 1973-retiring in 2000 AD. Ex-secretary V.H. Panisheet (UK), Ilford 1986 -1989 work for Hindu charitable organisations to help blind people in India.

MR RABINDER BHANOT JP (Pharmacist-Chiropodist)

59A High Street, Wanstead, London, E11 2AE

PLACE OF BIRTH: Kenya, 30.1.61
MARITAL STATUS: Married
CHILDREN: Three (Pranav, Varun, Ravina)
COLLEGE: Liverpool School of Pharmacy
ACADEMIC QUALIFICATIONS: BSc Hons
PROFESSIONAL QUALIFICATIONS: MSSCLA, MBCLA, MRPharms, JP
HOBBIES AND INTERESTS: Squash, football, reading, light music
PERSONAL PROFILE: I am a pharmacist, chiropodist, run a wholesale pharmaceutical company and a childrens day nursery employing about twenty staff. I am a magistrate at Stratford Magistrates Court, a school governor and I am a member of the executive board of the Ilford Hindu Centre (VHP).

MR SIRI NIWAS BHARDWAJ (Educationalist-Walker)

40 Whitehall Lane, Buckhurst Hill, IG9 5JG

PLACE OF BIRTH: India, 1.1.29
MARITAL STATUS: Married
CHILDREN: Six (Vijay, Ajay, Bharat, Rakesh, Asha, Rashmi)
COLLEGE: SOAS, London
ACADEMIC QUALIFICATIONS: BA Hons South Asian Studies
PROFESSIONAL QUALIFICATIONS: Teachers Certificate from Kenya
DIRECTORSHIPS: The Bharadwaj Trust
MEMBERSHIPS: Life member ISKCON, Watford, Lands-End-John 'O' Groat's Association, The Ramblers Association, Stratford Hindu Centre
HOBBIES AND INTERESTS: Distance walking, oil painting, reading, travelling
PERSONAL PROFILE: I am a keen walker and educationalist. In 1996 I walked a 1000 miles across Britain to raise money for the Bharadwaj Trust. In 1997 I walked from Calcutta to Amritsar, to celebrate 50 years of Indian Independence, followed by a walk in Eire, in 1998, between Dublin and Inniscarthy.
NOMINATED BY: K K Singh

DR BHOLA NATH BHARGAVA (Education)

President, Hindu Society (Hillingdon),

PLACE OF BIRTH: India, 13.2.30
MARITAL STATUS: Widower
CHILDREN: Two (Kapil, Shruti)
COLLEGE: Salford, Manchester
ACADEMIC QUALIFICATIONS: PhD, MSc
PROFESSIONAL QUALIFICATIONS: Post Graduate Diploma in Chemical Technology
PERSONAL PROFILE: In the UK since 1962. President India Society now Hindu Society. Hindu international development inspirer. Published Hindu community news Shakti Hindi Weekly. Hindu news of Hindu society (now Hindu Bharti). Organised national and international conferences on Hindi education matters for young people.
NOMINATED BY: Pandit K C Krishnatreya

MR PARAG BHARGAVA (Editor)

Managing Director, Cupid (Worldwide) Ltd, 83 South Road, Southall, UB1 1SQ

PLACE OF BIRTH: Bucks, 26.2.66
MARITAL STATUS: Married
COLLEGE: Kingston University
ACADEMIC QUALIFICATIONS: BSc Physics in Microelectronics & Computing
PROFESSIONAL QUALIFICATIONS: Certificate of Retail Excellence
DIRECTORSHIPS: Cupid (Worldwide) Ltd, Vis Media International
MEMBERSHIPS: Lions Club London-Hendon (President)
HONOURS/AWARDS: Melvin Jones Fellowship-Highest award within Lions International
HOBBIES AND INTERESTS: Singing, TV, socialising, charity work
EMAIL: parag@cupid.demon.co.uk
WEB SITE: www.cupid.demon.co.uk
PERSONAL PROFILE: Active within the community doing much charity work and business wise. Helping many through this unique publication which is complemented by singles parties. Creative, lively and young spirited to achieve results throughout. A keen helper and promoter for all sects of the Asian community.

MR RAMESHWAR NATH BHARGAVA
(CONSULTANT MARRIAGE BUREAU)

Managing Partner, Suman Marriage Bureau, 83 South Road, Southall, UB1 1SQ

PLACE OF BIRTH: Pakistan, 2.6.36
MARITAL STATUS: Married
CHILDREN: Two (Parag, Purva)
COLLEGE: BA Economics
DIRECTORSHIPS: Chairman-Cupid Worldwide Ltd
MEMBERSHIPS: Secretary: Punjabi Society of British Isles. IPS, ISS
HONOURS/AWARDS: Shiromani Award, Mother India Award
HOBBIES AND INTERESTS: Entertaining, socialising, cricket, sport in general
PERSONAL PROFILE: Service to humanity with devotion and dedication, our dedicated service has brought happiness to 6000 couples. Instrumental in bringing about an integration of the popularity, some very successful inter-caste marriages but also inter-religious marriages. Have raised charity funds for various deserving causes.

MRS SUMAN BHARGAVA (MANAGING DIRECTOR)

Suman Marriage Bureau, 83 South road, Southall, UB1 1SQ

PLACE OF BIRTH: India
MARITAL STATUS: Married
CHILDREN: Two (Parag, Purva)
COLLEGE: Agra University
ACADEMIC QUALIFICATIONS: MA Hindi Literature, Tabla Vishrad
DIRECTORSHIPS: Suman Marriage Bureau International
MEMBERSHIPS: Hindu Cultural Society, International Punjabee Society, Punjabi Society of British Isles
HONOURS/AWARDS: Mother India Award, Pride of India Gold Medal Award, Mahilla Shiromani Award
HOBBIES AND INTERESTS: Poetry, reading, music, cultural events
PERSONAL PROFILE: In 1972, established the Suman Marriage Bureau, alongside a welfare advisory service and an Anti-Dowery Society. Through my commitment to community have arranged over 6000 marriages and saved several others. As a result, have been the recipient of various awards for keeping Asian culture and tradition alive in the west.

MR IQBAL BHARIJ (HEALTH CONSULTANT)

Legal Protection Consultants, 128 Brent Road, Southall, UB2 5LD

PLACE OF BIRTH: India, 22.2.52
MARITAL STATUS: Married
CHILDREN: One (Kishan)
COLLEGE: Punjab University
ACADEMIC QUALIFICATIONS: MA, BA
PROFESSIONAL QUALIFICATIONS: MASC, BSYA (Reflex); (Irid); (Auri)
DIRECTORSHIPS: Hon. Managing Director
MEMBERSHIPS: MASC, BSYA
HONOURS/AWARDS: Alliance award
HOBBIES AND INTERESTS: Photography, meeting people; charitable, humanitarian work
PERSONAL PROFILE: Iqbal Bharij is a health consultant and a man of great vision. Amongst the academics he has gained a reputation as a 'remarkable man of great wisdom'. He has been engaged in humanitarian and peace promoting endeavours for last two decades. He has addressed audiences in Europe, Asia and Africa.

DR AJIT SINGH BHART (CORPORATE LAWYER)

Legal Consultant, Bhart & Associates, Bhart House, Stratton Fields, 51 Montgomery Road, Caversfield, Bicester, OX6 9FG

PLACE OF BIRTH: India, 26.2.38
MARITAL STATUS: Married
CHILDREN: Five (Jatinder, Satwant, Pinder, Jasbir, Gurbux)
COLLEGE: Punjab, London, US
ACADEMIC QUALIFICATIONS: BBA, LL.B, Post-Grad Labour Laws, PhD
PROFESSIONAL QUALIFICATIONS: Incorporate financial accountant. Law graduate
DIRECTORSHIPS: Stratton Fields Management Company - Immigration Information Bureau. British Institute of Mgmt.
MEMBERSHIPS: Fellow Institute of Financial Accountants
HONOURS/AWARDS: National Best Speech Award, Best Project Award industrial relations. Mother Gold India Award
HOBBIES AND INTERESTS: Gardening, cricket, writing
PERSONAL PROFILE: Councillor Caversfield Council, elected member of East Berks Community Health Council, Mental Health Appeals Manager of NHS Trust, Board member of Grendon, Springhill and Bullingdon Prisons, Lay inspector of Bucks County Council's Inspection Units, lay inspector of Oxford Police Stations and chairman Anglo-Asian Conservative Society.
NOMINATED BY: Jatinder S Bhart

DR BALWANT RAI BHARTI (LECTURER)

Family Support Officer, 33 Rosemary Crescent West, Goldthorn Park, Wolverhampton, WV4 5AP

PLACE OF BIRTH: India, 7.3.57
MARITAL STATUS: Married
CHILDREN: Four (Sunita, Anita, Balraj, Neelam)
COLLEGE: Punjab University, LSJ, University of Wolverhampton
ACADEMIC QUALIFICATIONS: BA Hons, MA, M.Phil, PhD
PROFESSIONAL QUALIFICATIONS: MBA, TESOC, Cert Ed, TCFE
DIRECTORSHIPS: Ravi Education and Training Institute
MEMBERSHIPS: For various NGO's
HONOURS/AWARDS: Guru Ravidass International Award 1997
HOBBIES AND INTERESTS: Economic development for Dalit community
PERSONAL PROFILE: I have a special interest promoting the cause of social upliftment, economic development of the (untouchables) Dalit community. I have contributed various articles/journals to raise awareness for community welfare issues. Donated £4000 to the Temple after teaching English classes in Wolverhampton.

DR CHITRA BHARUCHA (CONSULTANT HEMATOLOGIST)

DEP. MED. DIR/DEP CH EXE, Northern Ireland Blood, N.I. Blood Trans. Service, Lisburn Road, Belfast, BT9 7AL

PLACE OF BIRTH: India
MARITAL STATUS: Married
CHILDREN: Two (Anita, Tara)
COLLEGE: Christian Medical College
ACADEMIC QUALIFICATIONS: Vellore MBBS FRCPATH
HOBBIES AND INTERESTS: Hillwalking, badminton, cycling
PERSONAL PROFILE: Past president-Medical Women's Federation.
Currently-Member of Council. BBC-N Ireland-Council of Lepra.

DR HOSHANG BHARUCHA (CONSULTANT PATHOLOGIST)

Senior Lecturer, Queens University and Royal Victoria Hospital, Dept of Pathology, Grosvenor Road, Belfast, BT12 6BL

PLACE OF BIRTH: Bombay
MARITAL STATUS: Married
CHILDREN: Two (Anita, Tara)
COLLEGE: Christian Medical College
ACADEMIC QUALIFICATIONS: Vellore
PROFESSIONAL QUALIFICATIONS: MBBS, MD, FRCPath
HOBBIES AND INTERESTS: Badminton, photography, cycling, hillwalking
PERSONAL PROFILE: Asbestos related disease has been main professional interest and contribution.

MR AMIR BHATIA OBE (FINANCE COMPANY CHAIRMAN)

Chairman, The Forbes Trust, 9 Artillery Lane, London, E1 7LP

PLACE OF BIRTH: Dar-Es-Salaam, 18.3.32
MARITAL STATUS: Married
CHILDREN: Three (Parvin, Gulshan, Nina)
DIRECTORSHIPS: Oxfam, St Christophers Hospice, National Lotteries, Charity Board
MEMBERSHIPS: Local Investment Fund London East Training & Entreprises Council, Chairman-SITPRO
HONOURS/AWARDS: OBE
EMAIL: abhatia@casley.co.uk
PERSONAL PROFILE: Chairman of a finance company and working as a board member on various charities. Board member of National Lotteries Charity Board and recently appointed as chairman of SITPRO by DTI.
NOMINATED BY: Bertie Mann, Government Office For London

'In 1972, established the Suman Marriage Bureau, alongside a welfare advisory service and an Anti-Dowery Society. Have arranged over 6000 marriages'

SUMAN BHARGAVA

ANJALI BHATIA (ARTIST)

Singer, Wija Records,

PERSONAL PROFILE: Besides laying down her smooth, seductive vocals, Anjali's talents extend beyond that of a mere chanteuse. Anjali decided that the only way she could produce the sound she wanted was to do it on her own. As a former Voodoo Queen, Anjali Bhatia has already been daubed 'DIY's Princess of Power' by I-D magazine for moving effortlessly to the similarly DIY ethic of the dance generation.

MR AKASH BHATT (ARTIST)

6 Blunham Court, Harrowdene Road, Wembley, HA0 2JN

PLACE OF BIRTH: Leicester, 14.1.72
MARITAL STATUS: Single
COLLEGE: University of Westminster
ACADEMIC QUALIFICATIONS: Illustration BA Hons, Illustration MA in progress, St Martins School of Art
HONOURS/AWARDS: BP Travel Award 1997 and BP Commendation 1999
HOBBIES AND INTERESTS: Painting
PERSONAL PROFILE: Winner of BP Travel Award 1997. Travelled to Fiji to research second generation Fijian Indians and their integration into Fijian society. Resulted in own solo show at the National Portrait Gallery in 1998 titled 'Out of Fiji'. Highly commended this year at the National Portrait Gallery BP Portrait Award. Currently working on research for next exhibition studying identity of second generation British Asians.

MRS GORANDE BHATT JP (MANAGER)

Dental Practice, 2nd Floor, 144 -150 High Rd, Medical Centre, Willesden, London, NW10 2PJ

PLACE OF BIRTH: India, 11.10.57
MARITAL STATUS: Married
CHILDREN: Two (Unnati, Yash)
COLLEGE: Bombay Uni, LSE
ACADEMIC QUALIFICATIONS: MA, DEd, Dip. Man.Sc
MEMBERSHIPS: Federation of Small Businesses. Magistrates Assoc.
HOBBIES AND INTERESTS: Batik painting, Indian dancing.
PERSONAL PROFILE: I enjoy performing public duties in my capacity as a Justice of the Peace, a member of social security appeals tribunal and disability appeals tribunal. A member of the board of visitors. I also serve as a school governor within Harrow. I am currently the president of Federation of Brahmins Associations of Europe-an umbrella organisation for Brahmins within Europe.
NOMINATED BY: Dr Mayur Bhatt

MRS LAVANGIKA BHATT (NURSE-RTD)

PLACE OF BIRTH: India, 15.8.22
MARITAL STATUS: Married
CHILDREN: Four (Kiran, Chetana, Alaka, Manish)
COLLEGE: Bombay, India
ACADEMIC QUALIFICATIONS: BASTC and SRN (State registered nurse)
PERSONAL PROFILE: Graduated at age 32 after three children, (BA), trained for teacher training at 38. Town councillor in Tanzania. MOSHI 1955-57. Did nursing at 45 years of age (SRN). Worked in New York SRN and worked in the UK as a sister for nine years..
NOMINATED BY: Virendra Bhatt

DR MAYUR BHATT (DENTIST)

Dr Bhatt & Associates, 2nd Floor, Medical Centre,, 144-150 High Road, London, NW10 2PJ

PLACE OF BIRTH: Uganda, 5.11.50
MARITAL STATUS: Married
CHILDREN: Two (Unnati, Yash)
COLLEGE: Gujarat University
ACADEMIC QUALIFICATIONS: BDS, DGDP, RCS (Eng)
PROFESSIONAL QUALIFICATIONS: Govt Dental Hospital, India. Associate in three general dental practices, London. Own dental practice London
MEMBERSHIPS: British Dental Assoc., Anglo Asian Odontological Group
HOBBIES AND INTERESTS: Cricket, outings, theatre
PERSONAL PROFILE: I am very active within dental and local politics. Within dental world I sit on various committees. I am an adviser to a health authority. I also do consultancy for Dental Protection Society. I am also serving on BOV, Commissioner of Taxes and getting involved in the local community.

MR VIRENDRA BHATT (CHEMIST-RTD)

81 Alpine Drive, Wardle, Rochdale, OL12 9NY

PLACE OF BIRTH: India, 18.3.18
MARITAL STATUS: Married
CHILDREN: Four (Kiran, Chetna, Alaka, Manish)
COLLEGE: Bombay India
ACADEMIC QUALIFICATIONS: Musician, All India Radio Artist
PROFESSIONAL QUALIFICATIONS: Chemical Technology
HOBBIES AND INTERESTS: Music, performing artist
PERSONAL PROFILE: Invited to errect and establish a textile processing factory in Tanganyika (MOSHI) from Bombay, and another in Trika, Kenya was the only textile chemist of Indian origin 1952-1965.

MRS ARATI BHATTACHARYA (TEACHER-RTD)

Phalguni, 4 St Clair Close, Clayhall, Ilford, IG5 0PA

PLACE OF BIRTH: Calcutta, 15.10.33
MARITAL STATUS: Married
CHILDREN: One (Uttiya)
COLLEGE: Calcutta University
ACADEMIC QUALIFICATIONS: MA
PROFESSIONAL QUALIFICATIONS: Diploma in Rabindra Music
DIRECTORSHIPS: Teacher / Director Phalguni (School of Bengali Music)
MEMBERSHIPS: Havering Arts Council, Hornchurch
HOBBIES AND INTERESTS: Vocal music (modern & classical)
PERSONAL PROFILE: Founder teacher and director of Phalguni (School of Bengali Music). Teacher of Bengali music at Bharatiya Vidya Bhavan from 1980-1991. Directed a number of musical programmes at Queens Theatre; Vidya Bhavan, Tagore Centre and in various schools and colleges in London and outskirts. Used to broadcast music from Calcutta Radio Centre.
NOMINATED BY: Sharon Aitkin

MR SAKHI BHATTACHARYA (LECTURER-RTD)

4 St Clair Close, Clayhall, Ilford, IG5 0PA

PLACE OF BIRTH: India, 1.2.31
MARITAL STATUS: Married
CHILDREN: One (Uttiya)
COLLEGE: Santiniketan (Visva-Bharati)
ACADEMIC QUALIFICATIONS: MA (First Class)
PROFESSIONAL QUALIFICATIONS: Trained (UK) for teaching ESL (English as a second language)
HOBBIES AND INTERESTS: Reading, writing
PERSONAL PROFILE: Directed plays (English and Bengali) at the Queens Theatre and University Institute Hall, London. Secretary: Phalguni (School of Asian Music and Language). Ex-founder president of Tagore Centre. Edited a number of books on Tagore, published by Tagore Centre UK. Published books on poetry and plays in Bengali and English.
NOMINATED BY: A Bhattachariya

Besides laying down her smooth, seductive vocals, Anjali's talents extend beyond that of a mere chanteuse

ANJALI BHATIA

Founder teacher and director of Phalguni (School of Bengali Music)

ARATI BHATTACHARYA

MR BIPLAB BIJAY BHATTACHARYYA
(CHARTERED ACCOUNTANT)

Partner, Hacker Young Chartered Accountants, St Alphage House,, 2 Fore Street, London, EC2Y 5DH

PLACE OF BIRTH: Bangladesh, 25.11.44
MARITAL STATUS: Married
CHILDREN: Two (Shermina, Selina)
COLLEGE: University of Calcutta
ACADEMIC QUALIFICATIONS: BSc
PROFESSIONAL QUALIFICATIONS: FCA
MEMBERSHIPS: Fellow Institute of Chartered Accountants
HONOURS/AWARDS: International Excellence 1991, Glory of India 1993
HOBBIES AND INTERESTS: Cricket, Tagore songs, TV
PERSONAL PROFILE: After qualifying in 1973 spent five years with the London office of a top accounting firm, Ernst and Young. Joined Hacker Young, a top 25 firm of chartered accountants in 1978 and became a partner in 1982. A member of the firm's executive committee and head of its Asian Business Community Division.

MR AQUEEL BHATTI (STUDENT)

International Badminton Player,

PLACE OF BIRTH: Manchester, 12.6.80
COLLEGE: Loreto College
ACADEMIC QUALIFICATIONS: Passed GCSE's, Studying for A-Levels
HONOURS/AWARDS: Has obtained over 180 medals and trophies in matches and tournaments
HOBBIES AND INTERESTS: Cricket, boxing, snooker, tennis, football
PERSONAL PROFILE: Since starting at the age of eight, Aqueel has won numerous local and national titles, in every respective age group until present day. He also holds a seven year unbeaten record in North West. Currently represents England U19 and hoping to break into the senior squads.

MR ASIF BHATTI (NATIONAL DIRECTOR)

National Director, Citycare International Limited, 18 Horse Leaze, Manor Way, Beckton, London, E6 6WJ

PLACE OF BIRTH: Pakistan, 4.6.49
MARITAL STATUS: Married
CHILDREN: Two (Ruby, Asher)
COLLEGE: Punjab University
ACADEMIC QUALIFICATIONS: 5 A-levels
PROFESSIONAL QUALIFICATIONS: NVQ Level II, Information & Technology
HONOURS/AWARDS: Gold Disc Winner
HOBBIES AND INTERESTS: Singing
PERSONAL PROFILE: I am a professional singer and musician. I have won a Gold Disc in an Asian song contest for all over Europe. I have made six albums.
NOMINATED BY: James Gill

CLLR CULDIPP SINGH BHATTI (TEACHER-RTD)

Leicester City Council, 27 Oakland Avenue, Leicester, LE4 7SG

PLACE OF BIRTH: India, 25.10.35
MARITAL STATUS: Married
CHILDREN: Three (Paul, Deepa, Roopa)
COLLEGE: Trent Polytechnics, AS College
ACADEMIC QUALIFICATIONS: BSc (Econ) Hons London, BA (Maths) Open University, BA Punjab
PROFESSIONAL QUALIFICATIONS: Certificate in Further Education Birmingham. PGCE Leicester.
HOBBIES AND INTERESTS: Reading, swimming, gardening
PERSONAL PROFILE: Councillor since 1983. Deputy Lord Mayor 1995 -96. Lord Mayor 1996 -97. Chair Navrator Committee for eight years. Chair of Property Services Sub Committee. Member of Policy Board, Policy Resources Committee. Education Committee. Arts and Leisure Committee and Regenerations Committee.

'I worked with a Canadian bank before embarking on an academic career. I have authored a number of books on management accounting'

DR ALNOOR BHIMANI

MR DARSHAN LALL BHATTI JP (TRAVEL CONSULTANT)

Sales Manager, Kohli Travel, 228 Woodlands Road, Charing Cross, Glasgow, G3 6LN

PLACE OF BIRTH: India, 15.3.39
MARITAL STATUS: Married
CHILDREN: Four (Kiran, Sunil, Satish, Raaj)
COLLEGE: Punjab University
ACADEMIC QUALIFICATIONS: Matriculation Certificate (TGWU) English Post C Certifcates (1,2 & 3)
PROFESSIONAL QUALIFICATIONS: Intermediate Cert. in Commercial Education, MRCT (College Ambala City)
MEMBERSHIPS: British Institute of Management, Fellow British Society of Commerce
HONOURS/AWARDS: Poet and Short Story Writer Award (All India Literary Council)
HOBBIES AND INTERESTS: Poetry and short story writer, keen interest in general well being of community
PERSONAL PROFILE: At present he is a Justice of the Peace and District Court judge in Scotland. He has been an associate member of the editorial board of 'Equality' published jointly by Strathcylde Community Relations Council and Scottish Immigrant Labour Council. He has also been a member on the Childrens Panels (a special kind of childrens courts). He is also a published poet pen name 'Noor Bhatti'.
NOMINATED BY: B S Karde

MR KHALID IQBAL BHATTI (ACCOUNTANT)

Co-ordinator (AFSCS), Asian Family Support and Conciliation Service LBWF, 89 Ruckholt Road, Leyton, London, E10 5NS

PLACE OF BIRTH: London, 3.7.69
MARITAL STATUS: Married
CHILDREN: One (Mohammad Fraz)
COLLEGE: Punjab University, Lahore
ACADEMIC QUALIFICATIONS: Bachelor of Commerce
PROFESSIONAL QUALIFICATIONS: HNC
DIRECTORSHIPS: Multi National Training Co. Royale Accountancy
MEMBERSHIPS: Labour Party
HONOURS/AWARDS: 'Leader of the Year ' 1987-1988 Among universities and colleges at Lahore
HOBBIES AND INTERESTS: Social work
PERSONAL PROFILE: Founder member of various organisations and held different posts in London East Asian Business Association, AYCA, Home Start LBWF, Black Community Consortium and Asian Centre LBWF. Advisor Children and Social Service Committees LBWF. Chair Asian Welfare Committee.
NOMINATED BY: Cllr Liaquat Ali

MR MOHAMMED TAJ BHATTI (TEACHER)

PLACE OF BIRTH: Pakistan, 25.10.37
MARITAL STATUS: Married
CHILDREN: Four (Nadeem, Ghazala, Sahdia, Sobia)
ACADEMIC QUALIFICATIONS: BA
PROFESSIONAL QUALIFICATIONS: B.Ed
HOBBIES AND INTERESTS: Reading, walking, community services
PERSONAL PROFILE: I am fond of community work and doing various services for the community. I worked hard during my life. This took the esteem of my family to the highest pitch.
NOMINATED BY: Mohammed S Kiani

DR ALNOOR BHIMANI (SENIOR LECTURER)

Senior Lecturer, London School of Economics, Department of Accounting & Finance, Houghton Street, London, WC2A 2AE

PLACE OF BIRTH: Africa, 26.7.58
MARITAL STATUS: Married
CHILDREN: Two (Sofina, Aliya)
COLLEGE: King's College-London, Cornell University, London School of Economics
ACADEMIC QUALIFICATIONS: BSc, MBA , PhD
PROFESSIONAL QUALIFICATIONS: Certified Management Accountant (CMA), Canada
HONOURS/AWARDS: Fulbright Scholar (1979-81), Aga Khan Foundation Scholar (1979-81)
HOBBIES AND INTERESTS: Theatre, opera, classical music concerts
EMAIL: a.bhimani@LSE.ac.uk
PERSONAL PROFILE: I undertook elementary schooling in Switzerland from the age of five followed by schooling in London through to undergraduate studies. Following MBA studies in the US, I worked with a Canadian bank before embarking on an academic career. I have authored a number of books on management accounting and am best known perhaps for my research on European cost management practices.
NOMINATED BY: Yvette Ankrah, London School of Economics & Science

MS NINA BHIRANGI (ACTRESS)

Waring & McKenna, 11 Gower Street, London

PLACE OF BIRTH: Essex, 4.2.76
MARITAL STATUS: Single
COLLEGE: Arts Educational London School
ACADEMIC QUALIFICATIONS: GCSE's Music B
French A Drama A
PROFESSIONAL QUALIFICATIONS: A-levels's
Media C, BTEC Perf. Arts Distinction, Three Year
Acting Diploma
HONOURS/AWARDS: Nominated BTEC
Student of the Year 1994'
HOBBIES AND INTERESTS: Fitness (gym)
PERSONAL PROFILE: I have always enjoyed performing on stage, in particular
acting. I consider myself very lucky to be able to pursue a career doing some-
thing that I love so much. I have always strived to do well in whatever I do and I
am proud to be recognised as an achiever!

CLLR TARSEEM SINGH BHOGAL (MANAGEMENT CONSULTANT)

**Mayor Boro Waltham Forest, Business
Management Training Centre,** 123 Dawlish
Road, Leyton, London, E10 6QW

PLACE OF BIRTH: India, 1.2.37
MARITAL STATUS: Married
CHILDREN: Two (Parminder Singh, Narinder
Singh)
COLLEGE: Punjab University
ACADEMIC QUALIFICATIONS: FFA, MIMGT
PROFESSIONAL QUALIFICATIONS: Fellow-The
Institute of Financial Accountants & Member of
the Institute of Management
MEMBERSHIPS: BMTC. Principal, Staff Training Centre. The Chartered Institute
of Bankers
HONOURS/AWARDS: Freeman-City of London, Association of Indian Banks in
the UK
HOBBIES AND INTERESTS: Reading and writing books on banking and man-
agement
PERSONAL PROFILE: Management consultant; Delivers training courses on
banking and personnel management. Elected councillor, London Borough of
Waltham Forest since 1990. Mayor (1998-99), deputy mayor (1997-98), chair-
Personnel Strategy Committee 1994-98, Planning and Development (1990-94),
Member of Management-WF Asian Business Association, chair: Indian Cultural
& Welfare Association, Past chair; Citizen Advice Bureau.

MS SUDHA BHUCHAR (ACTRESS-ARTISTIC DIRECTOR)

Writer, Tamasha Theatre Co, 11 Ronalds
Road, London, N51 1XJ

PLACE OF BIRTH: Tanzania
MARITAL STATUS: Married
CHILDREN: One
COLLEGE: Roehampton University
ACADEMIC QUALIFICATIONS: BA, Maths/
Sociology
DIRECTORSHIPS: Joint artistic director Tamasha
Theatre Co
PERSONAL PROFILE: Sudha has worked as an
actress for 15 years in theatre, TV and radio.
Credits include 'Family Pride', 'Network East' and 'Eastenders'. She has jointly
run the acclaimed Tamasha Theatre Co. for ten years and has written extensively
with Shaheen Khan for Radio 4 including the serial 'Girlies'.

MR TARLOCHAN SINGH BILGA JP
(ARTIST-PRODUCER-PROMOTER)

Managing Director, TSB Productions, 33
Booth Street, Handsworth, Birmingham, B21
0NH

PLACE OF BIRTH: India, 12.6.53
MARITAL STATUS: Married
CHILDREN: Three (Bhupinder Singh, Lakhvir
Singh, Harsharon Kaur)
COLLEGE: Warley College
PROFESSIONAL QUALIFICATIONS: Music
Business Management Dip 1988
MEMBERSHIPS: AMBAA, PRS, MCPS, MU,
PAMRA
HONOURS/AWARDS: Various music awards and Gold Disc.
HOBBIES AND INTERESTS: Football, music
PERSONAL PROFILE: One of the founders of bhangra music. Arrived UK 1965,
studied Upland Warley College, started music 'Bhujangy Group' in 1967.
Appeared on TV 1969 Guru Nank 500th Anniversary. Won many awards 1984.
Chairman Race Relations Advisory Commission. Appointed Justice of the Peace
1984. 1986 created Golden Star currently produce under my own record label.
NOMINATED BY: B S Sanghera

MS KASHMIR BILGAN (TRADE UNION OFFICIAL)

Regional Organiser, GMB, Yeoman Buildings,
18 Rutland Street, Leicester, LE1 1RD

PLACE OF BIRTH: India, 5.8.61
MARITAL STATUS: Married
CHILDREN: Four (Ruairi, Niall, Oisin, Aimee)
COLLEGE: Trent Polytechnic
ACADEMIC QUALIFICATIONS: Politics Degree,
Institute of Marketing Diploma
MEMBERSHIPS: Labour Party
HOBBIES AND INTERESTS: Environment, civil
liberties, arts, music
PERSONAL PROFILE: Active within the trade
union movement for 14 years. Appointed first female Asian paid official of GMB
Trade Union in 1995. Believes in democracy, civil liberties, fairness and equal
treatment. Specialist area is the promotion of greater participation in society by
people particularly women from the ethnic minorities.
NOMINATED BY: Allan Black, GMB-Britains General Union

MR KARAN BILIMORIA (MANAGING DIRECTOR)

Managing Director, Cobra Beer Ltd, 21 The
Coda Centre, 189 Munster Road, London, SW6
6AW

PLACE OF BIRTH: India, 26.11.61
MARITAL STATUS: Married
CHILDREN: Two (Kai, Zara)
COLLEGE: Cambridge University
ACADEMIC QUALIFICATIONS: BCom Hons,
MA (Law)
PROFESSIONAL QUALIFICATIONS: ACA
(England & Wales) Chartered Accountant
DIRECTORSHIPS: Cobra Beer Ltd
MEMBERSHIPS: Carlton Club, Hawks Club, Pitt Club, Delhi Gymkhana Club
HONOURS/AWARDS: Vice president Cambridge Union, Polo Blue Cambridge
HOBBIES AND INTERESTS: Polo, scuba diving, tennis, squash, golf
EMAIL: cobrabeer@cobrabeer.com
PERSONAL PROFILE: Karan Bilimoria has a passion for beer and Indian cuisine.
Horrified with fizzy bloating Euro-lagers served in Indian restaurants, he decided
to develop an Indian lager which perfectly complemented curry. Today Cobra is
the biggest selling bottled Indian lager in the UK and one of Britain's fastest
growing beer brands.

MR GOKUL DAS BINANI (CHAIRMAN)

Binani Group of Companies,

PLACE OF BIRTH: India, 9.8.54
MARITAL STATUS: Married
CHILDREN: Three (Puja, Vidhi, Yashvardham)
COLLEGE: University of Bombay
ACADEMIC QUALIFICATIONS: B Com Degree
PROFESSIONAL QUALIFICATIONS: BCom
DIRECTORSHIPS: India Copper Information
MEMBERSHIPS: Insititute of Directors,
Associate member of LME
HOBBIES AND INTERESTS: Cricket, football,
musicals
PERSONAL PROFILE: A dynamic, energetic and
dashing entrepreneur. Has vast experience in managing and controlling, trading
and manufacturing public and private limited companies. Excellent communica-
tor, reliable, responsible and an impressive track record.

MR DALBIR BIRRING (PLUMBER MERCHANT)

Director, Redbridge Plumbing Supplies, 562
Cranbrook Road, Gants Hill, Ilford, IG2 6RE

PLACE OF BIRTH: Birmingham, 8.6.68
MARITAL STATUS: Married
CHILDREN: Two (Jatinder, Harvir)
COLLEGE: Warley College
ACADEMIC QUALIFICATIONS: 3 O-Levels-
Geography, History and T/D
MEMBERSHIPS: NMBS
HOBBIES AND INTERESTS: Football, golf
PERSONAL PROFILE: I opened my business in
1996, put all my savings in to it, first year's
turnover was very poor about £6000. Last year, turnover was over £2 million. I
think a business is only as good as the person who runs it. If you put 100%
effort into it you will be rewarded.
NOMINATED BY: P Singh

MR JARNAIL SINGH BIRRING (DEVELOPMENT OFFICER)

Asian Over 60's Centre Normanton, 20 Marina Drive, Allenton, Derby, DE24 9DR

PLACE OF BIRTH: India, 21.8.49
MARITAL STATUS: Married
CHILDREN: Three (Johnel, Harnaik, Gurnaik)
COLLEGE: Punjab University
ACADEMIC QUALIFICATIONS: BA Honours
PROFESSIONAL QUALIFICATIONS: Social worker
HONOURS/AWARDS: Civic Award City of Derby
HOBBIES AND INTERESTS: Weightlifting, reading
PERSONAL PROFILE: Began powerlifting in 1970, won 200 championships two World, four European and 16 British: Two school governor, chair Buxton High Peak College for Equal Opp. Tec: Officer of European Powerlifting Org: Director/vice chair Law Centre in Derby.

MR JOGINDER BIRRING (MANAGING DIRECTOR)

Corporate Investigator, Millenium Associated Network Ltd, The Docklands, London, E3 5AN

PLACE OF BIRTH: Dartford, 11.9.67
MARITAL STATUS: Single
COLLEGE: City Way Rochester Kent
ACADEMIC QUALIFICATIONS: 8 O-Levels, 7 CSE's, BTEC General
PROFESSIONAL QUALIFICATIONS: BTEC National Business Studies
DIRECTORSHIPS: MAN Ltd and Top Overseas Projects Ltd (Mumbai)
MEMBERSHIPS: Members of US Security and Investigation Councils
HONOURS/AWARDS: Interviews on Star TV India, Zee TV UK. Articles in The Times of India.
HOBBIES AND INTERESTS: Travelling, music, internet, socialising, reading
EMAIL: mangroup@excite.com
PERSONAL PROFILE: Started Europe's first and only Asian corporate and private investigation company-merged with 'Tops Detectives and Security' In Mumbai, the largest security company in India. Formed joint venture Tops Overseas Projects and MAN Ltd. For Asians around the world who need help.
NOMINATED BY: Brendan Clarkson

DR GAUTAM BODIWALA JP (DOCTOR)

Head of Accident & Emergency, Leicester Royal Infirmary NHS Trust, Infirmary Square, Leicester, LE1 5WW

PLACE OF BIRTH: India, 11.10.43
MARITAL STATUS: Married
CHILDREN: Two (Dhaval, Janki)
COLLEGE: Gujarat University
PROFESSIONAL QUALIFICATIONS: MBBS, MS, FFAEM, FICS, FICA
MEMBERSHIPS: Faculty of A & E Medicine, British Assoc of A & E Medicine
HONOURS/AWARDS: Justice of the Peace, Man of the Year, Mother India Int Award. Listed in many biographical volumes.
PERSONAL PROFILE: Surgeon, Head of Accident and Emergency Dept., Leicester. High academic input, More than 50 publications and one book, national and international contributions. Contributed in many conferences pioneering work in faculty and association of A & E Medicine.

DR E W BRAVE (LABORATORY MANAGER)

Doctor, 80 St Johns Avenue, Harlesden, London, NW10 4EG

PLACE OF BIRTH: India, 12.4.39
MARITAL STATUS: Married
CHILDREN: Two (Sandra, Sedwick)
COLLEGE: University of Rajasthan
PROFESSIONAL QUALIFICATIONS: PhD
HONOURS/AWARDS: PhD
HOBBIES AND INTERESTS: Reading, jogging, entertaining
PERSONAL PROFILE: Graduated from University of Rajasthan in 1960 in science. Worked in India as a production manager/BP registered chemist in an allied chemical and fertiliser company. At present working in a university as a senior laboratory manager teaching and helping students in all technical areas of study up to PhD. research level. In my spare time both at home and university I help students in need especially Asian's, by counselling.

DR SANDRA BRAVE (PHARMACOLOGY)

Astra Charnwood, 10 Bradgate Road, Loughborough, Leicester, LE1 3PG

PLACE OF BIRTH: London, 10.7.69
MARITAL STATUS: Single
COLLEGE: Kings College London
ACADEMIC QUALIFICATIONS: BSc Biochemistry and Pharmacology
PROFESSIONAL QUALIFICATIONS: BSc, PhD Pharmacology
HONOURS/AWARDS: PhD
HOBBIES AND INTERESTS: Travelling, trekking, DIY, sports.
PERSONAL PROFILE: Achieved a first class joint honours BSc in Biochemistry and Pharmacology at King's College London, London University (1987-1990). Further obtained a PhD in Pharmacology at King's College London (1996-1998). Under a Fulbright Scholarship completed a two year post-doctoral study in pharmacology at the University of Nevada, Reno, US (1994-1996). Currently working for Astra Pharmaceuticals investigating novel treatments for inflammatory diseases (i.e. asthma).

MR KAILASH BUDHWAR (JOURNALIST-BROADCASTER)

Freelance, India Context, 42 Hindes Road, Harrow, HA1 1SL

PLACE OF BIRTH: India, 11.4.32
MARITAL STATUS: Married
CHILDREN: Four (Mamta, Archana, Abhinaya, Dhun)
COLLEGE: Allahabad
ACADEMIC QUALIFICATIONS: MA
PROFESSIONAL QUALIFICATIONS: Media & Films, News Broadcasting, Editorial and Management
DIRECTORSHIPS: Retired from BBC World Service as Head of Hindi and Tamil Sections.
MEMBERSHIPS: Radio Academy, Ex-Commonwealth Journalists Assoc, Indian Journalists
HONOURS/AWARDS: Royal Commonwealth Sec: Fellow Royal Society of Arts
HOBBIES AND INTERESTS: Stage, screen, performing arts, cultural events
PERSONAL PROFILE: International consultant, political analyst/commentator on current affairs. Acted as media advisor to government of India. Held charge of World Service broadcasts in the BBC. Was broadcaster in All India Radio; Artist in Prithvi Theatres. Also in teaching as head of department and senior house master in two public schools. Won several honours in academic, literary and cultural spheres.

DR SAYED SUBHAN BUKHARI (HOSPITAL CONSULTANT)

Consultant Microbiologist, Leicester Royal Infirmary NHS Trust, Sandringham Building, Leicester, LE1 5WW

PLACE OF BIRTH: Pakistan, 5.2.58
MARITAL STATUS: Married
CHILDREN: One (Zara)
COLLEGE: University of London
ACADEMIC QUALIFICATIONS: MSc
PROFESSIONAL QUALIFICATIONS: MBBS, DGUMED, Dip RCPath, MRCPath
MEMBERSHIPS: BMA, British Infection Society, Hospital Infection Society, AMM
HONOURS/AWARDS: Presidential Award 1983, Merit Scholarship 1986
HOBBIES AND INTERESTS: World history, ancient civilisation, charity work, protection of the environment
EMAIL: sayed.bukhari@public.path.msmail.lri
WEB SITE: tr-trent.nhs.uk
PERSONAL PROFILE: Multilingual, serious and sincere. Expertise in the control of antibiotic resistance. Prevention of hospital acquired infections and identification and treatment of superbugs. Interest in charity work and the promotion of modern education and technology amongst Asian population. Also interested in the management of stress, time and people. I strongly believe in the principle of equal opportunities and discourage discrimination.
NOMINATED BY: Mrs Asma Bukhari

DR CHARAN SINGH BUNGER (PHYSICIST-LECTURER)

Head of Physics, Dudley College of Technology, 8 St David's Grove, Handsworth Wood, Birmingham, B20 1BT

PLACE OF BIRTH: India, 6.5.42
MARITAL STATUS: Married
CHILDREN: Three (Kiran, Rajevinder, Jatinder)
COLLEGE: Aston University
ACADEMIC QUALIFICATIONS: BSc, MSc, PhD (Nuclear Physics)
PROFESSIONAL QUALIFICATIONS: C.Phys, M.Inst P, Institute of Physics, London
EMAIL: charan@bunger99.freeserve.co.uk
PERSONAL PROFILE: Born in a village, educated at Ramgarhia College, Phagwara. Migrated to England in 1968. Educated to PhD Aston/Birmingham Universities. Held technical posts in research joined Dudley College in 1981. Held many voluntary positions as community leader in UK.
NOMINATED BY: Kiran Bunger

MR KAM BURA (Producer-Songwriter)

Company Director, Sub Dub Records Ltd, PO Box 3340, Birmingham, B20 2NN

PLACE OF BIRTH: Birmingham, 31.12.69
MARITAL STATUS: Single
COLLEGE: Wolverhampton University
ACADEMIC QUALIFICATIONS: BA Hons, currently studying for MA
DIRECTORSHIPS: Sub Dub Records Ltd
MEMBERSHIPS: PRS, MCPS, PPL, MU, PAMRA, AUORA, BASCA
HONOURS/AWARDS: Brit Awards nominee 1993
HOBBIES AND INTERESTS: Music, sports, computing, web design
EMAIL: sub.dub@virgin.net
WEB SITE: www.subdub.com
PERSONAL PROFILE: Having been in the music industry for over ten years, I have recorded over 100 albums in my career. I have travelled the world three times with various acts such as Apache Indian, Stereo Nation and the usual bhangra bands. I have also performed on various hit albums for Bally Sagoo, Stereo Nation and Apache Indian.

MRS SAIDA KHATOON BUTT (Lecturer-Teacher)

Sufi Master, University Of Salford, 107 Barcicroft Road, Heaton, Stockport, SK4 3PJ

PLACE OF BIRTH: India, 21.7.39
MARITAL STATUS: Married
CHILDREN: Four (Sima, Hanif, Shahzad, Shahid)
COLLEGE: Karachi, Pakistan
PROFESSIONAL QUALIFICATIONS: Sufi Healer, Counselling, Writer
MEMBERSHIPS: Azeemia Sufi Order
HONOURS/AWARDS: Sufi Master
HOBBIES AND INTERESTS: Reading, gardening
PERSONAL PROFILE: External lecturer in Salford University. Patron Azeemia Sufi Order which has 20 meditation centres in England and Europe, 52 in the rest of the world. Editor, monthly magazine Roohani Digest, writer of 12 books. Social worker.

MR SANJIV BUTTOO (Broadcast Journalist)

Broadcaster, BBC Radio Leeds, Greystones, Manor Heath, Savils Park, Halifax, HX3 0SS

PLACE OF BIRTH: Halifax, 17.5.67
MARITAL STATUS: Married
CHILDREN: Two (Sakshi, Gitika)
COLLEGE: Keele University, Jacob Kraner
ACADEMIC QUALIFICATIONS: Degree in Business & Finance, Textile Technologies
PROFESSIONAL QUALIFICATIONS: Trained as a BBC journalist
HONOURS/AWARDS: Various Journalist awards and nominations
HOBBIES AND INTERESTS: Travel, family, current affairs.
PERSONAL PROFILE: I am an outgoing and lively person who likes to socialise. I love my career and started life in the army, then working as a sales manager. I was a 'special constable'. Work takes up most of my time, the rest I spend with my family. I try to go to India each year on holiday.
NOMINATED BY: Anjum Mir

'Having been in the music industry for over ten years, I have recorded over 100 albums in my career. I have travelled the world three times with various acts such as Apache Indian, Stereo Nation and the usual bhangra bands. I have also performed on various hit albums for Bally Sagoo, Stereo Nation and Apache Indian'

KAM BURA

Entrants in the Asians in the Millennium have been nominated for their achievements and contributions. You can nominate someone who deserves to be in the Who's Who of Asian Achievers 2000

Entries are free

Send in your nominations, including name, contact address and telephone number to:

Books Division, Ethnic Media Group, 148 Cambridge Heath Road, London E1 5QJ

10 years of service to the Asian community

April 20 1993: Pakistan cricketers hit the headlines after they are accused of a drugs and sex binge whilst on tour in the West Indies. Angry fans come out in support of their heroes, claiming the stars were framed as part of a continued hate-campaign by the British press. They are vindicated when all four players involved are later cleared of any wrong doing

MR JAMES CAAN (CHIEF EXECUTIVE)

Chief Executive, Alexander Mann Group, Alexander House, 9-11 Fulwood Place, London, WC1V 6HG

PLACE OF BIRTH: Pakistan, 28.12.60
MARITAL STATUS: Married
CHILDREN: Two (Jemma-Lia, Hannah)
DIRECTORSHIPS: Alexander Mann Associates, Humana Consulting, Humana International, Alexander Consulting
HOBBIES AND INTERESTS: Tennis, cars
EMAIL: james-caan@alexmann.com
PERSONAL PROFILE: Arguably one of the leading players in the global recruitment industry. With over 120 offices world-wide, founder and chief executive of Alexander Mann Group. Over 250 permanent staff and 1500 contract interim managers, with revenues of over £100M. Pioneered midrange executive search industry.

DR URMILA CAPOOR (DOCTOR)

Senior Partner, Doctor Capoor's Surgery, 28/26 Basildene Road, Hounslow West, TW4 7LE

PLACE OF BIRTH: Pakistan, 9.9.38
MARITAL STATUS: Widow
CHILDREN: Two (Rajan, Ujuala)
COLLEGE: Amritsar, India
ACADEMIC QUALIFICATIONS: MBBS, DRCOG, FPACert. DFFP
PROFESSIONAL QUALIFICATIONS: MBBS, DRCOG, FPACert., DFFP
DIRECTORSHIPS: General practitioner, senior principal since 1972
MEMBERSHIPS: Lions Club International. St Johns Ambulance
HOBBIES AND INTERESTS: Gardening, walking, music
PERSONAL PROFILE: Resident UK 1968 . Started general practice, with late Dr V N Capoor 1972. During his lifetime was actively involved in charities. Lions Club International (District Governor's wife). Working with Asian community 1982. Visited Italy during earthquake. Charity mercy mission. Daughter-doctor, son-financial consultant.

MR BALWANT SINGH CHADHA JP (SOCIAL WORKER)

Chair-Cumbernauld Area Cttee, North Lanarkshire Council, 19B Woodburn Way, Balloch, East Field, Cumbernauld, G68 9BJ

PLACE OF BIRTH: India, 2.4.38
MARITAL STATUS: Married
CHILDREN: Three (Cheryl, Hermeet, Svaraj)
COLLEGE: University
ACADEMIC QUALIFICATIONS: CQSW Diploma, BSc, MSc
PROFESSIONAL QUALIFICATIONS: Qualified social worker and mental health worker
MEMBERSHIPS: National Committee of Social Work Training
HOBBIES AND INTERESTS: Poetry, creative writing
PERSONAL PROFILE: Elected to North Lanarkshire Council since 1995 after four unsuccessful attempts. First Indian born and the only Indian councillor in Scotland. A member of Strathclyde Police Joint Board. Chair of various public bodies.

MS LOLITA CHAKRABARTI (ACTOR)

Peters Fraser & Dunlop, 5th Floor, The Chambers, Lots Road, Chelsea Harbour, London, SW10 0XF

PLACE OF BIRTH: Hull, 1.6.69
MARITAL STATUS: Married
COLLEGE: RADA
ACADEMIC QUALIFICATIONS: 10 O-Levels, 3 A-Levels
PROFESSIONAL QUALIFICATIONS: RADA Graduate
MEMBERSHIPS: Equity
PERSONAL PROFILE: Acting work-WPC Blake in 'The Bill', 'Midsummer Nights Dream' and 'Dragon' at Royal National Theatre. 'Twelfth Night' for Salisbury Playhouse and Edinburgh Lyceum. 'King Lear' for Talawa Theatre Company. I ran Ensemble Theatre company for two-years in which we did three productions. I am currently writing a three part TV drama with my husband.

MS REETA CHAKRABARTI (JOURNALIST)

BBC Community Affairs Correspondent,

PLACE OF BIRTH: Isleworth, 12.12.64
MARITAL STATUS: Married
CHILDREN: One (Daniel Ashoke Hamilton)
COLLEGE: Exeter College, Oxford
ACADEMIC QUALIFICATIONS: BA Hons English and French
EMAIL: reetachakrabarti@bbc.co.uk
PERSONAL PROFILE: I have worked in BBC Network News since 1991, after a short stint in local radio and regional newspapers. Since 1997 I've been the BBC's community affairs correspondent, covering race-related news stories for all national BBC television and radio outlets. Most recently I have worked extensively on the Stephen Lawrence inquiry.

DR DEBABRATA CHAKRABORTI MBE (DOCTOR)

4 Binham Road, South Wooton, Kings Lynn, Norfolk, PE30 3TB

PLACE OF BIRTH: India, 1.1.37
MARITAL STATUS: Married
CHILDREN: Two (Saptarshi, Debika)
COLLEGE: NRS Medical College
ACADEMIC QUALIFICATIONS: MBBS
PROFESSIONAL QUALIFICATIONS: DPM, FRC Psych
HONOURS/AWARDS: MBE (1997)
HOBBIES AND INTERESTS: Reading, writing, music, films, drama
PERSONAL PROFILE: Retired consultant psychiatrist, regional tutor. Wrote two leading articles in the British Medical Journal. Reviewed TV documentaries and books for the British Medical Journal.

MR GAUTAM CHAKRAVARTY (BUSINESSSMAN)

Director, Federation of Ambedkarite & Buddhist Orgs. UK, Milan House, 8 Kingsland Road, London, E2 8DA

PLACE OF BIRTH: India
MARITAL STATUS: Married
CHILDREN: One (Ashok)
COLLEGE: Gujarat University, London University
ACADEMIC QUALIFICATIONS: Graduate in Economics and read Law, History and Political Science in the UK
DIRECTORSHIPS: Company Director
MEMBERSHIPS: Federation of Ambedkarite & Buddhist organisations UK
HONOURS/AWARDS: International Ambedkar Award
HOBBIES AND INTERESTS: Reading, writing, travelling, co-ordination of developing community projects
EMAIL: c.gautam@milanhouse.demon.co.uk
PERSONAL PROFILE: Arrived in the UK from India in 1969 after graduating in economics. In England, read law, history, political science. Founder-general secretary of Dr Ambedkar Memorial Trust which was formed in 1972. Closely associated with the Ambedkarite and Buddhist movement within UK. To promote Dr Ambedkar Mission worldwide, often visit US, Canada, Germany, Italy, France, Netherland, Spain, India, Malaysia and Nepal. Currently heavily involved with co-ordination of projects for developing countries.

MR SANDIP CHAKRAVARTY (STUDENT)

103 London Road, Plaistow, London, E13 0DA

PLACE OF BIRTH: England, 22.12.77
MARITAL STATUS: Student
COLLEGE: Thames Valley University
ACADEMIC QUALIFICATIONS: BTEC National Diploma in Computer Studies
HOBBIES AND INTERESTS: Music, playing tabla
PERSONAL PROFILE: I have been playing tabla from a very young age. I performed at the Royal Albert Hall at the age of 16 representing Newham Academy of Music (Asian Section). I have performed in various countries such as America, India, Belgium, Luxembourg and Gran Canaria.

Arguably one of the leading players in the global recruitment industry. With over 120 offices world-wide, founder and chief executive of Alexander Mann Group

JAMES CAAN

MR CHAMAN LAL CHAMAN (Arts Advisor)

Arts Advisor, Arts, Events & Venues Services, 42 Lansbury Drive, Hayes, YB4 8SB

PLACE OF BIRTH: India, 15.5.34
MARITAL STATUS: Married
CHILDREN: Three (Anurita, Anil, Rajiv)
COLLEGE: Punjab University
PROFESSIONAL QUALIFICATIONS: Producer, Director Radio & TV Programmes
MEMBERSHIPS: Lions Club
HOBBIES AND INTERESTS: Walking, music, travelling
PERSONAL PROFILE: Writer/broadcaster. Author: Guthli A collection Punjabi poems. Co-editor: Slivers a multi-lingual anthology of Punjabi, Hindi, Urdu and Bangla poems with English translation. Lyricist of over 40 recorded songs. Worked with BBC Radio and TV, LBC Radio, Sunrise Radio and former head of Voice of Kenya.

MR JASWANT CHANA (Garage Proprietor)

Ravensden Service Station, No. 8 Swindale, Brickhill, Bedford, MK41 7TT

PLACE OF BIRTH: India, 5.12.49
MARITAL STATUS: Married
CHILDREN: Four (Kashmir, Parmjit, Kamljit, Ravinder)
HOBBIES AND INTERESTS: Fundraising for national, International causes through sport
PERSONAL PROFILE: Having built two successful businesses and a loving family environment over the last eight years I have dedicated my spare time to raising money for various causes and charities. A hardworking, cheerful and confident second generation Asian hoping to make a small difference to the lifes of the less fortunate.
NOMINATED BY: Miss Pritpal Bhogal

MR ANUJ CHANDE (Chartered Accountant)

Partner, Grant Thornton, Grant Thorton House, Melton Street, London, NW1 2EP

PLACE OF BIRTH: Tanzania, 22.9.59
MARITAL STATUS: Married
CHILDREN: One (Polomi)
COLLEGE: City Of London University
ACADEMIC QUALIFICATIONS: 13 O-level's, 3 A-level's, 1 S-level
PROFESSIONAL QUALIFICATIONS: Fellow Inst of Chartered Accountants
DIRECTORSHIPS: India Restaurants Ltd
HOBBIES AND INTERESTS: Painting, yoga, tennis
PERSONAL PROFILE: Having qualified in 1981 with Coopers Lybrand, Anuj spent two years in US with NCR. Previously in charge of management consultancy in the South East region, he now specialises in serving Asian businesses at Grant Thornton. He was one of the youngest partners in the country when appointed in 1990. Married to Nishma with one daughter Polomi.
NOMINATED BY: Dr Spinder Dhaliwal

MR RAM SINGH CHANDELLA (Photo-Journalist Rtd)

Portrait Photographer, 39 Beavers Lane, Hounslow, TW4 6EH

PLACE OF BIRTH: India, 5.11.32
MARITAL STATUS: Married
CHILDREN: Five (Ajit, Pradeep, Dilip, Ravindra Bala, Madhu Bala)
COLLEGE: Bundelkhand Degree College
ACADEMIC QUALIFICATIONS: BA, Part 1
PROFESSIONAL QUALIFICATIONS: LMPA, LBPPA. New York Institute of Photography (Graduation)
MEMBERSHIPS: National Union of Journalists
HONOURS/AWARDS: Daily Telegraph
HOBBIES AND INTERESTS: Photography, Indian classical music
PERSONAL PROFILE: Arrived with the ambition to become a photo-journalist. Won the Daily Telegraph award, encouraged by picture agencies from Germany and US. After about a year, armed with my press-cuttings, I applied for membership of National Union of Journalists. Got the NUJ card and soon was able to get the job of press-photographer.

CLLR UMESH CHANDER JP (Councillor)

Mayor, London Borough Ealing, The Mayor's Parlour, Ealing Town Hall, New Broadway, London, W5 2BY

PLACE OF BIRTH: India, 3.6.51
MARITAL STATUS: Married
CHILDREN: Two (Dinesh, Hitesh)
COLLEGE: Punjab University
ACADEMIC QUALIFICATIONS: BSc, BEd
PROFESSIONAL QUALIFICATIONS: Railway Inspector
MEMBERSHIPS: Magistrate Assoc. BDA, London Mayors Association, Hindu Temple Trust. RMT
HOBBIES AND INTERESTS: Cricket, tennis, table tennis, music
PERSONAL PROFILE: Umesh has been serving the local community for the last 22 years. Mayor of LB Ealing for 1998-99, deputy 1997-98, chair of Planning 1994-97, magistrate 1992 – , chair of staff committee at Featherstone High School. Also secretary of Shri Ram Temple.

CAPTAIN KANDIAH CHANDRAN MBE (Chief Executive)

Director-Secretary, Preset Education & Employment Charitable Trust, 2nd Floor Offices, 201 High Street, Acton, London, W3 9DD

PLACE OF BIRTH: Sri Lanka, 12.12.32
MARITAL STATUS: Married
CHILDREN: Three (Dr Siddhartha, Shankar, Chitra)
COLLEGE: University of Madras
ACADEMIC QUALIFICATIONS: BSc (Hon)
PROFESSIONAL QUALIFICATIONS: Trained Accountant
DIRECTORSHIPS: Preset Education & Employment Charitable Trust
HONOURS/AWARDS: Winner of Jack David Award for Black Achiever of the Year 1994, Honoured by the 1990 Trust in 1995, 1996 awarded an MBE
HOBBIES AND INTERESTS: Reading
PERSONAL PROFILE: Captain Chandran was born in Sri Lanka in 1932, educated in Colombo graduating with a Bachelor of Science Degree in Botany, Chemistry and Zoology at the University of Madras in 1956. He taught for a year at Trinity College in Sri Lanka before joining the army as a commissioned officer and at the time of his discharge in 1965 he had progressed to the rank of captain.
NOMINATED BY: Jasper Singh

DR QUDSIA CHANDRAN (General Practitioner)

Doctor, Drs TR & Q Chandran, Pantiles Medical Centre, Church Street, Ashfield, NG17 1EX

PLACE OF BIRTH: Pakistan
MARITAL STATUS: Married
CHILDREN: Three (Kannan Saleem, Parosha amd Ruban Karim)
COLLEGE: Fatima Jinnah Medical College
ACADEMIC QUALIFICATIONS: Lahore, Punjab and Pakistan
PROFESSIONAL QUALIFICATIONS: MBBS, DRCOG
MEMBERSHIPS: British Medical Association, Overseas Doctors Association, Conservative Medical Society , Sherwood & Ashfield Conservative Association
HONOURS/AWARDS: Women of the Year Award 1996 & 98
HOBBIES AND INTERESTS: Reading, travelling, attending medical conferences, theatre, cinema, badminton, cooking, swimming
PERSONAL PROFILE: Dr Qudsia Chandran practices as principal general practitioner and family planning officer with husband. Completed 30 years of uninterrupted practice together. She is chairman Sherwood Conservative Women's Committee and vice-chairman, Overseas Doctors Association. Spoken at Conservative Party conferences and women's conferences. Received Women of the Year Award in 1996 and 1998.

> Dr Qudsia Chandran practices as principal general practitioner and family planning officer with husband. Completed 30 years of uninterrupted practice together. She is chairman Sherwood Conservative Women's Committee and vice-chairman, Overseas Doctors Association

DR THAMBITHURAI RAJ CHANDRAN
(General Practitioner)

Principal, Commission For Racial Equality, Shalimar, 53 Sheepwalk Lane, Ravenshead, Nottingham, NG15 9FN

PLACE OF BIRTH: Sri Lankan (Malaysia), 29.9.38
MARITAL STATUS: Married
CHILDREN: Three (Kannan, Parosha, Ruban)
COLLEGE: Ceylon Medical College
ACADEMIC QUALIFICATIONS: MBBS (Sri Lanka) DRCOG (UK)
DIRECTORSHIPS: Manor Group Nursing Homes
MEMBERSHIPS: BMA, ODA, RCGB, FACA, Fellow Royal Society of Medicine
HOBBIES AND INTERESTS: Reading, travelling, race relations
PERSONAL PROFILE: Commissioner, CRE, former Conservative parliamentary candidate (Preston). Former Ashfield District councillor, Former chairman One Nation Forum, ODA (Trent), BMA Mansfield, Mansfield Medical Society. President Ashfield Conservative Association. Chairman, Brit-Asian Education Trust.
NOMINATED BY: Ms Hannah Davis, Commission for Racial Equality

MR JATINDER SINGH CHATHA (Student)

Deansfield High School, 2 Chillington Fields, East Park, Wolverhampton, WV1 2BY

PLACE OF BIRTH: Wolverhampton, 23.6.83
MARITAL STATUS: Single
COLLEGE: Deansfield High School
ACADEMIC QUALIFICATIONS: 9 GCSE's
MEMBERSHIPS: BOA-British Olympic Association, BAI-Birmingham Athletics Institute
HONOURS/AWARDS: 5 National Wrestling Championships, 10th in world U16's
HOBBIES AND INTERESTS: Sports, movies, religion, talking
EMAIL: junior@singh45freeserve.co.uk
PERSONAL PROFILE: I really enjoy sports and believe everyone should take part in a sport. I love winning and training. I started to wrestle when I was six years old because my brothers used to wrestle, therefore I did as well. My grandfather was also a wrestler in India. I hope to go to the Olympics and one day be a world champion.
NOMINATED BY: J E Ault, Midlands Region Olympic Wrestling Association

MR AMAL KUMAR CHATTERJEE (Neuro-Surgeon Rtd)

Royal Preston Hospital, Fulwood, Preston

PLACE OF BIRTH: Calcutta, 1.8.25
MARITAL STATUS: Married
CHILDREN: One (Dr Amit Kumar)
COLLEGE: Edinburgh University, Calcutta University
ACADEMIC QUALIFICATIONS: MBBS, DGO (Cal)
PROFESSIONAL QUALIFICATIONS: FRCS (Edinburgh)
DIRECTORSHIPS: Local chair (Medical)-REC, Community Health Council.
MEMBERSHIPS: British Neuro Surgical Society, North of England Neurological Association
HONOURS/AWARDS: Local president-Overseas Medical Association. Medal-Fellow of ODA
HOBBIES AND INTERESTS: Sports, writer, religious advisor and priest
PERSONAL PROFILE: Supporter of universal brotherhood. Very keen on peaceful co-existence. Hates controversies, confrontations and conflicts of any nature. Complete belief in spiritual upliftment.

DR DEBJANI CHATTERJEE (Writer-Poet)

11 Donnington Road, Sheffield, S2 2RF

PLACE OF BIRTH: India, 21.11.52
MARITAL STATUS: Married
COLLEGE: University-Kent, Lancaster, Cairo
ACADEMIC QUALIFICATIONS: BA, MA, PhD
HOBBIES AND INTERESTS: Myths & legends, travel, comparative religions
EMAIL: debanji.chatterjee@which.net
PERSONAL PROFILE: Chatterjee Debanji has lived and studied in many countries around the world prior to settling and marrying in England. Now a full time poet, writer of books for children and editor. She previously worked in education, marketing and as director of Racial Equality Councils in Sheffield and in Oxford.

DR SATYA SARAN CHATTERJEE OBE, JP
(Consultant Chest Physician)

Chairman, ODA News Reviews Ltd, 'March', 20 Macclesfield Road, Wilmslow, Stockport, SK9 2AP

PLACE OF BIRTH: India, 16.7.22
MARITAL STATUS: Married
CHILDREN: Three (Camille, Nigel, Petula)
COLLEGE: Patna, Medical College
ACADEMIC QUALIFICATIONS: MBBS
PROFESSIONAL QUALIFICATIONS: FRCP (Lon), FRCP (Ed), FRCP (USA)
DIRECTORSHIPS: ODA News Review Ltd
MEMBERSHIPS: Rotary, Indian Religious & Charitable Trust, CIO, CTAC
HONOURS/AWARDS: OBE
HOBBIES AND INTERESTS: Bridge, reading, gardening
PERSONAL PROFILE: I have been involved in race and community relations in UK since 1965 and am still involved both nationally and internationally. Awarded OBE in 1971 and appointed Justice of the Peace.

MISS NEELAM CHAUDHARI (Pharmacist-Teacher)

Singer-Songwriter, ARL-Record Label, 25 Zangwill Road, Blackheath, London, SE3 8EH

PLACE OF BIRTH: India, 25.5.59
MARITAL STATUS: Divorced
CHILDREN: One (Amrit Dev Berry)
COLLEGE: London School of Pharmacy
ACADEMIC QUALIFICATIONS: B.Pharm (Hon), Cert Ed, C & G (Music)
PROFESSIONAL QUALIFICATIONS: Pharmacist, Teacher, Composer, Music Engineer
DIRECTORSHIPS: President of Asianet 93-95
MEMBERSHIPS: RPhS, MU, PRS, BAC&S
HOBBIES AND INTERESTS: Swimming, charity performances, cross-over music, collaborations
PERSONAL PROFILE: Singer, songwriter, composer and producer of debut album 'Azaadi-Freedom' in English, Hindi and Punjabi, introducing the new GAZ sound. Eastern philosophy in English. Vocally trained by Jane Humphrey. Qualified pharmacist and teacher. Community work as president of Asianet, radio presenter, journalist and performer, single parent.

CLLR MOHAMMED HUSSAIN CHAUDHARY
(Teacher-Rtd)

Councillor, World Muslim Workers Federation (President), 83 Cranford Lane, Heston, Hounslow, TW5 9HQ

PLACE OF BIRTH: Pakistan, 15.10.33
MARITAL STATUS: Married
CHILDREN: Four (Nighat, Khalid, Tahir, Farhat)
COLLEGE: University of Nottingham
ACADEMIC QUALIFICATIONS: MA
PROFESSIONAL QUALIFICATIONS: BEd, PGCE
MEMBERSHIPS: Co-op, WMWF
HOBBIES AND INTERESTS: Swimming, keeping-fit, politics, community interests
PERSONAL PROFILE: Came to this country in 1965. Study in Nottingham, University. Teacher for 23 years. Elected first Muslim councillor in 1990, 94, 98. Elected chairman education committee. Attended a conference in Ankara (Turkey) and elected as president of World Muslim Worker's Federation. Actively involved in community pursuits internationally.

CLLR JAWAID IQBAL CHAUDHRY (Councillor)

City of Manchester, 3 Turnball Road, Manchester, M13 0PZ

PLACE OF BIRTH: Pakistan, 2.9.44
MARITAL STATUS: Married
CHILDREN: Four (Naeem, Nadeem, Naseem, Nielah)
COLLEGE: Post Graduate
ACADEMIC QUALIFICATIONS: 5 A-Level's
MEMBERSHIPS: Labour Party
HONOURS/AWARDS: Silver Rose
HOBBIES AND INTERESTS: Sports, politics
PERSONAL PROFILE: Representing Rusholme Ward Labour Party to promote the welfare and social services within the ethnic minority. Taking action effectively on issues raised by the ethnic minority. Secretary-Gorton Black Socialist Society, chair-UK Pakistan Welfare Society, secretary-Asians For Equality.

MR MUSHARRAF CHAUDHURY (Medical Research-Care)

Scientific Officer, Guy's King's College and St Thomas' Hospitals, 27 Linden House, Linden Grove, Nunhead, London, SE15 3QB

PLACE OF BIRTH: Bangladesh, 17.12.73
MARITAL STATUS: Single
COLLEGE: Southbank University, London University
ACADEMIC QUALIFICATIONS: BSc Hons Biotechnology, MSc Computing and Information Systems
PROFESSIONAL QUALIFICATIONS: National General Cert. Occupational Safety and Health. Radiation Protection Superviser. Chartered Biologist
MEMBERSHIPS: Inst. of Biology. Institute of Occuptional Safety and Health, Library Association
HONOURS/AWARDS: 15 Certificates of Merit
HOBBIES AND INTERESTS: Stock exchange, karate, current affairs, computing
PERSONAL PROFILE: Eldest son of Mr and Mrs Konor and Danara Chaudhury. I came to London in 1984 as there has been family roots since the Second World War. I love London and intend on being a helpful and useful member of the society through voluntary and public sector work.
NOMINATED BY: Mrs D B Chaudhury

JALAL-UDDIN CHAUDRY JP (Civil Engineer)

Chartered Civil Engineer, City of Edinburgh Council, 19 Market Street, Edinburgh, EH1

PLACE OF BIRTH: India, 8.10.43
MARITAL STATUS: Married
CHILDREN: Five (Jemshed, Gulraiz, Kamran, Maimuna, Hamaad)
COLLEGE: HW University-Edinburgh
ACADEMIC QUALIFICATIONS: BSc (Civil Eng), MSc (Highway Traffic)
PROFESSIONAL QUALIFICATIONS: MICE Chartered Civil Engineer
MEMBERSHIPS: Institute of Civil Engineers
HONOURS/AWARDS: Lothian Civic Award
HOBBIES AND INTERESTS: Politics, reading
PERSONAL PROFILE: Ex chair Lothian Racial Equality Council. Ex- chair Lothian Community Relations Council. Chair Pakistan Art and Literary Council, Scotland. Member of Police / Ethnic Minority Liaison Group. Vice president-Royal Hospital for Sick Children Committee.

MR ASHOK KUMAR CHAUHAN (Warrant Officer)

HM Forces (ARMY), Ethnic Minority Recruiting Team EMRT (Army), EMRT, Clayton Barracks, Thornhill Road, Aldershot, GU11 2BG

PLACE OF BIRTH: Kenya, 19.1.59
MARITAL STATUS: Married
CHILDREN: One (Pritie)
ACADEMIC QUALIFICATIONS: 2nd In Command EMRT
PROFESSIONAL QUALIFICATIONS: Advanced Educ Promotions Cert. First Aid Instructor, Hazmat Operator Cert.
HONOURS/AWARDS: Gulf War & Adjutant General's Commendation, Goschen Silver Medal for sporting achievements. Royal Artillery. Bosnia and UN (Cyprus) Medals.
HOBBIES AND INTERESTS: Active in all sports, promoting British Army, time with family, learning French
PERSONAL PROFILE: Born in Kenya, I moved to England in the 1970's. In 1977 I joined the Army and was posted to West Germany. I have served all over the world including various conflicts. Joined the EMRT in 1997 to act as a role model promoting the Army. The Chauhan family has been my main motivation.
NOMINATED BY: W R Harber The Army

> 'Born in Kenya, I moved to England in the 1970's. In 1977 I joined the Army and was posted to West Germany. I have served all over the world including various conflicts. Joined the EMRT in 1997 to act as a role model promoting the Army. The Chauhan family has been my main motivation'
>
> **ASHOK KUMAR CHAUHAN**

MR DALUBHAI RAGHABHAI CHAUHAN (Estate Agent)

Proprietor/Director, East Park Investments Ltd, 105 East Park Road, Leicester, LE5 4QD

PLACE OF BIRTH: India, 16.1.40
MARITAL STATUS: Married
CHILDREN: Four (Sunila Vagela, Mahendra, Dharmendra, Manhar)
COLLEGE: Bardoli High School, India
ACADEMIC QUALIFICATIONS: Non-Metric
PROFESSIONAL QUALIFICATIONS: FNAEA
DIRECTORSHIPS: Vice president Hindu Temple, Leicester
MEMBERSHIPS: Shree Sanatan Mandir, president of Shree UKRK Seva Samaj Community Association, committee member Shree Sanatan Mandir-Leicester
PERSONAL PROFILE: Member Race Relations Forum advising the Home Secretary. I enjoy helping others achieve what they felt they could not achieve and get great pleasure from all events linked to this. Helped organise the Navrati Festival at De Montfort Hall, where I was chief guest. Trustee of Gujarat Hindu Assoc. Governor of Shree UKRK Seva Samaj School, Bardoli, India. Vice-president Hindu Temple, Leicester. President of Shree UKRK Seve Samrij Community Association. Cttee Shree Sanatir Mandi, Leicester.
NOMINATED BY: Mr Maganbhai Patel

DR HUSEN CHAUHAN (Doctor)

General Practitioner, British Medical Association, 173 Stanwell Road, Ashford, TW15 3RQ

PLACE OF BIRTH: Radhanpur, 17.12.34
MARITAL STATUS: Married
ACADEMIC QUALIFICATIONS: MBBS, DPH
PROFESSIONAL QUALIFICATIONS: MBBS, DPH
MEMBERSHIPS: BMA, IMA, World Medical Association
HONOURS/AWARDS: Distinction In Medical Studies
HOBBIES AND INTERESTS: World travel, politics, tennis, reading, exercise, social meetings
PERSONAL PROFILE: I am 5'9" tall, well built. I work as a doctor with disadvantaged and disabled people. Medical advisor of the India Welfare Society.

MR RAMAN CHAUHAN (Counsellor)

Development Officer, Alcohol Advisory Counsellor, Swanswell House, Norton Street, Coventry, CV1 5FY

PLACE OF BIRTH: India, 8.8.48
MARITAL STATUS: Married
CHILDREN: Four (Nilam, Hema, Jasmine, Jason (passed away))
COLLEGE: Kadro High School
ACADEMIC QUALIFICATIONS: Qualified inspector & qualified counsellor
PROFESSIONAL QUALIFICATIONS: Presented 'paper' at International level, Prague and Delhi
HONOURS/AWARDS: Social Work Today Awards1993, Hind Ratar Award 96.
HOBBIES AND INTERESTS: Involvement in the community and family
PERSONAL PROFILE: Raman has been key to developing the AAS programme for the Asian community. A counsellor and development worker for the past nine years, he also chairs the Black Alcohol Workers Forum in Midlands, Also a panel member for Alcohol Concern Voluntary Training Scheme. I am the general secretary of the Shri Krishna Temple, played a major part to build a £1 million temple in Coventry. I have organised national and international religious and cultural programmes in Coventry, for example Morai Babu Kathan Shri Yeagna.

MRS VIJAYANTI BEN CHAUHAN JP (Community Management)

Project Manager, Alcohol & Drug Services, 23 Birch Avenue, Penwortham, Preston, PR1 0PB

PLACE OF BIRTH: Fiji Islands, 28.12.55
MARITAL STATUS: Married
CHILDREN: Two (Mayur, Amar)
ACADEMIC QUALIFICATIONS: M.Ed in Management of Community Education
PROFESSIONAL QUALIFICATIONS: Corporate Member of Institute of Personnel Development
DIRECTORSHIPS: Mobiplay
MEMBERSHIPS: Governor-Runshaw College, North British Housing Association, Gujarat Hindu Society. Preston Childsplay Committee member.
HONOURS/AWARDS: Justice of the Peace
HOBBIES AND INTERESTS: South Asian cultural promotion work. reading, travelling, craft and design work
PERSONAL PROFILE: Very active in empowering the local Black and ethnic minority communities utilising extensive experience, knowledge and skills in community development, community education and project management. Also involved in multi-faith, South Asian arts and cultural promotion activities at local and national level.
NOMINATED BY: S Singh MBE

MR AJINDER PAL SINGH CHAWLA (DIRECTOR)

Chairman, Nova of London Ltd, Chawlsons House, 191-193 Commercial Road, London, E1 2BT

PLACE OF BIRTH: India, 6.3.39
MARITAL STATUS: Married
CHILDREN: Three (Ajesh, Daveneet, Tahira)
COLLEGE: Dehli University
ACADEMIC QUALIFICATIONS: M.A. (Pol. Science)
PROFESSIONAL QUALIFICATIONS: BT (Batchelor of Teaching) Degree
HOBBIES AND INTERESTS: Socialising
PERSONAL PROFILE: Founder president Cambridge Sikh Society. Ex executive member Cambridge Community Relations Council. Executive member International Panjabi Society. Chairman Nova Group of COS.

MR SAMPURAN SINGH CHEEMA (CIVIL SERVANT-RTD)

President, Shiromani Akali Dal (UK), 48 Willowbrook Road, Southall, UB2 4RH

PLACE OF BIRTH: Pakistan, 6.5.28
MARITAL STATUS: Married
CHILDREN: Four (Neelamjeet Kaur, Sheelamjeet Kaur, Ravinderjeet Kaur, Surinderpal Singh)
ACADEMIC QUALIFICATIONS: BA, LL.B
PROFESSIONAL QUALIFICATIONS: Advocate
MEMBERSHIPS: Labour Party
HOBBIES AND INTERESTS: Reading, social, religious, political journalism
PERSONAL PROFILE: Practising lawyer in Rajasthan, India. Came to England in 1965. Done civil service, security jobs, took out one English weekly (Asian Times) and Punjabi weekly (Ajeet). Owned printing press. Devoted to Shriomani Akali Dal (UK).

MR AMAR SINGH CHHATWAL (CIVIL SERVANT-RTD)

World Sikh Foundation, 33 Wargrove Road, Harrow, HA2 8LL

PLACE OF BIRTH: Pakistan, 1.10.12
MARITAL STATUS: Widower
CHILDREN: Three (Mrs D Chopra, Mrs M Magan, Mrs B Bharana)
ACADEMIC QUALIFICATIONS: BA Hons in History
PROFESSIONAL QUALIFICATIONS: Editor of religious magazine
DIRECTORSHIPS: The Sikh Courier
HONOURS/AWARDS: Editor of the Year Award
HOBBIES AND INTERESTS: Proof reading articles, travelling
PERSONAL PROFILE: Mr Chhatwal has done numerous services for the community. Apart from editing The Sikh Courier. He has actively been president of Punjabi Society UK. He has been organising social functions, taking active part in community gatherings. He was awarded Editor of the Year Award in April 1998.

MR MOHINDER SINGH CHHINA (ELECTRICAL ENGINEER)

Councillor,

PLACE OF BIRTH: India, 1.1.36
MARITAL STATUS: Married
CHILDREN: Five
COLLEGE: Punjab University
ACADEMIC QUALIFICATIONS: Intermediate Science
PROFESSIONAL QUALIFICATIONS: Diploma in Electrical & Mechanical Eng.
DIRECTORSHIPS: Watford Palace Theatre
MEMBERSHIPS: British Indian Councillors Association, Founder of Watford Indian Association
HONOURS/AWARDS: Deputy Mayor (1990-91 & 1992-93). First Asian Mayor of Watford (1991-92). Watford Racial Equality Council.
HOBBIES AND INTERESTS: Helping local community, jogging, walking
PERSONAL PROFILE: Since my arrival from India to UK in 1963, I joined the Labour Party in 1968, also founded Watford Indian Association of Race Equality Council. I became the first Asian local councillor 1982-94 and 1998-99. 1991-92 I am sitting local school governor of Charles School and former chair and vice chair of the same school.

MR PARKASH SINGH CHIMA (COMPANY DIRECTOR-RTD)

Four Winds, 61 Church Lane, South Crosland, Huddersfield, HD4 7DD

PLACE OF BIRTH: India, 7.1.24
MARITAL STATUS: Married
CHILDREN: Three (Mohan, Gurchait, Gurnaik)
HOBBIES AND INTERESTS: Gardening, reading, socialising
PERSONAL PROFILE: Retired company director of Bon Marche ladies clothing retailer. Arrived from India July 1950. At present involved in various social and cultural activities. Member of the Sikh Yorkshire Forum, Indian Workers Association, Guru Nanak Sikh Temple, Huddersfield Sikh Leisure Centre.

MR MAKHDOOM AHMAD CHISHTI (PRINCIPAL OFFICER)

Principal Officer, Birmingham City Council, 7 Rolling Mill Close, Edgbaston, Birmingham, B5 7QD

PLACE OF BIRTH: Pakistan, 4.4.58
MARITAL STATUS: Married
CHILDREN: Five (Verdah, Furkhandah, Zahida, Kanwal, Fahid)
COLLEGE: Birmingham University, Aston University
ACADEMIC QUALIFICATIONS: Post Graduate in Public Sector
PROFESSIONAL QUALIFICATIONS: BSc Hons in Mechanical Engineering
DIRECTORSHIPS: The Development Agency (UK)
MEMBERSHIPS: ILAM
HONOURS/AWARDS: Black Workers
HOBBIES AND INTERESTS: Gardening, film making, volunteer work
PERSONAL PROFILE: Secondment to local government association UK. National Development Officer for National Kabaddi Association UK. Vice chairman-Scouts Development. Secretary-Pakistan Sports Forum. Past 15 years working voluntarily to raise profile of Kabaddi and our communities with white European people. Raised money for several appeals.

MR RATILAL CHHAGANLAL CHOHAN (GENERAL MANAGER)

General Manager, Indian Senior Citizens Centre, 348 Denton Lane, Chadderton, Oldham, OL9 8QE

PLACE OF BIRTH: India, 24.9.41
MARITAL STATUS: Married
CHILDREN: Five (Chetna, Renuka, Anant, Rishi, Ditesh)
ACADEMIC QUALIFICATIONS: Member of Institute of Supervisory Mgmt.
PROFESSIONAL QUALIFICATIONS: Supervisory Management
HOBBIES AND INTERESTS: Voluntary work for communities
PERSONAL PROFILE: I am a general secretary of the Hindu Council of north of UK. I am a president of India Culture Social Centre, Oldham. A president of Shree Rohit Kshatriya Samaj, UK. A charity with branches in London, Birmingham, Preston, Leicester, Bolton and Manchester.
NOMINATED BY: J P Riaja, Indian Senior Citizens Centre

MR ASHWANI KUMAR CHOPRA (ACTOR-MODEL)

TV Presenter, Namaste TV, 41 Ratby Close, Lower Earley, Reading, RG6 4ER

PLACE OF BIRTH: India, 28.6.54
MARITAL STATUS: Married
CHILDREN: Two (Sameera, Vikrant)
COLLEGE: University of Delhi
ACADEMIC QUALIFICATIONS: BA
PROFESSIONAL QUALIFICATIONS: Certificate in Export Management
MEMBERSHIPS: Equity British Actors Equity Association
HOBBIES AND INTERESTS: Volleyball, qualified referee, coach
PERSONAL PROFILE: Was a professional volleyball player. Was a sports presenter for TV Asia, Spectrum Radio. Acted in Hollywood film 'Monsoon'. Acted in several TV serials and films in UK, India and Pakistan. Modelled for several multinational companies in UK. At present working as a TV presenter for Namaste TV.

Retired company director of
Bon Marche ladies clothing retailer

PARKASH SINGH CHIMA

MR HUKAM CHAND CHOPRA (HEADTEACHER RTD)

38 Margaret Road, New Barnet, EN4 9NT

PLACE OF BIRTH: India, 8.4.33
MARITAL STATUS: Married
CHILDREN: One (Danish)
COLLEGE: Punjab University, London University
ACADEMIC QUALIFICATIONS: BA Hons, M Ed, MA (Lond)
PROFESSIONAL QUALIFICATIONS: MA Educational Psychology (Lond)
MEMBERSHIPS: Ex Member British Psychological Society
HOBBIES AND INTERESTS: Politics, travelling, reading, gardening
PERSONAL PROFILE: Have been active in politics for over 25 years, hold various positions in the party, have been councillor for a London borough. Work voluntarily for various voluntary organisations. Both wife and son are councillors.

MR KRISHAN CHOPRA (TEACHER-RTD)

Councillor, 37 Manor Avenue, Hounslow West, TW4 7JN

PLACE OF BIRTH: India, 27.12.32
MARITAL STATUS: Married
CHILDREN: Three (Bandna, Rajeev, Raji)
COLLEGE: MA, B.Ed
ACADEMIC QUALIFICATIONS: B.Ed
MEMBERSHIPS: President, Hindu Cultural Trust, Hounslow
HOBBIES AND INTERESTS: Swimming, social and religious work
PERSONAL PROFILE: Founder member of Hindu Temple Ram Mandir, Southall. Founder trustee Hindu Cultural Trust Centre, Hounslow. Ex-chair of Hounslow Vishwa Hindu Parishad. Governor of a school. Member of Hounslow Council and SACRE, Police and Ethnic Group, Community Health Council. Well known in West London Asian community.

DR SHELLEY CHOPRA (DENTIST)

The Funjabis (Asian Comedy Group), www.funjabis.com

PLACE OF BIRTH: Kenya, 13.6.70
MARITAL STATUS: Single
COLLEGE: Kings College, London
ACADEMIC QUALIFICATIONS: BDS
MEMBERSHIPS: British Equity Assocation, The Funjabis
HOBBIES AND INTERESTS: Cooking, theatre, travel, Asian comedy
EMAIL: shelley@funjabis.com
WEB SITE: www.funjabis.com
PERSONAL PROFILE: Shelley is a member of the Funjabis who within two years have played to almost 10,000 people including the Edinburgh Festival; Leicester Comedy Festival, Theatre, TV and radio. The Funjabis form part of "One Nation Under a Groove"-The UK's longest running Asian comedy production company.

MRS USHA KUMARI CHOPRA (EDUCATION ADVISOR)

Advisor Education, London Borough of Barnet, 38 Margaret Road, New Barnet, EN4 9NT

PLACE OF BIRTH: India, 3.12.35
MARITAL STATUS: Married
CHILDREN: One (Danish)
COLLEGE: Punjab University, London University
ACADEMIC QUALIFICATIONS: BA
PROFESSIONAL QUALIFICATIONS: Trained Teacher
MEMBERSHIPS: Various societies & voluntary organisations
HOBBIES AND INTERESTS: Music, painting, travelling, politics
PERSONAL PROFILE: First Asian woman elected mayor in Barnet. Elected councillor London Borough of Barnet since 1994. Elected mayor of Barnet 1998. Involved in various voluntary organisations. Voluntary work with the elderly people in the area.

MRS ANURADHA ROMA CHOUDHURY (LIBRARIAN)

Ethnic Minorities Librarian, Cardiff County Council Library Services, 2 Clos Yr Wenault, Rhiwbina, Cardiff, CF14 6TW

PLACE OF BIRTH: Calcutta, 13.8.39
MARITAL STATUS: Married
CHILDREN: Two (Purba Rajlakshmee, Pushaun Paal)
COLLEGE: Calcutta University
ACADEMIC QUALIFICATIONS: BA Hons-Sanskirt, MA Sanskrit, PGCE Teachers Training-Cardiff
PROFESSIONAL QUALIFICATIONS: Gita Bharati-Indian Music Degree-Gold Medalist
MEMBERSHIPS: Board of Trustees of Cadmad-Multicultural Arts Group
HONOURS/AWARDS: Gold Medal for Indian Music 1965, HTV Television made a 1/2 hour documentary-1988
HOBBIES AND INTERESTS: Singing, painting, writing, community / interfaith involvement, multicultural arts
PERSONAL PROFILE: Publications: A book on Tagore's music in Bengali 1987. Contributions to books on Hinduism: The Essential Teachings of Hinduism-Rider. Workshop-Themes in Religious Studies Series 3- Pinter. Attitude to Nature-Sacred Places. Part time tutor at City Literary Institute, London.

MR ATIQUE CHOUDHURY (RESTAURATEUR)

Proprietor, Yum Yum Thai Restaurant, 30 Stoke Newington Church Street, London, N16 0LU

PLACE OF BIRTH: St Albans, 5.5.63
MARITAL STATUS: Married
CHILDREN: One (Rishi)
DIRECTORSHIPS: Asian School of Catering
MEMBERSHIPS: Oriental Chef of The Year-Egon Ronays Guide 1996
HOBBIES AND INTERESTS: Badminton
PERSONAL PROFILE: Founding member of Thai Restaurant Association. Chairman of Hotels Catering Training Foundation. NVQ Asian Restaurant Project. Chair of Stoke Newington Restaurant Watch.

DR BISHNUPADA PAL CHOUDHURY (UNIVERSITY LECTURER-RTD.)

Freelance Lecturer, 2 Clos Yr Wenault, Rhiwbina, Cardiff, CF14 6TW

PLACE OF BIRTH: India, 12.4.31
MARITAL STATUS: Married
CHILDREN: Two (Purba Rajlakshmee, Pushaun Paal)
COLLEGE: Gauhati, Calcutta, Lucknow, Edinburgh
ACADEMIC QUALIFICATIONS: MBBS, DOMS, MS, PhD
PROFESSIONAL QUALIFICATIONS: MBBS, DOMS, MS, PhD
MEMBERSHIPS: Elected Fellow Royal Asiatic Society of Great Britain & Ireland
HOBBIES AND INTERESTS: Painting, writing, giving talks on Indian art
PERSONAL PROFILE: Lectured physiology at Cardiff University, Part time tutor on Indian Art, Cardiff University and City Literary Institute-London. Director of studies on Indian Art-Oxford University-1997. Director of the course on Indian Art-Cambridge University 1998.

MR FAIZUR RAHMAN CHOUDHURY MBE (AUTHOR)

PLACE OF BIRTH: Bangladesh
MARITAL STATUS: Married
CHILDREN: Four (Faiza, Kaifa, Hesan, Haifa)
ACADEMIC QUALIFICATIONS: Birmingham degree
DIRECTORSHIPS: Vice chairman of the Liberal Democrats
MEMBERSHIPS: Member of a valuation tribunal in Birmingham
HOBBIES AND INTERESTS: Local history, badminton, family activities, food columnist
PERSONAL PROFILE: Faizur is presently running two award winning restaurants-The Purple Rooms and Regards II. He is the author of an Asian cookbook. Mr Choudhury works very hard in the community locally and internationally, he also carried out relief work for the Bangladesh cyclone victims, including clothing, food and medicine. Received MBE June 1999 from HM the Queen for services to community relations/
NOMINATED BY: R F Choudhury

First Asian woman elected mayor in Barnet. Elected councillor London Borough of Barnet since 1994. Elected mayor of Barnet 1998.

USHA KUMARI CHOPRA

MR FOYSOL HUSSAIN CHOUDHURY (RESTAURATEUR)

Verandah Restaurant, 9 Logie Green Gardens, Edinburgh, EH7 4HE

PLACE OF BIRTH: Bangladesh, 5.1.69
MARITAL STATUS: Married
CHILDREN: One (Ikram Hussain)
COLLEGE: Heriot Watt University
PROFESSIONAL QUALIFICATIONS: MBA
MEMBERSHIPS: Founder of Dine Bangladesh Campaign
HOBBIES AND INTERESTS: Voluntary work, snooker, badminton
EMAIL: Foysol@aol.com

PERSONAL PROFILE: Mr Choudhury is one of Edinburgh's youngest established entrepreneurs. He is heavily involved in the field of race relations and voluntary work. He is always seeking new goals. He runs one of Scotland's most prestigious Bangladeshi restaurants in Edinburgh.- The Verandah. The restaurant has picked up many awards. Visited by stars such as Clint Eastwood and Sir Cliff Richard who have enjoyed its cuisine. He is also captain of the local Bangladeshi football team.
NOMINATED BY: Wali Tasar Uddin MBE JP

MISS HELEN CHOUDHURY (SUPERVISIOR EMPLOYMENT SERVICE)

Supervisor, Action For Employment, 22 Lisson Grove, Marylebone, London, NW1 6TT

PLACE OF BIRTH: London, 14.2.71
MARITAL STATUS: Engaged
COLLEGE: University of London, Middlesex University
ACADEMIC QUALIFICATIONS: Master of Laws (LLM in Public Law), BA Hons Law with Sociology
MEMBERSHIPS: Advisory member on the Education Appeals Board, Waltham Forest Council, RSPCA, EIF, WWF Animal Charities
HONOURS/AWARDS: Second prize for giant cartoon strip for WWF (1992). Graduate Management Award (1998) by Cityside Regeneration
HOBBIES AND INTERESTS: Animal welfare, Elvis Presley &1960's songs, voice impressions, landscape art
PERSONAL PROFILE: I am an academic individual with two degrees in Law. I enjoy fundraising and organising events for various animal charities, and I'm also on the Education Appeals Committee for Waltham Forest Council as an advisory member. I am a diligent worker with ambitions to pursue a doctorate in the future.
NOMINATED BY: Seamus R Ansbro

DR KABIR CHOUDHURY (CHAIRMAN)

Chairman, Travel Link Worldwide Ltd, 27 Osborn Street, London, E1 6TD

PLACE OF BIRTH: Bangladesh, 31.12.43
MARITAL STATUS: Married
CHILDREN: Two (Atie, Nadia)
COLLEGE: Dhaka University, Manchester University
ACADEMIC QUALIFICATIONS: BSc Hons, MSc, MS, PhD
DIRECTORSHIPS: Travel Link, Bangladesh British Chamber of Commerce
HOBBIES AND INTERESTS: Sports, squash
PERSONAL PROFILE: First Bangladeshi to have been adopted as a parliamentary candidate from Bethnal Green and Bow in the general election 1997, gaining the highest swing nationally. Keen in international development through trade, commerce and investment.

MR MOHIB CHOUDHURY (JOURNALIST)

Editor, Notun Din, 192-196 Hanbury Street, Brady Centre, London, E1

PLACE OF BIRTH: Bangladesh
MARITAL STATUS: Married
CHILDREN: Four (Liza, Mehdi, Noksea, Tanzil)
DIRECTORSHIPS: Notun Din, BBCC
HOBBIES AND INTERESTS: Badminton
EMAIL: mc@planeteast.co.uk
WEB SITE: www.planet.co.uk
PERSONAL PROFILE: President of Bangla Press Club London. Editor of Notun Din. He accompanied Prince Charles' visit to Bangladesh on 1997. A high profile community leader and successful businessman. Well known for his cultural activities. He has produced successful Bengali stage plays and is founder of a British-Bengali Education Trust.
NOMINATED BY: Shofi Ahmed, YGF

MS PURBA CHOUDHURY (ARTS PRESS & PR)

External Relations Officer, London Arts Board, Tel-020 7835 1125, email-purba@africa.u-net.com

PLACE OF BIRTH: India, 22.10.67
MARITAL STATUS: Single
COLLEGE: St Hilda's College, Oxford
ACADEMIC QUALIFICATIONS: BA Hons Psychology, Philosophy and Physiology
DIRECTORSHIPS: Redcliffe Close (Old Brompton Road) Management Ltd
MEMBERSHIPS: Arts Marketing Association
HOBBIES AND INTERESTS: Singing-Royal Liverpool Philharmonic choir, Welsh National Opera

PERSONAL PROFILE: Purba Choudhury's career spans both public and media relations and the 'other side of the fence'-as a BBC Radio 2 broadcaster and as a freelance journalist covering issues that interest her most :- the arts, travel and alternative health therapies.

MR SOHAIL MOKTADEIR CHOUDHURY
(FINANCE CONSULTANT)

RB Group of Companies, 67 Brick Lane, London, E1 6QL

PLACE OF BIRTH: Bangladesh
COLLEGE: London School of Economics
ACADEMIC QUALIFICATIONS: BA Hons Economics
DIRECTORSHIPS: RB and Associates, RB Promotions, RB Agencies
HOBBIES AND INTERESTS: Football, martial arts, promoting cultural activities
PERSONAL PROFILE: Sohail Choudhury is a leading financial consultant. His companies RB Groups stand at the leading edge of financial Bangla Town. Sohail climbed his career ladder from junior sales manager to branch manager in well known financial companies. He is a regular sponsor of major cultural events as well as chairman of East London based Baumont Football Club A team and B team.
NOMINATED BY: Shofi Ahmed

MR AHMED US SAMAD CHOWDHURY JP
(EDITOR-RESTAURATEUR)

Chairman/ Managing Director, Rajpoot & Group / Samad Group/Potrika, Rajpoot House, 4 Argyle Street, Bath, BA2 4BA

PLACE OF BIRTH: Bangladesh, 1.1.56
MARITAL STATUS: Married
CHILDREN: Three (Faheem, Danial, Tahmid)
COLLEGE: Bath / Bristol
ACADEMIC QUALIFICATIONS: Degree in Business Management
PROFESSIONAL QUALIFICATIONS: FISMM, FIM, FHCIMA
DIRECTORSHIPS: Founder-director, Bangladesh-British Chamber of Commerce
MEMBERSHIPS: Founder-Bangladesh Educational Trust, Fellow-Inst of Sales Mktg Mgmt, Hotel Catering Institutional Management Association Chairman: Britain-Bangladesh Friendship Society
HONOURS/AWARDS: Personality of the Year 1997, Justice of the Peace
HOBBIES AND INTERESTS: Charity work
PERSONAL PROFILE: Founder and trustee: Bangladesh House and Bangladesh Centre (Bristol), Editor and chairman-Potrika (Bengali Weekly). Runs large number of restaurants including world renowned 'Rajpoot' in Bath. (Les Routier ' Restaurant of the Year 1998'). Director: Samad Group including Kushiara composite knitwear industries in Bangladesh. Fellows of the following: Hotel Catering International Management Association. Institute of Sales Marketing Management, Institute of Management.

MR GHULAM AHMED CHOWDHURY (CIVIL SERVICE)

Community Liaison Officer, Northampton College Open Campus, 28 Margaret Street, Northampton, NN1 3BW

PLACE OF BIRTH: Bangladesh, 31.12.42
MARITAL STATUS: Married
CHILDREN: Three (Mizan, Shahnaz, Ayesha)
COLLEGE: Dhaka University
ACADEMIC QUALIFICATIONS: B.Com
PROFESSIONAL QUALIFICATIONS: Teaching certificates to teach adults (C&GT, RSA, Dip)
MEMBERSHIPS: Independent member of the Northamptonshire Police Authority
HOBBIES AND INTERESTS: Charity work, global economy, reading
PERSONAL PROFILE: I am an independent member of the Northamptonshire Police Authority since 1995 and reselected by the Home Secretary for further four years again from April 1999. I was chairman of the Bangladeshi Community, Northampton for eight years. I am employed by the Northampton College as their Community Liaison Officer.
NOMINATED BY: Mr B Miah

MR GOLAM SOBHAN CHOWDHURY (PROPERTY BUSINESS)

Harrow Bangladesh Welfare Association, 36 Montrose Road, Harrow, HA3 7DU

PLACE OF BIRTH: Bangladesh, 6.7.42
MARITAL STATUS: Married
CHILDREN: Two (Shahaz, Yasmin)
ACADEMIC QUALIFICATIONS: Bachelor of Commerce
HOBBIES AND INTERESTS: Play badminton, coin collecting
PERSONAL PROFILE: I run a Asian elderly day centre in Harrow on a voluntary basis for the last six years. I am an active member of Harrow East Tory Party. I also run my property business, and I am president of Harrow Bangladesh Welfare Association.
NOMINATED BY: Mrs H Chowdhury

MRS HARMINDER KAUR CHOWDHURY
(FOOD INSPECTOR)

Food Inspector, London Borough of Ealing, HSC Food Hygiene, 2 Inverness Road, Southall, UB2 5QG

PLACE OF BIRTH: India, 20.6.54
MARITAL STATUS: Married
CHILDREN: Two (Davinder, Rajinder)
COLLEGE: University of North East London
ACADEMIC QUALIFICATIONS: BA Hons Economics
PROFESSIONAL QUALIFICATIONS: Environmental Health Higher Certificate in Inspections of Food Premises. Advanced Food Hygiene Certificate. Health & Safety NCBOSH Certificate. LCCD. Auditor Certificate BETEC Environmental Health. Tutor Health & Safety.
HONOURS/AWARDS: Tutor Food Hygiene Merit Award Advanced Food Hygiene
HOBBIES AND INTERESTS: Swimming, art, cookery
PERSONAL PROFILE: Conducts food hygiene courses for the community in Punjabi, Hindi, Urdu and English, Understands cultural differences in cooking practices and helps businesses on environmental health issues.
NOMINATED BY: Rajinder S Chowdhury

MRS MORZINA CHOWDHURY (TEACHER)

13 Gayfere Road, Clayhall, Ilford, IG5 0JG

PLACE OF BIRTH: Bangladesh, 13.3.49
MARITAL STATUS: Married
CHILDREN: Two (Shahtab, Reshmin)
COLLEGE: Dhaka University
ACADEMIC QUALIFICATIONS: BA Hons, MA
HOBBIES AND INTERESTS: Reading, visiting countries and meeting new people
PERSONAL PROFILE: I am very active member of my local community, playing an instrumental role in launching various cultural organisations since their inception. I have served on Bengali International (BI)'s executive committee since 1978. Founded the Redbridge Women's Association in the 1980's. Founded and still vice-chair of Redbridge Bengali Association (1997). Amongst other activities, devote much time in organising many high profile cultural and charity functions.
NOMINATED BY: Rvime B Uddin

MISS RAHIMA MAZEDA KHANAM CHOWDHURY
(STUDENT)

PLACE OF BIRTH: London, 13.1.86
MARITAL STATUS: Single
COLLEGE: Mulberry School for Girls
HONOURS/AWARDS: Competitions, school subjects and sports
HOBBIES AND INTERESTS: Rounders, basketball
PERSONAL PROFILE: I am a 13 year old student at Mulberry School for Girls, I will be going into Year 9, my poetry has been published in the 'Spellbound' poetry book. I participated in a readathon raising money for charity. I was awarded many certificates from Mulberry School. My ambition is to become a teacher.

Conducts food hygiene courses for the community in Punjabi, Hindi, Urdu and English

HARMINDER KAUR CHOWDHURY

CLLR WAHIDUS SAMAD CHOWDHURY (BUSINESS)

Owner, 24 Ambleside Road, Kingsway, Bath, BA2 2LR

PLACE OF BIRTH: Bangladesh, 1.10.46
MARITAL STATUS: Married
CHILDREN: Five (Sonya, Tanya, Robi, Olly, Asif)
ACADEMIC QUALIFICATIONS: Matriculate
MEMBERSHIPS: MHCIMA (UK), MISMA (UK)
HOBBIES AND INTERESTS: Charity works, reading, watching sports
PERSONAL PROFILE: Son of late Delawar Hussain and Asya Khanam Chowdhury. Wife-Dewan Rahana Chowdhury, arrived here in 1964. A councillor, president Bangladesh Association (B&NEs) and Bangladesh Caterers Forum. Advisor Bangladesh Association Bristol Bath and West. Secretary Britain Bangladesh Friendship Society. Trustee-Mother and Child Charity. Founder-member Greater Dev Council. Member of British Bangladeshi Chamber of Commerce Sylhet.

MRS BILLQUEES CHOWDRY (SOCIAL WORKER)

Specialist Officer, Waltham Forest Social Services, Sensory Disability Team, 47 Gainsford Road, Walthamstow, London, E17 6QB

PLACE OF BIRTH: Pakistan, 21.10.52
MARITAL STATUS: Married
CHILDREN: Three (Mamoon, Sabina, Haroon)
COLLEGE: Karachi University
ACADEMIC QUALIFICATIONS: BA, SWA, BSL II, Communication Skills
PROFESSIONAL QUALIFICATIONS: Sensory Disability Awareness, Special skill to communicate with deaf community

HONOURS/AWARDS: BSL II
HOBBIES AND INTERESTS: Meeting famous people, Indian music, old films to collect
PERSONAL PROFILE: I have been involved in a special school for deaf children for 20 years. I have achieved Level II BSL to communicate. I have a strong faith caring for elderly people specially with sensory disabilities to me it is equal to pray five times a day. Being in a different culture is a triple jeopardy for Asian elderly with no hearing or sight.

MISS SABINA CHOWDRY (SOCIAL WORKER)

Newham Deaf Services Team, Cable House, 27A Romford Road, Stratford, London, E15 4LL

PLACE OF BIRTH: London, 14.2.76
MARITAL STATUS: Single
COLLEGE: University of East London
ACADEMIC QUALIFICATIONS: 3 A-Levels, 7 GCSE's, Cert in Deaf Studies. Four Certs in IT. BSL Stage 111

PROFESSIONAL QUALIFICATIONS: Undertaking Dip SW, Social Work Training, British Airways Level I & II Fare & Ticketing course (1997)
MEMBERSHIPS: CCTESW, BASW, RNID, BDA, Community Care
HONOURS/AWARDS: Certificate of Educational Award. (Highly commended) Flying Colour Award for hockey
HOBBIES AND INTERESTS: Enjoys hockey, dancing, theatre, reading books, films and meeting people, also enjoys working as TV/video presenter
EMAIL: sabina@mcmail.com
PERSONAL PROFILE: She gained recognition as a young Asian, deaf woman within society for her work with Asian deaf community. She found her work rewarding after encouraging people to make positive changes in their life. Through her work, she hopes to inspire others, particularly Asian deaf women to achieve and realise their potential.

MRS AMITA RANJANA CHRYSANTHOU (UNEMPLOYED)

C/- Books EMG, 148 Cambridge Heath Road, London, E1 5QJ

PLACE OF BIRTH: India, 14.5.45
MARITAL STATUS: Divorced
CHILDREN: Two (Alexis, Gina)
COLLEGE: Convent, Holland Park. Princeton
ACADEMIC QUALIFICATIONS: Six O-Levels, London Chamber of Commerce Cert Eng.
PROFESSIONAL QUALIFICATIONS: Was trained as a qualified consultant
MEMBERSHIPS: NACF. Support poetry establishments
HONOURS/AWARDS: Poetry Society's Cert of Merit. Credit (Senior), Bronze Medal for Excellence
HOBBIES AND INTERESTS: Art, film, music, theatre, painting, poetry, design, travel, swimming, tennis, speaking various languages
PERSONAL PROFILE: In London since 1954. Convent educated, eloped, married Chris, Greek/Cypriot, children Alexis, Gina. Helped create successful family business-restaurant/superstore QGS. PTA Representative. P/T Consultant for Coty, Estee Lauder, Pringle of Scotland. Artistic poet-organised coffee and couplets at the V&A promoting poets. Readings Riverside Studios. Volunteer for various charity institutions.
NOMINATED BY: Miss Gina Chrysanthou

MRS SHAMSUNNISA CONTRACTOR (Teacher-Rtd)

Chairperson, Muslim Women's Welfare Association, 116 Albert Road, Walthamstow, London, E17 7PU

PLACE OF BIRTH: India, 24.8.24
MARITAL STATUS: Married
CHILDREN: Two (Imtiyaz, Munawar Sultana)
COLLEGE: Bombay University
ACADEMIC QUALIFICATIONS: BABT
PROFESSIONAL QUALIFICATIONS: Teachers Training
DIRECTORSHIPS: Chairperson of MWWA
MEMBERSHIPS: Asia Link Network, Waltham Forest
HONOURS/AWARDS: Civic Award from London Borough of Waltham Forest
HOBBIES AND INTERESTS: Music, reading and Indian classical music
PERSONAL PROFILE: Worked as educational administrative officer for Bombay Municipal Corporation-India-1953-69. Worked as a teacher in London 1966-84 and 1987-94. I am the co-founder of Muslim Women's Welfare Association and chairperson since 1980. Co-founder of Asian Women's Refuge in Waltham Forest-still serving the local community.

MISS HAJERA COOVADIA (Make-Up Artist)

Producer, World in Fashion, 386 The Water Gardens, Norfolk Crescent, London, W2 2DL

PLACE OF BIRTH: South Africa
MARITAL STATUS: Single
COLLEGE: Kings College University, London
ACADEMIC QUALIFICATIONS: BDS / FABTL / MABTH . Make-up artist, Producer
PROFESSIONAL QUALIFICATIONS: Dental surgeon, Make-up artist, BBC TV, Beauty therapist, Producer
MEMBERSHIPS: many
HONOURS/AWARDS: Asian Film Academy Award-Best Make-up Artist
HOBBIES AND INTERESTS: Theatre, reading, tennis, yoga, meditation, working with charities
PERSONAL PROFILE: Dental surgeon, beauty therapist, make-up artist, hairdresser, producer and PA manager fashion shows. BBC TV London and Scotland. Film credits,-Charles and Diana, shocking accident such a long journey, 11 film awards. Awards-Oscar winner - shocking accident, Best Asian make-up artist. Make-up for Elizabeth Taylor and the late Richard Burton.

MRS CHARIKA RAJINI COREA (Teacher-Montessori)

Headteacher, 256 Buckhurst Way, Buckhurst Hill, IG9 6JG

PLACE OF BIRTH: Sri Lanka, 16.6.65
MARITAL STATUS: Married
CHILDREN: One (Charin)
COLLEGE: Sujatha College
ACADEMIC QUALIFICATIONS: Diploma in Montessori Education, Associate Trinity College London
HOBBIES AND INTERESTS: Travelling, music, reading
PERSONAL PROFILE: Charika Corea has been involved in the very heart of Montessori education in London. She was headteacher of Greengables Montessori School in Wapping. She proposes to open her own Montessori school shortly.

MR IVAN COREA (Journalist-Writer-Teacher)

Head of FE. PR and Marketing, Mulberry Further Education, 256 Buckhurst Way, Buckhurst Hill, IG9 6JG

PLACE OF BIRTH: Sri Lanka, 5.4.57
MARITAL STATUS: Married
CHILDREN: One (Charin)
COLLEGE: Brunel University, Greenwich University, University of London
ACADEMIC QUALIFICATIONS: Bachelor of Education Degree, Diploma in Journalism. Certificate of Education
MEMBERSHIPS: ITT, ATL, UK Secretary-UK Board of Control for Cricket in Sri Lanka
HONOURS/AWARDS: Nominated for-United Nations Media Peace Prize (1981), Travelex Travel Writers Awards (1996, 1997, 1998)
HOBBIES AND INTERESTS: Travelling, listening to classical, popular music, cricket, international relations
EMAIL: ivancorea@lineone.net
PERSONAL PROFILE: Ivan Corea has been promoting South Asia and their communities for many years. In a media career spanning 20 years he has met / interviewed the heads of state of India, Pakistan, Bangladesh, Sri Lanka, Maldives and the UK. He was a British delegate to a UN conference on civil conflict 1998.
NOMINATED BY: Shazna Begum Uddin

MRS MONICA COREA (Teacher Rtd)

28B De Burgh Road, Merton, London, SW19 1DV

PLACE OF BIRTH: Sri Lanka, 22.6.29
MARITAL STATUS: Married
CHILDREN: Three (Ivan, Vernon Junior, Ouida)
COLLEGE: Badulla Girls High School
ACADEMIC QUALIFICATIONS: English Assistant's Certificate
MEMBERSHIPS: Emmanuel Church Group, Church of Ceylon Group
HOBBIES AND INTERESTS: Gardening, writing
PERSONAL PROFILE: Monica Corea served the teaching profession in Sri Lanka for eight years at UVA College, Badulla. She is actively involved in church work in Wimbledon.

MR VERNON COREA (Radio Broadcasting)

Consultant-Trainer, British Broadcasting Corporation, 104 Dorien Road, Raynes Park, London, SW20 8EJ

PLACE OF BIRTH: Sri Lanka, 11.9.27
MARITAL STATUS: Married
CHILDREN: Three (Ivan, Vernon Junior, Ouida)
COLLEGE: Bishops College, Calcutta
ACADEMIC QUALIFICATIONS: Theology
PROFESSIONAL QUALIFICATIONS: BBC Management Training
DIRECTORSHIPS: Director Commercial Service and News SLBC
MEMBERSHIPS: International Institute of Communication
HOBBIES AND INTERESTS: Music, reading, cricket
PERSONAL PROFILE: Served at Radio Sri Lanka (Ceylon) as director of commercial broadcasting and director of news after a career as announcer; producer; compere; newsreader, programmes assistant, commercial assistant and business manager 1956-75. Ethnic minorities advisor to the British Broadcasting Corporation from 1978-88 Radio Worldwide.

Ivan Corea has been promoting South Asia and their communities for many years. In a media career spanning 20 years he has met / interviewed the heads of state of India, Pakistan, Bangladesh, Sri Lanka, Maldives and the UK. He was a British delegate to a UN conference on civil conflict 1998.

August 2 1994: England captain Mike Atherton is caught on camera tampering with the ball in a Test match against South Africa. It is the moment every Asian cricket fan has been waiting for. It follows a sustained British press hate-campaign against the Pakistan team, who are labelled 'ball tampering cheats'. How the tables have turned…

MISS RAMONA DA GOMA (CLUB OWNER)

Nite Club Owner, Blues West 14, 11 Russell Gardens, Kensington, London, W14 8EZ

PLACE OF BIRTH: Kenya, 20.10.54
MARITAL STATUS: Widow
COLLEGE: Kings College London
ACADEMIC QUALIFICATIONS: Degree in Entomology
HONOURS/AWARDS: Represented Kenya Nationally and Internationally at Table tennis
HOBBIES AND INTERESTS: National hunt horse-racing
PERSONAL PROFILE: Ramona began her career in Fleet Street working for The Times and Sunday Times, for both Roy Thomson and Rupert Murdoch and launched The Mail on Sunday for Associated Newspapers. In 1983 she launched her successful consultancy helping numerous organisations set up during launches. In 1994 Ramona set up Blues West 14, a very exclusive Blues and Jazz Club in Kensington.

MRS BHANUMATI DABHI (SOCIAL WORKER)

Mental Health, Coventry Social Service, 150 Avon Street, Coventry, CV2 3G

PLACE OF BIRTH: Tanzania, 22.5.43
MARITAL STATUS: Married
CHILDREN: One (Rina)
ACADEMIC QUALIFICATIONS: BA Hons in European Studies
HONOURS/AWARDS: Diploma in Social Work Practice
HOBBIES AND INTERESTS: Community work
PERSONAL PROFILE: I'm a qualified social worker in the field of mental health with older people. I'm a registered blind person, suffer with arthritis and I have lots of health problems but this does not stop me from working with Asian blind and disabled people. I started a group called Asian Blind Association. (Ed: Mrs Dabhi lost her sight ten years ago. After her struggle to adjust she went on to take a diploma course in social science and now plays a leading role in her community providing help for others.)

MISS RINA DABHI (SENIOR SUPPORT WORKER)

Senior Support Worker, City College, 150 Avon Street, Coventry, CV2 3GP

PLACE OF BIRTH: Coventry, 12.2.74
MARITAL STATUS: Single
COLLEGE: Unversity of Manchester
ACADEMIC QUALIFICATIONS: BA Hons European Studies
PROFESSIONAL QUALIFICATIONS: BA Hons
HONOURS/AWARDS: Baden-Powell Girl Guides, 10 GCSE 'A', 4 A-Levels
HOBBIES AND INTERESTS: Music, reading, community work
PERSONAL PROFILE: I am a Gujerati speaking Asian lady and have studied up to my A-Levels in Coventry. I also studied finance to degree level and I am in a full time job.
NOMINATED BY: B Dabhi

PROF DAVID DABYDEEN (PROFESSOR-WRITER)

Professor of Literature, University of Warwick, Centre for British Cultural Studies, University of Warwick, Coventry, CV4 7AL

PLACE OF BIRTH: Guyana, 9.12.59
MARITAL STATUS: Single
COLLEGE: Cambridge
ACADEMIC QUALIFICATIONS: BA Hons, MA, PhD
MEMBERSHIPS: Guyana's Ambassador to UNESCO
HONOURS/AWARDS: Commonwealth Poetry Prize 1984
HOBBIES AND INTERESTS: Travelling
PERSONAL PROFILE: Author of three books of poetry and four novels all published by Jonathon Cape. Author of two books on the English artist, William Hogarth. Professor of literature at Warwick University and Guyana's Ambassador to UNESCO. Author of several studies of Caribbean and Black British literature.

MR FEROZE AHMAD DADA (CHARTERED ACCOUNTANT)

Senior Partner, Freeman & Partners Chartered Accountants, 30 St James Street, London, SW1A 1HB

PLACE OF BIRTH: Pakistan, 21.4.52
MARITAL STATUS: Married
CHILDREN: Two (Sumaya, Nadir)
COLLEGE: Karachi
ACADEMIC QUALIFICATIONS: B.Comm
PROFESSIONAL QUALIFICATIONS: FCA, ATII, ACIA&G
DIRECTORSHIPS: FSI Group Plc, Brook Hotels Plc, European Middleware Cons Co Ltd, Reyker Investment Ltd
MEMBERSHIPS: Brondesbury Cricket Club
HOBBIES AND INTERESTS: Cricket
EMAIL: freemanslondon@compuserve.com
PERSONAL PROFILE: Senior partner, specialising in corporate audit and UK corporation tax with particular interest in tax planning for overseas companies and individuals setting up business in the UK. Author of: Interest relief for companies. Former lecturer in taxation.

MR HAROON A. DADA (COMPANY DIRECTOR)

Managing Director, Hadson-Sudan Stores, 197 Baker Street, London, NW1 6UY

PLACE OF BIRTH: Uganda, 8.1.47
MARITAL STATUS: Married
CHILDREN: Two (Arif, Mobina)
DIRECTORSHIPS: DADA Trading Co Ltd
MEMBERSHIPS: Lions Club of Finchley, Memon Foundation
HOBBIES AND INTERESTS: Helping others, travel, good food
PERSONAL PROFILE: For last forty years helping the needs of others less fortunate than ourselves.

DR JASHWANT SINGH DAHELE (UNIVERSITY TEACHER)

Head, Sensor Systems Group, Cranfield University, 8 Orchard Close, Charney Bassett, Wantage, OX12 0EP

PLACE OF BIRTH: India, 16.1.38
MARITAL STATUS: Married
CHILDREN: Two (Max Rakesh, Rebecca Maya)
COLLEGE: University of Hong Kong
ACADEMIC QUALIFICATIONS: PhD
PROFESSIONAL QUALIFICATIONS: Chartered Engineer (CEng), Fellow of the Institution of Electrical Engineers (F.IEE)
HOBBIES AND INTERESTS: Golf, walking, reading, music
EMAIL: dahele@rmcs.cranfield.ac.uk
PERSONAL PROFILE: Dr Dahele has worked at the Royal Military College of Science, Cranfield University, since 1985; Currently reader in radio frequency engineering and head of the Sensor Systems Group. He is a member of the University Senate and until 1995 was Dean of postgraduate studies.
NOMINATED BY: Prof F R Hartley, Cranfield University

MR MOHAMMED ALTAF DAJI (COMMUNITY CONSULTANT)

Development Officer, Kirklees Racial Equality Council, 22 Cedar Grove, Batley, WF17 6BY

PLACE OF BIRTH: Batley, 19.2.66
MARITAL STATUS: Married
COLLEGE: DABTAC
ACADEMIC QUALIFICATIONS: BTEC National, Public Admin, RSA Counselling
PROFESSIONAL QUALIFICATIONS: RSA Diploma (Working in a Multi Ethnic Society)
MEMBERSHIPS: Member of IMWS, Asian Youth Association
HOBBIES AND INTERESTS: Football, photography, poetry, community work
PERSONAL PROFILE: I have been involved with community work since the age of 16 years old. I have done a lot of work with the youth in my area. For the past eight years I have been working for the Racial Equality Council to help empower and organise the community and their centres in Kirklees. I also help consulting the police on racism in the police force.

Dr Dahele has worked at the Royal Military College of Science, Cranfield University, since 1985; Currently reader in radio frequency engineering and head of the Sensor Systems Group

DR ASHWANT SINGH DAHELE

MR MANECK ARDESHIR SOHRAB DALAL OBE
(Chairman)

'Tall Trees', Marlborough Road, Hampton, TW12 3RX

PLACE OF BIRTH: India, 24.12.18
MARITAL STATUS: Married
COLLEGE: Trinity Hall, Cambridge
ACADEMIC QUALIFICATIONS: MA
PROFESSIONAL QUALIFICATIONS: FCIT, FBIM, FRSA
DIRECTORSHIPS: MD Tata Ltd London (1977-88). Group Director, Bombay (1980) Chairman, Bharatiya Vidya Bhavan UK.
MEMBERSHIPS: Royal Overseas League, Hurlingham Club, Hawks Club, Cambridge
HOBBIES AND INTERESTS: Tennis, squash, reading (Captained Cambridge University in both sports)
PERSONAL PROFILE: He started Air India in the UK in 1948 at the age of 29. He has held a vast number senior posts included are: former president, Indian Chamber of Commerce GB; Indian Management Association UK. World Conference on Religions and Peace. Chairman: Foreign Airlines Association UK; Indian YMCA in London; Royal Overseas League; Northbrook Society; Indian Women's Association.
NOMINATED BY: Dr M N Nandakumara and Dr H V S Shastry

DR MOHINDER SINGH DANG (Eye Specialist)

Clinical Director, South Durham Health Care NHS Trust, "Mussoorie House", 8 Compton Grove, Darlington, DL3 9AZ

PLACE OF BIRTH: India, 2.4.46
MARITAL STATUS: Married
CHILDREN: Two (Neetika, Tarana)
COLLEGE: Punjab, Dublin, Edinburgh, London
ACADEMIC QUALIFICATIONS: MBBS, DOMS, MS, DO (Dub), DO (Lond)
PROFESSIONAL QUALIFICATIONS: FRCS (Edin), FRCOPhth
DIRECTORSHIPS: Director and Head of Department
MEMBERSHIPS: European & International Cataract & Refracvtive Society BMA, ODA
HONOURS/AWARDS: 1st Class First MS Ophthalmology 1973. International Excellence Award NRI. President of India Award 1962. Distinction Award Memorial Hospital 1996
HOBBIES AND INTERESTS: Golf, hillwalking, music
PERSONAL PROFILE: Arrived in UK after masters degree in ophthalmology 1974. Trained in London, Liverpool and Manchester before becoming consultant in 1983. Held chair of Medical Advisory Committee, Senior Medical Staff Committee. Office holder Indian Doctors of Cleveland Society, executive member Sikh Community Darlington and Durham County Racial Equality Council.

MRS SHIRLEY MIRIAM DANIEL (Education-Consultant)

ECIS Limited Company, 7 Churchill Avenue, Kenton, Harrow, HA3 0AX

PLACE OF BIRTH: India, 20.8.35
MARITAL STATUS: Widow
CHILDREN: One (Ravindra)
COLLEGE: Madras
ACADEMIC QUALIFICATIONS: Bachelor of Science
PROFESSIONAL QUALIFICATIONS: Bachelor of Teaching MA
DIRECTORSHIPS: AFETuK, Citizenship Foundation and Changemakers
MEMBERSHIPS: Member Royal Chemical Society, FRSA
HOBBIES AND INTERESTS: Singing, walking, travel
PERSONAL PROFILE: Head of science and chief examiner for many years. Currently inspector of schools and PGCE for Ofsted. PGCE subject tutor and provides inset in schools. Member of Ethnic Minority Advisory Committee for JSB 1991-96. Member ICSTIS 1994-97. Non-executive director of health authorities.

> From a junior in Bond Street to creative director at Vidal Sasoon. Dar left Sasoon to do photographic shoots and give seminars throughout Europe. Dar has performed his magic on the locks of some of the top models in the world
>
> **DAR**

MR IBRAHIM DAR (Hair Designer)

Hair Salon Owner, Dar Salon, 8 Broxholme House, New Kings Road, London, SW6 4AA

PLACE OF BIRTH: Malaysia, 29.3.53
MARITAL STATUS: Single
DIRECTORSHIPS: Dar Salon
MEMBERSHIPS: Fellowship of Hairdressers
HOBBIES AND INTERESTS: Fashion, music, travel, swimming, keep-fit
PERSONAL PROFILE: From a junior in Bond Street to creative director at Vidal Sasoon. Dar left Sasoon to do photographic shoots and give seminars throughout Europe. Dar has performed his magic on the locks of some of the top models in the world as well as on English and Asian actresses and his work has been published in Vogue, Harpers and Queen, Tatler and The Times. He now runs a successful salon on New Kings Road, Chelsea, which is frequented by foreign royals, Imran and Jemima Khan, Fiona Fullerton......
NOMINATED BY: Samina Saeed

MR MOHANSINH RATANSINH DARBAR (Admin Assistant)

London Playing Fields Society, 13 Egerton Road, Twickenham, TW2 7SL

PLACE OF BIRTH: Tanzania, 18.9.37
MARITAL STATUS: Married
CHILDREN: Three (Hitendrasinh, Dhirendrasinh, Nishaba)
ACADEMIC QUALIFICATIONS: Eight O-Levels
MEMBERSHIPS: Rajput Samaj of UK, EMAG Richmond Nagrik Mandal RSSC, MPCL
HOBBIES AND INTERESTS: Cricket, table tennis, social
PERSONAL PROFILE: Arrived in the UK June 1969. Office bearer Rajput Samaj of UK 1976-1981. 1983 continuing. Richmond Nagrik Mandal 1976-1985. 1987 continuing. Rajput Samaj Sports Club from 1981, continuing. Middlesex Premier Cricket League from 1995 continuing. EC member of Ethnic Minority Advisory Group from 1995, continuing.
NOMINATED BY: Dhiren Darbar and Dharmendrasinh Chauhan

DR BHAGABAT CHARAN DAS MBE
(Medical Specialist Rtd)

Chairman, Indian Senior Citizen's Centre, 67 Half Edge Lane, Eccles, Manchester, M30 9AZ

PLACE OF BIRTH: India, 3.8.20
MARITAL STATUS: Married
CHILDREN: Two (Pradeepta, Satya Sunder)
COLLEGE: Utkal
ACADEMIC QUALIFICATIONS: MBBS (With Best Graduate Gold Medal)
PROFESSIONAL QUALIFICATIONS: DTM&H (London University)
DIRECTORSHIPS: President Indian Association, Manchester (92-94)
MEMBERSHIPS: Executive member of Manchester Council for Community Relations, Age Concern, Voluntary Action
HONOURS/AWARDS: MBE-Queens Birthday Honours Award 1996. National Whitbread Volunteer Award 1994
HOBBIES AND INTERESTS: Volunteering, writing, reading, football
PERSONAL PROFILE: MBBS, (India) 1959. To England for post graduate study. Specialist in geriatric medicine for 25 years. Retired 1985, voluntary work for Asian elderly. Has established day centre (social and health care) for Indian elderly, running five days weekly. Still working voluntarily. Now chairman.
NOMINATED BY: Dr R F Mehta and Ratilal Chauhan

MR BIMAL KRISHNA DAS (Priest)

Public Relations Officer, Inter. Society for Krishna Consciousness, 5 Astra Court, King Georges Avenue, Watford, WD1 7TA

PLACE OF BIRTH: India, 26.1.65
MARITAL STATUS: Married
COLLEGE: University of Hertfordshire
ACADEMIC QUALIFICATIONS: BSc Hons Applied Chemistry
HOBBIES AND INTERESTS: Philosophy, current affairs
PERSONAL PROFILE: Was campaign manager for the campaign to stop the Hare Krishna Temple from closing down to the public. Secretary of National Council of Hindu Temples (UK). First Hindu chaplain in UK to be elected mayor of Barnet council. Member of SACRE (Standing Religious Council for Religious Education) for Hertfordshire.
NOMINATED BY: Angela Aery, Watford

MISS MENEKA DAS (Actor-Singer-Songwriter)

LWA, 18 Elliot Square, London, NW3 3SU

PLACE OF BIRTH: India
MARITAL STATUS: Single
COLLEGE: Allahabad University
ACADEMIC QUALIFICATIONS: BSc Home
Economics
PROFESSIONAL QUALIFICATIONS: Actor
MEMBERSHIPS: Equity, Musician's Union,
Performing Rights Society
HONOURS/AWARDS: All India Singing
Competition 1st prize (2yrs), All India School
Competition Elocution. North India Classical
Singing Competition. Gold Disc-Single Sales
100,000
HOBBIES AND INTERESTS: Piano, guitar, poetry, writing
EMAIL: menaka@gormacmusic.com
WEB SITE: www.gormacmusic.com.menaka
PERSONAL PROFILE: Meneka was one of the first Indian females in a West
End musical VOYEURZ, Whitehall Theatre. She was also one of the first Indian
females along with her sister Sheenu, in their group SPELLBOUND, to be signed
by a major record company. Meneka was in the award winning musical '14
Songs, 2 Weddings and a funeral' and has appeared in films, BBC and ITV.

DR SANKAR KUMAR DAS (Doctor)

**Consultant & Senior Lecturer, Sutton
Merton Health Authority Trust,** 62 Rose Hill,
Sutton, SM1 3EX

PLACE OF BIRTH: India, 1.12.33
MARITAL STATUS: Married
CHILDREN: Two (Shumit, Priya)
COLLEGE: Calcutta University, Royal College,
England
ACADEMIC QUALIFICATIONS: MB, BS, FRCP,
FCCP. MBBS, FRCP, FCCP
PROFESSIONAL QUALIFICATIONS: Doctor of
Medicine, Senior Lecturer, Univ. London
DIRECTORSHIPS: Medi-Inventors Associates, London
MEMBERSHIPS: Royal College, London, American College of Physicians
HONOURS/AWARDS: National Health Service, Mother India Inter 1995', Man
of the Year 1994', American Biological Society,
HOBBIES AND INTERESTS: USA Flyer
PERSONAL PROFILE: Capt (Rtd AME India). Inventor of physio-machine.
Published 100 papers, books and computer science. Medical officer Borough of
Sutton.

DR SEKHARJIT DATTA (Computer Scientist)

Academician, 2 Squirrel Way, Loughborough,
Leicester, LE11 3GP

PLACE OF BIRTH: India, 9.6.41
MARITAL STATUS: Married
CHILDREN: One (Shomik)
COLLEGE: Calcutta University, London
University
ACADEMIC QUALIFICATIONS: BSc (Cal), MSc
(Lond), PhD (Lond)
PROFESSIONAL QUALIFICATIONS: FIETE,
MBCS, AMIEE
MEMBERSHIPS: British Computer Society.
Institute of Electrical Engineers. British Machine Vision Association. SSAISB.
European Speech Communications Association. Australian Speech, Science &
Technology Association
HOBBIES AND INTERESTS: Tagore's music, Indian classical music
PERSONAL PROFILE: Dr Datta spent twenty years in various IT research at the
Research Centre of International Computers Limited, UK, where he worked as a
senior research consultant. In 1987 he joined Loughborough University as a
member of the academic staff. His current research interests lie in acoustic sig-
nal processing and pattern recognition.
NOMINATED BY: Veronica King, Loughborough University

> Trained for chartered accountancy with
> Price Waterhouse Coopers (1996-to
> date). Committee member of the
> Southern Chartered Accountants
> Student Society. Southampton
> university graduate
> (1992-96)
>
> **GIRA DAVDA**

MISS GIRA DAVDA (Chartered Accountant)

Senior Associate, PricewaterhouseCoopers,
5 Claremont End, Esher, KT10 9LZ

PLACE OF BIRTH: Surrey, 25.9.74
MARITAL STATUS: Single
COLLEGE: Southampton University
ACADEMIC QUALIFICATIONS: BSc Hons
Business Economics & Accountants
PROFESSIONAL QUALIFICATIONS: Chartered
Accountant
MEMBERSHIPS: Institute of Chartered
Accountants in England & Wales
HONOURS/AWARDS: Acting and Public
Speaking Gold Medal, Duke of Edinburgh-Silver
Award
HOBBIES AND INTERESTS: Watersports, travelling, acting
EMAIL: gira.p.davda@uk.pwc.global
PERSONAL PROFILE: Trained for chartered accountancy with Price Waterhouse
Coopers (1996-to date). Committee member of the Southern Chartered
Accountants Student Society. Southampton university graduate (1992-96).
Awarded a one year internship in US with Price Waterhouse Coopers. Attended
Cheltenham Ladies College (1985-92).

MISS TANVI DAVDA (Banking Consultant)

Senior Consultant, IBM UK, 5 Claremont End,
Esher, KT10 9LZ

PLACE OF BIRTH: Surrey, 5.9.72
MARITAL STATUS: Single
COLLEGE: University of London, London
Business School
ACADEMIC QUALIFICATIONS: BSc Chemistry,
MSc Finance
MEMBERSHIPS: Women in Banking & Finance,
English Speaking Union (ESU)
HONOURS/AWARDS: Best Public Speaker
(ESU)
HOBBIES AND INTERESTS: Public speaking, opera, scuba diving, travel
EMAIL: tanvi-davda@uk.ibmmail.com
PERSONAL PROFILE: 1983-1990, Cheltenham Ladies' College, Head of House.
College prefect. 1990-1993, University of London, BSc Chemistry. 1993-1996,
Credit Suisse First Boston senior options trader. (incl. 2 years in Singapore
office). 1996-1997, London Business School, MSc Finance. 1997 to date, IBM
UK banking consultant.

MR KISHOR DAVDRA (Certified Accountant)

**Company Secretary, Trade Mark Owners
Association Limited,** 95 Northumberland
Road, Harrow, HA2 7RA

PLACE OF BIRTH: Uganda, 19.5.50
MARITAL STATUS: Married
CHILDREN: Two (Nimisha, Parekh)
COLLEGE: MS University, Baroda, India
ACADEMIC QUALIFICATIONS: B.Comm Hons
PROFESSIONAL QUALIFICATIONS: FCCA
MEMBERSHIPS: Institute of Directors
HOBBIES AND INTERESTS: Social work
PERSONAL PROFILE: I started with the compa-
ny as a junior bookkeeper in 1972. Now I am one of the executive managers
responsible for the day to day running of the business.

AVA DE SOUZA (Actress)

**Therapist-(young autistic children), Frazer-
Skemp Management,** 7 Evelyn Road, Ham,
Richmond, TW10 7HU

PLACE OF BIRTH: UK, 5.2.58
MARITAL STATUS: Married
CHILDREN: One (Poppy)
COLLEGE: The Arts Educational
ACADEMIC QUALIFICATIONS: 8 O-Levels
MEMBERSHIPS: Equity
HOBBIES AND INTERESTS: Literature, theatre,
religion, children
PERSONAL PROFILE: Ava de Souza has worked
as an actor in theatre, television and film. Productions of interest include Circus
Lumiere (Lumiere and Son); Twelfth Night (Cherub); The Nutcracker (Sands
Films); Aurang-Zebe (Royal National Theatre Studio). Co founder of Little Blisters
children's theatre company and has increasingly been involved in working with
autistic children.

> 'I started with the company as a junior
> bookkeeper in 1972. Now I am one of
> the executive managers'
>
> **KISHOR DAVDRA**

MISS DAPHNE DE SOUZA (MARKETING MANAGER)

Health Education Authority, Trevelyn House, 30 Great Peter Street, London, SW1P 2HW

PLACE OF BIRTH: Tanzania, 15.7.67
MARITAL STATUS: Single
COLLEGE: University of London, Strathclyde University
ACADEMIC QUALIFICATIONS: BSc Hons-Biochemistry, MSc-Marketing
PROFESSIONAL QUALIFICATIONS: Dip M , MCIM
MEMBERSHIPS: Chartered Institute of Marketing
HONOURS/AWARDS: PR week, International Visual Communication
HOBBIES AND INTERESTS: Yoga
EMAIL: daphne.desouza.org.uk
PERSONAL PROFILE: Joined the Health Authority in 1996, pursuing commercial partnerships for a number of award winning public health awareness campaigns. Currently seconded, part-time to the charity Business In The Community to manage a government sponsored, two year national campaign, Drugs-The Business Agenda.
NOMINATED BY: Seynour Fortescue

MR RAMAN KUMAR DEGA (ORTHOPAEDIC SURGEON)

Consultant Orthopaedic Surgeon, Wexham Park and Heatherwood Hospitals, Princess Margaret Hospital, Osbourne Road, Windsor, SL4 3SJ

PLACE OF BIRTH: India, 6.9.62
MARITAL STATUS: Married
CHILDREN: Two (Nikhila, Anil)
COLLEGE: Karnatak University
ACADEMIC QUALIFICATIONS: MBBS, LMSSA, FRCS, FRCS (Orth)
PROFESSIONAL QUALIFICATIONS: MBBS, LMSSA, FRCS, FRCS (Orth)
MEMBERSHIPS: British Orthopaedic Association
HOBBIES AND INTERESTS: Sports, travel, wines
PERSONAL PROFILE: Young orthopaedic surgeon working in the Windsor area. Keen sportsman interested in tennis, cricket and rugby. Family man with two children.

MR JAMIL DEHLAVI (FILM PRODUCER)

Director, Dehlavi Films,

COLLEGE: Oxford University, Lincolns Inn, Columbia University
ACADEMIC QUALIFICATIONS: BA French Literature & Politics, MA Honour School of Jurisprudence, Barrister-at-Law
PROFESSIONAL QUALIFICATIONS: MFA Film Directing
PERSONAL PROFILE: Jamil Dehlavi read at Oxford and was called to the Bar at Lincoln's Inn. He then studied film at Colombia University and has produced and directed many international award-winning feature films including: Towers Of Silence; Blood Of Hussain; Born Of Fire; Immaculate Conception; Passion In The Desert and Jinnah.

DR SURENDRA INDER DEO (DOCTOR)

General Practitioner, Bridge House Healthcare Centre, 96 Umfreville Road, London, N4 1TL

PLACE OF BIRTH: Guyana, 5.8.57
MARITAL STATUS: Married
CHILDREN: Four (Satish, Devendra, Priya, Amit)
COLLEGE: University London
ACADEMIC QUALIFICATIONS: BSc Hons, MB, BS
PROFESSIONAL QUALIFICATIONS: MRCGP, DFFP
DIRECTORSHIPS: Quality Education and Development (Health Care)
MEMBERSHIPS: BMA, Small Practices Association, East Haringey Primary Care Group.
HOBBIES AND INTERESTS: Reading, walking
EMAIL: deo.bridgehouse@binternet.com
PERSONAL PROFILE: GP dermatologist, educator, researcher and administrator. Recently elected by my peers onto the newly formed Primary Care Group. Published and spoken on ethnic health issues to conferences. Working to raise awareness and understanding of ethnic health to promote better services and improved outcomes for our community.

MR JOHN DEOL (PRODUCER-TELEVISION)

Director, MTV Europe, Hawley Crescent, London, NW1 8TT

PLACE OF BIRTH: Birmingham, 30.6.69
MARITAL STATUS: Married
COLLEGE: University of East Anglia
ACADEMIC QUALIFICATIONS: BA Honours in Politics and Economics
HOBBIES AND INTERESTS: Music, football, literature
PERSONAL PROFILE: After working as a reporter for Sunrise Radio News in 1992, I moved into television, working on BBC 2 and Channel 4 shows. I joined MTV in 1995. I love music, its my driving force-clubbing and gigging. I hope one day to be a music video director, but I love what I do right now. My main ambition in life is to see West Bromwich Albion FC win the league!

MR KANOOBHAI DESAI (DIRECTOR-SECRETARY)

Director-Secretary, Barker Chemicals Ltd, 49 Falcon Road, Battersea, London, SW11 2PH

PLACE OF BIRTH: Tanzania, 16.7.28
MARITAL STATUS: Married
CHILDREN: Three (Neela, Bhavna, Bimal)
COLLEGE: University of Bombay
ACADEMIC QUALIFICATIONS: BSc, LL.B, Barrister-at-Law
PROFESSIONAL QUALIFICATIONS: Barrister
DIRECTORSHIPS: Barker Chemicals Ltd, AMK (Care Homes) Ltd
HOBBIES AND INTERESTS: Travel, drama, sports, jogging, tennis
PERSONAL PROFILE: Practised law in Dar-es-Salaam from 1952-71. Was treasurer of Tanganyika Law Society till 1971. Was expelled, revoking citizenship, because acted for Oscar Kambona who left for UK. Branch president, National Association of Patidar Samaj, secretary Sardar Patel Memorial Society. Trustee Nadiad Nagrik Mandal a registered charity.
NOMINATED BY: Pravinbhai N Amin

MR MADHUBHAI DESAI (PHARMACIST)

Director, Barker Chemicals Ltd, 18 Corspe Hill, Wimbledon, London, SW20 0HG

PLACE OF BIRTH: Tanzania, 7.9.26
MARITAL STATUS: Married
CHILDREN: Two (Dilip, Ashit)
COLLEGE: Bombay
ACADEMIC QUALIFICATIONS: BSc Hons, BSc (Tech)
PROFESSIONAL QUALIFICATIONS: M.R.Pharm.S
DIRECTORSHIPS: Barker Chemicals Ltd, AMK (Care Homes) Ltd
MEMBERSHIPS: Royal Pharmaceutical Society of GB
HOBBIES AND INTERESTS: Photography, painting, sports (golf)
PERSONAL PROFILE: Practised as pharmacist in Dar-es-Salaam 1952-65. Then in London, owned several pharmacies. Founder member Pharmaceutical Society in Tanzania. Treasurer Indian Professionals Association. Trustee National Association of Patidar Samaj. Active member and office bearer in Rotary Club of Battersea Park.
NOMINATED BY: Pravinbhai N Amin

MR RAJESH DESAI (MANAGING DIRECTOR)

Managing Director, Hunt and Rogers Automotive Ltd, , 55 Whitmore Road, Small Heath, Birmingham, B10 0NR

PLACE OF BIRTH: London, 11.2.66
MARITAL STATUS: Married
CHILDREN: One (Sheena)
COLLEGE: Central England Birmingham
ACADEMIC QUALIFICATIONS: ONC, HND, ENG MSc in Manufacturing Systems
PROFESSIONAL QUALIFICATIONS: MBA
HONOURS/AWARDS: Winner of National Training Award 1995
HOBBIES AND INTERESTS: Computers, football
EMAIL: rajdesai@waverider.co.uk
PERSONAL PROFILE: Achieved senior management status at age of 25 years dealing with major automotive clients. Achieved MSc and MBA through company sponsorship over seven year period. Winner of National Training Award for outstanding achievement. Successful manager for major international plc. In 1998 recruited by BMW group to work on £0.5 billion UK project. Currently acquired manufacturing company based in Birmingham.
NOMINATED BY: Mrs V Desai

MR SUMANTRAI DHIRUBHAI DESAI (Admin Officer)

Administrative Officer, 56 Princes Street, Kingsbury, London, NW9 9JD

PLACE OF BIRTH: India, 11.9.40
MARITAL STATUS: Married
CHILDREN: Two (Manisha, Vimal)
COLLEGE: Gujarat University India, M S University, Baroda, India
ACADEMIC QUALIFICATIONS: BA Special, MA Hons, B.Ed Honours
HONOURS/AWARDS: 1998 Brent Citizenship Award, London Borough of Brent
HOBBIES AND INTERESTS: Cultural and social activities, charity work, gardening
PERSONAL PROFILE: Arrived from India in 1964 with BA (Special), MA (Special) and B.Ed (Honours). Worked as president, secretary, treasurer, school governor and committee member in various voluntary and charity organisations including Brahmin Society BIA, Hindu Councils, NCGO and Asian Foundation for help amongst others. Received Brent Citizenship Award. Working for benefits agency for last 33 years. Two children-doctor and dentist.
NOMINATED BY: S Desai

DR SURENDRA DESAI (Doctor)

GP, Langbank Medical Centre, Rajamee, 85 Lyndhurst Avenue, Mossley Hill, Liverpool, L18 8AR

PLACE OF BIRTH: India, 7.2.43
MARITAL STATUS: Married
CHILDREN: Two (Dipal, Amee)
COLLEGE: B J Medical College, Ahmedbad
PROFESSIONAL QUALIFICATIONS: MBBS, MS
MEMBERSHIPS: GMC
HOBBIES AND INTERESTS: Reading, sports, travelling
PERSONAL PROFILE: Principal GP and senior partner in group of four doctors since July 1978. Involved in local health committees and medico-politics.

MR AMERJIT SINGH DEU (Actor-Producer)

12 Kingsbridge Avenue, Ealing Common, London, W3 9AJ

PLACE OF BIRTH: India, 3.9.60
MARITAL STATUS: Married
CHILDREN: Two (Gursimran, Jasleen)
COLLEGE: Webber Douglas Academy of Dramatic Art
ACADEMIC QUALIFICATIONS: Radio, TV, Electronics Engineering in Leeds
PROFESSIONAL QUALIFICATIONS: Drama Diploma
DIRECTORSHIPS: Equity, NPA
MEMBERSHIPS: Equity, NPA, CRE Media
HOBBIES AND INTERESTS: Sports, travel, theatre, cinema, food
PERSONAL PROFILE: Established radio, theatre, film and television actor for fifteen years whose credits include: Twelfth Night; Doctor Faustus; Romeo and Juliet; Eastenders-Dr Singh; Udam Singh-lead role BBC TV; Surgical; Elderado; Lead role in films: Caught; Mysteries of Dark Jungle. Produced a short film-funded by National Lottery : Appeal. Judge for Sony Award and CRE Media Awards.

MRS NILIMA DEVI (Kathak Dance)

Dancer-Teacher, Centre For Indian Classical Dance, 48-50 Churchill Street, Leicester, LE2 1FH

PLACE OF BIRTH: India, 23.7.53
MARITAL STATUS: Married
CHILDREN: Two (Martin Amresh, Hans Varun)
COLLEGE: Baroda University
ACADEMIC QUALIFICATIONS: B.Comm, B.Mus, M. Mus
PROFESSIONAL QUALIFICATIONS: M.Mus (Kathak)
DIRECTORSHIPS: Centre For Indian Classical Dance
MEMBERSHIPS: ADI & I Board of Directors
HONOURS/AWARDS: BT Dance Award 1996
HOBBIES AND INTERESTS: Indian dance, music
EMAIL: cicd@menski.demon.co.uk
PERSONAL PROFILE: Since 1980 Nilima Devi has built up the Centre for Indian Classical Dance in Leicester, (now a registered charity) and has become a national figure. Also involved in Sangeet Sabha the Asian branch of Leicestershire Arts. Produced many dance performances.
NOMINATED BY: Dr Werner Menski

MR BHAJAN SINGH DEVSI (Race Equality Consultant)

Cultural Awareness Advisor, Wolverhampton Health Care NHS Trust, 44 Himley Crescent, Goldthorn Park, Wolverhampton, WV4 5DE

PLACE OF BIRTH: India, 26.11.44
MARITAL STATUS: Married
CHILDREN: Three (Jaspall, Sarabjeet, Randeep)
COLLEGE: Wolverhampton, University of Aston
ACADEMIC QUALIFICATIONS: DBA, DMS, HND (MECM.ENG)
PROFESSIONAL QUALIFICATIONS: MI Mgt
HOBBIES AND INTERESTS: Reading, swimming, social and voluntary work
PERSONAL PROFILE: Studied engineering and management, worked in industry for twenty years. Since 1982, been working in the field of racial equality, as unit director/senior lecturer, freelance consultant. Currently working as a race and cultural advisor with NHS in the Black Country. Active community member of Wolverhampton Community Health Care, Asian Community Network, Wolverhampton Against Racial Harassment. Chair and vice chair school governing body. WREC- exec member.
NOMINATED BY: Hyacinth Rowe

MS MISRI DEY (Actress)

Howard Cooke Associates, 19 Coulson Street, Chelsea, London, SW3 3NA

PLACE OF BIRTH: London, 4.1.68
COLLEGE: Wadham College, Oxford University
ACADEMIC QUALIFICATIONS: BA Hons English, M.Phil Theatre
PROFESSIONAL QUALIFICATIONS: Bristol Old Vic Theatre School Graduate
MEMBERSHIPS: Equity
HONOURS/AWARDS: Prince of Wales Business Trust, Amsterdam Arts School Award
HOBBIES AND INTERESTS: Scuba diving, running
EMAIL: deitch-dey@lineone.net
PERSONAL PROFILE: Misri is a working actress in theatre, television and film. She graduated from Bristol Old Vic in 1998 and prior to that completed her Master of Philosophy in Theatre, Dance and Development. She works with theatre to entertain, educate and empower!

MR DHARAMBIR SINGH DHADYALLA (Musician Lecturer)

Artistic Director, Leeds College of Music, 4 Blake Grove, Leeds, LS7 3LT

PLACE OF BIRTH: Kenya, 24.6.58
MARITAL STATUS: Married
CHILDREN: Three (Surmeet, Upneet, Kaviraj)
COLLEGE: SOAS
ACADEMIC QUALIFICATIONS: MA (Area Studies)
HOBBIES AND INTERESTS: Spiritual topics
PERSONAL PROFILE: Lectures in North Indian music and artistic director for Leeds Centre for Indian music and dance. Performed as a sitarist in many major festivals and Arts Council (hundreds of projects). Adviser for Arts Council and regional arts boards with particular experience in music education.

MISS NAVDEEP DHALIWAL (Student-Athelete)

4 Morven Avenue, Bishopbriggs, Glasgow, G64 1SG

PLACE OF BIRTH: Glasgow, 30.11.77
MARITAL STATUS: Single
COLLEGE: Glasgow University
ACADEMIC QUALIFICATIONS: Studying for my BDS (2000)
HONOURS/AWARDS: Blue Award from university. Ex-British women's league junior athlete of the year
HOBBIES AND INTERESTS: Reading, music, travelling especially to India
PERSONAL PROFILE: Competed in shotputt (SP) and discus since I was 13. At 14 years I was British U-15 shotputt champion and ranked 2nd in discus. I have represented Scotland in 12 Internationals. I also hold two Scottish schools and two Scottish NATIVE records. In 1998 I represented GB in an U-23 international against France and Germany (in discus) in Germany.

'At 14 years I was British U-15 shotputt champion and ranked 2nd in discus'

NAVDEEP DHALIWAL

MR SHASHIKANT DHOLAKIA (TRADING STANDARDS OFFICER)

Senior Authorised Officer, Northamptonshire County Council, 20 Upper Havelock Street, Wellingborough, NN8 4PN

PLACE OF BIRTH: Kenya, 28.6.48
MARITAL STATUS: Married
CHILDREN: Three (Rita, Renu, Suraj)
MEMBERSHIPS: Institute of Trading Standards
HOBBIES AND INTERESTS: Cricket, reading
PERSONAL PROFILE: Elected as first Asian Borough of Wellingborough councillor in 1990. In May 1996 elected as mayor for the Borough of Wellingborough. Founder member of Wellingborough District Hindu Association and an activist to build a Hindu Temple and community centre in the town. Actively involved in all community affairs. Serving on statutory and volunteer bodies.

MR MAGANLAL LALJIBHAI DHORAJIA (CARPENTER RTD)

Shree Hindu Community Centre, 9 Manor Farm Road, Tyseley, Birmingham, B11 2HT

PLACE OF BIRTH: India, 11.11.25
MARITAL STATUS: Married
CHILDREN: Five (Sangeeta, Nilesh, Asmita, Sanjay, Kaushik)
HOBBIES AND INTERESTS: Community worker
PERSONAL PROFILE: In 1979 got involved as a volunteer to raise funds for a Hindu Temple in the local area. 1981 Shri Laxminargyana Mandir (Birmingham) was purchased. I have been heavily involved with the temple both on the committee and as a volunteer. I provide support to anybody who needs help during functions.
NOMINATED BY: Chandrakant Jansari

PROF DR KALVIR SINGH DHUGA
(NUCLEAR PHYSICS COMPUTATIONAL SERVICES)

Professor-Director, George Washington University, C/- 116 Bierton Road, Aylesbury, HP20 1EN

PLACE OF BIRTH: India, 14.12.54
MARITAL STATUS: Married
CHILDREN: Three (Arayna, Rakhyle, Ravneel)
COLLEGE: Birmingham
ACADEMIC QUALIFICATIONS: PhD Nuclear Physics
DIRECTORSHIPS: Dept of Computational Sciences
MEMBERSHIPS: Numerous Bodies
HOBBIES AND INTERESTS: Plays football, squash
PERSONAL PROFILE: Taught Kings College London, Prof. Los Alamos N Mexico, US. Prof. Nuclear Physics George Washington DC, US. Director-Dept of Computational Sciences. Published several publications.
NOMINATED BY: G K Gill

MISS VENU DHUPA (THEATRE PRODUCER)

Executive Director, Nottingham Playhouse,

PLACE OF BIRTH: Kenya, 13.2.63
COLLEGE: Loughborough University, Bloomfield Hills Educ Inst, US (Sociology & Performing Arts)
ACADEMIC QUALIFICATIONS: BA Hons Drama, Dip in Performing Arts (Drama Studio)
PROFESSIONAL QUALIFICATIONS: Performances Bristol Old Vic, Belgrade, Coventry, Cardiff and Glasgow. MainstreamTV. Film director. Venue manager. Assist producer & producer (Royal National Theatre)
DIRECTORSHIPS: Executive Director
MEMBERSHIPS: Half Moon Young People's Theatre
HOBBIES AND INTERESTS: Drama
PERSONAL PROFILE: Venu is a professional performer. Executive director-Nottingham Playhouse.
NOMINATED BY: Veronica King, Loughborough University

> 'I was adopted at birth by white parents living in a small village in Yorkshire and now at 24 years I am the first professional Asian footballer within the British game'
>
> **CHRISTOPHER JOHN DOLBY**

CLLR RASHID AHMED DIN (COMPUTER ENGINEER)

Councillor (Slough), 102 Montague Road, Slough, SL1 3RW

PLACE OF BIRTH: Pakistan, 21.1.65
MARITAL STATUS: Married
CHILDREN: Two (Hammad, Faraz)
COLLEGE: Langley
ACADEMIC QUALIFICATIONS: O-Levels, Maths, English, Physics
PROFESSIONAL QUALIFICATIONS: City & Guilds Electronics 224 Servicing
MEMBERSHIPS: Labour Party
HOBBIES AND INTERESTS: Cricket, squash, music (promotion)
PERSONAL PROFILE: I have been active in community politics being councillor in unitary authority and have managed internationally known singer the late Nusrat Fateh Ali Khan. New involvement in organising international tours of well known musicians and have expert knowledge of computers being a qualified hardware engineer. Keen interest in breeding rare birds.

MR RASSHIED ALI DIN (DESIGN CONSULTANT)

Managing Director, Din Associates, 32 St Oswalds Place, London, SE11 5JE

PLACE OF BIRTH: Salford, 8.4.56
MARITAL STATUS: Single
COLLEGE: Birmingham Polytechnic
ACADEMIC QUALIFICATIONS: BA Hons, Interior Design
PROFESSIONAL QUALIFICATIONS: Fellow Chartered Society Designers. FCSD. Fellow Royal Society Arts. FRSA
HONOURS/AWARDS: Harvey Nicols/Observer Magazine Young Business Person of the Year 1990
HOBBIES AND INTERESTS: Horse riding
PERSONAL PROFILE: Rasshied Din is a well known designer with a successful interior and graphic design consultancy employing 22 staff. Clients have included Harrods, V& A Museum, Liberty, Selfridges and Earl Spencer. Rasshied has appeared in numerous press articles and made many TV appearances. He has been invited to represent his industry and country in many initiatives such as Creative Britain, UK/LA and 'Designing, Shopping and Eating' in Hong Kong. He is presently writing a book-New Retail due 2000.
NOMINATED BY: Clare Hardman Wilson, The London Institute

MR AJAZ AHMED DITTA (LECTURER-YOUTH WORKER)

Support Teacher, 37 Bradshaw Street, Nelson, BB9 9BW

PLACE OF BIRTH: Burnley, 24.10.68
MARITAL STATUS: Single
COLLEGE: Bradford, H Field, Leeds, St Martins College, Lancaster University, Bainbridge University, US.
ACADEMIC QUALIFICATIONS: GCSE's OND Technology, HND Engineering
PROFESSIONAL QUALIFICATIONS: B.Ed Hons 2.1, Cert.Ed, PGC (Youth & Community), D.Hom.Medicine
HOBBIES AND INTERESTS: Sport, homeopathy, driving, socialising, tutoring, reading Islamic literature
PERSONAL PROFILE: Having experienced university and working life Mr Ditta is one in a million. As well as an active youth and community leader, he has specialised in lecturing, homeopathy and private tutoring. His broad expertise and knowledge has played a vital role in Lancashire and Yorkshire in being seen as a role model within the Asian community.
NOMINATED BY: Naunz Ahmed

MR CHRISTOPHER JOHN DOLBY (FOOTBALL COACH)

Semi-Pro Footballer, Rotherham United Football Club, 5 South Street, Greasbrough, Rotherham, S61 4PN

PLACE OF BIRTH: Dewsbury, 4.9.74
MARITAL STATUS: Single
PROFESSIONAL QUALIFICATIONS: FA Certificate UAFA-B, Coaching/Football qualifications
MEMBERSHIPS: PFA
HOBBIES AND INTERESTS: Exercising, eating out, socialising, reading
PERSONAL PROFILE: I was adopted at birth by white parents living in a small village in Yorkshire and now at 24 years I am the first professional Asian footballer within the British game. At present I am playing semi-professional football and coaching children at Rotherham United Football club.
NOMINATED BY: Adam Lidiuci

MR AMRIK SINGH DOSANJH (Postmaster Rtd)

Post Office Counters Ltd, 2 Lambert Avenue, Langley, Slough, SL3 7EB

PLACE OF BIRTH: India, 20.3.35
MARITAL STATUS: Married
CHILDREN: Two (Bhupinder, Kanwaljit)
COLLEGE: Doaba College, Jullundher India
ACADEMIC QUALIFICATIONS: Master of Arts, Bachelor of Teaching
PROFESSIONAL QUALIFICATIONS: Teacher Training
MEMBERSHIPS: Labour Party, Sikh Temple, Indian Welfare Association
HOBBIES AND INTERESTS: Reading, badminton, travelling, politics
PERSONAL PROFILE: Borough councillor. Founder chairman British Indian Councillors Association (BICA). Chair of Slough Race Equality Council. Retired manager Post Office Counters. Actively involved in community issues. Active supporter of family based society. Against positive discrimination, strong believer of honesty and integrity. Secular in approach, respectful towards all religions.

MR NARINDER (KRISS) DOSANJH (Actor)

Asian Academy of Performing Arts (AAPA), 5 Ballot Street, Sandwell, Birmingham, B66 3EX

PLACE OF BIRTH: India, 31.3.61
CHILDREN: Two (Priya, Nikita)
ACADEMIC QUALIFICATIONS: O and 8 A-Levels, Diploma
PROFESSIONAL QUALIFICATIONS: Postgraduate DCG
DIRECTORSHIPS: BITS, NETS, AAPA
MEMBERSHIPS: Equity
HOBBIES AND INTERESTS: Arts, writing, music, percusionist-community work
PERSONAL PROFILE: Experienced professional actor in all mediums-stage, TV, films and radio. Now also involved in production of theatre, films etc. Started in dance and music (playing drums). Puts in many hours in helping people in the community-old and young. Recent work includes-regular in 'Emmerdale', three feature films and a West End play.

CLLR KIRTI KUMAR DOSHI (Business Consultant)

Centre Director, Belgrave Business Enterprise Centre Ltd, 367 Gleneagles Avenue, Rushey Mead, Leicester, LE4 7YJ

PLACE OF BIRTH: Tanzania, 28.10.53
MARITAL STATUS: Married
CHILDREN: One (Jay)
COLLEGE: Sardar Patel University
ACADEMIC QUALIFICATIONS: B Comm
HOBBIES AND INTERESTS: Travel, stamp collection, semi classical music
PERSONAL PROFILE: Founder member of various voluntary organisations in Leicester. First Jain to be elected as a councillor in the UK. Have been chair of Leisure Services, Equal Opportunities, Personnel Committee and Social Services. Councillor for Crown Hills ward since 1991. One of the first graduates of Leicester Common Purpose.

JASMINE DOTIWALA (Presenter-Producer)

TV Personality, MTV Europe, Hawley Crescent, Camden, London, NW1 8TT

PLACE OF BIRTH: London, 9.1.70
MARITAL STATUS: Single
COLLEGE: Surrey University
ACADEMIC QUALIFICATIONS: BA Hons 2.1, 3 A-Levels, 7 O-Levels
PROFESSIONAL QUALIFICATIONS: Producer/Presenter
MEMBERSHIPS: Royal Academy of Arts / Dance
HONOURS/AWARDS: Royal Academy of Dance Teachers
HOBBIES AND INTERESTS: Theatre, film, skydiving, scuba diving
EMAIL: jasmine.dotiwala@MTVNE.com
PERSONAL PROFILE: I am a young Asian female who has managed to conquer my field, inspite of the lack of support from the Asian community, except Eastern Eye, who have supported my rise within my career. I love being of ethnic origin, it makes me a deep mysterious spirit which intrigues people.
NOMINATED BY: Chantelle Charles

MR KHALID JEEVANI DRABU (Orthopaedic Surgeon)

Consultant, BUPA Gatwick Park Hospital, , Povey Cross Road, Horley, RH5 0BB

PLACE OF BIRTH: Pakistan, 9.11.52
MARITAL STATUS: Married
CHILDREN: Two (Roshan, Moshin)
COLLEGE: St George's University of London
ACADEMIC QUALIFICATIONS: MBBS
PROFESSIONAL QUALIFICATIONS: FRCS
MEMBERSHIPS: British Orthopaedic Association. Royal College of Surgeons.
PERSONAL PROFILE: Born in Rawalpindi, Came to UK aged five years. Schooling in Manchester, University of London. Appointed consultant at Redhill Surrey in 1988 with special interest in joint replacement surgery. Regular major conferences hosted at Redhill by Mr Drabu on joint replacement surgery.

MR KHURSHID DRABU (Barrister)

Immigration Judge, Immigration Appellate Authority, Hillside, Main Road, Otterbourne, SO21 2HH

PLACE OF BIRTH: India, 8.3.46
MARITAL STATUS: Married
CHILDREN: Four (Aliya, Farrah, Hamza, Zayba)
ACADEMIC QUALIFICATIONS: BA Hons, LL.B
PROFESSIONAL QUALIFICATIONS: Barrister-at-Law, Inner Temple
DIRECTORSHIPS: Art Asia Ltd, Southampton
HOBBIES AND INTERESTS: Cricket, gardening, Asian music
EMAIL: drabuk@aol
PERSONAL PROFILE: Head of Litigation, former Commission for Racial Equality 1990-96. President (part time) Mental Health Review Tribunal, South Region (1988 to present). Justice of the Peace (1984-96). Legal advisor, Muslim Council of Britain. Chair, Kashmiri Association of Great Britain. Chair, Art Asia Ltd, Southampton.

MR DIAMOND DUGGAL (Producer Music)

Director, Sub Dub Records Ltd, PO Box 3340, Birmingham, B20 2NN

PLACE OF BIRTH: Birmingham, 12.4.69
MARITAL STATUS: Married
CHILDREN: One (Rohan)
DIRECTORSHIPS: Sub Dub Records Ltd
MEMBERSHIPS: PRS, MCPS, PPL, MU, PAMRA, AUORA, BASCA
HONOURS/AWARDS: Mercury Award Nominee1993, Ivor Novello Award 1994 and Brit Awards 1993
HOBBIES AND INTERESTS: Interior design, photography
EMAIL: sub.dub@virgin.net
WEB SITE: www.subdub.com
PERSONAL PROFILE: Simon and Diamond record producers, songwriters and re-mixers are renowned for the conception and creation of Apache Indian. They have had a stream of UK Top 20 hits with artists including Erasure, Maxi Priest, The Beat and Apache Indian amongst others. They are both directors of Sub Dub Records Ltd and boast artists such as Stereo Nation and Swami on their label.

MR SIMON DUGGAL (Producer Music)

Director, Sub Dub Records Ltd, PO Box 3340, Birmingham, B20 2NN

PLACE OF BIRTH: Birmingham, 18.3.67
MARITAL STATUS: Single
DIRECTORSHIPS: Sub Dub Records Ltd
MEMBERSHIPS: PRS, MCPS, PPL, MU, PAMRA, AUORA, BASCA
HONOURS/AWARDS: Mercury Award nominee 1993, Ivor Novello Award 1994 and Brit Awards 1993
HOBBIES AND INTERESTS: Graphic design, photography
EMAIL: sub.dub@virgin.net
WEB SITE: www.sub.dub.com
PERSONAL PROFILE: Simon and Diamond record producers and re-mixers are renowned for the conception and creation of Apache Indian. They have had a stream of UK Top 20 hits with artists including Erasure, Maxi Priest, The Beat and Apache Indian amongst others. They have also written, produced and re-mixed for many top Asian artists including Stereo Nation, Hans Raj Hans and Sardool. They are both directors of Sub Dub Records Ltd.

'I love being of ethnic origin, it makes me a deep mysterious spirit which intrigues people'

JASMINE DOTIWALA

DUTT

MR KALYAN KUMAR DUTT (LIBRARIAN)

Ethnic Services, London Borough of Ealing,
61 Mansfield Avenue, East Barnet, EN4 8QE

PLACE OF BIRTH: India, 5.4.38
MARITAL STATUS: Married
CHILDREN: One (Sanghamitra)
COLLEGE: Allahabad University
ACADEMIC QUALIFICATIONS: MA
PROFESSIONAL QUALIFICATIONS: BT, ALA
MEMBERSHIPS: The Library Association
HONOURS/AWARDS: Royal Charter Centenary Medal
HOBBIES AND INTERESTS: Cricket, photography, current affairs, travelling
PERSONAL PROFILE: In public libraries for over 30 years and specially serving ethnic minorities for the last 26 years. Founder member of ALAG (Asian Librarian and Advisers Group) and CILLA (Co-operative of Indic Language Library Authorities); Also secretary of ALAG. Through exhibitions, seminars and cultural activities encouraging ethnic minorities and the host community to widen their horizon of foreign cultures, as it is a two-way street.
NOMINATED BY: Bhadra Patel

MR VIJAY DUTT (SENIOR EDITOR)

Senior Editor-Managing, Hindustan Times Ltd, 65 Bretten Close, London, NW11 7HW

PLACE OF BIRTH: India, 23.10.45
MARITAL STATUS: Married
COLLEGE: Colvin College Lucknow University
ACADEMIC QUALIFICATIONS: MSc, LL.B, Diploma in Public Administration
PROFESSIONAL QUALIFICATIONS: Journalism-Specialism in editing-re-writing
MEMBERSHIPS: P.P. Rotary Club, Life member UP Vintage Car Club, Expt. International Living, India International Centre
HONOURS/AWARDS: National Journalism Award for independent courage.
HOBBIES AND INTERESTS: Reading, travelling, tennis, collecting matchboxes
EMAIL: vdutt@aol.com
PERSONAL PROFILE: After completing education, took over family business before foraying into journalism, which included different forms of the print media. Passion for travelling has taken me far and wide. Philanthropy, travels and social interaction helped friendships across the world and in investigative and analytical writing.

MOHAMED SHAIKH EAOYOR (Garments Retailer)

Owner, Euston Saree Centre, 25 Swallow Field, Albany Street, London, NW1 3PJ

PLACE OF BIRTH: Bangladesh, 11.2.59
MARITAL STATUS: Married
CHILDREN: Four (Shalma, Alom, Akbor, Mehdi (Mahima))
COLLEGE: Scunthorpe College
ACADEMIC QUALIFICATIONS: A-Level
DIRECTORSHIPS: Massala Indian Cuisine
MEMBERSHIPS: Conservative Party, Bengali Workers Association
HOBBIES AND INTERESTS: Politics, community work, football, reading, badminton
PERSONAL PROFILE: I am politically active and was a candidate for councillor in 1998 (Tower Hamlets). Currently secretary of Tower Hamlets Conservative Association. I aim to promote educational achievement amongst the Asian community. To this end I was school governor in Camden 1995-97. I'm currently secretary general of Sylhet Division Development Council.
NOMINATED BY: Mr Kiranchand Gudka

MISS HEATHER EMMANUEL (Actress-Riding Instructor)

Examiner & Judge, 6 Kinscroft Road, London, NW2 3QG

PLACE OF BIRTH: Sri Lanka
MARITAL STATUS: Married
CHILDREN: Two (Christopher, Sarah)
COLLEGE: RADA
ACADEMIC QUALIFICATIONS: Fellow Trinity College London (Speech & Drama), GCSE Japanese
PROFESSIONAL QUALIFICATIONS: BHSAI, Examiner & Judge, Judo 1st Dan
HONOURS/AWARDS: Free Training at RADA
HOBBIES AND INTERESTS: Horse-riding, pottery, woodwork, upholstery, cookery, guitar, judo, signing for the deaf. (Trained in all the above).
PERSONAL PROFILE: Orphaned at nine months and brought up by nuns. Arrived alone in England from Sri Lanka, worked my way through RADA. First engagement at Old Vic and then extensively on film, radio and TV playing many nationalities. Work on a voluntary basis with people with special needs and learning difficulties.

Entrants in the Asians in the Millennium have

been nominated for their achievements and

contributions. You can

nominate someone who

deserves to be in the

Who's Who of Asian Achievers 2000

Entries are free

Send in your nominations, including name,

contact address and telephone number to:

Books Division, Ethnic Media Group,

148 Cambridge Heath Road, London E1 5QJ

10 years of service to the Asian community

December 1 1992: Eastern Eye backs British Sikhs in their campaign for their religious rights after the EC rules that Sikh workers must replace their turbans with protective head gear

MS SOUAD FARESS (Actress)

Andrew Manson, Protocol, 2/7 Harbour Yard, Chelsea, London, SW10 0XD

PLACE OF BIRTH: Ghana
MARITAL STATUS: Divorced
COLLEGE: Guildhall School of Music and Drama
ACADEMIC QUALIFICATIONS: AGS M&D
PROFESSIONAL QUALIFICATIONS: AGS M&D
DIRECTORSHIPS: Ex-Joint Stock Theatre Co. Genus Production. Widedot Limited
MEMBERSHIPS: Equity
HONOURS/AWARDS: Best Supporting Actress-Asian Film Academy

HOBBIES AND INTERESTS: Music, art, people, writing, IT, film, theatre
PERSONAL PROFILE: I have had a consistently good career in the arts-in television, film, radio and theatre-a miracle of persistence-after an early start in business.

MRS GHAZALA YASMIN FAROOQ JP (Social Worker)

Commissioning Officer, Social Service Dept, Redvers House, Flat 2, Union Street, Sheffield, S1 2LQ

PLACE OF BIRTH: India
MARITAL STATUS: Married
CHILDREN: Four (Faraz, Zara, Saba, Hina (Twins))
COLLEGE: Sheffield University
ACADEMIC QUALIFICATIONS: MA in Cultural Studies
PROFESSIONAL QUALIFICATIONS: CQSW, Certificate in Social Work

MEMBERSHIPS: Appointed JP in 1997
HONOURS/AWARDS: Equal Opportunities Award in MA
HOBBIES AND INTERESTS: Reading, writing, poetry, socialising with friends
PERSONAL PROFILE: I was born and brought up in Mirpur Azad Kashmir. I came to Britain in 1977. I was training to be a doctor but my qualifications were not accepted in the, UK. I have had to work extremely hard to get where I am now. I am pleased that I am making a positive contribution to the wider society.
NOMINATED BY: Self

MS MARIA FERNANDES (Solicitor)

Partner, Fernandes Vaz Solicitors, 31 Snaresbrook Road, Stanmore, HA7 4QN

PLACE OF BIRTH: Kenya, 22.5.59
MARITAL STATUS: Married
CHILDREN: Two (Luke, Anjali)
COLLEGE: Cardiff University College
ACADEMIC QUALIFICATIONS: LLB Hons
PROFESSIONAL QUALIFICATIONS: Solicitor
DIRECTORSHIPS: President Mental Health Review Tribunal
MEMBERSHIPS: Council Member, Law Society. Equal Opportunities Committee Law Society. Equal Treatment Advisory Committe of Judicial Board.

HOBBIES AND INTERESTS: Reading, travelling, studies, people, cinema, theatre
PERSONAL PROFILE: Born in Kenya. Father was a lawyer. Came to UK as a young girl. Always interested in the law as a profession. Initially became a barrister but found it hard to obtain a permanent place-left to do a number of other jobs. Became a solicitor.

DR VASCO FERNANDES (Doctor)

Consultant Public Health Physician, Buckinghamshire Health Authority, , Verney House, Gatehouse Road, Aylesbury, HP19 3ET

PLACE OF BIRTH: Kenya, 19.9.50
MARITAL STATUS: Married
CHILDREN: Two (Clare, Mark)
COLLEGE: GS Medical / Bombay
ACADEMIC QUALIFICATIONS: MBBS (1975)
PROFESSIONAL QUALIFICATIONS: DCH (1979), MRCGP (1980), MFPHM (1985)
DIRECTORSHIPS: (Non- executive) Board Member, Public Health Laboratory Service, appointed by Minister of Health 1995 (re-appointed 1998).
MEMBERSHIPS: President Milton Keynes REC since 1993
HONOURS/AWARDS: Faculty of Public Health Medicine FFPHM
HOBBIES AND INTERESTS: Cricket, hockey, travelling, gardening
PERSONAL PROFILE: Specialised in general medical practice (1980) and public health medicine (1985), appointed Consultant (1985). Other activities: British Medical Association; Chair (Oxford Region); Member (National) Committee for Public Health Medicine and Community Health since 1989; Chair Milton Keynes Division since 1993. Overseas Doctors Association, Chair Milton Keynes Division 1989 -1998 currently treasurer.

MISS MEHRU FITTER (Senior Librarian)

Coventry Libraries Multicultural Services, 18 Mary Herbert Street, Cheylesmore, Coventry, CV3 5ER

PLACE OF BIRTH: Kenya, 20.3.43
MARITAL STATUS: Single
COLLEGE: Poona (India), Newcastle upon Tyne
ACADEMIC QUALIFICATIONS: BA Hons
PROFESSIONAL QUALIFICATIONS: Diploma in Education, Diploma in Librarianship
MEMBERSHIPS: Library Association
HONOURS/AWARDS: Royal Centenary Award from Library Association

HOBBIES AND INTERESTS: Reading, travel, founded Coventry Asian Literary Circle
PERSONAL PROFILE: Kenya born, Mehru, was recently awarded The Royal Centenary Medal by the Library Association for meeting the challenge of providing a library and information service to a culturally diverse society. An ex-teacher, Mehru has been kept busy by her membership of school governing bodies and cultural and interfaith groups.
NOMINATED BY: Miss R S Fitter

THE RT HON. BARONESS SHREELA FLATHER JP
(Conservative Life Peer)

DL Royal County of Berkshire, House of Lords, , Westminster, London, SW1A 0PW

PLACE OF BIRTH: India, 13.2.34
MARITAL STATUS: Married
CHILDREN: Two (Paul, Marcus)
COLLEGE: University College London
ACADEMIC QUALIFICATIONS: LL.B
PROFESSIONAL QUALIFICATIONS: Barrister-at-Law 1971, Fellow of University College, Honorary Doctor of Open University 1994
DIRECTORSHIPS: Meridian Broadcasting, Marie Stopes International. The Cable Corporation
MEMBERSHIPS: Council of St George's House, Windsor Castle, Council of Winston Churchill Memorial Trust
HONOURS/AWARDS: 1996 Asian of the Year Award. Made Deputy Lieutenant for the Royal County of Berkshire in 1994
HOBBIES AND INTERESTS: Reading, cinema
PERSONAL PROFILE: The Right Honourable The Baroness Flather of Windsor and Maidenhead was born Shreela Rai in Lahore, British India. She is married to Gary Flather QC and has two sons and was called to the Bar at Inner Temple. She began her career as a teacher and became active in voluntary and community work whilst teaching in Maidenhead. She went on to the Bench in 1971 and in 1976 was elected the first ethnic minority woman councillor in the United Kingdom. She became the first Asian woman Mayor in Britain 1986-Royal Borough of Windsor.

MR MADHUN KUMAR FOOLCHAND (Senior Lecturer)

University of Wolverhampton, 132a Mount Road, Penn, Wolverhampton, WV4 5RX

PLACE OF BIRTH: Mauritius, 10.3.50
MARITAL STATUS: Married
CHILDREN: Three (Hema, Kumar, Natnan)
COLLEGE: MPhil, BSc, DPSN, RMN, Cert Ed (FE) RM
ACADEMIC QUALIFICATIONS: RMN
MEMBERSHIPS: Health and Community Council Member-appointed by the Secretary of State for Health.
HOBBIES AND INTERESTS: Keep fit, sports, politics, current affairs
PERSONAL PROFILE: I am very active in my university in promoting anti-racist issues in the training of nurses, There is no doubt that I am also a role model for Asian and Black people. My other role is as an active member of the Community Health Council-again promoting anti-racist issues.

MISS ABIGAIL FREEMAN-PASK (Schoolgirl-Actress)

The Jackie Palmer Stage School Agency, 30 Daws Hill Lane, High Wycombe, HP11 1PW

PLACE OF BIRTH: Sri Lanka, 19.1.90
PROFESSIONAL QUALIFICATIONS: Stage work at Richmond Theatre and Theatre Royal, TV work
HOBBIES AND INTERESTS: Dancing, singing, swimming, skating
PERSONAL PROFILE: Abigail is a professional actress, singer and dancer. She has appeared in many professional stage productions as well as TV adverts and soap operas. She also regularly appears in cabarets at top London hotels. Her excellent progress at school is not affected by her stage and screen activities.

April 1 1993: The British may have ruled India for 200 years, but with the discovery of the genuine Koh-i-noor diamond in retired army officer Sergeant Jagjit Singh's attic, it finally looks like we're having the last laugh. Eminent Indian historian Professor Piggot-Brown told Eastern Eye: 'British history over the last 150 years will have to be rewritten'

MR SUNIL GADHIA (Solicitor)

Partner, Stephenson Harwood, One St Paul's, Churchyard, London, EC4M 8SH

PLACE OF BIRTH: Kenya, 10.10.65
MARITAL STATUS: Married
COLLEGE: Nottingham University
ACADEMIC QUALIFICATIONS: LLB Law Degree
PROFESSIONAL QUALIFICATIONS: Solicitors Proff. Exams
DIRECTORSHIPS: Law Society Trustees Ltd. Fulham Legal Advice Centre
MEMBERSHIPS: Labour Party
HOBBIES AND INTERESTS: Politics, reading
EMAIL: sunilgadhia@stephensonharwood.com
PERSONAL PROFILE: Became a partner at the age of 31 in the litigation department of well respected City law firm, Stephenson Harwood. Involved in many high profile cases. Active in a number of charitable legal projects. Also active in community affairs and a committed member of the Labour Party.
NOMINATED BY: Lord Janner of Braunstone

MRS NITU GADHVI (Singer)

Music Section, 15 Buckingham Gardens, Edgware, HA8 6NB

PERSONAL PROFILE: Popular singer done playback singing for films like 'Janbaaz' and 'Gandhi'. Travels over the world performing concerts.

MR ANTONY DAVID JALIL GAFOOR (Barrister)

Legal Advisor, Department of Trade & Industry, 83 Central Road, Sudbury, Wembley, HA0 2LQ

PLACE OF BIRTH: London, 7.4.60
MARITAL STATUS: Married
CHILDREN: Three (Alexander, Christopher, Ethan)
COLLEGE: University of West Indies, London Guildhall University
ACADEMIC QUALIFICATIONS: LL.B, LL.M, MA, (Business Law) Dip.Comm.Law. Dip EC Law. Cert. Air Law. Corporate, Investment and Copyright Law.
PROFESSIONAL QUALIFICATIONS: Barrister & Attorney – at – Law, Trinidad & Tobago
MEMBERSHIPS: Bar Assoc. for Commerce, Finance & Industry, International Bar Assoc. Admin, Law Bar Assoc. Assoc of Catholic Lawyers
HONOURS/AWARDS: Scouting, Law Moots, Silver Medal. Archcon Fraternity of St Stephens
HOBBIES AND INTERESTS: Church, Westminister Cathedral reader. Master of Ceremonies, St Georges, Wembley. Reading, cricket, music (Asian & classical)
PERSONAL PROFILE: Called to the Bar at Gray's Inn with honours. In 1987: pupillage and common law practice. Legal officer, Treasury Solicitors Department; 1988 – 1990; Principal legal officer, Treasury Solicitors Department 1990 – 1991, Legal adviser Department of Energy 1991 – 1992; legal adviser, Department of Trade and Industry Solicitors Office. 1992 – Present; Attorney – at – Law, Trinidad and Tobago.

MR NITIN GANATRA (Actor)

Magnolia Management,

PLACE OF BIRTH: Kenya, 21.2.68
MARITAL STATUS: Single
COLLEGE: Bristol Unversity
ACADEMIC QUALIFICATIONS: BA Hons Drama, Film and TV. Two – years in Italy with Jerzy Grotowski
PROFESSIONAL QUALIFICATIONS: Lead role in "Haroun and the Sea of Stories" (1994) Salman Rushdie. Lead role in "Guru in Seven"
HOBBIES AND INTERESTS: Painting, martial arts, music
PERSONAL PROFILE: Always had keen interest in diverse work in the arts. Trying to break the stereotypes of Asians in the arts with films like 'Guru in Seven'. Trained in martial arts, music and dance, classified as a multi – skilled actor. Would love to see Asian businesses supporting and funding the work of their children – the British Asians.

MR RAVIN J GANATRA (Actor)

Theatre Director, Actors Group, c/o Sandra Chalmers Harrow Road Agency, Poland Street, London

PLACE OF BIRTH: Tanzania, 8.3.69
MARITAL STATUS: Married
COLLEGE: Manchester Polytechnic School of Theatre
ACADEMIC QUALIFICATIONS: BA Hons Theatre Arts
MEMBERSHIPS: Equity
HOBBIES AND INTERESTS: Travelling, sports
PERSONAL PROFILE: Ravin has numerous stage, TV and radio credits over the past seven years. His passion lies in theatre, especially theatre with a voice. Currently working on a three year project for Tara Arts – 'Journey to the West', charting the journey of Asians, generations ago, from India to Africa then to England.

MR ATUL GANDHI (Managing Director)

Namaste Asian TV,

PLACE OF BIRTH: India, 17.8.64
MARITAL STATUS: Married
CHILDREN: One (Ashish Varun)
COLLEGE: Middlesex University
ACADEMIC QUALIFICATIONS: B.Eng Hons Electronics Eng
PROFESSIONAL QUALIFICATIONS: ACCA 2.1 Accounting
HOBBIES AND INTERESTS: Travel, golf, movies
EMAIL: atul.gandhi@virgin.net

DR JAGDISH GANDHI (Gynaecologist)

41 Moss Road, Billinge, WN5 7BT

PLACE OF BIRTH: India, 1.6.52
MARITAL STATUS: Married
CHILDREN: Two (Malik, Prapti)
COLLEGE: Gujarat University, India
ACADEMIC QUALIFICATIONS: MB, DGO, MD, LMSSA, MRCOG, MFFP
PROFESSIONAL QUALIFICATIONS: MB, DGO, MD, LMSSA, MRCOG, MFFP
HOBBIES AND INTERESTS: Photography
PERSONAL PROFILE: Professionally a gynaecologist, a family man with homeopathic practitioner wife and two children. High contributions in the wider NHS activities through various local, regional and national committees including central consultant and specialist committee and chairmanship of Non – Consultant Career Grade Doctors (NCCGD) Committee of Mersey Region. Aims to achieve better working conditions for NCCGD – majority of whom come from overseas, are largely disadvantaged and exploited.

MR DON GAZARA (Mechanical Engineer)

Chairman CED, Trico International Ltd, Wood Green Business Centre, Clarendon Road, London, N22

PLACE OF BIRTH: Sri Lanka, 16.5.47
MARITAL STATUS: Married
CHILDREN: Two (Anuka, Oshana)
COLLEGE: Huddersfield
ACADEMIC QUALIFICATIONS: Institute of Mechanical Engineers
DIRECTORSHIPS: Trico International, Trico Navigation
MEMBERSHIPS: WWPC
HOBBIES AND INTERESTS: Swimming, social work, shipping in developing nations
EMAIL: triscosl@slt.uk

MR MAHOMED IQBAL GELU (Insurance)

Director, Sterling Insurance Group Ltd, 6 Gilpin Avenue, East Sheen, London, SW14 8QY

PLACE OF BIRTH: Malawi, 5.6.50
MARITAL STATUS: Married
CHILDREN: Two (Samir Aman, Ghalib Hussein)
COLLEGE: Eastbourne College
DIRECTORSHIPS: Albion Insurance Co Ltd, Sterling Insurance Group Ltd
MEMBERSHIPS: Link in the House of Lords
HOBBIES AND INTERESTS: Travel, reading, music, food, arts, major sporting events
EMAIL: igelu@albion – ins.co.uk
PERSONAL PROFILE: Arrived in the UK in September 1959 from Malawi.

MR JOHN GEORGE (Doctor)

Adjudicating Medical Practitioner, 3 Harlech Close, Stroud, Rochester, ME2 3QP

PLACE OF BIRTH: India, 5.6.48
MARITAL STATUS: Married
CHILDREN: Three (Diane, Anna, John)
COLLEGE: Mysore University
ACADEMIC QUALIFICATIONS: MBBS
PROFESSIONAL QUALIFICATIONS: FRCS
MEMBERSHIPS: BMA Professional Committee
HOBBIES AND INTERESTS: Running, keep fit, travelling
PERSONAL PROFILE: Born and brought up in South India. Involved in various charity and youth associations. President Catholic Youth Association while studying medicine. Left India 1976 and worked in Nigeria for five years; Doing mainly surgical operations. I came to the UK in 1981, took FRCS and worked in several hospitals. Elected Professional Fee Committee member of British Medical Association.

TARIQUE GHAFFUR (Police Officer)

Assistant Chief Constable, Lancashire Constabulary, PO Box 77, Hutton, Preston, PR4 5SB

PLACE OF BIRTH: Uganda, 8.6.55
MARITAL STATUS: Married
CHILDREN: Two (Ambreen, Faraaz)
COLLEGE: Keele University
ACADEMIC QUALIFICATIONS: BA Hons, MA
MEMBERSHIPS: British Criminology Society
HOBBIES AND INTERESTS: Sport, squash, music
PERSONAL PROFILE: Tarique made history by becoming the highest ranking chief police officer in the British police service from minority ethnic community. Joined Greater Manchester Police in 1974 and has since worked in Leicestershire and now Lancashire. Has also worked in India, Jamaica and the FBI Academy US.
NOMINATED BY: Gerald O'Connell. Lancashire Constabulary

MRS USHA RANI GHAI (Liaison Worker-Tutor)

Sandwell Asian Family Support & Service, 101 Nine Elms Lane, Park Village, Wolverhampton, WV10 9AW

PLACE OF BIRTH: India, 21.1.52
MARITAL STATUS: Married
CHILDREN: Four
COLLEGE: University of Calcutta
ACADEMIC QUALIFICATIONS: BSc, ESOL Teacher Training, Swimming Teacher.
HOBBIES AND INTERESTS: Playing chess, music, swimming, meeting people
PERSONAL PROFILE: I am 47 years of age. I am running 'Chesta' Asian women's group in Wolverhampton voluntarily. I teach Asian music, languages, organise trips in England and Europe. I am working in Sandwell helping Asian families with filling in forms, advice with all sorts of problems and comfort women with emotional support.

MR TANVEER GHANI (Actor)

Felix De Wolfe, London

PLACE OF BIRTH: Pakistan, 15.7.60
MARITAL STATUS: Married
CHILDREN: One (Romany Kemp – Ghani)
COLLEGE: Central School of Speech and Drama
ACADEMIC QUALIFICATIONS: Speech and Drama Diploma
HOBBIES AND INTERESTS: Yoga, film, theatre
PERSONAL PROFILE: An actor who has worked in film, theatre and television for the last 18 years. Appearing in 'The Far Pavilions', ''Eastenders'', 'Family Pride', 'Bhaji on the Beach' and 'Tiger Bay'. One whose full potential has not yet been realised.

CLLR HARJINDER SINGH GHATORA (Aircraft Engineer)

Councillor, Slough Borough Council, 4 Merlin Close, Brands Hill, Slough, SL3 8QW

PLACE OF BIRTH: India, 24.8.44
MARITAL STATUS: Married
CHILDREN: Two (Kavinder Singh, Maninder Singh)
ACADEMIC QUALIFICATIONS: Higher Secondary
PROFESSIONAL QUALIFICATIONS: Aeromautical Engineering Certificate (AEC 4) CAA
DIRECTORSHIPS: Sunrise Rice and General Mills FZR Road Moga
MEMBERSHIPS: Labour Party, AEEU Trade Union
HOBBIES AND INTERESTS: Photography, arts
PERSONAL PROFILE: I have been a member of Labour Party for 18 years and I have lived in Branch Hill since 1987. Governor of two schools. Board member of Thames Valley Ground Work Trust. I started my career in the Indian Air Force (IAF). Left India in 1971, lived in Norway and then moved to England in 1976 and joined British Airways. In 1982 left BA to start my own business but due to some reason could not start. Managing partner Sunrise Rice and General Mill in Moga, family owned.

MR ONKAR SINGH GHATORE
(Aircraft Maintenance Worker)

Combat Karate UK, 14 St Georges Avenue, Southall, UB1 1PZ

PLACE OF BIRTH: Kenya, 6.2.61
MARITAL STATUS: Married
CHILDREN: One (Randhir Kaur)
ACADEMIC QUALIFICATIONS: B Tec Management Studies
PROFESSIONAL QUALIFICATIONS: Chief Instructor of Combat Karate UK
MEMBERSHIPS: Amateur Martial Arts Association of Great Britain
HONOURS/AWARDS: Voluntary Worker with Children LB Ealing
HOBBIES AND INTERESTS: Self defence, meditation, voluntary work in community
PERSONAL PROFILE: My life long ambitions are to build a better society where all faiths can live together. As a martial arts instructor I also teach meditation and discipline to over 100 children. Whole community and clubs in UK have benefited from my teachings. I am supported by London Borough of Ealing.
NOMINATED BY: Manmeet S Johal

DR ABDUS SABOOR KHAN GHAURI (Surgeon)

Speciality Registrar, Sunderland Royal General Hospital,

PLACE OF BIRTH: East Africa, 26.11.64
MARITAL STATUS: Married
CHILDREN: One (Nadia Munahil)
COLLEGE: Cambridge University, Oxford University
ACADEMIC QUALIFICATIONS: MA (Cantab), BM Bch (Oxon), FRCS (Eng)
PROFESSIONAL QUALIFICATIONS: Surgeon – FRCS
MEMBERSHIPS: Royal College of Surgeons, BMA
HOBBIES AND INTERESTS: Allround sportsman especially hockey. Played for Kingston Grammer School, Cambridge & Oxford (Oxbridge Blue)
PERSONAL PROFILE: Born in 1964 at Tabora (East Africa). Went to Kingston Grammar School: – Passed GCE., 12 O – Levels all with A grades and 3 A – Levels all with 'A' grades and one distinction. Was prefect at Kington Grammar School. Research interest vascular surgery. Special interest in venus leg ulceration. Son of Mr Nazim Ghauri MBE, have two brothers Shahid and Mabroor both have done well in UK, being accountant and computer consultant respectively.

Tarique made history by becoming the highest ranking chief police officer in the British police service from minority ethnic community

TARIQUE GHAFFUR

Was prefect at Kington Grammar School. Research interest vascular surgery. Special interest in venus leg ulceration. Son of Mr Nazim Ghauri MBE

ABDUS SABOOR KHAN GHAURI

MR NAZIM KHAN GHAURI MBE (SUPT OF POLICE – RTD)

General Secretary & Vice Chair, Asian Elderly Group, 'Felstead', Traps Lane, New Malden, KT3 4RU

PLACE OF BIRTH: India, 28.8.31
MARITAL STATUS: Married
CHILDREN: Three (Shahid Hameed, Mabroor, Dr A Saboor i)
COLLEGE: Punjab and Teacher Training College, Nairobi
ACADEMIC QUALIFICATIONS: Passed Gazetted Police Law Qualifying exams. MA. BM. FRES.
PROFESSIONAL QUALIFICATIONS: Law Qualifying Exams in Criminal Law, Law of Evidence, Administration.
DIRECTORSHIPS: Supt, Police (Retd)
MEMBERSHIPS: Member Joint Consultative Committee, Police Community Consultative Group.
HONOURS/AWARDS: MBE, Member of the British Empire (1998)
HOBBIES AND INTERESTS: Played hockey for Kenya and Tanzania. Social, community service
PERSONAL PROFILE: Born 1931 in a respected family of Abbottabad. Retired a superintendant police officer and came to the UK from Tanzania in 1988. Long outstanding active voluntary worker in UK. Have been chairman/vice chairman and general secretary of various ethnic organisations in the UK. Mayor of Merton's Award 1994 for Meritorious and Voluntary Service to the community. 1998 was honoured with MBE by HM Queen at Buckingham Palace for community service and community relations.
NOMINATED BY: Mr Amir Siddiqui and Ataul Mujeeb Rashed

MR SAAD GHAZI (CATERER)

Company Director, Impact Overseas Ltd, 552 London Road, Isleworth, TW7 4EP

PLACE OF BIRTH: Bangladesh, 14.2.44
MARITAL STATUS: Married
CHILDREN: Three (Shahnaz, Fahmida, Nafia)
COLLEGE: Studied at Hanley College, Coventry
ACADEMIC QUALIFICATIONS: Catering Management
PROFESSIONAL QUALIFICATIONS: Catering Higher Management
DIRECTORSHIPS: Chairman – Impact Overseas Ltd. Director
MEMBERSHIPS: Bangladesh British Chamber of Commerce London.
HOBBIES AND INTERESTS: Travelling, community work
PERSONAL PROFILE: President Sreemongal Shomity. Advisor Surrey Bangladesh Welfare Association. Advisor Bangladesh Caterers Association (Surrey Region).

DR ARUN CHANDRA GHOSH CLLR
(MEDICAL MICROBIOLOGIST)

Freelance Consultant / Adviser, Councillor LB Barnet APN Enterprises, 50 Talbot Crescent, Hendon, London, NW4 4HP

PLACE OF BIRTH: India, 15.9.37
MARITAL STATUS: Married
CHILDREN: One (Neiloy Shankar)
COLLEGE: Calcutta University, London University
ACADEMIC QUALIFICATIONS: BSc
PROFESSIONAL QUALIFICATIONS: BVSC&AH, MPhil (Lon)
DIRECTORSHIPS: APN Enterprises Ltd
MEMBERSHIPS: CBIOL, MIBIOL, Member SFAM, Ex Middx County Cricket Club
HONOURS/AWARDS: Medal for sharp shooting, Crest for representing college hockey team
HOBBIES AND INTERESTS: Sports, literature, travel, gardening, philately, music, cookery, amateur theatrical
PERSONAL PROFILE: Medical microbiologist/research scientist with wide experience in public health microbiology. Experienced research guide. Was member of WHO and EU Scientific Working Group. Appeared on BBC TV 9 O'clock News while investigating botulinum food poisoning. Visiting academic and adviser to Kalyani and other universities in Calcutta, India. Author / co – author of more than 20 publications including chapters and books.

> He was the founder of the Christmas Cracker Project, which has given thousands of young people direct entrepreneurial experience and which has raised over £5 million for charity
>
> **RAM GIDOOMAL CBE**

MS SHIULIE GHOSH (ITN REPORTER)

Home Affairs Specialist, Independent Television News, 200 Gray's Inn Road, London, WC1X 8XZ

PLACE OF BIRTH: Leeds, 28.9.68
MARITAL STATUS: Single
COLLEGE: University of Kent
ACADEMIC QUALIFICATIONS: BA Hons Law
HOBBIES AND INTERESTS: Scuba diving, horse riding, ski – ing, climbing
EMAIL: sghosh@msn.com
PERSONAL PROFILE: I worked extensively for BBC TV in the Midlands and the South – East before joining ITN and the flagship programme 'News at Ten' in January 1998. In 1997 I travelled around the world as a backpacker and travelling still remains my passion.

MRS SUSHMITA GHOSH (KATHAK ARTISTE)

Bhavan Centre, 126 Biggerstaff Road, Stratford, London, E15 2LX

PLACE OF BIRTH: India, 4.7.64
MARITAL STATUS: Married
CHILDREN: One (Tara)
COLLEGE: Delhi
ACADEMIC QUALIFICATIONS: Hons Degree Physics
PROFESSIONAL QUALIFICATIONS: Post Diploma Kathak Kendra Delhi
PERSONAL PROFILE: A dancer, choreographer and teacher of Kathak in the UK since 1990, Sushmita's work is well known for its traditional roots, while at the same time being relevant to contemporary British life. Sushmita was trained by renowned Guru Shri Munna Shukla, at the prestigious Kathak Kendra in New Delhi.

MR RAM GIDOOMAL CBE (CONSULTANCY MANAGEMENT)

Chairman, Winning Communication Partnership Ltd, PO Box 43, Sutton, SM2 5WL

DATE OF BIRTH: 23.12.50
MARITAL STATUS: Married
CHILDREN: Three
COLLEGE: London Imperial College
ACADEMIC QUALIFICATIONS: BSc Hons, ARCS, FRSA
DIRECTORSHIPS: Business Links
MEMBERSHIPS: Cabinet Office Better Regulation Task Force. Syntel Europe. Covent Garden Market Authority. Chair South Asian Development Partnership
HONOURS/AWARDS: CBE
HOBBIES AND INTERESTS: Community and charity work, writing
PERSONAL PROFILE: Partnership. Former UK Group Chief Executive of the Inlaks Group. Forced to leave East Africa as a virtually penniless refugee. Awarded a CBE in 1998. He chairs the Anti – Discrimination Sub Group. He was the founder of the Christmas Cracker Project, which has given thousands of young people direct entrepreneurial experience and which has raised over £5 million for charity. Has written the successful: Sari 'n' Chips. and The UK Maharajahs as well as many published research reports.

MRS ZERBANOO GIFFORD (AUTHOR-CAMPAIGNER)

Hon Director, ASHA Foundation, Herga House, London Road, Harrow on the Hill, HA1 3JJ

PLACE OF BIRTH: India, 11.5.50
MARITAL STATUS: Married
CHILDREN: Two (Mark, Alexander)
COLLEGE: Watford College, London School of Journalism, the Open University
ACADEMIC QUALIFICATIONS: Class 2.1 BA Hon Degree
MEMBERSHIPS: Independent Broadcasting Trust. Voluntary Arts Network. Patron of UN Year of Peace. Friend of Daycare Trust.. Patron of Asians Friends of the RSPCA . Member Race Relations Forum advising the Home Secretary
HONOURS/AWARDS: Freedom of the City of Lincoln, Nebraska (1987) (87), Nehru Centenary Award (89). Nominated Woman of Europe (1991) Fellow Royal Society of Arts (1992)
HOBBIES AND INTERESTS: Collecting antique embroidery
PERSONAL PROFILE: Founder – director – ASHA Foundation. Former director of the Anti – Slavery International, and director of Charities Aid Foundation India. Three times parliamentary candidate (1983 – 92) and councillor, LB Harrow (1982 – 86), chair Community Relations Panel. Author: The Golden Thread, Asian Experience of Post Raj Britain (1990), Dadabhai Naoroji (1992), Asian Presence in Europe (1995), Thomas Clarkson and the Campaign Against Slavery (1996) . Celebrating India (1998).

MR AMIT GILL (STUDENT)

176 Porter Road, Derby, DE23 6RF

PLACE OF BIRTH: Derby, 19.6.80
COLLEGE: Mackworth College
ACADEMIC QUALIFICATIONS: GCSE, GNVQ Intermediate, Advanced IT
MEMBERSHIPS: Young Poets Corner
HONOURS/AWARDS: LAMDA Exams Distinction
HOBBIES AND INTERESTS: Poetry, acting, dancing, kick boxing, reading
PERSONAL PROFILE: I am dyslexic, I always thought I could never achieve anything in my life, but I was wrong. I realised we all have a gift and we must discover what we are good at. My talent is poetry and I have achieved my dreams. Never give up and always believe in yourself.
NOMINATED BY: Jeetinder Singh Pabla

MR CHARAN SINGH GILL MBE
(MANAGING DIRECTOR-RESTAURATEUR)

Managing Director, Harlequin Leisure Group Ltd, 10 Clypeholm Road, Glasgow, G1 0QQ

PLACE OF BIRTH: India, 8.12.54
MARITAL STATUS: Married
CHILDREN: Five (Ceetl, Basant, Preetpal, Jaspreet, Sampuran)
DIRECTORSHIPS: Harlequin Restaurant Group Ltd, Harlequin Properties (Scotland) Ltd, Curries Direct Ltd, Celestial Sounds Ltd. HM DEV (Scotland) Ltd. Richmount Ltd. Ashoka Johnson Ltd

HONOURS/AWARDS: MBE (1998) Non – executive Director – Glasgow University Hospital, NHS Trust
HOBBIES AND INTERESTS: Family pursuits, current affairs
PERSONAL PROFILE: My part – time job became a full time obsession and I was delighted to receive an MBE in 1998 for services to the food industry. This could not have been possible without the support of my family, and the dedication of my loyal staff who helped realise my dreams.
NOMINATED BY: Katriona Allen

GURBANS KAUR GILL JP (PROPRIETOR GUEST HOUSES)

Justice of the Peace, Ambercourt Guest House, 116 Bierton Road, Aylesbury, HP20 1EN

PLACE OF BIRTH: India, 11.3.37
MARITAL STATUS: Widow
CHILDREN: Two (Rippy, Reenu)
COLLEGE: Punjab University
ACADEMIC QUALIFICATIONS: MA Economics B.Ed
PROFESSIONAL QUALIFICATIONS: B.Ed
DIRECTORSHIPS: Gill Properties
MEMBERSHIPS: Social Services Policy & Resources, Public Protection, Personnel Committees on County Council, Chair: School Governing Bodies
HONOURS/AWARDS: Appointed Justice of the Peace 1980
HOBBIES AND INTERESTS: Community work, writing poetry, politics.
PERSONAL PROFILE: Arrived in Britain May 1996. Justice of the Peace since 1980. County councillor (SDP) 1983. Elected three times SDP District and County councillor 1983 – 1991. Two poetry books published (Punjabi).
NOMINATED BY: R Gill

MR HARJIT SINGH GILL (SUB POSTMASTER)

Mayor of Baron, 155 Barton Street, Gloucester, GL1 4HT

PLACE OF BIRTH: India, 7.2.55
MARITAL STATUS: Married
CHILDREN: Two (Gurkamal Singh, Amrit Kaur)
COLLEGE: G N University, Punjab
ACADEMIC QUALIFICATIONS: MA, Pol.Sc
HOBBIES AND INTERESTS: Sports
PERSONAL PROFILE: Married for 21 years with Jasminder Gill MA Pol Sc, My wife is sub-postmaster in one post office and I am sub-postmaster in the other office. I played hockey for university, Rest of India, member of Hockey Umpire Association, Glos. Racial Equality Forum, Glos. Inter Faith, chairman Punjabi Association.
NOMINATED BY: Jaideep Sareen

MISS REENU GILL (PROPRIETOR)

Proprietor Guest House, American Airlines, Amber Court, 116 Bierton Road, Aylesbury, HP20 1EN

PLACE OF BIRTH: Middlesex, 8.10.66
MARITAL STATUS: Single
PERSONAL PROFILE: Has been active member of a political party, community work. In business since I was 18 years old. Was school governor, managing a guest house while working for American Airlines.
NOMINATED BY: Ian Page and Steve Cockford

MR SATNAM SINGH GILL (TEACHER)

Vice Principal, Newham Sixth Form College, Kentish Town, London, NW5 1SU

PLACE OF BIRTH: India, 10.12.54
MARITAL STATUS: Married
CHILDREN: One (Kam)
COLLEGE: University of London
ACADEMIC QUALIFICATIONS: BSc
PROFESSIONAL QUALIFICATIONS: PGCE
DIRECTORSHIPS: Novas Ouvertures Group. Vice chair Bridge Housing Group
HOBBIES AND INTERESTS: Education, social housing, politics
PERSONAL PROFILE: Bellevue School Bradford and University of London. Qualified teacher 1978. Councillor – Camden 1986 – 90. Chair of policy and resources 1987 – 90. Legal advisor to Camden Law Centre 1979 – 86. Personnel Director Hackney 1986 – 91. Vice principal Newham Sixth Form College 1991 – 98. Principal Working Mens College for Men and Women, 1999 onwards.

MS SEEMA GILL (INTERPRETER – TEACHER – POET)

Arts & Social Club,

PLACE OF BIRTH: India, 22.6.47
MARITAL STATUS: Divorced
CHILDREN: Two (Ajita Mona Sorensen, Astrid Maya Sorensen)
ACADEMIC QUALIFICATIONS: BA Political Science
PROFESSIONAL QUALIFICATIONS: Diploma in Journalism
HOBBIES AND INTERESTS: Writing, photography, organising, inspiring, activist, community work
PERSONAL PROFILE: Despite the hardship and permanent grief caused by the recent breakup of her 22-year old marriage, Seema continues to rise above the challenges and proves to be a remarkable source of inspiration to all the women she has touched. She has worked as a painter, photographer, journalist, language teacher, youth and community worker, as well as running workshops and the Arts and Social Club. Seema communicates effectively in six languages: Punjabi, Hindi, English, Danish, Urdu and Swahili.
NOMINATED BY: Howard W Frost

MR SHEEM S GILL (MULTICULTURAL HEALTH OFFICER)

Greater Glasgow Community & Mental Health Service, 10 Maple Road, Dumbreck, Glasgow, G41 5DB

PLACE OF BIRTH: India, 13.8.48
MARITAL STATUS: Married
CHILDREN: Four (Veni, Sharon, Vijay, Sanjay)
COLLEGE: Glasgow University
ACADEMIC QUALIFICATIONS: High school & Intermediate Punjab Uni & UP Board. RGN, RMN
PROFESSIONAL QUALIFICATIONS: Diploma in Management
DIRECTORSHIPS: S & D Gill Ltd
MEMBERSHIPS: Treasurer, Scottish Asian Christian Fellowship
HONOURS/AWARDS: Nurse 1996 Award, Commendation for Trans-cultural Psychiatric Care
HOBBIES AND INTERESTS: Music, movies, hillwalking & social events
PERSONAL PROFILE: Innitiated Transcultural Nursing Care in Glasgow which led to the trusts innovative multicultural health project and subsequent race equality policy – 1995. As co – ordinator of the project I remain committed to the development and delivery of culturally correct healthcare provision to an estimated 40,000 ethnic minority population of Greater Glasgow.
NOMINATED BY: Ishbel White

She has worked as a painter, photographer, journalist, language teacher, youth and community worker, as well as running workshops and the Arts and Social Club

SEEMA GILL

MR SUCHA SINGH GILL JP (Property-Restaurant)

Managing Director, Orbit Productions Ltd, 94 – 96 Duncan Road, Gillingham, ME7 4JX

PLACE OF BIRTH: India, 10.3.40
MARITAL STATUS: Married
CHILDREN: Three (Jatinder, Ricky, Ranyi)
COLLEGE: Sarhal Qazian
ACADEMIC QUALIFICATIONS: BA Mism. BOV,
PROFESSIONAL QUALIFICATIONS: Business Management , NVQ Level 4/5
DIRECTORSHIPS: Strood Water Front Community Association
MEMBERSHIPS: Racial Equality. Chair Kent Multicultural Community Nity Association
HONOURS/AWARDS: Invited to Buckingham Palace
HOBBIES AND INTERESTS: Music, community, voluntary work
PERSONAL PROFILE: Justice of the Peace, self employed. Sit on Family Proceedings Court. Member of Bench Mangement Committee. Board member of Orbit Housing Assoc. Royal Air Force has given me an office to advise people with problems. As chairman of KMCA, I deal with case work. Have high regard in the local community Nity.
NOMINATED BY: Cllr Dai Liyanage

MR CHRISTOPHER GLOVER (Actor-Writer-Director)

Morgan and Goodman, 31d Denbigh Place, Pimlico, London, SW1V 2HA

PLACE OF BIRTH: London, 29.11.64
MARITAL STATUS: Married
CHILDREN: One (Ailish)
COLLEGE: Queen's University
ACADEMIC QUALIFICATIONS: BA Hons Social Anthropology
DIRECTORSHIPS: Former Director of Tinderbox
MEMBERSHIPS: British Actors Equity Association
HOBBIES AND INTERESTS: Theatre, film, politics
EMAIL: cglover@connectfree.co.uk
PERSONAL PROFILE: Raised in London, he worked in Ireland for eight years. An original member of Tinderbox, an award winning company that has developed new and innovative work since 1988. Christopher has travelled extensively and written on ethnic and political conflict in Nicaragua. He has appeared in numerous films and TV programmes.

MISS SUSHMA GOBINDRAM (Solicitor)

Trainee Solicitor, 14 Mayfield Avenue, Ealing, London, W13 9LR

PLACE OF BIRTH: London, 7.5.72
MARITAL STATUS: Single
COLLEGE: Thames Valley University
ACADEMIC QUALIFICATIONS: LL.B – Law Degree
PROFESSIONAL QUALIFICATIONS: Post Graduate Diploma in Legal Practice
MEMBERSHIPS: Member of the Law Society
HONOURS/AWARDS: 1st Prize talent competition judge, Rajendra Kumar, 1st Prize Festival of Brent Diploma – Distinction in Dance
HOBBIES AND INTERESTS: Dance, swimming, Hindi movies
PERSONAL PROFILE: A talented young lady who is a trainee solicitor by profession, to qualify in September 1999. Is a professional classical/film dancer who has achieved a first class diploma in Bharat Natyam and won first prizes in many competitions. She has performed on TV and for dignitaries including Prince Charles.

DR SHANTHA GODAGAMA (Ayurvedic Doctor)

Director, Ayurvedic Medical Association UK, Ayurvedic Medical Centre, Panchakarma Clinic, The Hale Clinic, 7 Park Crescent, London, W1N 3HE

PLACE OF BIRTH: Sri Lanka, 11.11.45
MARITAL STATUS: Married
CHILDREN: Three (Suneth, Sujith, Sumudu)
COLLEGE: Colombo University
ACADEMIC QUALIFICATIONS: BA, MS, M BA.C
PROFESSIONAL QUALIFICATIONS: Bachelor of Ayurvedic Medicine
DIRECTORSHIPS: Ayurvedic Medical Association
MEMBERSHIPS: British Acupuncture Council – Ayurvedic Medical Association
HONOURS/AWARDS: DAG Hammerkjohd. Award for Complementary Medicine
HOBBIES AND INTERESTS: Cricket, author of the Handbook of Ayurveda
PERSONAL PROFILE: Founding president Ayurvedic Medical Association. Founder – Dean, Ayurvedic Medical College, London. International lecturer on complementary medicine. Ex – director of therapy Tyringham Clinic. Awarded Gold Medal for research by World Conference of Complementary Medicine. Invited to Buckingham Palace.
NOMINATED BY: Amardutt Dhiman

DR MAHESHWAR GODBOLE (Doctor)

Eye Specialist, Indian Classical Music Society, 11 Lowerfold Way, Healey, Rochdale, OL12 7HX

PLACE OF BIRTH: Burhanpur, 15.1.33
MARITAL STATUS: Married
CHILDREN: One (Vinata)
COLLEGE: Medical College, Nagpur
ACADEMIC QUALIFICATIONS: MBBS (Nagpur), DO (Conj) London
MEMBERSHIPS: Honorary Secretary , Indian Classical Music Society
HOBBIES AND INTERESTS: Music, languages, writing, painting
PERSONAL PROFILE: The Indian Classical Music Society presents performances by Pukka professional visiting musicians and dancers. I have been it's secretary for 21 years. We maintain punctuality and discipline. People say they like my introductions. I also lecture and write on related subjects. I owe it all to my wife Shibani.
NOMINATED BY: Sharon Aitkin

DR SHIBANI MAHESHWAR GODBOLE (Gynaecologist)

Executive Committee Member, 11 Lowerfold Way, Healey, Rochdale, OL127HX

PLACE OF BIRTH: India, 12.9.34
MARITAL STATUS: Married
CHILDREN: One (Vinata)
COLLEGE: Medical College, Nagpur
ACADEMIC QUALIFICATIONS: BSc, MBBS (Nagpur), D.Obst, RCOG (Lond)
HOBBIES AND INTERESTS: Cookery, literature
PERSONAL PROFILE: I am a Sangeet Visharad from Gwalior. I play sitar and I sing classical and light songs. Professionally I have performed in England and Wales. In India I also represented my university at Delhi Inter – provincial Youth Festival. I was treasurer of the Indian Classical Music Society.

MISS VINATA GODBOLE (Actress-Indian Dancer)

11 Lowerfold Way, Healey, Rochdale, OL12 7HX

PLACE OF BIRTH: Durham, 9.8.64
MARITAL STATUS: Single
COLLEGE: College of Fine Arts, Madras
ACADEMIC QUALIFICATIONS: O – Levels, 1st Class Diploma – Indian Dance
PROFESSIONAL QUALIFICATIONS: Diploma in Swedish Massage, Diploma in Post – Grad Acting from Guildford School of Acting
MEMBERSHIPS: WWF, Equity, RSPB, JWPT
HOBBIES AND INTERESTS: Wildlife, music, literature, swimming
PERSONAL PROFILE: Worked as a dancer since 1988. Performed LED workshops, lectured, choreographed and taught in art centres, schools, colleges and festivals in UK, US, Norway, Canada, Zimbabwe, Malaysia. Worked as an actress since 1994. Small parts in TV series, some stage work and produced my own drama work for schools.

MR JASBIR (JAZZ) GOHAL (Producer-Presenter)

Actor, Namaste Asian TV, 160 Lathom Road, East Ham, London, E6 2DZ

PLACE OF BIRTH: India
COLLEGE: University of East London
ACADEMIC QUALIFICATIONS: Graduated in Broadcast Journalism
PROFESSIONAL QUALIFICATIONS: Producer, Presenter, Editor, Cameraman, Actor, Writer
MEMBERSHIPS: British Equity and member Indian Senior Actors
HONOURS/AWARDS: Voluntary Organisations
HOBBIES AND INTERESTS: Child counsellor, charity work for the aged
PERSONAL PROFILE: Have acted in many Hindi films and TV serials as well as stage and modelled. Attended drama school, fluent in Hindi and Punjabi and can read and write Hindi. Enjoy writing and producing programmes and providing fresh and interesting ideas. Great sense of humour, enjoy working with different people, enjoy travel, sport, music and have fun with my work.

'Have acted in many Hindi films and TV serials as well as stage and modelled'

JASBIR (JAZZ) GOHAL

MR GURDEV SINGH GOLA (CIVIL SERVANT)

Supervisor, DSS, Gola Raj House, 150 Deepdale Road, Preston, PR1 6PY

PLACE OF BIRTH: London, 8.1.72
MARITAL STATUS: Single
ACADEMIC QUALIFICATIONS: 3 O – Levels, 2 A – Levels
HONOURS/AWARDS: Trophy for karate and swimming
HOBBIES AND INTERESTS: Weight training, swimming, jogging
PERSONAL PROFILE: Chef and civil servant. Proud to be a Sikh. Treasurer and committee member of Preston Gurdwara.
NOMINATED BY: Rajendra Singh

PARPOOR SINGH GOLA (STUDENT)

Legal Student, Preston College, Gola Raj House, 150 Deepdale Road, Preston, PR1 6PY

PLACE OF BIRTH: Preston, 21.9.82
MARITAL STATUS: Single
COLLEGE: Preston College
ACADEMIC QUALIFICATIONS: 7 GCSE's
PROFESSIONAL QUALIFICATIONS: Business Studies
HONOURS/AWARDS: 4 Trophies in Boxing
HOBBIES AND INTERESTS: Amateur boxer, weight training
PERSONAL PROFILE: Father is a former international wrestler. I am studying and hope to own my business as an accountant. I am a fitness fanatic.
NOMINATED BY: Rajendra Singh

MS AILEEN GONSALVES (ACTRESS)

Felix De Wolfe, Manfield House, 1 Southampton Street, London, WC2R 0LR

PLACE OF BIRTH: Kenya, 17.7.73
MARITAL STATUS: Single
COLLEGE: Central School of Speech and Drama
ACADEMIC QUALIFICATIONS: BA in Acting
HONOURS/AWARDS: Smith College Award for outstanding contribution to National Student Drama Festival
HOBBIES AND INTERESTS: Table tennis, netball, life drawing
PERSONAL PROFILE: Performed in many theatre productions. The highlight so far was starring as Nora in Iben's 'A Dolls House' – Young Vic Theatre. Television and radio for the BBC include 'The Red Oleander', 'Choices' and 'Roger Roger'. Films include 'I love my Mum' and 'Such a long journey'. Developing playwriting and directory skills.

MRS AZMINA GOVINDJI (CONSULTANT NUTRITIONIST)

Dietician, Littlecote, Frithwood Avenue, Northwood, HA6 3LX

PLACE OF BIRTH: East Africa
MARITAL STATUS: Married
CHILDREN: Two (Bizhan, Shazia)
COLLEGE: London University
ACADEMIC QUALIFICATIONS: BSc Upper 2nd Class. Hons in Nutrition. Dip in Dietetics. City & Guilds Teachers Certificate (Distinction)
PROFESSIONAL QUALIFICATIONS: Diploma in Dietetics, City & Guilds Teacher
MEMBERSHIPS: PR Committee of the British Dietetic Association
HONOURS/AWARDS: Ismaili Award for Professional Excellence, Letter of Commendation
HOBBIES AND INTERESTS: Entertaining, Neuro – linguistic programming NLP
PERSONAL PROFILE: Azmina has appeared as nutrition expert on ITV, BBC, Channel 5 and Zee TV. She originates cookbooks for Sainsbury's and Weightwatchers and also writes for Readers Digest and women's magazines. Her success is mainly due to her lively personality and creativity in her field.

Azmina has appeared as nutrition expert on ITV, BBC, Channel 5 and Zee TV. She originates cookbooks for Sainsbury's and Weightwatchers and also writes for Readers Digest and women's magazines

AZMINA GOVINDJI

DR HANUME THIMME GOWDA CLLR (GENERAL PRACTITIONER)

Mountain Road Medical Centre, 111 Mountain Road, Thornhill, Dewsbury, WF12 0BS

PLACE OF BIRTH: India, 1.5.38
MARITAL STATUS: Separated
CHILDREN: Five (Ramesh, Ravish, Rajesh, Rakesh, Sampath)
COLLEGE: Mysore, Karnatak, India
ACADEMIC QUALIFICATIONS: MBBS, MD, DTCD
PROFESSIONAL QUALIFICATIONS: MBBS, MD, DTCD
MEMBERSHIPS: BMA, RSM, Rotary International
HOBBIES AND INTERESTS: Hard working, walking, holiday
PERSONAL PROFILE: General practitioner since 1980. Labour councillor since 1988 to date – Kirklees Metropolitan Council. President Dewsbury Rotary International 1998 – 99. President BMA, Dewsbury 1998 – 99.

MR BALDEV KRISHAN GOYAL (CHARTERED ACCOUNTANT)

Own Business, B Goyal and Co, 81 Parkstone Avenue, Emerson Park, Hornchurch, RM11 3LT

PLACE OF BIRTH: India, 29.5.37
MARITAL STATUS: Married
CHILDREN: Two (Mina, Prem)
COLLEGE: Panjab, India
ACADEMIC QUALIFICATIONS: MA (Economics), MA (History), B.Ed
PROFESSIONAL QUALIFICATIONS: ACMA, FCCA
HOBBIES AND INTERESTS: Badminton, social work
PERSONAL PROFILE: Founder and chairman of Board of Trustees, Radha Krishna Temple, Stratford. Founder president Asian Welfare Society, Havering. Member Police Consultative Committee, Havering. Former chairman CRC (Havering). Hon Auditor Murugan Temple, East London, Luxmi Narayan Temple and various other charitable organisations.

MS ROBINDER KAUR GREWAL (TEACHER)

Teacher In Charge, Mulberry School For Girls, Richard Street, Commercial Road, London, E1 2JP

PLACE OF BIRTH: India, 6.9.52
MARITAL STATUS: Single
COLLEGE: University College, London
ACADEMIC QUALIFICATIONS: BA Hons English, MA, PGCE, TEFL
HOBBIES AND INTERESTS: Cinema, reading, music, restaurants
PERSONAL PROFILE: Robinder Kaur Grewal has been working with the local East End community for the last twelve years. She is an English teacher in Mulberry School For Girls. Robinder is also involved in the Somali school and Jagonari Women's Centre within the sphere of community education.
NOMINATED BY: Irina Hossain

MR AVTAR SINGH GROVER (PROPERTY INVESTOR)

Director, 'Courtlands', 119 Wolsey Road, Moor Park, Northwood, HA6 2EB

PLACE OF BIRTH: India, 27.7.35
MARITAL STATUS: Married
CHILDREN: Two (Kan, Kiran)
COLLEGE: Punjab University
ACADEMIC QUALIFICATIONS: BA Hons Economics
PROFESSIONAL QUALIFICATIONS: Member British Institute of Management
DIRECTORSHIPS: Acorn's Hotel
MEMBERSHIPS: BIM, Senior Vice – President of NRI – UK
HONOURS/AWARDS: Mother India Award1984, Shiromani Award 1990. Hind Rattan 1991
HOBBIES AND INTERESTS: Currrent affairs, travel
PERSONAL PROFILE: I am involved in social and business affairs serving the NRI UK community as a senior vice president and have been awarded for my community work by the president of India and others receiving Shiromani, Mother India and Hind Rattan Awards. I have a business in commercial property investments.
NOMINATED BY: Miss Kiran Grover

MRS CHARANJIT KAUR GROVER JP (Magistrate)

Justice of the Peace, Courtlands, 119 Wolsey Road, Moor Park, Northwood, HA6 2EB

PLACE OF BIRTH: India, 3.4.44
MARITAL STATUS: Married
CHILDREN: Two (Kanwarjit, Kiran)
COLLEGE: Delhi University
ACADEMIC QUALIFICATIONS: BA Degree
MEMBERSHIPS: Fellow of the RSA, National Carers Association. Member Ethnic Advisory Committee, Member of Community Health Council.
HONOURS/AWARDS: Appointment by the Secretary of State – Tribunal panel member
HOBBIES AND INTERESTS: Health issues, reading, yoga, keep fit, travel
PERSONAL PROFILE: As a magistrate in the adult, youth and family courts, I have become involved in many community issues. I have worked as a health educator for the ethnic communities dealing with issues including HIV/AIDS and facilitating in Asian languages.
NOMINATED BY: Kiran Grover

MR MOHAMED YUSUF GULAMHUSEIN JP (Accountant)

CAT Music Ltd, 81 The Mall, Southgate, London, N14 6LL

PLACE OF BIRTH: India, 26.12.38
MARITAL STATUS: Married
CHILDREN: Two (Zeenat, Nasreen)
COLLEGE: Bennett College
ACADEMIC QUALIFICATIONS: Diploma in Business Studies
PROFESSIONAL QUALIFICATIONS: Fellow of Institute of Financial Accountants
MEMBERSHIPS: Enfield Victim Support Scheme
HONOURS/AWARDS: Freedom of the City London
HOBBIES AND INTERESTS: Cinema, music, travelling
PERSONAL PROFILE: Arrived from Zanzibar and settled in London since 1964. Married to Farida in Nairobi in 1968. Had two daughters in 1969 and 1978. Worked as an accountant in the Commonwealth Secretariat for 16 years. Appointed Justice of the Peace in 1992. Took an early retirement in 1993. Working part – time as an accountant. Sit on the Bench in Enfield Magistrates' Court. Serve as a member of the North – West London's Valuation Tribunal and act as a mental health manager in a private hospital in Edmonton.

MR OM PRAKASH GULATI (Managing Director)

Managing Director, Welcome Travel, 55 – 57 Wells Street, London, W1P 3RA

PLACE OF BIRTH: Pakistan, 1.2.42
MARITAL STATUS: Married
CHILDREN: One (Mrs Sonia Sadh)
COLLEGE: Delhi
ACADEMIC QUALIFICATIONS: Science Graduate
MEMBERSHIPS: Nargis Dutt Relief & Research Charity, International Punjabi Society, Punjab Society of British Isles. Indian Association of Harrow. Bhartiya Vidhya Bhavan
HOBBIES AND INTERESTS: Music, yoga, reading
PERSONAL PROFILE: Mr Gulati is one of the highest profile figures in the Indian community in the UK and India. He started with an electronic business and diversified into the travel trade. Today he is Managing Director of Welcome Travel GSA for Air India with offices in the West End, Southall, Wembley, Birmingham and Manchester and an annual turnover of around £30 million. His remarkable success is the result of his dedication, self – reliance and dynamic business acumen.

> Mr Gulati is one of the highest profile figures in the Indian community in the UK and India. He started with an electronic business and diversified into the travel trade. Today he is Managing Director of Welcome Travel GSA for Air India with offices in the West End, Southall, Wembley, Birmingham and Manchester and an annual turnover of around £30 million

OM PRAKASH GULATI

DR M. AKHTAR GULFAM (Journalist-Model)

Chief Editor, Glamour Media Ltd, 20/3 Hawkhill, Edinburgh, EH7 6LA

PLACE OF BIRTH: Pakistan, 13.3.69
MARITAL STATUS: Married
COLLEGE: Cambridge University – Napier University
ACADEMIC QUALIFICATIONS: FSc, BSc
PROFESSIONAL QUALIFICATIONS: MSc, M.Phil, PhD Special Journalism
DIRECTORSHIPS: Director Glamour Media Ltd, British Ethnic Journalist and Broadcasters Association – PAWA
MEMBERSHIPS: British Actors Equity – National Union of Journalist – PJA
HONOURS/AWARDS: Pride of Performance, Gold Medal UNO Seminar, Gold Award Youth Society London. Best Model 1996/97
HOBBIES AND INTERESTS: Modelling
PERSONAL PROFILE: Scotland correspondent of The London Nation. Ex – senior sub editor The Nation. TV/radio presenter. Live concert, fashion show compare, organiser. Best Model of the Year 1996/97. Edinburgh Mela. Best Journalist of the Year.
NOMINATED BY: Masood Khan and Amin Malik

MR BHARAT KUMAR GUPTA (Investment)

Director, India Investments Plc, 11 Middle Row, London, W10 5AT

PLACE OF BIRTH: London, 21.8.79
MARITAL STATUS: Single
COLLEGE: London School of Economics in Political Science
ACADEMIC QUALIFICATIONS: Law Student
DIRECTORSHIPS: India Investments Plc
MEMBERSHIPS: India Welfare Society, Kensal Community Association
HONOURS/AWARDS: Best Student of Middle Row School
HOBBIES AND INTERESTS: Serving the community, collecting: coins, banknotes, stamps
PERSONAL PROFILE: Plays a very active part in serving the community through India Welfare Society in Kensal Community Association. Has a very good knowledge of computers and has computerised accounts and investments of his company in a very convenient way.

DR CHAMAN LALL GUPTA (General Practitioner)

Principal GP, Welling Medical Centre, 'Nikraj', 15 Wansuny Road, Bexley Village, Bexley, DA5 2DG

PLACE OF BIRTH: India, 17.8.38
MARITAL STATUS: Married
CHILDREN: Two (Rajesh, Nikesh)
COLLEGE: Punjab University
ACADEMIC QUALIFICATIONS: Science Intermediate. MBBS (Pun)
PROFESSIONAL QUALIFICATIONS: CIFP (London)
MEMBERSHIPS: IMA
HOBBIES AND INTERESTS: Films, music, swimming
PERSONAL PROFILE: I have been a general medical practitioner, both in India and UK for the last 38 years. I enjoy helping people.
NOMINATED BY: Neelam Chaudhari

DR NARENDRA KUMAR GUPTA (Teaching-Research)

Lecturer, Napier University, 66 Langton View, East Calder, Scotland, EH53 0RA

PLACE OF BIRTH: India, 11.9.47
MARITAL STATUS: Married
CHILDREN: Two (Vikas, Aditya)
COLLEGE: Patna, Ranchi, (India), UMIST, Brunel, Napier
ACADEMIC QUALIFICATIONS: BSc (Eng), DTSc, MTech, PhD MBA, C Eng, Miee, MIRSE, SMIEEE
PROFESSIONAL QUALIFICATIONS: CEng, MIEE, MIRSE. Senior member IEEE
MEMBERSHIPS: IEES Professional Group Committee, Science, Education and Management Section of the IEE, Scotland
HOBBIES AND INTERESTS: Reading, swimming, meeting people
PERSONAL PROFILE: Published over 50 papers in journals and conference proceedings. Chairman, PG Committee 55 (Education and Training) of IEE (Institution of Electrical Engineers): 1996 – 97 Member editorial advisory panels of Engineering Science and Education Journal and Engineering Management Journal. Have chaired committees and conference sessions and referred conference and journal papers.

RAMA PRAKASH GUPTA (COMMUNITY ACTIVIST)

17 Fennel Street, Loughborough, LE11 1UQ

PLACE OF BIRTH: India, 1.9.34
MARITAL STATUS: Single
COLLEGE: Dehli University, Punjab University
MEMBERSHIPS: Life member – Friends of the Earth, Greenpeace, India YHA, Youth Hostel Assoc. India. LM Henry Doubleday Research Association (research in organic farming) Ghandi Foundation.
HOBBIES AND INTERESTS: Walking, yoga, keep fit, environmental work, voluntary work, like planting trees, youth hosteling
PERSONAL PROFILE: Rama Gupta has lived in Loughborough since 1962. He devotes time and energy to local and national charities and various religious and social activities. He keeps fit regularly at the town's leisure centre, and is well – known for his involvement in environmental issues for the betterment of the community.

DR SURAJ NARAIN GUPTA (GENERAL PRACTITIONER)

The Surgery, 7 Salisbury Avenue, Barking, IG11 9XQ

PLACE OF BIRTH: India, 1.1.42
MARITAL STATUS: Married
CHILDREN: Two (Dr R Gupta, Mr Nikon Gupta)
ACADEMIC QUALIFICATIONS: BSc, MBBS, DTM&H, DTCD
MEMBERSHIPS: BMA, ODA, IMA
HONOURS/AWARDS: RDMT Scholarship. WHO scholarship
HOBBIES AND INTERESTS: Swimming, Indian music, travel
PERSONAL PROFILE: Arrived UK 1972, after hospital jobs settled as GP in Barking. Interested in most ethnic race issues and activities.

MR SURESH KUMAR GUPTA (FINANCIER)

Managing Director, India Investments Plc, 11 Middle Row, London, W10 5AT

PLACE OF BIRTH: India, 16.9.40
MARITAL STATUS: Married
CHILDREN: Two (Asha, Bharat)
COLLEGE: Delhi Polytechnic, India
ACADEMIC QUALIFICATIONS: DC
PROFESSIONAL QUALIFICATIONS: ALAM, MICFM, MIFM, FRAS, FRNS
DIRECTORSHIPS: Kensal Community Association
MEMBERSHIPS: India Welfare Society, Conservative Party. Bhartiya Vidya Bhavan. Fellow Royal Asiatic Society. Royal Numistatic Society. Institute of Factory Mgmt
HONOURS/AWARDS: Bronze and Gold Medal, Diploma in Public Speaking
HOBBIES AND INTERESTS: Collecting banknotes, coins and stamps, serving the community
PERSONAL PROFILE: Founded India Welfare Society in 1966. Served as secretary 1966 – 1986. Chairman 1986 – 1994 and president since 1994. Served as member of Kensington, Chelsea and Westminster Health Authority from 1984 – 1996 on being appointed by the Health Secretary. Served as lay visitor to police stations from 1987 – 1990 on being appointed by the Home Secretary. Vice Chairman of Kensington and Chelsea Police Consultative Committee 1985 – 1991 and currently a member. Associated with many charitable and voluntary organisations.
NOMINATED BY: India Welfare Society

MR NIHAL GURUSINGHE (CONSULTANT NEUROSURGEON)

Preston Acute Hospitals, 11 Moor Park Avenue, Preston, PR1 6AS

PLACE OF BIRTH: Sri Lanka, 30.10.46
MARITAL STATUS: Married
CHILDREN: Two (Dilnath, Lakmal)
COLLEGE: University of Ceylon, Colombo
ACADEMIC QUALIFICATIONS: MBBS, FRCSEd
PROFESSIONAL QUALIFICATIONS: MBBS, FRCSEd
MEMBERSHIPS: Society of British Neurological Surgeons
HOBBIES AND INTERESTS: Cricket
PERSONAL PROFILE: Came to UK in 1975. First Sri Lankan to become a consultant neurosurgeon in the UK.

Founded India Welfare Society in 1966. Served as secretary 1966 – 1986. Chairman 1986 – 1994 and president since 1994. Served as member of Kensington, Chelsea and Westminster Health Authority from 1984 – 1996 on being appointed by the Health Secretary. Served as lay visitor to police stations from 1987 – 1990 on being appointed by the Home Secretary. Vice Chairman of Kensington and Chelsea Police Consultative Committee 1985 – 1991 and currently a member. Associated with many charitable and voluntary organisations

SURESH KUMAR GUPTA

MR MOHAMMAD HABIB (Lecturer)

Schoolteacher, Westborough High School, 121 Lees Holms, Thornhill Lees, Dewsbury, WF12 0AX

PLACE OF BIRTH: Pakistan, 7.12.61
MARITAL STATUS: Married
CHILDREN: Three (Shoaib, Henna, Iqra)
ACADEMIC QUALIFICATIONS: MBA, BBA, PGCE
PROFESSIONAL QUALIFICATIONS: PGCE
MEMBERSHIPS: Salfia Advice Centre, Ghousa Mosque, Kirklees Law Centre
HONOURS/AWARDS: First Position in AK in SSC exams, Cash prizes
HOBBIES AND INTERESTS: Reading books, playing table tennis, working with voluntary organisations
PERSONAL PROFILE: Born in Pakistan. Educated in Pakistan. Did a computer course, then worked for a computer firm as a marketing executive. Employed as a senior lecturer in business. Worked for many religious organisations.

MS NILIMA RAHMAN HADI (Senior Officer)

Libraries Outreach, Grameen Plc, Unit 2 & 17, Osbourne Trading Centre, Busk Road, Oldham, OL9 6QZ

PLACE OF BIRTH: Hull, 12.6.76
MARITAL STATUS: Married
CHILDREN: One (Syeda Farah Ehasan)
ACADEMIC QUALIFICATIONS: LLB Hons-(being attained)
DIRECTORSHIPS: Director of Grameen Plc
HOBBIES AND INTERESTS: Badminton, current affairs, swimming
PERSONAL PROFILE: I am an active person in both my local community and the Asian community as a whole. I completed my A-Levels and got married halfway through my degree. I value my private life immensely and still have a keen interest in Asian arts. I dance, write, act and I also MC shows. My ambition is to become a lawyer, who can make a difference.
NOMINATED BY: Ms Jane Parkinson

MR BASHIR-UL HAFEEZ (Local Government Officer Rtd)

Councillor, 17 Abbotts Road, East Ham, London, E6 1LE

PLACE OF BIRTH: India, 29.6.34
MARITAL STATUS: Single
COLLEGE: FA Kashmir University
ACADEMIC QUALIFICATIONS: Diploma in Automobile Engineering
PROFESSIONAL QUALIFICATIONS: CAA London
MEMBERSHIPS: Retired Shop Steward NALGO
PERSONAL PROFILE: Newham councillor 1986-98. Chair of North East Evaluation Tribunal 1995-95. Chair London Home and Water Safety Council 1992-95. Vice-chair 1995-98. Chair and vice chair of Citizens Advice Bureau 1996-97. Vice-chair of General Purposes Committee 1994. Chair of Entertainment Licensing. Vice-chair of Planning 1995-96.

DR PREM BIKRAM HAMAL (Doctor)

Medical Consultant, Pinderfields & Pontefract NHS Trust, Trust Headquarters, Rowan House, Aberford Road, Wakefield, WF1 4DG

PLACE OF BIRTH: Nepal, 22.2.35
MARITAL STATUS: Married
CHILDREN: Three (Abhinna, Anokha, Bobby)
COLLEGE: Tri-Chandra College, Lucknow Medical
ACADEMIC QUALIFICATIONS: MBBS
PROFESSIONAL QUALIFICATIONS: MRC Path, DC, Path, LRCP, MRCS
DIRECTORSHIPS: West Yorkshire Laboratory
MEMBERSHIPS: BMA, Royal College of Pathologists
HONOURS/AWARDS: Fellowship in Pathology 1982
HOBBIES AND INTERESTS: Golf
PERSONAL PROFILE: Chairman of Nepalese Doctors' Association 1985-87. Chairman of Nepalese Association in Midlands and North 1993-97. Chairman of Overseas Doctors' Association, Wakefield 1981-91.

MS AQUEELA HAMEED (Epidemiologist)

Health Policy & Mgmt Consultant, Stockton International Family Centre, 70 Dovecot Street, Stockton-On-Tees, TS18 1LL

PLACE OF BIRTH: Middlesborough, 1.7.68
MARITAL STATUS: Married
COLLEGE: University of Newcastle, University of Durham
ACADEMIC QUALIFICATIONS: 9 O-Levels 2 A*, 2 A-Levels, BA joint Hons in Sociology and Social Policy
PROFESSIONAL QUALIFICATIONS: Post Graduate Diploma in Arabic, MSc in Public Health Medicine
DIRECTORSHIPS: Manager of the 'Multi-Ethnic Health and Health Care Forum'
MEMBERSHIPS: Cleveland Aids Support
HONOURS/AWARDS: Research Fellowship Long Distance Running
HOBBIES AND INTERESTS: Sport, travel, interior design
PERSONAL PROFILE: I was born and grew up in one of the deprived wards in Middlesborough and saw education as a means of escaping from poverty. My commitment to working with disadvantaged and oppressed communities have led me to far off fields such as military occupied Gaza Strip. Locally, I am known as a vital force in the fight for racial equality in the NHS and have played a pivotal role in the formation of the Multi-Ethnic Health & Health Care Forum and Sehat Ka Ghar in Stockton.
NOMINATED BY: Zarda Khan

MR SHEIKH HAMEED (Insurance Broker)

Proprietor, ARH Associates, 15 Newhall Place, 16-17 Newhall Hill, Birmingham, B1 3JH

PLACE OF BIRTH: Pakistan, 31.1.59
MARITAL STATUS: Married
CHILDREN: Three (Faiza Sabeen, Adeel Shehzad, Sana Jabeen)
COLLEGE: Wolverhampton University
ACADEMIC QUALIFICATIONS: 9 O-Levels, 3 A-Levels
PROFESSIONAL QUALIFICATIONS: BA Hons, AC II, MLIA
MEMBERSHIPS: LIA, MNAEA, AIIB, CII
HOBBIES AND INTERESTS: Current affairs, travelling, racket sports
PERSONAL PROFILE: Entered the insurance industry in the late 1970's after leaving the teaching profession. Gained valuable experience by working through the various departments of large national insurance companies before taking professional insurance exams. Established successful brokerage in Birmingham, dealing with all aspects of insurance, mortgage, finance and estate agency.
NOMINATED BY: Faiza Sabeen

MR TARIQUE HANIF (Property Development)

Director (Joint), J T Homes, TY Gwyn, 2 Grovelands Road, Spencers Wood, Reading, RG7 1DP

PLACE OF BIRTH: Reading, 8.10.71
MARITAL STATUS: Single
COLLEGE: London Guildhall University
ACADEMIC QUALIFICATIONS: Business Studies HND
DIRECTORSHIPS: Director with partner J T Homes
HOBBIES AND INTERESTS: Motor racing, weight-training
PERSONAL PROFILE: I believe not taking a risk, is a risk in itself; any obstacle is a challenge, every opportunity should be taken. This has made my property business successful. Fitness is essential, motivation and discipline are vital, a healthy body and mind sets your business above the rest of its kind. Believe, Become, Achieve.
NOMINATED BY: Bobby Wain

MISS JANIFAR JENNY YEASMIN HANNAN (Student)

PLACE OF BIRTH: London, 15.6.86
MARITAL STATUS: Single
HONOURS/AWARDS: Netball, swimming, attendance, athletics and commendation
HOBBIES AND INTERESTS: All sports, but basketball is my favourite
PERSONAL PROFILE: I go to Mulberry School for Girls and I will be in Year 9 in September 1999. When I grow up I want to be a nurse or a lawyer. I like playing all kinds of sport but my best game is basketball I like it because you can do slam dunk da funk. My favourite subjects are RS, PE, science, maths, dance and drama.

'I was born and grew up in one of the deprived wards in Middlesborough and saw education as a means of escaping from poverty'

AQUEELA HAMEED

MR VIDYA PARKASH HANSRANI (Businessman)

Wholesale Partner, 14 Westleigh Avenue, Leicester, LE3 0HG

PLACE OF BIRTH: India, 15.4.18
MARITAL STATUS: Married
CHILDREN: Two (Krishan Kumar, Kushal Kumari)
COLLEGE: DAV College Lahore
ACADEMIC QUALIFICATIONS: FSc 1935 -1937
HONOURS/AWARDS: Men of Achievement (50 Year Membership Awards of IWA)
HOBBIES AND INTERESTS: Reading, writing
PERSONAL PROFILE: Arrived in Britain from India May 1939. President Indian Workers Association Coventry 1940-49. President chairman India League Leicester 1962-75

MR ROBEEL HAQ (Student)

Presenter-Journalist, Sangam-BBC Radio Bristol,

PLACE OF BIRTH: Bristol, 2.4.79
MARITAL STATUS: Single
COLLEGE: University of Wales-Cardiff
ACADEMIC QUALIFICATIONS: Studying BA degree Journalism, Film and Broadcasting
PROFESSIONAL QUALIFICATIONS: Bollywood columnist. Co-presenter, Sangam BBC Radio Bristol
HOBBIES AND INTERESTS: Writing, watching films, music

EMAIL: robeelh@hotmail.com
PERSONAL PROFILE: Achievements at age 19: Co-presenters for weekly Asian radio show on BBC Radio Bristol (called 'Sangam'); Regular columnist for Snoop magazine; Written for various national newspapers; Editor for school year newspaper; Student of the year and student representative for governing body during secondary school.
NOMINATED BY: Nadia Haq

DR MUSTAFA HAQQANI (Doctor)

Consultant Histopathologist, National Health Service, 2 Davies Way, Lymm, WA13 0QW

PLACE OF BIRTH: India, 6.10.41
MARITAL STATUS: Married
CHILDREN: One (Ehsan)
COLLEGE: Osmania Medical College
PROFESSIONAL QUALIFICATIONS: MBBS, SPath and FRCPath
MEMBERSHIPS: Royal Society of Medicine, International Academy of Pathology, Fellow Royal College of Pathologists
HOBBIES AND INTERESTS: Chess, gardening, sports especially cricket
EMAIL: mhaqqani@aol.com
PERSONAL PROFILE: I have been working in the NHS for 30 years. I achieved the highest office in my field some 22 years ago. In recognition of my services I was given a merit award back in 1987. I have sub-specialised in pathology of liver and skin. To date I have been involved in some 30 publications.

DR M D ZAINUL HAQUE (Teacher)

Science Teacher, Mulberry School for Girls, Richard Street, Commercial Road, London, E1 2JP

PLACE OF BIRTH: India, 10.7.42
MARITAL STATUS: Married
CHILDREN: One (Ajay)
COLLEGE: Patna University (India), London and Nottingham Universities
ACADEMIC QUALIFICATIONS: MSc (Patna), PhD (London)
PROFESSIONAL QUALIFICATIONS: Certificate in Education (Nottingham)
HOBBIES AND INTERESTS: Photography, gardening, travelling
PERSONAL PROFILE: Born and educated in India. Taught in Bangladesh as a lecturer. Arrived in the UK in 1968. Followed a teachers' training course at Nottingham University. Undertook research work in the field of radiation botany. Awarded a PhD degree in 1982. Published nineteen papers in various scientific journals with Professor Godward.
NOMINATED BY: Hasna Uddin

MR THEKKUMMURI HARIDAS (Restaurateur)

Civil Servant, Sree Krishna, Hari Mandiram, 11 Sheephouse Way, New Malden, KT3 5PF

PLACE OF BIRTH: India, 18.5.51
MARITAL STATUS: Married
CHILDREN: Three (Vaishak Nair, Vinod Nair, Nilesh Nair)
COLLEGE: Maharaja's College
ACADEMIC QUALIFICATIONS: Sree Krishna College Graduate
PROFESSIONAL QUALIFICATIONS: Diploma in Catering
DIRECTORSHIPS: Malabar Junction, Kerala International Investment Co Ltd
MEMBERSHIPS: Kerala Federation for the Blind, Bharat Vidya Bhavan British Malayalalle Association, Hindu Society, Kala
HOBBIES AND INTERESTS: Reading, writing, watching snooker
EMAIL: tharisdas@aol.com
PERSONAL PROFILE: Born in Kerala in 1951 to father Bhaskaran Nair and mother Thankamma. After completing graduation from Kerala, came to UK in 1973. Have been a civil servant since then. After gaining diploma in catering, while in civil service, established business partnership in South Indian Restaurants-Ragam Sree Krishna, Malabar Junction, Pallavi and Kerala Bhavan. Promoting Kerala cuisine and tourism to Kerala.

DR ABU BAKAR AHMED HARUN (Chairman)

BNSA, 18 Tavern Street, Stowmarket, Suffolk, IP14 1PH

PLACE OF BIRTH: Bangladesh
MARITAL STATUS: Married
CHILDREN: Six
ACADEMIC QUALIFICATIONS: Dip Nat, BSc, PhD, GCGI, FSl Hons
PROFESSIONAL QUALIFICATIONS: MIMgt, FRSA and PhD
HOBBIES AND INTERESTS: Reading, community activities
PERSONAL PROFILE: Fellow of the Royal Society of Arts. Dr A B Harun is a high -profile, Bengali community leader. Many of his activities won recognition. A regular guest of BBC Radio in Suffolk. Dr Harun added to his success as a writer, journalist, businessman and as the chair of an accomplished organisation BNSA which was set up in 1984. It's a successful community venture.

MR ZIA AKHTAR HASHMI (Hotel Management)

Public Relation Manager, The Taj, 109 Lower Addiscombe Road, Croydon, CR0 6PU

PLACE OF BIRTH: Pakistan, 30.6.64
MARITAL STATUS: Single
COLLEGE: Punjab University. College of Accountancy, London
ACADEMIC QUALIFICATIONS: ACCA
PROFESSIONAL QUALIFICATIONS: Dip in Modern Management and Dip Hotel Management
MEMBERSHIPS: Hotel Management Association, Young Men's Association
HONOURS/AWARDS: Distinction from Jersey College
HOBBIES AND INTERESTS: Only to look after my family
PERSONAL PROFILE: I started my career as a businessman in Pakistan. Then I moved to Abu Dhabi. I worked eight years in Abu Dhabi in management positions including Hilton International Hotel. Now I am in London studying for MBA.
NOMINATED BY: Siraj Ul Islam

MR GHULAM HASSAN (Textile Manufacture)

Managing Director, Empress Quilts & Textiles, Empress House, Peel Lane, Cheetham Hill, Manchester, M8 8RJ

PLACE OF BIRTH: Pakistan, 11.9.57
MARITAL STATUS: Married
CHILDREN: Three (Imran, Kamran, Irfan)
PROFESSIONAL QUALIFICATIONS: Bedding Expert
DIRECTORSHIPS: Muslim Youth Foundation
HOBBIES AND INTERESTS: Sports all kinds
PERSONAL PROFILE: I am a dedicated businessman as well as a dedicated husband and father. I also enjoy many types of sports and enjoy social events very much. My home country Pakistan is also a very important aspect of my business and personal life.
NOMINATED BY: Imran Hussain

'I have been working in the NHS for 30 years.
I achieved the highest office in my field some 22 years ago'

DR MUSTAFA HAQQANI

MR MAHMOOD UL HASSAN (Clothing MFG)

Director, Hoigh Standard Ltd, 15-25 Exeter Street, Rochdale, OL11 1JN

PLACE OF BIRTH: Pakistan, 1.9.55
MARITAL STATUS: Married
CHILDREN: Four (Uzma, Zeeshan, Intisham, Rehan)
ACADEMIC QUALIFICATIONS: BSc Industrial Engg
HOBBIES AND INTERESTS: Cricket, football

NOMINATED BY: M Zaheer Iqbal

MR ALI MOHAMMED 'SAM' HAYDER (Student)

Producer, 41 Hooke House, Grove Road, Bow, London, E3 5TL

PLACE OF BIRTH: London, 28.4.84
MARITAL STATUS: Single
COLLEGE: Bow School
ACADEMIC QUALIFICATIONS: est 8 A-C's
MEMBERSHIPS: Olga Theatre Company
HONOURS/AWARDS: Outstanding Achievements Prolonged Success
HOBBIES AND INTERESTS: Art, ice skating, graphics, business, drama
PERSONAL PROFILE: I'm a hardworking student and a keen poet, so much that I've recently released a book, which has been highly successful. I'm trying to start up a company called Hayder Enterprises Inc. I'm an entrepreneur and I separate pleasure from pain.

MRS FOQIA HAYEE (Voluntary Sector Rtd)

212 Reigate Road, Bromley, BR1 5JW

DATE OF BIRTH: 13.3.46
MARITAL STATUS: Married
CHILDREN: Two (Momin Hassan, Bu'Hussain)
COLLEGE: University of Punjab, Lahore, Pakistan
ACADEMIC QUALIFICATIONS: BFA (1964), MFA (1968)-Graphic Design
PROFESSIONAL QUALIFICATIONS: TFLA (1986)-Goldsmiths College, London
MEMBERSHIPS: Soroptimist International, APWA, Horniman Park
HONOURS/AWARDS: Absailed down City Bank for fundraising (certificate)
HOBBIES AND INTERESTS: Reading, writing, designing, painting, speaking
PERSONAL PROFILE: My background is in race relations and teaching (as well as graphic design) and I am now actively involved in the voluntary sector. As Mayor of Lewisham, I initiated several schemes including: promoting intergenerational links, promoting parental involvement in schools and their children's education as well as improving parenting skills (especially for ethnic minorities). These are still running to this day. I started an orienteering project in local park absailing.

MR GEORGIE HAYES (Actor-Singer)

Rocky Horror Show, Helen Stafford Mangement, 14 Park Avenue, Bush Hill Park, Enfield, EN1 2HP

PLACE OF BIRTH: Pakistan, 4.4.52
MARITAL STATUS: Married
CHILDREN: One (Kim)
ACADEMIC QUALIFICATIONS: 6 GCSE's, 2 A-Levels
PROFESSIONAL QUALIFICATIONS: Trained Actor Centre, London.
MEMBERSHIPS: Equity
HOBBIES AND INTERESTS: Songwriting, music, food, squash

PERSONAL PROFILE: After several years in cabaret he now works in theatre and TV. He played the much-coveted role of 'Riff Raff' in the 25th Anniversary tour of 'The Rocky Horror Show'. He has appeared in 'Miss Saigon', 'Jesus Christ Superstar' in London, 'South Pacific' in Japan, 'Shakespeare' and 'Rock 'n' Roll' in Berlin.

> ' My background is in race relations and teaching (as well as graphic design) and I am now actively involved in the voluntary sector'

FOQIA HAYEE

MR ATMA HEER (Actor-Singer)

Geet The Mega Band, PO Box 185, Wolverhampton, WV3 4DN

PLACE OF BIRTH: India, 16.4.56
MARITAL STATUS: Married
COLLEGE: Bilston College
MEMBERSHIPS: Equity, Musician's Union, Indian Workers Association
HONOURS/AWARDS: Asian Song Contest Winner 1988, Best Newcomer 1990/91, Best Upcoming 1991/92
HOBBIES AND INTERESTS: Music, squash, kung fu, keep fit
PERSONAL PROFILE: Atma now a student of the world famous Punjabi singer Hans Raj Hans fronts the band as lead singer. Atma has a multitude of talents which have been demonstrated on vinyl and on both the big and small screens. His acting career has given him focus in a Punjabi feature called Joshiela Dushman, commercials in Pakistan, the US and numerous TV appearances.

DR ARJUN HIRANI TD (General Practitioner)

Senior Partner, 1 Farley Road, Leicester, LE2 3LD

PLACE OF BIRTH: India, 14.10.39
MARITAL STATUS: Married
CHILDREN: Two (Nikhil, Sacheen)
COLLEGE: SMS Medical College, Jaipur
ACADEMIC QUALIFICATIONS: MBBS, MFFP (RCOG). Instructing doctor: Family planning and sexual health.
PROFESSIONAL QUALIFICATIONS: SMO, RAMC (V) Territorial Decoration (TD)
DIRECTORSHIPS: Stoneycroft Hotels, Stage Hotels
MEMBERSHIPS: BMA, President Shruti Arts, Leicester
HONOURS/AWARDS: TD
HOBBIES AND INTERESTS: Fitness, squash, badminton, snooker, classical music, promoting performing arts and sports
PERSONAL PROFILE: Cambridge school cert 1965 in East Africa. MBBS 1966, Jaipur. General practice since 1968. Chartered founder member Charnwood Lions 1973-75. Captain, RAMC 1982. Major 1987. TD 1995. Founder and current president of Shruti Arts Leicester since 1983. Instructing Doctor of Faculty of Family Planning (RCOG & OBST) 1981. MFFP 1993. Radio presenter of classical music on Sabras Radio (Voluntary) since 1995. Active Major, Senior Medical Officer in RAMC (V).

MR DILIP HIRO (Author)

Journalist,

COLLEGE: State University of Virginia
ACADEMIC QUALIFICATIONS: Master's
PERSONAL PROFILE: Born in the Indian subcontinent, Dilip Hiro was educated in India, Britain and America, where he received a Master's degree at the State University of Virginia. He then settled in London in the mid-1960's and became a full-time writer, journalist and commentator. He has published 21 books.

MR ANAM HOQUE (Community Youth Worker)

Progressive Youth Organisation (PYO), 179-181 Whitechapel Road, Davenant Centre, London, E1 1DW

PLACE OF BIRTH: Bangladesh, 1.3.75
MARITAL STATUS: Single
COLLEGE: Tower Hamlets College, Goldsmiths University
ACADEMIC QUALIFICATIONS: 9 GCSE A-C, BTEC Nat. Dip in Social Care
PROFESSIONAL QUALIFICATIONS: Dip HE & BA in Community & Youth Work
DIRECTORSHIPS: Davenant Centre, Youth Empowerment Scheme
MEMBERSHIPS: Regional Assessor for Prince's Trust, Assessor for Princess of Wales Diamond Memorial Fund
HONOURS/AWARDS: Community Expedition Awards, Achievement Awards, Community Involvement Award
HOBBIES AND INTERESTS: Travelling abroad, adventurous activities, games, music, cinema, football, keyboard
PERSONAL PROFILE: My aim in life is to support those less fortunate than me. I enjoy helping young people develop bright and innovative projects which help themselves as well as others. I also want to aim high in my career and hope one day to set up my own youth/community consultancy agency. I hope to continue to develop and act as a role model for other young people in my community. Also, I want to be a councillor one day.
NOMINATED BY: Nurul Hussain

MRS ROSHAN HORABIN (VOLUNTARY WORKER-RTD)

Jasmine Cottage, 69 Seckford Street, Woodbridge, IP12 4LZ

PLACE OF BIRTH: India, 9.5.24
MARITAL STATUS: Widowed
CHILDREN: Three (Victoria, Susannah, Jennifer)
COLLEGE: Educated Senior, Cambridge (Bombay)
ACADEMIC QUALIFICATIONS: Sociology, London University 3 Years
PROFESSIONAL QUALIFICATIONS: Home Office Diploma, Cropwood Fellowship. Institute of Criminology
DIRECTORSHIPS: Founded Befriending Sub Comm Newbridge. Council Member Ipswich.
MEMBERSHIPS: Suffolk Commission for Racial Equality, Council Member Howard League Racial Reform
HONOURS/AWARDS: Fellow Royal Society of Arts. Trustee Prisoners Award
HOBBIES AND INTERESTS: Reading, music, travel
PERSONAL PROFILE: Voluntary work in penal affairs education. Worked during war, prisoners of war intelligence department. First ethnic governor, Board of Governors, Greycoat Hospital School and Queen Annes Caversham, New Bridge Befriending Prisoners, probation officer in the UK. Prince's Trust-Counsellor for CRUSE, Bereavement-Publication: Asians in Penal Institutions. Trustee Prisoners abroad.

MISS IRINA HOSSAIN (STUDENT)

Mulberry Sixth Form,

PLACE OF BIRTH: Bangladesh, 16.7.81
MARITAL STATUS: Single
COLLEGE: Mulberry Sixth Form
ACADEMIC QUALIFICATIONS: FE Business Student
HOBBIES AND INTERESTS: Listening to various types of music, socialising
PERSONAL PROFILE: I was a member of a British delegation to the United Nations for a UNIS Conference in New York in 1998. The theme of the conference was civil conflicts and its global effects. I also spoke on insights into mentoring to a group of Bank of America employees.
NOMINATED BY: Jahanara Begum

DR ZAMIR-UL HUDA (GENERAL PRACTITIONER)

'Azeem', 50 Killyman Road, Dungannon, Co Tyrone, BT71 6DE

PLACE OF BIRTH: Panipat, 15.12.41
MARITAL STATUS: Married
CHILDREN: Three (Uzma, Mohammed Sameer, Mohammed Azeem)
COLLEGE: King Edwards Medical College, Lahore
ACADEMIC QUALIFICATIONS: MBBS
PROFESSIONAL QUALIFICATIONS: MCM, MBMAS, MBSECH
HOBBIES AND INTERESTS: Photography, music
PERSONAL PROFILE: Came to the UK in 1971, General practitioner, special interest cardiology and paediatrics. Chairman, ODA, N.Ireland.

MR SUREKHA HULUGALLE (BUSINESS ANALYST)

Reckitt & Colman Plc, 1 Burlington Lane, Chiswick, London, W4 2RW

PLACE OF BIRTH: Sri Lanka, 26.4.67
MARITAL STATUS: Married
CHILDREN: One (Shanendra Samuel)
COLLEGE: National Institute of Business Management
ACADEMIC QUALIFICATIONS: Computer Systems Design
PROFESSIONAL QUALIFICATIONS: Systems Design
MEMBERSHIPS: Singapore Comp Society. IDPM
HOBBIES AND INTERESTS: Photography
PERSONAL PROFILE: IT manager for eight years in Reckitt and Colman Sri Lanka. Current position since July 98. Actively involved in church work. Heading a church in London as pastor.
NOMINATED BY: Elwin Allen

MR KHAN HUQ (CHAIR OF WREC)

City Westminster College, 46A Churton Street, London, SW1V 2LP

PLACE OF BIRTH: Bangladesh
MARITAL STATUS: Married
COLLEGE: City of Westminster College
ACADEMIC QUALIFICATIONS: BA. MA. LL B.
DIRECTORSHIPS: Cotestel Ltd, London
MEMBERSHIPS: Chair Westminster Race Equality Council 1993-96, Member, Kensington Chelsea & Westminster Health Council 1994-98
HOBBIES AND INTERESTS: Cooking, collecting 19th Century prints on South Asia and traditional hats of different nationalities: ceramics, video filming, travelling
PERSONAL PROFILE: Bengali news presenter on radio and television-Pakistan and Bangladesh (1969-73). School teacher Dhaka (1971-73). Executive Beximco Ltd Dhaka (1973-75) and manager (1975-76). Director Cotestel Ltd London (1976-80). Self-employed investment management since 1980. Chair Migrants Resource Centre, London (1993-94). Chair-Westminster REC (1994-98).

DR HASANAT MOHAMMAD HUSAIN
(HEAD OF BILINGUALISM)

Head of Bilingualism, London Borough of Tower Hamlets, Mulberry Place, 5 Clove Crescent, London, E14 2BE

PLACE OF BIRTH: Bangladesh, 16.11.49
MARITAL STATUS: Married
CHILDREN: Three (Shiheen, Adeeb, Naushin)
COLLEGE: Exeter University, Sussex University, Greenwich University
ACADEMIC QUALIFICATIONS: BSc Hons, MSc, PhD. Royal Society Post Doctorate
PROFESSIONAL QUALIFICATIONS: PGCE, CPhys, MInst P, AICTP
DIRECTORSHIPS: Trustee Parents Centre of East London
MEMBERSHIPS: Institute of Physics, Labour Party
HONOURS/AWARDS: A Commonwealth Scholar, Asian Film Academy Award 1995, Royal Society Post Doctorate Fellow
HOBBIES AND INTERESTS: Politics, community works, tennis, travel
PERSONAL PROFILE: Formerly, Associate Prof of Physics: University of Dhaka (B'Desh); Zambia; Sebha (Libya). Junior Associate to International Centre for Theoretical Physics (Italy). Chairperson Greater Sylhet Council (UK). Executive-National Governors' Council (UK). Founder trustee of UK. Bangladesh Education Trust (UK). Consultant to Bangladesh Caterers Association in the UK. Chair of governors. Blue Gate Field Infant and Junior School. Chair of Section -11 Campaign Group LBTH. Presently the head of bilingualism, LBTH.

MRS SHEHZAD HUSAIN (COOKERY CONSULTANT)

Author, 10 Pickwick Way, Chislehurst, BR7 6RZ

PLACE OF BIRTH: Pakistan, 23.5.52
MARITAL STATUS: Married
CHILDREN: Three (Humaira, Sumra, Asim)
PROFESSIONAL QUALIFICATIONS: Shehzad has taught cookery at Orpington Adult Education Centre and at the Cordon Bleu School in London. She is a regular contributor to various publications on Indian food/cooking
HOBBIES AND INTERESTS: Cookery, travel, music, reading
PERSONAL PROFILE: As a restaurant critic Shehzad has reviewed some of the topmost Pakistani and Indian eateries in London for television and general expert comment. Most of Shehzad's time is occupied in her role as a cookery consultant and advisor to Britain's Marks & Spencer on their extensive range of Indian foods. It would not be untrue to say that she has played a pivotal role in the astounding success of the M&S Indian food lines.

MR SYED NASIR HUSAIN (BANK OFFICER-RTD.)

Voluntary Manager, Bromley Racial Equality Council,

PLACE OF BIRTH: India, 3.7.39
MARITAL STATUS: Married
CHILDREN: Three (Shehla, Nazir, Dr Sheheryar)
COLLEGE: Karachi University
ACADEMIC QUALIFICATIONS: MA (Geography), MA (Sociology)
PROFESSIONAL QUALIFICATIONS: Institute of Bankers
HOBBIES AND INTERESTS: Reading

It would not be untrue to say that she has played a pivotal role in the astounding success of the M&S Indian food lines

SHEZAD HUSAIN

MR MEHDI HUSAINI (University Lecturer)

Middlesborough Law Centre, 42 Gore Sands, Acklam, Middlesborough, TS5 8UJ

PLACE OF BIRTH: India, 26.9.38
MARITAL STATUS: Married
COLLEGE: University of Lucknow, University of Reading, University of London
ACADEMIC QUALIFICATIONS: BSc, MSc, M.Phil, Cert.Ed
PROFESSIONAL QUALIFICATIONS: MInst P, C Phys
DIRECTORSHIPS: Middlesborough Law Centre
MEMBERSHIPS: University and College Lecturers Union
HOBBIES AND INTERESTS: Equal opportunities, race equality, badminton, table tennis, reading
PERSONAL PROFILE: Was member of North Tees Community Health Council. Ex chair Racial Equality Council, Cleveland. Home Office assessor on Race Relations Act. Ex governor of schools and colleges. Ex member Teachers Benevolent Fund. Voluntary service organisations, Cleveland. Labour Party member. Involved in community education. Involved in campaigning against racism.

DR AHMED ZULQARNAIN HUSSAIN (Veterinary Surgeon)

33 Tallack Road, Leyton, London, E10 7JR

PLACE OF BIRTH: Pakistan, 22.1.53
MARITAL STATUS: Married
CHILDREN: Three (Sadaf, Sabah, Umar)
COLLEGE: Glasgow University
ACADEMIC QUALIFICATIONS: MSc Poultry Science
PROFESSIONAL QUALIFICATIONS: Degree of Doctor of Veterinary Medicine
MEMBERSHIPS: World's Poultry Science Association. British Veterinary Poultry Association. World Veterinary Poultry Association.
HOBBIES AND INTERESTS: Book reading, walking, travelling
PERSONAL PROFILE: I came to UK in 1977 and married in 1984. I completed my Degree of Doctor of Veterinary Medicine in 1980 from Agricultural University, Faisalabad, Pakistan. I qualified my Master in Poultry Science in 1998 from Glasgow University.

CLLR AKHTAR HUSSAIN (Councillor)

Blackburn and Darwen Borough Council, Member's Room, Blackburn Council, Town Hall, Lancashire, BB1 7DY

MARITAL STATUS: Married
HOBBIES AND INTERESTS: Motto is: Faith Unity, Discipline
PERSONAL PROFILE: I came to UK in 1970. Over the last 30 years I have served my Asian community and my local council, Blackburn with Darwen Borough Council very well. I have worked with Rt Hon Jack Straw, Home Secretary MP for Blackburn for more than 25 years. I have worked with many community leaders and Blackburn councillors.

MS CORRINE HUSSAIN (Regional Transplant Coordinator)

Co-ordinator, South Thames Transplant Co-ordination Service, Kings Healthcare, London, SE22 8PT

PLACE OF BIRTH: Kent, 26.8.63
MARITAL STATUS: Divorced
CHILDREN: One (Hannah)
COLLEGE: BSc (Hons) Health Studies
PROFESSIONAL QUALIFICATIONS: RGN, Diploma in Professional Nursing Studies. ENB100/998
DIRECTORSHIPS: United Kingdom Transplant
MEMBERSHIPS: UK Transplant Co-odinators Association, North American Transplant Co-ordinators Organisattion
HONOURS/AWARDS: Altajir Trust Bursary, NATCO Travel Scholarship
HOBBIES AND INTERESTS: Antiques, philosophy
PERSONAL PROFILE: A dedicated and responsible professional who is adaptive and creative within a changing and challenging environment. I believe in empowering others to recognise, develop and achieve their potential and I see each day as a new learning experience.

MR IMRAN HUSSAIN (Manufacturer-Textiles)

Sales Manager, Empress Quilts & Textiles, Empress House, Peel Lane, Cheetham Hill, Manchester, M8 8RJ

PLACE OF BIRTH: Manchester, 2.8.76
MARITAL STATUS: Single
COLLEGE: St Johns Manchester
ACADEMIC QUALIFICATIONS: Business and Finance Diploma
DIRECTORSHIPS: Manager to sales rep.
MEMBERSHIPS: Muslim Youth Foundation
HOBBIES AND INTERESTS: All types of sport, music, cars (Ferrari)
PERSONAL PROFILE: I am the third generation in a line of committed businessmen established for more than 25 years. I have been lucky to be able to carry on the family business. School and college was a great experience and pleasure. In my spare time I love my sports, music and also cars.

DR MIAN FARRUKH HUSSAIN (Psychiatrist)

Consultant, 6 Cadnam Close, Canterbury, CT6 5SA

PLACE OF BIRTH: Pakistan, 26.12.40
MARITAL STATUS: Married
CHILDREN: Three (Omar, Mustafa, Usman)
COLLEGE: Dow Medical Karachi
ACADEMIC QUALIFICATIONS: MBBS, FRCPsych
PROFESSIONAL QUALIFICATIONS: DPM, MRC, Psych, DPM (Eire)
DIRECTORSHIPS: Consultant
MEMBERSHIPS: Rotary Club Canterbury
HONOURS/AWARDS: Health, Hunger, Humanity Award UNHCFR
HOBBIES AND INTERESTS: Poetry
PERSONAL PROFILE: Consultant psychiatrist. Fellow Royal Society Medicine. Registrar Royal Rotary Club, Canterbury Medico Legal Practice.

MISS NURUN NAHAR HUSSAIN (Student)

PLACE OF BIRTH: London, 31.7.86
MARITAL STATUS: Single
COLLEGE: Mulberry School for Girls
HONOURS/AWARDS: Readathon, Spellbound, swimming, athletics, 100% attendance and language
HOBBIES AND INTERESTS: Playing badminton, sports, watching television
PERSONAL PROFILE: I'm a 12 year old student at Mulberry School. A poem I wrote was published in a book. I have received many awards and certificates for a variety of subjects. My poem about Shadwell was chosen to be read in the opening of 'The Dream Garden'.

MR SHELIM HUSSAIN (Importer-Exporter)

Chairman/Managing Director, Euro Foods (UK) Ltd, Reeve's Land Park Est, Langland Way, Newport, NP9 0PT

PLACE OF BIRTH: Bangladesh, 20.2.73
MARITAL STATUS: Married
CHILDREN: One (Shah Anisah)
COLLEGE: Coleg Glan Hafren
ACADEMIC QUALIFICATIONS: 5 GCSE, above O Level equivalent
PROFESSIONAL QUALIFICATIONS: Diploma in Business Studies
DIRECTORSHIPS: Euro Foods (Croydon) Ltd, S&B Development. Euro Food C&C Ltd
MEMBERSHIPS: British Frozen Food Federation. British Bangladesh Chamber of Commerce
HOBBIES AND INTERESTS: Football, snooker, badminton
PERSONAL PROFILE: I started the business Euro Foods in 1991 with only £20 in my pocket. With hardwork and Gods help today I have a group of companies with turnover expected to be over US $30 million. This was achieved especially with the help of my two best friends-Rohim and Siful.
NOMINATED BY: Saif-Ul-Islam

'I started the business Euro Foods in 1991 with only £20 in my pocket. With hardwork and Gods help today I have a group of companies with turnover expected to be over $30 million'

SHELIM HUSSAIN

February 15 1994: Nineteen-year-old Mukhter Ahmed is savagely beaten in East London by a mob of 20 racists. Community leaders appeal for calm as fears of revenge attacks grow.The 'attempted murder' comes only a month after teenager Quddus Ali is left for dead following a racist attack

MS SEETA INDRANI (ACTOR)

Mayer & Eden Ltd, 34 Kingly Court, London, W1R 5LE

PLACE OF BIRTH: London
MARITAL STATUS: Single
CHILDREN: One (Milly)
HONOURS/AWARDS: 1996 Best Actress, 1995 Best Supporting Actress
HOBBIES AND INTERESTS: Flamenco dance, opera
PERSONAL PROFILE: Seeta played WPC Norika Datta to much critical acclaim in Thames TV's 'The Bill', for nine years. Other television appearances, too numerous to list, include Belinda in Dido and Aeneus, and the Screen 2 film 'Maria's Child'. On stage her work covers the spectrum from The Royal Shakespeare Company to the London cast of 'Cats'.

MR ASIF IQBAL (STUDENT)

Cash Traders, 123/125 Lawn Lane, Hemel Hempsted

PLACE OF BIRTH: Hemel Hampstead, 4.10.75
MARITAL STATUS: Single
COLLEGE: University of Central Lancashire
ACADEMIC QUALIFICATIONS: Final Year BA Hons, Deaf Studies
PROFESSIONAL QUALIFICATIONS: Access to higher education
HONOURS/AWARDS: Whitbread Award
PERSONAL PROFILE: He has had a successful life working very hard. He has helped the community to learn attitudes to become very positive towards anyone. He has been travelling to research his projects and help campaigning over issues. Received recognition from HM Queen Elizabeth for achievement. Asif is a deaf university student
NOMINATED BY: University of Central Lancashire

MR IFRAN IQBAL (SCHOOLBOY)

123 Lawn Lane, Hemel Hampstead, HP3 9HS

PLACE OF BIRTH: Hemel Hampstead, 17.6.85
HOBBIES AND INTERESTS: Cricket, reading, woodwork, music, dancing
PERSONAL PROFILE: At the early age of eleven Ifran earned the Bronze Award 1996-97 Certificate for good work and effort. Certificate of achievement autumn term 1996 with 32 commendations for good work and effort as well as the Double Bronze Award December 1996. In 1997 he earned the Double Silver Award and Siver Award with a total of 56 commendations.

IMRAN IQBAL (SCHOOLBOY)

Longdean School, Cash Traders, 123 Lawn Lane, Hemel Hampstead, HP3 9HS

PLACE OF BIRTH: Hemel Hampstead, 22.3.84
MARITAL STATUS: Single
HOBBIES AND INTERESTS: Cricket, football, acting, singing
PERSONAL PROFILE: Imran has received many school awards for good work and effort including Gold, Double Bronze and Sapphire (presented in recognition of 100 commendations).
NOMINATED BY: Asif Iqbal

NAHIM IQBAL (STUDENT)

Longdean School, Cash Traders, 123 Lawn Lane, Hemel Hampstead, HP3 9HS

PLACE OF BIRTH: Hemel Hampstead, 4.10.82
MARITAL STATUS: Single
COLLEGE: Longdean School
ACADEMIC QUALIFICATIONS: 3 A-Levels, PE, Business Studies, English
HOBBIES AND INTERESTS: Sports, football, basketball, badminton
PERSONAL PROFILE: Nahim at age twelve, in only his third game for his club, Leverstock Green Colts, hit 101-not out as the Under-13 cricket side beat Redbourn. He broke an 18-year cricket club record.
NOMINATED BY: Asif Iqbal

WASIM IQBAL (STUDENT)

Cash Traders, 123 Lawn Lane, Hemel Hampstead, HP3 9HS

PLACE OF BIRTH: Hemel Hampstead, 8.1.80
MARITAL STATUS: Single
COLLEGE: Watford College, West Herts
ACADEMIC QUALIFICATIONS: HND Business Management
PROFESSIONAL QUALIFICATIONS: Two A-Levels (Business Studies & Law)
HOBBIES AND INTERESTS: Cricket, football, martial arts
PERSONAL PROFILE: Wasim has played for Longdean School in the Lord's Taverners' Cricketer Colts Trophy for Schools.
NOMINATED BY: Asif Iqbal

MR ZAFAR IQBAL (MANAGING DIRECTOR)

123 Lawn Lane, Hemel Hampstead, HP3 9HS

PLACE OF BIRTH: Pakistan, 25.3.59
MARITAL STATUS: Married
CHILDREN: Five (Wasim, Nahim, Imran, Irfan, Zara)
COLLEGE: Acton
ACADEMIC QUALIFICATIONS: HNC Electronic Engineering
DIRECTORSHIPS: MD Albanbridge Property Services
HONOURS/AWARDS: 1st Degree Black Belt Karate
HOBBIES AND INTERESTS: Cricket, badminton, martial arts
PERSONAL PROFILE: After college worked as design engineer in various fields of electronics from Telecom, medical systems, MOD, control systems. 1985-Started property company, owned 15 properties by 1989. 1987-Opened 2 convenience stores. 1992- Opened large industrial pizza delivery outlet. 1996-Opened Cash Traders, buying and selling goods of value from gold to cars and trailers. Also teacher in martial arts and fitness training.

MR ANIL ISHANI (SOLICITOR)

Diplomat, Nurabad, 170 Malden Road, New Malden, KT3 6DS

PLACE OF BIRTH: Kenya, 26.10.37
MARITAL STATUS: Married
CHILDREN: Two (Shaheen, Karina)
COLLEGE: Law Society
ACADEMIC QUALIFICATIONS: Lawyer
PROFESSIONAL QUALIFICATIONS: FCI ARB
DIRECTORSHIPS: 3 Private Companies
HOBBIES AND INTERESTS: Politics, travel
PERSONAL PROFILE: Involved in social and charitable work for Asians in UK for 27 years. Senior partner in city firm of solicitors. President and chairman of various organisations.

MR LUTFALI KASSAM ISHANI (HOTEL CATERING RTD)

Mervyn Court Hotel, 58 Pelham Court, 145 Fulham Road, Chelsea, London, SW3 6SH

PLACE OF BIRTH: Kenya
MARITAL STATUS: Married
CHILDREN: Two (Dr ML Ishani, FL Ishani)
PROFESSIONAL QUALIFICATIONS: Owned businesses in Uganda, Kenya and UK
DIRECTORSHIPS: Uganda Transport Company
MEMBERSHIPS: Rotary Club
HOBBIES AND INTERESTS: Tennis, politics, community
PERSONAL PROFILE: Former President of Commonwealth Societies of Kenya (1959-1961). Former director of City College (1981-1992). Involved in various borough activities. Former chairman and trustee Asian Elders Welfare Council. Career Raj Hotel and businesses in shops and restaurant (oldest Indian restaurant in Europe).

CLLR NAZRUL ISLAM (COUNCILLOR-SOCIAL WORKER)

Scheme Officer, Worcester City Council, 24 Chestnut Walk, Worcester, WR1 1PR

PLACE OF BIRTH: Bangladesh, 30.12.75
MARITAL STATUS: Single
COLLEGE: Brunel University
ACADEMIC QUALIFICATIONS: BSE Hons in Social Work/Social Studies
PROFESSIONAL QUALIFICATIONS: BSE Hons
PERSONAL PROFILE: I have graduated as a social worker this year, with a BSc Hons degree. Youngest executive member for Worcester Racial Equality Council. Youngest councillor in Britain when I was elected this year. I have also been involved with various community activities.
NOMINATED BY: Mr Nigel Holland Hanbury, Worcester

MS NEERJA JAIN (Transplant Co-ordinator)

University Hospital NHS Trust, Ground Floor, Nuffield House, The Queen Elizabeth Hospital, Edgbaston, Birmingham, B15 2TH

PLACE OF BIRTH: India
CHILDREN: One (Shivaanjli)
COLLEGE: Open University
ACADEMIC QUALIFICATIONS: BSc Hons, Teaching Adults & FE Certificate (730)
PROFESSIONAL QUALIFICATIONS: RGN, ENB (136)
MEMBERSHIPS: Advisor to Dept of Health. Nephology in Practice/BRS Council. UKTCA.
HONOURS/AWARDS: Winner of the 1998-1989 British Renal Symposium National Achievement Award
HOBBIES AND INTERESTS: Aerobics, yoga, world travel
EMAIL: Neerja.Jain@university-b.wmids.nhs.uk
PERSONAL PROFILE: Neerja is the first Asian transplant co-ordinator in the UK making a difference to people's lives. She facilitates the transplant process, while providing education and support to patients and their relatives. She is an invited advisor to the Department of Health Campaign and South Asian Organ Donor Campaign. Neerja has won a prestigious national achievement award for her work.
NOMINATED BY: Media Moguls

MR RAMNIK JAIN (Statistician)

Department For Education And Employment, Caxton House, 6-12 Tothill Street, London, SW1H 9NF

PLACE OF BIRTH: India, 15.11.45
MARITAL STATUS: Married
CHILDREN: One (Rina)
COLLEGE: University of Aston
ACADEMIC QUALIFICATIONS: BSc Hons in Metallurgy
PROFESSIONAL QUALIFICATIONS: Chartered Statistician
MEMBERSHIPS: Royal Statistical Society
HOBBIES AND INTERESTS: Playing bridge, cricket
EMAIL: info@dfee.gov.uk
PERSONAL PROFILE: Basic schooling in India. Obtained BSc (Hons) in Metallurgy from Aston University. Also a chartered statistician and member of the Royal Statistical Society. Joined the Department for Education in 1973 and have worked in almost all areas of education statistics. Responsible for the production of the school and college performance tables when they were first introduced in 1992.
NOMINATED BY: Bernadette Hillon, DFEE

MR RAJAN JALAL (Consultant)

Greater London Bangladeshi Association, 65 Brick Lane, London, E1 6PU

PLACE OF BIRTH: Bangladesh, 16.10.59
MARITAL STATUS: Married
CHILDREN: Two (Aruna Uddin Anissa, Anwar Uddin Anim)
COLLEGE: Guildhall University
ACADEMIC QUALIFICATIONS: BA, DMS
HOBBIES AND INTERESTS: Badminton, theatre, travel
PERSONAL PROFILE: A Tower Hamlets community leader for the last 25 years. Councillor (former) of Tower Hamlets, chair of the regeneration committee and deputy leader. Parliamentary candidate.

> Neerja is the first Asian transplant co-ordinator in the UK making a difference to people's lives. She facilitates the transplant process, while providing education and support to patients and their relatives. She is an invited advisor to the Department of Health Campaign and South Asian Organ Donor Campaign

NEERJA JAIN

CLLR INDER SINGH JAMU (Driving Instructor)

Mayor, London Borough Barking, 16 Oval Road South, Dagenham, RM10 9DR

PLACE OF BIRTH: India, 22.10.37
MARITAL STATUS: Married
CHILDREN: Three (Harpreet Kaur Grewal, Amardeep Singh Jamu, Jagdeep Kaur Minhas)
COLLEGE: Khalsa College Amritsar
ACADEMIC QUALIFICATIONS: BSc Agriculture, ADII
PROFESSIONAL QUALIFICATIONS: Approved self-employed Driving Instructor
HOBBIES AND INTERESTS: Gardening
PERSONAL PROFILE: Migrated to UK 1966. Set up own driving school in 1984. Elected councillor for River Ward in 1988 and have remained in this position since. During my period in office I served on the following committees: Education, Establishment, Planning & Development, General Purposes, Social Services, Technical Services, Road Safety Council, and have been the council delegate to BHB Community Health Council from 1988-96. First Asian mayor May 1998 for the Borough of Barking and Dagenham.
NOMINATED BY: Amardeep Singh, Asian Welfare Association

DADI JANKI (Spiritual Leader)

Co-Adminstrative Head, Brahma Kumaris World Spiritual University, Global Co-Operation House, 65 Pound Lane, London, NW10 2HH

PLACE OF BIRTH: India
MARITAL STATUS: Single
DIRECTORSHIPS: Brahma Kumaris, Janki Foundation
MEMBERSHIPS: Keepers of Wisdom, World Congress of Faiths
HOBBIES AND INTERESTS: World peace
PERSONAL PROFILE: Born 1916. Driven by her vision of a better world, Dadi Janki has dedicated her life to the upliftment of humanity by bringing communities together both locally and globally. She works for good race relations, inter religious acceptance and respect, family values, value-based education programmes and helping people of all backgrounds and ages to develop greater self worth. She believes that our global crisis is at root a crisis of spiritual values.

MR CHANDRAKANT DAHYABHAI JANSARI (Accountant)

Management Accountant, Shree Jansari Gnati Mandal, 5 Glover Close, Hall Green, Birmingham, B28 0JG

PLACE OF BIRTH: Uganda, 17.11.45
MARITAL STATUS: Married
CHILDREN: Two (Mona, Dhiran)
COLLEGE: Uganda
ACADEMIC QUALIFICATIONS: Accountancy
HONOURS/AWARDS: In community service from 'Sevak'
PERSONAL PROFILE: As a founder of the Shree Jansari Gnati Mandal of Birmingham, and holder of the post of chairman for ten years, my personal vision is to give help, support and dedication to the community. To continue to raise our profile through positive reforms, with the valued assistance of other members.
NOMINATED BY: Kishore Vadhia

MR POPATLAL JARIWALA (Academic Rtd)

92 Hounslow Road, Feltham, TW14 0AX

PLACE OF BIRTH: India, 22.7.28
MARITAL STATUS: Married
CHILDREN: Four (Hemant, Kapil, Daksha Caroline, Bharati Angela)
COLLEGE: Bombay University, London University
ACADEMIC QUALIFICATIONS: M.Com, BSc, Econ, Dip FE, MIL
PROFESSIONAL QUALIFICATIONS: Incorporated Linguist, Institute of Linguists
MEMBERSHIPS: Labour Party, The Co-operative Party, Fabian Society, Gujarati Literary Academy, Amnesty International, CND, Liberty
HOBBIES AND INTERESTS: Languages, campaign for human rights and equal opportunities, citizens advice
PERSONAL PROFILE: I am retired from my main occupation as senior lecturer in economics at a College of further and higher education in London. I also served as a Justice of the Peace for nearly 20 years, having retired in July this year. I am president at Gujarati Literary Academy at present time. I have been active in the Labour Party since 1963 and the human rights movement. I contested European Parliamentary elections in 1979.

MRS ANNAND JASANI MBE (Broadcaster)

Producer / Presenter, BBC Radio Wales, Broadcasting House, Llandaff, Cardiff, CYQ5

PLACE OF BIRTH: India, 12.3.49
MARITAL STATUS: Married
CHILDREN: Two (Karishma, Maya)
COLLEGE: Dudley (Birmingham) & Cardiff University
ACADEMIC QUALIFICATIONS: B.Ed Hons
PROFESSIONAL QUALIFICATIONS: Equity Member
DIRECTORSHIPS: Chair of Mewn Cymru (Wales)
MEMBERSHIPS: Equity
HONOURS/AWARDS: MBE (1998), DJ Awards, Race in the Media CRE.
HOBBIES AND INTERESTS: Arts, music, reading, cooking, travelling
PERSONAL PROFILE: Annand Jasani, producer / presenter of 'A Voice for All', award winning BBC Radio Wales programme; born 1949, Girdaspur; brought up in Tanzania; settlement in Britain 1967; secretary/teacher 24 years; stage and television actress, singer and expert in Indian international cuisine; awarded MBE, 1998 for 30 years voluntary services to Asian communities in Wales and Britain.

DR BHARAT JASANI (Consultant Pathologist)

Senior Lecturer, University of Wales College of Medicine, Heath Park, Cardiff, CF4 4XN

PLACE OF BIRTH: Kenya, 20.1.47
MARITAL STATUS: Married
CHILDREN: Two (Karishma, Maya)
ACADEMIC QUALIFICATIONS: BSc Hons, PhD, MBChB, FRC.Path
PROFESSIONAL QUALIFICATIONS: FRC.Path
DIRECTORSHIPS: Director of Regional Immunocytochemistry and Molecular Pathology Unit
MEMBERSHIPS: Association of Clinical Pathologists, British Society for Immunology
HONOURS/AWARDS: Becton Dickinson Fellowship (Royal College of Pathologists)
HOBBIES AND INTERESTS: Sports (athletics/cricket), philosophy, languages, arts, drama, travel
EMAIL: wptbj@cf.ac.uk
PERSONAL PROFILE: Bharat Jasani, senior lecturer and consultant pathologist; born 1947 Nairobi, Kenya; settlement in Britain 1961; medical educator and cancer researcher; first Beckton Dickinson Fellowship, Royal College of Pathologists; merit award in Pathology ; inventor-3 British and US patents; author of textbook and over 400 research publications and abstracts in pathological sciences.

DR ASHOK JASHAPARA (Academic)

Chair of Department, University of Westminster, Department of Construction & Surveying, 35 Marylebone Road, London, NW1 5LS

PLACE OF BIRTH: Yemen, 14.1.62
MARITAL STATUS: Married
CHILDREN: One (Nicole)
COLLEGE: The City University, London
ACADEMIC QUALIFICATIONS: BSc Civil Engineering, MBA Business & Finance. Doctor of Business Administration.
PROFESSIONAL QUALIFICATIONS: European Engineer, Chartered Eng. Fellow of the Chartered Institute of Building. Fellow of the Institute of Civil Engineers.
MEMBERSHIPS: Member of the Institute of Management
HONOURS/AWARDS: Visiting Prof. at Arizona State University. UPC in Barcelona and COATTM in Madrid.
HOBBIES AND INTERESTS: Tenor saxophone, swimming, motorbikes, sketching
PERSONAL PROFILE: Dr Ashok Jashapara was the first person to be awarded 'Doctor of Business Administration' in Europe and he now leads one of the top construction schools in the UK. He has developed an international reputation as a visiting professor and is a leading authority in the field of 'The Learning Organisation'. He also acts as a management consultant to UK firms and publishes regularly in magazines, books and academic journals.

> Dr Ashok Jashapara was the first person to be awarded 'Doctor of Business Administration' in Europe and he now leads one of the top construction schools in the UK

HARINDER KAUR JASPAL (Broadcaster)

Producer/Presenter BBC 3 Counties Radio, Diamond Cable Television, Coventry

PLACE OF BIRTH: Malawi
MARITAL STATUS: Married
CHILDREN: Two (Rubita, Rajan)
HONOURS/AWARDS: Journalsitic Award, BMA Bronze Award
HOBBIES AND INTERESTS: Promoting cultural activities, Hindi films / music
PERSONAL PROFILE: Came to Britain with her parents in 1963 and is married and settled in Coventry. Describes herself as a multi-faceted achiever in business, media, health promotion and cultural awareness. Currently involved in health awareness/promotion and working as a producer/presenter for radio and television. But Harinder feels that running a home and bringing up two children as 'good human-beings' is the most important achievement.
NOMINATED BY: Rani Dhindsa

CLLR SHAM SINGH JASSAR (Councillor)

London Borough of Hounslow, The Civic Centre, Lampton Road, Hounslow, TW3 1DR

PLACE OF BIRTH: India, 5.4.38
MARITAL STATUS: Married
CHILDREN: Four (Sukhwinder Kaur, Jetinder Kaur, Satvinder Kaur, Rachittar Singh)
COLLEGE: Govt College Ludhiana, Punjab Univeristy
ACADEMIC QUALIFICATIONS: MA Economics
PROFESSIONAL QUALIFICATIONS: Lecturer in Indian. Accounts Adminstrator UK
MEMBERSHIPS: Guild of the City of London, IWA, Labour Party, Singh Sabha Gurwa.
HONOURS/AWARDS: Freedom of the City of London
HOBBIES AND INTERESTS: Travelling, gardening, DIY
PERSONAL PROFILE: I was a lecturer in India and came to UK in 1968 on priority employment voucher. After working in customs and excise for 6 months I joined the post office as a postal officer and retired 1996. I joined the Labour Party in 1972 and was elected as a councillor in 1986 for London Borough of Hounslow, Central Ward. I was deputy mayor in 1989-1990 and elected as mayor 1990-91. During that year I got the Freedom of the City of London.

MR ASAM JAVED (Student)

University of Huddersfield, School of Applied Science, Queensgate, Huddersfield, HD1 3DH

PLACE OF BIRTH: Bradford, 25.6.77
MARITAL STATUS: Single
COLLEGE: Huddersfield University
ACADEMIC QUALIFICATIONS: 9 GCSE's, GNVQ Advanced Level 2+3 Accounts, BSc Science Foundation Course
MEMBERSHIPS: Labour Party, The Prince's Trust, Bradford REC, Disabilities in the Millennium
HONOURS/AWARDS: T&A 'Race Relations Award'
HOBBIES AND INTERESTS: Voluntary / community work, fitness training
PERSONAL PROFILE: I am currently studying for BSc (Hons) in Biology. I have undertaken voluntary community work for the past four years. I have, as well as studying, worked voluntary for my community. I have been involved in the Bradford disturbances, trying to resolve the conflict situation. I have represented various positions on various committees. I have worked with the young, old, abled and disabled.
NOMINATED BY: Asama Javed

AVTAR SINGH JAWANDA (Social Worker)

PLACE OF BIRTH: India, 27.4.51
MARITAL STATUS: Married
CHILDREN: Four (Valjit, Rajbinder, Amerjeet, Charnjit)
HONOURS/AWARDS: 1992, Won European powerlifting championship and 4th place in the world, 1994 2nd place European powerlifting championship, 3 Gold medals, 1 Silver, 1 Bronze 1997-1998. Gained over 40 British powerlifting championships. Manav Sewa Awards 1997.
PERSONAL PROFILE: Avtar Singh Jawanda started his powerlifting and cross country running in 1972. He is well known for his charity and fund raising work. In 1997 he received the Manav Sewa Award/Service to Humanity Award from Baba Deep Singh Ji Shahid Charitable Society (regd) in Haryana, India for his immense charitable work.
NOMINATED BY: Rajbinder Jawanda

CLLR MUSTAFA KAMAL (Deputy Leader)

Councillor, Leicester County Council, 56 Barkby Thorpe Road, Leicester, LE4 7JA

PLACE OF BIRTH: India, 1.8.43
MARITAL STATUS: Married
CHILDREN: One (Arif)
COLLEGE: Punjab University
ACADEMIC QUALIFICATIONS: BA
MEMBERSHIPS: Police Authority, National Association of Black, Asian and Ethnic Minority Councillors
HOBBIES AND INTERESTS: Reading, swimming, cricket
PERSONAL PROFILE: Deputy leader of Leicester City Council and the chair of the Finance Committee reporting to full council on financial matters. I have been a city councillor for over 12 years and have represented some of the most financially and socially deprived members of the ethnic minority community. I strongly believe in community orientated multi-agency approaches in Leicester. Chair of subcommittee, Vice-chair of Policy & Resources Sub Committee, Chair of the Leicester Partnership against Crime and Disorder

DR SIKANDAR HAYAT KAMLANA (Psychiatrist)

Consultant Psychiatrist, Mental Health Division, 'Balcraig' , 33 Stainburn Road, Cumbria, Workington, CA14 1SW

PLACE OF BIRTH: Pakistan, 12.9.46
MARITAL STATUS: Married
CHILDREN: Two (Ameen, Shehneela)
COLLEGE: Punjab University
ACADEMIC QUALIFICATIONS: Hon. Senior Lecturer Newcastle University
PROFESSIONAL QUALIFICATIONS: MBBS, DPM, FRC Psych. Dip. Psychother, Dip. Psychopharmacother.
DIRECTORSHIPS: Clinical Leader
MEMBERSHIPS: Chairman of Hospital Consultants & Specialists Association (HCSA) Cleveland and Durham
HONOURS/AWARDS: Merit Certificate for setting high standards of clincial care. Hospital doctor award 1997.
HOBBIES AND INTERESTS: Tennis, badminton, gym, jogging, walking
PERSONAL PROFILE: Appointed Senior Consultant Psychiatrist/Psychotherapist. Hon senior lecturer, University of Newcastle and college tutor. Chairman of HCSA for Cleveland and Durham. Specialist advisor on professional performance committees (GMC). Medical officer for Home Office. Clinical assessor for NHS Complaints Procedures.

MR JAFFERHUSSEIN AKBARALI KAPASI OBE (Businessman)

Kapasi & Co, 27a Ross Walk, Belgrave, Leicester, LE4 5HH

PLACE OF BIRTH: Uganda, 26.1.50
MARITAL STATUS: Married
CHILDREN: Two (Rashida, Muffaddal)
COLLEGE: Sheffield University
PROFESSIONAL QUALIFICATIONS: AFA
DIRECTORSHIPS: Leicestershire Asian Business Association, Independent Housing Ombudsman, Non-executive Director, Fosse Health NHS Trust
MEMBERSHIPS: Chairman, Asra Midlands Housing Association
HONOURS/AWARDS: OBE for services to business, Sheikh International Dawoodi Bohra
HOBBIES AND INTERESTS: Table tennis, occasional golf
PERSONAL PROFILE: Born in Uganda, a Dawoodi Bohra Muslim. 1972 Idi Amin prompted Asian exodus. Qualified as an accountant and worked for several companies involved in textile and garments. Set up accountancy practice in 1986 developing interest in textile and garments. Founder of LABA, past director of LCCI and LTEC. Currently NED of Fosse Health Trust, Director of IHO,
NOMINATED BY: Vijay Asi, Asra Midland Housing

MR ANISH KAPOOR (Artist)

c/o Lisson Agency, 67 Lisson Street, London, NW1 5DA

PLACE OF BIRTH: India, 12.3.54
MARITAL STATUS: Married
CHILDREN: Two
COLLEGE: Hornsey College of Art, Chelsea School of Art
HONOURS/AWARDS: Turner Prize Award, Awarded an Honorary Fellowship at the London Institute Lives and Works in London
PERSONAL PROFILE: Public collections. De Pont Foundation, Museo National Centro de Arte Reina Sofia, Tate Gallery, Hiroshhorn Museum and Sculpture Garden, Museo d'Arte Contemporeana, Fukuoka City Museum, Museum of Modern Art.

DR DINESH KAPOOR (General Practitioner)

GP Principal, Grange Park Practice, Chrisbrooke, 36 The Drive, South Woodford, London, E18 2BL

PLACE OF BIRTH: Indore, 12.7.44
MARITAL STATUS: Married
CHILDREN: Two (Disha, Rajaj)
PROFESSIONAL QUALIFICATIONS: MBBS, DA (London)
HOBBIES AND INTERESTS: Swimming, tennis, stage acting
PERSONAL PROFILE: Senior partner in medical practice in Leyton, London with GP wife and a partner. Arrived in the UK in December 1974. GP since 1982. GP trainer. Vice chairman of Redbridge and Waltham Forest Local Medical Committee. President of Leyton Medical Society. Vice-president of Indian Medical Association GB. Social secretary of Waltham Forest Branch of British Medical Association. Social secretary London ODA.

RAJINDER NATH KAPOOR (Underwriter (Ins-Reins))

Managing Director, Underwriting Agencies Limited, 1stFloor (REAR), Alpine House, Honeypot Lane, Kingsbury, London, NW9 9RX

PLACE OF BIRTH: Kenya, 2.8.40
MARITAL STATUS: Married
CHILDREN: Two (Navneeta, Sanjay)
DIRECTORSHIPS: Various
MEMBERSHIPS: IMA (UK)-Treasurer, Raj Durbar-President
PERSONAL PROFILE: Raj is Managing Director of a new Raj Kapoor Underwriting Agency Ltd. In London Mr Kapoor underwrites and issues all policy documents on behalf of three organisations-The Colonia Baltica Insurance Ltd, Assicurazioni Generali Spa of Trieste and Lloyds of London.

DR SUKHBIR SINGH KAPOOR (Chief Editor)

Vice Chancellor, World Sikh University London, 10 College Road, Harrow, HA1 1BE

PLACE OF BIRTH: India, 21.11.37
MARITAL STATUS: Married
CHILDREN: Two (Preetbir Singh, Ramanbir Singh)
ACADEMIC QUALIFICATIONS: PhD, LL.M, M.Comm
PROFESSIONAL QUALIFICATIONS: FCMA, FCCA
HONOURS/AWARDS: Publications: 27 Books, 100 articles, Best Book Literary Award
HOBBIES AND INTERESTS: Reading, writing
PERSONAL PROFILE: I have published 27 books covering areas of economics, accounting and religion. My book 'Ideal Man' was given 'Shromani Award' by the president of India. Many other awards by US and Canadian ethnic organisations for books on Sikh religion. I am also chief editor of Sikh Courier International published from London.

MR ANNUP RAJ KAPUR (Schoolboy-Black Belt)

131 Wolverhampton Street, Darlaston, Walsall, WS10 8UE

PLACE OF BIRTH: Birmingham, 12.7.89
ACADEMIC QUALIFICATIONS: Still studying
PROFESSIONAL QUALIFICATIONS: 9 years old
MEMBERSHIPS: Member of English Karate Association
HONOURS/AWARDS: Was the youngest Brown Belt at age seven years now youngest Black Belt in UK
HOBBIES AND INTERESTS: Football, karate, computers, music
PERSONAL PROFILE: Annup took up martial arts at the age of five on the advice of the medical specialist who had been treating his asthma, which was getting worse. Annup felt that karate was helping this condition. He achieved his Brown Belt at the age of seven. He has recently achieved a Black Belt at the age of nine years and is now the youngest Black Belt in the Britain, possibly Europe. Annups health has vastly improved. He is the nephew of superstar 'Apache Indian'.
NOMINATED BY: Mr Ajay Kapur

He has recently achieved a Black Belt at the age of nine years

ANNUP RAJ KAPUR

MR STEVEN KAPUR (Performing Artist)

Director, Sunset Records Ltd, PO Box 2726, Birmingham, B75 6DE

PLACE OF BIRTH: Handsworth, 11.5.67
DIRECTORSHIPS: Sunset Records/Apache Indian Ltd
MEMBERSHIPS: Musicians Union, PRS
HONOURS/AWARDS: Music awards from various associations
HOBBIES AND INTERESTS: Snooker, pool, football, swimming, music
PERSONAL PROFILE: Apache Indian, first made headlines in 1992, with his debut album 'No Reservations', which introduced his original style of music by fusing bhangra and ragga. Since then 'The Original Indian Raggamuffin', has gone from strength to strength, with seven Top 40 hits; four Brit Awards nominations; a Mercury Music Prize nomination; his own show on Radio One; International Dance Awards; and an Ivor Novello nomination.

MR RASHID KARAPIET (Actor)

The Narrow Road Co,

PLACE OF BIRTH: India
MARITAL STATUS: Single
COLLEGE: Sussex
ACADEMIC QUALIFICATIONS: B.Ed Hons Assoc. Institute of Linguists (German)
PROFESSIONAL QUALIFICATIONS: Teachers Dip Central School of Speech & Drama
HOBBIES AND INTERESTS: Music, theatre
PERSONAL PROFILE: Teaching and acting have been my main professions in the UK. I regard myself as that very rare bird: a working actor.

MR FIAZ RAFIQ KAREEM (Writer-Author-Publisher)

Publisher, Health N Life Publishing, PO Box 204, Salford, Manchester, M5 4AY

PLACE OF BIRTH: Denmark, 28.11.75
MEMBERSHIPS: IMB Academy, Los Angeles, California
HONOURS/AWARDS: Published a bestseller book.
HOBBIES AND INTERESTS: Martial arts, writing, reading
PERSONAL PROFILE: Fiaz a student of Richard Bustillo (original Bruce Lee student) studied at the Los Angeles Academy-California. He has written for national and international magazines. He's author of a book (European edition) and will be co-authoring a second edition (worldwide edition). He's a publisher and founder of Health 'n Life Publishing. A company dedicated to producing unique and quality books. He also intends to go in other business directions.

MAMTA KASH (Actress)

Kerry Gardner Management, 7 St Georges Square, Pimlico, London, SW1 2HX

COLLEGE: London
ACADEMIC QUALIFICATIONS: BSc Hons Econ
PROFESSIONAL QUALIFICATIONS: Dance, Drama
HONOURS/AWARDS: Best Actress Cannes, FIPA Gold Award. BBC TV Shalom-Salaam, London Sari Princess, Giles Cooper R4 Award
PERSONAL PROFILE: Worked as leading lady in a number of plays both on stage, radio and TV for instance :- BBC TV-'Shalom', 'Shalaam', 'Casualty', 'Between the Lines', 'Hetty Wainthrope Angels'. ITV-Ruth Rendal Thriller, 'Emmerdale Farm', 'Duel', 'Pravinaa's Wedding'. Film-'Mountbatton The Last Viceroy'.

MISS FATIMA HASSANALI KASSAM (Freelance Writer)

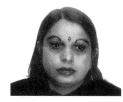

Scriptwriter, 43 Old Court House, Old Court Place, Kensington, London, W8 4PD

PLACE OF BIRTH: Blackpool, 5.6.59
MARITAL STATUS: Single
COLLEGE: School of Journalism, Carleton University, Ottawa University, Canada University
PROFESSIONAL QUALIFICATIONS: Diploma in Journalism, NCTJ
DIRECTORSHIPS: Proficiency Certificate ITU, Intro to TV presenting
MEMBERSHIPS: Royal TV Society London Screenwriters Workshop, Kensington & Chelsea Adult Education Cttee
HOBBIES AND INTERESTS: Health Clubs, cinema, theatre
PERSONAL PROFILE: 'West End-Girl', with attitude, former journalist and broadcaster. Taking Asian arts scene by storm writing short and feature film scripts to change and enhance the image of Asians and Blacks in Britain.

MR ISMAIL KASSAM (Accountant)

Proprietor Nursing Home, St Audreys Nursing Home, 19 Greenhill Close, Colehill, Wimborne, BH21 2RQ

PLACE OF BIRTH: Zanzibar, 17.1.38
MARITAL STATUS: Married
CHILDREN: Two (Tamgeza Begum, Salima Naaz)
COLLEGE: European University College
ACADEMIC QUALIFICATIONS: Bachelor of Arts, Degree in Business Admin
PROFESSIONAL QUALIFICATIONS: FFA, FMAAT, FFBA
PERSONAL PROFILE: Group accountant of Apple Corps Limited (Beatles Company) its subsidiaries and associated companies - May 1969 to June 1983. An honorary member of the (First) National Committee of the Aga Khan Foundation UK, a registered charity from January 1979 to December 1984. Honorary member of various Ismali community organisations.
NOMINATED BY: Miss Tameeza Begum Kassam

MR KARIM HASSANALI KASSAM (Solicitor)

Partner, Kenneth Elliot & Rowe, 109 Baker Street, London, W1M 1FE

PLACE OF BIRTH: Northumberland, 7.4.61
COLLEGE: Magdalene College Cambridge
ACADEMIC QUALIFICATIONS: MA Hons
PROFESSIONAL QUALIFICATIONS: Solicitor
HOBBIES AND INTERESTS: Arts, football, travel, reading
PERSONAL PROFILE: A modern Anglo Asian professional. A dynamic, commercially minded property lawyer based in the heart of London with a portfolio of entrepreneurial West End based commercial property clients. Many years of community service including chairmanship of the Ismali Legal Committee in London.
NOMINATED BY: Fatima Kassam

MR RATILAL K KATHRANI (Insurance)

Surveyor, J H Minet, H Park Chase, Wembley Park, HA9 8EH

PLACE OF BIRTH: India, 13.11.32
MARITAL STATUS: Married
CHILDREN: Three (Harsha, Hina, Ajay)
MEMBERSHIPS: Senior Citizen
PERSONAL PROFILE: I was a member and have held various posts in voluntary organisations: Lohana Community North London, Wembley (Brent) Lions Club, Hindu Council Brent, Brent Indian Association, Sawnvaya Parivar, Bharatiya Vidya Bhavan. I received Brent Citizenship Award in 1996 and Melvin Jones Fellow from Lions Club in 1995.

'The Original Indian Raggamuffin', has gone from strength to strength, with seven Top 40 hits; four Brit Awards nominations; a Mercury Music Prize nomination; his own show on Radio One; International Dance Awards; and an Ivor Novello nomination

STEVEN KAPUR

Group accountant of Apple Corps Limited (Beatles Company) its subsidiaries and associated companies - May 1969 to June 1983. An honorary member of the (First) National Committee of the Aga Khan Foundation UK

ISMAIL KASSAM

MRS GURDEV KAUR (TEACHING-WRITING)

Shromani Bal Sahitkar, HD Publishers, 180 Plantsbrook Road, Walmley, Sutton Coldfield, B761HL

PLACE OF BIRTH: India, 30.11.39
MARITAL STATUS: Married
CHILDREN: Three (Inderbir Kaur, Manpreet Singh, Gurinder Kaur)
COLLEGE: Punjab University India
ACADEMIC QUALIFICATIONS: MA
PROFESSIONAL QUALIFICATIONS: BEd, Sangeet Parveen, Sangeet Bhaskar
DIRECTORSHIPS: HD Publishers
MEMBERSHIPS: Chairperson-Sikh Nari Manch, Council of Sikh Gurdwaras, Birmingham
HONOURS/AWARDS: Shromani Award from Punjab Govt 1997
HOBBIES AND INTERESTS: Reading, community work, writing, singing, teaching, music
PERSONAL PROFILE: Shromani Bal Sahit award winner 1997 for writing childrens books. I have been honoured by Shromani Gurdwara Parbandhak Committee Amritsar twice-firstly for writing 'Sikh Hymns for Schools' first of its kind and second time for my 'talking books'. In April 1998 Delhi Gurdwara managing committee, honoured me for my work. Guru Nanak Dev University Amritsar, Quality Education Board Chandigarh and a number of local literary and religious organisations have honoured me from time to time.

MRS RANBIR KAUR (TEXTILE ARTIST)

Artist, Kiran Arts and Crafts,

PLACE OF BIRTH: India, 21.9.54
MARITAL STATUS: Married
CHILDREN: Three (Jaspreet, Prabhjeet, Kirandeep)
COLLEGE: Makere University Uganda
ACADEMIC QUALIFICATIONS: BA
PROFESSIONAL QUALIFICATIONS: BEd
MEMBERSHIPS: Birmingham Doll Maker Club
HONOURS/AWARDS: Eileen Trophy, Crystal Goblet, Best exhibition, Sandwell
HOBBIES AND INTERESTS: Making rag dolls
PERSONAL PROFILE: Arts and crafts runs as a family tradition in Ranbir's life. Over 60 exhibitions have been held and over 300 workshops have been arranged in England and Wales on arts, crafts and textiles. The outstanding display of Rangoli doll making, Asian embroidery, Indian block printing, Batik fabric painting and collage work has won acclaim and various facets of work are in constant demand. The work in this field has brought harmony and understanding in the communities.

DR RITA GULSHARAN KAUR (CERAMIC ENGINEER)

Mohawk Innovative Technology Inc, Courtney House, Courtney Drive, New Silksworth, Sunderland, SR3 1JS

PLACE OF BIRTH: Newcastle-U-Tyne, 17.1.70
ACADEMIC QUALIFICATIONS: BSc Hons Chemistry & Photographic Tech, 10 O-Levels 3 A-Levels
PROFESSIONAL QUALIFICATIONS: MSc, PhD Ceramics in Engineering. MSc Materials Engineering.
MEMBERSHIPS: Institute of Mechanical Engineering
HONOURS/AWARDS: Royal Academy of Engineering and British Council
HOBBIES AND INTERESTS: Swimming, playing chess, surfing the internet
PERSONAL PROFILE: On completing my MSc Materials Engineering at Sunderland University in Oct 1994, I was offered to do a PhD in ceramics/engineering by Brunel University and Castrol International in Dec 1994. I was awarded my PhD in April 1998 and have been offered a job as a ceramic engineer in America.

MS USHAWANT KAUR (POET-VISUAL ARTS)

Living Artists Movement, 18 Carlton Gate, Little London, Leeds, LS7 1HW

PLACE OF BIRTH: India, 30.6.40
MARITAL STATUS: Single
COLLEGE: Indian Universities
ACADEMIC QUALIFICATIONS: MA, BEd
PROFESSIONAL QUALIFICATIONS: BEd Teacher-Training, Three years parttime, fine art course
MEMBERSHIPS: Labour Party Leeds
HOBBIES AND INTERESTS: Poetry and visual arts (painting and drawing) craft
PERSONAL PROFILE: I founded Living Artists Movement. I am the daughter of a poet father and I am a poet and visual artist. I write poetry in English, Punjabi and Hindi languages. I have published one book 'Empty Shells' and I am going to publish a few more books in the near future.

DR JAGDISH KAUSHAL (JOURNALIST)

Editor, Amardeep Hindi Weekly, 2 Chapstow Road, London, W7 2BG

PLACE OF BIRTH: India, 29.8.32
MARITAL STATUS: Married
CHILDREN: Four (Balram, Krishan, Amardeep, Neelam)
COLLEGE: Punjab University
ACADEMIC QUALIFICATIONS: BA
PROFESSIONAL QUALIFICATIONS: ABMS, Banaras Hindu University
MEMBERSHIPS: ISKCON, EPS. Hindu Temple Trust, Southall.
HONOURS/AWARDS: Hindi Award in Vigyan Bhavan
HOBBIES AND INTERESTS: Yoga, meditation, reading, music, gardening
PERSONAL PROFILE: Very active in Asian social, cultural and spiritual field. Very good orator in Hindi, Urdu, Punjabi and English. Life member, patron and president of a few Indian societies. Invited by HM Queen Elizabeth to Buckingham Palace in Jubilee Year. Published a book, 'United we stand-Asians in Britain'

MR SYED KAZMI JP (LECTURER-RTD)

Deputy Director-Tertiary College, 4 Naseby Close, Mickleover, Derby, DE3 5QU

PLACE OF BIRTH: Pakistan, 2.4.34
MARITAL STATUS: Married
CHILDREN: Four (Amir, Majid, Asim, Farhat)
COLLEGE: Punjab University, Hull University-Open University
ACADEMIC QUALIFICATIONS: BSc, BA
PROFESSIONAL QUALIFICATIONS: BEd, PG + Diploma in Education
MEMBERSHIPS: Southern Derbyshire Community Health Council
HONOURS/AWARDS: Justice of the Peace
HOBBIES AND INTERESTS: Current affairs, voluntary work
PERSONAL PROFILE: Worked for four education authorities in England and retired as deputy director. I served Derby Council for Racial Equality as executive member and vice-chairman. Other voluntary work is my service to Pakistan Community Centre Derby as secretary and vice chairman, Pakistan Cultural Society-president, Southern Derbyshire Community Health Council member, Justice of the Peace.
NOMINATED BY: Dr Masjid Kazmi

MRS NARINDER KHABBRA (ASIAN LINK WORKER)

Prospect Associates, 28 Magpie Close, Forest Gate, London, E7 9DE

MARITAL STATUS: Married
PERSONAL PROFILE: Asian Link Worker for 'Cancer You Are Not Alone'. Set up Asian Cancer Support Group to aid Asian cancer sufferers. Care worker and warden for special projects. Course tutor for community education. Women's aid worker supporting women of domestic violence. Voluntary worker for a number of women's organisations.

DR FERDOUSE KHALEQUE (SOFTWARE CONSULTANT)

East-To-West, 46 Hare Lane, Hatfield, AL10 8PP

PLACE OF BIRTH: Bangladesh, 15.1.63
MARITAL STATUS: Married
COLLEGE: Imperial College, London
ACADEMIC QUALIFICATIONS: BSc Hons, PhD
PROFESSIONAL QUALIFICATIONS: MIEE, MIPhys, MIEEE
DIRECTORSHIPS: Managing Director (own company)
HONOURS/AWARDS: A-Level Awards, Many research papers and awards
HOBBIES AND INTERESTS: Travelling, cinema, internet, DIY
EMAIL: fkhaleque@btinternet.com
PERSONAL PROFILE: I run an internet consultancy firm specialising in product sales through the internet. Investing large sums of money learning the new technologies for a more progressive growth through the Millennium.

> 'I run an internet consultancy firm specialising in product sales through the internet. Investing large sums of money learning the new technologies for a more progressive growth'
>
> **DR FERDOUSE KHALEQUE**

CLLR GHAZANFER KHALID (Councillor)

Chair Disabilities Committee, Bradford Council, City Hall, Bradford, BD1

MARITAL STATUS: Married
CHILDREN: Four
PERSONAL PROFILE: Have been local councillor for past 12 years in Bradford. Have been involved in local community.

MISS BHOPINDER KAUR KHALSA (Student)

Volunteer, Hounslow Youth & Community Centre,

PLACE OF BIRTH: Birmingham, 17.9.79
MARITAL STATUS: Single
COLLEGE: Richmond & West Thames
ACADEMIC QUALIFICATIONS: A-Levels (4), FDVE Volunteer qualifications
PROFESSIONAL QUALIFICATIONS: First Aid, Diploma-Massaga and Yoga
MEMBERSHIPS: British Organisation of Sikh Students, National Union of Students, Neighbourhood Watch
HONOURS/AWARDS: Personality of the Year
HOBBIES AND INTERESTS: Martial arts, drama, sports, shopping, travelling
EMAIL: bkkhalsa@yahoo.com.uk
PERSONAL PROFILE: Miss Khalsa is an active member in her community and within the national volunteer sector, has membership to many organisations, e.g. Amnesty International, British Organisation of Sikh Students. She has represented her religion and community many times in the national and international media. Articles have been written about her being a positive role model. Her message-Have a happy, holy and healthy living, Love everybody and live in peace and justice.

MR PRITHVIPAL SINGH KHALSA (Managing Director)

Royale Glazing, 692b London Road, Isleworth, TW3 1PG

PLACE OF BIRTH: India, 15.6.54
MARITAL STATUS: Married
CHILDREN: Four (Bhopinder Kaur, Jasveer Kaur, Kulveer Kaur, Amritpal Singh)
MEMBERSHIPS: Community charities and volunteer work
HOBBIES AND INTERESTS: Martial arts, sports, travelling, weight training, singing to the praises of god
PERSONAL PROFILE: He is the managing director for Royale Glazing for the last 15 years since its establishment. He is a well known member of the Sikh community and recognised for his dedication and volunteer work both in the UK and internationally. He teaches the Sikh martial arts of Gatka and has an academy based in Southall.
NOMINATED BY: Bhopinder Kaur Khalsa

MR SARWAN SINGH KHALSA-SAGOO (Music Teacher)

137 Okehampton Crescent, Welling, DA16 1DH

PLACE OF BIRTH: Kenya, 24.11.56
MARITAL STATUS: Married
CHILDREN: Three (Rasital Kaur, Harkirat Singh, Sehanaj Kaur)
ACADEMIC QUALIFICATIONS: HND-Electro Mechanical Design Engineering
HOBBIES AND INTERESTS: Music-playing tabla, harmonium, violin, sport-badminton
PERSONAL PROFILE: I have taught semi-classical Indian music at several local venues for approximately fifteen years. I strongly believe that it is important to teach the younger generation about our rich culture, traditions and religion. When living in a western society it is easy to adopt the host culture and discard our own.
NOMINATED BY: Sukhwinder Kaur Khalsa-Sagoo

MR ALAUDDIN KHAN (Executive Rtd)

Merchant Marine, 12 Waverley Street, Coatbridge, Scotland, ML5 2BE

PLACE OF BIRTH: Scotland, 22.11.29
MARITAL STATUS: Widowed
CHILDREN: Four (Yasmine, Antoinette, Lowis, Anthony)
COLLEGE: Coatbridge Tech, Glasgow University
ACADEMIC QUALIFICATIONS: Post Grad-Endo Crinology, Philosophy-Biochemistry
PROFESSIONAL QUALIFICATIONS: NIMH
DIRECTORSHIPS: Executive-UPS-7 companies as companies stock inspector
MEMBERSHIPS: Ethnic Minority Group-vice-chair. Management committee Southside HA.
HONOURS/AWARDS: National Service Cup, L/GPL, National Service Medal
HOBBIES AND INTERESTS: Quran, Reading, TV, Carer Ethnic Minority Groups
PERSONAL PROFILE: Born in Coatbridge, 69 years age, of an ethnic origin parent, who came as an engineer and worked locally. I must be one of the first, if not the first generation of ethnic origin in Scotland. I started as an apprentice engineer at age 14 and have had a varied career. Merchant Marine Engineer Officer. Lord Hanson UPS, executive. Royal Liver Insurance, area inspector.
NOMINATED BY: Mohammed Kiani

MR ASAD AMIN KHAN (Medical Student)

Royal Free Medical School, 40 Greencroft Road, Heston, Hounslow, TW5 0BQ

PLACE OF BIRTH: Isleworth, 1.7.78
MARITAL STATUS: Single
COLLEGE: Royal Free and University College Medical School
ACADEMIC QUALIFICATIONS: 2nd year medical exam (MBBS)
PROFESSIONAL QUALIFICATIONS: 2nd year medical exam
HONOURS/AWARDS: Awarded many trophies in cricket and mathematics
HOBBIES AND INTERESTS: Cricket, squash, reading books, worldwide travel
PERSONAL PROFILE: All England Schools' Gold Award in Maths. Top grades GCSE O/A-Levels. Medicine, Royal Free Medical School. London Schools Cricket Championship. Rose Cup Cricket Award. Middx County U11, U15, U17. London Universities' team coached at Lords. Airlines World Cup in Sharjah and West Indies, to Pakistan this autumn Inshahllah. Ambition to play for England Inshahllah.
NOMINATED BY: Mr Ata R Khan

MS ASIFA JAHANARA KHAN (Senior Lecturer)

Centre Manager, City College Birmingham, 36 Coleshill Road, Hodge Hill, Birmingham, B36 8AA

PLACE OF BIRTH: Pakistan, 3.12.50
MARITAL STATUS: Married
CHILDREN: Three (Zafor, Amira, Asad)
COLLEGE: Punjab University, Wolverhampton University
ACADEMIC QUALIFICATIONS: Masters Degree, Punjab. (PGCE)
PROFESSIONAL QUALIFICATIONS: Teacher Training (UK), Counselling and Mgt Skills (UK)
DIRECTORSHIPS: Council of British Pakistanis, Roshini. Kasmiri & Pakistani Professionals Association.
MEMBERSHIPS: European Migrant Women's Forum. Pakistan Forum
HONOURS/AWARDS: Honourary chairships and directorships to various organisations
HOBBIES AND INTERESTS: Reading, badminton, rowing, keep fit
PERSONAL PROFILE: Born, brought up and married in Pakistan. Teaching experience three years in Pakistan, 14 years in the UK. Involvement in community work for 15 years. School governor for eight years, been nominated for JP position. Represented Pakistani British on Migrant Women's Forum in Europe. Friends and links across all races and nation's. Editor Biling weekly. Won two scholarships at secondary school and university level.
NOMINATED BY: Mr A Qayyum Chaudhary

'I strongly believe that it is important to teach the younger generation about our rich culture, traditions and religion'

SARWAN SINGH KHALSA-SAGOO

Born in Coatbridge, 69 years age, of an ethnic origin parent, who came as an engineer and worked locally. I must be one of the first, if not the first generation of ethnic origin in Scotland

ALAUDDIN KHAN

MR ATHAIR KHAN (Restauratuer)

Last days of the Raj Restaurant, Kells Lane, Low Fell, Gateshead, NE9 5HY

PLACE OF BIRTH: Bangladesh, 5.6.62
MARITAL STATUS: Married
CHILDREN: Four (Halema, Imran, Neelima, Mohima)
PROFESSIONAL QUALIFICATIONS: Business Management & Computer Studies
DIRECTORSHIPS: Last Days of the Raj Restaurant Ltd
MEMBERSHIPS: Chamber of Commerce, Labour Party
HONOURS/AWARDS: Restaurant of the Year since 1995. Numerous other awards for Quality.
HOBBIES AND INTERESTS: Improving my business
PERSONAL PROFILE: Athair Khan combines a busy family life with running his highly successful restaurant and takeaway. Launched in 1995, The Last Days of the Raj attracts a clientele who appreciate the fine cuisine and elegant surroundings. He is involved in supporting local and national charities and recently achieved acclaim with a place in the Top 100 Indian Restaurants by the Curry Club.
NOMINATED BY: Tony Noble

MR B HAKIM KHAN (Accountant)

Financial Administrator, Steerpike Limited, 62 Loftus Road, London, W12 7EL

PLACE OF BIRTH: Bangladesh, 18.9.46
MARITAL STATUS: Married
CHILDREN: One (Gali W H Khan)
ACADEMIC QUALIFICATIONS: Degree in Commerce
DIRECTORSHIPS: Beechtree Prop Ltd
HOBBIES AND INTERESTS: Reading books
EMAIL: hakimkhan@compuserve.com
PERSONAL PROFILE: Involved with music industry for over 20 years in the administration of financial and accounting matters. Dealing with intellectual copyright publishing, concert tours, records and videos.

MR FAROQUE KHAN (Actor-Teacher-Director)

John Markham Associates, 1A Oakwood Avenue, Purley, CR8 1AR

PLACE OF BIRTH: Uganda, 27.8.68
MARITAL STATUS: Single
COLLEGE: Strathclyde University
ACADEMIC QUALIFICATIONS: BA in Community Arts (with commendations)
PROFESSIONAL QUALIFICATIONS: Martial Arts Instructor, Movement Teacher
MEMBERSHIPS: Equity
HOBBIES AND INTERESTS: Martial arts, dancing, languages
PERSONAL PROFILE: Born in Uganda came to Britain in 1972. Grew up in Birmingham. Studied theatre in Glasgow and Paris. Began professional career as an actor and teacher in 1993. Have since worked and taught both national and internationally. Future plans include the forming my own company and training school.

MR FORHAD KHAN (Student)

Semi-Pro Footballer, c/o 9C Frederick Street, King's Cross, Camden, London, WC1X 0NF

PLACE OF BIRTH: London, 13.10.85
MARITAL STATUS: Single
COLLEGE: Holloway School
HONOURS/AWARDS: Best student of the term in tutor form and many trophies
HOBBIES AND INTERESTS: Playing football, pool, snooker, reading books
PERSONAL PROFILE: I play football for my school team, King's Cross Lithgow FC and semi professional club Hendon FC. I played in many national and international tournaments with my football clubs. I have had a trial with Leyton Orient FC under-13's. I want to become a professional footballer one day.

> Involved with music industry. Dealing with intellectual copyright publishing, concert tours, records and videos

B HAKIM KHAN

MR GMMH RAHMAN KHAN (Councillor)

Chair, Corporate Services, Haringey Council, 12 Linden Road, Tottenham, London, N15 3QB

PLACE OF BIRTH: Bangladesh, 31.8.40
MARITAL STATUS: Married
CHILDREN: Four (Hafizur, Saidur, Nasima, Najma)
COLLEGE: Dhaka University
ACADEMIC QUALIFICATIONS: MA (Second Class)
PROFESSIONAL QUALIFICATIONS: Passed part1 & 2 Banking Diploma examination-East Pakistan Bangladesh
DIRECTORSHIPS: Former Director of Council of Asian People
MEMBERSHIPS: Labour Party. Chair, Tottenham Black Socialist Society
HOBBIES AND INTERESTS: Ensuring equal opportunities, current affairs, reading, gardening
PERSONAL PROFILE: Since boyhood my ambition has been to serve the disadvantaged community to establish their rights. I started my working life in 1962 with State Bank of Pakistan and trained as banker and administrator. As chief accountant with a City bank in UK. Living in Haringey for over 20 years, have served on most community organisations.

MR IMRAN KHAN (Furniture Dealer)

Proprietor, Junaid Furnitures, 558 Romford Road, Manor Park, London, E12 5AF

PLACE OF BIRTH: Birmingham, 20.7.77
MARITAL STATUS: Single
MEMBERSHIPS: Member of the Overseas Pakistan Football Team (APSA)
HONOURS/AWARDS: Asian Football League, Goalkeeper of the Season 1997-98-99
HOBBIES AND INTERESTS: Racket sports, football, cricket
PERSONAL PROFILE: A humble secondhand furniture dealer. Plays football for Ahle Sunnah FC now known as London APSA. His commitment to the game is unquestionable and his success has earmarked him for a tour to his home country. Imran was headhunted by an organisation in Manchester to plays in goal against the touring Pakistan National team.

CLLR IMRAN AHMED KHAN (Business Development Officer)

Councillor (BMDC), Business Link, Bradford and District, 1 Princeville Street, Bradford, BD7 2AG

PLACE OF BIRTH: Bradford, 20.9.73
MARITAL STATUS: Single
COLLEGE: Leeds University
ACADEMIC QUALIFICATIONS: BSc Hons Technology Management, Masters-Business Admin (Mkting)
PROFESSIONAL QUALIFICATIONS: Licentiate-Inst. of Quality Assurance
DIRECTORSHIPS: Q.21. Association. Residential Study Centre
MEMBERSHIPS: Member of Labour Party
HOBBIES AND INTERESTS: Football, cricket, reading
PERSONAL PROFILE: Achieved 10 GCSE's and 2 A-Level's whilst attending Thornton Grammar School and went on to obtain an honours degree from University of Wales, Cardiff. Completed Masters Degree in Business Administration from Leeds University Business School. Now work for Business Link. I am also a Bradford City councillor representing University Ward.

MR JAVED KHAN (Director)

Director Development, City College Birmingham, Garretts Green Lane, Garretts Green, Birmingham, B33 0TS

PLACE OF BIRTH: High Wycombe, 31.7.63
MARITAL STATUS: Married
CHILDREN: Three (Muryum, Zaynah, Zarah)
COLLEGE: Salford University
ACADEMIC QUALIFICATIONS: BSc Mathematics, PGCE Teacher Training
DIRECTORSHIPS: Kashmiri and Pakistani Professionals Association
MEMBERSHIPS: Network for Black Managers of FE (NFBM)
HOBBIES AND INTERESTS: Cricket, current affairs
EMAIL: jkhan@citycol.co.uk
PERSONAL PROFILE: I am a British born Kashmiri with descendancy from Mirpur, Azad Kashmir (Pakistan). After completing my school education in an inner city comprehensive in Birmingham I spent four years in Manchester getting a maths degree and teachers training qualifications. After 14 years in education I am currently a member of my college's senior management team.
NOMINATED BY: Aamirah Hussain

DR KAMALUDDIN KHAN (Medical)

Lord Chancellors Medical Visitor, 59 Druidvsille Road, Liverpool, L18 3EW

PLACE OF BIRTH: India, 5.7.37
MARITAL STATUS: Married
CHILDREN: Three (Dr Salahuddin, Asif Kamal, Yousuf)
COLLEGE: Liverpool University
ACADEMIC QUALIFICATIONS: BSc, MBBS, Dpm, FRC Psych, PhD
PROFESSIONAL QUALIFICATIONS: BSc, MBBS, Dpm, FRCPsych, PhD
MEMBERSHIPS: Royal College of Psychiatrists
HOBBIES AND INTERESTS: Reading, travelling
PERSONAL PROFILE: Qualified from Lucknow Medical College in India 1960. Came to UK in 1969. Was consultant psychiatrist until 1995. As well as being Lord Chancellor's Medical Visitor and chairman of it's medical board. I am also medical member of Mental Health Review Tribunal and member of other committees.

MR KAMRAN KHAN (Student)

18 Stratton Road, Whalley Range, Manchester, M16 0BB

PLACE OF BIRTH: Manchester, 2.10.83
COLLEGE: Stretford High School
PERSONAL PROFILE: After winning numerous competitions throwing the hammer in athletics Kamran has represented Greater Manchester in the English schools championships (mini Olympics where over 50 countries compete). Kamran came second making him No 2 in England, the first Asian in his field. He has broken a 30-year record at his school.
NOMINATED BY: Zahida Parvez

MR MAHMOOD SHAFI KHAN (Lawyer)

Barrister, National Council of Pakistani Organisations, 103 Wexham Close, Luton, LU3 3TX

PLACE OF BIRTH: Dholpur, 16.7.28
MARITAL STATUS: Married
COLLEGE: Punjab, Karachi, Brunel University
ACADEMIC QUALIFICATIONS: BA, MA
PROFESSIONAL QUALIFICATIONS: LL.B, DILL, FETC, Cert Ed
DIRECTORSHIPS: Chairman of Council of Pakistani Organisations UK
MEMBERSHIPS: Honourable Society of Lincoln's Inn
HOBBIES AND INTERESTS: Music, theatre, social activities, radio broadcasting
PERSONAL PROFILE: Through organisations and personally have always fought against injustices/discriminations against ethnic minorities for the last forty years. Representations made before Home Office Select Committees and served on statutory/voluntary committees of health, education and employment etc. Training/lectures given to police authorities at Lancs, Yorks and Beds to develop understanding with ethnic minorities. Positions held as CRO/director and equal opportunities officer for local authority. At present practising as a barrister for human rights.

MR MAHTAB KHAN (Personnel Consultancy)

Employee Relations Manager, Birmingham City Council, 290 Oxhill Road, Handsworth, Birmingham, B4 7DQ

PLACE OF BIRTH: London, 27.4.64
MARITAL STATUS: Married
CHILDREN: Two (Omar, Jamila)
COLLEGE: Teeside Polytechnic
ACADEMIC QUALIFICATIONS: BSc Hons Social Studies Grad. Cert. Ed
PROFESSIONAL QUALIFICATIONS: Institute of Personnel & Development (IPD)
DIRECTORSHIPS: Chair of Aston Single Regeneration Budget Venture Board
MEMBERSHIPS: IPD and British Psychological Society
PERSONAL PROFILE: Mahtab is one of the few disabled Asians who has managed to achieve both academically and professionally despite the barriers he has had to face. In his spare time he undertakes freelance work as a management consultant as well as voluntary work in the community.
NOMINATED BY: Colin Clark, Birmingham City Council

Representing over 10,000 senior hospital doctors

MOHIB KHAN

MRS MEHER KHAN (Co-ordinator)

Muslim Women's Welfare Association, 425 Leabridge Road, Leyton, London, E10 7EA

PLACE OF BIRTH: India
MARITAL STATUS: Married
CHILDREN: Three (Zafer, Azher, Asher)
COLLEGE: Pakistan
ACADEMIC QUALIFICATIONS: Intermediate
PROFESSIONAL QUALIFICATIONS: Typist, Childcare with Special Needs, ESL, Computer Software
DIRECTORSHIPS: Institute of Overseas Pakistanis, Urdu Trust, Pakistani Anglo Sports Association.
MEMBERSHIPS: Unison, RSA
HONOURS/AWARDS: Ninth Finalist, Child Line Award
HOBBIES AND INTERESTS: Gardening, travelling
PERSONAL PROFILE: Founder member of Muslim Women's Welfare Association, Asian Women's Refuge, Asian Young Women's Refuge. First Asian women councillor to be elected in Waltham Forest. First women to be elected in history of Waltham Forest as deputy mayor. First Asian Muslim woman to be elected mayor in Britain. Always keen in promoting Asian women and culture. Actively supports all charitable causes within and outside Britain.

CLLR MOHAMMAD KHAN (Self-Employed)

55 Edmundson Street, Blackburn, BB2 1HL

PLACE OF BIRTH: Pakistan, 16.12.45
MARITAL STATUS: Married
COLLEGE: Garden College, Rawalpindi, Pakistan, Penn State University USA, Blackburn College of Technology
ACADEMIC QUALIFICATIONS: Diploma Business Management, City and Guilds of London Institute
PROFESSIONAL QUALIFICATIONS: Two Year Business Management Course
MEMBERSHIPS: Vice chair ELTEC Ethnic Minority Specialist Group. City Challenge. Blackburn Partnership. Single Regeneraation Budget. Member of the Management Committee, Member of the Police and Community Forum
HOBBIES AND INTERESTS: Reading
PERSONAL PROFILE: I came to this country in 1965. I studied textiles at Blackburn College. Subsequently, while working in the US, I succeeded in obtaining a business management qualification. For the past nine years I have played a leading role on the council to improve the quality of life for the residents of the borough.

MR MOHIB KHAN (Surgeon)

Associate Specialist, British Medical Association,

PLACE OF BIRTH: India, 1.1.44
MARITAL STATUS: Married
CHILDREN: One (Sana)
COLLEGE: Allahabad University
ACADEMIC QUALIFICATIONS: BSc
PROFESSIONAL QUALIFICATIONS: MBBS, FRCS
HOBBIES AND INTERESTS: Swimming, travelling, medical politics, fight against racial discrimination
PERSONAL PROFILE: Elected national chairman , BMA's Non-Consultant Career Grade Committee since 1996, representing over 10,000 senior hospital doctors. 80% are originally from overseas. Organised nationwide campaign to get the Specialist Medical Qualification Order changed, through parliament in 1997, resulting in 1500 doctors gaining access to the Specialist Register. Committed to fighting racial discrimination in the NHS.

MR MUHAMMAD MUNIR KHAN (Director WFREC)

Director, Waltham Forest Race Equality Council, 105 Falmouth Gardens, Redbridge, Ilford, IG4 5JJ

PLACE OF BIRTH: Pakistan, 4.5.41
MARITAL STATUS: Married
COLLEGE: University of Punjab, Lincoln's Inn
ACADEMIC QUALIFICATIONS: BA, LLB (Pb)
PROFESSIONAL QUALIFICATIONS: Lincoln's Inn, Barrister-at-Law
MEMBERSHIPS: Hon Society of Lincoln's Inn
HOBBIES AND INTERESTS: Reading, writing, TV, Asian music, gardening, walking
PERSONAL PROFILE: I held various community positions inter Alia; President, Inns of Courts Pakistan Society (1979-80); Chairperson All Faiths Association, Newham (1981-82). Legal advisor of various voluntary community organisations; specialist immigration and nationality laws and Islamic laws. Campaigns: Racial harassment and violence, establishment of religious spiritual services at Forest Healthcare Trust and Waltham Forest Disability Centre.

MUMTAZ KHAN (Community Development Officer)

290 Uxbridge Street, Burton-On-Trent, DE14 3JS

PLACE OF BIRTH: Pakistan, 5.12.46
MARITAL STATUS: Married
CHILDREN: Six (Shahid Mumtaz, Rashad Mumtaz, Firdous Mumtaz, Taj Mumtaz, Tab Mumtaz, Ni Mumtaz)
COLLEGE: Punjab University
ACADEMIC QUALIFICATIONS: Bachelor of Arts
HONOURS/AWARDS: Volunteer of the Year
HOBBIES AND INTERESTS: Local and national politics, music, community work
PERSONAL PROFILE: First Asian prospective councillor in the local council elections in 1987. Actively involved in the local communities assisting them with their welfare rights and offering general help from filling forms to representation at tribunals. Volunteer of the Year award winner. First Asian special police constable for Staffordshire Police.
NOMINATED BY: Silpazir Ahmed

DR MUTAHAR HUSSAIN KHAN (Hospital Consultancy)

Consultant Genito-Urinary Medicine, Mid Cheshire NHS Trust Crewe Cheshire, Shanti-Nir, 7 Aylesby Close, Knutsford, WA16 8AE

PLACE OF BIRTH: Bangladesh, 23.5.41
MARITAL STATUS: Married
CHILDREN: Three (Mahtab Hussain, Imtiaz Hussain, Ruwena Afroze)
COLLEGE: Dhaka Medical College, Dhaka University
ACADEMIC QUALIFICATIONS: MBBS 1964, Dip Ven 1971
PROFESSIONAL QUALIFICATIONS: Fellow World Health Organisation
HOBBIES AND INTERESTS: Music, reading, walking
PERSONAL PROFILE: Came to the UK 1969. Appointed as a full-time consultant in genito-urinary medicine in 1979. President Bangladesh Medical Association, UK 1988-1990. Former vice chairman Ethnic Minorities' Welfare and Community Organisation-Chester and North Wales and a Rotarian. Member professional organisations UK-BMA . MSSUD, BSSUD, BHIVA and in Europe IUSTI.

MR MUZAHID KHAN (Projects Officer)

Projects Officer, 138 Main Road, Westwood, Oldham, OL9 6JY

PLACE OF BIRTH: Bangladesh, 11.12.69
MARITAL STATUS: Married
CHILDREN: One (Syra)
COLLEGE: Manchester Metropolitan University
ACADEMIC QUALIFICATIONS: BA Hons Business Studies
MEMBERSHIPS: Peshkar Theatre Company, Royal Oldham Hospital Scanner Appeal, Sonnet
HONOURS/AWARDS: Recognition for voluntary work from HM Queen Elizabeth
HOBBIES AND INTERESTS: Football, networking, organising events, arranging tours of Asia, developing new initiatives.
EMAIL: mkhan@sonali.demon.co.uk
PERSONAL PROFILE: Born in Bangladesh, came to England in 1978. Educated in England, study part-time degree. Gained significant promotion at work to project officer for regeneration. Active in voluntary and community work. Received recognition from HM Queen Elizabeth for community work. I have written four successful lottery bids.
NOMINATED BY: N. Armstrong-Kersh, Royal Oldham Hospital

NADEEM KHAN (Editor)

Ethnic Media Group, 148 Cambridge Heath Road, London E1 5QJ

PLACE OF BIRTH: Birmingham, 3.1.68
MARITAL STATUS: Single
COLLEGE: Birmingham University
ACADEMIC QUALIFICATIONS: BSc Chemistry, MSc Scientific Computing and Scientific Information Technology
MEMBERSHIPS: Royal Society of Chemists, Birmingham Alumni Association, Newspaper Society
PERSONAL PROFILE: Currently Projects Director in the Books and Magazines Division at Ethnic Media Group. Formerly Editor of Eastern Eye and Asian Times newspapers and Business and Sports Editor for Daily Star newspaper in Beirut, Lebanon.

MR NAS KHAN (Sales Director)

Sales Director, Jennings, Yarm Road, Stockton-On-Tees, Cleveland, TS18 3RW

PLACE OF BIRTH: Pakistan, 31.12.59
MARITAL STATUS: Married
CHILDREN: Three (Natasha, Sairah, Sohail)
COLLEGE: Acklaim Sixth Form / Manchester University
ACADEMIC QUALIFICATIONS: 11 O-Levels, 3 A-Levels (Maths, English, Economics)
PROFESSIONAL QUALIFICATIONS: Accountant
DIRECTORSHIPS: Sales Director
MEMBERSHIPS: Chairman of the North East Ford Dealers Advertising Association.
WEB SITE: www.jennings-ford.co.uk
PERSONAL PROFILE: I joined the motor trade for a year out. Three years later I had been promoted through the ranks to non executive director for the Jennings Group. In 1992 I was instrumental in leading a management buy out becoming executive sales director expanding the group to six dealerships with further expansion due in 1999.

MR NAWAZ KHAN (Electrical Technician)

Team Leader, Muslim Association of Bradford, 32 Howard Street, Bradford, BD5 0BP

PLACE OF BIRTH: Pakistan, 29.9.68
MARITAL STATUS: Married
CHILDREN: Two (Sarah, M.Bilal)
MEMBERSHIPS: Secretary MAOB
HOBBIES AND INTERESTS: Serving the Muslim community

NOMINATED BY: Dr M.K Khan

MR RABNAWAZ KHAN (Head of Group)

Head of Group Systems Support, 14 Canton Walk, Macclesfield, SK11 7QN

PLACE OF BIRTH: Pakistan, 30.11.68
MARITAL STATUS: Married
CHILDREN: Two (Mohd Riasat, Sabrina)
COLLEGE: South Cheshire College, Crewe
ACADEMIC QUALIFICATIONS: BTec, National Diploma in Computer Studies
HOBBIES AND INTERESTS: Computing, cricket, keep fit
PERSONAL PROFILE: I am a 29 year old who has worked hard all my life to achieve success in my chosen career in computing despite having arrived in the UK in 1977 without any knowledge of the English language or culture at the age of nine.
NOMINATED BY: Noreen Khan , Macclesfield

CLLR RAJA ARIF KHAN JP (Sales Manager)

Councillor & JP, 57/59 Devonshire Road, Burnley, BB10 1AL

PLACE OF BIRTH: India, 30.6.46
MARITAL STATUS: Married
CHILDREN: Five
COLLEGE: Govt College
ACADEMIC QUALIFICATIONS: A-Level EQ
PROFESSIONAL QUALIFICATIONS: IT NVQ 2, A-Level standard in Pakistan
MEMBERSHIPS: Gen sec of local Lib Dem. Vice chair of Burnley and Pendle REC
HOBBIES AND INTERESTS: Reading, DIY, cricket, football, walking
PERSONAL PROFILE: Currently a local councillor and JP for the Burnley and Pendle Bench. As an active member of the community I have a number of commitments within voluntary organisations ie vice-chairman of the Burnley and Pendle REC and volunteer for Age Concern. My occupation is in the business sector as a sales manager.

'I joined the motor trade for a year out. Three years later I had been promoted through the ranks to non executive director for the Jennings Group. In 1992 I was instrumental in leading a management buy out'

NAS KHAN

MS SEEMA KHAN (Actress)

Aerobics Instructor, Clive Corner Associates, 75 Gloucester Road, Hampton, TW12 2UQ

PLACE OF BIRTH: Pakistan, 30.1.62
MARITAL STATUS: Divorced
CHILDREN: One (Sara)
COLLEGE: Roehampton Institute, Webber Douglas Academy. The City Lit.
ACADEMIC QUALIFICATIONS: 7 O-Levels and 3 A-Levels, Studying for BSc Sports & Exercise Science
PROFESSIONAL QUALIFICATIONS: P/Q, ACCA, RSA Exercise to Music, YMCA Fitness Trainer, YMCA Personal Trainer. Reebok Power Steo & Slide BASSC
MEMBERSHIPS: Equity, Fitness Professionals, Exercise Association, Reebok Alliance
HOBBIES AND INTERESTS: Stage combat, horse-riding, skiing
EMAIL: colin.ballantyne@virgin.net
PERSONAL PROFILE: On stage Seema has been involved in many Shakespearian productions with her last principal role as Reena in Saltley and Khahionian at the Birmingham Repertory Theatre. Television appearances include 'The Knock' 'Thief Taker' and 'Casualty'. She regularly teaches a variety of aerobics classes, instructs in a gym and is a personal fitness trainer.

CLLR DR SHAFI KHAN (Education Lecturer)

Mayor, Members Secretary, Croydon Town Hall, Mayors Parlour, Town Hall, Katherine Street, Croydon, CR0 1NX

PLACE OF BIRTH: Bangladesh, 5.2.54
MARITAL STATUS: Married
CHILDREN: One (Maria)
COLLEGE: Dhaka University
ACADEMIC QUALIFICATIONS: M Sc Civil Eng. Doctorate in Mathematical Physics
HOBBIES AND INTERESTS: Reading, tennis, current affairs
PERSONAL PROFILE: Dr Shafi Khan, who was the deputy mayor, took over as the first Asian mayor of Croydon on 17 May 1999. He played a leading role in establishing the Bangladesh Welfare Association's community centre and the opening of a Muslim burial ground in London's most populated borough. He is also a key figure in establishing the Asian Mela as an annual fixture.

SHAHEEN KHAN (Actress-Writer)

Lou Coulson,

PLACE OF BIRTH: Tanzania, 29.2.60
MARITAL STATUS: Married
CHILDREN: Two (Sophie, Nyla)
COLLEGE: Kingston University
ACADEMIC QUALIFICATIONS: BSc Hons Sociology
MEMBERSHIPS: Equity
HONOURS/AWARDS: Films I've been in 'Bhaji on the Beach', 'Flight', 'My Sister Wife'.
HOBBIES AND INTERESTS: Yoga, tennis, entertaining, collecting plates, pottery, skiing, theatre
PERSONAL PROFILE: I've been an actress since I was 16. First TV series was called 'Parosi-Neighbours'. Have done much theatre, TV and film work. Now co-write with Sudha Bhuchar.

MR SHASHA KHAN (Night Club Promotions)

Head Promoter, Poodle Chaos, 35A Windmill Road, Croydon, CR0 2XR

PLACE OF BIRTH: Islington, 14.3.72
MARITAL STATUS: Single
COLLEGE: Wolverhampton University
ACADEMIC QUALIFICATIONS: BA Hons Politics & Economics
HOBBIES AND INTERESTS: Deejaying, dance music
PERSONAL PROFILE: I am the head promoter of a night club promotions outfit by the name of Poodle Chaos. We have firmly established ourselves in the London house music scene by putting on parties at universities and nightclubs. In addition all our profits go to charities such as Amnesty International.
NOMINATED BY: James Saunders and Poodle Chaos

DR SHER AFZAL KHAN (Consultant Acupuncture)

Acupuncturist, Pakistan Welfare Association, 32 Malmesbury Road, Small Heath, Birmingham, B10 0JQ

PLACE OF BIRTH: Pakistan, 17.8.24
MARITAL STATUS: Married
CHILDREN: Four (Khalid, Shahid, Saeeda, Farkhanda)
COLLEGE: Punjab University, Chinese College of Acupuncture
ACADEMIC QUALIFICATIONS: Registered Medical Practitioner (Pakistan) Dr Acupuncture China
PROFESSIONAL QUALIFICATIONS: DHO, DHY and Dr Acupuncture. Registered Medical Practitioner (Pakistan)
DIRECTORSHIPS: Small Heath Forum and Rathbone Trust
MEMBERSHIPS: Labour Party, PWA, Muslim League Policing Cttee, UK. Pakistan Cultural Association
HONOURS/AWARDS: Highest award in acupunture , Republic of China
HOBBIES AND INTERESTS: Gardening, social services
PERSONAL PROFILE: Started cultural, social and political activities for Asians in 1958 to improve their status, dignity in jobs, business and social status, as well as equal rights and good community relations, acting as pioneer in these fields.
NOMINATED BY: M Ayyub, Muslim League UK

TARIQ AZIZ KHAN (Managing Director)

Midland Catering Company, MCC House, Warner Street, Digbeth, Birmingham B12 OJG

PLACE OF BIRTH: Pakistan, 1.12.56
MARITAL STATUS: Married
CHILDREN: Three (Sara, Nadira, Jamshed)
COLLEGE: Punjab University
ACADEMIC QUALIFICATIONS: BA Statistics
DIRECTORSHIPS: Midland Catering Company
MEMBERSHIPS:
HONOURS/AWARDS:
HOBBIES AND INTERESTS: Travelling, Sports, reading, social work.
PERSONAL PROFILE: Mr Khan moved from Gujuranwala, Pakistan to Frankfurt in 1977. After a spell at the American air base there, he set up a successful business. In 1984 he moved to Britain and a year later he began his catering business from his house. Now, Midland Catering Company is the market leader in the region and employs twenty people and his business is still growing. He is well known in the local community and dedicates a lot of his time to helping those less fortunate than himself. He believes in enjoying life to the maximum and his young, energetic and optimistic approach has been the secret of his success.

MR ZAHIRE KHAN (Software Engineer)

Software Engineer, Nabha Catering, 39 King Street, Maidenhead, SL6 1DZ

PLACE OF BIRTH: Slough, 27.7.70
MARITAL STATUS: Married
COLLEGE: Sunderland University
ACADEMIC QUALIFICATIONS: BSc Information Management
DIRECTORSHIPS: Nabha Catering
HONOURS/AWARDS: London Marathon Medal
HOBBIES AND INTERESTS: Computers, cricket, football, cars
PERSONAL PROFILE: At 26 I ran and completed the London Marathon and raised over £350 for a Third World charity. At 27 I own and run my own catering business in Berkshire. I also work in software for computer consultants 'Logica'. At 25 I set up and still run a cricket club called Elite Cricket Club, I have a Hons. degree in Computers and I love my parents and family. I'm cute and handsome so say the girls.
NOMINATED BY: Asam Dad

> He believes in enjoying life to the maximum and his young, energetic and optimistic approach to life has been the secret of his success
>
> **TARIQ AZIZ KHAN**

MR ZAKIR KHAN (COMMUNITY WORKER)

Co-ordinator, Futures 2000 +, Kingsley Hall, Powis Road, London, E3 3HJ

PLACE OF BIRTH: Bangladesh, 2.2.71
MARITAL STATUS: Married
CHILDREN: Two (Tania, Niyaz)
COLLEGE: University of East London
ACADEMIC QUALIFICATIONS: Diploma Careers Guidance
DIRECTORSHIPS: Millennium Development Corporation
MEMBERSHIPS: Bangladesh Football Association (UK)
HONOURS/AWARDS: Certificates from Mayor of Tower Hamlets Achievement Award, FA football Preliminary Award
HOBBIES AND INTERESTS: Football
PERSONAL PROFILE: A strong and resourceful individual with extensive managerial and frontline experience of numerous local authority and voluntary bodies. I have commitment to working with the local community, empowering local young people and developing both skills and avenues of opportunity. I have very strong interpersonal and communication skills.
NOMINATED BY: Salim Hussain, Bangladesh Football Association

MR AKRAM KHAN-CHEEMA (EDUCATION MANAGEMENT)

Managing Director, MAK-C Consultancy, 50 Oakwood Drive, Bingley, Bradford, BD16 4SJ

PLACE OF BIRTH: Kenya, 3.9.42
MARITAL STATUS: Married
CHILDREN: Three (Umar Manzoor, Fawzia Yasmin, Hamza Imran)
ACADEMIC QUALIFICATIONS: Cert Ed, DASE, M Phil
PROFESSIONAL QUALIFICATIONS: Business Masters (University of Bradford-Management Centre), OfSTED registered inspector
DIRECTORSHIPS: Panorama Enterprises, Bradford, FEF UK Ltd, AMS UK Ltd
MEMBERSHIPS: National Association of Educational Inspectors Advisers and Consultants, Institute of Management, Fellow of the Royal Society of Arts
HOBBIES AND INTERESTS: Watching good quality sports, activities, family life, community service, reading
EMAIL: akram@makcc.force9.co.uk
PERSONAL PROFILE: I came to England in 1960 for full time higher education and qualified as a teacher at Edge Hill College. I taught in several schools until 1979. In September 1979 I was appointed as an inspector of schools with the city of Birmingham. In October 1992 I established the MAK-C Consultancy offering education management, advisory and support services in the UK and overseas.
NOMINATED BY: J N Mirza

DR HARGUNDAS KHANCHANDANI
(MEDICAL PRACTITIONER RTD)

8 Ringwood Road, Luton, LU2 7BG

PLACE OF BIRTH: India, 10.4.23
MARITAL STATUS: Married
CHILDREN: Four (Dr Raj, Mr Vijay, Dr Baiju, Mr Neil)
COLLEGE: Mumbai
PROFESSIONAL QUALIFICATIONS: MBBS
HOBBIES AND INTERESTS: Coin/stamp collection, charity work, writing
PERSONAL PROFILE: Born in a village where there was no school. Still achieved to become a doctor. All my children are successful in their lives and prosperous. I served free for three months in a charitable hospital and organise eye camps in India. I am a trustee of Anandpur Durbar. I write books for charities to raise funds.

MR LALIT KHANNA (SOLICITOR)

London Borough of Waltham Forest, 1 Woodcote Drive, Orpington, BR6 8DB

PLACE OF BIRTH: Pakistan, 29.4.38
MARITAL STATUS: Married
CHILDREN: Two (Deepti, Sandeep)
COLLEGE: Law College UK, Delhi University
ACADEMIC QUALIFICATIONS: BA, LL.B, MBA
PROFESSIONAL QUALIFICATIONS: Advocate, Solicitor
MEMBERSHIPS: Member Law Society, Member Lions International. Royal Overseas League.
HONOURS/AWARDS: Awarded Samar Seva Star
HOBBIES AND INTERESTS: Community service, promotion of equal opps
PERSONAL PROFILE: Experienced employment specialist solicitor with excellent academic background. Came to UK in 1976. Former judge advocate (Navy). Awarded Samar Seva Star and GICA Operations Medal in Naval Operations. Spearheaded equal opportunities initiatives in local authority. Profile appeared in Equal Opportunity Review.

MISS SYEDA KHANOM (STUDENT)

Mulberry School For Girls,

PLACE OF BIRTH: Bangladesh, 21.4.82
MARITAL STATUS: Single
COLLEGE: Mulberry Sixth Form
ACADEMIC QUALIFICATIONS: GCSE A*, 6 A's and 4 B's
HOBBIES AND INTERESTS: Enjoy all sports, meeting different kinds of people
PERSONAL PROFILE: A confident Year 12 A-Level student and an outspoken teenager. I was chosen as part of the Mulberry delegation to represent Britain at the UN student conference in New York, March 1998. I am very ambitious, I hope to complete my A-level courses, go to university and then to conquer the business world.
NOMINATED BY: Alfa Khanom

BEGUM SYEDA SHORIFA KHANOM (BUSINESSWOMAN)

Proprieter, Euston Saree Centre, 100 Hampstead Road, West Euston, London, NW1 2NT

PLACE OF BIRTH: Bangladesh, 17.2.60
MARITAL STATUS: Married
CHILDREN: Four (Shalma, Alom, Akbor, Mehdi (Mahima))
DIRECTORSHIPS: Massala Indian Cuisine
MEMBERSHIPS: BWA
HOBBIES AND INTERESTS: TV, music, community work
PERSONAL PROFILE: I came to UK in 1979. As a housewife, I'm proud of myself. I run a boutique saree shop and a catering business in London. I am involved in community work and I am a member of the BWA Surma Community Centre in Camden. When I retire I wish to continue to serve the Asian community in Britain.
NOMINATED BY: Shaikh Eaoyor

DR BHUPAT RAY KHARA JP (DOCTOR)

Principal GP, 19 Toller Grove, Bradford, BD9 5NS

PLACE OF BIRTH: India, 18.9.34
MARITAL STATUS: Married
CHILDREN: Two (Dr Milan, Miss Mita)
COLLEGE: Calcutta
ACADEMIC QUALIFICATIONS: MBBS, DMRT
PROFESSIONAL QUALIFICATIONS: MBBS, DMRT Justice of the Peace
HONOURS/AWARDS: Justice of the Peace
HOBBIES AND INTERESTS: Travel
PERSONAL PROFILE: Hard working general practitioner for 38 years. Intelligent and very sociable. Appointed to Bench JP, first Asian in Bradford in 1969. Later established business of nursing homes, running three at the same time.

> 'I came to UK in 1979. As a housewife, I'm proud of myself. I run a boutique saree shop and a catering business in London'
>
> **BEGUM SYEDA SHORIFA KHANOM**

> 'Born in a village where there was no school. Still achieved to become a doctor'
>
> **DR HARGUNDAS KHANCHANDANI**

MR MADANLAL THAKOR KHAREGHAT
(Chartered Quantity Surveyor)

Assistant Director of Estates, Coventry University, Priory Street, Coventry, CV1 5FB

PLACE OF BIRTH: India, 1.3.53
MARITAL STATUS: Married
CHILDREN: Two
ACADEMIC QUALIFICATIONS: MSc in Construction Project Management
PROFESSIONAL QUALIFICATIONS: FRICS, FCIOB
MEMBERSHIPS: Fellow Institute of Chartered Builders, Fellow of the Royal Institute of Chartered Surveyors
PERSONAL PROFILE: Responsible for managing major capital building projects including new build, alterations and refurbishment works in excess of £20 million. Involved with Asian community work for over 25 years. Served as an honorary project co-ordinator on a community building project which received a national award (Community Enterprise Award in 1989). Served as an assessor on Community Enterprise Scheme for nine years.
NOMINATED BY: Michael Goldstein CBE, Coventry University

MR ABDUL KHAYUM (Project Management)

Project Development Manager, Rotherham Metropolitan Borough Council, 23 Firshill Road, Sheffield, S4 7BB

PLACE OF BIRTH: Pakistan, 13.7.59
MARITAL STATUS: Married
CHILDREN: Four (Zulfikar, Safrina, Naima, Niqash)
COLLEGE: Sheffield Polytechnic
ACADEMIC QUALIFICATIONS: 7 O-Levels, OND, ENG Technology. Teachers Certificate
PROFESSIONAL QUALIFICATIONS: Personnel Management IPM
MEMBERSHIPS: Institute of Personnel & Development
HOBBIES AND INTERESTS: Reading, voluntary charity work, driving, family, sports
PERSONAL PROFILE: Ten years working with Sheffield's voluntary and community organisations. First manager playing central role in establishing PMC/PEC. First chair-Black Community Forum. Former chair-multi-cultural education service and racial harassment project. Chair-Asian HA, School governing body, Police Liaison (K District). Secretary-Pakistan Promotional Forum. Performed sponsored parachute jump and raised £2200- for Imran Khan Cancer Appeal.

MR CHARANJIT SINGH KHEHRA (Senior Engineer)

Rover Group, 17 Gaveston Road, Leamington Spa, CV32 6EX

PLACE OF BIRTH: England, 17.4.64
MARITAL STATUS: Married
CHILDREN: Two (Manjinder, Amanveer)
PROFESSIONAL QUALIFICATIONS: UEFA 'B' Licence Football Coaching Qualification
HOBBIES AND INTERESTS: Music, football
PERSONAL PROFILE: Qualified as the first Sikh Asian in the world to gain UEFA 'B' Licence football coaching qualifications in May 1997. Due to take final UEFA 'A' Licence exam in 1999. Presently working as the only Sikh in a professional football club (Coventry City) as manager/coach in the youth academy.
NOMINATED BY: Bhajan Singh Aulak

MR ANIL KHOSLA (Town Planner)

Senior Assistant Director Environmental, London Borough of Hounslow, 4 Anthorne Close, Potters Bar, EN6 1RW

PLACE OF BIRTH: Kenya, 14.8.47
MARITAL STATUS: Married
CHILDREN: Two (Nikhil, Meera)
COLLEGE: London University
ACADEMIC QUALIFICATIONS: BSc (Econ), Dip TP Dip Trans.
PROFESSIONAL QUALIFICATIONS: MRTPI
MEMBERSHIPS: Royal Town Planning Institute. Royal Institute of Chartered Surveyors
HOBBIES AND INTERESTS: Tennis, Indian music
PERSONAL PROFILE: Studied at London School of Economics and then achieved professional qualifications in town planning. Worked in local government in London and country (Herts) for over 25 years. Heading a department of nearly 600 staff. Covering major regeneration of Feltham, Hounslow and Brentford. Also involved with London Heathrow's Terminal 5 inquiry.

CLLR ILYAS KHWAJA (Electrical Engineer-Rtd)

Councillor, 15 Denbigh Road, Hounslow, TW3 4DU

PLACE OF BIRTH: Gwallior State, 9.12.33
MARITAL STATUS: Married
CHILDREN: Two (Lubna, Nada)
COLLEGE: Karachi, Open University
ACADEMIC QUALIFICATIONS: BA Hon
PROFESSIONAL QUALIFICATIONS: BA Hon
DIRECTORSHIPS: Hounslow Law Centre Ltd, Hounslow Community Association Ltd
HOBBIES AND INTERESTS: Social & community work, politics, gardening and an interest in archeology
PERSONAL PROFILE: Ilyas has been living in Hounslow for the last forty two years, succeeded in gaining higher engineering qualifications and an honours degree. He was responsible for directly employed and contractor's technical staff for the planning and control of engineering projects. An active trade unionist, representing professionals, managers and specialist staff and has served as a chair of his trade union. Elected as a councillor in 1994.

DR MUHAMMAD SABIR KIANI (Doctor-Rtd)

Medical Practitioner, Communities United, 90 Copland Road, Glasgow, G51 2RR

PLACE OF BIRTH: Pakistan, 7.9.25
MARITAL STATUS: Married
CHILDREN: Five (M.Farooq, M.Zahoor, M.Khushnood, M.Haroon, Sameena Begum)
COLLEGE: Caldonald College, Paisley University
PROFESSIONAL QUALIFICATIONS: Electronic Engineer Hons Degree, BSc Hon
DIRECTORSHIPS: Scottish Homes, Glasgow
MEMBERSHIPS: Community Relations Council Glasgow
HONOURS/AWARDS: In Housing
HOBBIES AND INTERESTS: To help people in need
PERSONAL PROFILE: When I came to Britain 1961 I was refused a job being Black in Dudley, then I came to Glasgow. Here I got a job with Glasgow Transport. I also found various organisations to help the Asian, African Caribbean and Chinese communities. I have fought for five years to get Halal foods accepted and 12 years in housing to get a housing association started.
NOMINATED BY: Maggie Chetty

MS RUKHSANA JABEEN KIANI (Solicitor)

Principal, R Kiani Solicitors, 736 High Road, Leyton, London, E10 6AA

PLACE OF BIRTH: Pakistan, 30.5.59
MARITAL STATUS: Married
COLLEGE: London
ACADEMIC QUALIFICATIONS: LLM, BA Hons Law
PROFESSIONAL QUALIFICATIONS: Solicitor UK. Advocate Pakistan
MEMBERSHIPS: Chairperson of Home-Start LB Waltham Forest
HOBBIES AND INTERESTS: Photography, interior decorating, current affairs, travelling
EMAIL: kiani@talk21.com
PERSONAL PROFILE: Qualified UK lawyer of 14 years. Very dedicated and hardworking. In practise on own account after working in Central London with major national and international companies as their legal adviser. Very active in community social work in LB of Waltham Forest as chairperson of Home Start LBWF and assistant treasurer of Asian Centre LBWF. Very committed supporter.
NOMINATED BY: Khalid I Bhatti

DR ANANTA VENKATACHARY KIDAMBI
(Consultant Radiologist)

District General Hospital, 15 Hardwick Court, Hartlepool, TS24 9AH

PLACE OF BIRTH: India, 1.5.46
MARITAL STATUS: Married
CHILDREN: Two (Deepali, Ajay)
COLLEGE: Nagpur University, India
ACADEMIC QUALIFICATIONS: BSc, MBBS, DMRD, FRCR,(London) FFRRCSI (Dublin)
PROFESSIONAL QUALIFICATIONS: FRCR (London), FFRCSI (Dublin)
DIRECTORSHIPS: Previously Director of Acute Services & Medical Director
MEMBERSHIPS: BMA, Fellow Royal College of Radiologists
HOBBIES AND INTERESTS: Music, travel
PERSONAL PROFILE: Consultant radiologist in NHS over 20 years. Held senior positions in NHS: Clinical director; Director of Acute Services; Medical director; Acting Chief Executive; Also previously, chairman ODA in N.Ireland. Currently assessor in radiology for General Medical Council.

MS RANI ANNE KING (EDITOR-CIVIL SERVANT)

Editor, Department For Education And Employment, Feedback Magazine, Sanctuary Buildings, Gt Smith Street, London, SW1P 3BT

PLACE OF BIRTH: Bangkok, 25.10.50
MARITAL STATUS: Divorced
CHILDREN: Two (Justin, Julian)
ACADEMIC QUALIFICATIONS: 6 O-Level's
PROFESSIONAL QUALIFICATIONS: Various catering ones, housekeeping, catering, nutrition, hygiene
DIRECTORSHIPS: Tiger Lily Products Ltd, Hard Wok Cafe. King and Khan Enterprises.
HONOURS/AWARDS: Won Best Staff Magazine of the Year 1997.
HOBBIES AND INTERESTS: Cookery, writing, reading, enjoying life
EMAIL: info@dfee.gov.uk
PERSONAL PROFILE: I combine running several food related careers (including TV presentation), with my role as editor of the DfEE's staff magazine. A year ago we won a best magazine award (the first time for a government organisation). I am the first non-white woman editor in Whitehall.
NOMINATED BY: Bernadette Hillon, DFEE

KAPTIN KIRK (ARTIST)

Singer,

MEMBERSHIPS: PRS
HONOURS/AWARDS: Movie Bhangra Pop Award 1996
PERSONAL PROFILE: Apart from playing all over the country on the bhangra scene, Kaptin Kirk has also supported Toyah, Worlds Apart and Ultimate Kaos at mainstream gigs. He has been featured on various mainstream TV programmes, such as the Big Breakfast, Central News, Tribute to Bob Marley (Carlton) and Premier (Central TV). He had a big article in the Sun newspaper, the Sunday People and the Daily Star.

MR KUMARAVELU KIRUBAKARAN (CIVIL ENGINEER)

Director, The Institute of Civil Engineers, London Millennium Limited, 2 Borwick Avenue, London, E17 6RA

PLACE OF BIRTH: Sri Lanka, 17.1.48
MARITAL STATUS: Divorced
CHILDREN: One (Jessie)
COLLEGE: Hackney College
ACADEMIC QUALIFICATIONS: Auto Cad, Sel Tec, Dip in Mec. Eng.
PROFESSIONAL QUALIFICATIONS: BSc in Civil Engineering
DIRECTORSHIPS: Thames Limited and London Millennium Limited
MEMBERSHIPS: The Institution of Civil Engineers
HOBBIES AND INTERESTS: Interior design, fashion design, astrology, catering, magic, illusion
PERSONAL PROFILE: I was offered by 'Thames Water' a few thousands to buy the name 'Thames Limited' and I expect to get a good deal for the 'London Millennium Limited' name. I can compute mentally the first day of any millennium, century and decade in about 30 seconds. Ability to compute the day of any date. I drew the 'Solar system' with astrological symbols. Scale 1:20,000,000,000,000.
NOMINATED BY: Ms Kanak

MR SEWA SINGH KOHLI MBE (TRAVEL AGENT)

Director, Kohli Travels, 228 Woodland Road, Glasgow, G3 6LN

PLACE OF BIRTH: India, 13.5.19
MARITAL STATUS: Married
CHILDREN: Three (Pushpinder Kaur, Harpreet Singh, Aman Parkash Singh)
COLLEGE: Punjab University, Lahore
ACADEMIC QUALIFICATIONS: Honours in Oriental Languages
PROFESSIONAL QUALIFICATIONS: Passed four year course Institute of Shipping & Forwarding
DIRECTORSHIPS: Kohli Travel
MEMBERSHIPS: Chairperson Mel-Milaap Centre
HONOURS/AWARDS: MBE-Lifetime achiever award , Glasgow Chamber of Commerce
HOBBIES AND INTERESTS: Social, community work
PERSONAL PROFILE: I am founder member of Asian Arts and Mel-Milaap Elderly Day Care Centre Glasgow. Scottish Marriage Law was discriminatory against immigrants. After a prolonged struggle the law was changed. I was the main mover of this campaign.
NOMINATED BY: Mr G S Puri

MR DINESH KOTECHA (ACCOUNTANT-PROPERTY DIRECTOR)

County Property Officer, Northamptonshire County Council, Janki Nivas, 8 Watson Close, Wellingborough, NN8 5UH

PLACE OF BIRTH: Malawi, 29.7.56
MARITAL STATUS: Married
CHILDREN: One (Janki)
COLLEGE: Leicester University
ACADEMIC QUALIFICATIONS: Master of Business Administration
PROFESSIONAL QUALIFICATIONS: Certified Chartered Accountant
DIRECTORSHIPS: Non-exec director of Kettering General Hospital
MEMBERSHIPS: British Institute of Facilities Management
HOBBIES AND INTERESTS: Travelling, community/voluntary work, volleyball
PERSONAL PROFILE: Community leader and activist with over twenty years contribution to racial equality, Hindu community development and the voluntary sector. A qualified accountant and business graduate. Dinesh is a senior officer in local government and also a non-executive director of an NHS Trust Hospital.

MRS JAYMINI KOTECHA (SOCIAL WORKER)

Northants County Council Social Care & Health, Janki Nivas, 8 Watson Close, Wellingborough, NN8 5UH

PLACE OF BIRTH: Uganda, 8.3.60
MARITAL STATUS: Married
CHILDREN: One (Janki)
COLLEGE: Coventry University
ACADEMIC QUALIFICATIONS: Bachelor of Arts
PROFESSIONAL QUALIFICATIONS: Diploma in Social Work
HOBBIES AND INTERESTS: Travelling, cooking, walking, craft activities
PERSONAL PROFILE: Over 15 years experience of the voluntary and statutory sectors through racial equality, community development and child protective work. Led the establishment of a family centre and helped initiate several projects for Asian elders including a day centre and a sheltered accommodation scheme.

VINODKUMAR BHANULAL KOTECHA (COMMUNITY DEVELOPMENT)

Regional Co-Ordinator, Confedertion of Indian Organisations (UK), CIO, 24 Imperial House, St Nicholas Circle, Leicester, LE1 4LF

PLACE OF BIRTH: Uganda, 1.5.49
MARITAL STATUS: Married
CHILDREN: Two (Deepak, Sunil)
COLLEGE: Open University
ACADEMIC QUALIFICATIONS: Diploma in Pharmacy
PROFESSIONAL QUALIFICATIONS: Certificate in Management
DIRECTORSHIPS: Treasurer Asra Midland Housing Association.
MEMBERSHIPS: Trustee Age Concern Leicestershire & Rutland. Ex Lohana Boarder Association.
HOBBIES AND INTERESTS: Cricket, badminton, volleyball
PERSONAL PROFILE: Born and brought up in Buigiri, Uganda. Diploma in Pharmacy in India. Lived in Leicester since 1975. Developed extensive links with voluntary and statutory sector. Set up East West Community Project. Developed first Asian daycare centre in Leicestershire. Working as regional co-ordinator for Confederation of Indian Organisations (UK).
NOMINATED BY: S Raja

MR ABDUL KOYSOR (FOOTBALLER)

Junior Professional Footballer, c/o 9C Frederick Street, King's Cross, Camden, London, WC1X 0NF

PLACE OF BIRTH: Bangladesh, 7.4.86
MARITAL STATUS: Single
COLLEGE: Holloway School
HONOURS/AWARDS: School-Player of the Year, pupil of the term and many trophies
HOBBIES AND INTERESTS: I like playing football, snooker, pool, swimming
EMAIL: Ashrahman@hotmail.com
PERSONAL PROFILE: I have been playing football since the age of eight years old. I started playing for my school team and King's Cross Lithgow. My first professional club was Leyton Orient FC under-13's. I also play for district team, Camden and Islington. I have a personal boot sponsor, Puma UK.
NOMINATED BY: Ash Rahman

MR RANJIT KRISHNAMMA (Actor-Screenwriter)

Workshop Leader, Frazer-Skemp Management, Newclose House, Watergate Road, Newport, Isle Of Wight, PO30 1YP

PLACE OF BIRTH: Isle Of Wight, 16.10.59
MARITAL STATUS: Single
COLLEGE: Welsh College of Music and Drama
PROFESSIONAL QUALIFICATIONS: BEd, ACCA, DMS
HOBBIES AND INTERESTS: Sky diving, exploring the wild, scuba diving, bunjee jumping, guitar, marathons, running
PERSONAL PROFILE: Ranjit regularly appears in TV, film, theatre and radio. He has written and produced two plays for theatre and one full length screenplay. He is currently working on his debut novel. His greatest joy is leading courses such as Mastery for the Institute of Creativity.

PANDIT KESHAVA CHANDRA KRISHNATREYA
(Brahmin Priest)

Krishna Yoga Mandir, Mandir, 57 Balham Road, Edmonton, London, N9 7AH

PLACE OF BIRTH: India, 2.6.27
MARITAL STATUS: Married
CHILDREN: One (Divya)
COLLEGE: Allahabad University, London University
ACADEMIC QUALIFICATIONS: BA, MA (Geog), BEd, M.Ed, MA (Ed), DPEd, Indian DPEd
PROFESSIONAL QUALIFICATIONS: Sir William Houghton Research Scholar
DIRECTORSHIPS: Founder-Director Krishna Yoga Mandir

HONOURS/AWARDS: Hundreds
HOBBIES AND INTERESTS: Yoga, literary writing and poetry on Hinduism
PERSONAL PROFILE: My departed father was the founder of MMH College, Ghaziabad my birth town. After having finished education mostly from the University of Allahabad-India, taught in schools and colleges and served as PE supervisor-Delhi. Migrated in 1968. Taught up to A-Level; ILEA advisory teacher for Hinduism. No one can beat me on the scriptural knowledge of Hinduism, including yoga.

MR ASHOK KUMAR MP (Member of Parliament)

British Steel Technical Teeside Laboratories, Constituency Office, 6-8 Wilson Street, Guisborough, TS14 6NA

DATE OF BIRTH: 28.5.56
COLLEGE: Rykneld School for Boys, Derby, Aston University,
ACADEMIC QUALIFICATIONS: Chemical Engineering (BSc), Process Analysis and Control Theory (MSc), Fluid Mechanics (PhD)
PROFESSIONAL QUALIFICATIONS: Chartered Engineer, Institution of Chemical Engineers, Institute of Energy
MEMBERSHIPS: Research Fellow, Imperial College, London 1982-85, Councillor, Middlesborough Borough Council 1987-97. Member of Parliamentary Scientific Committee. Also member of PLP Trade and Industry Committee,
HOBBIES AND INTERESTS: Cricket, badminton, reading history and philosophy, listening to jazz
PERSONAL PROFILE: Member of Science and Technology Select Committee. Board Member of Parliamentary Office of Science and Technology (POST). PLP Treasury Committee, PLP Education and Employment Committee, PLP Job Creation Group. Secretary of All Party Parliamentary Group for the chemical industry. Secretary of All Party Parliamentary Group on Skin.

MR ASHOK KUMAR (Actor)

Sandra Griffin Management, 6 Ryde Place, Richmond Road, East Twickenham, TW1 2EH

PLACE OF BIRTH: Birmingham, 4.8.66
MARITAL STATUS: Married
CHILDREN: Four (Jamie, Hariet, Aaron, Mia)
COLLEGE: Redroof Theatre School
PROFESSIONAL QUALIFICATIONS: Teacher Diploma Drama
MEMBERSHIPS: Equity
HOBBIES AND INTERESTS: Swimming, riding
PERSONAL PROFILE: Determined to break down barriers within the film industry. Therefore creating a better understanding about alls equal, for equals.

MR PRAVESH KUMAR (Actor)

Magnolia Management, The Reduced Indian Film Co, 6 Trojan Court, 161 Willesden Lane, London, NW6 7SH

PLACE OF BIRTH: Slough, 9.9.70
MARITAL STATUS: Single
COLLEGE: Academy of Live & Recorded Arts
ACADEMIC QUALIFICATIONS: Actors Degree
EMAIL: prav60@aol.com
PERSONAL PROFILE: Pravesh has just completed his work with Tamasha's '14 Songs 2 Weddings and a Funeral' Based on the Bollywood Movie 'Hum Apke Hain Kaun' in which he played the lead 'Prem'. The company received 'BBC Achievement in Art' award. Pravesh has set up his own production company, producing two new plays into the Millennium-looking to move into film' Pravesh has a role in a Hollywood movie 'The perfumed garden', he is the lead. He has also worked extensively in theatre.

MR SURESH KUMAR (Travel Agent)

Chairman, Indra Travel, 791 Romford Road, Manor Park, London, E12 5AN

PLACE OF BIRTH: Essex, 15.2.63
MARITAL STATUS: Married
CHILDREN: Two (Megha Kumar, Ektaa Kumar)
COLLEGE: Seven Kings High School, Ilford
DIRECTORSHIPS: Chairman-Indra Travel, Ilford south Conservative Association
MEMBERSHIPS: ISCA, Redbridge Cultural Association, Redbridge Punjabi Centre
HONOURS/AWARDS: 1st prize for London Parade 1999 Redbridge, various awards and merits in sports, various awards for community work. Award for youth development in Redbridge. Punjab Centre for sports and services to all the communities of Redbridge
HOBBIES AND INTERESTS: Sports, politics, entertainment
PERSONAL PROFILE: A pioneer for the cause of the youth in arts and entertainment. Raises money for various charities and care and assistance for the elderly. Worked for all communities of Redbridge.

MR SURJIT KUMAR JP (Consultant-IFA)

1 Larkshall Road, Chingford, London, E4 7HS

PLACE OF BIRTH: Gujranwala, 1.11.40
MARITAL STATUS: Married
CHILDREN: Two (Sunil FRCS, Sanjoy MBBS)
ACADEMIC QUALIFICATIONS: MA
PROFESSIONAL QUALIFICATIONS: Fellow of the Institute of Management (FI Mgt.)
HONOURS/AWARDS: Silver Medalist Punjab University
HOBBIES AND INTERESTS: Oil painting, photography, gardening
EMAIL: kumar@surjit.demon.co.uk
PERSONAL PROFILE: Retired as a colonel from the Indian army. Now works as an Independent Financial Adviser for OWA Consultancy. Wife is a general practitioner. Elder son is an orthopaedic surgeon and the younger is a general practitioner (GP).

MS KRISHNA KUMARI-BOWLES (Actress)

Alvarez Management, 86 Muswell Road, Muswell Hill, London, N10 2BE

PLACE OF BIRTH: Kenya, 14.5.67
MARITAL STATUS: Married
COLLEGE: Rose Bruford College of Speech and Drama
ACADEMIC QUALIFICATIONS: BA Hons Theatre and Arts
MEMBERSHIPS: Equity, Musician's Union, Screenwriter Workshop
HOBBIES AND INTERESTS: Dance, drama, reading, horse-riding, fencing
EMAIL: karmaltd@aol.com
PERSONAL PROFILE: Working actress for eight years till present. After being trained at Rose Bruford College of Speech and Drama. Written many short films and two screenplays. Currently writing another and adapting one for theatre. Ten minute stage play was shortlisted for the Westminster Prize. Also performs Egyptian Dance.

August 22 1997: The world mourns the death of the qawwali king Nusrat Fateh Ali Khan. The maestro died in England whilst on route to the US for a kidney transplant. Tributes flood in for the irreplaceable performer who lost his life aged only 48

PROF SAJAL LAHIRI (PROFESSOR OF ECONOMICS)

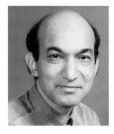

Professor of Economics, University Of Essex, 70 The Avenue, Wivenhoe Park, Colchester, CO7 9AL

PLACE OF BIRTH: India, 10.11.50
MARITAL STATUS: Married
CHILDREN: Three (Subhaneil, Onoshua, Naomi)
COLLEGE: Indian Statistical Institute
ACADEMIC QUALIFICATIONS: PhD
MEMBERSHIPS: Royal Economic Society, Econometric Society
HOBBIES AND INTERESTS: Music, reading
EMAIL: lahiri@essex.ac.uk

PERSONAL PROFILE: Educated in India and living in the UK since 1977. Has published several academic articles in leading international journals in economics. Chairing a Royal Society working party on ethnic representation in economics.
NOMINATED BY: Christine A Bartram, University of Essex

DR AMIR LAKHA (DOCTOR)

General Practitioner, KSIM Community of London, Wood Lane, PO Box 60, Stanmore, HA7 4FB

PLACE OF BIRTH: Kenya, 17.6.49
MARITAL STATUS: Married
CHILDREN: Three (Riyaz, Fatema, Mohammed)
COLLEGE: University of Nairobi
ACADEMIC QUALIFICATIONS: MB, Ch B, DPM (RCP Lond & RCS Eng)
PROFESSIONAL QUALIFICATIONS: MB, Ch B, DPM (RCP Lond & RCS Eng)
DIRECTORSHIPS: Mayfair Imperial Publishers

HONOURS/AWARDS: Husaini Medal
HOBBIES AND INTERESTS: Golf, tennis, writing, charity work
PERSONAL PROFILE: Dr Amir Lakha is a general practitioner with outstanding qualities in community work. Public speaking, charitable work and he has a vast network of friends in all communities worldwide. He established the Senior Citizens Association for Muslims. He was awarded the Husaini Medal for meritorious services to the Muslim community. Author of world renowned book. 'Heads you win-Tails you win.'

CLLR RAM PRAKASH LAKHA (COUNCILLOR)

Coventry City Council, 74 Harefield Road, Coventry, CV2 4BY

PLACE OF BIRTH: India, 4.1.49
MARITAL STATUS: Married
CHILDREN: Three (Amarpreet, Mandeep, Jagdeep)
COLLEGE: Ramgarhia College-Phagwara
ACADEMIC QUALIFICATIONS: BA Punjab University, Chandigarh
PROFESSIONAL QUALIFICATIONS: Supervisory Management
MEMBERSHIPS: Labour Party

HOBBIES AND INTERESTS: Civic/publicity/community hobbies-walking, reading
PERSONAL PROFILE: I was elected in May 1989 as councillor for Coventry City Council. I was ward secretary for Labour Party for few years and also vice chair of constituency Labour Party - and executive member of District Labour Party. I was chairman of voluntary sector and community committee and vice chair of property management committee for three years. I was secretary of Shri Guru Ravidass Temple for six years and national president of Shri Guru Ravidass Sabha UK in 1981-82.

MISS POONAM LAKHANI (STUDENT)

2 Epsom Road, Leicester, LE4 5DB

PLACE OF BIRTH: Leicester, 13.8.83
DIRECTORSHIPS: Teacher/director of various dance and drama pieces.
HOBBIES AND INTERESTS: Dance, community work, films, music, writing letters
PERSONAL PROFILE: I'm a unique youth as I've already acclaimed a high level of recognition for myself. I've scripted, directed and acted in bilingual dramas. I choreograph and teach dances which have been on television. I take initiative and lead in community activities and I'm one who's going to hit it big!
NOMINATED BY: Mr Tarsem S Dhillon

MR ARCHIE LAL (ACTOR)

Royal Shakespeare Company, 8 Bridge Street, Bretforton, Evesham, WR11 5SD

PLACE OF BIRTH: Glasgow, 4.11.62
MARITAL STATUS: Single
COLLEGE: East London Acting School
ACADEMIC QUALIFICATIONS: Diploma
DIRECTORSHIPS: Directed BTC sponsored by RSC
HOBBIES AND INTERESTS: Music, sport, poetry writing
PERSONAL PROFILE: I've always been interested in the arts, even at school I'd sing to the class at the first opportunity. After leaving school I travelled to Europe, the Middle East, Asia and the US. I attended drama school in 1988-91. I've been offered the present Eastern mix.

DR PYARE LAL (SURGEON)

Staff Surgeon A & E, The Hillingdon Hospital NHS Trust, Field Heath Road, Uxbridge, UB8 3NN

PLACE OF BIRTH: India, 15.5.46
MARITAL STATUS: Married
CHILDREN: Two (Rashmi, Prashant)
COLLEGE: King George's Medical College, Lucknow University
ACADEMIC QUALIFICATIONS: MBBS
PROFESSIONAL QUALIFICATIONS: FRCS (Edinburgh), FRCS (Glasgow), FRCS (Ireland), FICS (USA)

MEMBERSHIPS: Founder Member of World Association Hepato-Pancreato-Bilary Surgery, Member International Physicians for Nuclear Disarmament
HONOURS/AWARDS: Merit Award passing 1st Division UP Board High School
HOBBIES AND INTERESTS: Social work, politics, Indian music, cinema
PERSONAL PROFILE: Coming from a small village (Patari) in India. I graduated in medicine from King George's Medical College, Lucknow. After FRCS (UK) I worked as specialist surgeon in UK and Saudi Arabia. I take keen interest in progress and politics of India. Like millions of Indians I want to build a progressive, prosperous, strong, peaceful modern India-an India of our dreams.
NOMINATED BY: Prashant L Lal

MR TARSAME SINGH LALERIYA (RECORDING ARTIST)

Director, Sub Dub Records Ltd, PO Box 3340, Birmingham, B20 2NN

PLACE OF BIRTH: Coventry, 23.5.67
MARITAL STATUS: Married
CHILDREN: One (Serina)
ACADEMIC QUALIFICATIONS: 9 O-Levels, 2 A-Levels
DIRECTORSHIPS: Sub Dub Records Ltd
MEMBERSHIPS: PRS, MCPS, PPL, MU, PAMRA, AUORA BASCA
HONOURS/AWARDS: Best Mainstream Artist 1997 & 1998, Best Fusion Artist 1994 - UK Asian Pop Awards

HOBBIES AND INTERESTS: Swimming, painting, drawing, photography
EMAIL: sub.dub@virgin.net
WEB SITE: www.subdub.com
PERSONAL PROFILE: Tarsame Singh aka Taz, the artist formerly known as Johnny Zee. Described as the prince of bhangra pop fusion, a lyricist, composer and producer. He became the embodiment of the futuristic dimension of cross cultural music. His music is best described as a hybrid of Punjabi folk, Hindi and English fused with Western pop sensibility, infectious melodies and dynamic dance and RnB grooves.
NOMINATED BY: Kiran Lyall

MR LALI (SCHOOLBOY-DANCER)

DATE OF BIRTH: 10.2.87
COLLEGE: Studio Bollywood, The Harlequin Agency and Honey's Dance Academy
PERSONAL PROFILE: Has appeared on Zee TV, Asianet and Namaste TV both as a guest and as a performer and has attended many auditions for roles in films and television through his involvement with the Harlequin Agency and Theatre School. He also features in 'Spotlight'- the independent

NOMINATED BY: Indira Mahun

MR D B LALL (Chartered Accountant)

Partner: Lall Ondhia, Lall & Co, Chartered Accountants, 10 Station Road, Manor Park, London, E12 5BT

PLACE OF BIRTH: Bannu, 16.4.33
MARITAL STATUS: Married
CHILDREN: One (Deesha)
COLLEGE: Calcutta University
ACADEMIC QUALIFICATIONS: Bachelor of Science
PROFESSIONAL QUALIFICATIONS: Fellow of Institute of Chartered Accountants in England and Wales.
DIRECTORSHIPS: Crestwood Investments Plc
MEMBERSHIPS: Assoc. of Cost and Management Accountants
HOBBIES AND INTERESTS: Golf, reading
PERSONAL PROFILE: Founder chairman of Newham Asian Business Association. Senior vice-chairman of Newham Chamber of Commerce. Board member of East London Partnership.

MR ASHOK LAMBA (General Manager)

General Manager Term 1/2, Granada Retail Catering Ltd, Room 230 Terminal Two Office, Heathrow Airport, Hounslow, TW6 1QG

PLACE OF BIRTH: Kenya, 26.11.56
MARITAL STATUS: Married
CHILDREN: Two (Rohit, Nilesh)
COLLEGE: Slough College
ACADEMIC QUALIFICATIONS: C&G 706 1/2
PROFESSIONAL QUALIFICATIONS: Staff Trainer, Group Training Techniques, Beer Cellar Management, Quality through Hygenie
MEMBERSHIPS: Hindu temple
HONOURS/AWARDS: Company 20 years service
HOBBIES AND INTERESTS: Golf, football, cricket
PERSONAL PROFILE: Married age 42 with two children. Have worked for Forte/Granada catering for 22 years. Started as grill cook and worked at Heathrow, Luton and Southend Airports with various duties and job titles from headchef to general manager. At Heathrow Terminal 1 and Terminal 2. Looking after nine operations, 70 staff, 30,000 meals per week and £5.4 million turnover.
NOMINATED BY: Michael Pile, Granada Retail Catering

DR PUSHPA LATA (Research Scientist)

Adviser, 23 Salisbury Road, Forest Gate, London, E7 9JX

PLACE OF BIRTH: India, 1.5.42
MARITAL STATUS: Married
CHILDREN: Two (Ashish Singh, Ajay)
COLLEGE: QMC University, London University
ACADEMIC QUALIFICATIONS: BSc, MSc, PhD
PROFESSIONAL QUALIFICATIONS: PhD Cytogenetics in Roses
HONOURS/AWARDS: Published over 25 research papers in scientific journals
HOBBIES AND INTERESTS: Travel, photography, reading, sports
PERSONAL PROFILE: Born and educated in India. Worked as a scientist for 11 years before coming to UK in 1974. Completed PhD degree on 'Cytogenetics of Roses' from the University of London. Published over 25 research papers in International scientific journals. For last 14 years working with Citizens Advice Bureau Services.
NOMINATED BY: Dr S Ahmed

MR JOHN LEHAL (Political Lobbyist)

Parliamentary Researcher, House of Commons, 31 Great Peter Street, Westminster, London, SW1P 3LR

PLACE OF BIRTH: Hertfordshire, 1.4.73
MARITAL STATUS: Single
COLLEGE: Greenwich University, Cambridge University
ACADEMIC QUALIFICATIONS: BA Hons Economics, PGCE Mathematics
HOBBIES AND INTERESTS: Cinema, family and friends, following sport, current affairs
PERSONAL PROFILE: John was Labour's parliamentary candidate in North East Bedfordshire at the last general election. Aged 24, he was Labour's youngest parliamentary candidate in England. He achieved a swing of 15% and reduced the Tory majority to 5,000 votes in a rock solid Tory seat! John's experience at this young age has guaranteed a long future in British politics. For two years John worked as Parliamentary Researcher to the Labour MP for Luton South, Margaret Moran, before moving into public affairs.
NOMINATED BY: North East Bedfordshire Labour Party

MR JANDU LITTERWALA (International Lyricist)

Poet

PERSONAL PROFILE: Jandu Litterwala is a master of Punjabi songwriting. He started to write songs in 1968 following in his brother's footsteps. Now after three decades, countless hits and numerous accolades, his unique style of writing is more popular than ever. He has worked within Punjabi music to promote its language and culture through the world's best music directors and singers.

DR RAJINDER KAUR LOTAY (Doctor)

GP, 104 Moulsham Street, Chelmsford, CM2 0JG

PLACE OF BIRTH: India, 27.3.55
COLLEGE: Wales University, London University, Manchester University
ACADEMIC QUALIFICATIONS: MBBCh, MSc, PhD
PERSONAL PROFILE: Duke of Edinburgh Award 1973. Radio broadcaster Essex Radio Helpline 1982.

MR BADRUL LUDI (University Lecturer)

Senior Lecturer, London Guildhall University, Calcutta House, Old Castle Street, London, E1 7NT

PLACE OF BIRTH: Bangladesh, 31.12.51
MARITAL STATUS: Married
CHILDREN: Three (Selina, Atif, Sima)
COLLEGE: Bangladesh, London School of Accountancy, Greenwich University, London Guildhall University
ACADEMIC QUALIFICATIONS: B. Com, M.Com (Prel) Acctg Cert. Ed, PGCE
PROFESSIONAL QUALIFICATIONS: MAAT, ACEA, ABIM, AIDPM
DIRECTORSHIPS: Mitali Housing Assoc Ltd
HOBBIES AND INTERESTS: Music, reading, IT in small enterprises
EMAIL: ludi@lgu.ac.uk
WEB SITE: www.lgu.ac.uk
PERSONAL PROFILE: Involved in community work for over ten years. Treasurer, East London Bangladeshi Enterprise Agency. Treasurer, Jalalbad Overseas Organisation. Advisor Camden Bangladeshi Education Centre, Trustee, St. Hilda's Community East 1990-95.
NOMINATED BY: Shofi Ahmed, YGF

MR TONY SINGH LUTHER (Property Management)

Consultant, The Funjabis (Asian Comedy Group), www.funjabis.com

PLACE OF BIRTH: London, 9.3.65
MARITAL STATUS: Married
COLLEGE: University of Glamorgan
ACADEMIC QUALIFICATIONS: HND Accountancy
MEMBERSHIPS: Hampstead Garden Suburbs, Theatre Production Company, The Funjabis
HOBBIES AND INTERESTS: Theatre, stand-up Asian comedy
EMAIL: sody@funjabis.com
WEB SITE: www.funjabis.com
PERSONAL PROFILE: Tony is a member of the Funjabis who within two years, have performed to almost 10,000 people including the Edinburgh Festival, Leicester Comedy Festival, theatre TV and radio. Tony is also one of UK's leading Asian stand-up comedians. The Funjabis are part of 'One Nation Under a Groove'.

MISS PRIYA LYALL (Schoolgirl)

PLACE OF BIRTH: Sidcup, 11.2.90
COLLEGE: Longlands CP School
PROFESSIONAL QUALIFICATIONS: Swimming Certificates
MEMBERSHIPS: Brownies, St Johns Ambulance, School Choir
HOBBIES AND INTERESTS: Swimming, reading, bhangra, Indian films, dancing, writing Hindi songs, poems
PERSONAL PROFILE: When I was five, I had a poem published, called 'My Dad'. I did a dance in front of 500 people in Canada. I sang at the Royal Festival Hall last year and am going to sing there again this year. I am trying to write a film called 'Pooja Pooja Ta Thin Chor' for which I have already written two songs.
NOMINATED BY: Bimla Lyall

MR BASHIR AHMED MAAN JP (Councillor-Rtd)

Glasgow City Council, 8 Riverview Gardens, Glasgow, G5 8EL

PLACE OF BIRTH: Pakistan, 20.10.26
MARITAL STATUS: Divorced
CHILDREN: Four (Rashda, Tariq, Haimah, Aalya)
COLLEGE: Punjab University. Strathclyde University
ACADEMIC QUALIFICATIONS: MSc
DIRECTORSHIPS: Retired company director
MEMBERSHIPS: Fellow of the Royal Society of Arts and Commerce (FRSA)
HONOURS/AWARDS: Justice of the Peace 1968, Deputy Lord Lieutenant City of Glasgow.
HOBBIES AND INTERESTS: Golf, reading, writing
PERSONAL PROFILE: Active in the struggle for creation of Pakistan 1943-45. Settled in Glasgow 1953. Elected city councillor 1970. Magistrate of City of Glasgow 1971-74. Chair Police Committee 1973-75. Deputy chair, Commission for Racial Equality 1977-80. Chair Strathclyde Community Relations Council 1986-96. Joint governor, Christian Muslim Forum, Scotland 1995. Member Central Working Group. The Muslim Council of Britain.
NOMINATED BY: N A Arif, Scottish Pakistani Association

MR FARIDOON MADON MBE (Civil Service Rtd)

Active Campaigner, 1 Salisbury Mansions, St Ann's Road, London, N15 3JP

PLACE OF BIRTH: India, 20.12.30
MARITAL STATUS: Single
COLLEGE: Osmania University
ACADEMIC QUALIFICATIONS: MA, LL.B, B.Com
PROFESSIONAL QUALIFICATIONS: Ex-Advocate, AP Bar Council & Chartered Secretary
DIRECTORSHIPS: Tottenham Legal Advice Centre
MEMBERSHIPS: Haringey Racial Equality Council
HONOURS/AWARDS: MBE For Services to Community
HOBBIES AND INTERESTS: Community services, current affairs
PERSONAL PROFILE: First chairman of Haringey CRC. Elected to JCWI Executive, London Association of CRCs, GLARE and SCORE. Founder member and ex-vice chair of Haringey Community/Police Consultative Group; Life member ZTFE. Founder/President of North London Zoroastrian Association. Member CRE's Advisory Group on National Review of REC's. Member, Haringey CHC and first lay chair Voluntary Sector JCC.

DR SHIRIN MADON-MICHAEL (Lecturer)

London School of Economics & Political Science, Houghton Street, London, WC2A 2AE

PLACE OF BIRTH: London, 2.7.58
MARITAL STATUS: Married
CHILDREN: One (Priya Michael)
COLLEGE: Kingston University; Imperial College
ACADEMIC QUALIFICATIONS: BA (Econ), MSc Infotech, PhD Information Systems
PROFESSIONAL QUALIFICATIONS: Inst. of Linguists Associate Member (French)
PERSONAL PROFILE: Shirin Madon is a Parsee living in London. She is married with one child and works as a lecturer in information systems at the LSE. She researches the impact of information technology on developing countries focusing on India and has written several articles on the subject.
NOMINATED BY: Yvette Ankrah, London School of Economics & Science

CAPTAIN (DR) JAISHAN MAHAN (Captain-Doctor)

Army Medical Officer, Army, Garrison Officers Mess, Hospital Road, Aldershot, GU11 2AN

PLACE OF BIRTH: Sri Lanka, 9.3.74
MARITAL STATUS: Single
COLLEGE: University of Leicester
ACADEMIC QUALIFICATIONS: MBChB Medicine
PROFESSIONAL QUALIFICATIONS: ACLS, MIMMS, PHEC
MEMBERSHIPS: Basics
HONOURS/AWARDS: BBC Asia awards 98, Young Achievers Army Cadetship / Commission 1994
HOBBIES AND INTERESTS: Mountaineering, rowing, travel and scuba diving
PERSONAL PROFILE: Medicine has always been my career choice. However I also have many other interests. A keen mountaineer I have led expeditions to South America and Africa. I enjoy many sports in my free time but rowing is the main one. I am currently a doctor in the Army which I thoroughly enjoy.
NOMINATED BY: S Raja

MISS JESVIR KAUR MAHIL (Lecturer)

Management Consultant, College of International Awareness, 29 Birkbeck Avenue, Acton, London, W3 6HX

PLACE OF BIRTH: India, 31.5.61
MARITAL STATUS: Single
COLLEGE: Manchester University
ACADEMIC QUALIFICATIONS: BA Hons, RSA Dip.TEFL, MBA
PROFESSIONAL QUALIFICATIONS: MBA
DIRECTORSHIPS: College of International Awareness
HOBBIES AND INTERESTS: Photography, languages, travelling, dancing
PERSONAL PROFILE: Jesvir Mahil is the founder of the 'College of International Awareness' an educational organisation which aims to build bridges across nations through the power of friendships. With a BA (Hons) Degree in Psychology and an MBA. Jesvir has worked at an International level in education for 16 years in the UK, Spain, Italy and the US.

MR SAKANDER MAHMOOD (Business Administration)

9 Clevedon Road, Balsall Heath, Birmingham, B12 9HD

PLACE OF BIRTH: Pakistan, 29.10.55
MARITAL STATUS: Seperated
CHILDREN: Six
COLLEGE: East Birmingham College
ACADEMIC QUALIFICATIONS: NVQ 1/2 Business Administration
DIRECTORSHIPS: Mirpur Sports and Social Club
MEMBERSHIPS: Mirpur Sports and Social Club
HOBBIES AND INTERESTS: Sports-taking part and helping others take part
EMAIL: sakander@hotmail.com
PERSONAL PROFILE: Arrived in England in 1969 with no English. Grew up in inner city Birmingham. Educated myself after lengthy period of unemployment and illness. Now working hard to help the community to mix with host community. Have in the past worked with students union to set up cross-college network for ethnic minorities to liaise with each other. Runs a sports and social club for Mirpuri community.
NOMINATED BY: Brian Turner

MR RAIHAN N MAHMUD (Banker)

Chief Manager, Habib Bank Ltd, 100 Woodhall Gate, Pinner

PLACE OF BIRTH: Gojra, 10.8.42
MARITAL STATUS: Married
CHILDREN: Two (Farrukh H, Faheem T)
COLLEGE: Sind, Hydrabad
ACADEMIC QUALIFICATIONS: BA Hons 1st class, MA Economics
PROFESSIONAL QUALIFICATIONS: ACIB London
MEMBERSHIPS: Institute of Directors. BIFU. Various literary clubs.
HOBBIES AND INTERESTS: Religious history
PERSONAL PROFILE: Very successful banking career. Worked for BCCI for 17 years. Won a long and hard legal battle with the liquidators of BCCI. Made legal history, new employment law under my name Malik and Mahmud V BCCI in House of Lords. For BCCI employees Law report 27.6.97. H.L (E)3 1997

MR DEEPAK MAHTANI (Company Director)

International Director, South Asian Development Partnership, PO Box 43, Sutton, SM2 5WL

PLACE OF BIRTH: Hong Kong, 29.11.60
MARITAL STATUS: Married
CHILDREN: Two (Arun, Sanjay)
COLLEGE: Sophia University, Tokyo. American College. Switzerland
PROFESSIONAL QUALIFICATIONS: BA
DIRECTORSHIPS: Tradeways International Ltd, Winning Communcations Partnership Ltd
MEMBERSHIPS: London Chamber of Commerce, Emanuel Hospital Association. Exec Committee of Transplants in Mind.
HOBBIES AND INTERESTS: Reading, writing, travel, photography, speaking
PERSONAL PROFILE: Of Indian origin, lived in the Far East for 14 years and Switzerland for 14 years, speaks six languages. Runs two businesses, is a regular speaker at conferences and training seminars. Also active in a number of charities involved in health, development and education.

MR FAZAL SHARIFF MAJID-KHAN (Lawyer)

Managing Director, Air Travel Services, Air House, 91 Cricklewood Broadway, London, NW2 3JG

PLACE OF BIRTH: Pakistan, 19.9.56
MARITAL STATUS: Married
COLLEGE: Govt College Pew & University of London
ACADEMIC QUALIFICATIONS: BA Hons
PROFESSIONAL QUALIFICATIONS: LLB & Post Grad Diploma Aircraft Marketing
DIRECTORSHIPS: Parkline Ltd
MEMBERSHIPS: Executive Member of Labour Party
HOBBIES AND INTERESTS: Playing polo, travelling
PERSONAL PROFILE: I came to UK in 1979, got married to Mrs Mukhtar Majid-Khan and did work hard with Continental Airlines as an executive. Also worked in Asian community and got popular with own people and become executive member of the Labour Party.

CLLR NARENDRA MAKANJI (Councillor)

Haringey Council, 41 Darwin Road, Wood Green, London, N22 6PH

DATE OF BIRTH: 11.5.52
COLLEGE: University of Bradford
ACADEMIC QUALIFICATIONS: B Tech Honours
MEMBERSHIPS: Labour Party (1975), UNISON, Action for Southern Africa. Founder member of Black Sections 1983 and Black Socialist Society (1993)
PERSONAL PROFILE: Haringey councillor since 1982. I have held various positions within the council such as chair of finance, contracts and construction services committee etc. Involved in anti-racist campaigns at all levels since the mid-seventies. Currently chair National of Association of Direct Labour Organisation.
NOMINATED BY: Ansel Wong

MRS HAJRA MAKDA (Librarian-Author)

Freelance Correspondent, Leicester City Library, 1 French Road, Leicester

PLACE OF BIRTH: Malawi, 27.5.62
MARITAL STATUS: Married
CHILDREN: Two (Rizwaan, Junaid)
COLLEGE: St Wilfreds C of E School
PROFESSIONAL QUALIFICATIONS: 6 O-Levels, 3 A-Levels
MEMBERSHIPS: FMO
HONOURS/AWARDS: Previously appeared in Asian Whos Who
HOBBIES AND INTERESTS: Writing, reading, travelling, cooking
PERSONAL PROFILE: Mother-housewife. Author of cookery book 'Spice 'n' Easy'. Freelance correspondent for Leicester Mercury. Librarian for Leicester City Council. Member of Federation of Muslim Organisations. Community correspondent. Committee member of advisory board to hospitals. Voluntarily teaches English as a second language.

MR HEMRAJ DAHYA MAKWANA (Bank Official-Rtd)

Treasurer, Bachin Stores, Guildford Road, Westcott, Near Doking, RH4 3NG

PLACE OF BIRTH: Kenya, 14.12.35
MARITAL STATUS: Married
CHILDREN: Three (Naina, Ajay, Satish)
ACADEMIC QUALIFICATIONS: GCSE (Kenya) Cambridge
PROFESSIONAL QUALIFICATIONS: Associate of Inst of Bankers
MEMBERSHIPS: Jansari Organisations (UK)
HOBBIES AND INTERESTS: Literary-Running news letter for benefit of the community
PERSONAL PROFILE: Retired Barclays Bank official having held an executive post, privileged by very few Asians in 1980's. Been involved in social work since 1946. Founder member of many social and religious organisations in Kenya and in UK. Main force and executive member of Jan Kshatriya Sevak Mandal (UK) for last 26 years. Also involved in-Jansari Organisations UK uniting seven Jansari Mandals in UK. Assistant treasurer and editor of quarterly newsletter.

NOMINATED BY: Chandrakant Jansari

DR KAILASH CHAND MALHOTRA (Doctor)

Senior Partner, NHS, Stamford House, 2 Princess Street, Aston Under Lyne, OL6 9QH

PLACE OF BIRTH: India, 10.6.49
MARITAL STATUS: Married
CHILDREN: One (Aseem)
COLLEGE: Punjab University, Liverpool University
ACADEMIC QUALIFICATIONS: MBBS (Punjab), DTM+H (Liverpool)
PROFESSIONAL QUALIFICATIONS: MBBS, DTM+H
HOBBIES AND INTERESTS: Writing, reading
PERSONAL PROFILE: Medical secretary, West Pennine LMC, Regional representative BMA, GPC. Treasurer Internationa Hindi Convention.

MS ADEEBA MALIK (General Manager)

QED,

PLACE OF BIRTH: Bradford
MARITAL STATUS: Single
COLLEGE: Hull University / Open University
ACADEMIC QUALIFICATIONS: B Ed Hons, MA Education
DIRECTORSHIPS: Board member of the Yorkshire & Humber Regional Development Agency
MEMBERSHIPS: MECI, Soroptimist International
HONOURS/AWARDS: Yorkshire Young Achievers Award for Education and Training
HOBBIES AND INTERESTS: Dining out, music, current affairs
PERSONAL PROFILE: Member, University of Bradford. Trustee, Pukaar Foundation. Newly appointed board member of the Yorkshire and Humber Regional Development Agency. Member of the 'Yorkshire Young Achievers' Management Committee. Governor, Bellevue Girls Upper School, Bradford. Director, Spirit of Bradford. Member, Open University Steering Committee.

MR AFTAB MALIK (Postman)

Postman Sorter, 5 Anstey Road, Reading, RG1 7JR

PLACE OF BIRTH: Reading, 23.2.69
MARITAL STATUS: Married
CHILDREN: One (Ansia)
COLLEGE: Bradford College
ACADEMIC QUALIFICATIONS: BTEC General Diploma-Business & Finance
HONOURS/AWARDS: Perfect Attendance Award 1992. Fundraiser of the Year BT/RBC/Reading Chronicle Community Awards.
HOBBIES AND INTERESTS: Cycling, taking part in charity events.
PERSONAL PROFILE: Unlike myself, there are very few Asians who take part in fundraising activities. I hope my hardwork and achievements will get the message across to other Asians to do the same.
NOMINATED BY: Saeed Choudhary & Lakhbir Dhillon

MR AFZAL MALIK (Postmaster-Rtd)

Proprietor, Malik Post Office, 56 Chingford Mount Road, London, E4 9AA

PLACE OF BIRTH: Pakistan
MARITAL STATUS: Married
CHILDREN: Four (Imran, Sofia, Saba, Adnan)
COLLEGE: Punjab University
ACADEMIC QUALIFICATIONS: Graduate
PROFESSIONAL QUALIFICATIONS: Accountancy
DIRECTORSHIPS: Manager Mayfair and Marble Arch Post Offices
MEMBERSHIPS: General Secretary Waltham Forest Joint Council of Asian Organisations
HONOURS/AWARDS: Post Office Long Service and Efficiency Award for 35 years service
HOBBIES AND INTERESTS: Reading, general knowledge, current affairs, walking
PERSONAL PROFILE: First job as postman in London in 1963. Through hardwork and exams was promoted to postal officer within a year. Passed further exams. Appointed manager of Post Offices in Mayfair, Marble Arch and Portman Square. Also very active in local community. Past chairman of Waltham Forest CRC/REC. Received award for voluntary work in community. Retired postmaster.
NOMINATED BY: Imran

CLLR HANZALA MALIK JP (Councillor)

Sub Convenor of Education, City Council, Glasgow City Chambers, George Street, Glasgow, G2 1DU

PLACE OF BIRTH: Glasgow, 26.11.56
MARITAL STATUS: Married
CHILDREN: Two (Haaris, Marisa)
COLLEGE: University of Paisley
ACADEMIC QUALIFICATIONS: BSc Computing & Business Adminstration
DIRECTORSHIPS: Queens Cross Work Space
MEMBERSHIPS: Chair of West of Scotland Community Relations Council
HONOURS/AWARDS: Justice of the Peace
HOBBIES AND INTERESTS: Stamps, swimming, badminton, music, politics
EMAIL: hanzala.malik@ced.glasgow.gov.uk

NOMINATED BY: Dr D L Bhatti "Noor Bharti"

MR KRISHAN NARAYAN MALIK (Author)

Columnist,

PLACE OF BIRTH: India, 17.5.29
MARITAL STATUS: Married
CHILDREN: Two (Pawan, Anjan)
COLLEGE: Delhi University
ACADEMIC QUALIFICATIONS: MA History
MEMBERSHIPS: Royal Inst of International Affairs, Royal Commonwealth Society, Indian Journalists Association, National Union of Journalists, Press Club of India. Chelmsford Club (New Delhi)
HOBBIES AND INTERESTS: Reading, travel, aviation, Indian cuisine
PERSONAL PROFILE: European correspondent, Times of India, Research Associate, QEH University of Oxford; Senior Research Fellow, SOAS, University of London; President IJA-Europe, Chairman, Maitreya College, University of Delhi, SG. National Union of India; Publications; India and the United Kingdom and continuity in 1980's, co-editor, India and Britain-recent past and present challenges.

CLLR M. RAFIQUE MALIK (Director REC-Rtd)

Director (Honorary), Jinnah Community Development Trust, 87- 89 Abel Street, Burnley, BB10 1QD

PLACE OF BIRTH: Pakistan, 16.12.37
MARITAL STATUS: Married
CHILDREN: Seven (Zahid, Shahid, Jahanzaib, Shehryar, Zeeshan, Rifat, Sobia)
COLLEGE: Punjab University, Leeds University
ACADEMIC QUALIFICATIONS: BA
PROFESSIONAL QUALIFICATIONS: B Ed and PGCE
DIRECTORSHIPS: Director (Honorary) Jinnah Community Development Trust
PERSONAL PROFILE: Chairman Burnley & Pendle REC 1988-90. Director Blackburn REC 1984-97. Teacher in Burnley 1969-84. Member Race Relations Board 1969-76. Burnley Borough councillor 1976-date. Chairman Housing Community Member 1994-date. Deputy leader Burnley Council 1998-date. Chairman National Federation of Pakistani Assoc. UK 1969-72. Secretary Lancashire Council of Mosques 1989- date. Non-executive director Lancashire Ambulance Service NHS Trust 1997-date.

MR NASSER MALIK (Company Director)

Customer & Credit Director, Fine Art Developments Plc, 23 Baslow Grove, Heaton, Bradford, BD9 5JA

PLACE OF BIRTH: Pakistan, 28.12.62
MARITAL STATUS: Married
CHILDREN: Three (Sheraz, Munisa, Tanzeela)
COLLEGE: Leicester University, Bradford University
ACADEMIC QUALIFICATIONS: BA Hons, MBA
PROFESSIONAL QUALIFICATIONS: Inst. of Credit Management
DIRECTORSHIPS: Express Gifts Ltd; Roseway Ltd, MBA Ltd
MEMBERSHIPS: IOD, ICM
HOBBIES AND INTERESTS: Flying, golf, chess, squash
PERSONAL PROFILE: Institute of Directors, Association of MBA's. Institute of Credit Management. Bradford Eid Committee. Rotary Club. Junior Chamber of Commerce. Asian Enterprise Club

MR SHAHID MALIK (Independent Assessor)

Chief Executive, Haringey Regeneration Agency, Commission for Racial Equality, Elliot House, 10-12 Allington Street, London, SW1E 5EH

PLACE OF BIRTH: Burnley, 24.11.67
MARITAL STATUS: Single
COLLEGE: Southbank University, Durham University Business School
ACADEMIC QUALIFICATIONS: BA (Honours) Business Studies
PROFESSIONAL QUALIFICATIONS: Post Graduate Certificate in Business Counselling
DIRECTORSHIPS: Chairman, Board of Directors, National Urban Foundation. Commissioner CRE.
MEMBERSHIPS: FRSA, FIMgt,
HOBBIES AND INTERESTS: Current affairs, human rights, snooker, football, travel
EMAIL: sr_malik@hotmail.com
PERSONAL PROFILE: All of Shahid's work to date has been targeted at regenerating and empowering diverse inner city communities, and by doing so, helping and supporting those that are disadvantaged and excluded. By virtue of being the youngest and often first ethnic minority person in numerous roles, he has already broken down many race and age stereotypes that exist.
NOMINATED BY: Ushma Vyas

DHOLI GURCHARAN MALL (Dhol Player-Teacher)

Manager and Coach, Dhol Blasters and Nachda Sansaar, 195 Holyhead Road, Handsworth, Birmingham, B21 0AS

PLACE OF BIRTH: India, 8.3.52
MARITAL STATUS: Married
CHILDREN: Four (Novjoat K, Hurman, Satwant, Sunita)
COLLEGE: Handsworth Tech College
PROFESSIONAL QUALIFICATIONS: MECH Engineering (Tool maker and Service Engineer)
DIRECTORSHIPS: MB Recording Studio
MEMBERSHIPS: Asian Music Bhangra Arts Association
HONOURS/AWARDS: Best Personality and Best Dhol Player
HOBBIES AND INTERESTS: Keep fit, help to raise money for charities
PERSONAL PROFILE: From the start I was influenced by the unique rhythms of bhangra music. I am the first Dholi to have played with a live band on the UK bhangra scene. Most of my time is devoted to teaching the new generations of the UK both traditional bhangra dance and the Indian dhol at universities, schools etc. I have been all around the world on tours with various singing groups and dancing teams. I have just opened a Hair & Beauty Health Clinic 'B Handsome'.

MR RAZA MALLAL (Film-maker)

Director-Writer, Eyeline Productions, Highbank House, 83 Harehills Lane, Leeds, LS7 4HA

PLACE OF BIRTH: Pakistan, 13.7.59
MARITAL STATUS: Married
CHILDREN: Three (Onis, Sonya, Harris)
COLLEGE: Copenhagen
ACADEMIC QUALIFICATIONS: B.Com Business CEE Film Studies
PROFESSIONAL QUALIFICATIONS: Dip TV, Diploma in TV Production
DIRECTORSHIPS: Hall Place Studios Premier Productions
MEMBERSHIPS: BECTU
HONOURS/AWARDS: Bronze Dragon, Cracow 1990, Jury Grand Prize, Waterloss & Prix De Le Salamon
HOBBIES AND INTERESTS: Films, popular western, Asian music, computers
EMAIL: razamallal@hotmail.com
PERSONAL PROFILE: An award winning multi-talented writer/director who has made a whole range of films, in particular films which deal with issues affecting the ethnic minorities. In addition to production work Raza is actively involved in media education and he has tutored in numerous institutions. He is presently a lecturer in film direction at Leeds Met. University, as well as managing director of Eyeline Productions.
NOMINATED BY: John Thomas

> 'All of Shahid's work to date has been targeted at regenerating and empowering diverse inner city communities, and by doing so, helping and supporting those that are disadvantaged and excluded'
>
> **SHAHID MALIK**

MR MUHAMMED MATADAR (Teacher)

Blackburn Rovers, 1 Bold Street, Blackburn, BB1 7EL

PLACE OF BIRTH: Darwen, 26.2.77
MARITAL STATUS: Single
COLLEGE: Glamorgan University
ACADEMIC QUALIFICATIONS: BA Hons, PGCE, 3 A-Levels, 10 GCSE's
HONOURS/AWARDS: RFU Rugby, FA Teachers, Cricket Coach
HOBBIES AND INTERESTS: Sports, refereeing, music, keeping fit
PERSONAL PROFILE: I am the youngest Class 1 Asian referee in the country with aspirations to reach FIFA standards. I am a PE teacher in secondary education. Furthermore, I am secretary of the Asian Sports Association, Blackburn United FC and member of the Blackburn Multi-Racial Football Partnership at Blackburn Rovers FC where I am also the referees' appointments secretary for their youth academy.
NOMINATED BY: Gordon Taylor, Professional Footballers Asso.

MR AJMER SINGH MATHARU (Police Officer-Rtd)

Care Assistant, Leicester City Council, 147 Canon Street, Leicester, LE4 6NJ

PLACE OF BIRTH: India, 29.10.34
MARITAL STATUS: Married
CHILDREN: Five (Jaspreet Singh, Parveen Kaur, Jasminder Singh, Gurcharan Kaur, Jatinder Singh)
PROFESSIONAL QUALIFICATIONS: Federation of International Hockey Coach & Umpires, Senior Coach of English Hockey Association
MEMBERSHIPS: FIH, Institute of Advanced Motorists
PERSONAL PROFILE: Uganda police sub-inspector 1956 and retired as deputy superintendent 1968. First Sikh with turban to join British police 1970, Leicester. Uganda Hockey team captain 1960-1964. Qualified International hockey coach / umpire in 1964. Uganda Hockey National Coach up to 1968. Awarded Senior Coach of English Hockey 1976. Attended 1972 and 1992 Olympics and 1998 Hockey World Cup.

MR NIRMINDER MATHARU (Photographer)

Careers Advisor, Careers Bradford, 5 Wynford Mount, West Park, Leeds, LS16 6JH

PLACE OF BIRTH: India, 25.10.61
MARITAL STATUS: Married
CHILDREN: Three (Manita, Harvir, Inaik)
COLLEGE: Lancashire University, Huddersfield University
ACADEMIC QUALIFICATIONS: BA Hons Accounting & Finance
PROFESSIONAL QUALIFICATIONS: Diploma in Careers Guidance
DIRECTORSHIPS: Oriental Arts (Bradford)
(Charitable org. promoting Asian Arts)
MEMBERSHIPS: Asian Youth and Cultural Forum (Bfd)
HONOURS/AWARDS: Wedding / Portrait Awards
HOBBIES AND INTERESTS: Cinema, music, Dj's, reading, football
PERSONAL PROFILE: In my spare time I do a lot of voluntary work with disadvantaged young people, teaching them about photography and how to express their ideas / thoughts through film. I have produced an exhibition about positive role models (Asians) which has been displayed throughout the UK. I work for Careers Bradford advising ethnic minorities and other disadvantaged young people.
NOMINATED BY: Miss Frances Mangham

MR RAKESH MATHUR (Journalist)

Media Director, PO Box 25165, London, SW1V 3WH

PLACE OF BIRTH: India
MARITAL STATUS: Single
COLLEGE: Delhi and Bombay Universities
ACADEMIC QUALIFICATIONS: Post Graduate
PROFESSIONAL QUALIFICATIONS: Communication Arts
MEMBERSHIPS: FPA, Royal Television Society, RSA
HONOURS/AWARDS: Several
HOBBIES AND INTERESTS: Good food, wine, travels, internet, theatre
EMAIL: mathurrak@aol.com
PERSONAL PROFILE: Rakesh is multi-lingual. He feels at home in all cultures. He has widely travelled in Europe, Asia and the Americas. He has produced and directed a number of documentaries and worked for BBC, Paris Match and major media organisations.

MISS TANYA MATIN (Student)

PLACE OF BIRTH: London, 10.2.83
MARITAL STATUS: Single
HOBBIES AND INTERESTS: Travelling, acting, current affairs
PERSONAL PROFILE: I am a student studying for my GCSE's. I wish to pursue a career within the media. My interests are acting and current affairs. Recently I attended a United Nations conference in the US on human rights in which I participated. I have done some promotional work for the NSPCC and some advertising campaigns for leading companies.

MR AMIN MAWJI (Chartered Accountant)

Partner, Arthur Anderson & Co, 20 Old Bailey, London, EC4M 7BH

PLACE OF BIRTH: Kenya, 16.10.58
MARITAL STATUS: Married
CHILDREN: Two (Sophie Sarah, Sameer Adam)
COLLEGE: London School of Economics
ACADEMIC QUALIFICATIONS: BSc (Econ) Hons
PROFESSIONAL QUALIFICATIONS: FCA
MEMBERSHIPS: RAC Club
HOBBIES AND INTERESTS: Travel, eating out, Indian classical music
EMAIL: mawji@easynet.co.uk
PERSONAL PROFILE: Amin Mawji is head of Arthur Anderson's UK team specialising in serving the manufacturing sector. He has extensive experience of working with multinational and public companies and has advised on a number of mergers and acquisitions. He was educated at Queens College Taunton and graduated from the LSE.

MR JOHN MAYER (Composer-Violinist)

Professor of Composition, Indo Jazz Fusions, 17 Hermitage Road, London, N4 1DF

PLACE OF BIRTH: India, 28.10.30
MARITAL STATUS: Married
CHILDREN: Two (Jahan, Jonathan)
COLLEGE: Royal Academy of Music
PROFESSIONAL QUALIFICATIONS: ARAM
MEMBERSHIPS: MU, PRS, MCPS, CIMA
HONOURS/AWARDS: Winner of the Bombay Madrigal Scholarship
HOBBIES AND INTERESTS: Watching western films
PERSONAL PROFILE: John Mayer was the pioneer of the 'Fusion' of Indian and Western music with his ground breaking group 'Indo Jazz Fusions'. He has recorded for EMI, Polygram and Nimbus. He has written works for James Galway, Frich Gruenberg, Rohan de Sarami, the London Phillarmonic and London Symphony Orchestras.

MR SUKUMAR MAZUMDAR (Journalist)

Editor, Probashi Samachar, 20 Orchard Avenue, Southgate, London, N14 4ND

PLACE OF BIRTH: Bangladesh, 6.11.35
MARITAL STATUS: Married
CHILDREN: Two (Ila, Salil)
COLLEGE: Dhaka, Greenwich
ACADEMIC QUALIFICATIONS: BSc, PGCE
PROFESSIONAL QUALIFICATIONS: LJ, RJ and GPI
HOBBIES AND INTERESTS: Travelling, creative writing
PERSONAL PROFILE: I worked as a rubber technologist for ten years, then as a teacher for eight years. I edit and publish a Bengali magazine Probashi Samachar since 1979. Edit and publish an English magazine Asian Herald. General secretary Overseas Bengali Association. Governor Merry Hill School.

MR PANJABI MC (Music Producer)

Nachural Records,

PLACE OF BIRTH: Coventry
MARITAL STATUS: Single
COLLEGE: Coventry University, De Montford University
ACADEMIC QUALIFICATIONS: HND, Masters
HONOURS/AWARDS: Best album 98, Best producer, Best Single 98
HOBBIES AND INTERESTS: All types of music especially hip hop
PERSONAL PROFILE: The multi award winning all round music maker Panjabi MC. He released his first album in 1996 'Grassroots' which sold over 100,000 copies worldwide. His last album 'Legalised' became the fastest selling bhangra album of all time. Panjabi MC remains the indisputable pioneer of the sub-genre.
NOMINATED BY: Kiran Lyall

MR BRUCE MCNAIR (TOASTMASTER)

Self Employed, 155 Costons Lane, Greenford, UB6 9AD

PLACE OF BIRTH: India, 16.8.30
MARITAL STATUS: Married
CHILDREN: Three (Antoinette, Melanie, Justine)
COLLEGE: St Aloysius High School, India
ACADEMIC QUALIFICATIONS: Senior Cambridge
PROFESSIONAL QUALIFICATIONS: Fellow of the Guild of Professional Toastmasters
MEMBERSHIPS: Guild of Professional Toastmasters
HOBBIES AND INTERESTS: Family-local church, toastmastering
PERSONAL PROFILE: The first and only Asian-born professional toastmaster in the UK. Has officiated at royal occasions, and also with the Lord Mayor of London in Mansion House and the Guildhall. Has toastmastered civic banquets, dinner, dance, award ceremonies, cocktail parties, masonic functions, garden parties and weddings of nearly every culture.

ALHAJ TARA MEAH KHAN
(COMMUNITY ACTIVIST-BUSINESSMAN)

The Chair, Notun Din, Star of Bombay, 157 Westbourne Avenue, London, W11 2RS

PLACE OF BIRTH: Bangladesh, 20.8.31
MARITAL STATUS: Married
CHILDREN: Three (Jalal, Montaj, Husnara)
DIRECTORSHIPS: Notun Din
HONOURS/AWARDS: Awarded by National Manisa Porishad in Bangladesh
HOBBIES AND INTERESTS: Charity works
PERSONAL PROFILE: Chairman of Notun Din, a Bengali newsweekly. He rose to fame as a generous affluent senior community leader. Vice chair of BCA and other major Bengali organisations. His charity works here and in Bangladesh established him as a breakthrough community figure. He is a successful curry houses boss.

DR HARISH KUMAR MEHRA (SOCIAL SERVICES)

Planning Officer Equalities, Birmingham City Council, Social Services Dept, Louisa Ryland House, 44 Newhall Street, Birmingham, B3 3PL

PLACE OF BIRTH: India, 7.7.51
MARITAL STATUS: Married
CHILDREN: Two (Vasudha, Roohi)
COLLEGE: Birmingham University
ACADEMIC QUALIFICATIONS: PhD
PROFESSIONAL QUALIFICATIONS: Diploma in Social Work, Qualified Marriage Counsellor
DIRECTORSHIPS: MA, PhD and journalist
MEMBERSHIPS: National General Secretary of Asian Rationalist Society in Britain
HONOURS/AWARDS: East Midlands Art Council UK. Panjabi award for contributions to Panjabi literature
HOBBIES AND INTERESTS: Writing, social reforming
PERSONAL PROFILE: Harish Mehra came to Britain in 1973 after completing his BSc. He completed his Diploma in Social Work in 1984, and marriage guidance in 1987. He has worked in Coventry, Sandwell Social Services as a training officer and a principal officer in Northampton Social Services and Birmingham Education Department. Currently he is a planning officer and equalities in Birmingham Social Services. He has written seven books and his articles are published frequently in the UK and India.

DR ATUL MEHTA (DOCTOR)

Consultant, Dept of Haematology, Royal Free Hospital, London, NW3 2QG

PLACE OF BIRTH: Kenya, 14.1.54
MARITAL STATUS: Married
CHILDREN: One (Avani)
COLLEGE: Cambridge University, London University
ACADEMIC QUALIFICATIONS: MA, MD, MBBChin
PROFESSIONAL QUALIFICATIONS: FRCP, FRCPath, Dip Management
MEMBERSHIPS: British Society for Haematology, American Society for Haematology
PERSONAL PROFILE: Senior consultant in haematology at a large London teaching hospital. Author of more than 100 articles in all aspects of blood disease.

DR KHUSHRU M MEHTA OBE (GENERAL PRACTITIONER RTD)

52 Greenfield Avenue, Watford, WD1 5DN

PLACE OF BIRTH: India, 10.5.19
MARITAL STATUS: Married
CHILDREN: Four (Jamshed, Cyrus, Zeena, Roy)
COLLEGE: Bombay, Edinburgh
ACADEMIC QUALIFICATIONS: MBBS, FRCS
HONOURS/AWARDS: OBE, Paul Harris Fellow
HOBBIES AND INTERESTS: Rotary International
PERSONAL PROFILE: Senior Surgeon, Malaysia 1952-67. General Medical Practitioner 1967-90.

MR SITAL MEHTA (FASHION DESIGNER)

Senior Designer, GUS Home Shopping Ltd, Universal House, Devonshire Street, Manchester, M60 6EL

PLACE OF BIRTH: Kenya, 3.5.67
MARITAL STATUS: Single
COLLEGE: Central St Martins
ACADEMIC QUALIFICATIONS: (MA) Fashion Design CSM (MA)
PROFESSIONAL QUALIFICATIONS: CSM (MA)
HONOURS/AWARDS: Designer of the Year-BBC Clothes Show,
HOBBIES AND INTERESTS: Painting, music (singing), interior design, shows, ZEETV 20 minutes interview exhibitions
EMAIL: mehta.s.@gusco.com
PERSONAL PROFILE: After finishing my (MA) at St Martins I have worked for some of the leading high street retail outlets. Designing both menswear/womenswear also having won Designer of the Year award and having my range published in mail order home shopping catalogues. With 2 million copies distributed across Britain each year.
NOMINATED BY: Mita Mehta

MRS SARLA MEISURIA (CO-ORDINATOR)

Asian Deaf Women Association,

PLACE OF BIRTH: India, 11.2.66
MARITAL STATUS: Married
CHILDREN: Three (Vanisha, McTesh, Dipesh)
COLLEGE: Westham College, Newham College. Deafwork Holborn. City Lit. Holborm
ACADEMIC QUALIFICATIONS: P/T Youth Worker. Management Skills. Counselling Skills and Attitudes. British Sign Language 1+2
HONOURS/AWARDS: Cert. of Achievement, London Ethnic Minority Deaf Association, BT Young Deaf Achievers. International Women's Week for services to deaf Asian women.
HOBBIES AND INTERESTS: DIY, meeting people, fashion cloth, sewing, drawing, keep fit, weight training, swimming, jogging
PERSONAL PROFILE: I am an Asian women with a lot of ambition and aim in life but because of my disability (deafness) people do not believe in me and never thought I could make it. I understand the problems women with my kind of disability face every day of their lives, so I decided to set up this group in 1992 to reduce isolation of deaf Asian women. Now have seven staff.
NOMINATED BY: Lorla

MR ANAWAR BABUL MIAH (BARRISTER)

Raj Bari, Whislets Close, West Hunsbury, Northampton, NN4 9XB

PLACE OF BIRTH: Bangladesh, 22.4.72
MARITAL STATUS: Married
COLLEGE: Middlesex University
ACADEMIC QUALIFICATIONS: LLB Hons
DIRECTORSHIPS: Director, The Raj (UK) Ltd. Director, The Raj (GB) Ltd. Director, Haroon Group-Dhaka, Bangladesh.
MEMBERSHIPS: The Honourable Society of Lincolns Inn, The Association of Bangladeshi Lawyers
HOBBIES AND INTERESTS: Horse-riding, golf, travelling
PERSONAL PROFILE: Barrister (Lincoln's Inn). Consultant, J Cooper Solicitors-London. Consultant, Mian Law Associates-London. Vice Chair, Dame Colet House-London.
NOMINATED BY: Abdul Nur (Rouf)

'I am an Asian women with a lot of ambition and aim in life but because of my disability (deafness) people do not believe in me and never thought I could make it'

SARLA MEISURIA

MR HOSOUN MIAH (Restaurateur)

Manager, Thespians Indian Restaurant, 26 Sheep Street, Stratford-U-Avon, CV37 6EF

PLACE OF BIRTH: Bangladesh, 11.1.71
MARITAL STATUS: Single
MEMBERSHIPS: Guild of Master Craftsmen, The Taj Good Food Guide
HONOURS/AWARDS: Les Couiters
HOBBIES AND INTERESTS: Snooker, football, badminton
PERSONAL PROFILE: Willingness to learn, patient, calm. Interested in achieving and enjoying. I would like to introduce a new dimension of Indian cuisine to the western palate.
NOMINATED BY: H Miah

JUSNA BEGUM MIAH (Student)

PLACE OF BIRTH: London, 10.1.86
MARITAL STATUS: Single
HONOURS/AWARDS: PE, swimming, attendance and poems published
HOBBIES AND INTERESTS: Swimming, playing sports, watching TV, reading, any kind of books
PERSONAL PROFILE: My favourite subjects are art, English and food and playing sports like basketball. I love reading books. My favourite are horror books. My attendance is good. I have certificates for that. Also for PE and swimming. My poem was published in a book called Spellbound.

MISS RAJHANA BEGUM MIAH (Student)

PLACE OF BIRTH: London, 13.9.85
MARITAL STATUS: Single
COLLEGE: Mulberry School for Girls
HONOURS/AWARDS: 1st Star award in athletics and a readathon certificate
HOBBIES AND INTERESTS: Swimming, playing rounders
PERSONAL PROFILE: I'm a 13 year old student at Mulberry School. I will be in Year 9 in September. I received many certificates from Mulberry School. My poetry was published in the Spellbound poetry book. I raised money for charity and received a Readthon Certificate. When I leave school I want to be an actress.

MR SHAHID MIAH (Student)

Vice-President YARA, Youth Anti-Racist Alliance,

PLACE OF BIRTH: Bangladesh, 4.12.74
MARITAL STATUS: Single
COLLEGE: Middlesex University
ACADEMIC QUALIFICATIONS: GCSE (9), A-Levels, Art Foundation, Doing BA Hons
HOBBIES AND INTERESTS: Music, film and TV, playing basketball, keeping fit
EMAIL: sm49ers@cwan.net
PERSONAL PROFILE: Currently studying a BA Hons at Middlesex University, Shahid is vice-president of YARA. He is responsible for YARA projects including Media Conference (1996,1997 and 1998). Black Business and Employment Conference 1997 and RESPECT IT 98 (Information Technology Conference). He also worked on the EMMA awards 1999 .
NOMINATED BY: S Samra

MR SHOFIK MIAH (Student)

University College Suffolk, 12 Mountbatten Court, Ipswich, Suffolk, IP1 2NF

PLACE OF BIRTH: Ipswich, 3.3.76
MARITAL STATUS: Single
COLLEGE: University College Suffolk
ACADEMIC QUALIFICATIONS: GNVQ (Intermediate) Leisure & Tourism (merit); GNVQ (advanced) Business Studies
HONOURS/AWARDS: Community Sport Leader Award, Winning seven-a-side football tournament-held by IBCC.
HOBBIES AND INTERESTS: Play football, snooker, pool, badminton, archery
EMAIL: shofik@yahoo.com
PERSONAL PROFILE: An undergraduate, studying BA (Hons) Business Studies. Joined the Suffolk Constabulary as a special constable. Voluntary youth worker for Ipswich Bangladeshi Community Centre. Play for the Ipswich Bengali Football Team. Appeared on the 1998-2000 University College Suffolk Prospectus. Appearing in Asian national newspapers during the IBCC football tournament.
NOMINATED BY: Raj

MR SHOFIQUE MIAH (Chairman)

Community Trust, Brick Lane Community Trust, 320 Commercial Road, London, E1 2PY

PLACE OF BIRTH: Bangladesh, 1.7.54
MARITAL STATUS: Married
CHILDREN: Five (Nurul Islam..Reskona Begum)
DIRECTORSHIPS: Director of Tower Hamlets Law Centre
HONOURS/AWARDS: A terrace has been named after him in East London
HOBBIES AND INTERESTS: Communty activities
PERSONAL PROFILE: Community activist Shofique Miah is a well known name in East London's multicultural arena. A Bengali fighter successfully streamlined his activities on many East London community developments. To mark his contribution a terrace near Tower Bridge was named after him in 1996. He's a pioneering school governor.
NOMINATED BY: Shofi Ahmed

MISS NIGHAT MEHMUD MIAN (Solicitor)

Police Complaints Authority, 10 Great George Street, London, SW1P 3AE

PLACE OF BIRTH: Cleveland, 30.7.62
MARITAL STATUS: Single
COLLEGE: University of Birmingham
ACADEMIC QUALIFICATIONS: LLB Hons Law with French
PROFESSIONAL QUALIFICATIONS: Solicitor
DIRECTORSHIPS: Non-executive Director, North Birmingham NHS Mental Health Trust
MEMBERSHIPS: Law Society, Amnesty International, National Trust
HOBBIES AND INTERESTS: Reading, travelling, theatre, trekking
PERSONAL PROFILE: Parents: Mr Manzoor Alom Mian and Mrs Naziran Begum Mian, Educated at Teeside High School for Girls Eagelsclffe (1974-78). Acklam VI Form College (1978-80), After University (1980-84), Chester Law College (1984-85), articled with Edge and Ellison Solicitors Birmingham, qualified as solicitor 1989, Professional Indemnity Solicitor at Wansborough Birmingham (1991-94). Senior caseworker with office for Supervision of Solicitors (1994-98).

DR K B RAJ SINGH MINHAS (Management Trainer)

Fellow, Sheffield University, The Dore Moor House, Newfield Lane, Sheffield, S17 3DB

PLACE OF BIRTH: India, 29.10.42
MARITAL STATUS: Married
CHILDREN: Four (Deepika, Sharon, Karon, Akash)
COLLEGE: Sheffield University
ACADEMIC QUALIFICATIONS: PhD, MSc, DMS
PROFESSIONAL QUALIFICATIONS: FFA, MCIM, MI Mgmt
HOBBIES AND INTERESTS: Music, reading
EMAIL: RSMINHAS@sheffield.ac.uk
PERSONAL PROFILE: Researcher in consumer behaviour. Writer and author. Member: LITERATI CLUB. Awarded highest quality rating as a management researcher by ANBAR.

MR JEFF MIRZA (Stand-up Comedian)

Compere, MK Management, Battersea, London, SW11 1DJ

PLACE OF BIRTH: Ilford, 3.2.65
MARITAL STATUS: Married
CHILDREN: One (Ismena)
COLLEGE: Westminster, East London
ACADEMIC QUALIFICATIONS: B.Eng Hons, MSc Systems Engineering
HOBBIES AND INTERESTS: Cycling, swimming, watching Bollywood films
PERSONAL PROFILE: A regular contributor to Radio 4 and BBC's Live, Jeff Mirza is said to be 'Europe's Top Asian Comedian'. He has appeared on Comedy Nation, Eastern Mix, Zee TV and Asianet. Jeff holds workshops on comedy and is well known on the comedy circuit.

> Community activist Shofique Miah is a well known name in East London's multicultural arena. A Bengali fighter successfully streamlined his activities on many East London community developments

MISS NAZIA MIRZA (Student FT)

PT Lovaas Therapist, Windsor Fellowship, 47 Hackney Road, London, E2 7NX

PLACE OF BIRTH: Bradford, 16.1.77
MARITAL STATUS: Single
COLLEGE: Goldsmiths College-University of London
ACADEMIC QUALIFICATIONS: Reading for a BSc Hons. Psychology expected!
MEMBERSHIPS: Windsor Fellowship (organisation that provides management training for black and Asian students of high calibre)
PERSONAL PROFILE: As part of the Windsor Fellowship training programme I commenced my voluntary work as a Lovaas therapist (working with an autistic boy called Fred) in 1997, whilst in my second year at university. I still work with Fred alongside a team of five therapists supervised by the American Institute CARD (Centre for Autism and Related Disorders).

MISS SHAZIA MIRZA (Actress-Singer)

Science Teacher, Avanti Management, 27 Park Road, East Twickenham, TW1 2QD

PLACE OF BIRTH: Birmingham, 3.10.74
MARITAL STATUS: Single
COLLEGE: Rose Bruford College, Manchester University
ACADEMIC QUALIFICATIONS: 9 GCSE's, 5 A-Levels and 2 Degrees
PROFESSIONAL QUALIFICATIONS: Drama School, BSc
MEMBERSHIPS: Equity/ NUT
HOBBIES AND INTERESTS: Singing, piano, skiing, painting
PERSONAL PROFILE: I am an Asian actress, 24. Have done a lot of work in theatre and television. I also have two degrees and postgraduates and have been teaching physics, chemistry and biology in an East End comprehensive for three years. I have also spent three years at drama school (Rose Bruford, College). I have written and recorded my album and have my own stand-up comedy show.

MISS ANJUU MISRA (Actress-Presenter)

NSM, The Nightingale Centre, 8 Balham Hill, London, SW12 9EA

PLACE OF BIRTH: India, 31.5.64
MARITAL STATUS: Single
COLLEGE: University of Sussex
ACADEMIC QUALIFICATIONS: BA Bachelor of Arts, MSc Master of Science
MEMBERSHIPS: Equity
HOBBIES AND INTERESTS: Horse-riding, swimming, cycling, absailing, hillwalking
PERSONAL PROFILE: I have been very fortunate and privileged in my career because I have worked on such exciting productions as 'Eastenders', 'Family Pride', 'Network East', 'Dalziel and Pascoe', etc. I am very grateful to those directors/producers who had enough foresight not to let ethnicity get in the way of their casting criteria.

DR SURENDRA MISRA (Doctor)

General Practitioner, Greenhill Rise Medical Centre, Garden House, Pipewell, Kettering, NN14 0Q2

PLACE OF BIRTH: India, 2.1.49
MARITAL STATUS: Married
CHILDREN: Three (Angela, Sara, Krishna)
COLLEGE: Allahabad
ACADEMIC QUALIFICATIONS: BSc, MBBS, MS
MEMBERSHIPS: LMC, PCG
HOBBIES AND INTERESTS: Cooking
PERSONAL PROFILE: GP in Corby for 16 years. Actively involved in local politics and care. Extension of medical centre to offer alternative medicine. Aromotherapy, physio, accupunture and hypnotherapy.

MR VASANT MISTRY (Trustee Rtd)

40 Lodge Road, Rugby, CV21 2TF

PLACE OF BIRTH: India, 28.12.31
MARITAL STATUS: Married
CHILDREN: Four (Mahesh, Hemlata, Bharti, Priti)
HOBBIES AND INTERESTS: Reading and writing on social and cultural work
PERSONAL PROFILE: Served Indian community in Rugby from 1967. Established Indian Community Centre in Rugby and served as president/ secretary, treasurer and trustees. President and trustee Prajapatt Association. Ex member RRE Council Alcohol Advisory Service, Rugby Youth Club, HHS, CAB, SACRE, WEM and FORAM.

MR MANZOOR ELAHI MOGHAL JP (Financial Consultant)

Allied Dunbar, 1 Manor Close, Burbase, Leicester, LE10 2NL

MARITAL STATUS: Married
CHILDREN: Three (Nadeem, Zahir, Arif)
COLLEGE: Punjab University
ACADEMIC QUALIFICATIONS: BSc
PROFESSIONAL QUALIFICATIONS: FPC, MLIA (Dip)
DIRECTORSHIPS: British Asian Uganda Trust, Federation of Muslim Organisations (Lon) Ltd
MEMBERSHIPS: Life Insurance Association, Society of Financial Advisors, Magistrates Association
HONOURS/AWARDS: Uganda Independent Medal
HOBBIES AND INTERESTS: Broadcasting, writing, debating
EMAIL: memogal@hotmail.com
PERSONAL PROFILE: Chairman-Federation of Muslim Organisations-Leicester. Chairman of Leicester County Council Race Relation Committee 1986-99. Author broadcaster, Muslim scholar. Leading spokesman on race relations, Asian and Muslim issues, criminal justice system, Uganda etc. Part-time lecturer. Justice of the Peace.
NOMINATED BY: Veronica King, Loughborough University

HAFIZ ABDULLAH MOHAMMAD (Teacher)

LPC Student, London Guildhall University, 6 Rudstone House, Bromley High Street, London, E3 3AT

PLACE OF BIRTH: Bangladesh, 19.1.71
MARITAL STATUS: Married
COLLEGE: University of London
ACADEMIC QUALIFICATIONS: LLB Hons, PGCE (RE), MA Islamic Studies
PROFESSIONAL QUALIFICATIONS: Diploma in Legal Practise (LPC)
DIRECTORSHIPS: Darul Arqum Library
MEMBERSHIPS: Association of Muslim Lawyers
HONOURS/AWARDS: 1st Prize-National Essay Competition on Islamic law
HOBBIES AND INTERESTS: Community work in the fields of education and law
PERSONAL PROFILE: He came to Britain from Bangladesh in 1979. His qualifications include a Hafiz (memoriser) of the Qur'an. He taught RE and ESL in two schools. He will be completing his LPC in year 2000 to qualify as a solicitor. He was president of several Islamic societies, went on a relief convoy to Slovenia, published a 1st Prize essay on criminal law and several articles on Islam and was vice-chair of governors in a school. He is very active in the community.
NOMINATED BY: Kamal Uddin Ali

MR ASH MOHAMMAD (Managing Director)

Managing Director, Di-Log Test Equipment, Commercial Centre, East Lane, Wembley, HA9 7UW

PLACE OF BIRTH: Pakistan, 16.12.61
MARITAL STATUS: Married
CHILDREN: Two (Adam, Hannah)
COLLEGE: Bradford University
ACADEMIC QUALIFICATIONS: BSc Hons Mechanical Engineering
DIRECTORSHIPS: Non-executive Hammersmith & Fulham Workshop. Di-Log Test Equipment
PERSONAL PROFILE: After holding the position of managing director at Di-Log for two years. Ash set out to establish his own businesses, firstly starting an export agency and via a management buyout of an existing company he owns Di-Log Test Equipment based in Wembley.
NOMINATED BY: Syed Safiruddin, Pakistan Association

'GP in Corby for 16 years. Actively involved in local politics and care. Extension of medical centre to offer alternative medicine. Aromotherapy, physio, accupunture and hypnotherapy'

DR SURENDRA MISRA

MR KARAM CHAND MOHAN (Social Worker-Journalist)

Social Worker, Wandsworth Borough Council, 75 Cornwall Avenue, Southall, UB1 2TG

PLACE OF BIRTH: Babanpur, 20.7.52
MARITAL STATUS: Single
ACADEMIC QUALIFICATIONS: MA Political Science-CQSW-West London Institute of Higher Education
PROFESSIONAL QUALIFICATIONS: CQSW
MEMBERSHIPS: Secretary-Progressive Writers Association
HOBBIES AND INTERESTS: Music, reading, gardening
PERSONAL PROFILE: Came to UK in 1977. Worked for Civil Supplies Department in India. In UK worked as assistant editor for Punjab Times for seven years and was editor of Punjabi Darpan for four years. Also worked as freelance journalist. Author-Na Ghar De Ma Ghat De (Short Stories). Samen Maal Gallan (Interviews).

MRS SUDARSHON MOHINDRA JP (Community Activist)

Pensioner, Hindu Temple Cultural and Community Centre, 6 Tyneside Close, Aspley, Nottingham, NG8 5FX

PLACE OF BIRTH: East Africa, 15.3.33
MARITAL STATUS: Married
CHILDREN: Four (Anjali, Anita, Rajiv, Seema)
MEMBERSHIPS: Asian Arts Business Council
HONOURS/AWARDS: Citizen of Honour for Community Development
HOBBIES AND INTERESTS: Knitting, community work, the arts
PERSONAL PROFILE: Arrived from East Africa in 1965. Worked for Boots until 1995 and retired as a supervisor. Founder of Hindu Temple Nottingham and Kala Niketan Hindu School. Founder-trustee of Asian Arts Council. Achieved a lot for the community and busy as founder of Luncheon Club for the Hindu Senior Citizens.
NOMINATED BY: Devendra Sharma

MR MANSUR AHMED MOKIS (Divisional Manager)

98 Donald Street, Roath, Cardiff, CF2 4TR

PLACE OF BIRTH: Bangladesh, 31.12.70
MARITAL STATUS: Married
CHILDREN: Two (Rafiquzzaman, Rakibuzzaman)
COLLEGE: Dhaka University
ACADEMIC QUALIFICATIONS: Batchelor of Commerce
MEMBERSHIPS: President-South Wales Youth League. Gen Sec Cardiff Bangla School Management Committee. Organising secretary UK Bengali Journalists Assoc.
HONOURS/AWARDS: Distinguished Leadership Award from American Biographical Institution.
HOBBIES AND INTERESTS: Reading, journalism, voluntary work
PERSONAL PROFILE: I came to UK five years ago. Since my arrival have been actively involved in numerous community organisations and hold various positions. Have taken part in fundraising for Bangladesh Flood Relief. In Bangladesh I worked as a divisional manager for a life assurance company. Also actively involved and held various positions in many community organisations. Education secretary Greater Sylhet Welfare Council UK.
NOMINATED BY: Mr Mashahid Ali

DR BIJOY KRISHNA MONDAL (Consultant Physician)

Clinical Director, Rotherham General Hospitals NHS Trust, Shanti Niketan, Sitwell Grove, Rotherham, S60 3AY

PLACE OF BIRTH: India, 28.9.40
MARITAL STATUS: Married
CHILDREN: Three (Bipasha, Bidisha, Krishnendu)
COLLEGE: Royal Colleges
PROFESSIONAL QUALIFICATIONS: MB, FRCP (London), FRCP (Edin), FRCP (Glasgow), DT, M+H (Liverpool)
DIRECTORSHIPS: Clinical Director
MEMBERSHIPS: BMA, ODA, BAS
HONOURS/AWARDS: B Award
HOBBIES AND INTERESTS: Gardening, photography, travel
PERSONAL PROFILE: President of Rotherham Parkinson's Disease Society, ex Chairman of BMA Rotherham Division. Author of numerous articles in professional journals.

MRS DOLLY MONDAL (Lecturer)

Castle College, Granville Road, Sheffield

PLACE OF BIRTH: India, 9.9.49
MARITAL STATUS: Married
CHILDREN: Three (Bipasha, Bidisha, Krishnendu)
COLLEGE: Calcutta University
ACADEMIC QUALIFICATIONS: BA
PROFESSIONAL QUALIFICATIONS: Teacher Training
DIRECTORSHIPS: Director of Nursing Home. Secretary of Cultural Centre
MEMBERSHIPS: NATFHE. Udayan Cultural Centre
HOBBIES AND INTERESTS: Reading, music, dance, art, travel, cooking
PERSONAL PROFILE: Co-author of the poetry book 'Kabitanjali'. Numerous articles in cultural journals. Secretary of the Udayan Cultural Centre, Co-Writer of the 'Raymond-William Prize Winner Book'. 'Barbed Lines'

MR CLAUDE AJIT MORAES (Director JCWI)

CRE Commissioner, Joint Council for the Welfare of Immigrants,

PLACE OF BIRTH: South Yemen
MARITAL STATUS: Partner
COLLEGE: LSE, University of London, University of Dundee
ACADEMIC QUALIFICATIONS: LL.B (Law), MSc
PROFESSIONAL QUALIFICATIONS: Lawyer
HONOURS/AWARDS: Fellow, Royal Society of Arts (FRSA)
PERSONAL PROFILE: Commissioner for the Commission for Racial Equality (appointed 1998). Director, Joint Council for the Welfare of Immigrants (JCWI) (1992-) National Officer TUC (1989-92). Political advisor, House of Commons (1987-89). Parliamentary candidate (Labour, Harrow West 1992)
NOMINATED BY: Jane Horwood, JCWI

MRS RASHIDA MORBIWALLA (Businesswoman)

Jameel Store "One Stop Islamic Shop", 71 Berners Street, Highfields, Leicester, LE2 0FU

PLACE OF BIRTH: Tanzania, 25.1.49
MARITAL STATUS: Married
COLLEGE: Wigston College
ACADEMIC QUALIFICATIONS: Business Administration
HOBBIES AND INTERESTS: Garment designing, cooking, keeping fit, travelling
PERSONAL PROFILE: Rashida Morbiwalla runs a successful Islamic boutique -Jameel Store in Leicester. She is a religious teacher, accomplished cook, keep fit enthusiast, good singer, able speaker and life and soul of parties and gatherings. She wants to see woman succeed in business. She beams enthusiasm.

MR FIYAZ MUGHAL (Social Policy Development)

Project Manager, The Youth One Stop Shop, 6 Caxton Road, Wood Green, London, N22 6TB

PLACE OF BIRTH: Uganda, 14.9.71
MARITAL STATUS: Single
ACADEMIC QUALIFICATIONS: 2 O-Levels, 8 GCE's, 3 A-Levels
PROFESSIONAL QUALIFICATIONS: BSc-Neuroscience
HONOURS/AWARDS: Honours (BS-Neuroscience)
HOBBIES AND INTERESTS: Weight training, swimming, aerobic exercises, running
EMAIL: fiyaz.mughal@which.net
PERSONAL PROFILE: I am a social policy/service development officer with the Haringey CAB which involves fundraising, responding to social policy issues, supporting project development in service delivery and developing research methods. I am also project manager of Youth One Stop Shop, this involves fundraising, human and financial resource management and recruitment, financial planning and budgeting, and raising the profile of the service through both local and national press.
NOMINATED BY: Ushma Vyas

> Rashida Morbiwalla runs a successful Islamic boutique -Jameel Store in Leicester. She is a religious teacher and accomplished cook

DR SYEDA-MASOODA MUKHTAR
(BUSINESS STRATEGIST INTL.)

Manchester Business School, Cheshire, M33 4EN

PLACE OF BIRTH: Pakistan
MARITAL STATUS: Single
ACADEMIC QUALIFICATIONS: BSc (Econ)-M.Phil (Econ)-P.Dip (BIT)-PhD (Bus Admin)-FRSA
DIRECTORSHIPS: Non-Exec Director-NCHA Plc
MEMBERSHIPS: IMDA, AGB, Fellow Royal Society of Arts and Commerce
HONOURS/AWARDS: Youngest among top 100 business women of the year 1993 in the NW of England
HOBBIES AND INTERESTS: Enjoys travelling
PERSONAL PROFILE: Born in Pakistan, spent early childhood in the Middle East, educated in Europe. Now work internationally. Specialisms include business development and strategic management. Widely publicised and high profile work on women business owners and managers. Serves on the board of NCHA Plc.
NOMINATED BY: Karen Gabay, Manchester Business School

MR BIMAN MULLICK (ADVERTISING DESIGNER)

Publicity Consultant, 33 Stillness Road, London, SE23 1NG

PLACE OF BIRTH: India, 16.2.36
MARITAL STATUS: Married
CHILDREN: One (Sandra)
PROFESSIONAL QUALIFICATIONS: MCSD,FSTD
MEMBERSHIPS: Chartered Soc of Designers. Fellow of the Society Typographic Designers.
HONOURS/AWARDS: International Gold Medal for Brit. Gandhi Stamp. WHO Award for posters,1988
HOBBIES AND INTERESTS: Music
PERSONAL PROFILE: The first overseas designer to design a British postage stamp. Designed the first set of postage stamps for Bangladesh. Author of 'Hanuman Saves the Prince' and other picture books which are published by leading British publishers including Oxford University Press and Cambridge University Press. Currently creating original art and design using computers.

MR GUL AHMED MUN (CHILD-FAMILY THERAPIST)

Social Worker,

PLACE OF BIRTH: India, 13.1.39
MARITAL STATUS: Married
CHILDREN: Three (Safia-Amber, Jainab, Aisha)
COLLEGE: Karachi University, Bristol University
ACADEMIC QUALIFICATIONS: B.Comm, (KAR) CRSW (London), ACRSW (Bristol)
PROFESSIONAL QUALIFICATIONS: Certificate and Res.Soc Work
HOBBIES AND INTERESTS: Travelling, photography, cooking
PERSONAL PROFILE: I have worked with Department of Health for 22 years where my job involved management training, counselling, therapy, education and PR.

MR SEPALE MUNASINGHE (BARRISTER)

235 London Road, Twickenham, TW1 1ES

PLACE OF BIRTH: Sri Lanka, 2.1.37
MARITAL STATUS: Married
CHILDREN: Two (Karin, Gitanjali)
PROFESSIONAL QUALIFICATIONS: Barrister (Lincoln's Inn), Attorney (Sri Lanka)
HOBBIES AND INTERESTS: Travel, cooking, music
PERSONAL PROFILE: Since 1986, have been a chairman of Social Security Appeals Tribunal, Disability Appeals Tribunal and Special Adjudicator Immigration Appeals Authority. Member public inquiry into riots in Handsworth, Birmingham 1986. Governor of a comprehensive school 1981. Lecturer and examiner in law. Assistant Commissioner, Parliamentary Boundary Commission 1995
NOMINATED BY: Neelam Chaudhari

> ## The first overseas designer to design a British postage stamp. Designed the first set of postage stamps for Bangladesh
>
> **MR BIMAN MULLICK**

CLLR PITAMBARUM MUNISAMY (NURSE-TUTOR RTD)

City Councillor, Gloucester County Council, 62 Hempsted Lane, Hempsted, Gloucester, GL2 5JN

PLACE OF BIRTH: Mauritius, 9.12.42
MARITAL STATUS: Widowed
CHILDREN: Two (Richard, David)
COLLEGE: Open University
ACADEMIC QUALIFICATIONS: BA
PROFESSIONAL QUALIFICATIONS: RGN, Dip N, OND, Cert Ed, Cert HSM
DIRECTORSHIPS: Afro-Caribbean Association Ltd
MEMBERSHIPS: Liberal Democrats
HOBBIES AND INTERESTS: Gardening
PERSONAL PROFILE: Mauritian born. Trained as a nurse in1967-Nurse teacher 1973. Retired 1992 joined Liberal Democrat Party. First ever black councillor elected in Gloucester City Council in May 1995. Liberal Democrat candidate at 1997 General Election in Gloucester.
NOMINATED BY: EMG

DR GHULAM MURSHID (TEACHING-BROADCASTING)

Bengali Service, BBC World Service, Bush House, London, WC2B 4PH

PLACE OF BIRTH: Bangladesh, 31.3.40
MARITAL STATUS: Married
CHILDREN: two (Antu Panini, Amita Gargi Bipasha)
COLLEGE: Dhaka, Rajshahi, Melbourne
ACADEMIC QUALIFICATIONS: BA,MA, PhD
PROFESSIONAL QUALIFICATIONS: PhD
MEMBERSHIPS: Fellow, Bangla Academy
HONOURS/AWARDS: Bangla Academy Prize for Literature 1982
HOBBIES AND INTERESTS: Research, writing
PERSONAL PROFILE: Researcher, author and broadcaster. Published 14 books mainly on Bengali socio-cultural history (18th and 19th Centuries) and literature. Was professor of Bengali at Rajshahi University.
NOMINATED BY: Miss Shireen Khanom

CLLR KUMAR MURSHID (SENIOR MANAGER)

Consultant-Councillor, London Borough of Tower Hamlets, 19 New Row, Covent Garden, London, WC2

PLACE OF BIRTH: Bangladesh, 10.7.55
MARITAL STATUS: Married
CHILDREN: Two (Tanhim, Adrian)
COLLEGE: CSPS, Warsaw, City University London
ACADEMIC QUALIFICATIONS: MSc in Economics / CPE (Continuing legal studies)
PROFESSIONAL QUALIFICATIONS: Top managers qualification through local government management board
DIRECTORSHIPS: Tale of India Ltd
MEMBERSHIPS: Labour Party, The National Assembly Against Racism
HOBBIES AND INTERESTS: Politics, current affairs, travelling, literature
PERSONAL PROFILE: Sixteen years of involvement in community development and equality work in East London. Head of Policy and Equality at LBTH January, 1998. Local councillor in LBTH since May 1998. Chair, National Assembly Against Racism and Youth Action Scheme.

MR SACHDEV MUSAFIR (EXPORT AGENT)

Managing Director, Onkar Trading Ltd, 38 Corringway, London, W5 3AA

PLACE OF BIRTH: India, 5.5.44
MARITAL STATUS: Married
COLLEGE: Delhi University
ACADEMIC QUALIFICATIONS: BA in Economics. National Diploma in Hotel Management
DIRECTORSHIPS: Onkar Trading Ltd
MEMBERSHIPS: International Punjabi Society. Khokhrain Biradari (UK)
EMAIL: musafirb@aol.com
PERSONAL PROFILE: Born in Amritsar, educated in Delhi and England, son of well known politician Giani Gurmukh Singh Musafir, ex-chief minister of Punjab. Came to England in 1964. Studied here for hotel management and obtained a national diploma. Currently running his own business in exports from Europe.

DR FAHERA SINDHU MUSAJI (RESEARCHER)

National Audit Office, Health VFM, 157-197 Buckingham Palace Road, London, SW1W 9SP

PLACE OF BIRTH: Birmingham, 5.11.67
MARITAL STATUS: Married
COLLEGE: Oxford, Somerville College
ACADEMIC QUALIFICATIONS: BSc, PGCE, MSc, D.Phil (PhD)
PROFESSIONAL QUALIFICATIONS: PGCE
HONOURS/AWARDS: SERC & RCN Scholorships
HOBBIES AND INTERESTS: Reading, Hindi pop and bhangra, movies, DIY, philosophy, theology, travel
PERSONAL PROFILE: After A -Levels I gained the highest First Class Hons in Maths in London. I then went onto teach and gained a scholarship to Somerville College, Oxford for a MSc and PhD in Medical Statistics. Having completed this in 1994 I joined the NAO as research methodologist where I advise on methodology and statistics of VFM audits of government departments. I have written numerous publications in my field and have presented my research to both national and international academic audiences.
NOMINATED BY: Tariq Ismail Musaji

MR SYED MOHAMMED MUSTAFA
(JOURNALIST-ADVERTISING AGENCY)

2 Baynes Close, Enfield, EN1 4BN

PLACE OF BIRTH: India, 26.11.29
MARITAL STATUS: Divorced
CHILDREN: One (Ayisha Anne)
COLLEGE: University of Karachi
ACADEMIC QUALIFICATIONS: BSc Commerce
DIRECTORSHIPS: SMI Advertising
MEMBERSHIPS: Ex-President Foreign Press Assoc. RAC Club. 100
HOBBIES AND INTERESTS: Politics, cooking
PERSONAL PROFILE: Came to UK 40 years ago. Born in Delhi. Started in Y&R Advertising Agency. I joined FPA and was elected to the committee in 1976. Became only third person from a Third World country to become president in 1982. Also in 1977 set up SMI Advertising-The first ethnic minority advertising agency in UK.

DR SAYED ABU MUZAFFAR (DOCTOR)

Exec. Divisional Director, OMYA UK Ltd, 16 Stockbridge Road, Elloughton, HU15 1HN

PLACE OF BIRTH: India, 22.1.44
MARITAL STATUS: Married
CHILDREN: Two (Jameel, Hassan Nabeel)
COLLEGE: Bradford University
ACADEMIC QUALIFICATIONS: BSc, PgD, PhD
PROFESSIONAL QUALIFICATIONS: Member Inst. of Mana Cement
MEMBERSHIPS: Assoc. of Institute of Directors
HONOURS/AWARDS: Full colours-Bradford University
HOBBIES AND INTERESTS: Badminton, music, walking
PERSONAL PROFILE: Senior management positions held in international companies, Blue Circle industries and Omya. Senior member of the university, chairman, and captain of Bradford University Badminton Club. Director of Omya Pension Funds, awards for sports and music. International traveller.

MR SARJIT SINGH MYRRPUREY MBE (DIRECTOR REC RTD)

102 Kingsley Road, Bishops Tachrook, Leamington Spa, CV33 9RZ

PLACE OF BIRTH: Uganda, 29.6.25
MARITAL STATUS: Married
CHILDREN: Six (Anand, Pushpinder, Jasbinder, Ravinder, Rajbir, Davinder Paul)
COLLEGE: Khalsa College / Punjab University
ACADEMIC QUALIFICATIONS: BA
PROFESSIONAL QUALIFICATIONS: NEBSS
DIRECTORSHIPS: Director Racial Equality Councils, Warwick District and County of West Glamorgan
MEMBERSHIPS: Institute of Public Relations, Ethnic Minority Community Forum, Warcs
HONOURS/AWARDS: MBE
HOBBIES AND INTERESTS: Poetry and playwriting, theatrical performances and reading
PERSONAL PROFILE: Sarjit Singh Myrrpurey, director of Racial Equality, England & Wales (Ret); first Asian collector of customs and excise, founder of first club for blacks, Asians and whites, Tanzania; settlement in Britain 1967; Community Relations 1972-1994; MBE in 1994; actor, playwright, poet and radio broadcaster of great talent.

Entrants in the Asians in the Millennium have

been nominated for their achievements and

contributions. You can

nominate someone who

deserves to be in the

Who's Who of Asian Achievers 2000

Entries are free

Send in your nominations, including name,

contact address and telephone number to:

Books Division, Ethnic Media Group,

148 Cambridge Heath Road, London E1 5QJ

DR ZENOBIA NADIRSHAW (CLINICAL PSYCHOLOGY)

Lead Clinician/ Head of Psychology, Brent, Kensington, Chelsea & Westmins. NHS, 20 Kingsbridge Road, London, W10 6PU

PLACE OF BIRTH: India
MARITAL STATUS: Married
COLLEGE: North-West Thames Region
ACADEMIC QUALIFICATIONS: MA in Applied Clinical Psy, Diploma in Clincal Psychol, PhD
PROFESSIONAL QUALIFICATIONS: Chartered Psychotherapist (UCCC)
DIRECTORSHIPS: Trustee of the Mental Health Foundation,
MEMBERSHIPS: Fellow of the Royal Society of Arts, Manufacture & Commerce, Associate Fellow of the British Psychological Society
HONOURS/AWARDS: Winner of the BPS Inequality of Opportunity Award 1996/97
HOBBIES AND INTERESTS: Theatre, music, dance, eating out, reading
PERSONAL PROFILE: Being involved in National Health Service work just under twenty-five years I am aware of inequality of opportunity and inequality of service to Asian people in healthcare, planning, provision and service delivery. I have lectured and published widely over the years and I am now in a position to effect change, influence policy practice and national strategy.

MS MARIUM NAFISA (NURSE-DEVELOPMENT CONSULTANT)

Health & Social Care Officer, Westminster Race Equality Council, 16 Kinsdale Road, Peckham, London, SE15 4HL

PLACE OF BIRTH: Bangladesh, 13.3.56
MARITAL STATUS: Single
COLLEGE: N.London
ACADEMIC QUALIFICATIONS: RGN, RM, BA, MA
PROFESSIONAL QUALIFICATIONS: Nurse, Midwife
MEMBERSHIPS: MEDACT, NEHM
HONOURS/AWARDS: Hope 1995
HOBBIES AND INTERESTS: Equality issues, writing, travelling, promoting peace
PERSONAL PROFILE: Nurse, midwife and community activist. Founder member-Medical Action for Nuclear Disarmament (MEDACT) Network of European Health Managers (NEHM). Primary Health Education and Care Society (Bangladesh). Winner of HOPE Prize 1995 for young health managers. Interest: Equality, poverty elimination. Writes on such subjects.

MISS PARMINDER K NAGRA (ACTOR)

Lisa Richards Agency, Haymarket House, 28-29 Haymarket, London, SW1Y 4SP

PLACE OF BIRTH: Leicester, 5.10.75
MARITAL STATUS: Single
ACADEMIC QUALIFICATIONS: A Level in Contemporary Dance & Theatre Studies
HOBBIES AND INTERESTS: Reading, keeping fit, singing, cinema, theatre
PERSONAL PROFILE: Parminder's credits include: The 'Asia Award' winning 'Fourteen songs, two weddings and a funeral' and 'Tainted Dawn'. Tamasha Theatre Company: 'Oh Sweet Sita'. Tara Arts; 'Skeleton'. Soho Theatre Company: 'Sleeping Beauty'. Theatre Royal Stratford East: 'Nimai'. Leicester Haymarket: 'Fair Ladies'. Royal National Theatre: 'Dancing Girls of Lahore' and 'The Whispering Tree' (BBC Radio 4); 'Turning World' (C4); 'King Girl' and 'Casualty' (BBC).

MR SANDEEP NAGRA (BASKETBALL PLAYER)

Rushey Mead School,

MARITAL STATUS: Single
HOBBIES AND INTERESTS: Basketball, sport
PERSONAL PROFILE: Brilliant basketball player. Invited to trial for England. Trains with Leicester Riders.
NOMINATED BY: J Acharya

MR TOMMY NAGRA (TELEVISION BROADCASTER)

Producer, BBC Television, BBC Birmingham, Room 719, Pebble Mill Road, Birmingham, B5 7QQ

PLACE OF BIRTH: Birmingham, 9.1.68
MARITAL STATUS: Married
COLLEGE: Sheffield Hallam University
ACADEMIC QUALIFICATIONS: BA Hons Communication Media Studies
MEMBERSHIPS: NUJ, BECTU
HONOURS/AWARDS: National Mentoring Consortum for African, Caribbean and Asian Students, World Fest Houston Film Award for Investigative Journalism 1997
HOBBIES AND INTERESTS: Liverpool Football Club, music, Sony playstation
EMAIL: tommy.nagra@bbc.co.uk
PERSONAL PROFILE: Currently producing a documentary series on the history of Sikhs. Also producer of BBC 2's award winning series 'East', past work includes: The mysterious death of Ricky Reel; Racism in the medical profession; the rise in Asian youth crime and the lack of Asian footballers. Also produced the first series of Asian youth shop-Cafe 21. Born in Handsworth, Birmingham and strongly committed to putting the Asian community in the spotlight.

MR KEWAL NAHAR (LECTURER)

Designated Lecturer, 20 Rupert Street, Woodlands, Glasgow, G4 9AR

PLACE OF BIRTH: India, 10.9.47
MARITAL STATUS: Married
CHILDREN: Three (Ketan, Keshav, Kishan)
COLLEGE: Heriot-Watt Edin
ACADEMIC QUALIFICATIONS: BSc Hon.2(i), Physics Post Graduate Diploma Comp Sci
HOBBIES AND INTERESTS: Music, metaphysics, poetry, singing
PERSONAL PROFILE: Came from India without any knowledge of English left school without any qualifications. Worked for two years, joined further education and then to university. Gained BSc (Hons) Physics, Post Graduate Diploma in Comp Sci, Post Graduate in Teaching Diploma. Now designated lecturer in a further education college. Co-author of two maths books.
NOMINATED BY: Dr Seth

MISS NAZMIN NAHER (STUDENT)

PLACE OF BIRTH: London, 18.4.86
MARITAL STATUS: Single
COLLEGE: Mulberry School for Girls
HONOURS/AWARDS: Dance, PE, swimming and attendance
HOBBIES AND INTERESTS: Dancing, going out with friends, doing homework
PERSONAL PROFILE: I'm a student at Mulberry School. Next year I'll be in Year 9. My best subject is dance, this is because I achieved a lot of awards and did dance in Stepney Green School Centre. When I grow up I hope to be a nurse or professional dance teacher.

MR SHAM LAL NAIB JP (HEADMASTER-INSPECTOR RTD)

Hindu Association, 34 Mercia Road, Maidenhead, SL6 3DR

PLACE OF BIRTH: Pakistan, 7.3.37
MARITAL STATUS: Married
CHILDREN: Three (Seema, Kumar, Kishore)
COLLEGE: Leicester, Nottingham, Punjab
ACADEMIC QUALIFICATIONS: MA, Dip. Ed
PROFESSIONAL QUALIFICATIONS: Diploma in Education
DIRECTORSHIPS: SDK Jewellers
MEMBERSHIPS: Hindu Association; Commission for Racial Equality
HOBBIES AND INTERESTS: Community work, writing, music, speaking
PERSONAL PROFILE: Founder Hindu Association / Temple, Wellingborough 1969 -87. Justice of the Peace; Education inspector 1987-91; Headmaster of two schools; vice-chair and chair Wellingborough Council for Racial Equality 1974-81; Past member BBC Radio Advisory Committee. President of UK Council of Hindu Temples. Chairman Ethnic Minority Governors Committee.

Headmaster of two schools; vice-chair and chair Wellingborough Council for Racial Equality 1974-81; Past member BBC Radio Advisory Committee. President of UK Council of Hindu Temples.

SHAM LAL NAIB JP

MR BALWANT NAIK (TEACHING-JOURNALISM)

Freelance Journalist, 48 Shackleton Road, Southall, UB1 2JB

PLACE OF BIRTH: India, 15.11.20
MARITAL STATUS: Married
CHILDREN: Five (Shirish, Yamini, Abhay, Shailendra, Rita)
COLLEGE: Bombay India
ACADEMIC QUALIFICATIONS: BA Hons; MA, FIAP
PROFESSIONAL QUALIFICATIONS: Dip Ed
DIRECTORSHIPS: Fellow International Academy of Poets, Life member: UK based Gujarati Literary Academy
MEMBERSHIPS: Award winning poet-Queens Jubilee,
HONOURS/AWARDS: International Authors and Writers-Who's Who 1982
HOBBIES AND INTERESTS: Reading, writing and travelling
PERSONAL PROFILE: Post graduate and creative writer-Prolific in Gujarati and English. Publications: poems, short story collections and novels-Latest 'Passage from Uganda'. Award winning poet, Queen's Jubilee 'An ode to this seat of Her Majesty'. Fellow international Academy of Poets. Poetry collections: Petals of Roses 'Nirzarah' (streamlets). Past president, Gujarati Literary Academy.
NOMINATED BY: Vipool Kalyani JP

MR JIGAR NAIK (STUDENT)

Captain U-15 Cricket, Rushey Mead School, 80 Marfitt Street, Leicester, LE4 6RN

MEMBERSHIPS: Leicestershire Schools Cricket Team
HONOURS/AWARDS: Leicestershire Player of the Year 1998
HOBBIES AND INTERESTS: All sports
PERSONAL PROFILE: Outstanding cricketer who has just recently been invited to trial for England.
NOMINATED BY: Mr J Acharya

MR MOHAMMAD NAJIB JP (BUSINESSMAN)

Store Owner, 466 Colne Road, Burnley, BB10 1TW

PLACE OF BIRTH: Pakistan, 1.2.50
CHILDREN: Four (Adil, Muddasgar, Hamayed, Aroop)
COLLEGE: Punjab
ACADEMIC QUALIFICATIONS: BA, B.Ed
MEMBERSHIPS: Jinnah CDS (Chairman)
HONOURS/AWARDS: Justice of the Peace
HOBBIES AND INTERESTS: Politics
PERSONAL PROFILE: I came to this country in 1978. Established my own business. Became Labour Party member 1982. Elected councillor in 1989. In 1993 elected councillor for Lancashire County Council. I was appointed Justice of the Peace 1990, Chairman of Jinnah Community Development Service.

MR YOGESH NAKARJA (SOFTWARE ENGINEER)

Configuration Manager, National Grid Plc, Bearwood Road, Sindlesham, RG41 5BN

PLACE OF BIRTH: Uganda, 28.6.58
MARITAL STATUS: Married
CHILDREN: Two (Sayona, Sayal)
COLLEGE: Brunel University
ACADEMIC QUALIFICATIONS: MSc Numerial Analysis, BSc Hons Mathematics with Management Applications
MEMBERSHIPS: Technical Representative-EMA (Engineers & Managers Association)
HONOURS/AWARDS: 1st Prize-Primary leaving school examinations, Uganda
HOBBIES AND INTERESTS: Fatherhood, cricket
PERSONAL PROFILE: A religious person with two noteworthy periods of full-time honorary work for Anoopam Mission-a charity of which I was an executive trustee (1979-89): 1981/82-Project Manager in Denham, Bucks to set up 16 acre place of worship.1987/88-Computer consultant at Mogri, India to pioneer and set up Information Technology Centre (ITC) for Anoopam Mission, India.

MR RAMESH NANDA (HOTELIER)

Resident Manager, St James's Court Hotel & Apt, Buckingham Gate, London, SW1E 6AF

PLACE OF BIRTH: Kenya, 4.6.42
MARITAL STATUS: Married
CHILDREN: Two (Vikram, Radhika)
PROFESSIONAL QUALIFICATIONS: AHCIMA
MEMBERSHIPS: Hotel & Catering Management Institute
HOBBIES AND INTERESTS: Reading, golf, tennis
PERSONAL PROFILE: Over twenty years of experience in management of various airlines, in operations, sales and marketing in UK and overseas. Member of Prince of Wales Youth Trust and Asian Business Network. Managing 5-Star hotel, for last 13 years.

DR MATTUR NARAYANAVADHANI NANDAKUMARA (EXECUTIVE DIRECTOR)

Bharatiya Vidya Bhavan,

PLACE OF BIRTH: India, 28.10.52
MARITAL STATUS: Married
CHILDREN: Two (Raghunandan, Sitalakshmi)
COLLEGE: Mysore University, London University (SOAS)
ACADEMIC QUALIFICATIONS: MA (Sanskrit), PhD (Devotional Litt.)
PROFESSIONAL QUALIFICATIONS: Teaching Sanskrit since 1977. Languages to read and write: Sanskrit, Kannada, English, Hindi, Tamil, Teluga, Gujarati
MEMBERSHIPS: Member of various academic bodies on religious education in various boroughs.
HOBBIES AND INTERESTS: Enjoys lecturing on Indian matters
PERSONAL PROFILE: As the Bhavan's academic director, has organised workshops, lecture demonstrations, covering all aspects of Indian art and culture such as: music and dance; concerts by top artistes; seminars on religious topics; lectures by visiting scholars. Was on the selector's panel of the Borough of Brent to select music teachers and has been instrumental in running Bhavan's academic courses at places such as Letchworth, Milton Keynes and Kingsbury.
NOMINATED BY: Dr H V S Shastry

MR SWATANTRA NANDANWAR (LECTURER)

Essex Couty Council, Members Suite, PO Box 11, County Hall, Chelmsford, CM1 1DT

PLACE OF BIRTH: India, 17.4.44
MARITAL STATUS: Married
CHILDREN: One (Swapana)
COLLEGE: Queen Mary College
ACADEMIC QUALIFICATIONS: BSc, Diploma in Law
PROFESSIONAL QUALIFICATIONS: PGCE
HOBBIES AND INTERESTS: Literature, art, music, watching sport
PERSONAL PROFILE: A lecturer in health science and social care. The only ethnic minority councillor serving on Essex County Council, with special interests in social services, education and enterprise. Secretary to the Essex Race Equality Council. A member of Hindu Samaj (Basildon), promoting social and cultural links within the Asian community.
NOMINATED BY: Viplav Nandanwar

MR SYED Z H HAIDER NAQVI (CHARTERED ACCOUNTANT)

Partner, Haider Naqvi & Co, Concept House, 225 Hale Lane, Edgware, HA8 9QF

PLACE OF BIRTH: Pakistan, 14.10.49
MARITAL STATUS: Married
CHILDREN: Two (Chantal Samreen, Sabrina Yasmeen)
COLLEGE: Karachi
ACADEMIC QUALIFICATIONS: B.Comm; MA (Economics)
PROFESSIONAL QUALIFICATIONS: FCA, FCCA, FCIS
DIRECTORSHIPS: HELPS Ltd, Concept Computers International Ltd, First Tax Shop Ltd
MEMBERSHIPS: RAC Club
HOBBIES AND INTERESTS: Urdu poet, (2 collections: sare-Gulberg-eHena & Dard-ki-Dahleez) snooker, chess
EMAIL: hnco786@aol.com
PERSONAL PROFILE: Apart from a brief period in commerce and industry I spent most of my professional career of over 25 years in public practice. I have tended to focus on audit and have written a manual on the subject. I founded Hendon and Edgware Local Practices Support Group and offer free and confidential consultation to sole practitioners.

DR BHOPINDER SINGH NARU MBE
(DOCTOR-DENTAL SURGEON)

Dental Practice, c/o Race Equality Council, MEA House 4th Floor, Ellison Place, Newcastle Upon Tyne

PLACE OF BIRTH: Kenya, 18.1.29
MARITAL STATUS: Married
CHILDREN: Three (Sucitan, Amar, Amrit)
COLLEGE: University of Durham. Kings College Newcastle, Medical School Newcastle
ACADEMIC QUALIFICATIONS: MB, BS (Dur), LDS (Dur)
PROFESSIONAL QUALIFICATIONS: Dip Med Acu (UK)

MEMBERSHIPS: BMA
HONOURS/AWARDS: Queen Silver Jubilee Medal Award. MBE 1998
HOBBIES AND INTERESTS: Portrait painting, sculpture, art, classical Indian music
PERSONAL PROFILE: Dental qualification 1957. Medical qualification 1964. Member of following: Past and Present Race Relations Board, CRC, Regional Health Authority, BBC Council, BBC Presenter. Hon Physician for Chinese Community. Awarded MBE for Community Service 1998. Appointed Police Surgeon to Northumbria Police 1979. Speaks English, Urdu, Hindi, Punjabi and Swahili.
NOMINATED BY: Jon Harte, BBC Newcastle

MRS BUSHRA NASIR (TEACHER)

Headteacher, Plashet School, Plashet Grove, East Ham, London, E6 1DG

PLACE OF BIRTH: Pakistan, 9.11.52
MARITAL STATUS: Married
CHILDREN: Three (Imran, Unjum, Aneela)
COLLEGE: Queen Mary College
ACADEMIC QUALIFICATIONS: BSc (Hon) London, PGCE
MEMBERSHIPS: NAHT, AMGS
HOBBIES AND INTERESTS: Reading, swimming, badminton, social work
PERSONAL PROFILE: Headteacher since April 1993 of an 11-16 secondary school with 1350 students. In the 1999 Ofsted report the school was rated at A*, putting it in top 5% of secondary schools in relation to achievement. Have spoken at a number of conferences related to raising achievement and development of ethnic minority teachers.
NOMINATED BY: Fatema R Shaikh

SHAZIA NASREEN (STUDENT)

Cash Traders, 123 Lawn Lane, Hemel Hempstead, HP3 9HS

PLACE OF BIRTH: Hemel Hempstead, 10.2.78
MARITAL STATUS: Single
COLLEGE: Northampton
ACADEMIC QUALIFICATIONS: Higher National Diploma Fashion
PROFESSIONAL QUALIFICATIONS: GNVQ Advanced Art & Design
HONOURS/AWARDS: Sir George Burns Award
HOBBIES AND INTERESTS: Fashion designer, badminton, travelling
PERSONAL PROFILE: Shazia is a very determined and remarkable young woman who has been profoundly deaf since birth. She recently completed an Intermediate GNVQ course in art and design and won £250 from the Sir George Burns Fund-(which was set up to help young people with special needs). Shazia also managed to find a place for her fashion design skills in the wardrobe department at the Palace Theatre Watford making costumes for the classic mystery 'Outward Bound" and for a summer school production. Shazia uses sign language and is supported by lipreaders and her communicator.
NOMINATED BY: Asif Iqbal

MR AVI NASSA (ACTOR-WRITER)

Artistic Director, Whispering Eyes Theatre Co, 20 Belsize Square, London, NW3 4HT

PLACE OF BIRTH: Jerusalem, 28.6.56
MARITAL STATUS: Single
MEMBERSHIPS: British Equity
HOBBIES AND INTERESTS: Travelling and languages, song, dance
PERSONAL PROFILE: I was born in Jerusalem to a Jewish Indian mother and Jewish Iraqi father. In my 20's set to travel the world and ended up 1985 in London establishing my theatre company, writing about Women from the Eastern world including a play about my mother's life 'Woman in the moon'.

MR NARINDER THAKUR NATH
(ADMINISTRATOR-ACCOUNTANT RTD)

8 Hadleigh Rise, Caversham, Reading, RG4 6RW

PLACE OF BIRTH: Kenya, 28.9.24
MARITAL STATUS: Widower
CHILDREN: Three (Dharmvir BSc, Anita (Comp.Tech), Geeta (MSc))
ACADEMIC QUALIFICATIONS: London Matriculation
DIRECTORSHIPS: Past Dir: Narsingh & Nath (Civil Engineers)
MEMBERSHIPS: British Engineers (AMINBE). Past Associate Member of Institution of British Engineers

HONOURS/AWARDS: Promotions in Employment
HOBBIES AND INTERESTS: Photography, travelling, short story writing
PERSONAL PROFILE: Phenomenal rise in employment. Became chief staff officer on railway construction project. Chief of administrative service in North Africa etc, Social: Active campaigner through Asian media system against caste and class systems. Topics discussed on Asian radio.

DR PATHIKONDA VISWAMBARA NATH MBE (DOCTOR)

Principle GP,

DATE OF BIRTH: 1.3.42
MARITAL STATUS: Married
CHILDREN: Two
COLLEGE: Mysore University,
ACADEMIC QUALIFICATIONS: MBBS, DLO London
PROFESSIONAL QUALIFICATIONS: Diploma in Acupuncture therapy,training in occupational medicine
MEMBERSHIPS: Lion's Club International, Falklands Islands Children's Aid

HONOURS/AWARDS: MBE
HOBBIES AND INTERESTS: Charity work
PERSONAL PROFILE: Dr Nath has helped financially in the setting up of an Institute of Religious Studies (Gita Mandir) in Kolar, India, to promote religious education. He personally financed the setting up of a charity eye hospital in Karnataka, India, providing a building worth £75,000, Fifty free cataract operations are carried out every month. Initiator of 'Stanleys of the World' he arranged for deaf and dumb children from the Falklands Islands to come to the England's Northeast for two-years training

MR GAVARAL MOHAMED NATHOO
(CHARTERED ACCOUNTANT)

Practitioner Financial Conlts, Gavar Nathoo & Co, 3 Quex Road, London, NW6 4QE

PLACE OF BIRTH: Tanzania, 30.4.34
MARITAL STATUS: Married
CHILDREN: Two (Tazmeen, Salma)
COLLEGE: ICAEW
PROFESSIONAL QUALIFICATIONS: FCA
DIRECTORSHIPS: Brent Business Venture Ltd, Europlay Ltd, Tanga Renunion Ltd
MEMBERSHIPS: Rotary Club of Hampstead, Brent & Harrow Chamber of Commerce
HOBBIES AND INTERESTS: Music, arts, travel
PERSONAL PROFILE: Past president-Brent Chamber of Commerce. Also-Hampstead Rotary Club. Past governor-Hampstead School. Treasurer-Wembley Crime Prevention Panel. Chairman-Tanga Reunion. Director-Brent Business Venture. Co-opted member: Disabilities Committee (Brent).

MS DIL NAVAZ (TV PRESENTER-JOURNALIST)

Christina Shepherd Ltd, 13 Radnor Walk, London, SW3 4BP

MARITAL STATUS: Single
PROFESSIONAL QUALIFICATIONS: LLAM and ALAM Hons
MEMBERSHIPS: Equity and NUJ
HOBBIES AND INTERESTS: Theatre, photography, reading, current affairs

DR JAI K NAYAR (MEDICINE)

World President Friends Circle International, 10 Bengeworth Road, Harrow, HA1 3SE

PLACE OF BIRTH: India
MARITAL STATUS: Married
CHILDREN: Three (Arun, Kiron, Anoop)
COLLEGE: Punjab and London
PROFESSIONAL QUALIFICATIONS: MBBS (PB), DTM&H (ENG)
MEMBERSHIPS: FCI India Association, IPS, PSA
HONOURS/AWARDS: Hind Rattan 1990, Mother India 1992
HOBBIES AND INTERESTS: Sports, socialising
PERSONAL PROFILE: Arrived in UK from Tanzania 1971. World president Friends Circle International, patron India Association Harrow. Patron Home and Abroad. Vice president Unity Forum. Member International Cultural Exchange and other organisations. IPS and PS. Awarded Hind Rattan Award 1990 and Mother India International Award 1992.
NOMINATED BY: K K Singh

LALI NAYAR (MEDIA PRESENTER)

Food Consultant,

PLACE OF BIRTH: India, 29.4.46
MARITAL STATUS: Married
CHILDREN: Two (Aj, Priti)
COLLEGE: Osimania University, India
ACADEMIC QUALIFICATIONS: Bachelor of Arts in English and History
PROFESSIONAL QUALIFICATIONS: Diploma in Fine Arts, Diploma Indian Cookery
MEMBERSHIPS: Guild of Food Writers and various others
HOBBIES AND INTERESTS: Cooking, travelling, gardening, reading, writing
PERSONAL PROFILE: Lali Nayar, voted UK's 'Indian Chef of the Year' 1993 is a home economist, author and charity worker. She was TV Asia's cookery presenter with her own shows 'Lali's Rasoi' and 'Lali's Khaana Khazana'. Her food related documentaries 'A taste of success' for Zee TV were a big success. Central TV invited her to join their team to do the cookery feature in 'Eastern Mix' series. Lali drove a van on a number of charity missions to Poland, Albania and Romania supplying hospitals and orphanages with medical aid.

MS FARAH NAZ (PSYCHOTHERAPIST)

Asian Counselling Co-ordinator, Asian Counselling Service, 54 Ormiston Road, London, SE10 0LN

PLACE OF BIRTH: Pakistan, 23.11.67
MARITAL STATUS: Single
COLLEGE: King's College, London University
ACADEMIC QUALIFICATIONS: BSc Hons, MSc (Psychiotherapy)
PROFESSIONAL QUALIFICATIONS: Counsellor, Diploma
MEMBERSHIPS: BAC
HOBBIES AND INTERESTS: Climbing, Thai kick-boxing, reading
PERSONAL PROFILE: Having trained and worked in mental health for eight years, I set up a free Asian counselling service. I have obtained funding to train unemployed Asians as counsellors who are now successfully working. I have modified the service approach which is unique, culturally sensitive and progressive!
NOMINATED BY: Maureen Robertson, MIND

MR NAZRUL ISLAM NAZ (POET)

4 Limscott House, Bruce Road, London, E3 3HR

PLACE OF BIRTH: Bangladesh, 25.3.59
MARITAL STATUS: Married
CHILDREN: Five (Shahrear, Shahnewaz, Shahnoor, Shaherzadi, Shahara)
COLLEGE: University College London, Reading
ACADEMIC QUALIFICATIONS: BSc Philosophy
HOBBIES AND INTERESTS: Reading
PERSONAL PROFILE: Poet-translator have translated modern Anglo-American poetry into Bangla. Published work in UK, US and Banlgadesh. Currently engaged into theories of poetics and epistomology.

RT REV. DR MICHAEL NAZIR-ALI (DIOCESAN BISHOP)

Bishop of Rochester, Church of England, Bishopscourt, 24 St Margarets Street, Rochester, ME1 1TS

PLACE OF BIRTH: Pakistan, 19.8.49
MARITAL STATUS: Married
CHILDREN: Two (Shamaoun (Shammy), Ross)
COLLEGE: Oxford University, Cambridge University
ACADEMIC QUALIFICATIONS: BA, BLIEE, MLitt, PhD
DIRECTORSHIPS: Christian Aid (up to 1998), Oxford Centre for Mission Studies etc
MEMBERSHIPS: The Communion and Role of Women in the Ordained Ministry. Anglican and Roman Catholic International Commission. Board of Mission of the General Synod of the Church of England. Inter faith Consultative Group. Chairman of Council of Trinity College, Bristol.
HOBBIES AND INTERESTS: Cricket, music, reading, television, playing scrabble
PERSONAL PROFILE: Michael has been a visiting lecturer in a number of universities and colleges in the UK, Canada, the US and Australia. He is now visiting Professor of Theology and Religious Studies at the University of Greenwich. He has travelled widely in Africa, Asia, Australia, Europe, North and South America. He is the 106th Bishop of Rochester and the first non-white Diocesan Bishop in the Church of England. He is the author of five books.
NOMINATED BY: EMG

MRS BALBIR KAUR NAZRAN (ACTIVITIES OFFICER)

Activities Officer,

PLACE OF BIRTH: Phillipines, 11.2.49
MARITAL STATUS: Married
CHILDREN: Three (Jeevan, Mithchy, Rajan)
ACADEMIC QUALIFICATIONS: Tutor for Indian Embroidery and Asian Dressmaking
MEMBERSHIPS: Embroiderys Guilds "Reiki" Organisation
HONOURS/AWARDS: Exhibits various projects in museums, V&A, Hangive Mughal exhibition.
HOBBIES AND INTERESTS: Music, arts and crafts
PERSONAL PROFILE: I have had a variety of jobs from running my own business to teaching, to my present role as an activities officer for Asian women in mental health services-the most challenging and rewarding job. Challenging in convincing patients and organisations in medical establishments that patients have immense talents and rewarding when their work is recognised on a national scale.
NOMINATED BY: Eleanor Viegas

MISS REEDAH NIJABAT (BARRISTER)

Director, ArRum Ltd, 44-48 Clerkenwell Road, London, EC1M 5PS

PLACE OF BIRTH: London, 9.11.70
MARITAL STATUS: Single
COLLEGE: London School of Economics
ACADEMIC QUALIFICATIONS: LL.B, LLM
PROFESSIONAL QUALIFICATIONS: Barrister-at-Law
DIRECTORSHIPS: ArRum Ltd
MEMBERSHIPS: London Chamber of Commerce, Lincoln's Inn, ArRum Private Members Club
HONOURS/AWARDS: 1989 Student of the Year, 1991 Launched WIN
HOBBIES AND INTERESTS: Riding, running, cycling, swimming, gym, painting, foreign films, theatre, arts, culture, photography, tai chi
PERSONAL PROFILE: Graduated from the London School of Economics having read Law LL.B and continued to read an LLM. Became member of Lincoln's Inn and was called to the Bar in 1995. Spent two years in management consulting with Roland Berger & Partner. Resigned in May 1997 to pursue my entrepreneurial aspirations. Researched concept of private members club for Muslim professionals, entrepreneurs and students. ArRum Social Club was launched in summer 1999.
NOMINATED BY: Mrs Gazala Parkar, Wood Green

'Researched concept of private members club for Muslim professionals, entrepreneurs and students. ArRum Social Club was launched in summer 1999'

REEDAH NIJABAT

MR KRISHAN KUMAR NIJHAWAN (CERAMIC SCIENTIST)

Consultant Ceramist, 4 Hazelmere Road, Kensington Fields, Northolt, UB5 6UJ

PLACE OF BIRTH: Pakistan, 24.7.12
MARITAL STATUS: Married
CHILDREN: Four (Kusum, Kumud, Anil, Arun)
COLLEGE: Punjab University, Benares University
ACADEMIC QUALIFICATIONS: Bsc, (Ph) Dip Ceram (Benar), Al Ceram (UK)
PROFESSIONAL QUALIFICATIONS: Supervisor Central Glass & Ceramic Institute (India). Technical Advisor.Ceramic Engineer.Ceramist. Consultant Ceramist.
MEMBERSHIPS: Fellow Royal Microsopical Society (Oxford) FRMS. Associate Institute of Ceramics (Stoke AIC. Member of the Brahma Kumaris, World Spiritual University
HONOURS/AWARDS: Granted patents in US, UK and Australia for Fundamental Research in Cermanics for the manufacture of synthetic Bone China 1971
HOBBIES AND INTERESTS: Photography,
PERSONAL PROFILE: Vast technical experience in research and manufacture over a period of several decades, for abrasives, artificial mineral teeth. Bone China tableware. High alumina refractories and ceramics in India. West Germany and the United Kingdom. Patents for manufacture of synthetic Bone China tableware in the United States, United Kingdom and Australia. Numerous research papers published worldwide.

MISS DINESHI NIRGUNANANTHAN (SCHOOLGIRL)

PLACE OF BIRTH: Sri Lanka, 7.3.94
ACADEMIC QUALIFICATIONS: IQ of 158 at the age of 3 (Mensa Test)
MEMBERSHIPS: Mensa, Helen O'Grady Drama Academy, Heathrow Gym Club
HONOURS/AWARDS: Swimming-5m, 10m, 25m, 50m, Ducking Grad 1,2 & 3 & Puffin Award
HOBBIES AND INTERESTS: Singing, reading, dancing, swimming
PERSONAL PROFILE: The youngest member of Mensa. Three year old Dineshi Nirgunananthan, of Sri Lankan descent, became the youngest member of Mensa in November 1997 with an IQ of 158. Dineshi falls within the brainiest 1% of the population. She also excels at piano, violin, tap, ballet, Indian dancing and swimming.
NOMINATED BY: Nix Nigunananthan, mother

MR ANTONY NIXON (COMPANY DIRECTOR/ ECONOMIST)

Business Management Consultants, A & M Nixon Enterprises,

PLACE OF BIRTH: Budaun, 25.11.32
MARITAL STATUS: Married
CHILDREN: Five (Caroline, Josephine, Marle, Sarah, Penelope)
COLLEGE: Manchester, Salford. Leeds Metro. University of Wales. Karachi. Peshawar
ACADEMIC QUALIFICATIONS: BA, MA(Econ), MSc (Pol Econ), ACP (Dip Edin), Post grad. Library & Inf Science. Dip Marketing
PROFESSIONAL QUALIFICATIONS: ALA (Chartered Librarian) ACP (Dip in Edin). Gold medal in public speaking.
DIRECTORSHIPS: Chairman PTFA Lancashire County1998-99. BHAF, Manchester.
MEMBERSHIPS: Racial Equality Council, Labour Party
HOBBIES AND INTERESTS: Foreign travel, reading and writing, economics, politics
EMAIL: anthony.nixon@zen.co.uk
PERSONAL PROFILE: Economist, company director. Business and management consultant A & M Nixon Enterprises. Director/trustee and chairman Finance and Audit Sub-Committee BHAF, Manchester 1998. Consultant Pedagogical University, Vilnius, Lithuania 1997. Managing director Costcutter Nixon Supermarket 1993-95. Visited 26 countries on business and voluntary work. I have recently been appointed chairman for the NHS Executive North West Region.

MR NARANJAN SINGH NOOR
(DIRECTOR OF COMMUNITY EDUCATION)

Pensioner, Progressive Writer's Association, 13 Rosemary Cresent West, Goldthorn Park, Wolverhampton, WV4 5AP

PLACE OF BIRTH: India, 6.1.33
MARITAL STATUS: Married
CHILDREN: Four (Navtej Singh, Newton Singh, Usha, Jasbir)
ACADEMIC QUALIFICATIONS: MA, MSc
PROFESSIONAL QUALIFICATIONS: BT, Dip Ed
DIRECTORSHIPS: Bilston Community College
MEMBERSHIPS: NATPFE
HONOURS/AWARDS: Best Writers Award (Foreign) from the language department, Punjab
HOBBIES AND INTERESTS: Poetry writing in Panjabi, English
PERSONAL PROFILE: Before retiring as a faculty head at Bilston Community College in 1997. I had worked as a teacher at all levels, as the president and general secretary of IWA, GB and at present. I am the general secretary of the Progressive Writers Association GB. I am the author of seven books of Punjabi poetry, two of English poetry and have written various articles in English and Punjabi. I've won various national and international awards.

MR HARMESH SINGH NOTAY
(PE TEACHER-FOOTBALL SCOUT)

7 Beechwood Road, Burley, Leeds, LS4 2LU

PLACE OF BIRTH: Leeds, 26.4.69
MARITAL STATUS: Married
COLLEGE: Leeds Met University
ACADEMIC QUALIFICATIONS: BA Hons Sport, Exercise and Leisure studies. NQT Post grad.
PROFESSIONAL QUALIFICATIONS: Post Graduate Certificate of Secondary Education (PGCE)
MEMBERSHIPS: NUT, NASC, FA, BTA, EBBA
HONOURS/AWARDS: Many coaching and sports awards.
HOBBIES AND INTERESTS: Indian 'remix', reggae, swing - all sports
EMAIL: 68609582@nmu.ac.uk
PERSONAL PROFILE: I am a football scout for Leeds United AFC (Youth Development Dept). I am also a PE teacher I thank my family and friends for their continuous support and prayers. I am convinced that our Asian brothers and sisters out there can succeed in their chosen profession in the Millennium.
NOMINATED BY: Manjit Gatanuda

'The youngest member of Mensa. Three year old Dineshi Nirgunananthan, of Sri Lankan descent, became the youngest member of Mensa in November 1997 with an IQ of 158'

DINESHI NIRGUNANANTHAN

Vast technical experience in research and manufacture over a period of several decades, for abrasives, artificial mineral teeth. Bone China tableware

KRISHAN KUMAR NIJHAWAN

MRS SATWANT PARMAR (Sitarist)

Music Teacher, 115 Clayhall Avenue, Clayhall, IG5 0PN

PLACE OF BIRTH: India, 1.10.42
MARITAL STATUS: Married
CHILDREN: Two (Sukhbir Singh, Simret)
COLLEGE: Punjab University
ACADEMIC QUALIFICATIONS: BA Masters Degree in Music (Bombay)
PROFESSIONAL QUALIFICATIONS: PGCE, University of East London
HOBBIES AND INTERESTS: Drawing, painting
PERSONAL PROFILE: I was a professor of music teaching to BA and MA classes in India. Learnt from various professors and sitarists also from Nikhil Banerjee. Came to UK in 1968. Performed in many universities and public places, Royal Albert Hall (along with 45 students), Vienna City and many more famous venues. Also worked for Income Tax for ten years, qualified as a tax officer in 1980. Started Indian music sitar, tabla and harmonium in London's many schools and colleges.

MR VENKATA ADITYA PARNANDI (Medical Student)

Room No 815, Neuawd Meirinnydd, Heath Park, Cardiff, CF4 4YS

PLACE OF BIRTH: UK, 4.7.78
MARITAL STATUS: Single
COLLEGE: University of Wales, College of Medicine
ACADEMIC QUALIFICATIONS: 9 GCSE's, 5 A-Levels
PROFESSIONAL QUALIFICATIONS: ALCM
MEMBERSHIPS: Mensa
HONOURS/AWARDS: Piano Awards
HOBBIES AND INTERESTS: Music, piano playing, harmonium, singing, reading
PERSONAL PROFILE: I was born and educated in the UK. I am currently in the third year of medicine at the University of Wales College of Medicine. I play the piano and harmonium. I am an associate of the London College of Music and have participated in national piano competitions. I am a member of the university choir and orchestra. I also participate in the university debating club. I am a member of Mensa.
NOMINATED BY: Mrs Aravinda Rao

SHRI JONIAH PARTHA-SARATHI (Teacher)

Faith Tutor (Hindu-Dharma), Interfaith Education Centre, Listerhills Road, Bradford, BD7 1HD

PLACE OF BIRTH: India, 10.1.36
MARITAL STATUS: Married
CHILDREN: Two (Shailaja, Sharda)
COLLEGE: Sri Shankara Vidya Peeth, Bradford Community College
ACADEMIC QUALIFICATIONS: Bharatiya Vidya Bhawan, Hindu Dharma ,Sanskrit,
PROFESSIONAL QUALIFICATIONS: Diploma in Community Religious Studies (Interfaith)
MEMBERSHIPS: Secretary Hindu Education Council (Yorkshire)
PERSONAL PROFILE: I was born and educated in Tamil Nadu, India. I am a Hindu community worker and I am engaged in interfaith dialogue. I am working as faith tutor (Hindu Dharma) in the Interfaith Education Centre Bradford. Teachers and pupils can contact me for information on Hindu Dharma through BT Campus World (Internet Resource Service)-Tel: 01847 890 027.

MR SHAZAD PARVEZ (Mail Order)

Manager, Bradford Moor Youth Sports Association, Manse Street, Laisterdyke Youth & Community Centre, Bradford, BD3 8RP

PLACE OF BIRTH: Pakistan, 6.6.59
MARITAL STATUS: Divorced
CHILDREN: Three (Ghazal, Neelam, Rukhsaar)
COLLEGE: College
PROFESSIONAL QUALIFICATIONS: GCSE History, English
HONOURS/AWARDS: Presented to HM Queen Elizabeth at Bradford City Stadium
HOBBIES AND INTERESTS: Football, travel, music, cinema
PERSONAL PROFILE: I have worked for Grattan Plc for 24 years. I'm also a football scout for Bradford City FC and a youth worker. I organised sporting activities for Asian community in Bradford. I enjoy all sports, music and travel.
NOMINATED BY: Sajja Mahmud

MRS BADRUN NESA PASHA (Social Worker)

Snr Education Social Worker, Education Dept, Bangladesh Womens Employment Resource Centre, 497 Coventry Road, Small Heath, Birmingham, B10 0JS

PLACE OF BIRTH: Bangladesh, 3.11.39
MARITAL STATUS: Widow
CHILDREN: Two (Tauhid, Eba)
COLLEGE: Leicester University
ACADEMIC QUALIFICATIONS: MA, Post Grad Dip. Social Policy and Administartion
PROFESSIONAL QUALIFICATIONS: Dip. Social Work . CQSW
MEMBERSHIPS: Community Care, BAPSCAN
HOBBIES AND INTERESTS: Reading, writing, gardening
PERSONAL PROFILE: I am a senior social worker employed by Birmingham City Council. Founder of Bangladesh Womens Association in 1971. Established a Bangla school for children and centre solely for Bangladeshi women in Birmingham for their education and training, leading them into employment. I am the executive member of North Birmingham Health Trust.
NOMINATED BY: Michael Whitehouse and Nilufa Rashid

SAHERA PASHA (Kathak Dancer)

64 Gloucester Gardens, Bayswater, London, W2 6BN

PLACE OF BIRTH: India
MARITAL STATUS: Married
COLLEGE: Anjumen School Bombay
HOBBIES AND INTERESTS: Music, reading, swimming, walking
PERSONAL PROFILE: I strongly believe in perseverance, endurance and prayer. The acclaimed Urdu poet Mohammad Iqbal wrote: "There is both power and peace in the hymns of the devoted. Salvation for the inhabitants of this world lies in love. Love is God's greatest gift to a human being" Love is the thread that runs through my work.

MR JAGDEEP SINGH PASSAN (Drug Action Advisor)

Advisor, Greater Manchester Drug Action Group, 201 Easterly Road, Leeds, LS8 2RB

PLACE OF BIRTH: Uganda, 12.10.65
MARITAL STATUS: Married
CHILDREN: Two (Gorave, Varun)
COLLEGE: Huddersfield Teeside University, Leeds University
ACADEMIC QUALIFICATIONS: HND, MCIH, PGD (Law), DMS (Management)
PROFESSIONAL QUALIFICATIONS: Chartered Institute of Housing
DIRECTORSHIPS: Unity Housing Association Leeds
MEMBERSHIPS: Law Society
HOBBIES AND INTERESTS: Snooker, music, relaxation
PERSONAL PROFILE: My role should be seen as assisting our communities to have specific and linguistically appropriate services by effecting change from the top level of decision makers. Thus, services are suitable to black communities. Liaison with top tier management to effect change. Developing and delivering training package. Liaison with service purchasers, providers and black communities. Working closely with all Greater Manchester DAT's. Assisting/focal point of working with agencies and voluntary sector.
NOMINATED BY: Mick Narayan Singh

MR TALWINDER SINGH PATARA (Chartered Accountant)

Partner, TS Patara & Co, Kensington House, 70 Arthur Road, Edgbaston, Birmingham, B15 2UW

PLACE OF BIRTH: India, 4.11.53
MARITAL STATUS: Married
COLLEGE: Aston University Birmingham
ACADEMIC QUALIFICATIONS: BSc Hons in Physics
PROFESSIONAL QUALIFICATIONS: Chartered Accountant-Fellow
DIRECTORSHIPS: Kensington Trading Co Ltd, Kingfisher Corporation Ltd
MEMBERSHIPS: President of Asian Business Club
HOBBIES AND INTERESTS: Golf, films, socialising, surfing the Internet
EMAIL: ts.patara@virgin .net
PERSONAL PROFILE: Runs chartered accountancy practise in the West Midlands catering for small and medium sized businesses. Chairman of Kingfisher Corporation Ltd a company which operates weddings and function halls. President of the Asian Business Club for the business and professional community from the Indian sub-continent. Founding director of Spice Media Ltd, which launched a national Asian lifestyle magazine called Spice.

MR ADAM HAFEJEE PATEL JP (COMPANY DIRECTOR)

Comet Cash & Carry Ltd,

PLACE OF BIRTH: India, 7.6.40
MARITAL STATUS: Married
CHILDREN: Eight (Ilyas, Shirin, Shamin, Imran, Sophia, Saleha, Imtyaz, Iqbal)
COLLEGE: MS University, Baroda
ACADEMIC QUALIFICATIONS: B.Com
DIRECTORSHIPS: Blackburn Partnership, East Lancs Training & Enterprise Council, Enterprise plc
MEMBERSHIPS: Labour Party
HONOURS/AWARDS: Life Time Achievement Award, Asian Image
HOBBIES AND INTERESTS: Football, gardening, community work, politics
PERSONAL PROFILE: Member of the Labour Party since first came to UK in 1966. Member of Christian/Muslim Inter-Faith Forum and it's joint Chairman with the Bishop of Blackburn, the Rt. Rev Alan Chesters. Trustee of West Brookhouse Community Centre. One of five national counsellors of Muslim Council of Britain
NOMINATED BY: Mr Mahmood Tantwala

MR ANWER IBRAHIM PATEL (PHARMACIST)

Director, Gorgemead Ltd, PO Box 69, Unit L, Kershaw Business Centre, Baldwin Street, Bolton, BL3 5BF

PLACE OF BIRTH: Kenya, 19.10.55
MARITAL STATUS: Married
CHILDREN: Two (Aziz, Arifa)
COLLEGE: Leicester
ACADEMIC QUALIFICATIONS: BSc Hons Pharmacy
PROFESSIONAL QUALIFICATIONS: MR Pharm M, I Phum M
HOBBIES AND INTERESTS: Cricket, football, snooker, reading
PERSONAL PROFILE: Directorships held: Aerobelt Ltd, Athertons Chemists Ltd, Basil Clarke Ltd, Central Pharmacy (Mexborough) Ltd, Cityfocus Ltd, Charles Hall Ltd, C J Wrigley Ltd, E A Draper Ltd, Gorgemead Ltd, Greenwoods Ltd, MA Harris Chemists Ltd, McLoughlin & Nixon Ltd, M D Robinsons Ltd, Norman Youles Dispensing Chemists Ltd, Primelight Ltd, Roocrofts (1923) Ltd, Scholes (Chemists) Ltd, Steven Isaacs (Chemists) Ltd, Thaneglade Ltd.

MR BABUBHAI ASHABHAI PATEL (FINANCIAL CONSULTANT)

BA Finance & Mortgage Co, 900 Garratt Lane, Tooting Broadway, London, SW17 0NB

PLACE OF BIRTH: India, 19.5.34
MARITAL STATUS: Married
CHILDREN: Two (Pratiksha, Kamlesh)
COLLEGE: Vidyanagar India
ACADEMIC QUALIFICATIONS: 1st Year Science
DIRECTORSHIPS: President National Association of Patidar Samaj
MEMBERSHIPS: The company is a member of Interlink Premier Network Ltd which is regulated by the Personal Investment Authority
HOBBIES AND INTERESTS: Cricket, world affairs, reading, mountaineering
PERSONAL PROFILE: BA Patel arrived in Britain from Kenya in 1970 and established BA Finance & Mortgage Co. He operated this venture from Trafalgar Square, London. The company specialises in arranging finance and mortgages for professional and business properties.
NOMINATED BY: Mr Pravinbhai N Amin

MR BHIKHU C PATEL (MANAGING DIRECTOR)

Waymade Healthcare Plc, Sovereign House, Miles Gray Road, Basildon, SS14 3FR

PLACE OF BIRTH: Kenya, 1.8.47
MARITAL STATUS: Married
CHILDREN: Three (Nimisha, Neeshe, Rishi)
COLLEGE: Bristol University
ACADEMIC QUALIFICATIONS: BA Arch. Dip Arch. RIBA
DIRECTORSHIPS: Waymade Health Care Plc
HONOURS/AWARDS: Several company awards
HOBBIES AND INTERESTS: Swimming, walking, travelling, reading
PERSONAL PROFILE: I arrived in UK in 1995 to study and qualify as an architect. After practising for a while, joined my brother to drive forward retail pharmacy and develop privately owned Waymade Healthcare Plc. Currently manage property portfolio, retail and Waymade Group. Turnover £150 million including retail.

MR BHUPENDRA PATEL (POSTMASTER)

10 High Street, Thrapston, Kettering, NN14 4TW

PLACE OF BIRTH: India, 17.12.52
MARITAL STATUS: Married
CHILDREN: Two (Anita, Chirag)
COLLEGE: Gujarat University India
ACADEMIC QUALIFICATIONS: BE (Chem)
PROFESSIONAL QUALIFICATIONS: Postmaster
HONOURS/AWARDS: Best Post Office Award in 1995
HOBBIES AND INTERESTS: Reading, politics, cricket
PERSONAL PROFILE: Locally the only Conservative councillor for five years and mayor of Thrapston during 1998-99. A president of our Patel Circle based in Wembley with 1200 life members. Very much active in local community. A school governor in local school. A member of the Hindu Association in Wellingborough, Northants.

MRS FARIDA PATEL (COMMUNITY LIAISON WORKER)

10 Thornhill Park Avenue, Dewsbury, WF12 0DA

PLACE OF BIRTH: South Africa, 19.6.49
MARITAL STATUS: Married
CHILDREN: Four (Ahmed, Fuzail, Arshad, Hasina)
COLLEGE: Studied in South Africa
ACADEMIC QUALIFICATIONS: GCSE and 3 A-Levels
PROFESSIONAL QUALIFICATIONS: Interpreter and RE
MEMBERSHIPS: Nationally involved ICRC with government MP and secretaries
HONOURS/AWARDS: For community services and on honours list invited by HM Queen Elizabeth to garden party, July 98
HOBBIES AND INTERESTS: Fundraising, sewing, organising trips for ladies, helping people
PERSONAL PROFILE: Community liaison worker at Birkdale High School, Dewsbury. On the ICRC-as a member in London with Iqbal Sacranie - on a national basis. Involved with the police locally, racial harrassment etc. A member on the religious council. Was a governor for 15 years in schools and advisers on various groups locally. Worked in the hospital maternity for nine years as Interpreter.
NOMINATED BY: James Bostwick

MRS INDIRA PATEL OBE (PROPERTY MANAGEMENT)

Manager, 278 Coombe Lane, West Wimbledon, London, SW20 0RW

PLACE OF BIRTH: Kenya, 27.3.46
MARITAL STATUS: Mrs
CHILDREN: Two (Kamal, Paresh)
COLLEGE: Cambridge
ACADEMIC QUALIFICATIONS: 8 O-Levels
PROFESSIONAL QUALIFICATIONS: Trained Teacher
MEMBERSHIPS: Fellow BPW International
HONOURS/AWARDS: OBE Order of Officer of British Empire
HOBBIES AND INTERESTS: Swimming, fundraising, holidays, conferences, flower arrangements
PERSONAL PROFILE: Came to UK in 1975 with two boys aged five and eight. Voluntary services since 1977. Producing leaflets on health, organising charities and speaking at national, international conferences. Speaks on violence against women, women and health, Beijing Draft Platform of Action.

MR JANAKBHAI PATEL (INSURANCE AGENT)

Director, National Association of Patidar Samaj, 19 Lewis Road, Finchley, London, N12 9NH

PLACE OF BIRTH: Kenya, 1.5.28
MARITAL STATUS: Married
CHILDREN: Two (Jaimini, Nishit)
ACADEMIC QUALIFICATIONS: Matric
PROFESSIONAL QUALIFICATIONS: HCS (Higher Civil Service), Kenya
DIRECTORSHIPS: JNJP Insurance Services
MEMBERSHIPS: NAPS, Saistra Samaj Gujarati Shahitya Academy
HOBBIES AND INTERESTS: Sports, reading, social events
PERSONAL PROFILE: Arrived in UK 1967 joined National Association of Patidar Samaj. Was president 1971-72, Trustee 1975 onwards. Executive member of Brent Indian Association. Also founded the Sojitra Samaj. President 1969-71 and trustee 1996 onwards. At the time of East African exodus helped many families to find suitable businesses and residential properties.
NOMINATED BY: Pravinbhai N Amin

MR KAMLESH PATEL (Principal Lecturer)

Director, Ethnicity & Health Unit, Faculty of Health, University of Central Lancashire, Preston, PR1 2HE

PLACE OF BIRTH: Kenya
MARITAL STATUS: Married
CHILDREN: Three (Hamish, Humara, Dru)
ACADEMIC QUALIFICATIONS: BTEC / Dip / SW
PROFESSIONAL QUALIFICATIONS: CQSW
DIRECTORSHIPS: MHAC-ISDD. Director of the Ethnicity and Health Unit-University of Central Lancashire.
HONOURS/AWARDS: Kamlesh has acquired over £1 million in consultancy, research and evaluation grants.
HOBBIES AND INTERESTS: Cricket
PERSONAL PROFILE: At the Ethnicity and Health Unit-University of Central Lancashire he is responsible for managing a multi-disciplinary team undertaking research, development and consultancy in health and social care; focusing on ethnicity, drugs, alcohol, mental health, HIV/AIDS and social exclusion. As a social worker, he has worked within a specialist statutory social services drugs team as well as managing a voluntary drugs agency providing day care, out-reach and residential services for over seven years.

EX MAYOR LATA K.D. PATEL (Businesswoman)

Mega Trading Co, Kusum Service Station, 33 Uxbridge Road, Hayes, UB4 0JN

PLACE OF BIRTH: India, 28.6.56
MARITAL STATUS: Married
CHILDREN: One (Krisna)
MEMBERSHIPS: Hindu International
HONOURS/AWARDS: Vishwa Gurjari Award 1991. Arch of India Award (NRI Inst. Detroit 1992) Also Woman of the Year Award. Mother of India Award 1992. International Woman Award.
PERSONAL PROFILE: Lata Patel is an institution. Her home is used as her surgery for everyone in the community. People of all religious persuasions, colour, caste and creed are attracted to her for guidance, counselling, or drawing upon her expertise and experience as a Indian woman in the world of business. She always appears serene in a white sari: although she works 15 hours a day, in addition to welcoming a host of visitors to her home each year. Lata Patel was the first Gujarati woman to be elected mayor (Brent 1996) in the UK

MR MUKHAND JAYANTILAL PATEL (Senior Civil Servant)

Head of Branch, Department of Education And Employment, DFEE, Room 770, Caxton House, Arthill Street, London, SW1H 9NF

PLACE OF BIRTH: India, 3.6.49
MARITAL STATUS: Married
CHILDREN: Two (Neil, Anuthka)
COLLEGE: London University
ACADEMIC QUALIFICATIONS: BSc
PROFESSIONAL QUALIFICATIONS: FCIBSE, CEng, MIMARH Eng, AMIEE
MEMBERSHIPS: Chairman of local Scouts Group
HOBBIES AND INTERESTS: Scouting, rambling
EMAIL: info@dfee.gov.uk
PERSONAL PROFILE: He is a member of the senior civil service and head of the Architects and Building Branch at the DfEE. He worked with consultants and PSA before joining DfEE in 1982. He sits on various BSI and other professional committees and is chairman of SCALA Technical Committee. In 1994/95 he was elected president of the Society of Chief Engineers.
NOMINATED BY: Bernadette Hillon, DFEE

CAPT MUKUNDRAY (MIKE) PATEL (Airline Pilot)

Captain, Azure 2000-Cineworld, PO Box 299, Edgware, HA8 5AF

PLACE OF BIRTH: Uganda, 7.12.52
MARITAL STATUS: Single
ACADEMIC QUALIFICATIONS: Ainst. Smm 1990-Airline Transport License
PROFESSIONAL QUALIFICATIONS: Command Pilot 1978
MEMBERSHIPS: IAOPA-US, Dip Pl, Founder member of Tantra-Mantra-Yantra
HONOURS/AWARDS: Dr of Spiritual Astro Consultant
HOBBIES AND INTERESTS: Flying, astro spiritual jogging, bird watching, going to Yatra, treking
PERSONAL PROFILE: Founder Member of UK's Multi-Cultural Centre for Tantra-Mantra-Yantra. Diploma in private investigations, management in International entertainment-Associate promoter for International concert 1980-81-91-98, member of Agro International press corps. doctor of spiritual counselling UK.
NOMINATED BY: Bernadette Hillon, DfEE

MS NAINA PATEL (Director)

Policy Research Insti. on Ageing & Ethnicity, University of Bradford-PRIAE,, Management Centre, Emm Lane, Bradford, BD9 4SL

PLACE OF BIRTH: Kenya, 1.6.58
MARITAL STATUS: Married
COLLEGE: Lancaster/Bradford/Birmingham
ACADEMIC QUALIFICATIONS: BA Hons Econ, PGCE, MSc, MBA
PROFESSIONAL QUALIFICATIONS: PGCE
MEMBERSHIPS: Institute of Race Relations
HOBBIES AND INTERESTS: Arts, hiking, travel, International cuisine
PERSONAL PROFILE: PRAIE is first such Institute in the UK producing on behalf of Royal Commission on long term care for the elderly, the UK report on Minority Ethnic Elders. Naina has pioneered developments in race equality in social work as an innovator, researcher, writer, public speaker and influencing policy nationally and internationally. Paul Boateng MP called her study on dementia 'Authoritative and Impressive'-2nd March 1998.

MR PRAVINBHAI M PATEL (Vice President)

PLACE OF BIRTH: Kenya
DIRECTORSHIPS: President of West London Branch of National Association of Patidar Samaj
HOBBIES AND INTERESTS: Cricket, golf
PERSONAL PROFILE: Born in Kenya, arrived in the UK in 1968 and owned a subpost office and a newspaper tobacconist business. He has also served Karamsad Samaj for past 17 years and is its current vice president. In his spare time he plays cricket and is keen in playing golf. He is a founder member of Dulwich Cricket Club and instrumental in formation of Ableman Cricket League now known as Quickstop Cricket League.
NOMINATED BY: Mr Pravinbhai N Amin

DR RAMESH ASHABHAI M PATEL (Medical Practitioner)

Director, VBUSSR Ltd, 32 Baldwyns Park, Bexley, DA5 2BA

PLACE OF BIRTH: Kenya, 25.11.34
MARITAL STATUS: Married
CHILDREN: Four (Sucheta, Urvi, Vera, Shakti)
COLLEGE: Amritsar Medical College, Punjab
ACADEMIC QUALIFICATIONS: MBBS, Dob Rcog. DA MFFP, Lic AC
DIRECTORSHIPS: Director of VBUSSR Ltd
MEMBERSHIPS: BMA, Indian Medical Association
HONOURS/AWARDS: Mother India 1994. International Gold Award 1995, International Business Award 1995. International Grand Award 1998. Marathon Runner.
HOBBIES AND INTERESTS: Sport: Was the first Asian to do New York and London Marathons
PERSONAL PROFILE: Medical Practitioner, hospital clinical assistant. Social worker, past president of Rotary Club Crayford 1120. South East Hindu Association Temple Woolwich, Greenwich Gujarati Samaj, Soor Sangam. Holder of Harris Fellowship/Rotary Club.

MR RAMESH B PATEL (Managing Director)

Managing Director, Mandeer Ltd Kusal Ltd, Flat 2A, King Edward Man, Grape Street, London, WC2H 8DX

PLACE OF BIRTH: Burma, 18.9.36
MARITAL STATUS: Married
CHILDREN: One (Kalpesh)
HONOURS/AWARDS: Hind Rattan Award 1991 presented to Ramesh in Delhi by India's Minister of Finance. A Proclamation from the Mayor of Gainsville Florida, US for the enormous contributions made.
PERSONAL PROFILE: A devoted ambassador of Indian culture, he is inspired by Ayurvedic principles of eternal knowledge and wisdom and has helped and healed many people from their ailments. His poetry is an ecstatic outpouring of joy, serenity and beauty, offering encouragement and hope.

> A devoted ambassador of Indian culture, he is inspired by Ayurvedic principles of eternal knowledge and wisdom
>
> **RAMESH B PATEL**

MR RAMESH U PATEL (CHEMIST)

Technical Director, Siri Vallabh Nidhi UK, 4 Winchester Avenue, London, NW9 9SY

PLACE OF BIRTH: India, 30.12.38
MARITAL STATUS: Married
CHILDREN: Three (Apexa, Dipexa, Vimal)
COLLEGE: Kanpur Sugar Tech
ACADEMIC QUALIFICATIONS: Ind. Chemist
PROFESSIONAL QUALIFICATIONS: Sugar, Food, Paint Technologist
HOBBIES AND INTERESTS: Stage management, produce ballet
PERSONAL PROFILE: Does lots of charity work. Produce Indian ballet. Done lots of stage management for drama and competition ballet. Lots of community work. Charity for War wants, blind etc.

MR SAID PATEL (TECHNICIAN)

Bolton College, 89 Randal Street, Daubhill, Bolton, BL3 4AG

PLACE OF BIRTH: Kenya, 29.7.49
MARITAL STATUS: Married
CHILDREN: Two (Wasim, Fazal)
COLLEGE: Bolton College
ACADEMIC QUALIFICATIONS: CGLI Electrical Installation Pt 1, 2, 3
PROFESSIONAL QUALIFICATIONS: 7307 F&A Teaching Cert Basic Skills, Teaching Cert, D32/33 Assessors Cert
HONOURS/AWARDS: Outstanding Adult Learners Award 1994

HOBBIES AND INTERESTS: Cricket umpire, voluntary work for the community
PERSONAL PROFILE: Came from Kenya at the age of 16 unable to read or write. Now teaches at Bolton College after gaining his two different teaching certificates and assessors certificate. In 1994 won the North West Outstanding Adult Learners Award. Said's photo appeared in Foreign and Commonwealth Office posters which were distributed through embassies and consulates overseas to show the current 'face' of Britain today.
NOMINATED BY: Wasim Patel

MR VIJAY PATEL (PHARMACIST)

Chief Executive, Waymade Healthcare Plc, Sovereign House, Miles Gray Road, Basildon, SS14 3FR

PLACE OF BIRTH: Kenya, 10.11.49
MARITAL STATUS: Married
CHILDREN: Two (Amit, Dipen)
COLLEGE: De Montford University
ACADEMIC QUALIFICATIONS: BSc (Pharm) MRPS
PROFESSIONAL QUALIFICATIONS: MRPS
DIRECTORSHIPS: Waymade Healthcare Plc
MEMBERSHIPS: Royal Pharmaceutical Society of Great Britain

HONOURS/AWARDS: Elected to Europe's Top 500 Dynamic Entrepreneurs 1996 and 1997 (A EU initiative to identify the 500 fastest growing companies in Europe)
HOBBIES AND INTERESTS: Country walking, swimming, travel
PERSONAL PROFILE: I arrived in UK in 1967 with a burning ambition to be successful. After qualifying as a pharmacist I opened my first retail pharmacy in 1975. This has now grown into Waymade Healthcare Plc supplying branded and generic prescription medicines to pharmacies throughout the country with projected sales of £150 million for 1999. Waymade Awards-1996 and 1997 Independent on Sunday / Price Waterhouse Independent 100 (Ranked 86th) and Middle Market (Ranked 22nd). 1998 Middle Marker (Ranked 42nd)

MR MANJI PATEL-VEKARIA (MANAGING DIRECTOR)

Managing Director, MP Media Services, 35 Heigham Road, East Ham, London, E6 2JL

PLACE OF BIRTH: India, 15.12.49
MARITAL STATUS: Married
CHILDREN: Two (Dinesh, Dinal)
COLLEGE: University of East London
ACADEMIC QUALIFICATIONS: BA Hons Business Studies
PROFESSIONAL QUALIFICATIONS: Member of the Institute of Management
DIRECTORSHIPS: London Young Managers
MEMBERSHIPS: Communication Workers Union. Communication Managers' Association. Newham REC. Vishwa Hindu Parishad (UK) Newham Branch.
HOBBIES AND INTERESTS: Proactive voluntary community worker dealing with educational and other issues affecting young people and travel, numismatics, philately (thematic)
PERSONAL PROFILE: An experienced director with strongly developed operational skills within a fast moving media service environment. I am able to liaise with people at all levels both internally and externally. I am also a disciplined and focussed professional able to achieve goals under pressure; friendly, helpful, discreet, tactful, hardworking, conscientious and eager to learn.
NOMINATED BY: Community Office

DR MADHU LATA PATHAK JP (DOCTOR)

General Practitioner, 84 Parkway, Gidea Park, Romford, RM2 5PL

PLACE OF BIRTH: India, 13.1.45
MARITAL STATUS: Married
CHILDREN: Two (Pankaj, Tarun)
COLLEGE: AMU Aligarh India
ACADEMIC QUALIFICATIONS: MRCGP, DCH, DA, LMSSA, DTM&H, Dip Law
PROFESSIONAL QUALIFICATIONS: MBBS
MEMBERSHIPS: Member BMA, Justices Club
HONOURS/AWARDS: Justice of the Peace (Barking Branch)
HOBBIES AND INTERESTS: Music, travel
PERSONAL PROFILE: After qualifying MBBS came to UK in 1968. Have worked in several hospitals in Department of Paediatrics. Full GP since 1984. Part-time secretary of local medical committee. President of Inner Wheel in 1989. First lady member of Ilford Rotary Club.
NOMINATED BY: EMG

DR SURESH KUMAR PATHAK (RESEARCH MEDICINE)

General Practitioner, 84 Parkway, Gidea Park, Romford, RM2 5PL

PLACE OF BIRTH: India, 1.3.41
MARITAL STATUS: Married
CHILDREN: Two (Pankaj, Tarun)
COLLEGE: GR Medical College, India
ACADEMIC QUALIFICATIONS: D Obstet, DFFP
PROFESSIONAL QUALIFICATIONS: MBBS
MEMBERSHIPS: Royal Society of Medicine, Dagenham Rotary Club. BMA.
HOBBIES AND INTERESTS: Travel, music, reading, research
PERSONAL PROFILE: GP in Romford since 1971. Came to UK in 1966. Actively involved in research in general practice. Also I am a part time research lecturer at Department of General Practice, Queen Mary and Westfield College University of London. Past president of Rotary Club of Dagenham. Actively involved in charity work. Has organised eye camps in India.

MR RAJINDER SINGH PATTWAL (RETAIL)

Owner, Sari Raj Clothing Retail / Manufacturer, 105 Second Avenue, Manor Park, London, E12 6EN

PLACE OF BIRTH: India, 1.1.46
MARITAL STATUS: Married
CHILDREN: Five (Chamk Singh, Ravinder, Sharmila, Sukhwant, Sutnam Kaur)
ACADEMIC QUALIFICATIONS: High School GCSE
PROFESSIONAL QUALIFICATIONS: Instructor Training Course, London
DIRECTORSHIPS: Proprietor
HONOURS/AWARDS: School, swimming, weightlifting (cups) and trophies
HOBBIES AND INTERESTS: Football
PERSONAL PROFILE: Came to UK, 12 years ago with parents, brothers and sisters. Had the benefit of comprehensive education, worked with father S.Chanan S.Pattwal. Hard work and progressed in present business.

LORD SWRAJ PAUL (CHAIRMAN)

Caparo Group Ltd, 103 Baker Street, London, W1M 1FD

PLACE OF BIRTH: India, 18.2.31
MARITAL STATUS: Married
CHILDREN: Four
COLLEGE: Massachusetts Inst of Technology
ACADEMIC QUALIFICATIONS: Masters Degree, Mechanical Engineering
DIRECTORSHIPS: Caparo Group Ltd
MEMBERSHIPS: MCC, RAC
HONOURS/AWARDS: Life Peerage(1996). Padma Bhushan
PERSONAL PROFILE: Came to UK in 1966 and in 1968 founded Caparo Group Ltd which specialises in the manufacture and supply of steel based engineering products. Caparo employs 4000 people. Awarded the Padma Bhushan by Government of India 1983. Raised to the Peerage as Baron Paul of Marylebone 1996.

> Came to UK in 1966 and in 1968 founded Caparo Group Ltd which specialises in the manufacture and supply of steel based engineering products.
>
> **LORD SWRAJ PAUL**

MRS PRIYA PAWAR (Indian Classical Dancer)

Choreographer-Dancer, Pushpalata Dance Company, 812 Great West Road, Osterley, TW7 5NA

PLACE OF BIRTH: India
CHILDREN: Two (Asarlani, Prashant)
PROFESSIONAL QUALIFICATIONS: Nritya Varidhi, Kathak Kendra
DIRECTORSHIPS: Pushpalata Dance Co
HOBBIES AND INTERESTS: Music, travelling
PERSONAL PROFILE: Started dancing at the age of four years. Got Visharad (BA) at the age of nine years. Performing internationally and teaching since the age of 14 years on behalf of Indian Goverment in India and abroad and continuing in Britain since 1980. Priya chooses her favourite items from the traditional repertoires of Kathak and Odissi classical styles.
NOMINATED BY: Sharon Aitkin

DR RAJ PERSAUD (Consultant Psychiatrist)

The Maudsley Hospital, Camberwell, London, SE5 5AE

PLACE OF BIRTH: Reading, 13.5.63
MARITAL STATUS: Married
COLLEGE: University College London
ACADEMIC QUALIFICATIONS: MBBS, MRCPsych, MPhil, Dip Phil, MSc, BSc, DHMSA
MEMBERSHIPS: Queens Tennis Club
HONOURS/AWARDS: Royal College of Psychiatrists Research Medal
HOBBIES AND INTERESTS: Tennis
PERSONAL PROFILE: Resident psychiatrist on Granada TV's 'This morning'. Writes regularly for Financial Times, Daily Telegraph, Independent and Daily Mail. Columnist for Cosmopolitan, Men's Health. Lectures for Open University,

MR SUKHJIT SINGH PHULL (Lawyer)

Director, Legal Protection Consultants, 71 Paxton Avenue, Slough, SL1 2SX

PLACE OF BIRTH: Pakistan, 22.9.46
MARITAL STATUS: Married
CHILDREN: Three (Kiranjit, Harsimrin, Karenjit)
COLLEGE: Polytechnic Wolverhampton
ACADEMIC QUALIFICATIONS: LLB Hons CNAA
PROFESSIONAL QUALIFICATIONS: LLB Hons CNAA
DIRECTORSHIPS: Director of Legal Protection Consultants
MEMBERSHIPS: Independent Legal Practitioners
HONOURS/AWARDS: Berkshire Health Award
HOBBIES AND INTERESTS: Badminton, reading, meditation, walking
PERSONAL PROFILE: Director for Legal Protection Consultants since 1994, senior REC and acting director. Hillingdon REC 1987-94. Manager/lawyer at Woodlands Advice Centre Glasgow 1982-87. Senior industrial chemist 1969-82. Legal advisor to Asian Community Association, school governor and vice chairman of governors.

DR JAYSHREE PILLAYE (General Practitioner)

Public Health Doctor,

PLACE OF BIRTH: South Africa
COLLEGE: University of Natal, Durban, South Africa
ACADEMIC QUALIFICATIONS: MBChB (South Africa), MSc (LSE) and DFFP Diploma (Faculty of Family Planning) DA (Germany)
DIRECTORSHIPS: Founder of the Professional African and Asian Women's Association, 1989
MEMBERSHIPS: Royal Society of Medicine, New York Academy of Sciences. Faculty of Family Planning, Reproductive Health Care of the Royal College of Gynaecologists.
HONOURS/AWARDS: Dux Meritus at School, Woman of the Year 1997
HOBBIES AND INTERESTS: Reading, studying history of Asians in South Africa, politics, cooking
EMAIL: jupiree@epulse.net
PERSONAL PROFILE: Dr Pillaye has pioneered work to promote ethnic minority health and women's issues. A qualified medical practitioner and public health doctor, Dr Pillaye has undertaken work in promoting sexual health, and in initiating HIV/AIDS prevention strategies for minority communities and refugees. She has worked for UNAIDS in Geneva, and contributed to an Experts Meeting held in Brussels to overcome the double discrimination and inequality facing black and migrant women in the labour market.

DR DOMINGOS PINTO OBE (Surgeon)

Consultant Surgeon, Tyrone County Hospital, 89 Kevlin Road, Omagh, BT78 1PQ

PLACE OF BIRTH: India, 26.11.37
MARITAL STATUS: Married
CHILDREN: Three (Anthony, Fiona, Boris)
COLLEGE: London Hospital Medical School, London University
ACADEMIC QUALIFICATIONS: MBBS, LRCP, MRCS, MS (London), FRCS, FRCSE, FRCSI
MEMBERSHIPS: Association of Surgeons of Great Britain and Ireland
HONOURS/AWARDS: OBE
HOBBIES AND INTERESTS: Golf, travelling
PERSONAL PROFILE: Rotarian, Omagh Rotary Club (past president). Past captain Omagh Golf Club. Deputy Leiuntenant of Tyrone.

MR BIPIN PITROLA (Trade Union Official)

Area Organiser, USDAW-Union of Shop Distributive & Allied Workers, Walter Padley House, 9 Raleigh Walk, Waterfront 2000, Atlantic Wharf, Cardiff, CF1 5LN

PLACE OF BIRTH: Africa, 23.10.64
MARITAL STATUS: Married
CHILDREN: Two (Mitesh, Kemi)
MEMBERSHIPS: Equality First, Welsh Asian Council, Gujarati Association, Cadmad, Bristol REC
HOBBIES AND INTERESTS: Karate, films, politics, meeting people
PERSONAL PROFILE: First and only Black trade union official in Wales and South West England. Member of Bristol REC, Equality First in Cardiff, CADMAD, Welsh Asian Council-Secretary, South Wales Gujarati Association-Secretary, Labour Party ward and CLP member, Ethnic Minority Officer 1996-97, Youngest member of Industrial Tribunal in Wales 1995-98. Member of Sanatan Dharm Mandhir.

DR BIPIN PONDA (General Practitioner)

Swanlow Medical Centre, 39 Beeston Drive, Winsford, CW7 1ER

PLACE OF BIRTH: India, 8.8.31
MARITAL STATUS: Married
CHILDREN: One (Nina)
COLLEGE: Bombay, Liverpool
ACADEMIC QUALIFICATIONS: MBBS, DTM&H
MEMBERSHIPS: Professional Hypnosis Society
HOBBIES AND INTERESTS: Snooker and chess, Indian poetry to literature
PERSONAL PROFILE: Local and borough councillor-20 years. Mayor of Winsford (twice) 1980 and 1983. President Rotary 1986. President Round Table 1971. President Conservative Club 12 years. Trustee Conservative Club. President Stooke Club 10 years. Ex deputy police surgeon DSS / adjudicator / examiner. General medical practice.

MR HS POONI (Senior Analyst Programmer)

130 Ashbourne Way, Kingspark, Bradford, BD2 1ER

PLACE OF BIRTH: India, 22.7.57
MARITAL STATUS: Married
CHILDREN: Two (Manpreet Singh, Gaganpreet Singh)
COLLEGE: Leeds University
ACADEMIC QUALIFICATIONS: BSc Hons Computing & Operational Research
HOBBIES AND INTERESTS: Volleyball, Indian music
PERSONAL PROFILE: Founder member of Sikh Parents Association and Yorkshire Sikh Forum. General secretary of the latter organisation. Active community influencer contributing to better communications between Yorkshire's diverse communities. Liaise regularly with MP's, government reps and other key bodies. Very knowledgeable on Sikh religion.

Resident psychiatrist on Granada TV's 'This morning'. Writes regularly for Financial Times, Daily Telegraph, Independent and Daily Mail. Columnist for Cosmopolitan, Men's Health

DR RAJ PERSAUD

MRS BALMATI POORAN-SINGH (Nurse Midwife Rtd)

President CHS, Caribbean Hindu Society, 16 Ostade Road, Brixton Hill, London, SW2 2BB

PLACE OF BIRTH: Guyana, 26.9.29
MARITAL STATUS: Single
COLLEGE: Blairmont Lutheran
ACADEMIC QUALIFICATIONS: Pupil Teachers Appointment. PTA
PROFESSIONAL QUALIFICATIONS: Resgistered Nurse Midwife-Guyana and London
MEMBERSHIPS: President Caribbean Hindu Society
HONOURS/AWARDS: President CHS 1988 -90, Re-elected president 1998 -1999
HOBBIES AND INTERESTS: Travelling, reading, visiting the sick
PERSONAL PROFILE: Arrived in Britain 1964. Qualified in London 1969 as a registered nurse. Retired Sister St Thomas' Hospital London. Interest in Hindu religion. Since retiring 11 years ago I have been engaged constantly in voluntary work eg. visiting the sick and reading the scriptures-Ramayana Gita to them.

MR ASHWIN KANTILAL POPAT (Optometrist)

Heaton Caffin Opticians, 121 Uxbridge Road, Rickmansworth, WD3 2DN

PLACE OF BIRTH: Kenya, 20.11.48
MARITAL STATUS: Married
CHILDREN: Two (Shaina, Anand)
COLLEGE: City University
ACADEMIC QUALIFICATIONS: BSc, FBCO
PROFESSIONAL QUALIFICATIONS: FBCO
MEMBERSHIPS: Association of Optometrists. Local Optical Committee Camden, Islington and Hillingdon
HONOURS/AWARDS: Trustee Anoopam Mission-Charity
HOBBIES AND INTERESTS: Badminton and music, reading and helping various charities, TV, jokes
PERSONAL PROFILE: I was born in Nairobi and came to UK in 1965 to do my A-Levels, followed by my degree in Optometry. I was invited to Buckingham Palace for the garden party in July 1998. I serve on the Ophthalmic Committees of Camden, Islington and Hillingdon.

MR GOPAL BHAI POPAT (Voluntary Work)

Secretary, Asian Foundation for Help, 102 Camrose Avenue, Edgware, HA8 6BX

PLACE OF BIRTH: India, 1.8.24
MARITAL STATUS: Married
CHILDREN: Five (Rasik, Bharat, Hitesh, Anila, Kusum)
HONOURS/AWARDS: Brent Citizen Award
HOBBIES AND INTERESTS: Social and community charity work
PERSONAL PROFILE: Born in India, in Uganda from 1934-72 own business. Moved to UK in 1972 since then has been doing full time charity work. Associated with many national and international organisations.
NOMINATED BY: Dial Sharma

MR VINOD BHAGWANJI POPAT (Managing Director)

Managing Director, Midland Broadcasting Corporation, MPK House, 233 Belgrave Road, Leicester, LE1 3HT

PLACE OF BIRTH: Malawi, 6.10.55
MARITAL STATUS: Married
CHILDREN: Two (Neil, Nir)
COLLEGE: University Tutorial College, London
ACADEMIC QUALIFICATIONS: A-Levels History, Economics
DIRECTORSHIPS: Middlesex Broadcasting Corp Ltd, Midland Broadcasting Corp Ltd
HOBBIES AND INTERESTS: Sports, music, media related issues
PERSONAL PROFILE: Born in Malawi and now settled in the UK. Amongst his high profile work includes charitable funds for the 'Friends of Malawi'. He was responsible for acquiring the first RSL for Leicester and successfully ran 'Radio Festival' to coincide with the festivities of the Diwali celebration in Leicestershire. Vinod has most recently bid for a bigger prize-television broadcasting-and was successful in obtaining Britain's first Asian Terrestrial television channel and launched 'MATV-Channel 6-The Channel of Choice' in 1999.
NOMINATED BY: Ms Marlena

DR ROOPENDRA KUMAR PRASAD (General Practitioner)

Lostock Hall Medical Centre, 410 Leyland Road, Lostock Hall, Preston, PR5 5SA

PLACE OF BIRTH: India, 1.6.42
MARITAL STATUS: Married
CHILDREN: Three (Catherine, Sanjay, Naomi)
ACADEMIC QUALIFICATIONS: MBBS, MS, FRCS, MRCGP
DIRECTORSHIPS: BMA, ODA
PERSONAL PROFILE: General Practitioner. Chairman of South Lancashire LMC and North West Regional LMC. Member Primary Care Group. Council member of Medical Defence Union and BMA. Vice chairman of ODA. Past chairman of Regional Medical Committee. Past member of FHSA District Management Board. Committee of Management Prescribers Journal.

MS USHA PRASHAR CBE (Chairman)

The Parole Board, Abell House, John Islip Street, London, SW1P 4LH

PLACE OF BIRTH: Kenya, 29.6.48
MARITAL STATUS: Married
COLLEGE: University of Leeds, Glasgow University
ACADEMIC QUALIFICATIONS: BA Hons and Dip Soc
DIRECTORSHIPS: Non Executive Director of Channel 4 Television
MEMBERSHIPS: Deputy Chairman National Literary Forum
HONOURS/AWARDS: CBE
HOBBIES AND INTERESTS: Music, golf, reading
PERSONAL PROFILE: Public policy and social policy expert with extensive experience of equal opportunities, race relations, criminal justice and the arts.
NOMINATED BY: Bertie Mann, Government Office For London

MR ASHOK KUMAR PURI (Travel & Insurance Agent)

Principal, Old Hill Travel & Insurance Services, 19 The Mount, Cradley Heath, Warley, B64 6NJ

PLACE OF BIRTH: India, 31.8.56
MARITAL STATUS: Married
CHILDREN: Three (Aman, Karuna, Amit)
COLLEGE: College in India
PROFESSIONAL QUALIFICATIONS: Gen Life Insurance Courses while working with Allied and Dunbar
MEMBERSHIPS: Gym
HONOURS/AWARDS: Hind Rattan Award and Nav Rattan Award
HOBBIES AND INTERESTS: Snooker, cricket, writing, of course gym
PERSONAL PROFILE: Writing articles in Hindi for Indian newspapers. Journalist, community social work, attending meetings for news, travel around the world, must have a holiday once in a year for relaxation and leave the working life behind. For community service I received Hind Rattan and Nav Rattan Awards. Love my India, parents, brothers, sisters and of course, my wife and kids.
NOMINATED BY: Mr M R Khan

MR GURDEEP SINGH PURI (Day Care Manager)

Glasgow City Council Social Work Dept, Anderston Mel-Milaap Centre, 134 Berkeley Street, Glasgow, G3 7HY

PLACE OF BIRTH: India, 28.6.58
MARITAL STATUS: Married
CHILDREN: Three (Manpreet Singh, Amanpreet Kaur, Puneet Puri)
COLLEGE: B.Com, MA, SVQ
HONOURS/AWARDS: Pride of Moga Awards (India)
HOBBIES AND INTERESTS: Writing, reading
PERSONAL PROFILE: I have been working with elderly and disabled people for the last three years and I am president of the International Panjabi Mini Kahani Munch for the last five years and the author of 12 books.
NOMINATED BY: Dr G S Pandohal

Public policy and social policy expert with extensive experience of equal opportunities, race relations, criminal justice and the arts

USHA PRASHAR CBE

MRS KAILASH PURI (Writer)

Director,

PLACE OF BIRTH: Pakistan
MARITAL STATUS: Married
CHILDREN: Three
PERSONAL PROFILE: Kailash Puri is a prolific and celebrated writer. Her first publication was a novel and short stories collection. Since then she has published six novels, three short story collections, three volumes of poetry, nine controversial books on sexology, three cookery books plus autobiography, anthologies and essays. In addition she is working as a columnist for Punjabi weeklies, Des Pardes and Sandesh. A wide range of radio and TV programmes are also to her credit.
NOMINATED BY: Councillor Jagjit Singh Taunque

MR OM PURI (Actor)

Conway Van Gelder Ltd,

PLACE OF BIRTH: India, 9.3.50
MARITAL STATUS: Married
CHILDREN: One (Ishaan)
COLLEGE: Khalsa College, Patiala
ACADEMIC QUALIFICATIONS: BA
PROFESSIONAL QUALIFICATIONS: Graduate National School of Drama, Delhi and Film Institute, Pune
HONOURS/AWARDS: Best Actor at Karlovy Vary and Brussels (International Film Fests)
HOBBIES AND INTERESTS: Travelling, gardening
PERSONAL PROFILE: Have had a long association with films, television and theatre, but specially acclaimed in cinema. Have earned a number of national and international awards and acted in films both in India, Hollywood, British and Canadian films. Honoured with the Padma Shri by the president of India and the National Award (twice), the Soviet Land Nehru Award. Apart from Karlaray, Vary and Brussels (in the international arena) have done a few landmark roles in the history of Indian Parallel Cinema.

Entrants in the Asians in the Millennium have

been nominated for their achievements and

contributions. You can

nominate someone who

deserves to be in the

Who's Who of Asian Achievers 2000

Entries are free

Send in your nominations, including name,

contact address and telephone number to:

Books Division, Ethnic Media Group,

148 Cambridge Heath Road, London E1 5QJ

MR PARVEZ QADIR (ACTOR)

Piccadilly Management, Unit 123, 23 New Mount Street, Manchester, M4 4DE

PLACE OF BIRTH: Rochdale, 15.11.69
MARITAL STATUS: Single
COLLEGE: Salford University
ACADEMIC QUALIFICATIONS: HND, Media Performance 2 A-Levels
MEMBERSHIPS: Equity
HOBBIES AND INTERESTS: Reading, travelling, cinema, eating
PERSONAL PROFILE: I have always been fascinated by the world of entertainment since watching Bollywood and Hollywood movies. Which led me to train in college and university in acting. Its a hard struggle but if you have the determination to succeed you will.
NOMINATED BY: Shaista Aziz

MR KHAWAR MEHMOOD QURESHI (BARRISTER)

Chambers of Lord Neill QC, 1 Hare Court, Temple, London, EC4Y 7BE

PLACE OF BIRTH: England, 13.4.66
MARITAL STATUS: Single
ACADEMIC QUALIFICATIONS: LLB, LLM (Cantab) First Class
PROFESSIONAL QUALIFICATIONS: Barrister-at-Law
HONOURS/AWARDS: Queen Mothers Scholar 1990, Colombos Prizewinners 1990
HOBBIES AND INTERESTS: Squash, riding
PERSONAL PROFILE: Practising in commercial, international and constitutional law. Legal adviser to Bosnian government Dayton peace talks. Lecturer in international law. Member, International Relations Committee, Bar Council. Chairman of Trustees, War Child.

CLLR MURAD QURESHI (COUNCILLOR)

Regeneration Officer, 45-47/3 Daventry Street, Marylebone, London, NW1 6TD

PLACE OF BIRTH: Manchester, 27.5.65
MARITAL STATUS: Single
COLLEGE: UEA & UCL
ACADEMIC QUALIFICATIONS: BA Hons Development Studies; MSc Environmental Economics
DIRECTORSHIPS: Eco-Ventures (UK) Ltd
MEMBERSHIPS: ICEA, IEM, APM and EARA
HOBBIES AND INTERESTS: Playing, watching football and cricket, eating out
EMAIL: muradqureshi@BTinternet.com
PERSONAL PROFILE: A councillor in Westminster and Labour group spokesman on the Environment and Leisure Committee. Professionally an economist and environmental auditor in the housing and regeneration field while undertaking overseas consultancies for the UNCHS.

DR SHAKEEL AHMED QURESHI
(CONSULTANT-PAEDIATRIC CARDIOLOGY)

Guys Hospital, Dept of Paediatric Cardiology, 11th Floor, Guy's Tower, St Thomas Street, London, SE1 9RT

PLACE OF BIRTH: Pakistan, 20.3.52
MARITAL STATUS: Married
CHILDREN: Four (Rahila Noreen, Sajid, Abid, Atif Imran)
COLLEGE: Manchester
ACADEMIC QUALIFICATIONS: MBChB
PROFESSIONAL QUALIFICATIONS: FRCP
HOBBIES AND INTERESTS: Travelling, lecturing
PERSONAL PROFILE: Major interest is non-surgical treatment of congenital heart disease for babies and children.

MR SHAMIM AHMED QURESHI (BARRISTER-AT-LAW)

All Saints Chambers, 9-11 Broad Street, Bristol

PLACE OF BIRTH: Pakistan, 28.2.60
MARITAL STATUS: Married
CHILDREN: Four
COLLEGE: University of West of England, Bristol
ACADEMIC QUALIFICATIONS: LLB Hons
PROFESSIONAL QUALIFICATIONS: Bar-at-Law
MEMBERSHIPS: Criminal Bar Association, Bar Council, Western Circuit, Pakistan Association (Bristol)
HOBBIES AND INTERESTS: Cricket, fitness training
PERSONAL PROFILE: Came to this country in 1965, grew up in South Yorkshire and eventually qualified as a barrister in 1982. I worked for five years in Crown Prosecution Service and have been in private practice since 1989, specialising in criminal and immigration law.

> ## Major interest is non-surgical treatment of congenital heart disease for babies and children.
>
> **DR SHAKEEL AHMED QURESHI**

> ## Practising in commercial, international and constitutional law. Legal adviser to Bosnian government Dayton peace talks. Lecturer in international law. Member, International Relations Committee, Bar Council. Chairman of Trustees, War Child
>
> **KHAWAR MEHMOOD QURESHI**

Britain's premier
Asian newspaper

hard news, for the
discerning reader

For subscription information call 0171 702 8012

MRS SUDESH RAHEJA (Consultant-Advisor)

Consultant, RAS Associates, 51 London Road, Stanmore, HA7 4PA

PLACE OF BIRTH: India, 16.11.42
MARITAL STATUS: Married
CHILDREN: Two (Vandna Sehgal, Anjna)
COLLEGE: Punjab University, India
ACADEMIC QUALIFICATIONS: BA Hons, Hindi, BA in English, History and Punjabi
PROFESSIONAL QUALIFICATIONS: Quality Assessor Ethnic Minority and Community Relations
HOBBIES AND INTERESTS: Reading, travelling, music, entertaining, community involvement
PERSONAL PROFILE: I am a consultant trainer on issues relating to managing diversity and equality of opportunity specialising in racial and cultural communication. Clients include the MOD, Metropolitan Police, local Police Division, local authorities, career services, Home Office, Health Service etc. I am a magistrate and the vice president of the Indian Association of Harrow. I sit on various committees to break the barriers and enhance the quality of life.

MR ALIUR RAHMAN (Kickboxer)

British & European Championship, Bengal Cottage & Kebabish, 1 Green Road & 95 Main Street, Leicester, LE9 6RA

PLACE OF BIRTH: Birmingham, 18.6.70
MARITAL STATUS: Married
CHILDREN: One (Zahida)
ACADEMIC QUALIFICATIONS: GCSE Grade C & D
PROFESSIONAL QUALIFICATIONS: WAKO & Kung Fu Black Belt, First Degree
MEMBERSHIPS: WAKO & MAJA
HONOURS/AWARDS: Six British Championships, European Champion and over 30 other championships
HOBBIES AND INTERESTS: Work out on the bags at gym
PERSONAL PROFILE: I started at the age of 13 years old. By the age of 18 I have two active British titles, European title and performances in two World title attempts. Now I would like to own a gym to train new champions.
NOMINATED BY: Family

MR ASHADUR RAHMAN (Youth Worker)

Trainee Youth Worker, King's Cross-Brunswick Neighbourhood Association, 9C Frederick Street, King's Cross, London, WC1X 0NF

PLACE OF BIRTH: Bangladesh, 20.7.81
MARITAL STATUS: Single
COLLEGE: Mary Ward Centre
ACADEMIC QUALIFICATIONS: English Support, Learning, GCSE PE (Sport Game)
PROFESSIONAL QUALIFICATIONS: FA Junior Team Managers Course, FA Coaching Certificate Course
HOBBIES AND INTERESTS: Playing snooker, pool, tennis, table tennis, working out in the gym
EMAIL: ashrahman@hotmail.com
PERSONAL PROFILE: I have started doing youth work and coaching, managing football clubs at the age of 16 years. I try my best for young Asian people by giving my views, so they can achieve their goals in the future. My dream is for someone I have helped and advised through their life to make the top grade of their dreams.
NOMINATED BY: Terry Singh

MR EHSANUR RAHMAN (Technical Engineer)

Alcatel Submarine Network, 88 Tomswood Hill, Hainault, IG6 2QH

PLACE OF BIRTH: Bangladesh, 28.2.71
MARITAL STATUS: Single
COLLEGE: University of Wales
ACADEMIC QUALIFICATIONS: BSc Hons
PROFESSIONAL QUALIFICATIONS: RICS soon going for MBA sponsored by the company
MEMBERSHIPS: Royal Institute of Chartered Surveyors (RICS)
HOBBIES AND INTERESTS: Football, chess, badminton
EMAIL: ehsanrahman@asn
PERSONAL PROFILE: Born in Bangladesh, educated in UK. Intend to go on for higher job and I am getting myself ready for it. Hope to be successful.

MR EHTESHAM RAHMAN (Software Developer)

Salerio Consultant, 110 Ltd, 88 Tomswood Hill, Hainault, IG6 2QH

PLACE OF BIRTH: UK, 3.7.72
MARITAL STATUS: Single
COLLEGE: Kingston University
ACADEMIC QUALIFICATIONS: BSc Hons Business Information Technology
HOBBIES AND INTERESTS: Snooker, football
PERSONAL PROFILE: Grew up in Bangladesh, ie first seven years, came to England for secondary education, university and now in IT profession, where I hope to specialise in financial products. Live with brothers and parents in Essex.
NOMINATED BY: Shamim Azad

MR EKRAMUR RAHMAN (Software Developer)

Dunn and Bradstreet, 88 Tomswood Hill, Hainault, IG6 2QH

PLACE OF BIRTH: Wolverhampton, 20.6.73
MARITAL STATUS: Single
COLLEGE: Manchester University
ACADEMIC QUALIFICATIONS: BSc Computing and Accounting
HOBBIES AND INTERESTS: Chess, basketball
PERSONAL PROFILE: Born in England, O and A-Levels in Kingston Grammar School. BSc Manchester University. Going for Business Administration.
NOMINATED BY: Shamim Azad

DR MOHAMMAD RAHMAN (Doctor)

General Practitioner, Ashmore Park Health Centre, Griffiths Drive, Wednesfield, Wolverhampton, WV11 2LH

PLACE OF BIRTH: Bangladesh, 15.9.38
MARITAL STATUS: Married
CHILDREN: Three (Imon, Rumon, Rita)
DIRECTORSHIPS: Director and Chairman of Wolverhampton Doctors on Call
MEMBERSHIPS: Overseas Doctors Association
HONOURS/AWARDS: Fellowship of Royal Society of Medicines, Fellowship ODA
HOBBIES AND INTERESTS: Travelling, movies, reading thrillers
PERSONAL PROFILE: President Bangladesh Cultural Society 1983-87. National general secretary Bangladesh Medical Association (UK) Ltd 1986-88. National president-Bangladesh Medical Association 1992-94, Chairman-Overseas Doctors Association Wolverhampton 1990-96. Present president Overseas Doctors Association Wolverhampton, vice chairman Wolverhampton LMC.

MR MOHIBUR RAHMAN (Graduate)

Take Away Manager, Gulshan Indian Take Away, 8 Christchurch Street, Ipswich, IP4 2DJ

PLACE OF BIRTH: Bangladesh, 2.10.74
MARITAL STATUS: Married
COLLEGE: University College, Suffolk
ACADEMIC QUALIFICATIONS: BA Hons Business Administration (2.2)
HONOURS/AWARDS: Commendation Awards at school, First Aid at school
HOBBIES AND INTERESTS: Football, reading, music (Indian), travelling
PERSONAL PROFILE: I graduated in business administration at University College in 1997. Currently I am working as the manager of our family business. Gulshan Indian Take Away but my goal is to go into chartered accountancy or work for a big city firm one day.
NOMINATED BY: Mr A Rahman

'I am a consultant trainer on issues relating to managing diversity and equality of opportunity specialising in racial and cultural communication. Clients include the MOD, Metropolitan Police, local Police Division, local authorities, career services, Home Office, Health Service'

SUDESH RAHEJA

MR AJIT SINGH RAI (TRUSTEE)

Ex-President, Indian Workers Association Southall, Community Advice Bureau, 19A The Green, Southall, UB2 4AH

PLACE OF BIRTH: India, 21.4.28
MARITAL STATUS: Married
CHILDREN: Five (HS, SS, RS, SS, RS)
COLLEGE: DAV College Jalandhar, Payal University
ACADEMIC QUALIFICATIONS: BA
PROFESSIONAL QUALIFICATIONS: Adviser in immigration matters

MR JOHN SINGH RAI (CONSULTANT)

IT Administrator, Creston, 56 Lime Tree Avenue, Dunchurch, Rugby, CV22 7QT

PLACE OF BIRTH: Coventry, 18.5.73
MARITAL STATUS: Single
COLLEGE: Coventry University
ACADEMIC QUALIFICATIONS: 1st Class Honours Business Studies
PROFESSIONAL QUALIFICATIONS: MCSE Consultant IT
HONOURS/AWARDS: Rugby College 1993 Award, Outstanding Achievement BTEC Business Studies, Cov Uni 1997 most successful student graduating from Business School
HOBBIES AND INTERESTS: Badminton, fencing, reading
PERSONAL PROFILE: Had a rare growth from the age of 18 months treated at Birmingham Childrens Hospital until 17 years of age. Lost a lot of schooling as a child. I feel I have achieved well in life so far and would like to use my success to help others who are not so fortunate.
NOMINATED BY: Elizabeth Rai

MR KULDIP RAI (PRINTER)

Director, Punjabi Post (Printers) Ltd, 277 Soho Road, Handsworth, Birmingham, B21 9SA

PLACE OF BIRTH: India, 30.4.39
MARITAL STATUS: Married
CHILDREN: Four (Meena, Parvina, Sandeep, Rekha)
ACADEMIC QUALIFICATIONS: Printing
PROFESSIONAL QUALIFICATIONS: Metric in India
HONOURS/AWARDS: Well known among the community
HOBBIES AND INTERESTS: Driving, reading, music, community work

DR SUDHARAM RAI (DOCTOR)

Principal-General Practice, Manor Care Group, Medical Complex, Rainworth, NG21 0JP

PLACE OF BIRTH: India, 19.8.43
MARITAL STATUS: Married
CHILDREN: Two (Nithin, Neema)
COLLEGE: Mysore University
ACADEMIC QUALIFICATIONS: MBBS, MFFP, FRSM
PROFESSIONAL QUALIFICATIONS: MBBS and MFFP
DIRECTORSHIPS: Managing Director, R & K Care Ltd, Manor Care Group
MEMBERSHIPS: Chairman, British Medical Association
HONOURS/AWARDS: President, Mansfield Medical Society
HOBBIES AND INTERESTS: Golf, travelling, medical politics
PERSONAL PROFILE: General practitioner, board member and vice chairman, Primary Care Group for GP's, Member Armed Forces Occupational Health and Community Care Committees. Police surgeon, Major Territorial Army, Chairman Overseas Doctors Association. President Mansfield Medical Society, Medical Assessor GMC.

> 'General practitioner, board member and vice chairman, Primary Care Group for GP's, Member Armed Forces Occupational Health and Community Care Committees'
>
> **DR SUDHARAM RAI**

MR PREM RAINDI (MANAGING DIRECTOR)

Managing Director, Premier World Trading Co Ltd, Premier House, Rolfe Street, Smethwick, Birmingham, B66 2AA

PLACE OF BIRTH: India, 1.9.44
MARITAL STATUS: Married
CHILDREN: Two (Manraj, Amandeep)
MEMBERSHIPS: Asian Trade Association-Trustee Sri Deshmesh Sikh Temple-vice president
HOBBIES AND INTERESTS: Business deals, manufacturing
PERSONAL PROFILE: Prem Raindi has been involved within the clothing industry for the past 30 years. Over the years he has achieved great heights within his profession and has helped many people gain employment and even begin their own business ventures. Although recently he has seen very bad times within his business he is still the same lighthearted gentleman everybody has known.

DR SATWANT KAUR RAIT JP (MANAGER)

Co-ordinator for Education, Leeds City Council, Leeds Education Dept, 10th Floor, Merrian House, Merrian Centre, Leeds, LS2 8DT

PLACE OF BIRTH: India, 10.5.42
MARITAL STATUS: Married
CHILDREN: Two (Greta, Jasjit)
COLLEGE: University of Loughborough, Leeds, Sheffield.
ACADEMIC QUALIFICATIONS: MA (History) Delhi University
PROFESSIONAL QUALIFICATIONS: PhD (Librarianship) Loughborough
MEMBERSHIPS: ALA (Associate of Library Association). Asian Cultural Centre, Bradford. Indian Women Association. Leeds Sikh Parents Association. Supreme Council of Sikhs of Leeds
HOBBIES AND INTERESTS: Walking, gardening, writing
PERSONAL PROFILE: Migrated to England from India in 1968. Author of Dictionary of Punjabi name elements (1984); Bibliography on Ethnic Minorities (1981), Punjab Rasri Kala and many research articles and reports. Served on many ethnic minority organisations and worked with learning with the community in art, fairs, sound and school themes. Appointed JP in 1986.
NOMINATED BY: Mrs Sagoo

MR JAGDEV SINGH RAIZADA (TEACHER)

31 Walton Close, Ernesford Grange, Coventry, CV3 2LJ

PLACE OF BIRTH: India, 25.5.36
MARITAL STATUS: Married
CHILDREN: Two (Ameesh, Asheesh)
COLLEGE: University and teachers training college
ACADEMIC QUALIFICATIONS: MA
PROFESSIONAL QUALIFICATIONS: Post Graduate Certificate in Education
DIRECTORSHIPS: Management Committee ASRA Coventry Housing Association
MEMBERSHIPS: Coventry Community Relations Council; Midlands Central Euro-constituency Conservative Council
PERSONAL PROFILE: Policy co-ordinator and advisor to Sanatan Dharam Hindu Society; One Nation Forum; Midlands Constituencies Liaison Committee; West Midlands Area Council; Executive Council Coventry Southeast Conservative Association.

MISS LAILA RAJA (PRESENTER-JOURNALIST)

7 Trafalgar Business Centre, 77-87 River Road, Barking, IG11 0EZ

PLACE OF BIRTH: Pakistan, 20.8.75
MARITAL STATUS: Single
COLLEGE: Queens. Medical (Nottingham)
ACADEMIC QUALIFICATIONS: BSc Hons Genetics
MEMBERSHIPS: Crystal Palace Sports Centre
HONOURS/AWARDS: Bronze and Silver Medal Trampolining
HOBBIES AND INTERESTS: Trampolining, horse-riding, ice skating, swimming
PERSONAL PROFILE: I started broadcasting at the age of 16 at various radio stations including GLR, Spectrum and Apna. Having established my name I began to present at Namaste and Asianet Television. I am also a freelance journalist. I feel more Asian women should be encouraged to come forward in the media.
NOMINATED BY: Fauzia Mirza

MS SUSHILA RAJA (TRAINING CONSULTANT)

Director, Syndicate Training Services Ltd, 13 Pickering Close, Leicester, LE4 6ER

PLACE OF BIRTH: Sri Lanka, 27.6.47
MARITAL STATUS: Divorced
CHILDREN: One (Dr Jaishan K Mahan)
COLLEGE: Middlesex University
ACADEMIC QUALIFICATIONS: MA
PROFESSIONAL QUALIFICATIONS: Certificate in Training
MEMBERSHIPS: Associate of Institute of Personnel Development
HOBBIES AND INTERESTS: Travel
PERSONAL PROFILE: Sushila Raja is a training consultant and director of Syndicate Training Services Ltd. She empowers women through training programmes in managing community organisations, women into management, training the trainer, mentoring programmes and capacity building projects. She set up projects for women in Sri Lanka, South Africa and Britain.
NOMINATED BY: Capt J K Mahan

MR DIPEN RAJYAGURU (INFORMATION-PUBLICITY OFFICER)

1990 Trust, Southbank Techno Park, 90 London Road, London, SE1 6LN

PLACE OF BIRTH: Uganda, 23.10.69
MARITAL STATUS: Single
COLLEGE: South Bank University
ACADEMIC QUALIFICATIONS: LL.B Hons
DIRECTORSHIPS: Founder and vice chair of Bangla 2000
HOBBIES AND INTERESTS: Reading, writing, swimming, Asian theatre
EMAIL: dipenr@hotmail.com
PERSONAL PROFILE: Dipen is the information and publicity officer for The 1990 Trust, a leading and award winning information and policy organisation, disseminating information and writing on key issues that effect the Black (African, Asian and Caribbean) communities. With his legal background he also undertakes casework and researches, advises and drafts legal documents for The 1990 Trust.
NOMINATED BY: Ushma Vyas

(REV) PANDIT HITENDRA M RAJYAGURU
(SOCIAL WORKER)

Hindu Pandit, Shri Vidhya Satsang Mandal, 37 Roberts Road, Leicester, LE4 5HG

PLACE OF BIRTH: Kenya, 15.1.60
MARITAL STATUS: Married
CHILDREN: Two (Kavita, Shyam)
ACADEMIC QUALIFICATIONS: MA, BSc
PROFESSIONAL QUALIFICATIONS: Pandit
MEMBERSHIPS: South London Brahmin Society, LBS, FHP, HRAES, Shri Vidhya Satsang Mandal
HONOURS/AWARDS: Hon Pandit of South London Brahmin Society
HOBBIES AND INTERESTS: Astrology, reading, japa, yoga
PERSONAL PROFILE: To create an oasis where it is demonstrated in daily practical life, the practicality, the immense value, and the perfect validity of the greatest ideas of mankind. Where truth has personality, divine love, a peace that passes understanding rules, every circumstance and situation of life, where matter and spirit are reconciled.

MR ABDOOL CADER RAMAN OBE
(CONSULTANT PSYCHIATRIST)

Peakfields, Gravel Castle Road, Barham, Canterbury, CT4 6QF

PLACE OF BIRTH: Mauritius, 19.6.20
MARITAL STATUS: Married
CHILDREN: Three (Karrim, Adam, David)
COLLEGE: Guys Hospital
PROFESSIONAL QUALIFICATIONS: FRCPsy
HONOURS/AWARDS: OBE
HOBBIES AND INTERESTS: Writing
PERSONAL PROFILE: Has been World Health Organisation consultant for years. Presided, WHO technical service on African psychiatric development. Has written an autobiographical book, published 1992 , 'Nola Paradise' I love You Mauritius.
NOMINATED BY: Rotary Club Canterbury

MS SAKUNTALA RAMANEE (ACTRESS)

Magnolia Management, 136 Hicks Avenue, Greenford

PLACE OF BIRTH: London, 26.10.61
CHILDREN: Two (Jay, Saritha)
COLLEGE: Kent University
ACADEMIC QUALIFICATIONS: BA Hons Drama
MEMBERSHIPS: Equity
EMAIL: pmat114@aol.com
PERSONAL PROFILE: A respected theatre performer Sakuntala has also appeared frequently in television, radio and cinema productions. Her work with Tara Arts, Tamasha, The Royal Court and National Theatre has been applauded by audiences, writers and her fellow performers alike.

MR KRISHNA RAMDEHOLL (HEAD OF YOUTH SERVICE)

Buckinghamshire Youth County Council, 4 Cliffview Road, Lewisham, London, SE13 7DD

PLACE OF BIRTH: London, 13.10.58
MARITAL STATUS: Common Law
CHILDREN: Four (Jacinta, Sataish, Janesh, Sukera)
COLLEGE: University of London, Goldsmiths College
ACADEMIC QUALIFICATIONS: MA Sociology-Research BA History/Sociology
PROFESSIONAL QUALIFICATIONS: Post Graduate Diploma in Youth and Community work 1991-96
DIRECTORSHIPS: Head of National Black Worker /Trainers Group 1991-96
MEMBERSHIPS: National Institution of Youth Community Education Officers
HONOURS/AWARDS: 1998-Anti bullying project for youth, 1997 Asian Youth Business Project
HOBBIES AND INTERESTS: Asian music, Asian sport, jazz
PERSONAL PROFILE: I have worked for 25 years in youth service in Greenwich, Lewisham, Tower Hamlets and Waltham Forest. In 1999 I will be one of three heads of youth service in the country as I take up a new post in Buckinghamshire. I have been committed and successful in bringing Asian youth and the community to play a part.
NOMINATED BY: Pam Donovan, Goldsmiths University of London

DR RAMNARACE RAMNARINE (ACADEMIC)

Senior Lecturer, University of North London, School of Communications Technology, 166-220 Holloway Road, London, N7 8DB

PLACE OF BIRTH: Trinidad, 29.7.41
MARITAL STATUS: Married
CHILDREN: One (Sean)
COLLEGE: Kings College
ACADEMIC QUALIFICATIONS: BSc Hons, MSc, PhD Physics
PROFESSIONAL QUALIFICATIONS: C.Eng
MEMBERSHIPS: MIEE
HONOURS/AWARDS: Senior Research Fellow at Kings College London
HOBBIES AND INTERESTS: Eastern philosophy, golf, reading, writing
EMAIL: r.ramnarine@unl.co.uk
PERSONAL PROFILE: Co-researcher for: body scanner infra red spectro photo met photon counter for macro molecules. Published 22 academic international papers, two books: officer in the Royal Air Force. Voluntary work-Bureau of Standards-chair of Electrical and Electronic Division. Secretary of ICCA London, UK Division: Also do gratis lectures in Eastern philosophy to various organisations.
NOMINATED BY: B S Virdee

MR BISHNAUTH RAMRAJ (SERVICE ENGINEER)

Service Engineer, B & J Domestic Appliances Repairs & Sales, 1 Warwick Road, Manor Park, London, E12 6QP

PLACE OF BIRTH: Guyana, 12.5.55
MARITAL STATUS: Married
CHILDREN: One (Indira)
COLLEGE: Southwest London
ACADEMIC QUALIFICATIONS: GCE, A-Level
PROFESSIONAL QUALIFICATIONS: Diploma
HOBBIES AND INTERESTS: Cricket, pools
PERSONAL PROFILE: After 22 years of opening the batting for Ford Cricket Club. I have scored the highest runs of 216 not out in the league (Dagenham Post Essex) for Ford CC in 45 overs and have scored over 1000 runs every season. I won the batting award in the league for 1998.
NOMINATED BY: Nix Nirgunananthan

MR SHAHBAZ RAMZAN (Community Safety Officer)

Community Safety Officer, Milaap Project (Voluntary Youth Group), 61 Hucklow Road, Sheffield, S5 6TB

PLACE OF BIRTH: Sheffield, 7.9.66
MARITAL STATUS: Married
CHILDREN: Two (Shahbaan, Usmaan)
COLLEGE: Sheff Hallam University
ACADEMIC QUALIFICATIONS: HND Business Studies, Post Grad, Social Policy, A-Level Urdu , English, Maths
DIRECTORSHIPS: MD, Express Results Ltd
MEMBERSHIPS: Milaap Project, Black Justice Project, National Equal Opportunities Network. Jammu Kashmir Liberation Front. Sheffield Racial Harassment Project.
HOBBIES AND INTERESTS: Youth work, snooker, pool, visiting places, current affairs, learning languages
PERSONAL PROFILE: Community Safety Officer-ten years. Qualified youth and community worker 1983, currently working on a voluntary basis. Founder member of Milaap Project 1997. Employment opportunity for young Asians to gain paid employment. Consultant on: equal opportunities, Managing Diversity, Investor in People, and Community Safety. Speaker on various national conferences: Finland, Luxembourg and London on Equal Opps / Black people and the criminal justice system.
NOMINATED BY: M Hussain

MR DILJIT RANA MBE (Hotelier & Property Developer)

Managing Director, Andras House Ltd,

DATE OF BIRTH: 20.9.38
MARITAL STATUS: Married
CHILDREN: Two
DIRECTORSHIPS: President-Belfast Chamber of Trade & Commerce 1992-93.
MEMBERSHIPS: Northern Ireland Chamber of Commerce & Industry, Founder and Chief Executive Indian Business Forum, Founder of the Indian Community Centre, CBI (NI) Council. IOD
HONOURS/AWARDS: Flax Trust Award 1997. NI Special Achievement Award in recognition of Mr Rana's efforts to keep Belfast City Centre business alive during the worst years of the Troubles. MBE 1996 for services to the community and industry Belfast.
PERSONAL PROFILE: Present business interests include catering, restaurants and hotel developments. I am the proprietor of the Holiday Inn Garden Court, Holiday Inn Express and Renshaws Hotel, Belfast. Future projects include Holiday Inn Core Brand Hotel at Shaws Bridge, Belfast and Cairndhu House in Larne. Set up and continues to fund the Rana Bursary in the School of Architecture in Queens University to encourage students to work on various developments and redevelopment's within Northern Ireland.

MR RANJIT SINGH RANA (Editor-Journalist)

Editor, Punjabi Guardian, 129 Soho Road, Handsworth, Birmingham, B21 9JT

PLACE OF BIRTH: India, 25.11.59
MARITAL STATUS: Married
CHILDREN: Four (Amrit, Himat, Kirat, Simrat)
COLLEGE: Punjab University, Patiala, Guru Nanak University
ACADEMIC QUALIFICATIONS: BA, MA (Punjab & History)
PROFESSIONAL QUALIFICATIONS: RSA Diploma in Teaching. Diploma in Journalism
DIRECTORSHIPS: General secretary, Punjabi Arts Council
MEMBERSHIPS: Punjabi Arts Council
HONOURS/AWARDS: Library Award 1994
HOBBIES AND INTERESTS: Writing, reading, tourism
PERSONAL PROFILE: My four poetry books are published by famous publishers in India. I won British Punjabi Literary Award 1994 organised by Punjabi Literary Society UK. Also a Birmingham Sikh Gurdwara Council Award 1996.

'Present business interests include catering, restaurants and hotel developments. I am the proprietor of the Holiday Inn Garden Court, Holiday Inn Express and Renshaws Hotel, Belfast'

DILJIT RANA MBE

MR SATVINDER RANA (Senior Government Officer)

Head of Equalities and Strategy, Birmingham City Council & BBC Radio, PO Box 2122, Baskerville House, Broad Street, Birmingham, B1 2NE

PLACE OF BIRTH: India
MARITAL STATUS: Married
CHILDREN: One (Kireet)
COLLEGE: Nottingham University
ACADEMIC QUALIFICATIONS: Master of Business Administration MBA
PROFESSIONAL QUALIFICATIONS: Diploma in Management Studies (DMS)
MEMBERSHIPS: British Institute of Management
HONOURS/AWARDS: Best Radio Programme, Favourite Radio Presenter
HOBBIES AND INTERESTS: Music, cinema, keeping fit, reading, travelling
PERSONAL PROFILE: Worked in local government for 14 years and is head of equalities and strategy for Birmingham City Council. One of the most senior Black / Asian local government officers in the country. Presents the award winning Aaj-Kal Show on BBC Radio Derby and writes for Spice magazine.

MR RAJESH KANU RAO (Cricketer)

Sussex County Cricket Club, 72 Woodstock Road, Wembley, HA0 4EX

PLACE OF BIRTH: London, 9.12.74
MARITAL STATUS: Single
COLLEGE: Manchester Met
ACADEMIC QUALIFICATIONS: BSc Sports Science (Studying for)
PROFESSIONAL QUALIFICATIONS: All Levels of cricket coaching
HONOURS/AWARDS: Gold Award Nat West Trophy, National Lord Taverners Youth Award
HOBBIES AND INTERESTS: Music (swing, soul, hip hop), football, reading sports biographies
EMAIL: rrao@rrao.freeserve.ac.uk
PERSONAL PROFILE: Twenty-four year old, right handed, batsman and leg-spin bowler. Has represented England at all youth levels. Holds record for highest individual score in one day cricket in Sussex CCC history . Potentially the best leg spin bowler in the country according to Shane Warne's coach and mentor Terry Jenner.

DR A M FAZ RASHID (Consultant Pathologist)

Dartford & Gravesham NHS Trust, 36 Red House Lane, Bexleyheath, DA6 8JD

PLACE OF BIRTH: Bangladesh, 29.12.37
MARITAL STATUS: Married
CHILDREN: Two (Tina, Samantha)
COLLEGE: University of Dhaka
ACADEMIC QUALIFICATIONS: MBBS
PROFESSIONAL QUALIFICATIONS: MSc (Path), FRCPath
MEMBERSHIPS: BMA, ACP and BSCC
HOBBIES AND INTERESTS: Computer, DIY, gardening, swimming, keep fit
EMAIL: aburashid@aol.com
PERSONAL PROFILE: Qualified 1961, training in pathology, became Ass. Prof. of Pathology, Institute of Postgradaute Medicine and Research, Dhaka, Bangladesh. Further training at the Institute of Pathology, Free University of Berlin, Germany 1974. Consultant pathologist since 1980. Director of pathology 1992-97. College Tutor, The Royal College of Pathologists, London. Chairman, BMA, Dartford, Gravesend and Medway Div., 1976-77. Chairman, BDMA, London and SE Region 1990-92.

MR BAJLOOR RASHID (Restaurateur)

Proprietor, Curry Garden, 31 Bank Street, Ashford, TN23 1DQ

PLACE OF BIRTH: Bangladesh, 28.5.62
MARITAL STATUS: Married
CHILDREN: Four (Tanveer, Thawheed, Nishat, Zarin)
COLLEGE: School
DIRECTORSHIPS: Bangladesh British Chamber of Commerce
MEMBERSHIPS: Bangladesh Caterers Association. Greater Sylhet Welfare Council UK
HOBBIES AND INTERESTS: Badminton, movies, socialising
PERSONAL PROFILE: I am a renowned businessman in Kent. My partnership business with my brother paid so well that I decided to discontinue my studies and became involved with wholesale trading of rice and spice then in several restaurants. I am involved with a property business and also a partner in international trade.

MRS KIRAN RATNA (Dancer)

Director, India Dance Wales, 22 Maesycoed Road, Heath, Cardiff, CF4 4HF

PLACE OF BIRTH: Kenya, 2.7.61
MARITAL STATUS: Married
CHILDREN: Two (Prashant, Vibha)
COLLEGE: University of Wales
ACADEMIC QUALIFICATIONS: BSc Hons Electrical and Electronics Engineering
PROFESSIONAL QUALIFICATIONS: MSc Systems Engineering
DIRECTORSHIPS: India Dance Wales
MEMBERSHIPS: Welsh Independent Dance, ADITI
HONOURS/AWARDS: Project funded by Arts Council of Wales International
HOBBIES AND INTERESTS: Initiatives fund, lottery fund in 1998-99
PERSONAL PROFILE: The pioneer of Indian dance in Wales formed first Indian dance company in Wales. 'The Kiran Ratna Co' in 1993. Now a company limited by guarantee is 'India Dance Wales' working in Wales and the South West.

MR HARMEGH SINGH RATTAN (Finance Officer Rtd.)

Civil Servant, 2 Lancing Road, Newbury Park, Ilford, IG2 7DR

PLACE OF BIRTH: India, 4.10.40
MARITAL STATUS: Married
CHILDREN: Two (Charnjeet, Sarvjeet)
COLLEGE: Kenya College
PROFESSIONAL QUALIFICATIONS: Accountancy
HONOURS/AWARDS: Namdev Award-received in 1980 for community service
HOBBIES AND INTERESTS: Politics, community service, football
PERSONAL PROFILE: Served on the Newham Race Relations Association and on Newham Police Community Consultative Group. Mr Rattan is a co-ordinator of Neighbourhood Watch in Redbridge. Chairman of Newbury Ward-Labour Party South .

MRS HINA RAVAL (Project Co-ordinator)

Project Co-ordinator, City Council, 17 Ashchurch Drive, Wollaton, Nottingham, NG8 2RB

PLACE OF BIRTH: Kenya, 5.12.52
MARITAL STATUS: Married
CHILDREN: Three (Jaymala, Neelam, Mitul)
COLLEGE: Ahmedabad University, Nottingham University
ACADEMIC QUALIFICATIONS: NVQ Level 3 in Customer Care
PROFESSIONAL QUALIFICATIONS: Word Processing
MEMBERSHIPS: Leicester Radio Listeners Club, Brahma Samaj Nottingham
HONOURS/AWARDS: Nottinghamshire County Council 1995, 1997
HOBBIES AND INTERESTS: Reading, singing
PERSONAL PROFILE: I am a very cool, calm, steady grounded person. Very helpful in many ways due to variety of experience. I am firm but flexible, also in different ways, depending on situation. I am hard working concientious worker. Consistent, reliable and happy-go-lucky.
NOMINATED BY: Bharat N Raval, Theatre Square Subway

MS SAFFIA RAWAT (Teacher)

Deputy Head of Year, Mulberry School For Girls, Richard Street, Commercial Road, London, E1 2JP

PLACE OF BIRTH: Burma, 31.8.66
MARITAL STATUS: Single
COLLEGE: University of Bradford
ACADEMIC QUALIFICATIONS: BSc Hons, PGCE
HOBBIES AND INTERESTS: Football, cricket, reading, cinema, socialising
PERSONAL PROFILE: I was born in Rangoon, Burma but came to this country at the age of three months. My schooling was completed in Bolton. I now work in the East End of London with mainly Bangladeshi students and hopefully through my work have inspired many of them to go to university.
NOMINATED BY: Tahera Begum Matin

MR SUJAN RAWTANI (Consultant Musician)

Consultant, Sujan Rawtani, 72 Preston Hill, Harrow, HA3 9SG

PLACE OF BIRTH: India, 27.4.25
MARITAL STATUS: Married
CHILDREN: Four (Maya, Nanak, Suniya, Satram)
COLLEGE: Pracheen Kala Kendra. Chandigarh
ACADEMIC QUALIFICATIONS: Sangeet Bhaskar (M.Music)
PROFESSIONAL QUALIFICATIONS: Music Therapy
DIRECTORSHIPS: Founder Director, Sindhi Art Circle
MEMBERSHIPS: Community Artist, Sindhu Samaj
HONOURS/AWARDS: First Prize in Tabla 1966, CSSCB India Government & Asian Film Academy, Carlton Sponsored Community Awards 1995
HOBBIES AND INTERESTS: Sponsor music, writing poetry
EMAIL: nrawtani@aol.com
PERSONAL PROFILE: Tutored Wandsworth music class and was honoured Ambassador of Unity (1987). Asian Film Academy Community Awards (1995). Music therapy classes at Gardner Hill unit Springfield Hospital. Contributions BBC Storytelling sound effects, Five O'Clock Special (German Radio). Holi with Shyam. 'Light the candles' Cambridge. Author Sadhwada, Wahakveechare, Art of Tabla prefaced by Pandit Ravishankar and Pandit Ramnarain.

MR MOHAMMED RAZAO (Probation Officer)

West Yorkshire Probation Service,

PLACE OF BIRTH: Pakistan, 29.3.56
MARITAL STATUS: Married
CHILDREN: Six (Minaal, Imtekhab, Swabu, Samina, Nosheena, Zubar)
COLLEGE: Sheffield University
ACADEMIC QUALIFICATIONS: BA Hons, CQSW (Student M.Phil)
PROFESSIONAL QUALIFICATIONS: CQSW
MEMBERSHIPS: Saifa-Voluntary Association Mosque
HOBBIES AND INTERESTS: Playing squash
PERSONAL PROFILE: Born in Pakistan (AK) educated in UK. Probation officer RRI. Elected councillor since 1996, for Labour Party.

CLLR ABDUL REHMAN (Governor Rtd)

Mayor of the City of Derby, Derby City Council, 38 Peartree Crescent, Derby, DE23 8RP

PLACE OF BIRTH: Pakistan, 12.3.36
MARITAL STATUS: Married
CHILDREN: Seven (Azra, Shazia, Habib, Nazia, Salma, Zara, Hafeez)
COLLEGE: Pakistan College, Lahore
MEMBERSHIPS: Pakistan Muslim Welfare Assoc. Derby, Derby Jamia Mosque (Founder chairman), Pakistan Community Assoc. (Former chairman), Pakistan Muslim Funeral Assoc.
HOBBIES AND INTERESTS: Member Liversage Trust, Member Derby Racial Equality Council
PERSONAL PROFILE: Born in Pakistan Abdul Rehman came to UK in 1960. He worked for many years as a bus driver retiring in 1993. In 1990 was elected Derby's first Muslim councillor and has represented Litchurch Ward since that time. Became the city's first Muslim mayor in May 1998. Governor of Peartree Infants Junior School

MR SAJJAD REHMAN (Community Consultant)

Trans-cultural Services Manager, Reading Borough Council, Department of Social Services, Civic Centre, Reading, RG1 7TH

PLACE OF BIRTH: India, 29.11.64
MARITAL STATUS: Married
COLLEGE: Bradford University
ACADEMIC QUALIFICATIONS: BTEC HND Computing and Information Systems Science
PROFESSIONAL QUALIFICATIONS: Diploma in Public Services Interpreting (Post Grad)
MEMBERSHIPS: MIL, MITI, member of Institute of Linguists
HOBBIES AND INTERESTS: Community work, computing, cricket, Zee TV
PERSONAL PROFILE: Only Asian ever to pass Institute of Linguists examination qualifying as the only Asian MIL from the Royal County of Berkshire. Currently manager of Reading Council and Trans-cultural Services. Responsible for councils projects with a focus on ethnic minorities. Also a consultant for International Police Staff Training College at Bramshile, UK.

Only Asian ever to pass Institute of Linguists examination qualifying as the only Asian MIL from the Royal County of Berkshire

SAJJAD REHMAN

DR SHAFIQ REHMAN (Hypnotist-Therapist)

Director, Centre for Hypnosis, PO Box 99, Manchester, M8 0JX

PLACE OF BIRTH: Pakistan, 3.12.64
MARITAL STATUS: Single
COLLEGE: University of Manchester
ACADEMIC QUALIFICATIONS: BA Hons, PhD, TEFL Cert
PROFESSIONAL QUALIFICATIONS: Diploma Clinical & Medical Hypnosis, Herbal Therapy Cert
DIRECTORSHIPS: Centre for Hypnosis. International Federation of Positive Hypnotists IFPH
MEMBERSHIPS: Federation of Ethical Stage Hypnotists FESH, Afro-Asian Society. Greenpeace.
HONOURS/AWARDS: Black Belt Kung Fu, Excellence Award (for Pain Control and Hypnosis). AIV, US
HOBBIES AND INTERESTS: Swimming, squash, horse-riding, countryside, music, travel
PERSONAL PROFILE: First Asian stage hypnotist to do 'Mind Magic' shows. Originator of 'Awake Trance Therapy' hypnotherapy without sleep and innovative techniques in hypnosis. Specialist in pain control and anaesthesia without drugs. Herbalist and healer. Teacher: positive use of hypnosis. Working to bring benefits of hypnosis and healing to Asians.
NOMINATED BY: Dr Abdul Razaq Zeria, Manchester

MRS LAKHVIR RELLON (Social Work-Management)

Development Manager, Northern Birmingham Mental Health Trust, Trust HQ, 71 Fentham Road, Erdington, Birmingham, B23 6AL

PLACE OF BIRTH: India, 27.9.63
MARITAL STATUS: Married
CHILDREN: Two (Amar, Hakam)
ACADEMIC QUALIFICATIONS: BA Law and Sociology
PROFESSIONAL QUALIFICATIONS: Diploma in Social Work / Diploma in Management
PERSONAL PROFILE: Asian Women's Centre-co-ordinator. Netherton Social Services Development-(community social worker). Halesowen SSD (social worker-children and families). Sandwell SSD (service co-ordinator-mental health). Save the Children Fund (Team manager hosted visit by President of SCF), Wrote book 'Minding your own business'. NSPCC, Team manager of Bal Raksha, family support service for Asian families in Leicester.
NOMINATED BY: Mr Lakhvir S Rellon

MR SHAHAB REZA (Accounting Technician)

Freelance Bookkeeper, Shahab Reza FIAB, PO Box 19, Stanmore, HA7 4YL

PLACE OF BIRTH: Pakistan, 15.9.62
MARITAL STATUS: Married
CHILDREN: Two (Abbas, Zainab)
COLLEGE: Greenhill College University Cambridge
PROFESSIONAL QUALIFICATIONS: FIAB, AAT Technician NVQ 4. BTEC GNVQ
MEMBERSHIPS: Fellow International Association Bookkeepers FIAB, AAT
HOBBIES AND INTERESTS: Jigsaw in 3D, information technology, reading
EMAIL: 786shahabreza@msa.com
PERSONAL PROFILE: I am profoundly deaf since birth. I am a freelance bookkeeper, accounting technician with eight clients in UK and abroad. My special needs is my own sign language interpreter (BSc) for clear communication with a number of hearing peoples/client business meeting. I have 18 years experience in various fields of industries, trade and financial positions.

DJ RITU (DJ-Radio Presenter)

Sasa Music, 309 Aberdeen House, 22-24 Highbury Grove, London, N5 2EA

PERSONAL PROFILE: Made her mark through infamous club 'Bombay Jungle': Co-founder and former head of A & R at Outcaste Records. Currently touring worldwide as an individual mixmaster, and with her highly acclaimed band 'The Asian Education'. Produces and presents weekly Asian show for BBC 3CR-also syndicated in Germany and Turkey. Renowned for her pioneering and professional approach across Asian music through the 1990's.
NOMINATED BY: Bushra Ahmed

MISS SERENA B ROBINS (Actress)

Guildford School of Music & Drama, Nadya Young Asian Drama Group, The Royal National Theatre, Upper Ground, London, SE1

PLACE OF BIRTH: London, 21.8.75
MARITAL STATUS: Single
COLLEGE: Guildhall School of Music and Drama
ACADEMIC QUALIFICATIONS: A-Level Art and English. O-Levels Drama, Art and English
PROFESSIONAL QUALIFICATIONS: Professional Actress BA Honours
MEMBERSHIPS: Fox Fellowship
HONOURS/AWARDS: BA Honours professional actress
HOBBIES AND INTERESTS: Drama, teaching, travel, theatre, carer
PERSONAL PROFILE: My work centres around diminishing social misunderstandings and repression within our community in Asia and Britain. Creating a dialogue with agencies and theatre groups for young Asians at the Royal National Theatre, London.

MR PRADIP KRISHNA 'ROY' ROHATGI
(Chartered Accountant)

International Consultant, Roy Rohatgi Associates, 43 Great Brownings, College Road, London, SE21 7HP

PLACE OF BIRTH: India, 10.11.39
MARITAL STATUS: Married
COLLEGE: University College London
ACADEMIC QUALIFICATIONS: B.Com (Cal), BSc (Econ)
PROFESSIONAL QUALIFICATIONS: FCA (E&W), FCA (India)
DIRECTORSHIPS: Governor International Students House London
MEMBERSHIPS: IOD, Oriental Club, Royal Overseas League, International Fiscal Assoc., International Tax Planning Assoc., Strategic Planning Society
HOBBIES AND INTERESTS: Golf, classical guitar, travel
EMAIL: roy@ltpa.org
PERSONAL PROFILE: Arthur Andersen 1970-1994 (24 years). Retired as managing partner, India and partner in London office; International tax and strategy consultant. Specialist on doing business in India. Recently appointed adjunct professor in international taxation in Regent University of Law, US.

MR MAHMOUD A ROUF (Accountant)

M A Rouf & Co, 1st Floor, 68 Brick Lane, London, E1 6RL

PLACE OF BIRTH: Bangladesh, 30.11.46
MARITAL STATUS: Married
CHILDREN: Two (Sohani, Raziq)
COLLEGE: Dhaka University
ACADEMIC QUALIFICATIONS: B.Com
HOBBIES AND INTERESTS: Part-time columnist, reporter
PERSONAL PROFILE: Mahmoud Rouf is an accountant, running his own practice since 1976 and involved with community works ever since. At present chairman of: Brick Lane Business Association: Banglatown Development Forum: Davenant Community Centre: Ethnic Minority Enterprise Project. Mahmoud is devoted to develop ethnic businesses through fighting institutionalised and organised discrimination.
NOMINATED BY: M Bodrul Mozid

MR MOHAMMED ABDUR ROUF (Restaurateur)

Owner, Diamond Properties (UK),

PLACE OF BIRTH: Bangladesh
COLLEGE: Dhaka, Dundee
ACADEMIC QUALIFICATIONS: Textile Engineer
DIRECTORSHIPS: Balaka Bangladeshi Restaurant, President of the Bangladesh Association for Dundee
MEMBERSHIPS: Member of the British Trade Delegate
HONOURS/AWARDS: Nominated as Best Indian Restaurant in Scotland (1995) by the Good Curry Restaurant Guide
HOBBIES AND INTERESTS: Golf, cricket, fundraising
PERSONAL PROFILE: Abdur Rouf came to Scotland in the early 1970's to further his studies in textile at Dundee, but has diversified his business interests and created several successful business concerns which are now solid and properous interests. He is Regional President of Scotland for the Bangladesh-British Chamber of Commerce.
NOMINATED BY: Lord Provost of Dundee

CLLR NIRMAL ROY (LECTURER)

Councillor, London Borough of Camden, 74 Gordon Mansions, Torrington Place, London, WC1E 7HH

PLACE OF BIRTH: West Bengal, 1.5.35
MARITAL STATUS: Married
CHILDREN: Two (Tumin, Dilip)
COLLEGE: University College, Institute of Education, London
ACADEMIC QUALIFICATIONS: MSc
PROFESSIONAL QUALIFICATIONS: British and international sociological Assoc.
DIRECTORSHIPS: Chair-NEC Local Authorities Action for Southern Africa
MEMBERSHIPS: Oxfam, War on Want, Age Concern, Third World First, Covent Garden Trust, Groundwork-Camden
HOBBIES AND INTERESTS: Cinema, theatre, concert, tennis, cricket
PERSONAL PROFILE: Been a councillor for 19 years. Hold important positions as the chair of planning, equalities and public health committees. Been vice-chair for eduction, leisure and policy resources committees. Worked as a lecturer and as the principal policy adviser in local government. Keen on raising minorities issues and concerns. Mayor of Camden (1990-91).

MRS SUKLA ROY (TEACHER)

Science Teacher, Mulberry School for Girls, Science Department, Richard Street, London, E1 2JP

PLACE OF BIRTH: India, 1.2.52
MARITAL STATUS: Married
CHILDREN: Three (Curie, Somali, Sreedeep)
ACADEMIC QUALIFICATIONS: BSc, MSc
PROFESSIONAL QUALIFICATIONS: BSc, MSc
HOBBIES AND INTERESTS: Gardening, socialising, the arts and craft
PERSONAL PROFILE: I was born and brought up in India. After completing my master degree, I got married and came to England in 1974. We are settled in England and raised our three children over the years. Since 1987, I started my teaching career and I am working hard alongside my commitments towards the family. I act as a positive role model in science and I am determined in raising the achievements of pupils.
NOMINATED BY: Hasina Khatun

CLLR MADHU RUPAREL (COUNCILLOR)

Medway Council, 28 Tintagel Manor, Skinner Street, Gillingham, ME7 1LH

PLACE OF BIRTH: Kenya, 9.12.41
MARITAL STATUS: Married
CHILDREN: Two (Ketan, Sonya)
MEMBERSHIPS: Liberal Democrats
HOBBIES AND INTERESTS: Travel, international cuisine
PERSONAL PROFILE: Madhu spent his life in the hotel industry, starting at the Ambassador Hotel in Kenya and rising to head buyer at London's Savoy. The first EM manager in the prestigious Savoy Group. For a short while he owned a small hotel in Somerset before retiring due to ill health. Moving back to Kent he is now a Liberal Democrat councillor on Medway Council.

MR MAHENDRA HIRJI RUPARELL (PROPERTY MANAGEMENT)

Proprieter, Sunrise Estates, 9 Vane Close, Kenton, Harrow, HA3 9XD

PLACE OF BIRTH: Tanzania, 23.5.43
MARITAL STATUS: Married
MEMBERSHIPS: Lohana community, North London
HONOURS/AWARDS: Melvin Jones Fellow for Dedicated Humanitarian Services
HOBBIES AND INTERESTS: Collecting paper cuttings
PERSONAL PROFILE: Worked for number of years in charitable organisations. Past president of Lions Club of Enfield. Recipient of renowned Melvin Jones Award for dedicated humanitarian services from Lions Club International Foundation.

MR SHANTOO RUPARELL MBE (SOLICITOR)

SH Ruparell Solicitors, Alperton House, Bridgewater Road, Alperton, HA0 1EH

PLACE OF BIRTH: Tanzania, 5.12.32
MARITAL STATUS: Married
CHILDREN: Two (Saloni, Amit)
COLLEGE: The Law Society
ACADEMIC QUALIFICATIONS: Solicitor of Supreme Court
PROFESSIONAL QUALIFICATIONS: Barrister-at-Law, Solicitor
MEMBERSHIPS: Vice chairman-Bhavan
HONOURS/AWARDS: MBE
HOBBIES AND INTERESTS: Fund-raising for charities
PERSONAL PROFILE: Honorary solicitor to many charitable institutions. Vice Director of Central Middlesex Hospital Trustee. Sardar Patel Memorial Society.

BIBI RUSSELL (DESIGNER)

Founder-Bibi Productions,

PLACE OF BIRTH: Chittagong, 19.8.50
MARITAL STATUS: Divorced
CHILDREN: Two (Omar, Bickey)
COLLEGE: London College of Fashion
ACADEMIC QUALIFICATIONS: Degree in Design and Textiles
PROFESSIONAL QUALIFICATIONS: Designer and Handloom Textile Expert
HOBBIES AND INTERESTS: Art, music, reading
PERSONAL PROFILE: In many ways Bibi is a unique person in Bangladesh. Her height alone (5'10") sets her apart. She studied at the London College of Fashion, where she obtained a degree in design and textiles in 1975. Today she is considered an expert in creative arts and crafts in Bangladesh despite spending so much time in Europe. She began 'Street Children' project to provide children the opportunity to sell newspapers, flowers and candy instead of begging to survive.
NOMINATED BY: Clare Hardman Wilson, The London Institute

'In many ways Bibi is a unique person in Bangladesh. Her height alone (5'10") sets her apart. She studied at the London College of Fashion, where she obtained a degree in design and textiles in 1975. Today she is considered an expert in creative arts and crafts in Bangladesh despite spending so much time in Europe. She began 'Street Children' project to provide children the opportunity to sell newspapers, flowers and candy instead of begging to survive'

BIBI RUSSELL

The Black Who's Who

Order your copy now. Call: 0171 702 8012

MISS IMTIAZ SADIQ (Ethnic Minority Dev. Officer)

GAVO Newport Resource Centre, 35 Commercial Road, Newport, NP20 2PB

PLACE OF BIRTH: Pakistan, 6.5.67
MARITAL STATUS: Single
COLLEGE: University of Wales, Caeleron
ACADEMIC QUALIFICATIONS: BA Cultural Studies
MEMBERSHIPS: BAWSO Black Association of Women Step Up, SEWREC South East Wales Racial Equality Council.
HONOURS/AWARDS: Young Adult Achiever-Recognised by Buckingham Palace-for achievement in race equality field
HOBBIES AND INTERESTS: Photography, filmmaking
PERSONAL PROFILE: Primarily, my interests and achievements lie within the role of community activist. This role incorporates work with minority ethnic women's groups. I see my main strength as being a dynamic motivating force behind these women's aspirations, whether it be individual or group focused.

MR SHAHED SADULLAH (Journalist)

Editor-The News-London, Jang Publications, 1 Sanctuary Street, London, SE1 1ED

PLACE OF BIRTH: India, 1.10.44
MARITAL STATUS: Married
CHILDREN: Two (Shaiza, Asif)
COLLEGE: Dhaka University
ACADEMIC QUALIFICATIONS: Honours in English, First Class First
PROFESSIONAL QUALIFICATIONS: Graduated from Civil Service Academy, Lahore, main subjects Law, Economics & Public Admin
MEMBERSHIPS: MCC, Mensa, The High IQ Society
HOBBIES AND INTERESTS: Cricket, reading, South Asian politics
PERSONAL PROFILE: Qualified for the civil service of Pakistan in 1967 by standing first in the countrywide central superior services exam open to everyone. After serving on various posts in the government of Pakistan, was posted to the Pakistan High Commission in London. Subsequently left the service and took up journalism becoming editor of Imran Khan's magazine Cricket Life. After a brief stint in South magazine, came to Jang.

MR MOHAMMED SAEED (Human Resources Manager)

Human Resources-UK, Reuters Group Plc, Human Resources Management, 85 Fleet Street, London, EC4P 4AJ

PLACE OF BIRTH: India, 20.4.69
MARITAL STATUS: Married
CHILDREN: Two (Mohammed Avas, Aisha Anwar)
COLLEGE: London
ACADEMIC QUALIFICATIONS: BA, MA Human Resources Management
PROFESSIONAL QUALIFICATIONS: Graduate
HOBBIES AND INTERESTS: All sports, cricket
PERSONAL PROFILE: As a professional human resources manager, I specialise HR strategy, employment law, mergers and acquisitions. I spend most of my free time with my family and follow the fortunes of Manchester United FC and Pakistan cricket team. An ardent student of the Naqshbandi Tariqat of Islam.
NOMINATED BY: P Anwar

MR SYED SAFIRUDDIN JP (Chartered Engineer)

17 Menlove Avenue, Allerton, Liverpool, L18 2EH

PLACE OF BIRTH: India, 4.1.28
MARITAL STATUS: Married
CHILDREN: Four
COLLEGE: Patna, Lahore, UK
MEMBERSHIPS: Chairman of Afro-Asian Caribbean Standing Committee, President of the Pakistan Association Liverpool, Chairman of MASCO. Broadcasting Trust.
HOBBIES AND INTERESTS: Gardening, travelling, photography
PERSONAL PROFILE: Arrived in the UK in 1962 from Pakistan. Offices held: president of the Pakistan Association, former chairman of Merseyside CRC, former RRB member, Post Conference Constituent Committee. 'Black People in Britain The Way Forward'. Hon. sec Institution of Electrical Engineers Merseyside. Founder of Pakistan Centre.
NOMINATED BY: Mr J L Singh, MASCO

MR DEV SAGOO (Actor-Director-Presenter)

Chairman Arts Media Luton, 20 Torquay Drive, Leagrave, Luton, LU4 9LN

PLACE OF BIRTH: Uganda, 24.2.52
MARITAL STATUS: Married
CHILDREN: Three (Amar, Roshni, Shaan)
COLLEGE: London Academy of Music and Dramatic Arts
ACADEMIC QUALIFICATIONS: Dramatic Arts Graduate
PROFESSIONAL QUALIFICATIONS: Drama Tutor/ Director
MEMBERSHIPS: British Actors Equity Association
HONOURS/AWARDS: Best Supporting Actor TV 'Family Pride', Asian Film Academy
HOBBIES AND INTERESTS: Poetry, singing, compere, live show host
PERSONAL PROFILE: In 1997 completed 25 professional years in showbiz. Mentioning some work; RSC, Royal National Theatre etc. 'Jewel in the Crown'. 'Playschool' presenter. 'Prime Suspect'. 'Albion Market'. 'Family-Pride'. 'Grange Hill'. Main host TV Asia /Zee four years: Breakfast Show. Anchored programmes; 'Euro-Zindagi'. Hosted documentary 'Uganda Revisited'. Telethon Earthquake Appeal. Chairman Artezium Arts / Media-Luton. Plus many films.

MR GURNAM SINGH SAHNI (Director)

Touchstone Imports Limited, 6 Heron Trading Estate, Alliance Road, London, W3 0RA

PLACE OF BIRTH: Pakistan, 8.8.27
MARITAL STATUS: Married
CHILDREN: Three (Veena, Arvinder, Raffial)
COLLEGE: Khalsa College
ACADEMIC QUALIFICATIONS: BA
DIRECTORSHIPS: Touchstone Imports Limited
MEMBERSHIPS: Patron International Punjabi Society Europe 1997 -. President Central Gurdwara London 1994-.
HONOURS/AWARDS: Hind Rattan Award 1994
PERSONAL PROFILE: Patron International Punjabi Society Europe 1997-. Recipient of Hind Rattan Award 1994. Joint Secretary International Punjabi Society UK 1994-96. President Central Gurdwara London 1994. Founder President Khukhrain Community UK 1993-98.

MR TRILOCHAN SINGH SAHNI (Proprietor)

Shannalles, 16 Chelmsford Square, London, NW10 3AR

PLACE OF BIRTH: Pakistan, 10.11.35
MARITAL STATUS: Married
CHILDREN: Two (Amritpal Singh, Simmi)
COLLEGE: Agra University
ACADEMIC QUALIFICATIONS: MA (Economics)
DIRECTORSHIPS: Owner, Shannalles (import/export/wholesale clothing)
MEMBERSHIPS: Life Member Punjabi Society and International Punjabi Society.
HONOURS/AWARDS: President of India Award for gallantry and meritorious service, governor's commendation. Best Senior Under Officer, 7th UP Battalion, National Cadet Corp.
HOBBIES AND INTERESTS: Reading, writing
PERSONAL PROFILE: Life member and treasurer Punjabi Society of British Isles. General secretary Central Gurdwara (London), general secretary Biradari (UK). Ex vice president Puthohar Biradari (UK). Ex finance secretary Sikh Forum UK.
NOMINATED BY: K K Singh

MR GURDIAL SINGH SAHOTA (Community Activist)

84 Walbrook Road, Derby, DE23 8RY

PLACE OF BIRTH: India, 25.3.33
MARITAL STATUS: Married
CHILDREN: One (Herminder Kaur)
HOBBIES AND INTERESTS: Cricket, gardening, writing, helping others
PERSONAL PROFILE: Head chairman of Indian Welfare Organisation in Derby. This involves voluntarily helping others with social service / security issues, updating passports, visa's, puts great effort into helping people who have any disabilities. Very well known in his local community and is respected dearly by his daughter, son-in-law and three grandchildren.
NOMINATED BY: Mrs H Kaur

MR AJAB SAMRAH SINGH (Art Director)

Creative Head, Saatchi & Saatchi Advertising, 8 Killyon Road, London, SW8 2XT

PLACE OF BIRTH: Birmingham, 22.9.64
MARITAL STATUS: Married
COLLEGE: Stourbridge College of Art
ACADEMIC QUALIFICATIONS: Degree in Advertising and Design
DIRECTORSHIPS: Saatchi & Saatchi, Museum of London
HONOURS/AWARDS: Campaign Poster Awards (Silver), European Poster Awards (Gold), Campaign Press Awards (Gold and Silvers), Creative Circle Gold Award. National newspaper Awards (Gold, 4 Silvers) Canne Awards (2 Golds), British Diversity Awards
HOBBIES AND INTERESTS: Photography, art
PERSONAL PROFILE: A first generation Sikh who was born and raised in the Black Country. My parents taught me the value of hardwork and a good education. They inspire me everyday of my life, quite simply I am driven by the huge debt I owe them. Received Designers and Art Directors. 26 Commendations award.

DR AJEET SINGH (Doctor)

Consultant Anaesthetist, NHS, Larbreck, Cawston, Rugby, CV22 7RY

PLACE OF BIRTH: Pakistan, 6.6.35
MARITAL STATUS: Married
CHILDREN: Three (Varjeet, Aarti, Vineeta)
COLLEGE: KG. Med. College, Lucknow, India
PROFESSIONAL QUALIFICATIONS: MBBS, DA, FFARCS
MEMBERSHIPS: Professional Societies, Rotary Club of Coventry Jubliee
HOBBIES AND INTERESTS: Golf, broadcasting, music
EMAIL: a.singh@pipemedia.co.uk
PERSONAL PROFILE: Came to UK in 1968. Appointed consultant anaesthetist 1972. For six-years promoted Asian programmes on local radio station.

MISS AMRIT KUMARI DHIGPAL KAUR SINGH
(Artist-Illustrating-Curator)

Twin Studio, 27 Eleanor Road, Bidston, Wirral, L43 7QN

PLACE OF BIRTH: London, 18.2.66
MARITAL STATUS: Single
COLLEGE: Liverpool University College, Chester University
ACADEMIC QUALIFICATIONS: BA Hons Combined Studies: Comparative Religion, Ecclesiastical History, 20th Century Art History
PROFESSIONAL QUALIFICATIONS: Member of the Manchester Academy of Fine Arts
MEMBERSHIPS: Manchester Academy of Fine Arts
HONOURS/AWARDS: Award for most outstanding Two-Dimensional Award, North West Arts Board 'Travel Bursary Award'
HOBBIES AND INTERESTS: Play flute, karate, music
PERSONAL PROFILE: 'Considered as the freshest of the New British Artists' (Daily Telegraph) Amrit has exhibited widely in the UK and abroad as one half of the 'Twin' artist partnership known as 'Twin Studio' whose award winning paintings of multicultural Britain have continued to receive high public profile and International media acclaim.

CLLR BALBIR SINGH JP (Chairman)

President, Bradford Racial Eqaulity Council, 19 Spring Hill, Wrose, Shipley, BD18 1ND

PLACE OF BIRTH: India, 28.6.37
MARITAL STATUS: Married
CHILDREN: Two (Kulvinder, Jatinder)
COLLEGE: Punjab University, India
ACADEMIC QUALIFICATIONS: BA, B Ed
PROFESSIONAL QUALIFICATIONS: Business Management
DIRECTORSHIPS: Shipley College
HONOURS/AWARDS: Gold Award for Community Services by BT
HOBBIES AND INTERESTS: Sports, politics, TV documentaries, walking
PERSONAL PROFILE: Elected councillor 1986-94. Justice of the Peace. Chairman BFO Racial Equality Council. President of Trustee of Family Service Unit. Governor of local college. President of Bradford Sikh Parents Association.

BHUJANGEY BALBIR SINGH (Bhangra Musician)

PERSONAL PROFILE: Bhujangey bhangra group are the pioneers of bhangra music in the UK. Although artists like Kuldip Manak, Surinder Shinda and Surinder Kaur were household names for many first generation Asians, it wasn't until Birmingham's Bhujangey group got their act together that the real foundations of bhangra music in Britain were laid. Hit songs include 'Peeni Ae Vilayti' and 'Akh Lar Gayi'.

MR BALDEV SINGH (Managing Director)

Hardwar Cut Price Stores, 362 Paisley Road West, Glasgow, G5 1BG

PLACE OF BIRTH: India, 5.4.32
MARITAL STATUS: Married
CHILDREN: Six (H Singh, S Singh, P Singh, K Singh, R Kaur, H Kaur)
PERSONAL PROFILE: After various labouring posts we decided on a retail shop. All our family are involved in our shops. We now have a healthy empire in South Side of Glasgow. The family are also involved in helping in the Sikh temples and other charity work.
NOMINATED BY: Muhammad Sabir Kiani

MS DALJIT KAUR SINGH (Artistic Director)

Co-ordinator, Jeet Community Arts, 2 Ismay Court, Elliman Avenue, Slough, SL2 5BX

PLACE OF BIRTH: Malawi, 1.11.62
CHILDREN: One
HOBBIES AND INTERESTS: Dance, music, cooking, reading
PERSONAL PROFILE: Compassionate, experienced dance / exercise instructor, performer, artistic director and single parent working towards providing Asian dance for relaxation, exercise and therapy. Creating access to the arts for Asian and cross-cultural women focusing on elderly women/men with disabilities, and women with mental health problems who need access to people and communities.
NOMINATED BY: Jeet Daljit K Singh

MR EUROPE SINGH (Educational Broadcaster)

Commissioning Executive, BBC Television, BBC White City, 201 Wood Lane, London, W12 7TS

PLACE OF BIRTH: Manchester, 17.11.48
MARITAL STATUS: Single
CHILDREN: Two (Martha, Seth)
COLLEGE: Dundee University, London University, Exeter University
ACADEMIC QUALIFICATIONS: BSc, PGCE, M Ed
PROFESSIONAL QUALIFICATIONS: PGCE. Advanced Training Certificate
DIRECTORSHIPS: Public Broadcasting for a Multicultural Europe (PBME)
MEMBERSHIPS: Oxfam Association, Governor Pimlico School
HOBBIES AND INTERESTS: Race relations, history, bridge, tennis, cooking, travel
PERSONAL PROFILE: Born in Manchester of Sikh parents, he was educated at Dundee, Exeter and London Universities. He has taught for fourteen years and has been an advisory teacher at ILEA. For the last nine years he has worked at the BBC. Currently seconded part-time to develop the University for Industry.
NOMINATED BY: Robert Albury, BBC

Bhujangey bhangra group are the pioneers of bhangra music in the UK. Although artists like Kuldip Manak, Surinder Shinda and Surinder Kaur were household names for many first generation

BHUJANGEY BALBIR SINGH

MR GULAB SINGH MBE (Manager NHS)

Health Promotion Manager, North West Lancashire Health Promotion Unit, 12 Holmfield Road, Fulwood, Preston, PR2 8EP

PLACE OF BIRTH: Liverpool, 24.2.55
MARITAL STATUS: Married
CHILDREN: Three (Balvinder Kaur, Gurcharan Singh, Deepak Singh)
COLLEGE: University of Central Lancashire
ACADEMIC QUALIFICATIONS: NHS Management
DIRECTORSHIPS: Chair of Preston Racial Equality Council
MEMBERSHIPS: SHEPS (Society of Health Education and Promotion Specialists) and UNISON
HONOURS/AWARDS: MBE and Bronze Award
HOBBIES AND INTERESTS: Keep fit, football, walking, Indian music
EMAIL: gulab@cablenet.co.uk
PERSONAL PROFILE: Over 25 years service in the NHS, dealt with sensitive issues appertaining to Black and Asian communities at a local and national level (drugs, sexual health - HIV/AIDS). In my voluntary capacity I have served on various committees such as local authority, schools, Gurdwaras, REC's and other voluntary organisations.

MR GURPARSHAD 'RICKY' SINGH (Cabbie)

Owner, 47 Second Avenue, Manor Park, London, E12 6EJ

PLACE OF BIRTH: London, 2.12.73
MARITAL STATUS: Single
HONOURS/AWARDS: Boxing Trophies
HOBBIES AND INTERESTS: Boxing, swimming, fitness
PERSONAL PROFILE: Lived in Preston since 1979, now resident in London. Was vice-president of Sikh Gurdwara. Now strict in boxing training for 'Don't try this at home' (TV)'. Missed being on 'Gladiators' by one point. Aims to be a TV star soon. Ricky took just 40 seconds to wrap up his first ever amateur bout for Preston Fulwood Boxing Club in a senior lightweight contest.
NOMINATED BY: Rajendra Singh

MR HARMANDER SINGH (Local Government Officer)

Corporate Strategy Officer, London Borough of Tower Hamlets, Town Hall, Corporate Strategy Team, 1st Floor, Mulberry Place, 5 Clove Cresent, London, E14 2BG

PLACE OF BIRTH: India, 27.7.59
MARITAL STATUS: Married
CHILDREN: Four (Sandeep Kaur, Jasvir Singh, Baldeep Kaur, Tarlochan Singh)
COLLEGE: North East London Polytechnic
ACADEMIC QUALIFICATIONS: Production Engineering
PROFESSIONAL QUALIFICATIONS: D32 & D33 (NVQ Assessor - currently undertaking)
MEMBERSHIPS: Institute of Public Service Management
HOBBIES AND INTERESTS: Current affairs, DIY, sports
PERSONAL PROFILE: 16 years public service, concentrating on social policy. Voluntary sector development consultant. School governor and OFSTED Inspector, Magistrate since 1993, youth worker and management team member, Lay assessor of registered homes. Fundraiser for charities mainly by running marathons. Established national charities and served on VCC/ITC and assessed UK bids for NLCB.
NOMINATED BY: B K Saund

PROF HARMINDAR SINGH (Professor Rtd)

Sikh Divine Fellowship,

PLACE OF BIRTH: Pakistan, 1.8.16
MARITAL STATUS: Married
CHILDREN: Two (Hardip Singh, Baldip Kaur)
COLLEGE: MA (English)
ACADEMIC QUALIFICATIONS: MA (English), BA (French), J D Diploma in Journalism
DIRECTORSHIPS: Vice-president of World Congress of Faiths. Co-chair UK International Inter-faith organisation World Conference of Religion on Peace.
MEMBERSHIPS: Religious Panel of Amnesty International
HONOURS/AWARDS: Shiromani Award given by Vice president of India . Nominated for International Inter-Faith, Oxford
PERSONAL PROFILE: For the last about 25 years Professor Harmindar Singh has been very active in the fields of race relations, Inter-Faith Movement, religious education and Sikh Studies (Theology etc.) in the UK with a view to maintaining harmony and goodwill between various religions and ethnic communities. In recognition of his work he was one of the first Indians nominated by the government as a member of the Home Secretary's Advisory Council on Race Relations at its inception in 1976. He served it for about six years.

MR JAGTAR SINGH (Fire Officer)

Senior Divisional Officer, West Midlands Fire Service, Lancaster Circus, Queensway, Birmingham, B

PLACE OF BIRTH: India, 4.2.54
MARITAL STATUS: Married
CHILDREN: Two (Rumandip Kaur, Dewear Singh)
COLLEGE: Birmingham Polytechnic
ACADEMIC QUALIFICATIONS: BA Hons
PROFESSIONAL QUALIFICATIONS: Member of Institute of Fire Engineers
HOBBIES AND INTERESTS: Cricket, football, charity Rumania with Aid
PERSONAL PROFILE: I have worked for the Fire Service now for over 21 years and have achieved one of the highest ranks in the service. I believe I am the most senior Asian officer in the British Fire Service. I am very proud of that and am hoping for more Black firefighters to join the service and more to achieve senior positions of influence.
NOMINATED BY: John Wildman, West Midlands Fire Service

MR JASWANT SINGH MBE (Social Worker)

Senior Practitioner, 3 Mansfield Street, Riverside, Cardiff, CF1 8EE

PLACE OF BIRTH: Pakistan, 9.8.38
MARITAL STATUS: Married
CHILDREN: Six (Harjeet Kaur, Dharampal Kaur, Guru Shabad Singh, Harsaroop Kaur, Panna Singh, Jaspreet Singh)
PROFESSIONAL QUALIFICATIONS: City & Guild in Radio and TV, CQSW
HONOURS/AWARDS: MBE
HOBBIES AND INTERESTS: Cricket, rugby

MRS JUGDISH SINGH (Volunteer-Housewife)

Conflict/Change, 42 Ramsay Road, Forest Gate, London, E7 9EW

PLACE OF BIRTH: Cleveland, 27.1.53
MARITAL STATUS: Married
CHILDREN: Four (Ozzi - Gobind)
COLLEGE: New Vick - East ham
ACADEMIC QUALIFICATIONS: NVQ in Meditation
HONOURS/AWARDS: My first poem was published, it was about Princess Diana
HOBBIES AND INTERESTS: Writing, poetry, community work, reading
PERSONAL PROFILE: Volunteer - mediator - working in Newham and Waltham Forest. Also with Asian women. As a befriender - I like supporting the community. I wrote a poem which was inspired, after reading the effects of young Asian women in UK who commit self harm. My first poem was dedicated to Princess Diana.
NOMINATED BY: Ozzi

MR KRISHAN KUMAR SINGH (Author - Journalist)

Editor, Park Publications, 1 Park Close, Dollis Hill Avenue, London, NW2 6RQ

PLACE OF BIRTH: India, 2.12.15
MARITAL STATUS: Married
CHILDREN: Three (Vijay, Nalini, Arun)
COLLEGE: Panjab University
ACADEMIC QUALIFICATIONS: Bachelor of Arts
PROFESSIONAL QUALIFICATIONS: CAIIB (Bombay), CAA (London)
DIRECTORSHIPS: Park Publications
HONOURS/AWARDS: Hind Rattan Award from Indian Finance Minister. From Croydon College, Gold Medal from Punjabee Society of British Isles. Indian Professional Assoc.
PERSONAL PROFILE: Patron Punjabee Society of the British Isles. Patron of Hindu Centre, London. Chairman - Forum for Indian TV Viewers. General secretary, Punjab Unity Forum. Senior vice president India Association (UK). Chairman, Board of Trustees, Hindu College, London.

'I have worked for the Fire Service now for over 21 years and have achieved one of the highest ranks in the service. I believe I am the most senior Asian officer in the British Fire Service'

MR JAGTAR SINGH

DR KUMAR SINGH (Doctor)

Prison Medical Officer,

PLACE OF BIRTH: India, 12.9.44
MARITAL STATUS: Married
CHILDREN: Three (Bhavna, Chetna, Vickram Kumar)
COLLEGE: Prince of Wales Medical
ACADEMIC QUALIFICATIONS: MBBS
PROFESSIONAL QUALIFICATIONS: Did full vocational training in general practice 1977-79 Captain in British Army 1985 - 87
MEMBERSHIPS: BMA, ODA, WASA & MCC Member for two terms
HOBBIES AND INTERESTS: Badminton
PERSONAL PROFILE: Came to the UK in 1977 to train in radiology but in the absence of limited opening did a full vocational training after hospital jobs in orthopaedics. Short term locums.

MR MANJIT SINGH (Director)

Security Officer, M J Security Services (UK) Limited, 217 East Park Road, Leicester, LE5 5AZ

PLACE OF BIRTH: India, 10.3.50
MARITAL STATUS: Married
CHILDREN: Four (Satminder, Jatinder, Gulninder Kaur, Daljinder Kaur)
COLLEGE: Guru Nanak University, Amritsar
ACADEMIC QUALIFICATIONS: MA, B.Ed
PROFESSIONAL QUALIFICATIONS: Bodyguard for VIP's
DIRECTORSHIPS: Director for MJ Security Services (UK) Limited

MEMBERSHIPS: LABA
HONOURS/AWARDS: 20 World records in the Guinness Book of Records
HOBBIES AND INTERESTS: Weight-training
PERSONAL PROFILE: Manjit Singh is the first Asian to get his name in the Guinness Book of Records in the field of sports. Currently holds 20 world records in the Guinness Book of Records.
NOMINATED BY: Premjit Sidhu

HIS HONOUR JUDGE MOTA SINGH QC LLD (Judge)

Southwark Crown Court, 1 English Grounds, London, SE1 2EH

PLACE OF BIRTH: Kenya, 26.7.30
CHILDREN: Three (Satvinder, Jaswinder, Paramjeet)
COLLEGE: Lincoln's Inn
PROFESSIONAL QUALIFICATIONS: Examiner of the Supreme Court. QC 1978. Recorder 1979. Circuit Judge 1982
MEMBERSHIPS: MCC. Race Relations Board. London Rent Assessment Committee.
HONOURS/AWARDS: LL D GN University Australia
HOBBIES AND INTERESTS: Reading, Patron, Sutton Lawn Tennis Assoc, Anne Frank Education Trust; St George's Hospital, Tooting and Swaminarayan Hindu Temple, Neasden
PERSONAL PROFILE: When Ugandan Asians were expelled by Idi Amin in early 1970's I was nominated as sole representative on their behalf to approach the United Nations in connection with their claim for compensation for the loss of their properties. In September 1998 I was appointed by the Sikh religious authorities in Amritsar, India, Chairman of the European Section of the World Sikh Council, a body set up in Amritsar following a gathering of Sikhs from all over the world.

MISS RABINDRA KUMARI DHIGPAL KAUR SINGH (Artist-Illustrator-Curator)

Twin Studio, 27 Eleanor Road, Bidston, Wirral, L43 7QN

PLACE OF BIRTH: London, 18.2.66
MARITAL STATUS: Single
COLLEGE: Liverpool University College Chester
ACADEMIC QUALIFICATIONS: BA Hons Combined Studies: Comparative Religion, Ecclesiastical History, 20th Century Art History
PROFESSIONAL QUALIFICATIONS: 2nd Dan (Level) Black Belt in Go Ju Ryu Karate
MEMBERSHIPS: Manchester Academy of Fine Arts
HONOURS/AWARDS: Punjab Academy of GB (1991), Nominee for Best New Talent (1997), Individual Artists' Development Award (1994). Major awards won each year since 1985
HOBBIES AND INTERESTS: Piano, karate, music
PERSONAL PROFILE: Rabindra represents the other half of the artist 'Duo' 'Twin Studio', whose modern Indian miniatures have challenged the Eurocentric tendency of contemporary art practice and academia. They are the subject of a fine art publication, two arts documentaries, and are held in both private and public collections worldwide.

MR RAJENDRA 'REG' SINGH (Catering Representative)

150 Deepdale Road, Preston, PR1 6PY

DATE OF BIRTH: 2.9.42
MARITAL STATUS: Married
COLLEGE: Shoreditch Comprehensive School
ACADEMIC QUALIFICATIONS: 5 GCE O-Levels, 2 GCE A-Levels
MEMBERSHIPS: Neighbourhood Watch, Victims Support, Preston Conservative Club, Preston Police and Community Forum
HOBBIES AND INTERESTS: Boxing, wrestling, martial arts, swimming, athletics, weight lifting, travel
PERSONAL PROFILE: I can speak Punjabi, Hindustani, Urdu and English. I was a liaison officer and also an Interpreter for the ethnic community acting for the police for Inner London sections at the Criminal Crown Court. I was treasurer and general secretary at Sikh Temple. I am now the president of the Sikh Temple. I was on the Parent Teacher Association at Northlands High School and am now parent governor both at Deepdale Junior School and Moor Park High School and also a club committee member of the Royal Anti Diluvan Order of Buffaloes.
NOMINATED BY: S Labh Singh

MR RANJIT SINGH (Teacher Rtd)

111 Standard Road, Hounslow, TW4 7AY

PLACE OF BIRTH: India, 6.4.30
MARITAL STATUS: Married
CHILDREN: Two (Jatinder Kaur, Yadivindra Singh)
PROFESSIONAL QUALIFICATIONS: Retired teacher/co-ordinator of community languages for London Borough of Ealing
MEMBERSHIPS: Executive member of the CRC (previously vice chairman)
PERSONAL PROFILE: Positions held - Ex-general secretary of Gurdwara Sri Guru Singh Sabha Southall. Has served on the governing bodies of various schools. Previously chairman of Hounslow Heath junior and infants schools. Vice chairman of Ethnic Minorities Liaison Sub-Group. Appointed a lay visitor by the local Labour Party, serving in various committees. Founder executive of Gurdwara Sri Guru Singh Sabha Hounslow and its president 1979-1998. Ex -president Immigrant Teachers Association UK.

PROF RITI SINGH (Academic)

Deputy Head, School of Mechanical Engineering, Cranfield University, Cranfield, Bedford, MK43 0AL

PLACE OF BIRTH: India, 4.3.41
MARITAL STATUS: Married
CHILDREN: Three (Sunil, Vijay, Arjun)
COLLEGE: St Stephen's College, University of Delhi, Imperial College London
ACADEMIC QUALIFICATIONS: BSc (First Class Honours), DIC
PROFESSIONAL QUALIFICATIONS: CEng, FIMechE, FRAeS, FIDGTE
DIRECTORSHIPS: Gas Turbine Technology Centre. University Technology Centre in Gas Turbine Combustion & Performance Engineering, University Technology. Chair Propulsion Committee.
MEMBERSHIPS: Propulsion Committee, Inst. of Mechanical Engineers Academic Editor, Aircraft Engineering and Aerospace Technology Journal
HOBBIES AND INTERESTS: Reading, bridge, chess, walking, technology, strategy, futures, technology globalisation
EMAIL: r.singh@cranfield.ac.uk
PERSONAL PROFILE: Professor Singh, deputy head, School of Mechanical Engineering has 35 years experience in gas turbines, with senior appointments in Rolls-Royce, ABB, Sweden, and was chief engineer at Kongsberg Gas Turbines, Norway. He has consulted for forty organisations in over twenty countries. He has made keynote speeches at major international conferences.
NOMINATED BY: Prof F R Hartley, Vice Chancellor, Cranfield University

> Manjit Singh is the first Asian to get his name in the Guinness Book of Records in the field of sports.
> Currently he holds 20 world records

DR SHYAM PRATAP SINGH (Consultant Cardiologist)

Senior Lecturer, University of Birmingham, 101 Westfield Road, Edgbaston, Birmingham, B15 3JE

PLACE OF BIRTH: India, 4.4.32
MARITAL STATUS: Divorced
CHILDREN: Three (Kishan, Paul, Sheila)
COLLEGE: Lucknow University
ACADEMIC QUALIFICATIONS: MBBS, FRCP (UK1971)
PROFESSIONAL QUALIFICATIONS: PLAB & MB Examiner MRCP (UK)
DIRECTORSHIPS: Ex director of Cardiothoric Unit Birmingham Children's Hospital
MEMBERSHIPS: Fellow University Birmingham. MCC. Senior Fellow Harvard University US (1963)
HONOURS/AWARDS: Chancellors Award given by Kenneth Clarke (Chancellor1993) for excellence
HOBBIES AND INTERESTS: Cricket
PERSONAL PROFILE: First Indian to be appointed consultant cardiologist in UK (1967). Visiting scientist Mayo Clinic (US) 1967. Visiting cardiologist Stockholm (1968). Extra ordinary member British Cardiac Society, Association of European Cardiologist. I represent UK on the subgroup of European Society which advises EU countries grown up congenital heart disease (GUHD). Author of 100 publications in International journals: BMA Journal, US Inst of Cardiology; Lancet. Co-author three books on cardiovascular medicine.

MR TERRY SINGH (Freelance Soccer Coach)

Soccer Guru, Soccer Promotions & Coaching Organisations, , 45 Galleywood Drive, Leicester, LE4 0NH

PLACE OF BIRTH: Leicester, 18.2.69
MARITAL STATUS: Married
CHILDREN: One (Charanpreet Kaur)
COLLEGE: Loughborough University
ACADEMIC QUALIFICATIONS: Sports Studies Degree
PROFESSIONAL QUALIFICATIONS: FA Qualified Coach
DIRECTORSHIPS: Soccer Coaching Organisation
MEMBERSHIPS: FA Coaches Associations
HONOURS/AWARDS: FA Recognition, Contribution to football in the community, Top 100 People in British Football
HOBBIES AND INTERESTS: Relaxing, music, any sporting activities
EMAIL: M - 07970 317 203
PERSONAL PROFILE: Soccer Guru Terry Singh. Former Leicester City trialist. Former Leicester City football community coach (five years). Only Asian soccer coach to be involved with a professional club. Only Asian in the top 100 people in British football. Coached the Official Indian World Cup Team. Involved with the first ever Mega Mela at NEC Birmingham. Organised Soccer Skills Roadshow across Britain to find the top three skilful players.
NOMINATED BY: Vinod Kotecha, Leicester

MR TJINDER SINGH (Artist)

Singer, Wiija Records,

HONOURS/AWARDS: Mercury Music Prize Nomination, MTV Award Nomination, Q Award Nomination and Ivor Novello Award Nomination
PERSONAL PROFILE: 'Brimful of Asha' single - released in February crashed into the chart at No 1 knocking Celine Dion off the top - has sold 575,000 copies to date, making it one of the Top 20 best selling singles of the year. 'When I was Born For The Seventh Time' has gone Gold & has now sold over 100,000 copies in the UK.

Brimful of Asha' single - released in February crashed into the chart at No 1 knocking Celine Dion off the top - has sold 575,000 copies to date

TJINDER SINGH

MRS YVONNE SINGH (Senior Lecturer Rtd)

University of Greenwich, 3 Hollies Close, Gibsons Hill, London, SW16 3EF

PLACE OF BIRTH: India, 19.6.39
MARITAL STATUS: Married
CHILDREN: Two (Shehnaz, Sudhir)
COLLEGE: London University
ACADEMIC QUALIFICATIONS: BA Agra Univ 1962, MA Psychology London Uni 1983
PROFESSIONAL QUALIFICATIONS: Dip Child Development 1975, Diploma in Teacher Education
DIRECTORSHIPS: Chair Child Dev. Society (London University 74-75)
MEMBERSHIPS: 1989 - Chair South London Indian Council, Croydon REC 1987-89. Chair Educ Sub Cttee 1988. Member & Advisor to various committees, Member of Health Authority Croydon
HOBBIES AND INTERESTS: Reading, outdoor sports, computers, foreign travel
EMAIL: sudhir@platinum.demon.co.uk
PERSONAL PROFILE: Arrived in England August 1964. Worked with six Indian families in Southall teaching children to speak English and integrate into school system. Taught in school for partially sighted children for ten years. Proceeded to Avery Hill College Eltham as lecturer in special education (now University of Greenwich). Course co-ordinator for B.Ed Hons 'Children with Severe Learning Difficulties'. Published summary of thesis in 'Journal of Mental Deficiency'.

MRS GOMTI DEVI SINGHANIA (Director)

Simportex Ltd, 2nd Floor, Mitre House, 177-183 Regent Street, London, W1R 7FB

PLACE OF BIRTH: India, 24.3.44
MARITAL STATUS: Married
CHILDREN: Two (Ashok Kumar, Anita Kumari)
DIRECTORSHIPS: Simportex Ltd

MR VISHWA NATH SINGHANIA (Managing Director)

Simportex Ltd, 2nd Floor, Mitre House, 177-183 Regent Street, London, W1R 7FB

PLACE OF BIRTH: India, 15.3.37
MARITAL STATUS: Married
CHILDREN: Two (Ashok Kumar, Anita Kumari)
COLLEGE: St Andrews College, Gorakhpur University
ACADEMIC QUALIFICATIONS: B.Com, MA (Econ)
DIRECTORSHIPS: Simportex Ltd
EMAIL: vnsinghania@simportex.com
PERSONAL PROFILE: Having completed academics in India, came to London in 1961. After further training, joined a textile company for few years then started his own company in 1964 trading in textiles, soft commodities and then removed to metal trading. Also worked as voluntary trustee of the Verkateshwara Temple Trust in the UK - Birmingham.

DR ASWINEE KUMAR SINHA (Doctor Rtd.)

National Health Service, 33 Kilworth Avenue, Southend-On-Sea, SS1 2DS

PLACE OF BIRTH: India, 21.2.33
MARITAL STATUS: Married
CHILDREN: Two (Rachana, Manas)
COLLEGE: Calcutta University
ACADEMIC QUALIFICATIONS: BSc (Calcutta), MBBS (Calcutta), MRCP
PROFESSIONAL QUALIFICATIONS: MBBS. DCH (Lon) DTM&H (Liverpool)
MEMBERSHIPS: BMA, British Association for Sports Medicine, British Association for Immediate Care, Fellow of the Royal Society of Tropical Medicine. Country Gentleman's Association. Rotary Club.
HOBBIES AND INTERESTS: Driving, gardening, travelling, photography
PERSONAL PROFILE: Came to UK 1959; Worked in hospitals in England, Scotland and Wales for 11 years; Expatriate medical officer from UK to Sierra Leone (West Africa) for six years. GP in Southend-on-Sea for 23 years. Hon. Medical Officer for Southend Football Club since 1976. Hon. Medical Officer for Commonwealth Games in Edinburgh. Now doing locum work for general practitioners who are ill or on holidays.

SIVASAKTI SIVANESAN (Music Lecturer)

Music Teacher, Bharatiya Vidya Bhavan, Flat A, Basement Barons Court House, Barons Court Road, London, W14 9DS

PLACE OF BIRTH: Jaffna, 21.2.57
MARITAL STATUS: Married
COLLEGE: Ramanathan College
ACADEMIC QUALIFICATIONS: GCE A/L
PROFESSIONAL QUALIFICATIONS: Sangeetha Ratnam Sangeetha Vidwan
DIRECTORSHIPS: Vani Fine Arts Society Catford
HONOURS/AWARDS: 'Vidwan'
HOBBIES AND INTERESTS: Travelling, music, dance, any fine arts
PERSONAL PROFILE: Sivasakti learnt from many traditional teachers at an early age. Graduated from Tamil Nadu Government Music College. Was lecturer at Sri Lanka University, Jaffna. At present teaches Karnatic music and veena at the Bharatiya Vidya Bhavan, where she trains students to performance level and beyond and singing for dance. She has performed throughout the world and appeared on TV. She founded the Vani Fine Arts Society, London and released audio cassettes and CDs both as teaching aids and for listening pleasure.

MISS NINA SMALLEY (Research Assistant)

Project Officer, University of Glamorgan, Educational Development Unit, Pontypridd, CF37 1DL

PLACE OF BIRTH: Birmingham, 8.12.73
MARITAL STATUS: Single
COLLEGE: University of Glamorgan
ACADEMIC QUALIFICATIONS: BSc Hons Psychology with Criminal Justice
MEMBERSHIPS: SAGSET
HONOURS/AWARDS: Adult Learners Award 1998
HOBBIES AND INTERESTS: Computers, science fiction, art, swimming
PERSONAL PROFILE: I won the 1998 Adult Learners Award from the National Institute for Adult Continuing Education. This recognised my role in helping students across all subjects and levels with their educational needs including time management, essay writing and information technology. I undertook this role alongside study for my degree.
NOMINATED BY: Prof John Dixon, University Of Glamorgan

MR SOWARAN SINGH SOAR JP (Electrical Engineer Rtd)

Govt Servant, MOD, 97 Ilkeston Road, Lenton, Nottingham, NG7

PLACE OF BIRTH: India, 15.4.32
MARITAL STATUS: Married
CHILDREN: Four (Ravinder Kaur, Kanwal Kaur, Veena Kaur, Tanjot Singh)
ACADEMIC QUALIFICATIONS: AMIEE (London), MIED (London)
MEMBERSHIPS: Associate Member Institute of Electrical Engineers
PERSONAL PROFILE: Came to this country in 1958 - got into Commonwealth Citizens Consultative Committee - predecessor of the present Racial Equality Council in which I was chairman in early 70's. Founder member and sometimes official of three Sikh Temples in Nottingham. Appointed first Sikh Justice of the Peace in Nottinghamshire. Assisted charity commission to organise fair elections in oldest and largest Sikh temple in Nottingham. Presently representing local Afro-Caribbean Asian Forum.
NOMINATED BY: Davinder Panesar

MR WIMAL SOCKANANTHAN (Lawyer)

Broadcaster, Wimal & Co Solicitors, 727 London Road, Thornton Heath, Croydon, CR7 6AU

PLACE OF BIRTH: Sri Lanka, 30.6.44
MARITAL STATUS: Married
CHILDREN: One (Sowjana)
COLLEGE: Ceylon Law School
ACADEMIC QUALIFICATIONS: Lawyer, Sri Lanka
PROFESSIONAL QUALIFICATIONS: Solicitor, Supreme Court of England and Wales
DIRECTORSHIPS: TRT - Tamil Radio and TV
MEMBERSHIPS: Chairman GA Trust
HOBBIES AND INTERESTS: Drama, acting, music, broadcasting
PERSONAL PROFILE: A solicitor practising in the UK since 1976. Firm: Wimal & Co. Wife: Pathma (also a solicitor). Daughter: Sowjana (18). Well known in Tamil media circle as a producer and newsreader in Radio Ceylon (SLBC). Now freelance broadcaster with the BBC Worldservice Tamil. Associated with TRT Group currently broadcasting 24 Hour Tamil TV all over Europe.

CLLR ANSUYA SODHA (Lecturer Marketing)

Mangement Consultant, Vishnu Marketing and Management Consultancy, 47 Glenmere Avenue, Mill Hill, London, NW7 2LT

PLACE OF BIRTH: Kenya, 27.3.43
MARITAL STATUS: Married
CHILDREN: Two (Sandip, Nina)
COLLEGE: Middlesex University
ACADEMIC QUALIFICATIONS: MBA
PROFESSIONAL QUALIFICATIONS: Dip Chartered Institute of Marketing
MEMBERSHIPS: Association of Master in Business Administration. Electricity Consumers Committee
HOBBIES AND INTERESTS: Community work, health, fitness, travel
EMAIL: Ansuya@Vishnumarketing .demon.co.uk
PERSONAL PROFILE: Community work. Chair Barnet Racial Equality Council. Chair North London Mentoring Project. Vice chair DSO. Chair of Welsh Harp Joint Consultative Committee. College lecturer since 1975. Tutor at Open Business School. CIM Examiner Equal Opportunity Co-ordinator.

CLLR PAUL SINGH SOHAL (Resins Technician)

Borough Councillor, 31 The Normans, Wexham Court Estate, Slough, SL2 5TT

PLACE OF BIRTH: India, 1.1.51
MARITAL STATUS: Married
CHILDREN: Two (Mandeep, Sandeep Singh)
COLLEGE: Punjab University
ACADEMIC QUALIFICATIONS: BA
DIRECTORSHIPS: Non-executive director NHS Trust
MEMBERSHIPS: Race Equality Council. Asian Community Association
HOBBIES AND INTERESTS: Voluntary work, debating current issues, photography etc
PERSONAL PROFILE: Member of Berkshire County Council and Thames Valley Police Authority from May 1989 to March 1998. Currently member of Slough Borough Council. Non-executive director of NHS Trust. Chair of Board of Governors of LEA Infant School. National charities Lottery Board's south-east region's committee member. Major achievement setting up a Drop-in Centre for Asian elderly.

CLLR MOHAN SINGH SOKHAL JP (Councillor)

45 Hall Lee Fold, off Holy Bank Road, Lindley, Huddersfield, HD3 3NX

PLACE OF BIRTH: India, 13.6.43
MARITAL STATUS: Married
CHILDREN: Four (Baljit, Ravinder K, Jagdip K, Parminder K)
COLLEGE: Punjab University
ACADEMIC QUALIFICATIONS: BA
MEMBERSHIPS: Kirklees Racial Equality Council Management Committee, Vice president of the Huddersfield Indian Workers Association. Labour Party. Trade Unionist - Branch Treasurer
PERSONAL PROFILE: I am married man with four grown up children. I came to England in 1966. I joined the Labour Party to see Britain as a modern, more equal and fair society, having seen all these gross inequalities and poverty in India. I have been Labour councillor for over ten years on Kirklees MC having been first elected on 20 April 1989. I represent Kirklees on West Yorks Police Authority. I am a Justice of the Peace and member of TGWU.

MR MARCUS JAYANT SOLANKI (Mental Nurse)

RMN Day Centre Manager, Wesley Hall Community Project, 14 Horston Road, Leicester, LE2 0GH

PLACE OF BIRTH: India, 2.5.58
MARITAL STATUS: Married
CHILDREN: Two (James Jonathon, Naomi Joy)
COLLEGE: Charles Frears
ACADEMIC QUALIFICATIONS: SEN (M) RMN Registered Mental Nurse
PROFESSIONAL QUALIFICATIONS: RMN, BA Hon Health 2nd year student.
MEMBERSHIPS: UK CC Health Forum. Ex chairman, secretary. treasurer. Media spokesperson
HONOURS/AWARDS: Health of Nation Award
HOBBIES AND INTERESTS: Travelling, collecting antiques, serving community, spending time with family
PERSONAL PROFILE: 15 years area health service, 10 years community health. Specialist in mental health care (25 years service). Professional appointment in hospital and community projects. Founder member of Asian Elders Health Forum. In 1995 former manager of the first Asian Elders Project Ashram Leha 1991-95. Served Adhar and Aakash - LEFAP Project (voluntary). Age Concern Post 1995-96. Lecturer broadcaster, translator (community).
NOMINATED BY: Dr Valerie Mahett MBE

MR VIJAY SOLANKI (Marketing)

Marketing Manager, Capital Radio, 30 Leicester Square, London, WC2H 7LA

PLACE OF BIRTH: Kenya, 31.12.68
MARITAL STATUS: Single
COLLEGE: Newcastle University
ACADEMIC QUALIFICATIONS: 12 O-Levels, 5 A-Levels, BSc Hons Psychology
MEMBERSHIPS: Marketing Society
HONOURS/AWARDS: Design Award 1983
HOBBIES AND INTERESTS: Walking, politics, music
EMAIL: vijay.solanki@capital.radio.co.uk

PERSONAL PROFILE: Vijay Solanki started university studying medicine. His real passion was psychology and marketing. He worked for Procter & Gamble and Lever Brothers from 1992 - 1997. Vijay then ran a new product development team at Bisto Foods. He joined Capital Radio as marketing manager in 1999.

MR DALJIT SINGH SOND (Business Rtd)

No 1 Shirts, 33 Moor Road, Stanley, Wakefield, WF3 4EL

PLACE OF BIRTH: India, 1.5.24
MARITAL STATUS: Married
CHILDREN: Six (Raghbir Singh, Surinder Kaur, Kuldeep Kaur, Rajinder, Narinder, Permindar)
COLLEGE: Punjab University
ACADEMIC QUALIFICATIONS: Matriculation
HONOURS/AWARDS: Invited to Buckingham Palace garden party
HOBBIES AND INTERESTS: Community service, teaching, religious education

PERSONAL PROFILE: I have always worked for the general welfare of the Asian communities. General secretary of the Sikhs in Great Britain's central committee 1968-69. General secretary Northern Council of the Sikh Temple in 1975-76. Organised Vaisakhi processions in 1958. Race Relations Council 1969 as an active member. General secretary the Sikh Temple for seven years.
NOMINATED BY: Dr S K Rait J.P.

MR RANJIT SONDHI CBE (College Lecturer)

BBC Governor, BBC, c/o Westhill College, Selly Oak, Birmingham, B29 6LL

PLACE OF BIRTH: India, 22.10.50
MARITAL STATUS: Married
CHILDREN: Two (Maya, Kabir)
COLLEGE: University of Birmingham
ACADEMIC QUALIFICATIONS: BSc Hons
DIRECTORSHIPS: National Primary Trust, Birmingham Health Authority
MEMBERSHIPS: Fellow of Royal Society of Arts. Member, Lunar Society . Radio Authority . Independent Broadcasting Authority.

HONOURS/AWARDS: CBE
HOBBIES AND INTERESTS: Ancient history, travel
PERSONAL PROFILE: Previously: Director Asian Resource Centre, Deputy Chairman, CRE, Chairman, Refugee Employment Training Education Forum. Presently: Governor of the BBC and Chairman of English National Forum. Director of Birmingham Health Authority, member of Home Secretary, Race Relations Forum, member of Disability Rights Task Force.

MR RAMESH KUMAR SONI (Journalist)

Milap Weekly, 30 Staffard Cripps House, Clem Attlee Court, London, SW6 7RK

PLACE OF BIRTH: India, 1.2.38
MARITAL STATUS: Married
CHILDREN: Three (Neeru, Seema, Dyal)
COLLEGE: New Delhi
ACADEMIC QUALIFICATIONS: MA
PERSONAL PROFILE: I am publishing two Indian newspapers Milap and Navin Weekly for the benefit of the Indian community. I have been publishing these papers since 1965.

'For the last 28 years I have been involved with teaching and community work'

MANJULA PAUL SOOD

MS SEEMA SONI (Travel)

Director/Marketing Manager, Dreamers Paradise, 21 Grafton Street, Mayfair, London, W1X 3LD

PLACE OF BIRTH: UK, 23.2.65
MARITAL STATUS: Married
CHILDREN: One (Deepak)
COLLEGE: Westminster College
ACADEMIC QUALIFICATIONS: HND Management
HOBBIES AND INTERESTS: Travel, cooking, sci fi
EMAIL: seema.galaxy@binternet.com

PERSONAL PROFILE: Very enterprising and always on the lookout for anything new or dynamic to help people make their dreams come true ie Space Travel, exotic islands, celebrities etc. I do a lot of charity work simply because I love kids and animals. I am basically 'mad' and almost always take a challenge and good for a laugh.

DR SUSHIL SONI (Archivist)

Project Archivist, Suffolk County Council Libraries & Heritage Dept, 72 Belmont Road, Pinewood, Ipswich, IP2 9XT

PLACE OF BIRTH: India, 30.12.36
MARITAL STATUS: Married
CHILDREN: Three (Rohit, Manoj, Sheetal)
COLLEGE: Delhi (India) Durham (UK)
ACADEMIC QUALIFICATIONS: MA (History), PhD (History) Durham
PROFESSIONAL QUALIFICATIONS: Diploma in Archives and Management
MEMBERSHIPS: Society of Archivists. Labour Party. SACRE. SIFRE. UNISON
HOBBIES AND INTERESTS: Reading, writing, community welfare, participation in political and religious activities
PERSONAL PROFILE: PhD from Durham University in 'Administration of Punjabi 1849-59' in 1965. Worked for Suffolk County Council since 1967. Currently senior archivist in the records office of the council's library and heritage department. Parish councillor for Pinewood, since 1986 and chairman 1994-96. Founder member of Ipswich and Suffolk Indian Association 1976 and Ipswich and Suffolk CRE Equality (1977). Chair of European Panel 1986 -1994. Secretary Black Members Group 1989 to date. Co-opted to SACRE,
NOMINATED BY: H S Minhas

MR MANISH SOOD (Programme Manger)

Lottery Youth Programme, Wellingborough District Hindu Association, 44 Belgrave Road, Belgrave, Leicester, LE4 SA

PLACE OF BIRTH: Leicester, 11.7.71
MARITAL STATUS: Single
COLLEGE: South Bank University
ACADEMIC QUALIFICATIONS: BA Hons, MBA
PROFESSIONAL QUALIFICATIONS: MBA, AHCIMA
MEMBERSHIPS: AMBA, AHCIMA, MECA
HONOURS/AWARDS: Community Care Award
HOBBIES AND INTERESTS: Reading, learning different languages, working to the best of my ability
PERSONAL PROFILE: Having specialised in the areas of hotel management as my first degree and focused on marketing, human resource management, environmental management and international business during the MBA, I intend to pursue a long term career in senior management with a large multinational company. I also want to help the community.
NOMINATED BY: Janti Patel

MS MANJULA PAUL SOOD (Teacher Rtd)

Councillor, Leicester City Council, B1, Members Area, New Walk Centre, Leicester, LE1 62G

PLACE OF BIRTH: India, 23.12.45
MARITAL STATUS: Widow
CHILDREN: Two (Manish, Mitesh)
ACADEMIC QUALIFICATIONS: BA Hons, MA Sociology
PROFESSIONAL QUALIFICATIONS: Teachers Qualification
DIRECTORSHIPS: NHS Trust, Non exec Glenfield Hospital
MEMBERSHIPS: Chair of the NAARI Leicester Enterprise Training Scheme, Leicester Council of Faiths
HOBBIES AND INTERESTS: To hold charities, voluntary work, reading spirituality
PERSONAL PROFILE: For the last 28 years I have been involved with teaching and community work. Worked for the needs of diverse communities, women and youth are my personal interests. Raised money for charities. Vice chair of Social Services and Education.

MR MANOJ SOOD (Promoter)

Diwali Show Promotions, 59 Trowell Avenue, Wollaton, Nottingham, NG8 2DW

PLACE OF BIRTH: Canada, 19.11.74
MARITAL STATUS: Single
COLLEGE: Queen Mary and Westfield College (University of London)
ACADEMIC QUALIFICATIONS: BSc Hons Economics & Econ Studies
PROFESSIONAL QUALIFICATIONS: Young Enterprise, Basic Numeracy
HOBBIES AND INTERESTS: Reading, socialising, playing sport, business

PERSONAL PROFILE: A dedicated and meticulous planner and entrepreneur who enjoys fresh challenges. A hard worker with a 'can do' winning attitude. Enjoys Indian cinema and art. Very sports orientated, partaking in the Khalsa football tournaments in the summer. Though most of all - love my family.
NOMINATED BY: Ushma Vyas

MS GITA SOOTARSING (Consultancy)

Prinicpal, Amber Consultants,

PLACE OF BIRTH: Mauritius, 16.6.49
COLLEGE: University of Westminster
ACADEMIC QUALIFICATIONS: HNC Business Studies, Post Grad Diploma and Personnel Management
PROFESSIONAL QUALIFICATIONS: MIPD and AIMG
DIRECTORSHIPS: Commissioner CRE, Vice chair Essex Police Authority
MEMBERSHIPS: Panel Member - Employment Tribunals
HONOURS/AWARDS: Small Business - High Flyer Windrush 1999
HOBBIES AND INTERESTS: Art, travel, gardens, dancing, theatre
EMAIL: gitas@compuserve.com
PERSONAL PROFILE: Following a success broadly - based career with the Bank of England. Gita started her own consultancy which covers policies, practices, management development, social research and mentoring etc. She is a regular conference speaker in the UK and abroad and combines her work with public service. She recently won a High Flyer's Award at the Windrush 99 Awards.

MISS IMANE SOUISI (Schoolgirl-Actress)

School, The Jackie Palmer Stage School Agency,

PLACE OF BIRTH: Wycombe, 26.7.86
COLLEGE: Furze Platt School
ACADEMIC QUALIFICATIONS: Tap Dancer, Jazz, Drama, Ballat and Irish
PROFESSIONAL QUALIFICATIONS: Actress and Dance
HONOURS/AWARDS: School Awards and Dancing Awards
HOBBIES AND INTERESTS: Dancing, singing, reading

DR NAGAN SRINIVASAN (Doctor)

PLACE OF BIRTH: India
MARITAL STATUS: Married
CHILDREN: Two (Uma Nandhini, Srinandhan)
COLLEGE: Bangalore University, India
ACADEMIC QUALIFICATIONS: MBBS Degree
PROFESSIONAL QUALIFICATIONS: MBBS
MEMBERSHIPS: Chairman of Oxford Dravidian Amnesty Council UK, President of Federation of Ambedkarites and Buddhists Organisation
HOBBIES AND INTERESTS: Photography, current affairs, reading, travelling, comparative religious philosophy, trans-cultural psychiatric issues
EMAIL: sarvasinni@aol.com
PERSONAL PROFILE: Born in Kolar Goldfields, educated in Bangalore, arrived in UK for training in medicine. Have been deeply involved in the socio-religious activities and campaign against human rights violation on the down trodden in India. Have been running a charitable trust to help in the educational needs of the down trodden children.

MR ASHOK KUMAR SRIVASTAVA (Actor-Tennis Coach)

Researcher, Innerspace, c/o Stiven Christie Management, Richmond Buildings, 80A Dean Street, London, W1V 4AD

PLACE OF BIRTH: Pakistan, 21.10.62
MARITAL STATUS: Single
CHILDREN: One (Nitesh Kumar)
COLLEGE: Middlesex University Business School
ACADEMIC QUALIFICATIONS: MBA, NVQ, HND, USPTR (Qualified coach)
MEMBERSHIPS: Equity, AMBA, ALTC, PLTC, USPTR
HONOURS/AWARDS: Equity Mixed Doubles Champions 1995, Equity Mens Doubles Runner Up 1997, Equity Mens Doubles Champions 1998
HOBBIES AND INTERESTS: Tennis, football, golf, squash, hockey, snooker, pool, cinema, driving, music, travel, photography, electronics, antiques, toy collector
PERSONAL PROFILE: Born in Karachi, Pakistan. Emigrated to Glasgow, where he spent most of his childhood and youth. Graduated as a civil engineer from Glasgow College of Technology. Moved to London ten years ago. He gained an MBA from Middlesex University Business School whilst residng in London. When he is not acting or tennis coaching, he works as a part-time researcher at Middlesex University Business School, and to date he has had three research papers published, with respect to gaining a potential PhD.

MRS SUKHVINDER KAUR STUBBS
(Manager - Policymaker)

Chief Executive, The Runnymede Trust, 133 Aldergate Street, London, EC1A 4JA

PLACE OF BIRTH: India, 25.10.62
MARITAL STATUS: Married
COLLEGE: Oxford University
ACADEMIC QUALIFICATIONS: MA (Oxon)
PROFESSIONAL QUALIFICATIONS: Dip Marketing MBA
DIRECTORSHIPS: Demos; Refugee Council; Queen Mary's NHS Trust; Black Country Development Corporation
MEMBERSHIPS: Fellow : RSA; British American Project
HOBBIES AND INTERESTS: Mountain hiking, adventure travel, European cinema
EMAIL: sukhvinderstubbs@hotmail. com
PERSONAL PROFILE: Sukhvinder grew up in Handsworth, Birmingham and went on to study at Oxford where she gained the top University prize and met her husband David. In her current post, Sukhvinder is Deputy to the Minister on an Education Task Force and works closely with government departments and the Cabinet Office. Sukhvinder is a regular speaker and writer on management issues, cultural diversity, politics, European women's issues and was listed in the Evening Times 100 powerful women.

MR BABULAL V SUDRA (President Rtd)

Secretary, Gujarati Senior Citizen Welfare Association (Redbridge),

PLACE OF BIRTH: Kenya, 6.7.31
MARITAL STATUS: Married
CHILDREN: Four (Jayshukh, Ashok, Dilip, Sona)
PROFESSIONAL QUALIFICATIONS: Electrician
PERSONAL PROFILE: President of Shree Vishva Karma Vainsh Society London since 1992. Secretary Gujarati Senior Citizen Welfare Association (Redbridge) since 1992. I do all these as a voluntary services for our community. Came in this country in 1970 from Uganda where I was working for a subsidiary of ICI as an electrician.

NOMINATED BY: G K Dattani

Following a success broadly - based career with the Bank of England. Gita started her own consultancy which covers policies, practices, management development, social research and mentoring etc. She is a regular conference speaker in the UK and abroad and combines her work with public service

GITA SOOTARSING

DR DIWAKAR SUKUL (CLINICAL PSYCHOLOGIST)

Director, Kamkus - Multi Dimensional Health Care, Training & Research Centre, 100 Harley Street, London, W1N 1AF

PLACE OF BIRTH: India
MARITAL STATUS: Married
CHILDREN: One (Divya)
ACADEMIC QUALIFICATIONS: PhD (Psychology)
PROFESSIONAL QUALIFICATIONS: MA (Clin Psy), PGDBM, Dip Addictive Behaviour, Dip Hypnotherapy, Psychotherapy, NLP
DIRECTORSHIPS: Kamkus, Ethnocon, GMU

MEMBERSHIPS: Several
HONOURS/AWARDS: MD (Alternative Medicines), Who's Who of the Year 1995 (American Bio SNS - US) Certificate of Merit. International Dictionary of Biographies - Cambridge
HOBBIES AND INTERESTS: Judo, acting, poetry, reading, music
PERSONAL PROFILE: Dr Diwakar Sukul hails from Delhi, India. He trained as a clinical psychologist. He arrived in the UK in 1990 for further studies and experience in British psychiatry. He studied hypnotherapy, NLP and addictive behaviour in UK. In 1991 he joined Turning Point Southall Alcohol Advisory Service as project manager where he pioneered the integration of complementary/alternative medicine for the treatment of addiction. Dr Sukul has appeared on BBC TV, Zee TV and several cable TV and radio programmes on holistic medicine.

REV. DR SUMANA - SIRI (MEDICAL DOCTOR-BUDDHIST MONK)

Executive Director, Buddhist Realists' Vihara, 85 Highworth Road, New Southgate, London, N11 2SN

PLACE OF BIRTH: Malaysia, 31.12.52
COLLEGE: University of Sri Lanka, Oxford University
ACADEMIC QUALIFICATIONS: Dip in Buddhist Studies, BA Hons Now . M Th (Oxford)
PROFESSIONAL QUALIFICATIONS: Doctor in Homoeopathy, Doctor in Naturopathy, Dip in Homoeopathy
DIRECTORSHIPS: Executive Director - Buddhist Realists' Centres, London, Italy, Malaysia and Germany
MEMBERSHIPS: International Association of Historians of Asia, Oxford Union, The Oxford Society
HONOURS/AWARDS: Fellow - British Institute of Homoeopathy
HOBBIES AND INTERESTS: Social issues, dialogues, medical ethics, public speeches, inter-racial communication
PERSONAL PROFILE: Born and bred in Singapore and Malaysia educated in Sri Lanka and UK. Currently research scholar at Oxford University. Doctor in homeopathy and naturopathic medicine. Founder of the Buddhist Realist Movement Worldwide. Sociologist and historian of Asia, communicative in ten languages, interested in human affairs.
NOMINATED BY: Rev D Wimala

MR DALVIR SINGH SUMMAN (BROADCASTER)

Radio Presenter, 19 Dyngs Walk, Smethwick, Warley, B66 7DU

PLACE OF BIRTH: India, 27.10.58
MARITAL STATUS: Married
CHILDREN: Two (Kavita, Kanwal)
COLLEGE: Bilston College, Sedwell College
ACADEMIC QUALIFICATIONS: GCE, A-Level, Dip Com lang
PROFESSIONAL QUALIFICATIONS: Dip Welfare Studies, Punjabi O-Level
MEMBERSHIPS: Punjabi Kala Munch, Punjabi Kavi Mandle. NUJ
HONOURS/AWARDS: Broadcasting award, West Mids Police (Special Constable)
HOBBIES AND INTERESTS: Special constable, music, photography, writing short stories, poetry
PERSONAL PROFILE: Punjabi poet, presenter, broadcaster, journalist, singer, community worker, special constable for ten years West Midlands Police. Worked at Walsall Social Services - Worked hard for community betterment.

Dr Diwakar Sukul hails from Delhi, India. He trained as a clinical psychologist. He arrived in the UK in 1990 for further studies and experience in British psychiatry. He studied hypnotherapy, NLP and addictive behaviour in UK

MR ARUN KUMAR SWARUP (MORTGAGE-INSURANCE CONSULTANT)

Financial Adviser, Allied Dunbar, 22 St Pauls Hill, Winchester, SO22 4AB

PLACE OF BIRTH: India, 4.6.38
MARITAL STATUS: Married
CHILDREN: Three (Anita, Anil, Nina)
COLLEGE: Calcutta
PROFESSIONAL QUALIFICATIONS: Fellow of the Institute of Chartered Accountants. Financial Planning Certificate Chartered Insurance Institiue.
MEMBERSHIPS: Winchester Tennis and Squash Club and Littleton Tennis Club
HOBBIES AND INTERESTS: Tennis, bridge, cricket, swimming
PERSONAL PROFILE: Arrived in UK from India in 1976. Helped many from the ethnic community to set up their own business and purchase properties. As an experienced financial consultant can assist with raising capital/funding for purchase of businesses and investment, commercial and residential properties.

MR BOBBY AYYUS SYED (PR - MARKETING)

Accounts Director, Hearsay Communications Worldwide Ltd,

PLACE OF BIRTH: Pakistan, 13.9.62
MARITAL STATUS: Single
COLLEGE: University of London
ACADEMIC QUALIFICATIONS: BSc Social Science, BA Hon International Relations, MA
PROFESSIONAL QUALIFICATIONS: MA Politics (SOAS)
DIRECTORSHIPS: Institute of Directors
MEMBERSHIPS: Associate member of Institute of Public Relations
HOBBIES AND INTERESTS: Scuba diving, horse riding, films
PERSONAL PROFILE: Booby Ayyus Syed is a graduate of BSc (Hons) Social Science, BA (Hons) International Relations and MA in Area Studies (South Asia) from the School of Oriental and African Studies (University of London). Following graduation he worked as a diplomatic marketing consultant at SOAS and set up a training course for diplomats. He was responsible for marketing and promotion as well as lecturing, research and diplomatic liaison.

MRS SHAHEEN SYED (PUBLISHER)

Proprietor, The Muslim Matriimonial, Empire House, Empire Way, Wembley, HA9 0EW

PLACE OF BIRTH: India, 18.2.42
MARITAL STATUS: Married
CHILDREN: Four (Mohammed, Ahmed, Asghar, Zaw)
ACADEMIC QUALIFICATIONS: BSc
PROFESSIONAL QUALIFICATIONS: Secretary to Roy Hattersley MP
HOBBIES AND INTERESTS: Getting people married, family events
EMAIL: syeda@musmat.demon.co.uk
PERSONAL PROFILE: The Muslim Matrimonial was formed over two years ago as a service to the Muslim community in the UK. Previously I was the constituency secretary of Roy Hattersley MP. I hope to see Muslim Matrimonial as a household name in the near future.

MRS SULTANA SYED (EDUCATION WELFARE OFFICER)

Muslim Women Organisation, 75 Elvaston Road, Wollaton, Nottingham, NG8 1JS

PLACE OF BIRTH: India, 29.11.47
CHILDREN: Three (Nadeem, Naveed, Nabeel)
COLLEGE: Karachi University
ACADEMIC QUALIFICATIONS: BSc
PROFESSIONAL QUALIFICATIONS: Community and Youth Work. Teaching South Asian Languages. Management Training
MEMBERSHIPS: President of Muslim Women's Organisation
HONOURS/AWARDS: Vol Work, Community Study and Community Care
HOBBIES AND INTERESTS: Gardening, reading, swimming, politics, community work
PERSONAL PROFILE: Came to UK in 1968. Set up Ladies Circle 72. Founded Asian Women's Project. Supervision JIPAC Project 1983-86. Language teacher 1973-88. ESL Co-ordinator 1982-88. Full time worker for LEA as education liaison / welfare officer 1986-98. Created Muslim Women's Organisation and Muslim Women's Centre was established in 1987. Nominated Midland Woman of the Year 1985. Nottingham Asian Arts Council and Asian and Afro Caribbean Forums Executive Committee member. IT Consultant, doctor, student.
NOMINATED BY: Mrs S Ahmad

January 25 1994: Controversial scenes in the Gurinder Chadha's film, Bhaji On The Beach, are labelled blasphemous, vulgar and offensive'. However, the film billed as a 'comical daytrip to Blackpool by a group of Asian women' is a huge hit with mainstream audiences. Chadha defends the film as a 'vibrant an varied insight' into British Asian lives

MR ABDUL BARI TALUKDER (Compliance Inspector)

Compliance Inspector, Newham Contribution Agency, Inland Revenue, Jubilee House, Farthingale Walk, Stratford, E15 1BR

PLACE OF BIRTH: Bangladesh, 13.11.38
MARITAL STATUS: Married
CHILDREN: Four (Rumman, Tamanna, Farzana, Faisal)
COLLEGE: Cambridge, Manchester, Southampton
ACADEMIC QUALIFICATIONS: Masters Degree Banking
MEMBERSHIPS: PCS

HOBBIES AND INTERESTS: Current affairs
PERSONAL PROFILE: Came to this country on 14.1.64. Entered British civil service on open competitions as an executive officer on 1967. Went to Buckingham Palace on 17.7.85. Community work – vice chair of a secondary school. Employed as Compliance Officer of Tax Office on 14.4.99.

MR ASHWIN KUMAR TANNA (Pharmacist)

33 Panmure Road, Sydenham, London, SE26 6NB

PLACE OF BIRTH: Tanzania, 29.1.45
MARITAL STATUS: Married
CHILDREN: Two (Anand, Asha)
COLLEGE: University of Sunderland
ACADEMIC QUALIFICATIONS: BSc
PROFESSIONAL QUALIFICATIONS: FRPharms
DIRECTORSHIPS: Own chemist business – Sailmead Ltd
MEMBERSHIPS: Chair – Lordship Lane Traders Assoc, East Dulwich Action Group

HONOURS/AWARDS: 1992 – Designated Fellow of Royal Pharm. Society, 1997 – Southwark Council
HOBBIES AND INTERESTS: Gardening, reading, politics
PERSONAL PROFILE: After graduation, purchased a business in Lordship Lane 1973 to date. While running the business, I served the community and profession by serving as governor of local schools, forming East Dulwich Action Group and Lordship Lane Traders Association and being on the council of the professional body.

MR MOHAMMED TARIQ (Trading Standards Officer)

Enforcement Officer, Birmingham City Council, 115 – 157 Corporation Street, Birmingham, B4 6PH

PLACE OF BIRTH: Pakistan, 30.10.67
MARITAL STATUS: Single
COLLEGE: Matthew Bolton College Further Education
PROFESSIONAL QUALIFICATIONS: Business and Finance
HOBBIES AND INTERESTS: Cricket, football, swimming, watching documentaries
PERSONAL PROFILE: My biggest achievement was when I appeared on a BBC national documentary 'The Fraud Squad' I feel that this was a major achievement not just for me but for the citizens of Birmingham, in particular the Asian community. I felt really proud to be part of a major prime time documentary.
NOMINATED BY: Saima Qureshi

CLLR JAGJIT SINGH TAUNQUE (Councillor)

Community Liaison Officer, 127 Petersfield Road, Hall Green, Birmingham, B28 0BG

PLACE OF BIRTH: India, 11.10.34
MARITAL STATUS: Married
CHILDREN: Two (Pavnit Kaur, Mandip Singh)
COLLEGE: Birmingham University
ACADEMIC QUALIFICATIONS: BSc
DIRECTORSHIPS: Birmingham Focus on Blindness Board BRID . Chair of India Club.
MEMBERSHIPS: Member of the Labour Party and Trade Union. GMC. Birmingham Civic Society. Punjab Literary Circle

HOBBIES AND INTERESTS: Economic policy, housing, education and environmental health, hockey, badminton
PERSONAL PROFILE: He is chairman of the Health and Social Welfare Committee of Birmingham Community Relations Council and an executive member of its India Club, chairman of the Birmingham Punjabi Cultural Centre. Vice chairman of the Punjabi Literary Circle. In 1985 he founded Birmingham's first drop – in centre for elderly ethnic people.
NOMINATED BY: Satinder Kaur

MRS SATINDER KAUR TAUNQUE (Teacher)

127 Petersfield Road, Hall Green, Birmingham, B28 0BG

PLACE OF BIRTH: India
MARITAL STATUS: Married
CHILDREN: Two (Pavnit Kaur, Mandip Singh)
COLLEGE: Wolverhampton University
ACADEMIC QUALIFICATIONS: BA, BT
PROFESSIONAL QUALIFICATIONS: PGCE

NOMINATED BY: Jagjit Singh Taunque

CLLR VIRENDRA KUMAR TEWARI (Banking – Rtd)

Director, Kamkus – Multi Dimensional Health Care, Kamkus, 100 Harley Street, London, W1N 1AF

PLACE OF BIRTH: India, 3.7.39
CHILDREN: One (Sheila)
COLLEGE: Agra University, Edinburgh University
ACADEMIC QUALIFICATIONS: BSc
DIRECTORSHIPS: Osprey Computer Systems
PERSONAL PROFILE: Came from India in 1959 to study engineering. Worked in computing and then in banking (computer section) followed by promotions in retail banking. Took early retirement in 1992 to help community. Went into politics and was elected councillor in 1994 and again 1998.

MS RASHMI THAKAR (Sales-Marketing Manager)

Manager, Grim's Dyke Hotel, Old Redding, Harrow Weald, HA3 6SH

PLACE OF BIRTH: Uganda, 13.7.59
MARITAL STATUS: Ms
CHILDREN: One (Shivani)
COLLEGE: London College
ACADEMIC QUALIFICATIONS: 3 A-Levels, 8 O-Levels
PROFESSIONAL QUALIFICATIONS: Public Relations
HOBBIES AND INTERESTS: Indian philosophy, drama, music
PERSONAL PROFILE: Sales and marketing co – ordinator at Grim's Dyke Hotel. Only Asian woman who is part of senior management team. Friends in high society – Personal friend of the Puris, the Madhwanis, the Noons, the Maneks, the Zaiwallas in the UK. Devotee of Shree Morari Babu. Runs a successful partnership involved in commercial properties and hotels.
NOMINATED BY: Sarah Laiwalla

MR SUBHASH THAKER (Director of Sales)

Director of Sales & Marketing, The Taj Group of Hotels, St James Court, Buckingham Palace, London, SW1E 6AP

PLACE OF BIRTH: India, 26.12.49
MARITAL STATUS: Married
CHILDREN: Two (Siddharth, Namrata)
COLLEGE: Delhi University
ACADEMIC QUALIFICATIONS: BA, Post Graduate in Marketing, Diploma in Direct Marketing
PROFESSIONAL QUALIFICATIONS: Management and Direct Marketing
MEMBERSHIPS: Charter Institute of Marketing, Institute of Direct Marketing. Hotel Industry Marketing Group
HOBBIES AND INTERESTS: Management issues, architecture, travel, philosophy
PERSONAL PROFILE: In depth experience in marketing of consumer durables and service industry with wide interest in issues covering management, philosophy and different cultures.

Sales and marketing co-ordinator at Grim's Dyke Hotel. Only Asian woman who is part of senior management team. Friends in high society – personal friend of the Puris, the Madhwanis, the Noons, the Maneks,

RASHMI THAKAR

MR NAVINBHAI RUGNATH THAKERAR (DIRECTOR)

Director, Bi – Rite, 9 Rushmoor Close, Pinner, HA5 2HF

PLACE OF BIRTH: Kenya, 6.9.35
MARITAL STATUS: Married
CHILDREN: Two (Rekha, Pulin)
COLLEGE: Bhavans, Andheri, India
ACADEMIC QUALIFICATIONS: BSc
HOBBIES AND INTERESTS: Social work
PERSONAL PROFILE: I was president of Lohana Community North London. Vice president of Lohana Community Greater London. I do social work and have for over 40 years, ie arrange marriages.

CLLR JIM THAKOORDIN (EDUCATION CONSULTANT)

Director, Equality Training & Management, 310 Manor Road, Woodside, Near Caddington, Luton, LU1 4DN

PLACE OF BIRTH: Guyana, 6.8.43
MARITAL STATUS: Married
CHILDREN: Two (Michael, Jane)
COLLEGE: Essex, Warwick, London and Hertfordshire University
ACADEMIC QUALIFICATIONS: Diploma Oxford, BA Hons PGCE, MBA
PROFESSIONAL QUALIFICATIONS: Qualified Teacher and Business Consultant and Health Trust Board

MEMBERSHIPS: Labour Party National Policy Forum Commission for Education and Employment
HONOURS/AWARDS: Various community awards
HOBBIES AND INTERESTS: Politics, gardening, country music
PERSONAL PROFILE: Jim Thakoordin, born in Guyana 1943, arrived in Britain in 1961. County councillor and active in community affairs. Labour parliamentary candidate. Past regional trade union official. Governor of Cranfield and Luton Universities. Non – executive director of Health Trust, member of Labour Commission for Education and Employment and national policy forum. Written several books and manages own consultancy business. Victim Support and Further Education Funding Council.

MR ROHAN THAKRAR (PRODUCT CONTROLLER)

Product Controller, Greenwich Natwest, South Harrow, London

PLACE OF BIRTH: London, 1.10.75
MARITAL STATUS: Single
COLLEGE: Nottingham Trent University
ACADEMIC QUALIFICATIONS: BA Hons Accounting and Finance 1st Class
PROFESSIONAL QUALIFICATIONS: CIMA Stage 3 Qualified
HONOURS/AWARDS: Best Performing Student in Final Year
HOBBIES AND INTERESTS: Sport, movies, family, follow financial markets, sleeping
PERSONAL PROFILE: I'm a keen upcoming Asian Millennium Man. Year 2000 will be the most successful year for me and my family. Look out for me, listen for my name, I'm on the way.
NOMINATED BY: RS Chowdhury

MR SUBHASH KANJI THAKRAR (CHARTERED ACCOUNTANT)

SK Thakrar & Co Chartered Accountants, Thakrar House, 113 Woolwich High Street, London, SE18 6DN

PLACE OF BIRTH: Uganda, 18.6.48
MARITAL STATUS: Married
CHILDREN: Two (Rishi, Rupa)
COLLEGE: London Guildhall University
ACADEMIC QUALIFICATIONS: Experience in Accounting Field
PROFESSIONAL QUALIFICATIONS: Fellow of Institute of Chartered Accountants
DIRECTORSHIPS: Health Authority 1996. Trustee/Director Inveileaver Lodge – a charity.
MEMBERSHIPS: Past president – Woolwich Lions Club. Woolwich Rotary Club
HONOURS/AWARDS: Personal satisfaction
HOBBIES AND INTERESTS: Reading, charity work, property, business developments
PERSONAL PROFILE: Came to UK 1967. Qualified as an accountant 1972. Aduiting 1974 – own practice started 1976 – family practice now. Founder and first auditor (joint) Lohana Community of UK and South London. Trustee for Stroke Prevention Fund at Brook Hospital, Member of Lions Rotary Clubs. Local Chamber of Commerce and various activities. Involved as auditors to local Hindu and Sikh temples and others. Non – executive director – Bexley and Greenwich Health Authority for some 15 years. Loves to help people!

MR KEEKIRA THAMMAIAH (COUNCILLOR RTD)

Lecturer, 26 Longcroft Road, Canons Park, Edgware, HA8 6RR

PLACE OF BIRTH: India, 10.2.35
MARITAL STATUS: Married
CHILDREN: One (Ponnu)
COLLEGE: Bangalore University
ACADEMIC QUALIFICATIONS: MA, LLB
PROFESSIONAL QUALIFICATIONS: Law
HOBBIES AND INTERESTS: Community work, politics
PERSONAL PROFILE: Came to this country in 1964 took up teaching and now retired. Member of National Union of Teachers and University and College Lecturers Union. Executive member of Council for Racial Equality and Citizens Advice Bureau in Harrow. Active member of Labour Party. Elected as a councillor in London Borough in 1994 and again in 1998. At present member of Education Committee and Chairman of the Grants Committee.

MR GURBAX SINGH THEATHI (ARTIST)

Painter (RTD), 66 Norwood Road, Southall, UB2 4DP

PLACE OF BIRTH: India, 11.10.23
MARITAL STATUS: Widower
CHILDREN: Five
ACADEMIC QUALIFICATIONS: Fine Art
PROFESSIONAL QUALIFICATIONS: Metric
HONOURS/AWARDS: Asian Film Awards 1996 (UK)
HOBBIES AND INTERESTS: Art (Painting)
PERSONAL PROFILE: I did metric and after that I got training one year Lahore, Pakistan. One year after that I joined the Punjab Government Calico Printing Association. Served at the American Embassy then I came to the UK in 1981 and I won the Asian Film Award 1996.
NOMINATED BY: Preeti Arora

MR GURBACHAN SINGH THIND (FINANCIAL CONSULTANT)

Former Mayor 1998 – 99, Thind & Co, 35 Trent Road, Langley, Slough, SL3 8AW

PLACE OF BIRTH: India, 2.5.40
MARITAL STATUS: Married
CHILDREN: Two (Mohnish Kaur, Rajeshpal Singh)
COLLEGE: London University
ACADEMIC QUALIFICATIONS: BA
PROFESSIONAL QUALIFICATIONS: B.Ed
DIRECTORSHIPS: Thind & Co, London
MEMBERSHIPS: Ex President Guru Gobind Singh Foundation, London
HONOURS/AWARDS: President Award of India
HOBBIES AND INTERESTS: Hockey, politics
PERSONAL PROFILE: I was chief advisor to Chief Minister Gurpaur Singh in Punjab India in 1967-71. I became a councillor in Slough in 1991. In 1997 I was honoured as deputy mayor and in 1998 – 99 as mayor of Slough. I was the first mayor of new unitary council with £115 million budget 1998 – 1999.

MISS NATALIE TINN – NGYUTIN (ACTRESS)

CAM London,

PLACE OF BIRTH: London, 31.5.73
MARITAL STATUS: Single
COLLEGE: Mountview Theatre School
ACADEMIC QUALIFICATIONS: Acting and Musical Theatre Diploma
PROFESSIONAL QUALIFICATIONS: Four years in the profession
MEMBERSHIPS: Equity
PERSONAL PROFILE: Tiger Lilly in 'Peter Pan' for The Royal National Theatre. Cheryl in 'Made in England' written by Parv Bancil. Smokey Joes Cafe and Fame West End. Commercial for Jerry Springer and Carphone Warehouse, Douglas for the BBC. Film: – 'What rat's won't do'.

'I'm a keen upcoming Asian Millennium Man. Year 2000 will be the most successful year for me and my family. Look out for me, listen for my name, I'm on the way'

ROHAN THAKRAR

MR CYRUS RUSTOM TODIWALA (Restaurateur)

Executive Chief/Proprietor, Cafe Spice Ltd, Cafe Spice Namaste, 16 Prescot Street, London, E1 8AZ

PLACE OF BIRTH: India, 16.10.56
MARITAL STATUS: Married
CHILDREN: Two (Jamsheed, Hormuzd)
COLLEGE: Bombay
ACADEMIC QUALIFICATIONS: Diploma in Hotel Management., Bombay
PROFESSIONAL QUALIFICATIONS: Only experience plus few certificates
DIRECTORSHIPS: Cafe Spice Ltd, Namaste of London Ltd
HONOURS/AWARDS: Best Indian Chef in the UK 1992, 1993, 1995, 1996
HOBBIES AND INTERESTS: Cooking, gardening, DIY, repair and restoration of clock and watches, conservation
PERSONAL PROFILE: Highly acclaimed master chef and owner of Cafe Spice Ltd and Cafe Spice Namaste. The restaurant is considered one of the best in Britain and has won many awards. Cyrus published his own book. Won the National Training Award. The first ever Indian restaurant to have won. His contribution to the industry is invaluable.

MR ABDUL AZIZ TOKI (Project Coordinator)

Marylebone Bangladesh Society, 54 Chetwode House, Grendon Street, Lisson Green Estate, London, NW8 8SR

PLACE OF BIRTH: Bangladesh, 3.4.60
MARITAL STATUS: Married
CHILDREN: Three (Romena, Abu Taher, Abu Sorwar)
COLLEGE: Chitagong University
ACADEMIC QUALIFICATIONS: BA
PROFESSIONAL QUALIFICATIONS: Advanced Diploma in Organisation. Management Certificate
MEMBERSHIPS: European Migrant Forum, Voluntary Service Overseas, Westminster Race Equality Council.
HOBBIES AND INTERESTS: Creative writing, reading, travelling, sports
PERSONAL PROFILE: Editor – fortnightly, Bangladesh (1984-85). Editor monthly (revolution) Germany (1987). Assistant teacher – DM High School. Assistant secretary – Chittagong Divisional Scout (1984-86). Writer. Last scene (drama) 'Ulta Bozhilere Ram' (storybook) 'Ami Ki Manush' (poetry).

DR ASHWINI KUMAR TREHAN (Consultant Gynaecologist)

Dewsbury District Hospital, Halifax Road, Dewsbury, WF1 3 4HS

PLACE OF BIRTH: India, 23.7.51
MARITAL STATUS: Married
CHILDREN: Two (Pooja, Abhishek)
COLLEGE: Ranchi University, India
ACADEMIC QUALIFICATIONS: MBBS
PROFESSIONAL QUALIFICATIONS: MBBS, DRCOG, FRCOG, FRCS (Edin)
MEMBERSHIPS: RCOG (England), BSGE RC of Surgeons (Edin), ISGE
HONOURS/AWARDS: Gold Medal in Surgery
HOBBIES AND INTERESTS: Gardening
PERSONAL PROFILE: Ashwini Trehan, consultant gynaecologist has successfully pioneered keyhole hysterectomies. It is the only hospital in the country offering this unique service which allows women to go home just 24 hours after having the surgery and the technique has an amazing success rate with very low complications, one of the very lowest in the country.
NOMINATED BY: Poonam Trehan

MR SHANKER TRIVEDI (Vice President)

Vice President, Sun Microsystems (UK), Newlyn, Shinfield Road, Reading, RG2 7BE

PLACE OF BIRTH: Birmingham, 8.11.56
MARITAL STATUS: Married
CHILDREN: Two (Nikhil, Tara)
COLLEGE: IIT (Delhi), IIM (Calcutta)
ACADEMIC QUALIFICATIONS: MS (Computer Science), MBA
DIRECTORSHIPS: Sun Microsystems
MEMBERSHIPS: Institute of Directors; Institute of Management; Royal Overseas League
HONOURS/AWARDS: Gold Medal (IIM Calcutta)
HOBBIES AND INTERESTS: Cricket, crosswords, reading, sailing
EMAIL: shanker.trivedi@uk.sun.com
PERSONAL PROFILE: Professional manager in hi-tech industry with experience in large multi-nationals (IBM, ICM and SUN) as well as small start-ups. Extensive marketing sales technology and general management experience. Educated at IIT and IIM.

MR PREM TULSIANI (Events Organisation)

Managing Director, DS Promotions, 35 Sovereign House, 19 – 23 Fitzroy Street, London, W1P 5AB

PLACE OF BIRTH: London, 3.7.76
MARITAL STATUS: Single
COLLEGE: Kings College London
ACADEMIC QUALIFICATIONS: BSc Honours Mathematics and Management
DIRECTORSHIPS: DS Promotions, Premier Trading Ltd
HOBBIES AND INTERESTS: Travel, music, socialising, computing
PERSONAL PROFILE: Started organising events for Asian students three years ago. Promoted at all the major clubs in London. Recently organised a Diwali show at the Wembley Conference Centre for over 2500 people. In the process of setting up a family run entertainment organisation to cater for all ages in the Asian community.
NOMINATED BY: Ushma Vyas, Shaista Aziz

> Ashwini Trehan, consultant gynaecologist has successfully pioneered keyhole hysterectomies. It is the only hospital in the country offering this unique service which allows women to go home just 24 hours after having the surgery and the technique has an amazing success rate with very low complications, one of the very lowest in the country

> Highly acclaimed master chef and owner of Cafe Spice Ltd and Cafe Spice Namaste. The restaurant is considered one of the best in Britain and has won many awards.

CYRUS RUSTOM TODIWALA

10 years of service to the Asian community

June 5 1998: Tensions in the the sub continent rise as India and Pakistan carry out nuclear tests within weeks of each other. As the world condemns both countries, British Asians call for an 'end to the madness'

CLLR ALA UDDIN (LECTURER)

Deputy Leader Council, London Borough of Tower Hamlets, 51 Kingward House, Hanbury Street, London, E1 5JR

PLACE OF BIRTH: Bangladesh, 4.12.52
MARITAL STATUS: Married
CHILDREN: Three (F Ahmed (Ms), F Ahmed (Mr), F Ahmed (Master))
COLLEGE: Polytechnic of Central London
ACADEMIC QUALIFICATIONS: BA Hons. Social Science
PROFESSIONAL QUALIFICATIONS: Lecturer (FE College)
DIRECTORSHIPS: Six organisations including the NHS Trust
MEMBERSHIPS: Six organisations including Labour Party
HOBBIES AND INTERESTS: Discussions, travelling
PERSONAL PROFILE: I am an elected councillor and deputy leader of Tower Hamlets council. I have worked with London wide organisations, local and national organisations to promote interests of Asian communities and improve their position in this society. I am a committed politican to address local problems and raise issues of national importance that could affect the Asian community in Britain today.

THE RT. HON. BARONESS UDDIN (WORKING PEER)

House of Lords,

PLACE OF BIRTH: Bangladesh, 17.7.59
MARITAL STATUS: Married
CHILDREN: Five (Shamim, Sabid, Shareef, Tasneem, Shakeeb)
COLLEGE: North London University
MEMBERSHIPS: Commonwealth Parliamentary Association, Inter Parliamentary Union. All Party on Children-Health, Education and Employment
HOBBIES AND INTERESTS: Family, community work, International affairs, women, politics
PERSONAL PROFILE: Involved in community work in Tower Hamlets in the areas of women, health, education, race relations and disability issues. International affairs. Councillor for Wapping eight years, deputy leader of Tower Hamlets Council for two years.
NOMINATED BY: The Runnymede Trust, Sukhvinder Stubbs

MISS JULI BEGUM UDDIN (SCHOOLGIRL)

PLACE OF BIRTH: London, 12.7.86
COLLEGE: Mulberry School for Girls
HONOURS/AWARDS: PE, swimming
HOBBIES AND INTERESTS: Rounders, basketball, watching TV
PERSONAL PROFILE: My name is Juli I am 12 years old and I am a student in Mulberry School. I enjoyed helping to research the Who's Who 1999.

MR MOHAMMED FOIZ UDDIN
(COMMUNITY DEVELOPMENT OFFICER)

Community Development Officer, Birmingham City Council, 18 Gainsborough Road, Great Barr, Birmingham, B421NA

PLACE OF BIRTH: Bangladesh, 5.5.62
MARITAL STATUS: Married
CHILDREN: One (Sujat)
COLLEGE: Chittagong University, Dhaka University
ACADEMIC QUALIFICATIONS: B Com M.Com
PROFESSIONAL QUALIFICATIONS: Diploma in Banking
DIRECTORSHIPS: LEA School Governor
MEMBERSHIPS: Member of European Forum UNISON, active member of the Labour Party, patron of National Training Academy in Bangladesh
HOBBIES AND INTERESTS: Enjoy setting up new ideas, themes, badminton, chess, Bengali music
PERSONAL PROFILE: Born and brought up in Sylhet in Bangladesh, I received my early education in the village. I am a graduate of the universities of Chittagong and Dhaka. I served as a bank official for six years. Migrated to the UK in mid-1990's and experienced first hand the shortage of community workers. I started my career as a voluntary community worker and later on became the first umbrella group community development officer for Birmingham City Council.

MR ANSAR AHMED ULLAH (COMMUNITY WORKER)

Nirmul Committee, London Borough of Tower Hamlets, Mulberry Place, 5 Clove Crescent, London, E14 2BG

PLACE OF BIRTH: Alampur
MARITAL STATUS: Married
CHILDREN: One (Taramon Chandona Yasmin)
HOBBIES AND INTERESTS: Rave music
PERSONAL PROFILE: Anti racist campaigner. Community worker in the field of social and cultural education.

MR BALBIR SINGH UPPAL JP (CHAIRMAN)

Manager, Sikh Leisure Centre, Prospect Street, Springwood, Huddersfield, HD1 2NX

PLACE OF BIRTH: India, 4.8.56
MARITAL STATUS: Married
CHILDREN: Two (Manraj, Balraj)
COLLEGE: Huddersfield Polytechnic
ACADEMIC QUALIFICATIONS: Higher National Diploma in Electrical & Electronic Engineering
PROFESSIONAL QUALIFICATIONS: Associate of the Institute of Electrical Engineers
DIRECTORSHIPS: Sadeh Lok Housing Association. Huddersfield Pride Ltd.
MEMBERSHIPS: Institute of Electrical Engineers. Magistrates Association
HONOURS/AWARDS: 'CRE' Bursary to study in US, Justice of the Peace
HOBBIES AND INTERESTS: Glider pilot, enjoy football, swimming
PERSONAL PROFILE: Came to the UK in 1962. Qualified in engineering. Managed a retail business for six years, also managed the Indian Workers Association of Huddersfield for five years. Set-up three major projects in Huddersfield: Ray Street Enterprise Centre; Sadeh Lok Housing Association and Sikh Leisure Centre. Current chairman of Sadeh Lok Housing Association since 1997. Appointed Justice of the Peace in 1989.

MR PARAMJIT UPPAL (MANAGEMENT CONSULTANT)

Director, Arthur Anderson Business Consulting, 16A Malvern Road, Maidenhead, SL6 7RH

PLACE OF BIRTH: India, 8.8.67
MARITAL STATUS: Married
CHILDREN: Two (Lakhita, Paven)
COLLEGE: University of Manchester
ACADEMIC QUALIFICATIONS: 1st Class Honours BSc and Master of Engineering
PROFESSIONAL QUALIFICATIONS: Chartered Accountant
DIRECTORSHIPS: The PHL Partnership Ltd
MEMBERSHIPS: British Computer Society
HONOURS/AWARDS: BT Research Scholorship
HOBBIES AND INTERESTS: Golf, travel, Punjabi culture, children, IT
EMAIL: puppal@btinternat.com
WEB SITE: www.phlpartnership.com
PERSONAL PROFILE: Emigrated to England aged eight. Started school, not yet speaking any English, left with best grades. Finally obtaining first class honours. Started career with Anderson Consulting. Now a director with Arthur Anderson Business Consulting. At the same time running a marriage matchmaking service with my wife for Punjabi people.
NOMINATED BY: Harbinder K Uppal

> 'Obtained a first class honours degree. Started career with Anderson Consulting. Now a director with Arthur Anderson Business Consulting. At the same time running a marriage match-making service with my wife for Punjabi people'

PARAMJIT UPPAL

An exciting new weekly supplement dedicated to Black and Asian public sector professionals nationwide.

Are you keen to keep abreast of current issues in the public sector perspective?
Looking for a new job that matches your professional skills and qualifications?
If the answer is yes, then look no further than Public Sector.
Every week we bring you topical news and opinions from all sections of the public sector
from nursing to teaching, from social work to volunteering.

Public Sector, free every week with Asian Times & Caribbean Times

For subscription information contact: EMG, 1st Floor,
148 Cambridge Heath Road, London E1 5QJ Telephone 0171 702 8012 and ask for Monique or Yvonne

PROF PANKAJ VADGAMA (Doctor)

Prof Clinical Biochemistry, University of Manchester, 4 The Sidings, Worsley, Manchester, M28 2QD

PLACE OF BIRTH: Kenya, 16.2.48
MARITAL STATUS: Married
CHILDREN: Three (Reena, Rooshin, Preeya)
COLLEGE: Newcastle-upon-Tyne
ACADEMIC QUALIFICATIONS: MBBS, BSc (1), PhD
PROFESSIONAL QUALIFICATIONS: FRCPath, C Chem, FRSC
MEMBERSHIPS: Association Clinical
Biochemists, EPSRC Medical Engineering College 1994
HONOURS/AWARDS: IEE Education Science and Educational Journal Prize 1994
HOBBIES AND INTERESTS: Reading, walking
PERSONAL PROFILE: Qualified in medicine 1971, after house jobs was demonstrator in histopathology and took up a registrar appointment in clinical biochemistry at the Royal Victoria Infirmary Newcastle. Appointed MRC Training Fellow 1977-80, after a period in the NHS became Director of Biosensor Group of Newcastle University. Research interests: biochemical monitoring, biomaterials and biosensors.

DR VINOD VASHRAM VADHER (Electrical Engineering)

Senior Lecturer, Loughborough University, Ashby Road, Loughborough, LE11 3TU

PLACE OF BIRTH: Kenya, 6.2.50
MARITAL STATUS: Married
CHILDREN: Two (Nilesh, Sailesh)
COLLEGE: Aston, Imperial, Loughborough
ACADEMIC QUALIFICATIONS: BSc 1st Class Hons, M Phil, DIC, PhD, MBA
PROFESSIONAL QUALIFICATIONS: Chartered Electrical & Mechanical Engineer
MEMBERSHIPS: MIEE, MIMECHE, MIEEE, Eur Ing, C Eng
HONOURS/AWARDS: IEE prize for highest marks in BSc exams-University of Aston
HOBBIES AND INTERESTS: Classical music, movies, history, philosophy, science
EMAIL: v.v.vadher@lboro.ac.uk
PERSONAL PROFILE: Arrived in UK in June 1967 from Kenya. I did my studies at Loughborough Tech College, Aston University, Imperial College and Loughborough University. I hope to continue to progress in research, publications and teaching.
NOMINATED BY: Veronica King, Loughborough University

MR KISHOR VADHIA (Shoe Repairer)

Self Employed, 133 Cole Valley Road, Hall Green, Birmingham, B28 0DG

PLACE OF BIRTH: Kenya, 4.6.54
MARITAL STATUS: Married
CHILDREN: Three (Manish, Chetan, Bhavik)
HONOURS/AWARDS: One award from small organisation for charitable work
HOBBIES AND INTERESTS: Charity work, helping others, community work
PERSONAL PROFILE: Vice president of Shree Jensari Conetti Mandal Birmingham for the last ten years, PRO Jansari Organisation UK.
Substantial contribution in the community by organising many charity shows in the UK. Founded a charity group called 'Aadhunik' with six other fine artists. Donations received are sent to India for the sole benefit of destitute people, homeless widows, children and stray animals. Most outstanding achievement was to build five houses for homeless leprosy families in Delhi.
NOMINATED BY: Chandrakant Jansari

DR ARUN VAIDYANATHAN (Research Scientist)

Industrial Chemist, 10 The Linx, Bletchley, Milton Keynes, MK3 6JN

PLACE OF BIRTH: India, 2.5.38
MARITAL STATUS: Married
CHILDREN: Three (Mina, Rajini, Anjali)
ACADEMIC QUALIFICATIONS: BSc (Madras), BScTech (Bombay), MSc Tech (Bombay)
PROFESSIONAL QUALIFICATIONS: PhD (Leeds), BA (Open), PG. Dip. IT (De Montford) FETC (City & Guilds) PG Dip. Pollution Control, CNAA
MEMBERSHIPS: Fellow of the Chemical Society
HONOURS/AWARDS: Leeds University Studentship to do PhD (1966-68)
HOBBIES AND INTERESTS: Cricket, badminton, stamp collection
PERSONAL PROFILE: First Asian school governor in Milton Keynes (1980); chairperson of Milton Keynes CRE (1985); executive member of Milton Keynes Police Committee (1982); lay visitor to Milton Keynes police station. Worked as research fellow at the Open University and author of several research papers in chemistry. Published articles on 'Bhopal Chemical Disaster', 'Brandt Commission' in New Scientist. Regular contributor to Eastern Eye and Asian Voice.
NOMINATED BY: H Patel

MR BABAR VAQAS (Student Doctor)

13 Argyll Place, Barnwood, Gloucester, GL2 0QS

PLACE OF BIRTH: Huddersfield, 21.11.78
MARITAL STATUS: Single
COLLEGE: University of Bristol
ACADEMIC QUALIFICATIONS: GCSE's 10 A*s, A-Levels, 4 A's
MEMBERSHIPS: BMA
HONOURS/AWARDS: R. Wofinden prize for excellent performance in 1st year exams at university
HOBBIES AND INTERESTS: Tennis, reading, religion, community work
PERSONAL PROFILE: Achieved all 10 A* at GCSE (1995), highest exam score ever at one of the best schools (Grammar) in the South West (est 1666), 4 A's at A-Level and gained first position and prize in the first year of medicine at Bristol University. Will complete Neuroscience BSc in one year and plan to become a neuro surgeon.
NOMINATED BY: Mrs Nasreen Akhtar

MR SHAILESH VARA (Solicitor)

Cameron McKenna, Mitre House, 160 Aldersgate Street, London, EG1A 4DD

PLACE OF BIRTH: Uganda
MARITAL STATUS: Single
COLLEGE: Brunel University
ACADEMIC QUALIFICATIONS: LL.B
DIRECTORSHIPS: Vice-president Small Business Bureau
HOBBIES AND INTERESTS: Cricket, Tae Kwondo (Black Belt), travel
PERSONAL PROFILE: Conservative parliamentary candidate in General Election 1997. Executive committee Association of Conservative Parliamentary Candidates 1998. Executive committee Society of Conservative Lawyers 1991. Previously worked in Hong Kong as business consultant to US companies. Regular speaker on radio, television, conferences and corporate training seminars. Cricket-played for England in Legal Rest of the World versus Legal India in New Delhi, Nov 1997.

INDIRA VARMA (Actress)

Marina Martin Associates,

PLACE OF BIRTH: Bath, 27.9.73
COLLEGE: RADA
PROFESSIONAL QUALIFICATIONS: Piano grade 7, Oboe grade 5, French (bi-lingual), German A-Level. Fencing proficiency certificate. Skiing and ballet
MEMBERSHIPS: Regent's Park Zoo, Equity and Greenpeace
HOBBIES AND INTERESTS: Piano, food, embroidery, skiing, swimming, glass blowing
PERSONAL PROFILE: Theatre, film and television work includes 'Othello' (Bianca), 'As You Like It' (Phoebe), 'House of Bernarda Alba' (Bernada), 'Kama Sutra' (co-lead), 'Phoenix' (Maneet). 'Psychos' (Martine) and 'The Grove' (Emma).

MR NAVIN VARMA (Hotelier-Developer)

Owner-Director, NKV Property Holdings, 9 Royal Terrace, Edinburgh, Scotland, EH7 5AB

PLACE OF BIRTH: Kenya, 3.3.56
MARITAL STATUS: Married
CHILDREN: One (Natasha)
HOBBIES AND INTERESTS: Motor racing, football
EMAIL: frederickhouse@ednet.co.uk
PERSONAL PROFILE: Started in 1990. Since then built and operated five hotels. Sold two, one to Stakis Hotels and one to private company. Expanded into retail parks near Glasgow in 1997. New venture for 1999, bought 16 self catering apartments. Assets worth £8.5 million. Recently featured on Asianet TV. More success in Edinburgh with the new parliament.

'Conservative parliamentary candidate in General Election 1997. Executive committee Association of Conservative Parliamentary Candidates 1998'

SHAILESH VARA

MRS THANRAM RAMA VARMA (DOCTOR)

Reader-Assist Professor, St Anthony's Hospital, No 3 Wood Cote Drive, Purley, CR8 3PD

PLACE OF BIRTH: India, 2.10.38
MARITAL STATUS: Married
CHILDREN: Two (Meena, Sunil)
COLLEGE: Madras, India
ACADEMIC QUALIFICATIONS: FRCOG, FRCS, PhD-London
PROFESSIONAL QUALIFICATIONS: Medical Doctor FRCS, FRCOG, PhD
DIRECTORSHIPS: Was Clinical Director, Assisted Conception Unit-St George's Hospital
MEMBERSHIPS: Royal College of Obstetrics. Royal College of Surgeons and Gynaecology. Committees for Equal Opportunities for women and ethnic minorities in the national health.
HONOURS/AWARDS: Edinburgh several awards were given
HOBBIES AND INTERESTS: Music, travelling, classical dancing
PERSONAL PROFILE: I was the first female surgeon (O&G) appointed in a large medical school as consultant and senior lecturer to St Georges Medical School. I was first woman doctor to be a member of the Board of Obstetrics and Gynaecology in the University of London. First female doctor from the ethnic minority who took St George's Hospital before the Industrial Tribunal-twice-and won both cases. Have been invited to Madras to setup a medical centre of excellence for women and children.

MR KEITH VAZ MP (BARRISTER)

Parliamentary Secretary, House Of Commons, Westminster, London, SW1A 0AA

PLACE OF BIRTH: Yemen, 26.11.56
MARITAL STATUS: Married
CHILDREN: Two (Luke, Anjali)
COLLEGE: Cambridge University
PROFESSIONAL QUALIFICATIONS: Barrister
HONOURS/AWARDS: Asian of the Year 1988-89
PERSONAL PROFILE: Elected MP for Leicester East in 1987 the first Asian in 50 years to be in parliament. Shadow Minister for recreation and planning 1992-97; Parliamentary Private Secretary to the Attorney-General since 1997. Governor, Commonwealth Institute; Hon. president Asian Business Network; Hon. president National Organisation of Asian Businesses.

CLLR MERLYN VAZ (COUNCILLOR)

Chair-Senior Citizens Forum, Leicester City Council, 153 Scraptoft Lane, Leicester, LE5 2FF

PLACE OF BIRTH: India, 29.8.29
CHILDREN: Three (Keith Vaz, Valerie Vaz, Penny McConnell)
COLLEGE: Sidney Webb College
PROFESSIONAL QUALIFICATIONS: Teachers
PERSONAL PROFILE: First Asian woman councillor in the history of Leicester city; elected in Charnwood, Leicester in 1989; re-elected 1991 and 1994; Chair, Property Services Committee of Leicester City Council 1991-1994; Chair, Senior Citizens Committee 1994. Trustee, Sahara Trust, Author ' The Olympians'.

MS VALERIE CAROL MARIAN VAZ (LAWYER)

65 Main Street, Bushby, Leicester, LE7 9PL

PLACE OF BIRTH: Yemen, 7.12.54
MARITAL STATUS: Married
CHILDREN: One (Liberty India Rose)
COLLEGE: London University
ACADEMIC QUALIFICATIONS: BSc Hons 2:1 (Main field Biochemistry)
PROFESSIONAL QUALIFICATIONS: Common professional examination solicitors, final exam (Law).
MEMBERSHIPS: Labour Party; SERA; Law Society; Equity Association of Women Solicitors
HOBBIES AND INTERESTS: Gardening, photography, piano, guitar
EMAIL: valerievaz@libertyindiarose
PERSONAL PROFILE: Qualified as solicitor 1984; Founded Townsend Vaz Solicitors. Deputy district judge 1996. Presenter / Interview BBC TV Network East. School governor. Member Ealing Health Authority (three years). Councillor London Borough of Ealing 1986-90; Deputy leader 1988. Parliamentary candidate general election 1987 Twickenham candidate European Elections 1999. Columnist-Eastern Eye.

DR GUDUGUNTLA VENKATESHAM (DOCTOR)

General Practitioner, Chiswick Health Centre, Fishers Lane, Chiswick, W4 1RX

PLACE OF BIRTH: India, 1.11.48
MARITAL STATUS: Married
CHILDREN: Two (Preethi,Vinai Chandra)
COLLEGE: Osmania
ACADEMIC QUALIFICATIONS: MBBS, JCPTGP, MFFP
MEMBERSHIPS: BMA, ODA
HOBBIES AND INTERESTS: Stamp collection
PERSONAL PROFILE: Arrived UK 1974, member of BMA and ODA since 1974, treasurer ODA, N W Thames 1989-92, treasurer Osmania Medical Graduates Association in UK 1991-95; fundraising secretary Sri Venkateshwara (Balaji) Temple of UK since 1995 and permanent trustee 1998.

DR SRIRAMA S VENUGOPAL OBE (DOCTOR)

Principal GP, Overseas Doctors Assoc. UK, 24 Melville Road, Edgbaston, Birmingham, B16 9JT

PLACE OF BIRTH: India, 14.5.33
MARITAL STATUS: Married
CHILDREN: Two (Arun, Anu)
COLLEGE: Osmania Hyderabad
ACADEMIC QUALIFICATIONS: BSc, MBBS, DMRD, FRCGP, DRMD
PROFESSIONAL QUALIFICATIONS: FRCGP, FRIPHH, FRSH, MFPHM, FRSM
DIRECTORSHIPS: Overseas Doctors News Review
MEMBERSHIPS: ODA, BMA, GMC, RCGP, Royal Society Medicine
HONOURS/AWARDS: OBE
HOBBIES AND INTERESTS: Music, gardening
PERSONAL PROFILE: GP Principal for 34 years. Former president Overseas Doctors Association, Member of GMC and other Royal Colleges. Worked to eliminate racism in medical profession. Worked for migrants in EU.

MR DEEPAK VERMA (ACTOR)

Playwright, 63 Cassland Road, Hackney, London, E9 7AL

PLACE OF BIRTH: India
MARITAL STATUS: Single
COLLEGE: Central School of Drama
ACADEMIC QUALIFICATIONS: Speech and Drama Graduate
DIRECTORSHIPS: Pukka Nasha Ltd
HONOURS/AWARDS: Prince of Wales Trust Role Model/Asian of the Year 1995
HOBBIES AND INTERESTS: Theatre, reading, music production, travelling
PERSONAL PROFILE: First Asian to do opera in Covent Garden. Acted in 'Eastenders' for five and a half years as non-stereotype Asian. Acted, directed and written plays. Have own music company. Speak, read and write Punjabi. Also sings and is recording a musical album.
NOMINATED BY: R K Verma

MR JATINDER VERMA (ARTISTIC DIRECTOR)

Tara Arts, 356 Garratt Lane, London, SW18 4ES

PLACE OF BIRTH: Tanzania, 17.7.54
COLLEGE: York University, Sussex University
ACADEMIC QUALIFICATIONS: BA, MA History
HONOURS/AWARDS: 1990 Time Out Special Award for Outstanding Contribution to London Theatre and Bonding of British, European and Asian Cultures
EMAIL: jatinder@tara-arts.com
PERSONAL PROFILE: Co-founder and artistic director of Tara Arts, which has since 1977 been the leading Asian theatre company in the UK. Jatinder has directed, written and adapted most of Tara's productions, which have ranged from contemporary plays to the classics of the world stage. He is also a regular contributor to UK radio and TV (BBC World Service, BBC Open University) and is often called upon as a specialist cultural commentator by the media. Jatinder has also been part of the Poverty Commission set up by CHANNEL 4.

'First Asian to do opera in Covent Garden. Acted in 'Eastenders' for five and a half years as non-stereotype Asian. Acted, directed and written plays'

DEEPAK VERMA

CLLR MEHAR VERMA (Councillor)

County Councillor, City & County of Swansea, 22 Glynderwen Close, Sketty, Swansea, SA2 8EQ

PLACE OF BIRTH: India, 15.8.31
MARITAL STATUS: Married
CHILDREN: Two (Mohinder, Dhirendra)
COLLEGE: Punjab
ACADEMIC QUALIFICATIONS: MA, M.ED, AFBPS's
PROFESSIONAL QUALIFICATIONS: MA, M.ED and AFBPS's
HOBBIES AND INTERESTS: Current affairs, gardening, yoga
PERSONAL PROFILE: County councillor since May 89. Founder chairman Indian Society SW Wales. Trustee Swansea Council of Voluntary Services. Member of Governors University of Wales Swansea. Board Member Swansea Local Health Group. Chairman Quality Assurance Council of Education.

MRS RAMESH VERMA (Teacher)

Project Manager, EKTA Project, Neighbourhood Care Project, 60 Roll Gardens, Gants Hill, Ilford, IG2 6TW

PLACE OF BIRTH: Tanzania, 17.7.42
MARITAL STATUS: Widow
CHILDREN: Two (Deepak, Nagesh)
COLLEGE: Teachers College, Dar-es-Salam
ACADEMIC QUALIFICATIONS: HSc, BEd
PROFESSIONAL QUALIFICATIONS: Teachers Training
HONOURS/AWARDS: National Caring Awards
HOBBIES AND INTERESTS: Reading, gardening, sewing, travelling, volunteering
PERSONAL PROFILE: Worked for Asian elders and their carers for 20 years. Campaigned for their rights in England and Europe. Worked closely with statutory agencies to provide culturally and religiously sensitive services. Raised awareness among Asian elders to take up services provided. Reduced their isolation by befriending them.
NOMINATED BY: ETKA Project and Jay Rashid

MISS VEENA VERMA (Social Worker)

115 West End Road, Southall, UB1 1JF

PLACE OF BIRTH: India, 2.10.60
MARITAL STATUS: Single
COLLEGE: Brunel University
ACADEMIC QUALIFICATIONS: BA. BEd, Dip in Social Work
HOBBIES AND INTERESTS: Writing short stories, poetry
PERSONAL PROFILE: Punjabi writer. A short storybook published in 1994. One book for poetry and another for short stories under publication . I write about women, especially Asian. I am well known in the society for my daring writings.

MRS NALINI VIBHUTI (Business Manager)

Kaveri Communications, Nandi Hill, Longwood, Walderslade, Chatham, ME5 9JG

PLACE OF BIRTH: India, 5.10.52
MARITAL STATUS: Married
CHILDREN: Two (Rashmi, Mayur)
COLLEGE: Karnataka University
ACADEMIC QUALIFICATIONS: MA India
DIRECTORSHIPS: Kannala Balaga UK,
MEMBERSHIPS: Mid Kent Conservative Association
HOBBIES AND INTERESTS: Painting, decorating, entertaining, travel
PERSONAL PROFILE: Patron and promoter of Vimochana Charity for destitute children in India. Organise social and cultural gatherings. Promote artists from India to increase awareness of Indian culture.

'Patron and promoter of Vimochana Charity for destitute children in India. Organise social and cultural gatherings. Promote artists from India to increase awareness of Indian culture'

NALINI VIBHUTI

DR RAVI VIBHUTI (Medical Practitioner)

The Churchill Clinic, 94 Churchill Avenue, Chatham, ME5 9JG

PLACE OF BIRTH: India, 9.4.49
MARITAL STATUS: Married
CHILDREN: Two (Rashmi, Mayur)
COLLEGE: Karnataka Medical College, College Hubli India.
PROFESSIONAL QUALIFICATIONS: MBBS
MEMBERSHIPS: BMA, Kannala Balaga UK, Mid Kent Conservative Association
HOBBIES AND INTERESTS: Travel, reading, meeting people
PERSONAL PROFILE: Founder secretary of Kannala Balaga of UK. Patron and promoter of Vimochana Charity for destitute children in Karnataka India. Secretary of British Medical Association, Dartford, Gravesend and Medway Division. Patron of Mid Kent Conservative Association.

KALAMANDALAM K N VIJAYAKUMAR
(Kathakali Actor)

Director, Kala Chethena Kathakali Company, 1 Holland Road, Woolstone, Southampton, SO19 9SW

PLACE OF BIRTH: India, 1.10.57
MARITAL STATUS: Married
CHILDREN: One (Billy)
COLLEGE: Kerala Kalamandalam
ACADEMIC QUALIFICATIONS: Kalamandalam Diploma and Post Graduate
PROFESSIONAL QUALIFICATIONS: Kathakali Actor from Kerala Kalamandalam
DIRECTORSHIPS: Kala Chethena Kathakali Company
HONOURS/AWARDS: Central Government of India Award
HOBBIES AND INTERESTS: Travel, other cultures, gardening
PERSONAL PROFILE: I have performed internationally since 1982 with the Kerala Kalamandalam and as an independent artist. Co-founded the Kala Chethena Kathakali Company in 1987 and have brought Kathakali to thousands of people in the UK, Europe, Brazil, Indonesia and Scandinavia. I am committed to developing any awareness of Kathakali.
NOMINATED BY: Sharon Aitkin

MR KANAPATHIPILLAI VIJAYARATNAM
(Engineering Consultant)

Director, Rosebury Consulting Ltd,

PLACE OF BIRTH: Analaitivu, 10.5.48
MARITAL STATUS: Married
COLLEGE: Imperial College, London
ACADEMICS QUALIFICATIONS: M Eng, MSc (London), DIC, BSc (Eng) Hons
PROFESSIONAL QUALIFICATIONS: MICE, MASCE, MCIWEM, MIWA, C Eng, MIHA, MIWRA, MSRA, MICOSE, MIEEE
HONOURS/AWARDS: Scholarship by UK Govt (1976), NATO Adv Study Institute (81)
HOBBIES AND INTERESTS: Golf, cricket, writing, reading, fine arts, travel, broader education of engineers
EMAIL: cwee12345@aol.com
WEB SITE: www.vijayaratnam.com
PERSONAL PROFILE: 25 years worldwide experience in civil engineering, water and environmental engineering. Expertise as project manager, project team leader, principal engineer and resident engineer for multi-disciplinary engineering and management. Plan, study, design construction and commissioning of large and small engineering projects. Specialising in environmental based projects

PARMINDER VIR (Producer)

Formation Films, PO Box 3635, Harlesden, London, NW10 5BW

DATE OF BIRTH: 16.2.55
MARITAL STATUS: Married
CHILDREN: Two (Mala, Anyon)
DIRECTORSHIPS: Formation Films Ltd
MEMBERSHIPS: Tricycle Theatre, Board of Directors, Cultural Diversity, Arts Council of England, Women in Film and Television Board.
PERSONAL PROFILE: Parminder Vir is an independent film and television producer. Her first feature film was 'Babymother' made for Channel Four Film Four. She is also working for Carlton Television as consultant to the director of programmes, developing a strategy for mainstreaming Black and Asian talent on and behind the screen.
NOMINATED BY: Ansel wong

DR BAL SINGH VIRDEE (SENIOR LECTURER)

Senior Lecturer, University of North London, 166-220 Holloway Road, London, N7 8DB

PLACE OF BIRTH: Uganda, 12.5.63
MARITAL STATUS: Married
COLLEGE: University of Leeds
ACADEMIC QUALIFICATIONS: BSc Hons, MPhil, PhD
PROFESSIONAL QUALIFICATIONS: C Eng
MEMBERSHIPS: MIEE, New York Academy of Sciences
HOBBIES AND INTERESTS: Reading, travelling, jogging, making exotic foods
PERSONAL PROFILE: Dr Virdee specialises in the area of high frequency wireless communications. He has done extensive research and development work in this area and hence has published several scientific papers in this area. He has been invited to chair international conferences overseas. He enjoys travelling and in particular meeting different people and experiencing different cultures. He also enjoys having a challenging outlook on life.
NOMINATED BY: Dr R Ramnarine, University of North London

MANJEET SINGH VIRDEE (LIGHTING DESIGN ENGINEER)

Lighting Design Engineer, Leicester City Council, 5 The Common, Evington, Leicester, LE5 6EA

PLACE OF BIRTH: Kenya, 30.12.53
MARITAL STATUS: Married
CHILDREN: Three (Gurpal, Mandeep, Sukhjit)
COLLEGE: Loughborough University, De Montfort University
ACADEMIC QUALIFICATIONS: HNC in Electrical and Electronic Engineering
MEMBERSHIPS: The Institute of Lighting Engineers
HOBBIES AND INTERESTS: Football, keep fit activities
EMAIL: mvirdee@freeserve.com
PERSONAL PROFILE: I am 45 years of age married with three children ages 16, 14 and 13. My work in the Asian community has been with the under -10's to under- 16's football players, in encouraging youngsters to compete at a higher level and arrange trials at professional clubs. I am currently the youth secretary for Khalsa Football Federation UK and chairman of GNG FC Leicester.

MS HARVEY VIRDI (ACTRESS)

LWA, 18 Elliott Square, London, NW3 3SU

PERSONAL PROFILE: Trained at the Academy Drama School, various experience, including theatre, TV, film and radio. Experienced in devising and starring on writing / directing.

MR SURJIT SINGH VIRDI (PROJECT OFFICER)

Sikh Community & Youth Service, 348 Soho Road, Handsworth, Birmingham, B21 9QL

PLACE OF BIRTH: Birmingham, 10.6.68
MARITAL STATUS: Single
COLLEGE: UCE Birmingham
ACADEMIC QUALIFICATIONS: BSc in Computing
PROFESSIONAL QUALIFICATIONS: C&G 7307 in Adult Education
MEMBERSHIPS: BNC TCCC-BEBI Nanaki Charitable Trust Leisure and Learning Centre
HONOURS/AWARDS: Student of the Year award
HOBBIES AND INTERESTS: Travel, computing, teaching
EMAIL: surjitvirdi@yahoo.com
PERSONAL PROFILE: Surjit has secured numerous funds for community based projects which have included, educational funds for undergraduates. He secured a large amount of funds and resources for three years from the National Lottery in just four months of being in his present post. He appreciates life and what the world has to offer.
NOMINATED BY: Bimla Lyall

MR HARDISH VIRK (WRITER-DIRECTOR-ACTOR)

Freelance Arts Practitioner, Multi Arts Nation Ltd, 5 Syndnall Fields, Coventry, CV6 6NQ

PLACE OF BIRTH: Coventry, 9.3.71
MARITAL STATUS: Single
COLLEGE: Coventry University
ACADEMIC QUALIFICATIONS: 7 O-Levels, 2 A-Levels
DIRECTORSHIPS: Multi Arts Nation Theatre
HOBBIES AND INTERESTS: Writing, travelling, reading, meeting new people, films, music
EMAIL: hvirk@aol.com.uk
PERSONAL PROFILE: Hardish Virk has worked in mainstream and community arts; dance, music and theatre, as a writer, director and actor. He has also been in two Hollywood movies. Hardish has facilitated many community arts projects, working with young people and South Asian people. He is also a DJ.
NOMINATED BY: Paven Virk

MISS JASVIR VIRK (WRITER-RADIO PRESENTER)

PLACE OF BIRTH: Pakistan, 1.2.48
MARITAL STATUS: Single
CHILDREN: Three (Hardish, Paven, Manjinder)
ACADEMIC QUALIFICATIONS: Arts Diploma
HOBBIES AND INTERESTS: Indian dance, performing music, keeping fit, writing, reading, travelling
PERSONAL PROFILE: Jasvir Virk is a writer, radio presenter and performer. She has written three books; two books depicting lives of Asian women in England and her autobiography. She presents a Panjabi show on Radio XL. Jasvir has also participated in national theatre and reading shows.
NOMINATED BY: Hardish Virk

MS LAKHBIR VIRK (UNIVERSITY DIRECTOR)

Director, Leeds Metropolitan University, Fairfax Hall, Beckett Park, Leeds, LS1 3QS

PLACE OF BIRTH: India, 27.1.60
MARITAL STATUS: Divorced
COLLEGE: University College Cardiff
ACADEMIC QUALIFICATIONS: BA Hons English, MBA
DIRECTORSHIPS: KAAMYABI, KCETA, Centre for Race, Culture and Education.
HOBBIES AND INTERESTS: Literature, history, art, cinema, theology
PERSONAL PROFILE: Came to Britain after completing secondary schooling. Trained as a teacher. Have worked extensively in statutory and voluntary sectors in areas of anti racism and black feminism. More recently have focused primarily upon race and education-higher education, the schools sector and community education. Have extensive network of educationships across Europe dedicated to combating racism and xenophobia through education.
NOMINATED BY: Emma Leech

MISS MANJINDER VIRK (ACTRESS-DANCER)

Artistic Director/Performer, Pangran Dance Theatre, Principal Artistes Agency, 4 Paddington Street, Marylebone, London, W1M 3LA

PLACE OF BIRTH: Coventry, 5.11.73
MARITAL STATUS: Single
COLLEGE: De Montfort University
ACADEMIC QUALIFICATIONS: BTec in Performing Arts, BA Hons in Performing Arts
MEMBERSHIPS: Equity
HOBBIES AND INTERESTS: Music (guitar), martial arts, travelling, writing
EMAIL: manjinderv@hotmail.com
PERSONAL PROFILE: Working professionally in the arts for six years. Artistic director of 'Pangran Dance Theatre'. Directed three productions-'Tanz', 'Exploration of loss' and 'Fear of Glass'. Toured nationally and internationally. Performed with several theatre companies including: Red Ladder, Roundabout, Proper Job, Multi Arts Nation, Women in Theatre and Belgrave Theatre.
NOMINATED BY: Jasvir Virk

'Dr Virdee specialises in the area of high frequency wireless communications. He has done extensive research and development work in this area and hence has published several scientific papers in this area'

DR BAL SINGH VIRDEE

MISS PAVEN VIRK (ACTRESS)

Writer-Director, Watermans Arts Centre, Sandra Boyce Management, 1 Kingsway House, Albion Road, London, N16 0TA

PLACE OF BIRTH: Leicester, 10.12.74
MARITAL STATUS: Single
COLLEGE: Coventry University of Performing Arts
PERSONAL PROFILE: Actress, writer and artistic director of her own theatre company 'Second Generation'. Plays produced include 'Girlie Talk', 'Boy meets Girl'. Directing credits include 'Manny and Jake' (Belgrade Theatre), 'Jubilee Park' (A devised musical), 'Dear Mary' (A Radio Play). Acting credits include 'Casualty' BBC1, 'Blazed' C4. Currently touring, 'Dont look at my sister', 'Innit' and 'Arrange That Marriage'
NOMINATED BY: Jasvir Virk

MRS BHARTI VYAS (HOLISTIC BEAUTY THERAPIST)

Propreitor, Bharti Vyas Holistic Therapy & Beauty Salons, Bharti Vyas Enterprises, 24 Chiltern Street, London, W1M 1PF

PLACE OF BIRTH: Kenya, 3.11.43
MARITAL STATUS: Married
CHILDREN: Two (Shailu, Priti)
COLLEGE: Ray Cochrane Beauty College
ACADEMIC QUALIFICATIONS: BABTEC, CIDESCO, Laser Therapy, Magnet Therapy, Semi Permanent Make Up
PROFESSIONAL QUALIFICATIONS: Written two books
DIRECTORSHIPS: Sole Proprietor of two businesses
MEMBERSHIPS: DIP MIAF, MAA, Holistic Therapists
HONOURS/AWARDS: Zest, Now, Harpers and Queen, Top Sante, Marie Clare, Daily Telegraph all noted her as one of Britain's top therapists
HOBBIES AND INTERESTS: Enjoys dancing, swimming, travelling
EMAIL: bhartivyas@aol.com
PERSONAL PROFILE: Bharti has been instrumental and innovative in influencing changes in attitudes to beauty and well being. Practising therapy for 20 years-treating dignitaries and celebrities. The author of two books, her own unique therapy system and she owns two highly successful salons in Mayfair, London. She is extensively featured in the national and International media.

Entrants in the Asians in the Millennium have been nominated for their achievements and contributions. You can nominate someone who deserves to be in the Who's Who of Asian Achievers 2000

Entries are free

Send in your nominations, including name, contact address and telephone number to: Books Division, Ethnic Media Group, 148 Cambridge Heath Road, London E1 5QJ

DR TALIB WARSI (Marketing Director)

Manufacture International Recipe Ready Meals, S&A Foods, Sir Francis Ley Industrial Park, 37 Shaftsbury Street South, Derby, DE23 8YH

PLACE OF BIRTH: India, 1.1.47
MARITAL STATUS: Married
CHILDREN: Two (Sadiq, Abid)
COLLEGE: Prince of Wales
ACADEMIC QUALIFICATIONS: MB, BF
MEMBERSHIPS: Network Derby, St Johns Ambulance
HONOURS/AWARDS: Contributed to winning many awards for company including: British Quality Food & Drink Award-overall winner, 1994,. Food Manufacture Awards-Most Innovative New Product UK,1994,. Derbyshire Innovative Award, 1994. ADAS/Sunday Telegraph Food & Drink Awards-Silver, 1995
HOBBIES AND INTERESTS: Painting, travelling, music
PERSONAL PROFILE: Talib Warsi is a highly creative and dynamic individual. Working closely with his wife, Talib has contributed greatly to the success of S&A Foods. Talib is an ideas driven, 'people person' who is constantly aiming for the next big innovation-be it in food manufacturing or a completely new sector. Other awards received include: East Midlands Competitiveness Awards 1996. NatWest/ Sunday Times Business Awards-Finalist. 1997. Food Processing Awards-Company of the Year-Runner up, 1998

MS THUSHANI WEERASEKERA (Actress)

Actorum Ltd, 3rd Floor, 21 Foley Street, London, W1P 7LH

PLACE OF BIRTH: London
MARITAL STATUS: Single
COLLEGE: University of London
ACADEMIC QUALIFICATIONS: Animal Physiology BSc
PERSONAL PROFILE: Theatre includes: 'Suppliants' (The Gate Theatre). 'How high is up?' SLAP (Crucible Studio, Sheffield) Television includes: Casualty, Network East (BBC TV). Film includes: 'An arranged irony', 'A circle red' and 'Little England'. I am currently writing my second play.

MR ANDREW WEWAGE-DEP (Commissioned Officer Rtd)

Civil Servant, Ark, 31 Ridge Avenue, Letchworth, SG6 1PR

PLACE OF BIRTH: Sri Lanka, 10.4.33
MARITAL STATUS: Married
CHILDREN: Two (Khushlani, Khushil)
COLLEGE: Trinity College, London
ACADEMIC QUALIFICATIONS: Matriculate
PROFESSIONAL QUALIFICATIONS: LTCL (Teach), LTCL (Perf), ATCL
MEMBERSHIPS: MIPM, Memb STSD, Life Member RAFA
HONOURS/AWARDS: Gold Medals, Trophies, Diplomas, Certificates-For Speech and Drama
HOBBIES AND INTERESTS: Freelance writing, music, theatre
PERSONAL PROFILE: Arrived here in 1975 to join Irvin Great Britain, the parachute manufacturer. Returned to Sri Lanka for a spell in broadcasting with Sri Lanka Broadcasting Corporation. Backed by wife Ratnavalie, studied theory of music, with distinction. Retired finally after 18 meritorious years with the DHSS.

PROF NARIN CHANDRA WICKRAMASINGHE (Professor)

Professor Cardiff University, Cardiff University, 24 Liwynypia Road, Lisrane, Cardiff, CF4 5SY

PLACE OF BIRTH: Sri Lanka, 20.1.39
MARITAL STATUS: Married
CHILDREN: Three (Anil, Kamala, Janaki)
COLLEGE: Cambridge University
ACADEMIC QUALIFICATIONS: ScD, PhD, MA
PROFESSIONAL QUALIFICATIONS: FRAS, FIMA, C Math, FRSA
HONOURS/AWARDS: Numerous International Awards
HOBBIES AND INTERESTS: Photgraphy, poetry, walking
PERSONAL PROFILE: Sri Lankan born astronomer, mathematician and writer. Former Fellow of Jesus College Cambridge. Professor of Applied Mathematics and Astronomy at Cardiff since 1973. Author of over 20 books, co-propounder with Sir Fred Hoyle of the cosmic theory of life. Internationally renowned for contributions to theory of cosmic dust, comets and origin of life.

MRS PRIYA WICKRAMSINGHE (Teacher-Writer)

Part-time Teacher, South Glamorgan Education Authority, 24 Llwynypia Road, Lisvane, Cardiff, CF4 5SY

PLACE OF BIRTH: Sri Lanka, 4.7.45
MARITAL STATUS: Married
CHILDREN: Three (Anil, Kamala, Janaki)
COLLEGE: University of Ceylon. University of Wales, Cardiff
ACADEMIC QUALIFICATIONS: ATCL (pianofork)
PROFESSIONAL QUALIFICATIONS: Further Education Teaching Certificate, Diploma TEFL
HONOURS/AWARDS: Cordon Bleu/Independent Cook of the Year (1993)
HOBBIES AND INTERESTS: Travelling, food, theatre, classical music, walking
EMAIL: xdw20@dial.pipex.com
WEB SITE: dspace.dial.pipex.com/nelum
PERSONAL PROFILE: Sri Lankan born, cookery writer, author of 'Spicy and Delicious', 'Oriental Cookbook' and 'Leith's Book of Indian' and 'Sri Lankan Cooking'. Winner of Cordon Bleu / Independent cookery competition in 1993. A part time teacher and guest lecturer at the Leith's School of Food and Wine. Made several TV appearances on Yorkshire TV 'Farmhouse Kitchens'.

MR KUMARJIT WIJESURIYA (Solicitor-Licensed Conveyor)

Principal, Suriya & Douglas, Ilford Chambers, 11 Chapel Road, Ilford, IG1 2AF

PLACE OF BIRTH: Sri Lanka, 25.7.57
MARITAL STATUS: Married
CHILDREN: Two (Julian, Sophie)
COLLEGE: College of Law
ACADEMIC QUALIFICATIONS: Solicitor
PROFESSIONAL QUALIFICATIONS: Solicitor
DIRECTORSHIPS: Jabhill Properties Ltd, Eden Developments Ltd
MEMBERSHIPS: (MCC) Marylebone Cricket Club, Wentworth Golf Club
HOBBIES AND INTERESTS: Cricket, golf, table tennis, all ball sports, theatre, travelling
PERSONAL PROFILE: Property lawyer employing 13 employees, established 1982. Property/new house developer with NHBC registration employing 20 sub-contractors at any one time. Suffolk Minor County Cricketer since 1994 (capped 1996). MCC full playing member. Capped club cricket conference. Represented player toured South Africa, Australia and Zimbabwe and selector. Captain Finchley Cricket Club.

DR KULSUM WINSHIP (Non-Executive Director)

Medical Practitioner Rtd, 1 Dudley Road, Finchley, London, N3 2QR

PLACE OF BIRTH: Kenya, 26.10.30
MARITAL STATUS: Married
CHILDREN: Two (Anna Zuleika, Julian Abdulla)
COLLEGE: Royal College of Surgeons in Ireland
ACADEMIC QUALIFICATIONS: LRCP & SI
PROFESSIONAL QUALIFICATIONS: FRCPE, FFPHM, FFPM
DIRECTORSHIPS: Non-Executive Director Barnet Healthcare NHS Trust
MEMBERSHIPS: Commonwealth Countries League (NGO) Educational Charity, Member Barnet Breast Cancer Advisory Committee
HONOURS/AWARDS: Fellow of RSA Patron, Barnet Cancer Care
HOBBIES AND INTERESTS: Arts, education, women's health-breast cancer
PERSONAL PROFILE: Came to the UK in 1947. Studied medicine in Eire. Specialised in child health. Joined Department of Health in 1974-first Asian woman appointed as a senior medical officer. Past council member Breast Cancer Care. School governor of school for severely learning disabled pupils.

MR ANSEL WONG (Education)

Vice-Principal, Morley College, The Ajoupa, 68 Buchanan Gardens, Kensal Green, London, NW10 5AE

PLACE OF BIRTH: Trinidad, 4.10.45
MARITAL STATUS: Married
CHILDREN: Six (Sandra, Malaika, Suilin, Kamilah, Khadifa, Cyntac)
COLLEGE: IoE, Hull University, Brunel University
ACADEMIC QUALIFICATIONS: BA Hons, Dip Ed, M.Ed
DIRECTORSHIPS: Open Channels, Notting Hill Carnival Trust, Cultural Co-operation
HOBBIES AND INTERESTS: Theatre, music, arts
EMAIL: ansel.wong@virgin.net

MR ANDREAS YACOUB (POLICE OFFICER)

Positive Action Team, Metropolitan Police Service, 28 Aybrook Street, London, W1M 3JL

PLACE OF BIRTH: Austria, 8.11.61
MARITAL STATUS: Married
COLLEGE: Guildford Technical College
ACADEMIC QUALIFICATIONS: 10 O-Levels, 3 A-Levels
PROFESSIONAL QUALIFICATIONS: 15 years as constable in Met Police
HONOURS/AWARDS: British Diversity Awards 'Gold' for ' Awareness Work' in Ethnic Minority Recruitment
HOBBIES AND INTERESTS: Painting, tennis, squash, football, golf, travelling
PERSONAL PROFILE: Joined the Metropolitan Police in 1983. In 1994 co-founded the Positive Action Team, unique in it's field, dedicated to encouraging and supporting Black and Asian people in joining London's police service. As a result the numbers of ethnic minority officers have doubled in this short time. Want to achieve far more.

MR PRAKASH YADAGUDDE (DANCE TEACHER)

Choreographer, Bharataiya Vidya Bhavan, Flat 1, 18 Barons Court Road, West Kensington, London, W14 9DT

PLACE OF BIRTH: India, 9.5.57
MARITAL STATUS: Married
CHILDREN: Two (Akshay, Avinash)
COLLEGE: Bangalore
ACADEMIC QUALIFICATIONS: BA Diploma in Kathak Dance
PROFESSIONAL QUALIFICATIONS: Bharatanatyam South Indian Classical Dance, Choreography Post graduation
HONOURS/AWARDS: Sringaramani
HOBBIES AND INTERESTS: Football
PERSONAL PROFILE: Sri Prakash Yadagudde is a performer, teacher and choreographer of international repute. He graduated in Bharatanatyam from Bangalore University and has studied dance and choreography under many distinguished dance gurus. Sri Prakash, a fine teacher, has not only trained many students to professional standard but also presented numerous group and solo pieces performing in India, Europe, North America and Australia. Since 1984 teaching at Bhavan Centre.

MRS MAMTA YADAV (EDUCATION ADVISER)

Community Support Officer, South Lancashire Council, 24 Falkland Street, Glasgow, G12 9PR

PLACE OF BIRTH: India, 8.2.58
MARITAL STATUS: Married
CHILDREN: Two (Yesha, Hemang)
ACADEMIC QUALIFICATIONS: MA Sociology, MSc in Cultural Management
PROFESSIONAL QUALIFICATIONS: LL.B. Sangeet Prabhakar in Vocal Music, tabla and Kathak dance
DIRECTORSHIPS: Ex-Centre for Contemporary Arts
MEMBERSHIPS: Scottish Arts Council - Dance & Mime Committee and Ethnic Minorties Arts
HONOURS/AWARDS: First in India in cultural programmes (NCERT) and many others.
HOBBIES AND INTERESTS: Singing, giving concerts, entertaining elderly and handicapped, watching TV, listening to good music, eating
PERSONAL PROFILE: Arrived in UK in 1986, worked as Asian Arts co-ordinator to promote South Asian Arts in education as part of curriculum. Rose to become development officer to promote multicultural anti racist perspective in schools and now working as an adviser in SLC advising on equality issues and other mainstream responsibilities. Performed on national TV/radio in India. Gave innumerable solo concerts all over Scotland. Performed for Channel 4.

'Joined the Metropolitan Police in 1983. In 1994 co-founded the Positive Action Team, unique in it's field, dedicated to encouraging and supporting Black and Asian people in joining London's police service'

ANDREAS YACOUB

PROF PRADEEP YADAV (PROFESSOR)

Professor of Finance, University 0f Strathclyde SIRIF, Curran Street, 100 Cathedral Street, Glasgow, G4 0LN

PLACE OF BIRTH: India, 31.8.53
MARITAL STATUS: Married
CHILDREN: Two (Yesha, Hemang)
COLLEGE: University of Strathclyde
ACADEMIC QUALIFICATIONS: BA Hons Physics, MSc (Physics), MSc (Financial Studies), PhD (Finance)
DIRECTORSHIPS: Director and CEO, Scottish Institute for Research in Investment and Finance (SIRIF)
MEMBERSHIPS: British Accountancy Association, European Finance Association, American Finance Association, International Financial Management Association.
HONOURS/AWARDS: INQUIRE Outstanding Paper Award 1989, Chicago Board of Trade Outstanding Paper Award 1993, ICAEW Academic Fellow 1992
HOBBIES AND INTERESTS: Travelling, writing
EMAIL: p.k.yadav@strath.ac.uk
PERSONAL PROFILE: Pradeep Yadav entered academic finance in 1988 after ten years in senior public sector management positions. He moved from lecturer to senior lecturer to professor in five years, and to head of department in seven years. He has about 35 articles published/presented in leading International finance outlets; has been ICAEW Academic Fellow; and has won outstanding paper awards from INQUIRE and the Chicago Board of Trade. He specialises in futures and options.
NOMINATED BY: University of Strathclyde

MISS MEHMOODA YAHOR (HEALTH CARE WORKER)

BRI Maternity Unit, 33 Ryan Street, West Bowling, Bradford, BD5 7DE

PLACE OF BIRTH: India, 22.10.64
PROFESSIONAL QUALIFICATIONS: NVQ Level 3 Childcare, First Aid
HONOURS/AWARDS: Certificates
HOBBIES AND INTERESTS: Cooking, sewing, films, songs, going out meeting new friends
PERSONAL PROFILE: Ideal partner: Someone loving and caring. Loves music, films, travelling, cooking, sewing, meeting people. Hates waking up in the morning. Best actor Shah Rukh Khan, best actresses Kajol. Ambition wanted to be a teacher. Message: Be happy enjoy your life.
NOMINATED BY: Ranjit

CLLR MOHAMMAD YAQOOB (BUS DRIVER)

Bus Driver, Bradford Traveller, 148 Rochester Street, Bradford Moor, Bradford, BD3 8AU

PLACE OF BIRTH: Pakistan, 3.2.48
MARITAL STATUS: Married
CHILDREN: Two (Shabana, Shareena)
COLLEGE: Blackburn Technical College
ACADEMIC QUALIFICATIONS: Dip in Textiles, College Diploma, City/Guild Textiles
PROFESSIONAL QUALIFICATIONS: Supervisory study in transport
MEMBERSHIPS: Labour Party, TGWU
HOBBIES AND INTERESTS: Cricket, snooker, reading
PERSONAL PROFILE: I have been employed in public transport primarily and a trade union representative for eighteen years. Dealing with employer and community has led me to take a more representative community role. I wish to serve to the very best of my ability regardless of colour, religion or background.

MR MANICKAM YOGESWARAN (LECTURER-SINGER)

Composer, Asian School of Arts,

PLACE OF BIRTH: Sri Lanka, 3.3.59
MARITAL STATUS: Single
ACADEMIC QUALIFICATIONS: Institute of Cost and Management Accountants
PROFESSIONAL QUALIFICATIONS: CIMA
DIRECTORSHIPS: Director of Asian School of Arts London
MEMBERSHIPS: Musician Union. Petron Member - Hamsadwani - Madras.
HONOURS/AWARDS: 'Kalai Mamani', 'Suranaya Devan', 'Tamil Isai Lavarasu', 'Amirtha Gana Prava'.
HOBBIES AND INTERESTS: Nature, yoga and teaching integrating Karnatic music with other World music.
PERSONAL PROFILE: Concert vocalist-Karnatic Music Mirdangist, flutist, concerts, Europe, Scandinavia and Canada. Regular appearances in the December Music Festival, Madras. Lead singer 'Dissidenten' Indipop-Europe, US and Canada. Visiting lecturer Goldsmith University. Recorded many CD's in classical and fusion music. Music for dance companies 'Shobana', 'Narthani' and in Europe. Composed background score for documentary 'Serendipty'. Singing with Western classical composers Olando Gough, Chloe Goodchild and Jocelyn Brook.

MR MORGAN YOUNG (ACTOR-DIRECTOR)

Producer/Choreographer, Michael Rose Ltd, The Dairy, Throop Road, Holdenhurst, Bournemouth, Dorset, BH8 0DL

PLACE OF BIRTH: Basingstoke, 8.10.55
MARITAL STATUS: Single
COLLEGE: DBCPA-Performing Arts
ACADEMIC QUALIFICATIONS: 8 GCSE
PROFESSIONAL QUALIFICATIONS: Various RAD/STD Dance Awards, 20 Years professional experience
DIRECTORSHIPS: Michael Rose Ltd, TAP Dogs UK Ltd, Marlene UK Ltd
MEMBERSHIPS: Advisory Board Member DBCPA
HONOURS/AWARDS: TMA Nominations - Best Touring Shows, Olivier Nominations ' Marlene ' Lyric Theatre
HOBBIES AND INTERESTS: Old English houses and gardens, castles, dogs, pets
PERSONAL PROFILE: Actor, director, choreographer, producer: Producing includes: 'Sweet charity'; 'Victoria Palace'; 'Marlene'; Lyric Theatre. Touring: 'Hot Shoe Shuffle'; 'TAP Dogs'. Directorial National Tour: 'Tom Foolery'; 'Singing in the Rain'; 'Me and My Girl'; Lincoln Theatre, Royal. Choreographer: 'Sophisticated Ladies', Gielguid Theatre, YMWLI, Central TV. Actor: Rep includes Manchester, Colchester, Nottingham, West End.

MR ALTAF YUSUF (BUSINESS DEVELOPMENT OFFICER)

Business Development Officer, Lancashire Constabulary, PO Box 77, Hutton, Preston, PR4 5SB

PLACE OF BIRTH: Preston, 30.5.67
COLLEGE: Preston College
ACADEMIC QUALIFICATIONS: GCSE's, B'TEC NAT-Public Administration
MEMBERSHIPS: Institute of Charity Fundraising Managers, Lancashire Juvenile Liaison Association, Lancashire Black Police Association
HOBBIES AND INTERESTS: Football, charity, community work
PERSONAL PROFILE: During my ten years with Lancashire Police I have been promoted three times. In my current role as business development officer I have created many partnerships between the Asian community and police. I am very respected in the community through my involvement in voluntary community work, in particular raising, organising relief and for the poor throughout the world.
NOMINATED BY: Paul Reynolds, Chief Inspector

'During my ten years with Lancashire Police I have been promoted three times. In my current role as business development officer I have created many partnerships between the Asian community and police'

ALTAF YUSUF

Entrants in the Asians in the Millennium have

been nominated for their achievements and

contributions. You can

nominate someone who

deserves to be in the

Who's Who of Asian Achievers 2000

Entries are free

Send in your nominations, including name,

contact address and telephone number to:

Books Division, Ethnic Media Group,

148 Cambridge Heath Road, London E1 5QJ

MR NADHIM ZAHAWI (SALES DIRECTOR)

European Sales, Smith & Brooks Ltd, 46 Highlands Heath, Putney, London, SW15 3TX

PLACE OF BIRTH: Kurdistan, 2.6.67
MARITAL STATUS: Single
COLLEGE: University College London
ACADEMIC QUALIFICATIONS: BSc Hons Eng
PROFESSIONAL QUALIFICATIONS: Chemical Engineer
DIRECTORSHIPS: Clinical Diagnostics & Control Ltd
MEMBERSHIPS: Anabells Club
HOBBIES AND INTERESTS: Horse-riding, cinema
EMAIL: nadhim.zahawi@smithbrooks.co.uk
PERSONAL PROFILE: Elected councillor London Borough of Wandsworth 1994. Fought Erith and Thamesmead for the Conservative Party in 1997 General Election.

MR SAROSH ZAIWALLA (SOLICITOR)

Senior Partner, Zaiwallia & Co-Solicitors, 33 Chancery Lane, London, WC2A 1ZZ

PLACE OF BIRTH: India, 27.9.47
MARITAL STATUS: Single
CHILDREN: Two (Freya, Varun)
COLLEGE: University of Bombay
ACADEMIC QUALIFICATIONS: BCom, LLB
PROFESSIONAL QUALIFICATIONS: Solicitor
MEMBERSHIPS: Law Society. Maritime Arbitrators' Assocaition. Baltic Exchange London. International Court of Arbitration. (Paris & London). London Maritime Arbitrators Association
PERSONAL PROFILE: Member of the International Court of Arbitration at the International Chamber of Commerce, president of the Society of the Lotus Children, co-convener Asian Business Breakfast Club in the House of Commons. Specialist in international commercial contracts, maritime disputes, immigration and nationality cases

MR ANTONY ZAKI (ACTOR-PRODUCER)

Magnolia Management, Flat 12, Elgin Court, 16 Montepelier Road, Ealing, London, W5 2QP

PLACE OF BIRTH: Pakistan, 25.12.68
MARITAL STATUS: Single
ACADEMIC QUALIFICATIONS: 4 A-Levels, 10 O-Levels
PROFESSIONAL QUALIFICATIONS: Dip in Drama
HONOURS/AWARDS: New Producer Alliance Critics Award. Best supporting actor gypsy magic. Aga Khan Foundation Award for Excellence in Arts
HOBBIES AND INTERESTS: Flying, diving
EMAIL: azaki@cwcom.net
WEB SITE: www.netspin.co.uk
PERSONAL PROFILE: Worked in TV from 'Poirot' to 'Young Indiana Jones'. Films: 'Gypsy Magic'- Best picture winner Montepelier first lead. 'Guru in Seven'-Co-producer and co-star. Co-starred in 'The Journey' with Roshan Seth and Saeed Jaffrey. Diana's Love interest in film, 'People's Princess'-East film.

MR MISBAH ZAMAL (JOURNALIST)

Presenter, Sunrise Radio, Sunrise House, Sunrise Road, Southall, UB2 4AU

PLACE OF BIRTH: Bangladesh, 1.7.61
MARITAL STATUS: Married
CHILDREN: Four
PROFESSIONAL QUALIFICATIONS: Certificate in Broadcasting Journalism
HOBBIES AND INTERESTS: Cultural activities
PERSONAL PROFILE: Successful journalist and Sunrise radio presenter. His Bengali programme on Sunrise Radio was the first Bengali programme. It's a very popular programme at the moment. He is the assistant editor of a Bengali weekly. He also promotes musical events.
NOMINATED BY: Shofi Ahmed

MR ISHAQUE HASSAN ZERIA (SPIRITUAL HEALER)

10 Queens Drive, Prestwich, Manchester, M25 0HQ

PLACE OF BIRTH: India, 31.12.29
MARITAL STATUS: Married
CHILDREN: Two (Mohammad Nazir, Abdul Razaq)
HOBBIES AND INTERESTS: Enjoys travelling and giving medical and religious advice to people in the UK and abroad
PERSONAL PROFILE: Mr Zeria, is better known as Maulana Ishaque by all who know him, out of respect. Maulana Ishaque came to the UK in 1969 and worked for an engineering insurance consultant in Manchester until 1990, when because of his eye problem (he lost his sight completely in the last two years), took early retirement. People from all over the UK have been consulting Maulana Ishaque with their problems. Both medical and religious.

PROF DR ALIMUDDIN ZUMLA
(CONSULTANT PHYSICIAN-UNIVERSITY DON)

Director-Reader- Consultant, Royal Free and University College Medical School, 46 Cleveland Street, London, W1P 6DB

PLACE OF BIRTH: Zambia, 15.5.55
MARITAL STATUS: Married
CHILDREN: Three (Aadeela, Musa, Adam)
COLLEGE: Zambia, London and Royal College of Physicians
ACADEMIC QUALIFICATIONS: Bsc,(Distinction), MB.CHB Hons, MSc (Distinction), PhD, MRCP, FRCP
DIRECTORSHIPS: UCL, Bloomsbury Wellcome Tropical Centre, Unza-Uclms TB/HIV Project. Visiting Professor Uni Zambia
MEMBERSHIPS: British Society for Study of Infection, Royal Society of Tropical Medicine and Hygeine, Institute of Biology. British Society for Immunology. Trustee and Scientific Adviser for 'TB Alert'.
HONOURS/AWARDS: Murgatroyd Prize,1991, Woodruff Medal for Excellence in Medicine,1987
HOBBIES AND INTERESTS: Career counselling, philately, medical writing, generating political, material support for medical research, cricket
EMAIL: a.zumla@ucl.ac.uk
PERSONAL PROFILE: Distinguished, star-studded career in medicine and science. Internationally renowned for his contributions to medical research, training and educational activities in infectious diseases, tropical medicine, AIDS and tuberculosis. Has a broad and philosophical outlook towards life and a deep commitment to assisting East and Central African countries. Has published several popular medical text books and over 100 articles in medical journals.

DR DEREK ZUTSHI (CONSULTANT PHYSICIAN)

Medical Consultant Physician, 36 Eton Court, Eton Avenue, Hampstead, London, NW3 3HJ

PLACE OF BIRTH: London, 26.4.30
MARITAL STATUS: Married
COLLEGE: University of Bristol
ACADEMIC QUALIFICATIONS: MB ChB
PROFESSIONAL QUALIFICATIONS: FRCP (London)
MEMBERSHIPS: Royal Society of Medicine, Royal Society for Arts, Royal Society for Asian Affairs, Worshipful Society of Apotheories Athenaeum
HONOURS/AWARDS: Hon Fellowship Hunterian Society, Hon LLD (University of Bristol 1999)
HOBBIES AND INTERESTS: Travel, archaelogy, wine, opera
PERSONAL PROFILE: Career: NHS, Civil Service and Independent Tribunal Service. Member Court Council and formerly chairman Convocation, University of Bristol. Previously president Hunterian Society. Deputy chairman Board of Governors, Tottenham College of Technology. Chairman Board of Trustees, Hindu Centre. Festival Council of Indian Organisations. Honorary secretary British Association for Rheurnathology and Rehabilitation.

People from all over the UK have been consulting Maulana Ishaque with their problems. Both medical and religious

SHAQUE HASSAN ZERIA

Distinguished, star-studded career in medicine and science. Internationally renowned for his contributions to medical research, training and educational activities in infectious diseases, tropical medicine, AIDS and tuberculosis

BEGUM SYEDA SHORIFA KHANOM

Late Entries - Page Guide

QAMAR AHMED (FREELANCE JOURNALIST)

Broadcaster, Self Employed, 20 Woodstock Grove, London, W12 8LE

PLACE OF BIRTH: India, 23.10.37
MARITAL STATUS: Single
COLLEGE: Sind University, Pakistan
ACADEMIC QUALIFICATIONS: Bachelor of Arts,
PROFESSIONAL QUALIFICATIONS: Diploma in Journalism, London School of Journalism
MEMBERSHIPS: Cricket Writer's Club, England, United Cricket Board of South Africa
HONOURS/AWARDS: Pakistan Association of Statisticians and Scorer's Award
HOBBIES AND INTERESTS: Cooking, photography
PERSONAL PROFILE: Covered cricket test matches for every cricket playing country's newspapers including: The Daily Telegraph, The Times, The Guardian, Sunday Times, Dawn (Pakistan), The Hindu (India), Nation (Barbados), Reuters, BBC, ABC (Australia). TV: New Zealand, West Indies, Pakistan, South Africa, covered 257 tests, 476 one-day games and contributed to the Oxford Biographical Dictionary.

MS TANZEEM AHMED (POLICY OFFICER)

Policy Officer, Confederation of Indian Organisations, 5 Westminster Bridge Road, London, SE1 7XW

PLACE OF BIRTH: India, 21.4.65
MARITAL STATUS: Married
CHILDREN: One (Younus Mukadam)
ACADEMIC QUALIFICATIONS: BSc Psychology
MEMBERSHIPS: British Psychology Society
HOBBIES AND INTERESTS: Reading, travelling
EMAIL: cio@gn.apc.org
PERSONAL PROFILE: I came to this country as a refugee from Uganda. Having a background in psychology, I started work as a researcher. Later I moved on to work in the voluntary sector. My main achievements have been to profile the needs of Asian people and the voluntary sector through publications, presentations, representation on committees and other foray.

MISS FARJANA ALI (STUDENT)

PLACE OF BIRTH: Single, 20.5.86
MARITAL STATUS: Single
COLLEGE: Mulberry School for Girls
HONOURS/AWARDS: Swimming certificate, netball certificate
HOBBIES AND INTERESTS: Sports, playing computer games
PERSONAL PROFILE: I have achieved a lot of different certificates for swimming and athletics. I have also won a poetry competition. My poem 'Moonlight' was published in a book called Spellbound which contained a lot of other chosen poems.

MISS SAJIA ALI (STUDENT)

PLACE OF BIRTH: London, 23.11.85
MARITAL STATUS: Single
COLLEGE: Mulberry School for Girls
HONOURS/AWARDS: Certificates for netball, swimming and basketball
HOBBIES AND INTERESTS: Sports, playing computer games
PERSONAL PROFILE: I have been awarded certificates for a variety of activities like sports and projects. My hope for the future is to get a really good job, so that I can earn some money and enjoy myself.

MR SOHAIL ANJUM (PHOTOGRAPHER)

Picture Editor, Ethnic Media Group, 1st Floor, 148 Cambridge Heath Road, London, E1 5QJ

PLACE OF BIRTH: South London, 24.7.72
MARITAL STATUS: Single and available!
COLLEGE: University of North London
ACADEMIC QUALIFICATIONS: Degree - Mass Communication and Tourism Studies
MEMBERSHIPS: National Union of Journalists
HOBBIES AND INTERESTS: Arts, cinema, theatre, web designing
EMAIL: sohail@easynet.co.uk/sanjum@aol.com
WEB SITE: http://easyweb.easynet.co.uk
PERSONAL PROFILE: Being a photographer I meet lots of politicians, celebrities and musicians. The best photographic experience I encountered was covering the Junoon concert in Wembley 1998. In the future I would like to eventually bring out my own magazine.

MR MOHAMMED ASLAM (DIRECTOR)

Kingsland Supermarket, 98 Kingsland High Street, Dalston, London, E8 2NS

PLACE OF BIRTH: Kashmir, 10.11.53
MARITAL STATUS: Married
CHILDREN: Five (Rukhsana, Parwez, Farzana, Tasleem, Shabana)
COLLEGE: Dadyal, Mirpur
ACADEMIC QUALIFICATIONS: BA Degree
PROFESSIONAL QUALIFICATIONS: Business
DIRECTORSHIPS: Company Management
MEMBERSHIPS: Labour Party, Arts Council
HONOURS/AWARDS: Diploma in Acting
HOBBIES AND INTERESTS: Showbiz, music, travel
PERSONAL PROFILE: Succeed in business, managing supermarket. Also involved in show business, with an interest in politics and music.

PARV BANCIL (PLAYWRIGHT)

Mel Kenyon, Casarotto Ramsay Ltd, National House, 60-66 Wardour Street, London, W1V 4ND

PLACE OF BIRTH: Tanzania, 7.2.67
MARITAL STATUS: Married
HONOURS/AWARDS: BBC Radio 4 Young Playwrights Festival 1991
PERSONAL PROFILE: I began writing plays in 1986 for a company based in Hounslow, Hac Theatre. After the company lost its funding in 1989. I became a freelance writer and I have written over 13 plays. I am currently under commission at the Royal Court Theatre. Also I am working on projects for BBC and CH4.

SABIRA BEGUMUDDIN (STUDENT)

PLACE OF BIRTH: London
COLLEGE: Mulberry School for Girls
HONOURS/AWARDS: Swimming certificate, Spellbound certificate
HOBBIES AND INTERESTS: Collecting magazines, books
PERSONAL PROFILE: I go to Mulberry School for Girls. In year 2000 I'm going to be in Year 9. I am 13. I love collecting magazines to read. My favourite subject is RS. I really love going to school. I want to be a singer. I have worked on a poem which was published in Spellbound. I have loads of ambitions. I would like to be a nurse or dance teacher. I would also like to be a social worker or a TV presenter.

MR AMARJEET SINGH BHAMRA (HOLISTIC PRACTITIONER)

Atma Institute Ltd, PO Box 1551, Windsor, SL4 1TZ

PLACE OF BIRTH: Kenya
MARITAL STATUS: Married
CHILDREN: Four
ACADEMIC QUALIFICATIONS: MBA, ITEC, IIHHT
PROFESSIONAL QUALIFICATIONS: MInst M, MBIM
HONOURS/AWARDS: Regional, national and international awards
HOBBIES AND INTERESTS: Holistic medicine
PERSONAL PROFILE: Pioneer in research, development and marketing holistic medicine in Europe. Founder ASA (Aids Action South Asia).

MRS AMRIT-KAUR BHAMRA (ARTIST - PRINCIPAL)

Atma - Institute Ltd, PO Box 1551, Windsor, SL4 1TZ

PLACE OF BIRTH: Kenya
MARITAL STATUS: Married
CHILDREN: Four
ACADEMIC QUALIFICATIONS: ITEC, IIHHT
PROFESSIONAL QUALIFICATIONS: Equity member
HONOURS/AWARDS: Regional, national and international in medicine
HOBBIES AND INTERESTS: Holistic medicine, arts, dance
PERSONAL PROFILE: Founder of hoslitic - medicine college in Europe. Founder of Apna Punjab Gidda Group.
NOMINATED BY: Amarjeet Singh

'Being a photographer I meet lots of politicians, celebrities and musicians. The best photographic experience I encountered was covering the Junoon concert in Wembley 1998. In the future I would like to eventually bring out my own magazine'

SOHAIL ANJUM

MR KULWANT SINGH BHAMRAH (SINGER)

Apna Group, 18 Cubley Road, Hall Green, Birmingham, B28 8EH

HONOURS/AWARDS: Awarded 8 Gold and Platinum disks for outstanding sales of their 10 albums over 12 years.
HOBBIES AND INTERESTS: Writing, composing and arranging music
PERSONAL PROFILE: Apna Group continues where Apna Sangeet, a band of the 1980's, left off, pioneering into uncharted waters of the global stage and recording ground breaking albums. The first album under the Apna Group banner became the first British Bhangra act to go on tour in Australia and New Zealand.

MR SUDARSHAN KUMAR BHATIA (HOTEL BUSINESS)

Chair Trustee, Hindu Society,

PLACE OF BIRTH: India, 24.11.49
ACADEMIC QUALIFICATIONS: MSc (Physics)
PROFESSIONAL QUALIFICATIONS: Hotel business
HOBBIES AND INTERESTS: Community service
PERSONAL PROFILE: Active community worker in organisations ISKCON, Vishwa Hindu Kendra, Southall, Amritvani and Hindu Society.

MR HASSAN BHATTI (WHOLESALE MANAGER)

Punjab Textiles, Unit 13, Barrett Industrial Estate, Park Avenue, Southall, UB1 1PP

PLACE OF BIRTH: Pakistan, 28.8.68
MARITAL STATUS: Married
CHILDREN: Three (Qasim, Zara, Zayn)
COLLEGE: Southbank University
ACADEMIC QUALIFICATIONS: BA Hons Business and Finance, 7 O-Levels, 3 A-Levels
HONOURS/AWARDS: 1998 NEC Birmingham Mega Mela Award for Best Stall, 1997 Wembley Conference Centre Award for Best Designer Wedding Wear
HOBBIES AND INTERESTS: Cricket, squash
EMAIL: enquires@punjab-textiles.co.uk
WEB SITE: www.punjab-textiles.co.uk
PERSONAL PROFILE: Punjab Textiles was first established 30 years ago. At first it was a fabric shop with just one stall, since then it has expanded to a ready-made designer boutique on Southall Broadway.

DR SWAMINATH DANDAPANI (MANAGEMENT CONSULTANT)

Managing Director, S D Enterprises Ltd, , 103 Wembley Park Drive, Wembley, HA9 8HG

PLACE OF BIRTH: India, 23.6.21
MARITAL STATUS: Married
CHILDREN: Three (Ravi, Vidya, Shankar)
COLLEGE: Madras, Naspur, Netherlands
ACADEMIC QUALIFICATIONS: MA, PhD, Dip Soc.Work
PROFESSIONAL QUALIFICATIONS: Dip Soc Policy
DIRECTORSHIPS: S D Enterprises Ltd
MEMBERSHIPS: Fellow Institute of Management. Fellow Institute Sales Management. Fellow Institute of Administration
HONOURS/AWARDS: Visihta Seva Medal - government of India, National award from government of Bahrain
EMAIL: dandpani@diran.co.uk
PERSONAL PROFILE: Sociologist, author of ten books - one translated in Swahili and one translated in Rumanian. Seven years with the Ministry of Defence, 30 years in PTY in India. Ten years with United Nations and 15 years as a management consultant.

MR DINESH DHAMIJA (CHAIRMAN)

Flight Bookers Plc, 177 Tottenham Court Road, London, W1P OLX

PLACE OF BIRTH: Australia, 28.3.50
MARITAL STATUS: Married
CHILDREN: Two (Biren, Darun)
COLLEGE: Fitzwilliam, Cambridge
ACADEMIC QUALIFICATIONS: MA (Cantab)
DIRECTORSHIPS: Many
MEMBERSHIPS: RAC, Oxford and Cambridge Club, Wentworth Golf Club, Hawks Club
HOBBIES AND INTERESTS: Golf, travelling
EMAIL: dinesh@flighbookers.net
WEB SITE: www.flighbookers.net
PERSONAL PROFILE: Started his travel business in 1980 and now employs 220 people with annual sales of £52 million. Flightbookers is now the 10th largest scheduled airline business in the UK.

CLLR KABAL SINGH DHILLON (TEACHER)

Chair of Education, London Borough of Waltham Forest, 122 Colchester Road, Leyton, London, E10 6HD

PLACE OF BIRTH: India, 1.1.37
MARITAL STATUS: Married
CHILDREN: Three (Miss A N Dhillon, Dr P S Dhillon, Master G S Dhillon)
COLLEGE: University of London
ACADEMIC QUALIFICATIONS: MSc
PROFESSIONAL QUALIFICATIONS: PGCE
PERSONAL PROFILE: I teach in a college. My wife is also a teacher, my daughter gained BSc in Pharmacy from Queen's University, Belfast. Second child, son, studied medicine in Saint Bart. London, third child starts A-Levels. I have been a Labour councillor of LBWF since 1994. Now I am chair of education.

MR JAZ DHINGRA (MUSIC PRODUCER-DJ)

LL Cool Singh, Metropolis Management, 55 The Broadway, Southall, UB1 1JY

PERSONAL PROFILE: Jaz Dhingra better known as 'LL Cool Singh' started his musical career as a DJ at the age of 16. He got his first break into producing music with the collective album of music producers known as 'Hidden Treasure'. He then released 'Da Live Session', which went straight to number one in the Eastern Eye UK Top Ten Charts. Now at the age of 22 LL Cool Singh is currently working on his next album.

MR HARISH KARSAN DHOKIA (SENIOR LECTURER)

Community Development Manager, Coventry Technical College, The Butts, Coventry, CV1 3GD

PLACE OF BIRTH: Kenya
MARITAL STATUS: Married
CHILDREN: Two (Nimesh, Rajesh)
ACADEMIC QUALIFICATIONS: HNC in Chemistry, Bachelor of Education, Post Graduate Diploma, RSA Diploma, Cert in TESOL
PROFESSIONAL QUALIFICATIONS: Advanced Diploma in Public Health and Hygiene, Diploma in British Institute of Innkeeping, JNC Certificate in Youth and Community Work
DIRECTORSHIPS: Ethnic Minority Alliance: ACHAL (ASRA Coventry) Housing Association: and HK Dhokia & Associates
MEMBERSHIPS: Magistrates Association, British Institute of Innkeepers, CYWU, NATHFE, Lions Club International, Shree Krishna Temple (Coventry), Bharat Samaj (Rugby)
HONOURS/AWARDS: Hind Ratan
HOBBIES AND INTERESTS: Reading history and theology, research interests in social anthropology, table tennis, badminton, enjoys cycling
PERSONAL PROFILE: Harish Dhokia is a prominent member of the Black and Asian community in Coventry who for over 20 years has been actively involved in several local, regional, national and International organisations. He also serves on several executive boards and is an advisor on issues of education and training. Harish Dhokia has also served as a magistrate since 1989 and is honoured to have been elected in 1995, the youngest president of the local Hindu temple for two years running. He is member of the Court of the University of Warwick.
NOMINATED BY: Davinder Panesar

MR MOHAN SINGH DHRAMRAIT
(RADIO SPECTRUM ENGINEER)

Radiocommunications Agency (DTI), 24 Beulah Road, Thronton Heath, CR7 8JE

PLACE OF BIRTH: BA, Fiji, 22.3.40
MARITAL STATUS: Married
CHILDREN: Two (Jagjit Kaur, Inderjit Singh)
COLLEGE: Norwood Technical College - London
ACADEMIC QUALIFICATIONS: Diploma in Eletronics and Radio
PROFESSIONAL QUALIFICATIONS: Associate Member of Institute of Electrical Engineers
MEMBERSHIPS: IMPS
HONOURS/AWARDS: Radiocommunications Agency Award,
HOBBIES AND INTERESTS: Gardening, photography, community, interest in racial equality
EMAIL: mohan.dharmrait@itu.int
PERSONAL PROFILE: I work in international radio spectrum engineering, representing the UK (government and industry), in international fora and chairing several international committees. I have also played an active role in the trade union movement over the past thirty years, specialising in employment law and equal opportunities.
NOMINATED BY: William H Brett IPMS

Apna Group continues where Apna Sangeet, a band of the 1980's, left off, pioneering into uncharted waters of the global stage

KULWANT SINGH BHAMRAH

MR RAJ GHAI (MARKETING DIRECTOR)

Media Moguls, 65-67 Wembley Hill Road, Wembley, HA9 8BD

PLACE OF BIRTH: India, 27.3.66
MARITAL STATUS: Single
HONOURS/AWARDS: Numerous
HOBBIES AND INTERESTS: Cooking, music
EMAIL: raj@mediamoguls.com
WEB SITE: www.mediamoguls.com
PERSONAL PROFILE: One of the most familiar faces within Asian media. He first appeared on Spectrum Radio breakfast show in 1989. After a successful three years and behind the scenes at TV Asia, Raj moved to Zee TV. Raj is one of the directors of Media Moguls, a PR and marketing agency. His expertise within the Asian music industry is reflected in the large number of mainstream record labels that use Media Moguls to promote their artists.
NOMINATED BY: Pedro

MR KULVINDER GHIR (ACTOR-WRITER)

Peters, Fraser & Dunlop,

PLACE OF BIRTH: Kenya, 10.8.73
MARITAL STATUS: Vegetarian!
COLLEGE: Drama School
MEMBERSHIPS: Equity
HONOURS/AWARDS: LWT Plays on Stage Award, BAFTA Nomination
HOBBIES AND INTERESTS: Football, cricket, martial arts, kung-fu fighting
NOMINATED BY: Kiran Lyall

MRS SUNITA GOLVALA (DANCE DIRECTOR)

Nava - Kala Dance Academy, 211 Ranelagh Court, Regency Walk, Croydon, CR0 7UW

PLACE OF BIRTH: India, 9.10.35
MARITAL STATUS: Married
CHILDREN: Two
HOBBIES AND INTERESTS: Reading, choreography, drama, yoga
PERSONAL PROFILE: To promote understanding and appreciation of Indian dance art in the community at large and endeavour to place Indian dance in the mainstream of British artistic activities.

MR GARY GURMEET (MANAGING DIRECTOR)

Southnews Plc, 89 Eastworth Road, Chertsey, KT16 8DX

PLACE OF BIRTH: Kenya, 4.5.51
MARITAL STATUS: Married
CHILDREN: Two (Adam, Gary)
PERSONAL PROFILE: Managing Director of Southnews Plc, Parent company of Ethnic Media Group. Southnews publishes 60 local newspapers in the South East.

MR IMRAN HAFEEZ (STUDENT-PT LIBRARIAN)

Sat Assistant, Bradford Police Club for Young People, 9 Agar Street, Girlington, Bradford, BD8 9QL

PLACE OF BIRTH: Bradford, 9.9.82
MARITAL STATUS: Single
ACADEMIC QUALIFICATIONS: Studying 9 GCSE's
PROFESSIONAL QUALIFICATIONS: Silver Medal Life Saving, Bronze Duke of Edinburgh Award, NBC Leadership, First Aid Certificates
DIRECTORSHIPS: President of the Kaamyaab Keystone and Community Action Group
MEMBERSHIPS: National Association of Boys Clubs (NBC), National Association of Boys Clubs and Clubs for Young People
HONOURS/AWARDS: Lions International regional and district level, Work to Play Scheme Award
HOBBIES AND INTERESTS: Football, basketball, poetry, cricket, snooker, table tennis, badminton
PERSONAL PROFILE: I am a 16 year old student at Rhodesway Upper School studying the final year of my GCSE. I am hoping to do my A-Levels and go into social work. I am actively involved in my community, working voluntarily and will be for many years to come.

> One of the most familiar faces within Asian media. He first appeared on Spectrum Radio breakfast show in 1989

RAJ GHAI

MR ABDUL AZIZ HAFEZI (SOLICITOR)

Partner, Merricks Solicitors, Fountain House, 130 Fenchurch Street, London, EC3M 5JJ

PLACE OF BIRTH: India, 2.1.65
MARITAL STATUS: Married
CHILDREN: Three (Ammaarah, Hannah, Ahmed Umer)
COLLEGE: Leicester Polytechnic
ACADEMIC QUALIFICATIONS: BSc
MEMBERSHIPS: The Law Society
HOBBIES AND INTERESTS: Family, India, charity, sport
PERSONAL PROFILE: Born Gujarat, India. Admitted 1986 as partner at Merricks specialising in insurance related litigation. Runs a charity for two districts in Gujarat, India. Strong advocate for assimilation and working in a secular society.

MR MUJIBUL ISLAM (DESKTOP PUBLISHER)

Graphic Designer, Ethnic Media Group,

PLACE OF BIRTH: Bangladesh, 25.12.72
MARITAL STATUS: Single
COLLEGE: London Guildhall University
ACADEMIC QUALIFICATIONS: BA Hon Design, A-Levels, 8 GCSE
DIRECTORSHIPS: Bangladesh Youth Movement
MEMBERSHIPS: NUJ, BYM
HONOURS/AWARDS: Duke of Edinburgh Award - Graphic Designer of the Year-S News
HOBBIES AND INTERESTS: Sports, fast cars, design, good lifestyle
PERSONAL PROFILE: Graduated in 1997 in BA Design, acquiring a 2:1 status. Currently employed by Southnews plc as magazine designer for one of their leading newspapers. For the past five consecutive years I have been an active chairperson for the Bangladesh Youth Movement, one of the largest voluntary Bangladesh organisations in the UK.

MADHUR JAFFREY (ACTRESS)

Conway Van Gelder Ltd, 3rd Floor, 18-21 Jermyn Street, London, SW1Y 6HP

PLACE OF BIRTH: India
MARITAL STATUS: Married
CHILDREN: Three
COLLEGE: Delhi University, RADA
ACADEMIC QUALIFICATIONS: Maj Eng. RADA Honours Diploma
HONOURS/AWARDS: Silver bear, best actress award for Shakespeare Wallah
PERSONAL PROFILE: Theatre: 'East Dance at Dum Dum'. Broadway: 'The Guide'; 'Conduct Unbecoming'; Television includes: 'Peacock Spring'; 'Firm Friends'; 'Love Match'; 'A Wanted Man', 'The Bloodless Arena'. English Films: 'The Assam Garden'; 'Heat and Dust'; 'Autobiography of a princess'; 'Guru' and 'Shakespeare Wallah'.

MR MOHAMMED JAHIR HUSSAIN MIAH (ENGINEER)

Technical Support Advisor, GCI Limited,

PLACE OF BIRTH: London, 22.9.72
MARITAL STATUS: Single
COLLEGE: Salford University
ACADEMIC QUALIFICATIONS: B Eng Hons
PROFESSIONAL QUALIFICATIONS: Engineering Designers Corporate Status
DIRECTORSHIPS: GCI Ltd, Bengie Engineering Ltd
MEMBERSHIPS: IMEACE, Institute of Engineering Designers
HONOURS/AWARDS: Student Awards
HOBBIES AND INTERESTS: Engineering journals, designing, sport all kinds
EMAIL: mmiah570177@aol.com
PERSONAL PROFILE: I am one of the eleven people and the first Asian to have completed B Eng Honours European Engineering course. I have worked for several big companies (BNFL, AEA) and I am a director of companies in UK and Bangladesh. I used to play basketball for Manchester Giants and achieved plenty of championships with other clubs

MISS CHARMAINE JAYETILLEKE (ACCOUNTANT)

14 Conifer Way, Hayes, UB3 2HL

PLACE OF BIRTH: Sri Lanka
MARITAL STATUS: Single
ACADEMIC QUALIFICATIONS: CIMA, Diploma in Marketing and Media
HOBBIES AND INTERESTS: Meeting people, travel, theatre, films
PERSONAL PROFILE: Represented Sri Lanka in Japan to market and advertise Ceylon Tea. In London formed Sri Lanka Christian Association to bring all Sri Lankans under one umbrella. Over 40 children previously denied an education are being sponsored by the SLCIA. Held first ever beauty pageant in London and over 20 fashion shows with Eastern and Western clothes.

MR NINDER JOHAL (Managing Director)

Nachural Records,

PLACE OF BIRTH: Birmingham
MARITAL STATUS: Married
CHILDREN: One (Amar)
COLLEGE: Aston University
ACADEMIC QUALIFICATIONS: BA Hons in Accountancy and Finance, Masters Business Administration
DIRECTORSHIPS: Nachural Records, Aston Acoustic
MEMBERSHIPS: Association of Chartered Certified Accountants (ACCA)
HONOURS/AWARDS: Young Asian Business Person 1997
HOBBIES AND INTERESTS: Football, cricket, tennis, badminton, reading, bhangra music

MR ASHVIN KUMAR JOSHI (Actor)

Henry's Agency, 53 Westnury, Rochford, SS4 1UL

PLACE OF BIRTH: Dar-es-Salaam
MARITAL STATUS: Married
COLLEGE: Birmingham Theatre School
MEMBERSHIPS: Equity
HOBBIES AND INTERESTS: Sport : badminton, squash, football, horse-riding, swimming
PERSONAL PROFILE: Qualified computer analyst trained as an actor with appearances in association with English Shakespeare and for Birmingham Old Rep, Leicester Haymarket and Nottingham Playhouse with extensive touring experience for Tara Arts. Films include: 'The Dance of Shiva'; 'Strings' and 'Memsaab Rita' for BBC.
NOMINATED BY: Vic Leach, Henry's Agency

MR SAYED JAIN KARWANI
(President - Afghan Action Cttee.)

Society of Afghan Residents in the UK, 51 York Road, Acton, London, W3 6TS

PLACE OF BIRTH: Afganistan, 7.7.30
MARITAL STATUS: Married
CHILDREN: 17 (Fahim, Natki, Monir, Shinki, Hosi, Burmal, Emal, Mukhtar, Ahmad, Nazir, Pary, Shir, Belal, Nessar)
COLLEGE: Mirwais College, Kandahar, Afghanistan
ACADEMIC QUALIFICATIONS: Baccalaureat in Teaching
PROFESSIONAL QUALIFICATIONS: Diplomas in Librarianship and Aircraft Warehousing 1962-83
DIRECTORSHIPS: Chair (1982-94), President (1994-98), Society of Afghan Residents in the UK
HONOURS/AWARDS: Whitbread Volunteer Action Award 1995
HOBBIES AND INTERESTS: Afghan Culture
PERSONAL PROFILE: Leader of Afghan Exile Community in UK. Founder of Society of Afghan Residents in the UK. Founder and president of Afghan Action Committee International. Founder of Helping Hand for Afghan Refugees, UK. Resident since 1978. British citizen internationally renowned in Afghan community.

MISS SHUBA KHAN (Student)

PLACE OF BIRTH: London, 29.3.86
MARITAL STATUS: Single
COLLEGE: Mulberry School for Girls
HONOURS/AWARDS: Certificate for swimming
HOBBIES AND INTERESTS: Sports, swimming, watching TV, playing
PERSONAL PROFILE: I have achieved a lot during the year. I am hoping to get a good job so that when I grow up I can earn a lot of money. I am quite good at maths and sport. I got a certificate because I have done well in PE and maths. I am good at listening to instructions and good at concentrating in class.

WADUD ISMA KHATUN (Student)

PLACE OF BIRTH: England, 10.10.85
MARITAL STATUS: Single
COLLEGE: Mulberry School for Girls
HONOURS/AWARDS: Certificate for athletics and swimming.
HOBBIES AND INTERESTS: I like swimming
PERSONAL PROFILE: I am a student in Mulberry School for Girls I am going to be in Year 9 in 2000. I want to be a doctor or a lawyer.

MISS DILSHAD KHOT (Comedian)

Dhanak Group,

PLACE OF BIRTH: Kenya
MARITAL STATUS: Single
COLLEGE: University of Central England
ACADEMIC QUALIFICATIONS: Degree in Social Work
MEMBERSHIPS: BASW
HONOURS/AWARDS: Certificate in semi final for Daily Telegraph - Open Mic Award
HOBBIES AND INTERESTS: Finding peace, telling jokes, poetry, singing

DR HARPREET SINGH KOHLI (Public Health Consultant)

Consultant in Public Health Medicine, Glasgow University, 13 Selborne Road, Glasgow, G13 1QG

PLACE OF BIRTH: India, 14.2.57
MARITAL STATUS: Married
CHILDREN: Four (Siobhan, Maya, Ciaran, Nisha)
COLLEGE: Edinburgh University
ACADEMIC QUALIFICATIONS: BSc,MBChB, MPH
PROFESSIONAL QUALIFICATIONS: DRCOG, MRCGP, FFPHM
HOBBIES AND INTERESTS: Watching Celtic FC, golf, reading
EMAIL: hskohli@dinmed.gla.ac.uk
PERSONAL PROFILE: I was born in Delhi and came to Glasgow when I was five years old. After completing my medical degree I trained in general practice and then specialised in public health medicine. Having children of mixed parentage. I believe strongly in a society which is multi-cultural and anti-racist.
NOMINATED BY: G S Puri

MR GURCHETAN KOONER
(Quality Controller-British Champion)

PLACE OF BIRTH: UK, 26.11.71
MARITAL STATUS: Married
COLLEGE: Wolverhampton
ACADEMIC QUALIFICATIONS: 8 GCSE's, 3 A-Levels, 1 HND, 1 BA Degree
PERSONAL PROFILE: Three times British Wrestling Champion, 85 Kg category. Only Non Registered Indian (NRI) to win a major tournament in Punjab. Represented GB at many internationals. Commonwealth Silver Medalist.
NOMINATED BY: J E Ault, Midlands Region Olympic Wrestling Association

DR RAJ KUMAR (Economist)

Special Adviser (Economic), Economic Legal Advisory Services, 18 Denison Close, Hampstead Garden, London, N2 0JT

PLACE OF BIRTH: Malaysia, 23.12.47
MARITAL STATUS: Single
COLLEGE: University of Edinburgh
ACADEMIC QUALIFICATIONS: PhD Economics
MEMBERSHIPS: Institute of contemporary arts
HONOURS/AWARDS: University of Edinburgh Fellowship, University of Malaysia Entrance Scholarship
HOBBIES AND INTERESTS: Travel, reading, writing, cinema, cookery, internet
EMAIL: r.kumar@commonwealth.int
PERSONAL PROFILE: Dr Kumar is programme leader for the Commonwealth Secretariat's debt advisory programme and has been an advisor to more than 30 governments in debt management and natural resource development. He is an international speaker and author of numerous articles on the subject of economic development and has published two books.
NOMINATED BY: Mohinder Puri

MR MANOJ LADWA (Corporate Lawyer)

Singhania and Co, 24 Buckingham Gate, London, SW1E 6LB

PLACE OF BIRTH: Birmingham, 1.6.73
MARITAL STATUS: Single
COLLEGE: London School of Economics
ACADEMIC QUALIFICATIONS: LL.B Hons, Post Graduate in Legal Practice
PROFESSIONAL QUALIFICATIONS: Advocate, Admitted to the Indian Bar
DIRECTORSHIPS: Communications Director of HSS (UK) - National Charity
MEMBERSHIPS: The Law Society, The Bar Council of Maharastra and Goa, World Council of Hindus, Friends of India Society International
HONOURS/AWARDS: Recognition by Her Majesty The Queen for social service and promotion of Indo-British relations 1998
HOBBIES AND INTERESTS: British and Indian politics, modern history, media relations
PERSONAL PROFILE: Founder and former president of the National Hindu Students Forum. Advises numerous social, political organisations on media strategy. Acts for NRI's and foreign investors on Indian corporate transactions. Regularly invited on radio and television. Guest columnist for various ethnic and Indian publications.

Three times British Wrestling Champion, 85 Kg category. Only Non Registered Indian to win a major tournament in Punjab

GURCHETAN KOONER

MR LALI MAHUN (Student)

Teen Haseen,

PLACE OF BIRTH: India, 10.2.87
COLLEGE: Woodbridge High School
ACADEMIC QUALIFICATIONS: Still at school
PROFESSIONAL QUALIFICATIONS: Won many awards & trophies for dancing. professional dancer
HONOURS/AWARDS: Recognition as a professional dancer
HOBBIES AND INTERESTS: Dancing, music, singing, cycling, football
PERSONAL PROFILE: Lali has received recognition within the Asian community as a professional dancer. With the formation of his dance group - Teen Haseen - he has managed to achieve much success and respect. The group work extremely hard and do all their own choreography while studying at the same time.

DR A A MALIK (Solicitor)

Senior Partner, Malik Law Associates Solicitors, Malik House, 233 Bethnal Green Road, London, E2 6AB

ACADEMIC QUALIFICATIONS: MA (History), MA (Pol. Science), MA (Urdu), LL.B, JD
PROFESSIONAL QUALIFICATIONS: Barrister-at-Law
EMAIL: solicitors@malik-law.demon.co.uk
PERSONAL PROFILE: Dr Malik is the founder and senior partner of Malik Law Associates, solicitors. In just a few years Malik Law Associates has become one of the UK's leading firms of solicitors in the field of immigration law. Dr Malik is also author of a few books including: British Immigration Law: A Simple Guide.

MR MOHAMMAD ZULFIKHAR MALIK (Sales Manager)

Punjab Textiles, 8 The Broadway, Southall, UB1 1PS

PLACE OF BIRTH: Nairobi, 13.8.69
MARITAL STATUS: Married
CHILDREN: Three (Rabia, Sabir, Mustafah)
COLLEGE: Acton College
ACADEMIC QUALIFICATIONS: 4 O-Levels, 2 A-Levels
DIRECTORSHIPS: Punjab Textiles
HONOURS/AWARDS: 1998 NEC Birmingham Mega Mela Award for Best Stall, 1997 Wembley Conference Centre Award for Best Designer Wedding Wear
HOBBIES AND INTERESTS: Swimming, cricket
EMAIL: enquires@punjab-textiles.co.uk
WEB SITE: www.punjab-textiles.co.uk
PERSONAL PROFILE: At this present moment Punjab Textiles is the largest retailer and wholesaler for 54 outlets in the UK. Punjab Textiles is renowned for its designs, styles and colours all available at affordable prices.

CLLR SARDUL SINGH MARWA MBE JP (Councillor)

Marwason, 16 Statham Drive, Edgbaston, Birmingham, B16 0TF

PLACE OF BIRTH: India, 11.5.47
MARITAL STATUS: Married
CHILDREN: Three (Amardeep Singh, Amarpal Singh, Sandeep Singh)
COLLEGE: Handsworth College
ACADEMIC QUALIFICATIONS: DIP Ed
PROFESSIONAL QUALIFICATIONS: Electrical Engineer. Computer Technician
DIRECTORSHIPS: Marwason
MEMBERSHIPS: International Panjabi Society. The Lunar Society. Birmingham Liberal Democrats Campaign Group
HONOURS/AWARDS: MBE, Justice of the Peace
HOBBIES AND INTERESTS: Music, reading, travel, keeping fit
PERSONAL PROFILE: An ambitious and hardworking individual, a good communicator with excellent inter-personal skills, excellent public speaker. Is able to motivate others to give their best. He is a quick learner and readily picks up new skills or techniques. Mr Marwa is popular with all ethnic groups and is capable of relating to all sections of the community. In recognition of his achievements, he was awarded the MBE in 1990 New Year Honours List.

Born in Bombay in 1969, sister of His Highness Maharajah of Karauli, Rajasthan, school and university in Jaipur, India. Present research doctorate in art and historical studies of Indian palaces

PRINCESS SHRUTI KUMARI MEDTIA

MR AJIT SINGH MEDTIA (Property Developer)

Managing Director, Red Lion Construction, Hartford House, Wellington Road, Oldham, OL8 4DD

PLACE OF BIRTH: Oldham, 11.9.68
MARITAL STATUS: Married
COLLEGE: Imperial College, University of London
ACADEMIC QUALIFICATIONS: B Eng Hons
PROFESSIONAL QUALIFICATIONS: ACGI (Associate of the City and Guilds Institute London)
DIRECTORSHIPS: Red Lion Construction
MEMBERSHIPS: Institute of Civil Engineers
HONOURS/AWARDS: Best O-Level prize and school head boy
HOBBIES AND INTERESTS: Business, travel, politics, arts, sports - polo, cricket, tennis, charity work in India
PERSONAL PROFILE: Born in Oldham in 1968, childhood raised in India (Rajasthan/Gujarat) on former ruling great Grandfather's estate. School and university in England. Successful multi-million pound business career as property developer after brief spell as a merchant banker in London. Passion for polo, politics and ecological issues. Set up educational trust for welfare of under-privileged children in India. Elected vice-president of Asian Business Association, and governor of College.

PRINCESS SHRUTI KUMARI MEDTIA (Academic)

PhD Research Study, University of Rajasthan, Hartford House, Wellington Road, Oldham, OL8 4DD

PLACE OF BIRTH: Bombay, 19.12.69
MARITAL STATUS: Married
COLLEGE: University of Rajasthan
ACADEMIC QUALIFICATIONS: BA Arts, MA Fine Arts & Music
PROFESSIONAL QUALIFICATIONS: PhD Research ongoing
HOBBIES AND INTERESTS: Asian music and art, philosophy and charitable works
PERSONAL PROFILE: Born in Bombay in 1969, sister of His Highness Maharajah of Karauli, Rajasthan, school and university in Jaipur, India. Present research doctorate in art and historical studies of Indian palaces. Married in 1995 to Ajit Singh Medtia. Featured in the National Geographical. Now resides in Britain. Involvement in local charity work, arts and classical music and promotion of Indian history, religion and culture.

MEENAKSHI (Artist)

Singer, Kismet Records,

PLACE OF BIRTH: India
ACADEMIC QUALIFICATIONS: MA Music
HOBBIES AND INTERESTS: Singing Hindi and Punjabi songs
PERSONAL PROFILE: Meenakshi the latest up and coming singer has been signed to Kismet Records for five albums in Jan 1999. She is already an established singer in India. She featured on 'The Yardies' album with 'Bajre Di Rakhi'. She will also feature on Jett Jagpal's + The Specialist albums before recording her solo album 'That Feeling Later'.

MR MALKIS MIAH (VIP-Manager)

Welfare Secretary, Awami League, Gulshen Restaurant, 18b Sheep Street, Northampton, NN1 2LU

PLACE OF BIRTH: Bangladesh, 25.12.58
MARITAL STATUS: Married
CHILDREN: Five (Abdul Rahman, Shahana Begum, Shuhena Begum, Rumena Miah, Kosru Miah)
DIRECTORSHIPS: Awami League co-ordinator, Welfare Secretary, Bangladesh Cricket Team Agent
MEMBERSHIPS: Awami - League Northants
HOBBIES AND INTERESTS: Meeting people - (social activities)
PERSONAL PROFILE: In 1970, I came to Britain with my family and we settled in Northampton. In 1986 I became a businessman in my hometown. In 1989, I was elected as a sports secretary for the community centre. In 1995 I joined the Conservative Party and in 1996, I became the co-ordinator of Awami League of Northampton. I became an agent for the Bangladesh cricket team in 1999.
NOMINATED BY: A Rahman

CLLR LAKHBIR SINGH MINHAS (Inspector)

Councillor,

PLACE OF BIRTH: Pakistan, 19.11.33
MARITAL STATUS: Married
CHILDREN: Two (Sukhjinder Singh, Kulwinder Singh)
COLLEGE: Punjab University
PROFESSIONAL QUALIFICATIONS: Management
DIRECTORSHIPS: Own factories in India
HONOURS/AWARDS: Deputy and mayor of Slough
HOBBIES AND INTERESTS: Meeting and helping in the community
PERSONAL PROFILE: I have devoted over 20 years of my life towards public services. I have been awarded with the honour of being the first Citizen of Slough in 1977 and 1998 as mayor of Slough. In my year of office quite a lot was achieved such as: unitary authority; athletic track; and rebuilding the social centre. Being a family man I am proud of my sons and the family, they are doing well in their electronics field.

MR KRISHAN KUMAR MITTAL (Interpreter-Translator)

PLACE OF BIRTH: Pakistan, 15.10.35
MARITAL STATUS: Widower
COLLEGE: Aligarh, India, Sheffield, Leeds and York
ACADEMIC QUALIFICATIONS: BA, ND, CE, DSEN and MA
PROFESSIONAL QUALIFICATIONS: Teacher, part-time lecturer. Modern Arts and Languages
MEMBERSHIPS: Founder member of Hindu Cultural Society of Bradford 1967, Member of the Bradford NHS Trust Spiritual and Religious Care Team.
HOBBIES AND INTERESTS: Writing, voluntary work
PERSONAL PROFILE: In 1947 from Pakistan as a refugee to India. 1964 to UK on an employment voucher. Hindi teaching volunteer for Hindu Cultural Society of Bradford. Politically Labour Party supporter. Ex-teacher and part-time lecturer: modern arts and languages.
NOMINATED BY: Vijay Bansal

CLLR MAN MOHAN (Sociologist)

Councillor, Linacre College Oxford, Town Hall, London Borough of Lewisham, London, SE6

PLACE OF BIRTH: India, 5.1.25
MARITAL STATUS: Married
COLLEGE: Columbia University, Oxford University
ACADEMIC QUALIFICATIONS: B Litt, D Phil
PROFESSIONAL QUALIFICATIONS: Sociologist and demographer
MEMBERSHIPS: British Sociological Association, Labour Party
HOBBIES AND INTERESTS: Climbing, gardening

CLLR ABDUL GAFOOR MULLA (Councillor)

Chair - Equality, London Borough of Hackney, 14 Warneford Street, Hackney, London, E9 7NG

PLACE OF BIRTH: India, 14.11.37
MARITAL STATUS: Married
CHILDREN: Seven (Farida, Hamida, Zahida, Mohamed Farouk, Abeda, Sakiha, Rehmatulla)
ACADEMIC QUALIFICATIONS: Kenya Preliminary equivalent SSC
PROFESSIONAL QUALIFICATIONS: Driver. Speaks Gujrati, Hindi, Punjabi, Swahili and Urdu.
DIRECTORSHIPS: Trustee of Hackney Muslim Council
MEMBERSHIPS: Labour Party. CRE. Gujrat Muslim Association
HOBBIES AND INTERESTS: Driving, poetry, reading, counselling, voluntary worker, walking, playing computer games
PERSONAL PROFILE: Muslim born in India - married living in London Borough of Hackney since 1967 where I am an elected Labour councillor - (1986). Bus driver for 25 years. Lead member on equality in Hackney Council. Heavily involved in community issues. Can speak Gujrati, Hindi, Punjabi, Swahili and Urdu. Loves poetry and Quawali.

MISS AISHA NASIB (Journalist)

Editor EMag, Ethnic Media Group,

PLACE OF BIRTH: Staffordshire, 17.3.75
COLLEGE: University East London
ACADEMIC QUALIFICATIONS: BA Hons Media
PROFESSIONAL QUALIFICATIONS: BBC Core Skills 1,2,3
HONOURS/AWARDS: Favourite Radio Presenter UK Asian Pop and Dance Award
HOBBIES AND INTERESTS: Socialising, travelling, entertaining, reading, music
PERSONAL PROFILE: I am a very competitive person. I thrive on a challenge, always working to my best ability. I get myself involved with everything at all times. I enjoy all types of music in particular Hindi. I enjoy meeting new and different people. Always the first to make a joke of things. I was born to party.

MOHAMMED MISKIN NASIM (Civil-Building Engineer)

Vice Chair Education, 12 Waverley Road, Walthamstow, London, E17 3LQ

PLACE OF BIRTH: Pakistan, 14.7.36
MARITAL STATUS: Married
CHILDREN: Five (Azra, Rehn, Rizwan, Farzana, Farhan Khyber)
COLLEGE: Karachi
ACADEMIC QUALIFICATIONS: BA
PROFESSIONAL QUALIFICATIONS: Civil & Building, North East London Poly Technic
DIRECTORSHIPS: Future career service
HOBBIES AND INTERESTS: Reading
PERSONAL PROFILE: General secretary LGC, chair Education Committee, vice chair Education Committee. deputy whip Labour Group. Representation on education committee ie Muslim, Hindu and Sikh.

MR MOHAMMED SHAH NEWAZ (Projects Manager)

Oldham Sixth Form College, 79 Prospect Road, Oldham, OL9 6LG

PLACE OF BIRTH: Bangladesh, 16.12.71
MARITAL STATUS: Married
CHILDREN: Two (Shah Sarwar Newaz, Nishat Tasneem Shah)
COLLEGE: The University of Findlay, Ohio, USA
ACADEMIC QUALIFICATIONS: BSc Hons (two years out of three)
PROFESSIONAL QUALIFICATIONS: Further and Adult Teaching Certificate
DIRECTORSHIPS: Trinity College certificate in teaching English
HONOURS/AWARDS: City and Guild Vocational Assessor Award
HOBBIES AND INTERESTS: Reading, travelling, community work, swimming
EMAIL: sn2@oldham-sfc.ac.uk
PERSONAL PROFILE: I came to the UK in 1993. During the past four years I have gained experience in community development work through my role as an active community worker, adviser at CAB, member at the Ethnic Minority Working Party for OMBC and joint secretary for Greater Sylhet Development Council UK. I started my career as an ESOL tutor and through my hard work I have been promoted to projects manager at the Oldham Sixth Form College.
NOMINATED BY: Kim Clifford

MR SHAHID KHAN NIAZI (Vice President)

Resident Vice President, Citi Bank N.A, 123 Headstone Lane, N.Harrow, HA2 6JS

PLACE OF BIRTH: Pakistan, 15.11.60
MARITAL STATUS: Married
CHILDREN: Two
COLLEGE: Aitchison College, Lahore, Los Angeles, US, Claremont Graduate School
ACADEMIC QUALIFICATIONS: MBA Marketing, BSc Finance
PROFESSIONAL QUALIFICATIONS: Investment Advice Certificate, Securities Institute UK
MEMBERSHIPS: Pakistani Bankers Association, Investment Management Regulatory Organ. UK
HOBBIES AND INTERESTS: Horse-riding, polo

MR ZAHOOR AHMAD NIAZI (Editor)

Daily Jung, 1 Sanctuary Street, London, SE1 1ED

PLACE OF BIRTH: Karachi, 1.1.45
MARITAL STATUS: Married
CHILDREN: Five (Kashif, Faisal, Anas, Ashar, Ms Eram)
ACADEMIC QUALIFICATIONS: MA Journalism
MEMBERSHIPS: NUJ
HONOURS/AWARDS: Gold medal awarded by Pakistani community in Denmark
HOBBIES AND INTERESTS: Reading, Walking
EMAIL: jang@globalnet.co.uk
PERSONAL PROFILE: Working as journalist since 1967, widely travelled to cover international events. Actively involved in community affairs. Held number of posts in trade union (PFUJ and KUJ). Presently elected president of Pakistan Journalist Association UK.

> I have devoted over 20 years of my life towards public services. I have been awarded with the honour of being the first Citizen of Slough in 1977 and 1998 as mayor of Slough
>
> **LAKHBIR SINGH MINHAS**

MR C D PATEL (Chartered Accountant)

Managing Director, Kensington International Hotels, 4 Templeton Place, London, SW5 9LZ

PLACE OF BIRTH: Fiji
MARITAL STATUS: Married
COLLEGE: Institute of CA
ACADEMIC QUALIFICATIONS: Chartered Accountant
PROFESSIONAL QUALIFICATIONS: ATII
DIRECTORSHIPS: Ciddy Ltd
MEMBERSHIPS: Institute of Taxation
HOBBIES AND INTERESTS: Travel, arts, reading
PERSONAL PROFILE: In hotels and real estates business since 1975. Chairman of Earls Court Hoteliers Organisation.

MR PETER E PERERA (Chartered Engineer)

Engineering Consultant, 43 Hillside Avenue, Woodford Green, IG8 7QU

PLACE OF BIRTH: Sri Lanka, 1.8.32
MARITAL STATUS: Married
CHILDREN: Two (Chrys, Anouska)
COLLEGE: St Joseph's College, Ceylon University . Faraday House Eng College, London
ACADEMIC QUALIFICATIONS: DFH - Graduate
DIRECTORSHIPS: Building Engineering Services - London Borough of Camden, Chief Services Engineer
MEMBERSHIPS: Institution of Electrical Engineers, Radio Society of Great Britain
HOBBIES AND INTERESTS: Amateur radio, music, sport, travel
EMAIL: pperera@compuserve.com
PERSONAL PROFILE: Former chief electrical engineer for the London Borough of Redbridge 1972-1985. Introduced innovation and change in public service engineering services. Presently - engineering consultant on energy management and communications specialising satellite communications technology. Actively engaged in promoting science and technology in education. Established Satellite Tracking and Radio Communications Centre in Overseas School.

MR PREM PRAKASH MBE (Chairman)

Asian News International, Apt 1, 39 Portland Place, London, W1N 3AG

PLACE OF BIRTH: India, 15.2.32
MARITAL STATUS: Married
CHILDREN: Two (Sanju Prakash, Seema Kukreja)
COLLEGE: University of Delhi
ACADEMIC QUALIFICATIONS: BA
PROFESSIONAL QUALIFICATIONS: Author, journalist
DIRECTORSHIPS: ANI Media Plc, Asian Vision Pvt Ltd, Sita Travels
MEMBERSHIPS: National Liberal Club, India Journalists Association
HONOURS/AWARDS: MBE, President of India's Gold Medal for documentaries.
HOBBIES AND INTERESTS: Photgraphy, travel, economics
EMAIL: ani@btinternet.co.uk
PERSONAL PROFILE: Pioneered TV journalism in India. Launched Asia's first multi-media news agency Asian News International or ANI. Today ANI is one the three global TV news agencies. The text service is subscribed by newspapers all over the world. The Queen honoured Prem Prakash with an MBE in 1997 for contributions to the growth of TV News industry in India and the UK.

MISS HAFSA QUADIR (Student)

DATE OF BIRTH: 21.11.85
MARITAL STATUS: Single
COLLEGE: Mulberry School for Girls
HONOURS/AWARDS: Attendance, PE and swimming
HOBBIES AND INTERESTS: Watching television, playing on the computer
PERSONAL PROFILE: I am a student in Mulberry School, I am going on to Year 9. I wrote a poem in Year 7 which has been published in a book Spellbound and I'm a good student who is confident in everything and tries hard in everything and I'm good at reading and spelling.

MISS ANJNA RAHEJA (Managing Director)

Media Moguls, 65-67 Wembley Hill Road, Wembley, HA9 8DP

PLACE OF BIRTH: London, 24.7.65
MARITAL STATUS: Single
COLLEGE: Oxford
ACADEMIC QUALIFICATIONS: BA Hons (Oxon) Experimental Psychology
DIRECTORSHIPS: Media Moguls
HOBBIES AND INTERESTS: Cooking, travel, sailing, reading
EMAIL: anjna@mediamoguls.com
WEB SITE: www.mediamogul.com
PERSONAL PROFILE: An Oxford graduate, Anjna left university to pursue a career in PR and marketing. In 1993 she set up her own PR and Marketing Agency, Media Moguls. Since its inception Media Moguls has grown from a one woman band to a twelve strong team of dedicated and passionate people.
NOMINATED BY: Pedro

SUFIYA RAHMAN (Student)

PLACE OF BIRTH: London, 22.5.86
MARITAL STATUS: Single
HONOURS/AWARDS: Swimming, attendance and PE
HOBBIES AND INTERESTS: Dancing, listening to music, going out with friends
PERSONAL PROFILE: I am a student in Mulberry. Next year I am in Year 9. My best subject is dance because I like dance movements, I also love performing. When I grow up I want to be a pilot, learn how the plane works and go around the world.

REV PUJYA SHREE RAMBAPA (Babaji)

PLACE OF BIRTH: India
DIRECTORSHIPS: Founder Jignyasu Satsang Mandal, Rambapa Sadhu Seva Trust, Maruti Rambaba Seva Trust
HONOURS/AWARDS: Title 'Saint of the Thames' by the Garavi Gujarat Newspaper
HOBBIES AND INTERESTS: His challenge is 'God never leaves the burden of his debt on anybody while they are doing his work, so go forward without any fear or doubt. Be sure that it will all be in surplus eventually'.
PERSONAL PROFILE: Shree Rambapa is 77 years old. His face is ever radiating love for everyone, and he is a walking Pratima of unlimited energy who can put youngsters to shame. Dressed in white, he has a shawl draped over his shoulder and a mala around his neck. His service's has reached masses through three trusts, namely Jignyasu Satsang Seva Trust, Rambapa Sadhu Seva Trust and Maruti Rambaba Seva Trust in India.

MR RAVI RATTAN (Dental Legal Adviser)

211 Wembley Hill Road, Wembley Park, HA9 8EL

DATE OF BIRTH: 18.10.62
MARITAL STATUS: Married
CHILDREN: One (Asha)
COLLEGE: University of London, University College Hospital Dental School
ACADEMIC QUALIFICATIONS: LDSRCS, Pg Dip DPM
PROFESSIONAL QUALIFICATIONS: LDSRCS, Pg Dip DPM
MEMBERSHIPS: Hertfordshire LDC, BDA, Northwest Thames LAPRAP committee.
PERSONAL PROFILE: Dental advisor to Ealing, Hammersmith and Hounslow Health Authorities. I have participated in the occasional interview for BBC Radio World Service on clinical dental topics.

KRISHAN RADIA (Schoolboy)

HONOURS/AWARDS: Official 'Guinness Book of Records' the youngest ever to obtain a GCSE (subject Information Technology Grade C
PERSONAL PROFILE: Aged just six years old, Krishan hit the headlines in August 1998 when he became the youngest ever to obtain a GCSE. He received the news live on television before an audience of six million. His mother, Neeta enrolled him at nearby Ryde College after she bought the family a computer. College tutors were so impressed with his grasp of technology that they asked his parents to let him enter the GCSE exam - the rest is history.

MR KRISH (KUMAR) RAVAL (Research Scholar)

PLACE OF BIRTH: Ethiopia, 2.4.72
COLLEGE: University of Sheffield
ACADEMIC QUALIFICATIONS: LLB Hons Research Scholar, Medical and Bioethical Law. Bachelor of Laws Degree (Class 2, Division 1)
DIRECTORSHIPS: Director of Training and Development, The Cambridge Union Society
HOBBIES AND INTERESTS: Writing
PERSONAL PROFILE: Written several articles on issues of diversity and culture for various university, community and non-governmental organisation periodicals. Recently profiled in the Malta Independent Magazine.
NOMINATED BY: Mrs B Gardiner BA

Aged just six years old, Krishan hit the headlines in August 1998 when he became the youngest ever to obtain a GCSE

KRISHAN RADIA

MRS J RAVICHANDRAN (MANAGING DIRECTOR)

Flower Power, 337 Bethnal Green Road, Bethnal Green, London, E2 6LG

PLACE OF BIRTH: Singapore, 4.5.62
MARITAL STATUS: Married
CHILDREN: Three (Prakash, Malar, Ashok)
COLLEGE: Barking College
ACADEMIC QUALIFICATIONS: NVQ 2 in Floristry
DIRECTORSHIPS: Flower Power
HOBBIES AND INTERESTS: Reading, badminton, tennis
PERSONAL PROFILE: First became involved in floristry two and a half years ago, since then have qualified as a florist and now own florist.

MR AZIZ REHMAN (BUSINESS FACILITATOR)

Huddersfield Pride, Mid Yorkshire Chamber of Commerce, Wakefield Road, Aspley, Huddersfield

MEMBERSHIPS: Huddersfield Small Business Network
PERSONAL PROFILE: Aziz was appointed by Huddersfield Pride to co-ordinate the setting up and running of Huddersfield Small Business Network. Based at the Mid Yorkshire Chamber of Commerce Aziz sees his role as a facilitator. He runs seminars specifically for small businesses which deals with theory and practise.

MR JITENDERPAL SINGH SAHNI (DIRECTOR)

VIP Computer Centre Ltd,, Unit B, Canalside North, John Gilbert Way, Manchester, M17 1UP

PLACE OF BIRTH: India, 22.4.66
MARITAL STATUS: Married
PROFESSIONAL QUALIFICATIONS: Institute of Directors
DIRECTORSHIPS: VIP Computer Centre Ltd, Commsport Ltd
MEMBERSHIPS: Institute of Directors
HOBBIES AND INTERESTS: Badminton, computers
EMAIL: jatti@vip-computers.co.uk
PERSONAL PROFILE: Aged 33, Jitender 'Jatti' Sahni came to Britain from Kuwait in 1990. With just one staff member, he established VIP Computer Centre Limited, a distributor of computers and components to the resale trade. Since then the company has grown to become one of the largest of its type in the UK with projected turnover for 1999 expected to be in the region of £84 million.

MISS JAEE SAMANT (TEAM LEADER-CIVIL SERVANT)

New Deal Policy, Department of Education And Employment, 30 Regency Lodge, Adelaide Road, Swiss Cottage, London, NW3 5EE

PLACE OF BIRTH: India, 8.3.67
MARITAL STATUS: Single
COLLEGE: University of Oxford (UK)
ACADEMIC QUALIFICATIONS: MA
MEMBERSHIPS: Fellow of Royal Society of Arts
HONOURS/AWARDS: Dame Henrietta Barnet Bequest Award
HOBBIES AND INTERESTS: Reading, theatre, cinema, music, travel
EMAIL: info@dfee.gov.uk
PERSONAL PROFILE: Jaee feels that one of her greatest achievements was being selected for the Civil Service Fast Stream. She was made Private Secretary to the Rt. Hon Michael Portillo, Secretary of State for Employment and Private Secretary to Rt. Hon Gillian Shephard, Secretary of State for Education and Employment. Jaee has worked voluntarily in a leper treatment home in Bombay
NOMINATED BY: Bernadette Hillon, DFEE

MR NIRMAL SINGH SEKHON (MANAGING DIRECTOR)

Nirmal Razai Mart & Co Ltd, Northfield Works, Carlisle Terrace, Bradford, BD8 8AS

PLACE OF BIRTH: India, 1.1.52
MARITAL STATUS: Married
CHILDREN: Two (Iqbel, Narinder)
COLLEGE: Jallinder High School Bhoughar
ACADEMIC QUALIFICATIONS: Matriculation
PROFESSIONAL QUALIFICATIONS: English, Punjabi, Hindi and Urdu
DIRECTORSHIPS: Nirmal Razai Mart Co. MD & CEO Yorkshire Fibre Filling Co
MEMBERSHIPS: Chairman of Trustee of Guru Gobind Singh Sikh Temple. Vice chair East West Conservative Assoc. Governor Buttershaw Upper School
HONOURS/AWARDS: Chair Yorkshire Sikh Forum. Bradford West Crime Prevention Panel
PERSONAL PROFILE: Since 1971 I have been a member of many police community panels, and have promoted liaison between the Sikh community and the police. I have been invited to meet with chief constable and senior police officers to give advice on Sikh community affairs. I am a member of the Police and Community Abuse Panel, where I play an important role to appraise the police regarding the needs of the battered women and absconded girls. Also member of Bradford Asian Business Association and Drugs Action Team.
NOMINATED BY: Sharon Aitkin

MR OWAIS SHAH (CRICKETER PROFESSIONAL)

Batsman, Middlesex County Cricket Club,

PLACE OF BIRTH: Pakistan, 22.10.78
MARITAL STATUS: Single
COLLEGE: Westminster (Harrow)
ACADEMIC QUALIFICATIONS: 8 GCSE's, 2 A-Levels currently doing business degree
PROFESSIONAL QUALIFICATIONS: Cricket Coach Level 2
HOBBIES AND INTERESTS: Music, cinema, friends
PERSONAL PROFILE: Cricketer playing for Middlesex 1XI. England 'A' tours to Australia and Sri Lanka. World Cup (winners) ENG U19 Captain.

MR PRAVIN SHAH JP (FINANCE AND HOUSING OFFICER)

Local Govt Officer, 150 Cheyneys Avenue, Edgware, HA8 6SC

PLACE OF BIRTH: Kenya, 13.7.48
MARITAL STATUS: Married
CHILDREN: Two (Simi, Dipi)
COLLEGE: University of London
ACADEMIC QUALIFICATIONS: BSc Hons, IPSM
PROFESSIONAL QUALIFICATIONS: IPSM
MEMBERSHIPS: Chartered Institute of Housing
HONOURS/AWARDS: Justice of the Peace
HOBBIES AND INTERESTS: Politics, travel, welfare work
EMAIL: pravin@shah.unisonfree.net
PERSONAL PROFILE: Justice of the Peace in Harrow. Chairman of Harrow Asian Action Group. Secretary of Harrow Council for Racial Justice. Member of Labour Party. Ex-councillor for London Borough of Harrow. Branch officer for Brent Unison local government branch. Have been involved in human rights and race issues.
NOMINATED BY: Dipi Shah

MISS SUHELI (EMILY) SHAHID (STUDENT)

PLACE OF BIRTH: London, 4.2.86
MARITAL STATUS: Single
COLLEGE: Mulberry School for Girls
HONOURS/AWARDS: Swimming certificate, Spellbound poem certificate
HOBBIES AND INTERESTS: Sports, reading, listening to music, watching TV
PERSONAL PROFILE: The things I've achieved are : I've won a poem competition which then got published in a book called Spellbound, along with other poems written by young poets in East London. I also won many puppet competitions in primary school.

MR HARI MOHAN SHARMA (DIRECTOR)

HMS Estates and Lettings, 384 - D Northolt Road, South Harrow, HA2 8EX

PLACE OF BIRTH: India, 10.7.36
MARITAL STATUS: Married
CHILDREN: Two (Reema, Neil)
COLLEGE: Agra University
ACADEMIC QUALIFICATIONS: MA Econ
HOBBIES AND INTERESTS: Music, travel, social, reading, poetry
PERSONAL PROFILE: Pleasant, social, religious, community help organising recitings and stage shows etc.

MR DEVENDRA KANT SHARMA (ARCHITECT)

Chairman, Hindu Temple Community & Cultural Centre,

PLACE OF BIRTH: India, 10.9.40
MARITAL STATUS: Married
CHILDREN: Two (Miss Punam Sharm, Mr Akshay Sharma)
COLLEGE: Sir JJ School of Architecture, Bombay
PROFESSIONAL QUALIFICATIONS: Dip Architecture
MEMBERSHIPS: Associate member of Indian Institute of Architects AIIA
PERSONAL PROFILE: Chairman of the Hindu Temple since June 1996. EC Member of Nottingham Racial Equality Council since 1987. EC Member of Hindu Temple from 1985-87. Secretary Brahmin Welfare Association from 1988-1994. Govenor of South Notts college for three years.

HEMA SHARMA (ARTIST)

Singer, Kismet Records,

PLACE OF BIRTH: India
PERSONAL PROFILE: Recorded first track at the age of 14, Gallan Gurrian, which was on PMC's Legalised album, then it was remixed on '2 Lethal Desi'. Hema's new album is to be released in Dec 99. It will be produced by Panjabi MC on Kismet Records.

DR PUSHI SHARMA (Doctor)

Senior Medical Officer, Regional Health Authority, Hillingdon, 6 Westwood Avenue, South Harrow, HA2 8NS

PLACE OF BIRTH: India, 6.2.39
MARITAL STATUS: Married
CHILDREN: Two (Reema, Neil)
ACADEMIC QUALIFICATIONS: MBBS
PROFESSIONAL QUALIFICATIONS: MBBS and DGO
MEMBERSHIPS: British Medical Association
HOBBIES AND INTERESTS: Cooking, profession, social, music
PERSONAL PROFILE: I am a pleasant and professional being and I enjoy helping society as a whole.

MR SUKSHINDER SHINDA (Music Producer)

Moviebox Ltd, 786 Coventry Road, Small Heath, Birmingham, B10 0TX

PERSONAL PROFILE: Sukshinder Shinda is the music producers' producer. He has brought brilliance, articulation and clarity of texture to some of the biggest and greatest bhangra albums of his generation. Sukshinder has worked with some of the finest vocal talents to take them on to another level. He has that rare gift to construct a melody straight from his heart and place it comfortably into his listeners' inner most consciousness.

MR NAVJOT SINGH (General Manager.)

Daimler Chrysler, Marlborough Court, Sunrise Parkway, Linford Wood, Milton Keynes, MK14 6YR

PLACE OF BIRTH: Birmingham, 13.4.70
MARITAL STATUS: Single
COLLEGE: University of Newcastle-upon-Tyne, University of Bradford Management Centre
ACADEMIC QUALIFICATIONS: Degree, Diploma Management Studies
PROFESSIONAL QUALIFICATIONS: MBA in Marketing Management
MEMBERSHIPS: Chartered Institute of Marketing, Institute of Direct Marketing
HONOURS/AWARDS: Innovation Award for Financial Management 1999, Venture Capital Award 1995
HOBBIES AND INTERESTS: Socialising, badminton, football, travel

MS TEJI SINGH (Public Relations-Company Director)

Sterling Enterprises, Shakespeare House, 168 Lavender Hill, London, SW11 5TF

PLACE OF BIRTH: East Africa, 23.7.63
MARITAL STATUS: Single
DIRECTORSHIPS: Sterling Enterprises
PERSONAL PROFILE: I've been an established and recognised face in the media since 1992 where I began as a news anchor for TV Asia's flagship news programmes. I have since built on my professional reputation and experience to form my own company - Sterling PR & Productions, which currently boasts a prolific list of ethnic and mainstream clients.

MR NIRANJAN SINGHANIA (Producer-Director)

Photoniks Video Productions, PO Box 431, Harrow, HA3 5ED

PLACE OF BIRTH: Tanzania, 2.3.59
MARITAL STATUS: Married
ACADEMIC QUALIFICATIONS: Education in Tanzania and India
PROFESSIONAL QUALIFICATIONS: Media Studies
HONOURS/AWARDS: Social Photographer 1981, Commercial Photographic 1982
HOBBIES AND INTERESTS: Rifle shooting, chess, mountaineering, wildlife photography
PERSONAL PROFILE: Founder and executive director of the Friends Society Photographers Club. Life member Lohana Community North London. Member Lions Club International.

> A highly talented and experienced news cameraman, Bhasker Solanki has filmed news reports in over 50 countries

MR BHASKER SOLANKI (News Cameraman-Video Producer)

BBC Senior News Cameraman, BBC News, Wood Lane, London, W12

HONOURS/AWARDS: Special Commendation - Royal Television Society 1992, Order of Mother Teresa - Awarded by President of Albania 1992, Amnesty International News coverage of Burundi 1994
HOBBIES AND INTERESTS: Technology, cinema, Asian arts
PERSONAL PROFILE: A highly talented and experienced news cameraman, Bhasker Solanki has filmed news reports in over 50 countries around the globe including many of the worlds major conflicts. Solanki has covered historical events like Tiannanamen Square, the Kurdish refugee crisis, famine in Sudan and Somalia, civil wars in the former Yugoslavia, Rwanda, Zaire and Northern Ireland.

MR PARESH SOLANKI (Journalist-Broadcaster)

Editor, BBC Asian Programmes, BBC Birmingham, Pebble Mill Road, Birmingham, B5 7QQ

MEMBERSHIPS: Royal Television Society, British Psychological Society
HONOURS/AWARDS: Worldfest Silver and Bronze, RTS Regional, New York Festival, 2nd at Prix Iris and various other for BBC Asian Programmes Unit
HOBBIES AND INTERESTS: Technolog, cinema, asian arts
PERSONAL PROFILE: Solanki's programme credits include: series producer/executive producer of the Asian arts and entertainment flagship 'Network East' and the international award winning current affairs strand 'East'. He has been an executive producer for a wide range of programmes including 'Cafe 21', 'Network East Big Talk', Independence Concerts and Independence Series and a number of top documentaries including 'Jinnah', 'Sikhs', 'Malaya' and 'Burma'.

MR RANJIT SOOD (Restaurateur)

Managing Director, Joint Cater Ltd, T/A The Woodlands Restaurants, 148 Regents Park Road, London, NW1 8XW

PLACE OF BIRTH: India, 18.7.47
MARITAL STATUS: Married
CHILDREN: Two (Rajat, Sapna)
COLLEGE: Punjab University
ACADEMIC QUALIFICATIONS: B.Com
PROFESSIONAL QUALIFICATIONS: Accountant
DIRECTORSHIPS: Joint Cater Ltd
HOBBIES AND INTERESTS: Reading, chess, tennis
PERSONAL PROFILE: Came to London in 1970 to study chartered accountancy. Started Woodlands in 1981 and developed into a chain. Opened branches in Singapore and two Italian restaurants in 1999. Also have a property company with various interests. Pioneer of South Indian vegetarian cuisine in UK.

MR NABIL SOUSSI (Schoolboy-Actor)

The Jackie Palmer Stage School Agency, 30 Daws Hill Lane, High Wycombe, HP11 1PW

PLACE OF BIRTH: Wycombe, 31.10.90
COLLEGE: Clayton Combinds
ACADEMIC QUALIFICATIONS: Actor
HONOURS/AWARDS: School Report
HOBBIES AND INTERESTS: Dancing, drama, bike riding, reading

MR SUBHASH VITHALDAS THAKRAR
(Chartered Accountant)

Senior Partner, Blackstone Franks, "Ganga Nivas", Cygnet Close, Northwood, HA6 2TA

PLACE OF BIRTH: Uganda, 10.7.55
MARITAL STATUS: Married
CHILDREN: Two (Ravi, Kavita)
COLLEGE: Birmingham
ACADEMIC QUALIFICATIONS: B.Com (Acc)
PROFESSIONAL QUALIFICATIONS: FCA, MBIM and FRSA
DIRECTORSHIPS: Blackstones Consultancy Ltd
MEMBERSHIPS: Member of OFWAT, Regulator of water industry, Member of Asian Business Association Committee of London Chamber
HOBBIES AND INTERESTS: Keep fit, gym, cycling
EMAIL: sthakrar@blackstone-franks.co.uk
PERSONAL PROFILE: Active in charitable activities. Part of committee of British Uganda Trust. Organiser of events for the Disraeli Club. Joint author to a number of business/tax books. I give lectures on business matters. Mentioned as premier accounting firm in Ram Gidoomal's book - 'UK Asian Maharajas'.

MISS JULFA BEGUM UDDIN (Student)

PLACE OF BIRTH: London, 14.10.85
MARITAL STATUS: Single
COLLEGE: Mulberry School for Girls
HONOURS/AWARDS: Netball, raising money for charity, Spellbound poem published
HOBBIES AND INTERESTS: Football, singing, basketball
PERSONAL PROFILE: I go to Mulberry School and will be in Year 9 in September. When I grow up I want to be a pilot or a doctor. I like football and other sports. I support Man Utd. I play netball for Mulberry School.

MISS NADIRA UDDIN (Student)

PLACE OF BIRTH: London, 19.3.86
MARITAL STATUS: Single
COLLEGE: Mulberry School for Girls
HONOURS/AWARDS: Swimming, athletics and basketball
HOBBIES AND INTERESTS: Football, basketball
PERSONAL PROFILE: I am a Mulberry School student. I am going to be in Year 9 next year. This year I was involved in a poetry project called Spellbound. I wrote a poem called 'The ant and the dove'. My favourite subject is RE. When I leave school I would like to be a journalist.

MR WALI TASAR UDDIN MBE JP (Director)

Bangladesh - British Chamber of Commerce UK, Shapla-Bhaban, 312 Lanark Road, Edinburgh, EH14 2LJ

PLACE OF BIRTH: Bangladesh, 17.4.52
MARITAL STATUS: Married
CHILDREN: Five (Hafiza, Suhaly, Shahan, Suhan, Ruhaly)
COLLEGE: Putney College
ACADEMIC QUALIFICATIONS: HNC
PROFESSIONAL QUALIFICATIONS: MBIM, FINST, SMM
DIRECTORSHIPS: Frontline Int, Air Ser Ltd, Universal Coba Corps Ltd
MEMBERSHIPS: Edinburgh Merchant Ltd, Member of the British Institute of Management
HONOURS/AWARDS: MBE, Young Scots of the Year
HOBBIES AND INTERESTS: Community service, football, watching TV for sport
EMAIL: waliuddin@aol.com
PERSONAL PROFILE: Britain's first Bangladeshi Consul-General in Scotland, chairman of Commonwealth Society Edinburgh. In 1992 the International Junior Chamber of Commerce awarded Young Scotland Award 1984. First Bangladeshi appointed Justice of the Peace in Scotland 1995. Awarded Member of the British Empire (MBE).
NOMINATED BY: Foysol Hussain Choudhury

MR SHREERAM VIDYARTHI (Writer-Publisher)

Editor, Indiawise, Borden Villa, Borden Lane, Sittingbourne, ME10 1BY

PLACE OF BIRTH: India, 7.10.38
MARITAL STATUS: Married
CHILDREN: Three (Anurag, Nachiketa, Madhumita)
COLLEGE: Finished Education
ACADEMIC QUALIFICATIONS: BA Hons Drama, CA, BA Music
PROFESSIONAL QUALIFICATIONS: Is an actor, and is an accountant
DIRECTORSHIPS: Directors
WEB SITE: www.indiawise.com
PERSONAL PROFILE: A seasoned journalist and broadcaster (active since 1956), I hold an MA in Eng Litt, have been writing in Hindi and English regularly. Ran a specialist bookshop - Books from India in London for 22 years.

MISS ANDREA JANE WILLIAMS (Singer)

Amas Internet, Amas@orangenet.co.uk

PLACE OF BIRTH: Pakistan, 18.6.57
MARITAL STATUS: Single
COLLEGE: Kilburn College
ACADEMIC QUALIFICATIONS: Baces Award creative writing
HONOURS/AWARDS: International Library Poetry Award
HOBBIES AND INTERESTS: Singing, songwriting, dancing
EMAIL: amas@orangenet.co.uk
WEB SITE: www.geocities.com/southbench
PERSONAL PROFILE: I would like to promote East-West relations due to my Anglo-Indian descent. Also to launch my own brand name cosmetics and fashion range. To have a hit record and my book published.

MISS ROUJEE YASMIN (Student)

DATE OF BIRTH: 24.4.86
MARITAL STATUS: Single
COLLEGE: Mulberry School for Girls
HOBBIES AND INTERESTS: Pop music, art (drawing)
PERSONAL PROFILE: I am student from Mulberry School. One of my poems was published in the Spellbound poetry book. I won third prize in the metropolice story competition when I was in primary school. I took part in the readathon sponsorship collection and was given a certificate.

Entrants in the Asians in the Millennium have been nominated for their achievements and contributions. You can nominate someone who deserves to be in the Who's Who of Asian Achievers 2000

Entries are free

Send in your nominations, including name, contact address and telephone number to: Books Division, Ethnic Media Group,

This list comprises the top 200 Asian individuals or close families in Britain as measured by their identifiable wealth. Those who qualify for the list include families from India, Pakistan, Bangladesh, Sri Lanka and East Africa or their children. We have included certain Non-Resident Indians (NRIs) who have made London their home.

We measure only assets we can identify - mainly business - through their accounts filed at Companies House, or their holdings in quoted companies. We have no access to bank accounts and do not attempt to compromise their privacy in this way.

Business assets are valued on the following grounds:

1) stakes in quoted companies are valued on their rating at the end of 1998 as published in The Financial Times.

2) It is much more difficult to value private companies. Where possible, we have tried to base a valuation on the prevailing price/earning ratio for a sector or an equivalent quoted company. Frequently this is impossible as profits in private

RULES OF ENGAGEMENT

companies are usually much lower as owners, quite legitimately, plough the profits back into the business rather than hand them over to the Inland Revenue. This has meant almost adopting a case-by-case basis, particularly with the many cash & carry businesses in the list with high turnovers and low profits. We have sought to achieve a balance in our valuations for these between turnover and profitability. We apologise in advance to those who may not agree with our assessment of their wealth.

3) Frequently, the holding companies or the majority shareholders in many of the Asian-owned businesses are companies or trusts based in Jersey or other so-called tax havens. We have uniformly assumed these to be part of the controlling family stake and valued the family accordingly.

4) Family stakes are pooled and in such instances we list the main family members with the words 'and family' to follow.

In addition, as this is a sensitive issue within families, we do try to break down the individual stakes in the family entry.

We do not rely on gossip or other tittle-tattle in compiling. Most of the information about individuals and their families has been gleaned from public sources such company accounts lodged in Companies House, quoted company documents lodged with the Stock Exchange.

We only use private information about individuals if it has been freely given for this list or if it has been published already in a reputable newspaper, magazine or reference work.

Wealth Code

Britain's richest Asians are listed in the following styles:

Position
Name age

Occupation
£ Value (last year's value)

The Asian audit 1999

A BUSINESSMAN in the know said, only half in jest, that "there are enough candidates in Leicester alone to fill Eastern Eye's rich list." We have resisted the temptation. But the observation, unscientific but intuitively spot-on, illustrates a wider truth.

Many British-Asians continue to thrive in Leicester, London and other cities, which, in the vernacular, 'have been dusted down with the brown pound'. This is, of course, the 'brown pound' of the small army of British-Asian shopkeepers, food manufacturers, wholesalers, distributors and other business risk-takers.

Gordon Brown, the chancellor, would scarcely disagree. He told a breakfast meeting of Asian businessmen that they were a credit to the country. Many of the breakfasting businessmen were from east Africa and their "dusting down of inner-city Britain" has produced a highstreet that, typically, resembles a south Asian city.

Or, as the Economist said in a rather more globally relevant context, "the success of Asian incomers will make Britain in 1999 resemble [multicultural] California". It said Asian families (especially those from east Africa) will be better off than the average white in the year ahead. The proportion of Asians attending UK universities will be higher than that of indigenous whites; and they will, on average, achieve higher grades. The typical British economist and business school graduate will soon be Asian.

The re-building of Britain has at its margins a business class that, in the third year of Britain's Richest Asian 200, shows no sign of losing steam. This year's list has a collective value of £7.5bn, a big rise on last year.

It is a mixed bag. The top 50 account for £6.bn and the bottom 50 just £250m. By sector the leading area of business by the number of entries is industry and manufacturing with 41, valued collectively at £3,545m, though it is dominated by the the the top four - the Hinduja family, Lakshmi Mittal, Lord Paul and the Madhavani family.

The next three highest ranking sectors are more representative of the broader community. Food retailing and production and cash and carry has 31 entries valued at £693m. Next is its commercial cousin, distribution and wholesale, with 30 entries valued at £274m; it

includes the UK's leading Asian grocer, Sir Anwar Pervez, the newly-knighted boss of Bestway (valued at £120m). Retailing, including fashion, follows, with 29 entires but valued at a total of £674m. The fastest-growing sector is computers, telecoms and information technology, with 16 entries valued at £410m.

What's the secret? Charan Sohal of Orbit International, a small Birmingham-based fashion company, reckons he knows. "The Asian philosophy is to work for the next generation. We (elders) have laid down the foundation and it is up to our ambitious sons to build the skyscraper for the next generation."

If there is a common thread uniting many entries in this year's listing, it is the question of succession. This concern has illustrated itself at various levels.

Foremost is the emergence of a second generation of British-Asians who are either taking charge or at least making special contributions. Charan Sohal's three sons, Inderjit, Rajinder and Sarrjit, are guiding the company founded by their father. It is is valued at £10m and, despite operating in a sector where margins are low, the brothers' ambitions are vaulting.

Angard Paul, the youngest of three sons of Lord Paul, the Labour peer and industrialist, has made his mark in a field as far removed from the family steel business as could be. Paul was co-producer of *Lock, Stock and Two Smoking Barrels*, the surprise British film success of 1998. The Harrow-educated Paul invested a reported £500,000 in a film with a total budget of £1m. The film took £11.2m at the box office, making it Britain's biggest financial film success of the year. Paul's desk is now full of film scripts, besides the more traditional steel, motor and manufacturing proposals.

The dilemma over succession was most clearly illustrated at Noon Products. Its owner, G K Noon, aged 62, decided the best course for growth was to sell out to a listed company, W T Foods, rather than pass on the reigns to his two daughters.

The stock market is a new arena for Noon and others such as Mike Jatania, who launched a new venture capital-backed company to carry on where Lornamead, his family-owned cosmetics firm, left off. His aim, he says, is to be the "boss of my own stock-market listed company within 3-5 years".

He may view with special interest the

damage wrought by the stock market on Ispat International, the company largely owned by Mittal, who this year slips to No. 2 behind the Hinduja family.

Although Ispat International made a significant acquisition in the US last year, the company's share price took a plundering. From a launch price of $27 in the summer of 1997, the price sank at one point last year to about $7. Mittal and his wife, Usha, are valued at £1,200m, down from £2,000 last year.

The Hinduja brothers, the top family after two years in the second berth, will regret that their year was defined by a row over their offer to underwrite a part of the Millennium Dome project, and not for business.

Subhash Chandra, owner of Zee-TV, rises to No 3 in a year when the Asian television battle took shape in the UK. Sony TV was launched, the first real competition to Zee TV, and Asianet was kicked off the airwaves in bits of east London, the first casualty of an increasingly competitive sector.

There were other casualties too. Rueben Singh is omitted from the list after the sale of his retail chain, Miss Attitude, raised doubts about his valuation.

We live in a global economy so this year we include the top Indian businesses in the US. Several million people of south Asian origin live in the US.

Their achievement is considerable, though it is less a function of immigration as has been the case in the UK. Instead, US Indians' success is the product of higher education and a migration into industry and information technology.

The impact has been spectacular. Amazon.Com and Microsoft recently paid several hundred million dollars each for two IT companies founded by expatriate Indians in California.

The fastest-growing Indian-owned company in the US was Intercontinental Software Solutions, founded by Haridas Kesavan and Mohan Viddam Reddy. The company's 1997 revenues totalled $3.75m, a 177 per cent on 1996.

On the Columbus Day weekend, the main public holiday in the US, Kesavan and Reddy were working at their factory.

Silicon Valley does not seem such as long way from Leicester, after all. ■

Hindujas in high spirits

1st
SRICHAND, 63, & GOPI, 59,
HINDUJA
AND FAMILY
Finance, industry, oil and telecoms
£1.3bn (£1.2bn)

● Srichand Hinduja is the patriarch of the global trading, oil and banking family, which this year is the new No 1 in the Top 200.

Yet politics rather than business earned the family attention last year. Their offer to underwrite the Spirit Zone, one of 14 zones comprising the £758m Millennium Dome, caused a political stink, taking the gloss of their rise from No 2 to the apex with a valuation of £1.3bn.

SP, as he is universally known, and Gopi Hinduja are two of four brothers who run a world trading, finance and industrial group from London, with a strong focus on India. The business was started by their father, who made his fortune in trading in Iran. Sangam, the Hinduja holding company, was named after the popular Hindi film, which their father distributed profitably in Iran.

Senior sources say the brothers are toying with the idea of selling stakes in some businesses following unsolicited offers. They may be tempted so as to plough more resources into their telecoms interests, the business that most excites the family. Yet talk of a retreat from any of the three key areas in which they operate in India is premature. The year ahead could be a watershed if only a fraction of the speculation about their 'refocusing' materialises.

At the heart of the family's manufacturing interests is Ashok Leyland, a vehicle-maker based in southern India. Sources say the brothers have declined a $1bn offer from a US volume car manufacturer anxious to gain a foothold in the Indian market. The same sources say a price of $200m has also been placed on the Astra pharmaceuticals business.

The family's cable television network is now one of the largest in India and is valued by bankers at $600m. Internet, data processing and telephony services are being piggy-backed on the cable network, an example of the convergence of media and telecoms that is driving so much change in the sector worldwide. In Bangalore, the family is also pumping resources into its software operations, on which they pin great hope.

Other industrial holdings include Gulf Oil International, which was bought for $280m in 1984 and is now expanding into China, Latin America and the far east, and Indian Chemical Corporation. The family has a $1.4bn joint venture power project with the UK's National Power. The brothers have received offers for their stake, say sources, and are apparently torn over whether to see through the project, one of several prestige schemes assigned 'fast-track' status by the Indian government, or sell at a premium. Similarly, investors have offered $200m for a 20 per cent stake in the family's finance and leasing division in India, say sources.

This speculation will keep the brothers busy and they presumably could have done without the fuss over the Spirit Dome. SP insists his £6m offer was designed to promote 'multicultural understanding'. In the event SP's desire, fashioned by a personal piety, was obscured by the political fall-out.

The row focused on the role of the

responsible minister at the time, Peter Mandelson, and the fact that the offer had come from Asian/Hindu billionaires.

Mandelson was accused of courting the family. He insisted he was championing the Dome, not actively soliciting funds.

At the time, Mandelson denied he would be compromised if he were seen to be raising money from businesses he was supposed to regulate as trade minister. (He later resigned for not disclosing a loan from a cabinet colleague.) In any case, both Church and parliamentarians were annoyed that a celebration marking 2,000 years of Christianity was being undermined by donations from secretive, devout Hindu businessmen.

The Church's discomfort was made worse by the fact that the Hindujas' offer emerged in the week of Diwali, the festival of light, the major Hindu festival. This concurrence was an unintended triumph of Hindu PR, though few at the Swaminayaran Mandir, the Hindus' spiritual heartland in north London, would interpret the events in such a benign way.

There may yet to be a final, defining twist. In December it was announced that the Dome would, after all, be fundamentally Christian in character. An account of the life of Jesus would be presented at the Spirit Zone, which would also have its own 'contemplation area'.

At the time of writing, the Hindujas had yet to make a formal commitment. It is thought improbable that the brothers, hardly proselytizers for their faith and for whom 'multi-faith harmony is pivotal, would subscribe to an event which celebrates the triumphalism of a single faith.

"We feel that we should focus to the maximum on multicultural understanding. We are all human beings. All faiths are not different - people created a lot of differences," SP has said.

He may well have asked himself, privately, why he bothered in the first place. That question has been overlooked in the furore. The brothers had been working on a more ambitious "monument to mutual inter-faith understanding". This was the £100m multi-cultural park near Peterborough, known as Concordia. But the project was abandoned after it failed to win Millennium funding. The Zone - politically-sensitive and unlikely to flop - presented an opportunity to revive the ideas underpinning Concordia. That encouraged the brothers, who saw it as the perfect vehicle on which to pin their idea. Their assumption seemed reasonable enough given the broader aims of the Dome - at least until the late reassertion of Christianity at its heart.■

Up and down year for steel baron

2nd
LAKSHMI MITTAL, 48
Steel
£1.2bn (£2bn)

● At home and at work, acquisitions marked the Mittal year. That will only partly mask the disappointment of a severe slump in the share price of Ispat International, the family's listed company. Lakshmi Mittal therefore loses his top slot, slipping into second place with a £1.2bn tag.

Nevertheless, there was much to admire. In December, Lakshmi Mittal's son and heir, Aditya, married his Wharton colleague, Megha. The four-day ceremony in Calcutta, with performers including film idol Shah Rukh Khan, was breathtaking even by the standards of moneyed-India.

Aditya is a director at the steel empire built up by his father, now the world's fourth biggest steelmaker. His primary role is strategy and acquisition and his new bride, who like Aditya has an MBA, may join her husband in the business.

At work, Mittal's LNM group, which incorporates the quoted Ispat International as well as the family's privately owned companies, continued the programme of expansion that has earned him the name of a latter-day Andrew Carnegie, the 19th century steel baron.

Mittal is the founder and majority shareholder in London-based Ispat International. The company was partially floated in 1997 on the New York and Amsterdam stock exchanges.

But the stock market volatility, Asian economic flu and fear of deflation in commodity prices have hit the price hard. From a launch price of $27, the share price at one point touched $7.

At December 1998, Mittal's Ispat holding (84 per cent) was worth $800m. Proceeds from the partial floatation in 1997 and a repaid loan add $430m. His private steel interests add perhaps another $530m. Private interests, property and cash add another $240m taking him to $2bn, or £1,200m.

Mittal remains a relatively anonymous figure narrowly defined by his wealth and Hampstead residency. This caricature is unfair to a man who, away from his Berkeley Square corporate headquarters, appears free of affectation. He is often seen on the social circuit of expatriate Indians and is described by friends as warm and unpretentious. This, as one Indian hostess remarked, is fortunate as it tends to put at ease assembled admirers in the marbled rooms where Mittal is entertained.

Mittal made his name in Indonesia where he settled after a childhood in Calcutta...

The admiration is, of course, deserved. After the disappointment of losing out in the race to buy Sidor, the Venezuelan state steel company in 1997, Mittal finally caught his big catch.

Last May, Ispat International paid £857m ($1.43bn) for Inland Steel, the sixth largest US steel-maker. The purchase made Ispat the eighth biggest steel producer in the world. The US deal was an important strategic breakthrough: the US is the largest steel market in the world and the Inland acquisition is a crucial fit in Mittal's ambition to become the pre-eminent global steel producer. With manufacturing plant in eight countries, Mittal is now the only truly global steel operator.

Ispat expects to produce some 19m tonnes of steel this year at plants in Mexico, Trinidad and Tobago, Canada, Germany, Ireland and the US. Mittal also privately owns plants in Kazakhstan and Indonesia, where he started his career two decades ago.

The Inland deal was quickly followed in June with the purchase of a one-third stake in Westfalische Drahtindustrie, a German maker of steel wire. This strengthens Ispat's hands in making high-value wire rods for products such as fasteners and ropes. A month later, Ispat was in the running for Co-Steel Sheerness, the UK arm of the Canadian Co-Steel multinational.

Mittal made his name in Indonesia, where he settled after a childhood in Calcutta. In India, he studied accountancy at the city's best college, and steel production at the feet of his father, Mohan Lal, who ran a small family-owned steel mill. Though he has lived outside India for 23 years, he still acknowledges the legacy of his Indian roots.

"Being Indian is a real advantage. You learn a lot about bridging differences and reaching compromises when you grow up in a country with over 300 languages and ethnic groups," he told *Fortune* magazine.

This attitude has underpinned his business strategy, which has been built on buying run-down, inefficient plants and reviving them through scrupulous and tough mangement and cost-saving production.

There have been some unexpected benefits too. At the giant Ispat-owned Karmet Kombinat plant in Timurtau, Kazakstan, the co-mingling between Indians and Kazaks has yielded rare cross-cultural benefits.

The local hotel has learnt to cook vegetarian dishes (the Indian managers hated the local Kazak cuisine), while the (whisky-loving) Indians have learned to drink vodka. Production has doubled at Karmet. ■

Good news for Zee's Chandra

3rd

SUBHASH CHANDRA, 48

Media

£450m (£450m)

● Subhash Chandra is an Indian television magnate who made his fortune in trading. He may now make his name as the man who stole a march on Rupert Murdoch in the huge Indian market.

Chandra describes as 'cool' the relationship between Zee and Murdoch's News Corp, which in 1994 paid a reported $47.5m for a 49.8 per cent share in Asia Today Ltd, the broadcaster of Zee TV. The tone of the relationship was perhaps set at the time when Chandra and his partners in ATL responded to Murdoch's suggestion of a full takeover by saying: "India's not for sale".

It was not a propitious start. The relationship has now come full circle with Chandra offering to buy out Murdoch for an undisclosed sum but at a considerable multiple to what the US magnate originally paid. "It's not going to work out and that's why we have said that it is better that we buy you out and then you do your things, you are free and we are free.

As India's closed economy was opening up in the early 1990s, Chandra's alliance with Murdoch carried huge symbolic resonance: it illustrated corporate India's internationalisation, and in an industry of the future.

"We have made a proposition to buy them out. We have already offered to take over their interests (in India). They have not responded," said Chandra in a remarkably candid assessment of a relationship that has clearly soured.

So frosty has the relationship become that Chandra speaks of legal action. "I don't know what is going in their minds...this partnership doesn't last because they are in violation of...shareholders agreements. So we are going to take action on those issues.

"I feel that Murdoch has not been able to really focus on India ... he's the victim of a lot of external forces, those who didn't want this to happen."

This is a reference to the vested interests - Chandra among them but including a large chunk of the domestic media - which opposes the entry of foreign media groups into the Indian market. As ever in India, this commercial opposition has been wrapped in a nationalist flag which goes by the name of 'swadeshi'.

"I strongly feel that foreign ownership has to be restricted," he says. "I strongly feel that controls should remain in the national hands." He says, for example, that explosive inter-communal issues that led to the deaths of thousands were "blown out of proportion" by foreign broadcasters and that Indians would have dealt with the subject more responsibly.

'Murdoch has not been able to really focus on India ... he's the victim of a lot of external forces...'

He offers the television oligarch's defence of the kind of programming deemed as corrupting "Indian mores", the very argument used by politicians to keep out foreign media. "We have to provide what is required in the competitive scenario," he says.

So what has gone wrong with Zee and News Corp? Five years ago, Murdoch, newly installed as the owner of Star TV, the largest satellite broadcaster in Asia, arrived in India amid great expectations. He met political rulers, industry titans, even the fabled cable-wallahs who controlled the cable distribution sector (after initially declining their invitation to talk).

Though India is a huge English-speaking market, many believe Murdoch underestimated the importance of indigenous programmes. News Corp is not strong on indigenous programming; Zee is. This has given local broadcasters an edge in production, a key advantage, and has dented Murdoch's charge into India, as well as that of other western broadcasters such as Carlton.

"Maybe they thought they were going on the right track," said Chandra. "I wouldn't like to comment on where they've gone wrong. I feel perhaps the culture of News Corp is to have a total control, whereas this partnership emphasised that we will do everything in joint partnership."

Chandra's remarkably bold comments reflect his position of strength. He is the undisputed television magnate of India though he displays few of the caricature signs commonly associated with media barons.

That may be because Chandra made his fortune in selling rice to Russians before migrating to television. He runs a diversified conglomerate and sees television as just another business.

He talks of the convergence of telecoms and media that is overhauling the industry worldwide in a measured way. Rarely does he display the passion of a Murdoch or CNN's Ted Turner and evangalise about 'popular choice', 'programming' and '24-hour broadcasting'.

He remains guarded, too when discussing the creative fine-tuning of programming. "I like to watch the news," he says, much as a corporate executive might say after a long day at the office.

The toil at the office has been fruitful. Two years ago bankers valued his Zee Multimedia Worldwide at £450m. Given the growing investor appetite for media ventures, that valuation may now be conservative. But we stick with it as the 1998 turmoil in Asia has played havoc with many assumptions on stock market valuations.

Chandra also owns the first Disney-type entertainment park in India and a large canning machinery operation. He has invested £20m, he says, in Britain. Asia TV Limited, his British subsidiary, pushed up profits from £646,000 to

4th

LORD PAUL, 68,
& FAMILY
Industry

£325m (£500m)

● A difficult year for the steel industry is reflected in the lower valuation for Caparo, the steel empire built up by Swraj Paul, since he came to Britain over 33 years ago. Lord Paul is now taking a back seat in the business, with day to day control in the hands of his three sons.

But slowing down seems to be an anathema to the 68-year old peer, who is carving out a new career into politics. He is becoming an adept member of the House of Lords, where he sits on the Labour benches. If the Lords are reformed, it will be people like Lord Paul who will be needed in the second chamber. But he is no poodle; he has severely criticised the government's sponsorship of British industry, about which he feels passionately. Lord Paul now reckons Caparo is worth around £325m in the current climate. His 1997 figures showing £24m operating profits on £542m sales underpin this valuation.

£857,000 on sales up from £9.5m to £11.9m in the year to March 1997. This year Chandra is looking to exploit the digital revolution that is transforming the global telecoms industry.

He plans to launch a clutch of new channels on Zee TV, his UK operation, which is just settling down after another morale sapping year. But Chandra is not dismayed. He is the fourth owner of a station which has seen several reincarnations since it was launched as TV Asia nearly a decade ago.

With an exciting digital world at his fingertips, Chandra does not envisage a fifth change of ownership. ■

5th
FELIX GROVIT, 56
Finance
£300m (£300m)

● The birth of the Euro may prove to be a major threat to Felix Grovit, the low-key owner of the Chequepoint chain of bureaux de change. Grovit, born in India as Fareed Ismail, eschewed a career at the Bar to move into proper-

6th=
JASMINDER SINGH, 47, & FAMILY
Hotels
£200m (£150m)

● "It's the company I want to see in the papers, not individuals." Nothing in the 15 years since Jasminder Singh made his remarks has made him change his mind.

Singh is one of the UK's biggest independent hoteliers. Yet he remains an intensely private individual in contrast to the high-profile characters the hotel industry invariably throws up. He rarely gives interviews. Instead he lets the success of his £200m Edwardian Hotel group speak for itself.

In 1997 Edwardian made £10m profit on sales of £74.9m. The Singh family owns around 86.6 per cent of the ordinary and deferred shares. The business is easily worth its £224m of net assets. We value the Singh stake at £194m. Other assets take the family to £200m.

Singh's reflections on his business strategy were made to the Catering Times in the early 1980s. Yet they remain pertinent today. He emerges as a businessman with a common sense approach to the trade; someone who views risk-taking not in the cavalier manner of a Donald Trump but with a quiet methodical approach that reflects the accountant in him.

He is cast as a generous employer who while disdainful of unions, supports his staff and upholds the principle of meritocracy. Finally, in many crucial areas of company development, he emerges as simply years ahead of his Asian contemporaries.

His business strategy is straightforward and has changed little. "The policy we adopted was to take over run-down properties and upgrade them to the highest standard possible, and it has certainly paid divi-

ty. He sold up his property empire in 1974 just before a property meltdown and set up Chequepoint instead. He has never looked back. By the mid-1990s, he had 130 bureaux in 11 countries, and in his last interview with the Mail on Sunday, Grovit said he planned to grow the business to 200 branches. Most of the 60 British branches are in the London area. Grovit family trusts own Chequepoint through Inver Trust

dends for us over the past few years."

This approach is as evident at his most recent acquisition, the Skyway Hotel near Heathrow airport, as it was when he bought and developed The Savoy Court in central London. The Savoy Court was his first purchase individually - Singh and his uncle Satinder Vohra had been partners before parting ways amicably - and the one that gave his Edwardian group a real kick-start in the early 1980s.

"It had been run down for 40 years and was reaching the end of its lease, which was a good reason for the previous owners not bothering to spend money on refurbishing it. We took the view that if we could improve the property and the market rental situation to the freeholders without them having to spend anything then we could get a renewal of the lease. That is exactly what happened."

Singh came to London from Nairobi in

Corporation, which has seen its net assets grow to around £270m by the early 1990s. We stick with last year's valuation of £300m for Grovit while we wait and see what effect the Euro will have on Chequepoint's business. Despite the threat, Grovit is quite relaxed about it and indeed supported the staunchly pro-European Europa Times in the early 1990s.

1970. Four years later he qualified as an accountant. But after a spell in the City and working in his own practice, he sought the advice of his uncle, Satinder Vohra, a noted hotelier with Sarvova Hotels.

Vohra gave Singh a tough 18-month crash course in running a hotel, which the young trainee would later describe as "useful".

The two relatives went into partnership together and bought the Edwardian Hotel in Harrington Gardens, London. After 18 months they sold the hotel and bought another, the Vanderbilt.

Singh's affection for the Vanderbilt was deep. "It has one of the most impressive facades in London, occupying one whole block on a prime site in Cromwell Road." He would later buy out his uncle's interest in the Vanderbilt. They are now friendly rivals.

Today Singh has seven hotels in central London, trading under the Edwardian Hotel Group umbrella, with 1,110 rooms. All the hotels are four or five-star. His latest acquisition has taken him out of central London. He plans to spend between £15m-£20m upgrading the Skyway Hotel, which he bought from Trusthouse Forte for £35m.

On the issue of flotation, Singh's views in the early 1980s still ring true today as many Asian-founded businesses consider whether to relinquish ownership through a sale to outside parties or pass the business onto the next generation.

The Edwardian group remains privately owned, but Singh's discussion of a possible float 15 years ago indicates how forward looking he was. "We have been looking at the stock market for some time and I would have thought we would provoke interest if we arrived there. If we were to go public and if our control was diluted, then any company considering a take-over would have to show they could produce the same sort of returns. But we would try to maintain the controlling stake in any deal if we went public," he said.

Singh remarked in the CT interview that the Edwardian group was not a family-run business but one built on meritocracy. That is strikingly true today: the group employs talented professionals and though there are some family members in key roles, the senior management is less obviously dominated by relatives.

His strong attachment to the country where he has made his fortune emerges strongly. "We are a British company, backed by British money... and we work by British business methods."

On his success he said: "It has come after a modest outlay and from that we have built up a company that is on a par with most of the smaller publicly quoted hotel groups."

6th=
TOM SINGH, 49
Fashion retailing
£200m (£150m)

● The £330m flotation of New Look, the Weymouth-based fashion chain duly took place last June just before the stock market turmoil of the summer. For Tom Singh, the flotation was the culmination of 30 years' hard work. A keep-fit enthusiast, he started New Look, a womenswear retailer, in 1969 with some money borrowed from his parents, who emigrated to the West Country from India in the late 1940s when Singh was a baby. He had planned to float in 1994 but called it off, angry with the City's modest pricing. In 1996, a large stake in the business was sold to City institutions for £170m. Singh and his family trusts retained a stake while receiving some £105m cash for the majority of their shares. Mindful of earlier City criticism, Singh took-on some high-powered executives on board to run the company while retaining the role of commercial managing director. It seems to have worked. While rival retailers who floated at the same time have seen their shares savaged, New Look's shares had only fallen 5.5p from their 165p offer price by the year end, or just over 3%. Indeed, in the six months to September

1998, New Look reported profits up 21%. It is even taking customers from such vaunted high street names such as M&S. As a result, Singh's remaining stake in New Look was worth almost £92m at the start of 1999. After-tax and allowing for past salaries and dividends, we reckon he is easily worth £200m.

8th
MANUBHAI MADHVANI, 70, & FAMILY
Plantations and trade
£150m (£150m)

● The gradual rebuilding of the Ugandan economy under the government of President Yoweri Museveni has been helped by returning Ugandan Asians keen to put the nightmare years of the Amin government behind them. In the lead has been the Madhvani family led by 69-year old Manubhai Madhvani, one of four brothers who ran a huge business empire in Uganda until their expulsion in 1972. Now based in London, they have rebuilt their conglomerate ranging from breweries to sugar factories and tea plantations. They have also invested in new areas such as tourism and computer software. Forbes, the influential US business magazine puts their fortune at about £140m as long ago as 1994.
Cautiously, given the volatility of world markets, we have only moved slightly forward to £150m despite all their impressive work in Uganda

9th=
GULU LALVANI, 59
Consumer electronics
£120m (£60m)

● An authoritative report in *The Sunday Telegraph* last September suggested that Gulu Lalvani was planning an £80m flotation of his Binatone consumer electronics business.

That price seems fair in the light of Binatone's £4m profit and £80m sales in the year to March 1998. Binatone - named after his sister, Bina, was set up in 1960 when Lalvani and his brother Partap started importing cheap pocket radios from Hong Kong. Lalvani is from Karachi and came to Britain as a student.

With Partap, he started in business selling imitation pearl necklaces from Hong Kong. It was when these went out of fashion that he turned to consumer electronics. It was Lalvani who helped Alan Sugar start in business in 1966. He allowed the 19-year old Sugar, who had just walked out of his job as a delivery boy, to take a week's supply of Binatone products on credit. Sugar sold the lot in one day and paid Lalvani that evening. Sugar took another consignment the next day - and the rest is history. In 1989, Lalvani bought out Partap and

now owns all of Binatone. He was briefly in the news in the summer of 1997 when the tabloid press reported that he took Princess Diana out to a nightclub less than three months before her death.

The proceeds from the sale of his 9% stake in Amstrad in early 1998, his other assets including a Belgravia home, a sumptuous Hong Kong penthouse, and at least four other homes give him a valuation of at least £120m.

9th=
SIR ANWAR PERVEZ, 64
Food distribution
£120m (£120m)

● Not many farmer's sons from Rawalpindi are able to send their sons to Eton and also receive a knighthood. But then Sir Anwar Pervez, knighted in the recent New Year's

Honours List, has worked his way to the top the hard way. He came to England in 1956 and worked as a Bradford bus conductor before opening his first convenience store in London's Earl's Court. That was in 1962. From those humble beginnings, he has built up the Bestway business. Based in West London, Bestway is now the second largest cash and carry operation in the UK. In the year to June 1998, Bestway made £24m profit on sales of £670m. It is easily worth £200m on these figures. Pervez and his

family trusts own around half the shares. With other assets and past salaries/dividends, he is easily worth £120m. His knighthood came for services to the food industry and for his charitable work. Part of Bestway's profits go to the Bestway Foundation, which provides equipment for schools in needy areas and sponsors foreign students in the UK.

11th
VIJAY, 49, & BHIKHU PATEL, 51
Pharmaceuticals
£113m (£25m)

● The National Pharmacy Association is undergoing something of a facelift. More than half its 11,000 members are Asians.

Pharmacy is popular among Asian because it combines a professional training, immense business opportunities and self employment. The outlook has been particularly promising in recent years.

Kirit Patel, who owns the Day Lewis chain of 35 pharmacies in southern England, is vice chairman of the NPA. He says the Asian network helped him acquire his first pharmacy.

A similar impetus helped Vijay Patel, Britain's top pharmacist. He has made the successful transition from dispensing drugs to running a large chain of pharmacies. "I always wanted to be in business so that I could control my destiny," he says.

Vijay Patel is chief executive of Waymade, an Essex-based pharmaceutical wholesale business which he runs with his brother, Bhikhu. In 1997, Waymade's profits rose 250 per cent to £5.3m on sales up 65 per cent at £85.5m. When 1998 figures are produced they are likely to show £8.1m profit on sales of £134.5m. It is easily worth £91m on these figures and is 100 per cent owned by the two brothers. They also own Chemys, a £17m sales chemists chain worth £8.75m, and have £13.75m of other assets, including commercial property.

Waymade is often featured in listings for the fastest growing companies, dynamic entrepreneurs etc. Three years ago Waymade came 86th in a national newspaper's top 100 fast-growing privately-owned companies.

"Bloody rich. That's what I always wanted to be," Vijay told *Enterprise* magazine.

It was an ambition driven by the difficult circumstances of their arrival in the UK from Kenya in the early 1970s. The brothers lost their father when they were small children and they were raised by their mother. They attribute much of their success to her strong leadership.

Vijay studied at night school and then university before opting for pharmacy rather than medicine because it offered greater scope for business. He opened his first chemist's shop in Leigh-on-Sea with a loan guaranteed by an uncle.

Bhikhu was an architect but was drawn into his brother's more appealing business. They teamed up and expanded the one shop to 15, all in Essex. This became the basis for Waymade, which was set up in 1984.

In the early days Vijay concentrated on sales and Bhikhu on finances. In fact, when it came to sales, Vijay, the younger by two years, was a driven man. He was able to buy bulk goods more cheaply than from his regular wholesale suppliers. So he started selling to his retail rivals and kept a small margin. The growth was exponential and laid the seeds for Waymade.

His customers include small village chemists and Boots, the multiple, where he once turned down a job in favour of a smaller group which allowed him to complete his training.

Waymade still specialises in marketing and distributing prescription medicines and manufacturing surgical products and medical devices. Its main market is domestic, but it is exporting more now. The company is broadly divided into four divisions - medicines, distribution, and manufacture of dressings and bandages. The final one is "innovative medical devices", which covers a portfolio of branded prescription products acquired through licensing and marketing agreements and joint ventures.

The brothers recently launched an own brand label called Sovereign. They plan to buy drugs developed by multinationals, which are selling under pressure of costs or because the lines do not fit into their global strategy.

Vijay has not fully exorcised the pharmacist in him. He is behind the counter every Saturday, helping serve customers at the chain of chemists he owns. This helps him keep in touch with the customer - "the single most important person in the business."

12th=
RATILAL CHANDARIA, 63
Industry
£100m (£100m)

● Chandaria is one of three East African brothers who control Comcraft, a low-key industrial group with extensive steel, chemical and plastic interests in 40 countries. In Britain, one of their major operations is the Mainetti coat hanger manufacturing business based in the Scottish borders. Despite the fact that profits at the business fell from £3.9m in 1996 to £2.8m in 1997, on sales down £21m at £28.9m, we stick with our very conservative £100m valuation of last year. Sources have suggested that the Chandarias' whole empire could be worth close to £1 billion. But as we cannot measure the level of debt in the disparate empire, we cautiously stick with £100m, however conservative that may be.

12th=
TAHIR MOHSAN, 28, & FAMILY
Computers
£100m (£50m)

● Mohsan, one of the youngest managing directors in business, has led a low profile life - until now. He was recently reported to

have met Prince Charles at Buckingham Palace. At the same time, Mohsan's company, Time Computers, is advertising its wares on television as well as through the press. But who is Mohsan? His rise in our listing is due in no small measure to his elder brother, Dr Tariq Mohammed, a Pakistani-born doctor. In the mid-1980s, worried that his younger brother - then a teenager living in Blackburn - would get up to mischief, Mohammed determined to start a business that would keep idle hands busy. In 1987, Time Computers was born as a mail order business with Mohsan as managing director. The business, which was initially based at their parents' corner shop, grew so fast that the home was filled with computers in every room. Today, Time is a major business selling computers by mail order from purpose built premises in Burnley and Blackburn. The holding company, Granville Technology, saw its profits soar to £6.2m on sales of £103.3m in the year to June 1997. It is easily worth £100m and is owned by Mohsan and his family.

12th=
SONU SHIVDASANI, 32, & FAMILY
Leisure and industry
£100m (£100m)

● The son of the late Indoo and Mrs Lakshmi Shivdasani, 32-year old Sonu comes from a successful Sindhi family with a major empire embracing industrial and food plants in Nigeria, tea estates in India and vineyards in France. They also have a finance house in Geneva. Eton and Oxford-educated Sonu was born in London, and is carving out a career on his own in the leisure sector, with developments in the Maldives and Thailand. Inlaks Holdings, the main business, is registered in the Virgin Isles. In Britain, they have some business interests including Homac Seafood, based in Edinburgh, with £1m of assets. The scale of the family wealth may be gauged from Sonu's West London home, which was valued at £5.5m in 1997. The family are generous donors to charity via the Inlaks Foundation started in 1976, which is registered in Liechtenstein. A £100m valuation is probably a tad conservative but we stick with that until more information becomes available.

12th=
RASIKLAL THAKRAR, 61, & FAMILY
Retailing
£100m (£13m)

● Last year we were guilty of a major undervaluation of the Thakrar family. First we assumed that the family did not own all the company (they do) and secondly the profits have roared ahead at Ciro Citterio, the men's fashion chain. The Birmingham-based company made £7.4m profit on sales of £84m in the year to January 1998, double its 1997 figure. In the year to January 1999, it should make £8.5m on sales of £90m. On these figures it is easily worth £95m even in today's climate. We add £5m to the Thakrar family wealth for property and other assets. Not bad for someone who started in business in 1973 with his first Leon Allan men's wear shop in Birmingham a year after being expelled from Uganda by Idi Amin.

16th
MIKE JATANIA, 34, & FAMILY
Cosmetics and beauty products
£90m (£12m)

● Jatania is chief executive of Lornamead, a London-based company specialising in hair and skin care products. He is one of four brothers who came to Britain in 1969 from Uganda before the Amin terror. His three brothers - George, Vin and Danny - are also heavily involved in the company, which specialises in buying brands from multinationals and marketing them internationally. Last year, they acquired the Harmony hair spray brand off Unilever, the number two in Britain, for an undisclosed sum, though industry estimates put the price at £25m. With their international network, the Jatanias can push Harmony into 65 countries as well as in the British market. They aim to repeat the Harmony strategy with other brands that are currently rather neglected in the portfolios of multinationals. To help speed the process, they have formed a new company for acquisitions called EMVI, with heavyweight venture capital backing from Alchemy Partners, who have taken a 33.3% stake in the company, leaving the Jatanias with 66.7%. With this focused approach to brands, the brothers are aiming to build a business that could float on the stock market within the next 3 to 5 years valued at perhaps £200m. Last year the Jatania businesses made around £5m profit world-wide. Valued on a par with rival cosmetics and skin care businesses, their operations are currently worth perhaps £90m.

17th
NAT PURI, 59
Industry
£85m (£85m)

● Nat Puri, the East Midlands industrialist, knows he has a battle on his hands. While 1997 was a good year for his four main companies, Melton Medes, Conder Structures, Blugilt Holdings and Melham, 1998 proved more difficult with profits falling. Under the pressure of increased competition from cheap imports and suffering from the high pound, Puri is determined to become more competitive and says he must improve the bottom line by £6m to survive in 1999. He knows what he is talking about. An Indian-born maths graduate, he came to Britain in 1966 and trained as an engineer. In 1975, he started his own business as a consulting engineer and has since built up Nottingham-based Melton Medes and his other companies into one of the largest private industrial groups in Britain. In 1997, the total pre-tax

profits of the four businesses reached £15m, of which £13m is attributable to Puri. These figures easily justify last year's £85m valuation which we stick with in the light of lower company values in the industrial sector and Puri's comments about the 1998 figures.

18th
HUMAYUN MUGHAL, 46
Computers
£72m (£45m)

● Mughal arrived in Britain 25 years ago with just £15 in his pocket from his native Pakistan. After studying electronics at Liverpool University, he worked for a major electronics company. In 1979, he started Akhter Group, a computer operation. The Harlow based company was planning a stock market float in the summer of 1997, which would have valued it at around £60m,

but Mughal called it off because of stock market conditions. The business is performing strongly and should make at least £5m profit in 1998-99. We value the company at around £85m on these figures. That values Mughal's 84.6% stake at nearly £72m.

19th
RASHMI THAKRAR, 54
Rice imports
£70m (£30m)

● Business is going nicely for the 'rice king' of Britain. He has over half the market through his company Tilda Rice, which continues to enjoy a high profile thanks to the television adverts featuring well-known actress and author, Madhur Jaffrey. Tilda enjoys the benefits of a modern plant and private jetty in Essex. Thakrar and his family was expelled from Uganda in 1972 by Idi Amin.

In the latest accounts we saw, for the

year to June 1996, Thakrar's main holding company, Braunstone Properties, saw a sharp increase in profits to £5.8m on £91m sales. We value it slightly less than the ratio for quoted food companies at around £70m.

20th
JAMES CAAN, 38
Recruitment consultancy
£61m (£3.4m)

● Another serious undervaluation last year. James Caan founded the Alexander Mann business in 1985 when he identified and filled a gap in the British recruitment market by introducing executive search to the middle management sector. This was followed by the explosion in information technology in the early 1990s when Caan saw an untapped market in the flexible IT workforce. He also successfully introduced

a partnership culture into his organisation enabling top executives to become equity partners in the growing Alexander Mann Group.

His strategies have enabled the company to sustain 100% growth year on year over the past five years, culminating in 1998 revenues of over £80m with profits exceeding £6m, and a network of over 120 offices worldwide. Caan's stake in his various businesses is valued at around £54m, with other assets of £7m. Virgin Fast Track recently included one of Caan's business interests in its league table of the top 100 fastest growing companies in the UK. A group with such an impressive growth record is a prime candidate for a UK stock market flotation. At only 38, Caan's ambitions have clearly not peaked.

21st=
IQBAL AHMED, 42, & FAMILY
Food production
£60m (new entry)

● Ahmed is chairman and managing director of two separate companies,

Seafood Marketing International and Iqbal Brothers, both based in Manchester. He owns the businesses with his two brothers, Kamal and Bilal. The family is from Bangladesh.

They began Iqbal in 1976 and Seafood Marketing, which trades under the Seamark name, 15 years later. Seamark processes shrimps under its

own brand name and exports them throughout the EU and other countries. They were awarded a Queen's Award for Exports last year. Iqbal, which is largely UK-based in its activities, also wholesales other foodstuffs. On the back of profits of around £4m in 1998, we value Seamark at around £50m on a par with equivalent quoted companies. Adding in Iqbal Brothers (a partnership) takes the Ahmed asset wealth to perhaps £60m.

21st=
LORD, 68, & APURV BAGRI, 39
Metal trading
£60m (£80m)

● Profits at Minmetco, the Bagri holding company for the family's metal trading interests, moved up marginally in the year to March 1998, from £2.8m to just over £3m on turnover down around £13m at £176m. Valued on a par with other quoted 'financial' businesses, these figures value Minmetco at £44m - roughly its net asset figure. Lord Bagri, chairman of the London Metal Exchange knows all about metal trading. Born into a middle class family in Calcutta in 1930, he has been in the business as an apprentice, then an employee and finally on his own since the age of 15. He came to Britain at 19, eventually setting up his own company, Metdist, and joined the LME's management committee in 1973. He was elevated to the LME's main board in 1983, becoming chairman in 1992. Bagri was widely admired for the way that the exchange emerged unscathed from the Sumitomo scandal in which a rogue Japanese copper trader ran up losses of £2.4 billion. This work and the charitable efforts of the Bagri Foundation led to his peerage. The family business is now largely run by his son, Apurv. We reckon that other assets and past dividends - £6.75m in 1998 alone - take the Bagris to £60m.

21st=
GURCHAIT, 49, & GURNAIK CHIMA, 40
Retailing
£60m (£50m)

● Press reports in recent months have speculated on the possible flotation of the Chima brothers' Bon Marche fashion chain based in Huddersfield. But the reports have been dismissed as pure speculation by the company, though if the business were to think about a stock market quote, it would be a very attractive investment. The business was started as a market operation in East Anglia by their father Parkash Chima, and his sons joined their cousin to develop a market operation in northern England. They opened their first shop in Doncaster in 1985 and are expanding at 25 stores a year to reach a 400 branch target in the UK. Their cousin was bought out in 1996 and the Chima brothers own all the shares. They remain as directors but have taken some top class retail managers from BhS and Body Shop to grow the business. Though profits grew by around £500,000 to £4.48m on sales of nearly £8m at £81.5m, we only raise last year's valuation by £10m.

21st=
SHAMI AHMED, 36
Fashion and property
£60m (£60m)

● The first signs of Shami Ahmed's new business strategy were apparent in January when he took small stakes in the retailers House of Fraser and Austin Reed. His plans include investing a further £5m from his personal fortune. Ahmed is reckoned to be moving into underperforming retail and property companies to turn them round. It is 12 years since he started the Legendary Joe Fashion empire, having built up his early business experience from working on his father's market stalls in the North West. The family had moved to the area from Pakistan when Ahmed was two and he left school at the earliest opportunity to go into business.

The Joe Bloggs group - which besides the Joe Bloggs jeans business also includes household names such as Gabicci and Elizabeth Emanuel - turned over in excess of £50m last year. The Joe Bloggs brand name gives it at least a £30m valuation. Ahmed's more recent forays into property add at least £30m.

Ahmed's unique business style - in particular his bitter bust-up with high society designer Elizabeth Emanuel - was memorably portrayed in a BBC documentary on great corporate battles of the 1990s.

Ahmed emerged much as his image con-

sultants might have wished - northern working-class, iconoclastic, brutal and a winner. Emanuel, whose business was rescued by Ahmed, must have wished she had never set eyes on him, still less join him in a business.

The tempestuous relationship collapsed under the burden of a yawning divide between two driven individuals: it was a confrontation between north and south; high fashion and mass production; immigrant and establishment.

Emanuel, who has dressed Belgravia's finest, said her creativity was emasculated after Ahmed forced her to move to Wembley, the heartland of Hindu Gujaratis, where saris, not ballgowns, form the fashion landscape. This was a provocative instruction, guaranteed to make Emanuel implode. The designer felt disoriented working in a 'studio' surrounded by terraces of semis, newsagents and grocers. She moaned that she could not deliver the lovely silk dresses that made her so desirable in old-money Belgravia.

"I just could not work in Wembley," she said, in a comment resonating with sub-text. She had ventured into a world that proved a fashion, commercial and geographic disaster. The two parted company, with Ahmed retaining the brand-name.

25th
RAJAN KUMAR, 37, & FAMILY
Fashion
£50m (£50m)

● In a recent interview, Rajan Kumar said 'Of course there is talk of recession.' But he added: 'We find that our business is increasing quite well at the moment.' He runs the Rajan Group, a Manchester-based fashion business which supplies middle-market stores such as New Look. The Rajan Group also has its own labels and designs such as Whispering Smith and Iron Hammer. The business was started in 1967 by his father, Lal Kumar, who had started out on a Chorley market stall. Rajan Kumar joined in 1981 after taking a business studies degree from Salford University. We value the company at over £40m on the back of £1.3m profit and sales of £38.9m in the year to March 1998. Other assets take the Kumar family to £50m.

Food king Noon sells up

26th=
GULAM NOON, 61
Food production
£40m (£25m)

● G K Noon has always been a standard bearer for the Asian business community. But his decision to sell the business that made his fortune has raised eyebrows. As with most things he undertakes, the sale proved to be an enduring talking point.

In December Noon, who was awarded the MBE three years ago, was paid £50m in cash and stock (£7.5m is linked to profit targets up to March 2000) for the sale of Noon Products to W T Foods, a diversified ethnic foods group based in Hertfordshire. After tax and allowing for other assets, he is worth around £40m.

The deal was a "reverse takeover". Typically, small and dynamic companies often "reverse" into a larger target company when they want to acquire a stock market listing but are unable, or reluctant, to do it alone. The Noon deal was the largest takeover of a Asian-founded company in the UK.

Noon Products is arguably the best-known Asian franchise in the UK. W T Foods has grown mostly by acquisition and has had its eye on Noon Products for several years: the Noon acquisition was its third purchase of an ethnic foods producer since April 1997.

The sale struck a chord in the community. Asian companies in the UK cherish the principle of family ownership of businesses. They argue that this is not only socially and culturally beneficial; it also affords commercial advantages.

Why did Noon sell? Noon, pictured with his wife, Mohini, says he sold because this was the only way the business could grow. He was keen to protect and develop the enviable franchise; Sainsbury buys some 70 per cent of his output. He says the decision was his alone though he did consult his brother.

Observers say Noon's decision was guided by a central factor: would the

business continue to grow in the hands of his family but without his presence. The answer was "no".

The synergies between WT and Noon Products were compelling, say Noon and Keith Stott, chairman of W T Foods. WT Foods has an established distribution network in southern Europe and believes it can extract value and savings from Noon. Centralised marketing will produce savings, for example. The management strongly denies speculation of job cuts among the 500 mostly Asian staff.

It is thought that a labour issue at the company, which arose last year when a small group of workers demanded union recognition, may have influenced Noon's decision to sell. Earlier this year Noon recognised the workers' demands for full union recognition, ahead of new legislation.

Noon's daughter, Zeenat Harnal, who has worked alongside her father since the firm was started a decade ago, said the labour dispute soured relations with the workers.

The showdown hurt Noon, who is regarded as a benevolent employer. "We are like a family here," says Harnal.

The mood may have changed but the line-up remains the same. Under the terms of the deal Noon and his senior management, including his brother and daughter, will remain with the company for at least two years. Noon, as one of WT Foods' largest shareholders, has been appointed a non-executive director

of W T Foods.

The sale raised broader questions in the Asian community, where Noon is an advocate of the Asian family-owned business. Supporters of this principle argue that by concentrating ownership and management in the hands of a small family core, decision-making is centralised and, in practice, speedier. Strategic decisions, whether arrived at in the boardroom, the temple, the mosque or at home, are quickly enacted, invariably by relatives.

Will the sale set a trend? Opinion is divided. Traditionalists argue that the new generation is unquestionably qualified to take over and point to several examples of smooth transitions. Critics say Noon's sale is an implicit admission that his daughters and brother, though faithful servants, are not dynamic growers of a business.

Harnal admits she was disappointed not to have been given the opportunity to grow the business. She now accepts her father's decision, and strongly denies that her sex disqualified her for the top job. "It had nothing to do with his decision to sell. It was irrelevant."

The traditionalists say that at times of stock market uncertainty, family ownership is a bulwark that is commercially appealing.

The modernisers say a pyramid management structure is no longer desirable, and even commercially wilful. They say it leads precisely to the Noon predicament: there was no one considered fit to take over.

This camp argues that many Asian businesses are now mature and need to look beyond the family. They need working capital to expand and realistically that can only come from the stock market, and not the family. Similarly, they are no longer dependent for either recruitment or business on a narrow ethnic source. They employ senior executives from outside the community and are open to new ideas.

These and complimentery changes such as diversification and greater compliance with trends in corporate governance, help Asian businesses integrate with the mainstream.

Noon says he has taken a brave decision but one that does not leave him completely adrift. Business is in his blood. He retains the franchise for Noon Restaurants, the outlets that he started three years ago at Heathrow Airport. Noon's youngest daughter, Zamin Sekhon, who was horrified by the sale, runs the restaurant and has no intention of letting this business slip through the family fingers.

26th=
NARESH, 57, & MAHESH PATEL, 50
Food retailing and film processing
£40m (£45m)

● We cut the value of the Patel brothers by £5m this year, reflecting both the slight fall in profits at their main holding company for their Europa food retailing interests and the lower values for food groups this year. In the year to September 1997, Adminstore saw its profits fall from £2.8m to £2.6m though sales were up nearly £5m at £68.4m. In 1985 the two Kenyan-born brothers bought up an old

food business and re-named it Europa. In 1997, Europa took over the Cullens convenience store group for £7.4m. The business is worth perhaps £40m, which values the 80% stake held by the Patels and their family trusts at perhaps £36m. We add £4m for their stake in the Colorama film processing business, where profits and sales in the year to September 1997 were only slightly down on last year at £226,000 and £16m respectively.

28th
JOHN MATTO, 50
Textiles
£36m (£30m)

● Matto, who hails from Punjab, was 15 before he could read. His first business venture was a coffee bar. But he is now a major force in the British textile industry through his Grasshopper Holdings. Based in Wolverhampton, Grasshopper is a major babywear supplier. and a model employer. Matto, who owns all the shares in the business, attributes his success to "hard work, dedication...finding a niche market...and not having too many chiefs." It works.

In the year to June 1997, Grasshopper made £3.6m profit and is worth at least £30m as a result. We add £6m for other assets and property.

29th=
SHIRAZALI DHARAMSHI, 50, & FAMILY
Property and paper
£35m (£40m)

● The apparent £5m fall in our valuation of the Dharamshi family actually belies what was a pretty good year for their main paper-making business based in Leicester.

LPC is a very successful family-owned company which makes disposable paper products, operates chemists shops and deals in property.

Incorporated in 1988, its profits rose from £2.8m to £3.2m on sales up from £50.8m to £51.4m in the year to September 1997.

But with lower company valuations in the paper sector this year, we cut the value of the business to around £35m despite its good performance. Sorry.

29th=
AMARJIT SANDHU, 62, & FAMILY
Wholesale
£35m (£35m)

● Amarjit Sandhu started in business in Hong Kong in 1972 but has been investing heavily in Glasgow since 1985. He has two Scottish companies, ABS (Scotland) and Saraki (UK) and a Hong Kong business IPJ Agencies. He divides his time between Scotland and Hong Kong. The three businesses have between them sales of well over £30m. Sandhu says he pays "a lot of money to the Inland Revenue" and reckons the three are worth around £35m. We still agree.

29th=
NISSIM MUSRY, 71, & FAMILY
Textiles
£35m (new entry)

● The Musry family owns about half the shares in Wrengate, a Manchester textiles importer and processor. Nissim Musry is chairman of the company, which was founded in 1974. Wrengate made pre-tax profits of £6.1m on sales of £87m in the year to April 1997. It has a strong balance sheet and is worth £70m.

29th=
ANIL RUIA, 42, & FAMILY
Textiles
£35m (£35m)

We still reckon that Anil Ruia and his family interests own around a half of Wrengate, the textile importer and processor based in Manchester where Nissim Musry (qv.) and his interests own the other half. At least half the shares are held by Gibraltar-based companies. Wrengate made pre-tax profits of £6.1m on sales of £87m in the year to March 1997. It has a strong balance sheet and is worth £70m.

29th=
PERWEEN 42 & DR TALIB WARSI, 52
Food manufacturing
£35m (£45m)

● The Millennium Bug should hold no fear for Perween Warsi. As she revealed in The Sunday Times last October, her company, S&A Foods has invested £750,000 in a millennium compliant system that links S&A much more closely with key

customers and suppliers. In 18 months, the company has gone from being heavily dependent on manual operations to automation where no paper at all is generated in the order and supply chain. This is the sort of careful far-sighted planning that has helped Mrs Warsi to an MBE in the 1997 honours list and the 1996 award of Woman Entrepreneur of the Year. Yet she could have remained as the wife of a Derby GP has she not despaired of ever finding a decent samosa in her local supermarket in Derby. She married her husband Talib at the age of 17 in an arranged marriage and in 1975, came to Britain, living first in Wales and later Derby. She started making her own samosas and, today, she has turned that simple idea into a major food firm, S & A Foods (named after the initials of her two sons).

As the business grew, she sold a 70% stake to the now defunct Hughes Group to finance a new factory. When Hughes went into receivership, she had to show potential buyers round the factory before she was able to secure funding from 3i to buy back her 70% stake from Hughes for £1m. The venture capital firm also took a 30% stake itself which was a shrewd move. In 1997, S&A Foods increased profits by £500,000 to £2.78m on sales up £10m at £30.8m. Last year we were a little bit over enthusiastic in our valuation. Also food companies are not as valuable this year and despite the profits increase, we reckon a £50m valuation for

the business is fair. That values the stake held by Perween Warsi and her husband at £35m. Mrs Warsi recently rejected speculation that S&A was in merger talks with W T Foods, the acquisitive listed company which recently bought Noon Products. She said she valued her independence.

29th=
FAKHRUDDIN SUTERWALLA, 60, & FAMILY
Food processing
£35m (£20m)

● Fakhruddin Sutterwalla and his four brothers - Hatim, Siraj, Mansoor and Iqbal - continue to prosper as the pioneers of ethnic branded foods. The TRS Cash & Carry business was started by their father, Taher, but the expansion is due to the sons. This year we have found some more of their businesses and five separate TRS companies we have identified made around £2.7m profit on £99m sales in 1996 and 1997. On these figures, the business assets are conservatively worth £35m.

35th=
GULSHEN BHATIA, 65, & FAMILY
Hotels
£30m (£12m)

● Having found the main Bhatia family company we are now in a position to raise the valuation of the formidable Mrs Bhatia and her family. A widow from Tanzania, who invested her life savings in a small London hotel 15 years ago, Mrs Bhatia executed a series of deals which left her with Great Western Hotel next to Paddington Station. Muirgold Limited, the family holding company, made a £2.7m profit on sales of £10.28m in the year to February 1998. Valued on a par with quoted leisure companies, it would be worth over £30m on these figures. We value the Bhatia family at this level.

35th=
MAQ RASUL, 45
Retailing
£30m (£40m)

● A £1m fall in profits at Global Video and lower company valuations leads us to cut the value of Maq Rasul by £10m this year. Faisalabad-born Rasul came to Glasgow in 1964 as a child, and despite a tough upbringing in the Gorbals as one of 11 children, he went to university, graduating with a civil engineering degree in 1976. He scraped the money together to start a

grocery shop in 1977 and moved into video rentals after selling that business for £100,000. Global, his Glasgow-based company, is now expanding into England. But in 1997, profits fell by £1m to £2.7m though sales were up to £25.9m. Valued on a par with equivalent quoted retailers puts a £35m value on the company. 3i, the venture capital group, is now a shareholder, but Rasul and his family trusts own most of the shares. He is easily worth £30m.

35th=
MONI VARMA, 50
Rice production
£30m (£10m)

● Indian-born Moni Varma was raised in Malawi where he went into business making barbed wire. He developed strong trading links with Europe and other parts of Africa before moving to Britain in 1983 and worked as a steel and commodity trader. He was approached by Indian relatives to explore rice trading opportunities in England. he saw a gap in the market and set up a rice milling operation in West London. But having outgrown that site, he built an ultra-modern facility at Rochester in Kent, complete with its own jetty. After four years, this site has reached full capacity and a £6m investment is planned to double capacity. Five years ago, Varma set up his own milling and procurement operation in India to secure a supply of quality rice for which the British have a growing appetite. He had to overcome fierce opposition from Indian bureaucracy and rival rice businesses, but prevailed in the end. In all the Veetee Group made £2.75m profit on sales of around £49m in its global operations in 1997-98. With his other businesses ranging from paint manufacturing to cashew nut farming, he is easily worth £30m.

35th=
RAMESH SACHDEV, 53
Healthcare
£30m (£15m)

● Sachdev, a chartered accountant and property dealer, started nursing home operator Life Style Care in 1987. A planned stock market float was called off in 1994 when the stock market weakened. Last year Sachdev finally sold the company making around £25m for his family's 85% stake. The company was re-named Ultima, but Sachdev has kept the Life Style Care name and started a new nursing home business. He also has property interests through Britannic Trustees, a North London-based company worth around £5m. In all Sachdev is easily worth £30m.

35th=
JATTI, 32, & AVNEET SAHNI, 28
Computers
£30m (£20m)

● Husband and wife team Jatti and Avneet Sahni came to Britain from Kuwait in 1990. Based in Manchester, they have built up VIP Computer Centre into one of Britain's fastest-growing companies. They own all the shares in the business which distributes computer components. In its last filed accounts for the year to October 1997, VIP made £1.95m pre-tax profits on sales of £72.3m. In the current year, profits will hit £2.1m on £84m of sales. It is easily worth £30m on these figures. Jatti Sahni reckons VIP's success is down to a philosophy of "learning through trust." He learnt UK business practices through working closely with non-Asian management in trustful two-way relationships. He adds: "If non-Asians went to India - or anywhere else in the world - to establish a business, we'd think them rather stupid if they did not recruit from, and work close-

ly, with the local talent." Sensible advice.

35th=
NIRMAL SETHIA, 57, & FAMILY
Property
£30m (new entry)

● Nirmal Sethia is chairman of N. Sethia (London) Limited, a property letting company based in the City. Incorporated in 1975, the business is totally owned by Sethia and his family.

In the year to July 1997, N. Sethia (London) made a £2.46m profit on sales of £30m. On these figures, it is easily worth over £25m. We add £5m for other assets including dividends of £1.28m taken by the Sethia family in 1996 and again in 1997.

35th=
TEJ, 34, & BOBBY DHILLON, 30
Hotels
£30m (£20m)

● Tej Dhillon is actively looking to build up the family hotel assets by a chunky acquisition. He tried to buy hotels last year but refused to pay the crazy prices being demanded. The recession may help to

bring prices down to more realistic levels.

Tej, a London University graduate, worked in the City before starting his own hotel and property business with his sister. It must have been in their blood. Their late father came to Britain from India in 1952 with

around £3 in his pocket and started a restaurant business. In 1998, Dhillon Property Developments, with seven hotels and numerous other properties, made around £1.7m post-tax profits and is easily worth £25m on these figures. A property portfolio adds another £5m.

35th=
KIRIT, 46, & MEENA PATHAK, 42
Spices
£30m (£30m)

● Profits at Worldwing Investments, the holding company for the Patak Spices business grew sharply in the year to September

1997, from £384,000 to £770,000 on sales up over £5m at nearly £29m. In 1994 Patak Spices headed a list of top selling brands and has never looked back publicity-wise.

The business is owned and run by husband and wife team, Kirit and Meena Pathak from a factory in Wigan. Despite the growth in profits and sales, we stick with last year's £30m.

43rd=
ABDUL ALIMAHOMED, 59, & FAMILY
Packaging
£28m (£15m)

● Abdul Alimahomed emigrated from Malawi with just £2,000 in his pocket in 1974. Today he is chairman of Euro Packaging PLC, a Birmingham-based manufacturer of paper bags and plastic carrier bags incorporated in 1977. His family own all of Euro Packaging. Despite the low rating for the packaging sector, it is easily worth £15m on the back of £2.05m profit and sales of £42.8m in 1997.

Other businesses add £5m while the family own properties worth some £8m.

43rd=
DILJIT RANA, 60
Property and hotels
£28m (£10m)

● Diljit Rana started Andras House, a Belfast-based property and hotel group in 1991. It has benefited from the current peace settlement in Northern Ireland and is leading the way with some bold developments. Andras House, 100% owned by the Rana family, is expecting to make £1m

profit on £6m of sales in 1998. With a strong asset base it is easily worth £26m. We add £2m for other assets.

45th=
ABDUL BHATTI, 63, & FAMILY
Food distribution
£26m (£23m)

● Abdul Bhatti is a director of the Bestway cash-and-carry business, which was started in 1976 by newly-knighted Anwar Pervez (qv.). Bhatti and his family have a 12.98% stake in the West London-based company which we value at around £200m, somewhat less than the food retailing average on the back of £24m profit and sales of £670m in the year to June 1998.

45th=
ADALAT, 64, & ARSHAD CHAUD-HARY, 38
Food distribution
£26m (£23m)

● Adalat and Arshad Chaudhary are both directors of Bestway. Between them they have a 12.98% stake in the West London-based company which we value conservatively at around £200m.

48th=
DINESH CHANDARIA, 48, & FAMILY
Paper
£25m (£30m)

● Dinesh Chandaria comes from a family of Kenyan paper-makers. The family decided to diversify into the UK and, in 1990, bought the Otley-based Garnett paper-making business for over £15m. Chandaria is chairman of the

holding company, Eldridge Investments. Despite higher profits at Garnett of £660,000 on sales slightly down at £18.6m in the year to September 1997, company values are lower (particularly in paper) and we value it at £10m. We add around £15m for Kenyan assets.

45th=
MOHAMMED SHEIKH, 62
Food distribution
£26m (new entry)

● Yet another of the Bestway millionaires, Sheikh is a director of Sir Anwar Pervez's (qv.) Bestway cash-and-carry operation.

Sheikh has an 12.98% stake in the fast-growing business which made £24m profit on sales of £670m in the year to June 1998. We value Bestway at around £200m on these figures, a conservative valuation.

48th=
ANANT, 50, & VIPIN SHAH, 55
Banking
£25m (£25m)

● Anant Shah and his brother Vipin run Meghraj Bank, a private bank established by their father, Meghji Pethraj Shah. It specialises in serving the needs of the Asian community. The Shahs hail from Kenya and Anant was educated at the LSE. The bank's shareholder funds rose slightly in the year to June 1997 from £11.72m to £11.76m. The bank is very cautious, having reduced the risk within its loan portfolio. and cut its gearing. We still value the Shahs at last year's £25m.

50th=
TOM, 67, & MELBA 62, CORREIA
Leisure
£24m (new entry)

● Tom and Melba Correia, a husband and wife team who hail from Goa and later went to Uganda, arrived in Britain in the early 1970s. In the mid-1970s, they took over the Hayes & Jarvis tour operator which dates back to 1852. Through hard work, they built up the up-market tour operator to the point where it sent 70,000 people a year off to exotic climes at around £850 per head. In June 1998, they sold the company to First Choice for £24m. They are off to manage a Caribbean hotel business.

50th=
SATINDER GULHATI, 54, & FAMILY
Hotels
£24m (£15m)

● Gulhati is a director of Edwardian, the private hotel group which operates luxury hotels in and around London. The group was founded by major shareholder Jasminder Singh (qv.). Gulhati and his family trusts have 10.85% of the company. Edwardian is easily worth its £224m net assets in 1997, when it made £10m profit on sales of £74.9m. That values the Gulhati family stake at £24.3m.

50th=
MUKESH, 49, & RAKESH SEHGAL 47
Fashionwear
£24m (£45m)

● Brothers Mukesh and Rakesh Sehgal set up Visage Holdings in 1981. The South

Shields-based business has grown by importing and distributing wholesale fashionwear. The Sehgals considered a float on the stock market and in the early 1990s rejected four takeover bids. In the year to January 1997, Visage made after-tax profits of £1.5m, nearly half the previous year, on sales up £20m to £97m. It is worth £23.5m. The Sehgals own all the shares.

53rd
ZAMEER CHOUDREY, 41, & FAMILY
Food distribution
£23m (new entry)

● Choudrey, an accountant by training, is finance director of the Bestway cash-and-carry business. With his family, he has an 11.45% stake in the fast-growing company worth around £200m on the back of £24m profits and sales of £670m in the year to June 1998.

54th=
GURBACHAN, 62, & SANDY CHADHA ,30
Electronic goods and property
£22m (£15m)

● Gurbachan Chadha arrived in Britain from India in the early 1970s, and started Supreme Imports in 1975, dealing mainly in electronics goods at the time. He also started a property business in the early 1980s. His son, Sandy, now runs the Manchester-based business, which now deals mainly with branded consumable products. It made net

profits of over £1m on sales of £12.6m in 1997-98 and is easily worth £12m. Other business and property assets take the Chadhas to £22m.

54th=
BHARAT MEHTA, 46,
Pharmaceuticals
£22m (£15m)

● Bharat Mehta runs Necessity Supplies, a pharmaceutical wholesaler based in Uxbridge, West London. The business which was incorporated in 1986, made £3.2m profit on sales of £47.5m in the year to June 1997. Mehta has a 30% stake but all the shares are owned by his family. They live modestly and take little out of the company in dividends or salaries, and Necessity Supplies only employed 17 staff at its June 1997 year end. We value it at £22m on these figures.

56th
SUNIL WICKREMERATNE, 34
Recruitment services
£21m (new entry)

● Wickremeratne, known as Wicks to his colleagues, is of Sri Lankan descent. An economics graduate from University College London, he runs Progressive Computer Recruitment, Britain's fastest-growing company, according to the 1998 Virgin Fast Track 100 He started as a management trainee in an IT recruitment agency. In 1990, Wickremeratne started Progressive backed by his then employers and has never looked back. In the 14 months to November 1997 it made £2.75m profit. Sales of £68m are forecast in 1998 and we value it at around £60m as a result. He owns a third of the equity worth perhaps £20m, while he also has 26% of another recruitment business called Pathway, which is worth around £4m. In all, we value Wickremeratne at £21m.

57th=
PRABHU SUDHAKAR, 63
Construction
£20m (£40m)

● Pell Frischmann, the engineering consultancy where highly qualified consulting engineer, Prabhu Sudhaker , has a 40% stake (including trusts) has seen a sharp slowdown in its fortunes. In the year to

March 1997, profits fell sharply to £1m on sales of £18.3m. But the company does have a strong balance sheet and £34.9m of net assets. It is worth perhaps £50m, valuing Prabhu's 40% stake at £20m.

57th=
HARPAL MATHARU 42, & FAMILY
Hotels
£20m (new entry)

● Harpal Matharu is managing director of Global Grange Limited, a London-based hotel operator. The business was incorporated in 1980 and has grown rapidly. In the year to March 1997, Global made £992,000 profit on sales of £9.36m. We value it slightly above its £19.6m of net assets. Matharu has a 33% stake himself but all the shares are held by other family members who sit as directors.

57th=
PRAMOD MITTAL
Industry
£20m (new entry)

● Pramod Mittal is the younger brother of steel magnate, Lakshmi Mittal. Like his elder brother, Pramod has moved to London and lives in Mayfair. He is also heavily involved in the family's steel business, which is quite distinct from Lakshmi Mittal's operations. Ispat Industries, as it is called, is worth around $60m, of which the Mittal family has 25%. Pramod Mittal's share and his other assets give him a valuation of around £20m.

57th=
MUKHTAR MOHIDIN, 46
Lottery winner
£20m (£20m)

● A former factory worker from Blackburn, Mohidin was the first major winner on the National Lottery with a £17.8m win on 10 December 1994. He now lives in the Home Counties under an alias to escape the pressures of his good fortune. We reckon that even if he is spending money quite freely (and there are no reports in the tabloid press of that), interest on his capital will have taken Mohidin to £20m.

57th=
RAJESH PASSI
Fashion goods
£20m (£20m)

● Passi is chairman and the main shareholder in By Design, a Manchester-based importer and distributor of fashion goods. (Family trusts own the rest of the shares.) The business was incorporated in 1980. In the year to April 1997, By Design's pre-tax profits were £1.347m on sales of £43.4m. On these figures it is easily worth £20m.

57th=
GIRISH REDDY, 44
Finance
£20m (£10m)

● Reddy is a partner in Goldman Sachs, the US investment bank, who works in the bank's London equities division. As a partner, he would have been far richer had the Goldman Sachs flotation gone ahead last autumn. But the float was called off following stock market turmoil. The floatation has been revived and could be completed by the end of this year. In any case, as a partner, Reddy owns a stake which is still worth £20m.

With greater liquidity in the shares, it could be worth double or treble that sum. Reddy's elevation to partnership and wealth was reported in the British press (17/10/96). He heads Goldman's derivatives operation and is an Indian national.

57th=
MOHAMED SAWAR, 48
Textiles
£20m (new entry)

● Mohamed Sawas owns all of Swordward,

a Bolton-based textiles company incorporated in 1981. It made £2.9m profit on sales of £24.5m in 1997. But it does have quite high gearing and is worth around £20m on these figures.

57th=
KANWALJIT, 62,
& KALVINDER SIDHU, 35
Fashionwear
£20m (£15m)

● Kanwaljit and Kalvinder Sidhu are chairman and managing director respectively of Palmier, a London-based distributor of ladies clothing incorporated in 1986. The business is doing nicely, turning in pre-tax profits of £1.4m on sales of £26.5m in the year to March 1997. Palmier is worth around £15m on these figures. The Sidhus own all the shares in the company. They also own West End Fashions, worth £5m on profits of £289,000 and £2.1m sales in the year to March 1997.

57th=
RASHID TAYUB, 50
Cash & carry
£20m (£20m)

● Sales are motoring along at Crown Crest, the Leicester-based cash and carry operation owned by Rashid Tayub. He came to Britain from Malawi in 1976 and started a small store in Huddersfield which has grown into a major operation. In the year to March 1998 sales at Crown Crest rose from £35.8m to £50.8m, while profits grew from £700,000 to £1.1m. With lower company values this year, the rise in profits only means we stick at last year's £20m valuation.

57th=
ANOOP VOHRA, 68, & FAMILY
Hotels
£20m (£5m)

● Kenyan-born Anoop Vohra is a hotelier with interests in London. His family owns the Rembrandt Hotel via an Isle of Man company, Kilkenny Ltd and had other hotels such as the Reubens and the Washington, which were sold in 1997 at the top of the market. Before the sale, three companies where the Vohras were directors had sales of over £16m and operating profits of £3.8m. In 1998, they were on the acquisition trail again and bought hotels for over £16m. We were

somewhat low in our valuation last year and we raise it to £20m - still a cautious figure as we are not sure of the level of debt in the businesses.

67th=
MUNIR AHMAD, 56, & FAMILY
Cash & carry
£15m (£20m)

● Munir Ahmad and his two brothers each own a third of Tyne Tees Cash & Carry, a Middlesbrough-based business. It was incorporated in 1980 and operates cash and carry depots. In 1997, the company saw its profits fall from £17,000 to £7,000 though sales rose from £56.7m to £58.2m. But adding in directors' emoluments of around £1.7m as part of the profit figure, the business is easily worth £15m this year.

67th=
MOEZ DAYA, 40
Telecommunications
£15m (£12m)

● Kenyan-born Daya is an engineering consultant and director of telecoms group Mobile Systems International. He was part of a team which put up £100,000 to start the firm in 1990. In September 1996, a US investor paid £36m for a 20% stake. The deal valued the company at £180m. Daya's stake plus the after-tax proceeds from his share of the sale bring him to £12m. We raise the value this year as mobile phone business values have risen sharply in recent months.

67th=
DINESH, 48, & TANI DHAMIJA, 47
Travel agency
£15m (£12m)

● Sales are booming at Flight Bookers, the London-based travel agency owned by Dinesh and Tani Dhamija through a Jersey-based company, Sebira Holdings. They also own Dabin Travel, which is worth around £3m on the back of £543,000 profit. In 1997, Flight Bookers sales rose by nearly £10m to £47.2m, though profits were marginally lower at £325,000. With the travel trade still looking in reasonable shape we stick with last year's £12m valuation for the business adding £3m for Dabin.

**67th=
RAMESH
DEWAN, 51**
Property
£15m (£15m)

● Ramesh Dewan has interests in property and publishing, but his fortune largely stems from building factories. Trans-Britannia built 200 factories in a mere eight years.

Dewan is a prominent Liberal Democrat supporter. In assessing his wealth we have looked at the accounts of over 30 companies where Dewan is a director and/or shareholder. Some were 1996 and others were later 1997 accounts. In all they have total net assets of around £13.9m. With past salaries thrown in, we cautiously stick with last year's £15m valuation.

**67th=
MADHUSUDAN, 52, & RANJAN
KOTECHA, 51**
Cash & carry
£15m (£20m)

● The Kotechas own Barking Cash & Carry, an Essex-based wholesaler of pre packed food and drinks merchandise to trade customers. Madhusudan Kotecha is a director of the company, though Ranjan Kotecha resigned from the board in May 1995. Barking Cash & Carry was one of the best performing private companies in a recent survey by Management Today magazine. In 1997, sales shot up £20m to £114.8m, though profits fell from £1.1m to £743,000. With lower company values this year, we value Barking at £15m.

**67th=
GOKUL BINANI, 44**
Finance
£15m (£15m)

● Gokul Binani is managing director of Metal Traders, a privately-owned metal commodities trader with strong Indian links. We reckon the Binani family owns all the shares directly or through a Jersey trust. The company trades in dollars and made a small profit of $82,000 on $76m sales in the year to June 1996. No dividend was paid though it paid dividends of nearly £5m in 1993. We reckon it is still worth £10m. Other asserts take the Binanis easily to £15m.

**67th=
DR AVTAR LIT, 48**
Media
£15m (£20m)

Lit is well known in the Asian community for his radio station, based in West London. Sunrise, a subsidiary of Asian Broadcasting Corporation, was incorporated in 1989. In 1996 it made just under £500,000 profit on sales of £1.7m. In 1997, Lit was looking for £700,000 profit. Cautiously we reckon the business is worth over £10m on these figures though Lit reckons it is worth much more and has turned down bids over £20m.

But these are uncertain times. He is expanding the business into Sri Lanka and we add at least £5m for these assets. Interestingly, Lit has been carefully paring back his gearing in recent years, a smart move if there is a recession looming.

67th=
AJIT PATEL
Pharmaceuticals
£15m (new entry)

● There are four Patels on the board of Goldshield, the distributor of healthcare products that was floated on the stock exchange in June.

Ajit Patel, the chairman and chief executive, admits he was "quietly concerned" about the City's possible adverse reaction to the "Patel presence". In the event, his concerns were unfounded. The Croydon-based company was successfully listed with a valuation of £57.9m. With other assets Patel, who says a decade ago "I was on my knees business-wise", is easily worth £15m. "I had many concerns that the board was overweight (with Patels) and that this might cause problems," he said, recalling the pre-flotation presentations to financial institutions. But these concerns were outweighed by his confidence in the business. "The business was solidly structured and would stand up to scrutiny; and we had great confidence in our presentations."

The City has traditionally been cool to businesses that were heavily reliant on a single individual or family. In contrast, Asian businesses view these structures as valuable. In recent years, both camps have softened the stances. Goldshields' flotation is one consequence.

The last Patel to have made such a striking impact on the City was Arunbhai Patel in the 1980s. He was an ambitious accountant who in an audacious move bought a large chain of newsagents in a heavily leveraged deal. Many in the City were surprised and their fears were realised. Arunbhai Patel had overstretched himself and ultimately paid the price.

Ajit Patel is aware of the parallels. As the boss of a publicly listed company he has already been panned in the City press for refusing to split the jobs of chairman and chief executive, in defiance of the Cadbury code on corporate governance. This concentration of decision-making on a single individual, say observers, is a leaf from the Arunbhai Patel book of corporate management.

Ajit Patel is a pharmacist who ran

his own outlet for seven years until 1991. Two years earlier he has borrowed heavily to buy out his partner in a business turning over £500,000 annually. The ink was barely dry when recession hit. "It was very bad timing," he said.

He had been looking for new opportunities to ease his parlous commercial condition. Pharmacy was comfortable but hardly challenging and he wanted something more creative. He opened a printing business but with little success. Then he retreated to his own industry, where he says opportunities were arising in healthcare distribution.

Several factors were forcing this change. The National Health Service was undergoing overhaul; at the same time, multinational drugs companies such as Glaxo and SmithKline Beecham were restructuring as competition intensified. This new mood of deregulation excited Patel. "The big companies no longer wanted to retain less well performing drugs lines because of the high overheads; at the same time there was huge growth in over-the-counter sales as patents expired and generic products emerged.

This presented opportunities for smaller distributors. In 1991 Patel set up Goldshield under the government's Business Expansion Scheme. He attracted some 40 investors - rising to 110 and

mostly Asians - who between 1991-93 invested £1.3m. "They were investing in my confidence."

The first year was very bad but the turning point came in the second year when Patel bought from Glaxo the rights to Neonoclex, a treatment for blood pressure. "Glaxo was off-loading many drugs lines and I was competing against 30 rivals. Somehow I persuaded the licensing manager at Glaxo that Neonoclex would be safe in my hands."

Although multinationals' proprietorial interest in a drug ceases once the license is sold, as the developers of the drug (which is usually sold with a good market franchise) their reputation is still on the line. That is why they like to sell to companies that will nurture the drug with strong advertising and good distribution.

The next seven years, which included the sale of his pharmacy in 1994, saw growth gallop as Goldshield expanded its portfolio to some 30 pharmaceutical lines and more than 400 healthcare products. Turnover rose sharply to more than £20m.

By the mid-1990s, Patel had decided that strategically it was in the company's interests to float. In part this was to honour a pledge to his original investors that he would "provide them with an exit".

There were three options: sell to a company within the industry but this was ruled out because it would not provide good value; buy back the shares; or go to the stock exchange.

"At the flotation price, for every one pound invested by the original backers, they earned £360 - tax-free because of the BES status. Since then only 11 investors have cashed in, a measure of the shared optimism."

For his part, Patel retained 5.745m shares in the company, which at 245.5p a share (December 1998) are worth £14.1m. He also sold £360,000 worth of shares at the float. Breakneck growth has whetted his ambitions. As the largest mail-order distributor of healthcare products, Patel is now considering opening healthcare centres in high streets. That, he says, would mean that within two years he would have won a place both in the City and in city centres. ■

67th=
JAYANTILAL GANDHI, 47, & FAMILY
Food production
£15m (£15m)

● Jayantilal Gandhi heads a family-owned business empire based in London's East End which supplies ethnic food and drink to the catering trade.

The booming business was started as a partnership in the 1960s and the first of the three family companies, Gandhi Oriental Foods, was formed in 1971. The other two businesses, GOF International and Gandhi Wine (Suppliers), are more recent. Together, they made around £500,000 profit on £16.5m of sales in the year to April 1997.

With other assets added, we value Gandhi and his family at £15m.

67th=
BHARAT SHAH 49 & FAMILY
Pharmaceuticals
£15m (£10m)

● Bharat Shah chairs Sigma, a private pharmaceutical distributor based in London. There are six Shahs on the board, though only three are shareholders. Each of these three, led by Bharat Shah, has a third of the equity. In the year to August 1998, sales at Sigma rose by £20m to £60m, while profits rose to £700,000. The whole pharmaceuticals sector is more highly valued this year and the company would easily command a £15m price tag on these figures.

Sigma is currently the largest generic drug wholesaler in the UK, commanding around 15 per cent of the market.

67th=
ANWAR PATEL, 44, & FAMILY
Chemists
£15m (new entry)

● Anwar Patel is company secretary and a director of Gorgemead Ltd, a retail chemists business based in Bolton. The business - started in 1979 - made a loss of £190,000 on sales of £13.3m in the year to August 1997. But if we add the majority of the directors £557,000 salaries to the bottom line, Gorgemead would be

67th=
JITENDRA RUIA, 56, & FAMILY
Textiles
£15m (£15m)
● Jitendra Ruia runs Ruia Holdings, an importer and processor of textiles based in Manchester. All the shares are held by the Ruia family, either directly or via a Channel Islands trust. We value the company at around £15m, the same as last year. In the year to April 1998, the group returned to profit making £1.3m on sales of £31.6m. The company paid out £1m in dividends but the highest paid director's salary fell from £1.09m to £414,000. With lower company values however, we stick with £15m.

worth perhaps £5m. Patel owns half the business. We reckon that Patel and his family also own the holding company for Manchester-based Scholes (Chemists) which is worth £12m on the back of £918,000 profit on sales of £17.36m in the year to August 1997.

67th=
MOHAMMED ZAFAR, 42
Industry
£15m (£3m)

● At the age of 17, Mohammed Zafar borrowed money and set up his own small children's wear shop in Yorkshire. It proved a major success and he added ladies' wear to his range. Five years after

starting his shop, he had built up sufficient capital to start a bed manufacturing plant. He offered a first class service including seven day delivery and expanded the operation into an old mill. By the early 1980s, he noticed that old mills were coming up for sale very cheaply and went into property as well. He now has 20 mills. His commercial property portfolio is doing well and is valued at around £6m. He is also building a new 100,000 square foot bed factory in Batley which when it becomes operational at the end of the year, will propel his Hick Lane Bedding business to sixth in the league of independent bed manufacturers in the UK.

Hick Lane is worth around £7m on

the back of £500,000 profit and sales of £7m forecast in the current year.

With other assets and property, we value Zafar at £15m, much higher than last year's miserly £3m. Sorry for the undervaluation.

67th=
MAHENDRA SHAH, 53, & FAMILY
Pharmaceuticals
£15m (£10m)

● Mahendra Shah is managing director and company secretary of GD Cooper & Co, a pharmaceutical goods wholesaler based in Croydon, Surrey. The business was established in 1978 and its main subsidiaries are Anchor Pharmacy Ltd and Dexpharm Ltd.

In the year to the end of August 1997, GD Cooper made a £775,735 profit (32% up on 1996). With higher values in that sector, we value the company at around £15m. There are five Shahs on the board and each has a 20% stake in the company.

67th=
HARSHADRAI PATEL, 55
Pharmaceuticals
£15m (£4m)

● Harshadrai Patel is a director of Interport Ltd, a distributor of pharmaceutical products based in South London.

The company was incorporated in 1981 and he owns all the shares. In the year to March 1998, Interport saw a sharp rise in profits from £246,076 to £782,000 on sales nearly doubled at £13m. A strong balance sheet and operating in a well regarded sector give the company and Patel a £15m valuation this year.

82nd
AJAZ AHMED, 25
Computers & Media
£14m (£8m)

● Ahmed became interested in computers and marketing as an 11-year old growing up in Berkshire. After school, he went into marketing before going to university and dropping out.

In 1993, he launched Internet consul-

tancy AKQA New Media based in central London. Ahmed owns 95% of AKQA which is set to achieve a £10m turnover in 1998. As a result it is the UK' s largest independent new media design agency. He has been offered multiples of the company's turnover, though he now reckons the business is worth £14m as he told the BBC in a recent programme. We agree.

83rd=
LIYAKAT, 49, & SULTAN ASARIA, 48
Food and industry
£13m (£10m)

● The Asarias are directors of Pride Oil Products, a family-owned company which imports and distributes edible oils. Based in the shadow of Wembley stadium, the business was incorporated in 1976 and the Asarias own all the shares. They also own London Drums & Cans, a drum and can maker which we missed last year. Their business assets are worth £12m on the back of a forecast £900,000 profit on sales of £27.5m in 1998-99. Other assets take them to around £13m.

83rd=
TRILOK WOUHRA, 62, & FAMILY
Cash & carry
£13m (£11m)

● Trilok Wouhra is managing director of

East End Foods, a family-owned wholesale food distributor based in Birmingham which has sharply improved its performance in its latest 1998 accounts. It was established in 1972 and there are five members of the Wouhra family on the board. In the year to March 1998, East End sharply increased profits from £427,000 to £613,401 on sales up over £2.5m to £60.8m. It would easily be

worth £12m on these figures even in the current climate. We add £1m for other family assets.

85th=
KISHORE PAGRANI, 36, & FAMILY
Food
£12m (£10m)

● Pagrani is managing director of private family-controlled food distributor T Choithram. The business was incorporated in 1960 and is best known for its Natco range of spices, produced in a new Wembley factory.

T Choitram, which is controlled from the British Virgin Isles, made a £349,000 profit on sales of £24.4m in 1997. It is worth £10m on these figures in today's climate. The higher profits offset lower company values in the sector. We did not include another Pagrani company last year, Giant Exports, worth £3m on the back of £205,000 profit and sales of £5.8m. It has quite high gearing though.

85th=
AJMAIR BHULLAR, 50, & FAMILY
Textiles
£12m (£30m)

● A difficult time for Wetherby Fashions, the Leeds-based textiles group where Ajmair Bhullar is a director and the largest individual shareholder with 45% of the shares (the rest are in family hands). With a 64.6% fall in pre-tax profits to just £830,000 on sales up by nearly 9% at £30.2m in the year to April 1997, Wetherby Fashions' margins were eroded.

We value the business at around £12m on these figures. The company has recently moved into clothes wholesaling which may help future results.

85th=
ZAHIR, 43, & SHAFINDA DAMJI, 42
Petrol retailer
£12m (£15m)

● Tanzanian-born Zahir and Shafinda Damji are directors of Trackform, a private garage and petrol retailer based in southwest London. Trackform, incorporated in 1981, is worth about £12m, based on profits of £910,000 and sales of £36.8m in the year to August 1997. Despite this slight rise in profits, the petrol retailing and garage sector has fallen in value this year, hence the downgrading. The Damjis are joint owners.

85th=
ASHOK KALLUMPRAM, 40, & FAMILY
Textiles
£12m (£12m)

● A slight rise in profits at Premier Textiles to £887,000 on sales of £17.6m in the year to June 1997 helps keep Ashok Kallumpram and his family at the same £12m level in this list as last year. Kallumpram is a director of Premier, a Manchester-based textiles importer, where a large number of the shares are held in family trusts. Premier was incorporated in 1981. We value the business and Kallumpram family at around £12m.

85th=
RABNAWAZ KHAN, 70, & FAMILY
Property
£12m (£4m)

● Rabnawaz Khan has a 40% stake in Baseasset Ltd, a holding company based in Chertsey, Surrey. Its subsidiaries are involved in property and it was incorporated in 1983. The rest of the Khan family have a 55% stake in the company.

Baseasset saw its profits surge from £228,000 to £700,000 on sales of £2.6m in the year to March 1998. With a strong balance sheet and no borrowings, it is easily worth £12m on these figures, a healthy rise on last year. Well done.

90th=
INDERJIT AHLUWALIA, 38, & FAMILY
Computers
£10m (new entry)

● Inderjit Ahluwalia is managing director of Anix Group, a Bristol-based computer software and maintenance company.

Incorporated in 1989, Anix has grown fast in recent years, with sales up from £2.6m in 1993 to £12.1m in 1997 - a 361% rise. With profits of £603,000 in 1997 a valuation of perhaps £20m is realistic given the high ratings in the computer software sector. Ahluwalia and his family own just over half of Anix's shares.

90th=
SUKHPAL AHLUWALIA, 40, & FAMILY
Car parts

£10m (new entry)
● Sukhpal Aluwalia is managing director of Euro Car Parts, a fast-growing Wembley-based company which acts as a wholesaler of motor car parts and accessories.

The business was incorporated in 1992 and in the year to October 1997, saw its profits rise from £203,000 to over £1m on sales up by nearly £3.5m at £25.3m. We assume the Ahluwalia family own all the business even though its ultimate parent, Nirmal Limited, is Isle of Man-based. We value the company and Ahluwalia family at £10m on these figures.

90th=
BASHIR AHMED
Cash & carry
£10m (£10m)

● Bashir Ahmed is managing director of BA Cash & Carry, a Cardiff-based food wholesaler and retailer. He owns 97% of the shares in the business which was incorporated in 1979.

In the year to February 1998, the business saw its profits move up marginally to £758,000 on sales up over £2m to £67m.

Despite the rise in profits, we value the business and Ahmed at last year's £10m as food company values are lower this year.

90th=
DAMODAR CHANRAI, 55
Industry
£10m (£10m)

● Chanrai heads a business dating back to Victorian times with interests in glass, textiles and real estate. He works with his brothers, Vinod, Pita and Pishu. They fund the Chanrai Foundation, which supports many Asian charities. In the year to March 1998, their company, Chanrai International recovered somewhat with sales up from £5.4m to £13.5m.

Losses fell sharply from £476,000 to just £85,000. We keep the Chanrai's value at last year's £10m until profits return. We recognise that the £10m valuation is underpinned by overseas assets which are difficult to value. We may be conservative here.

90th=
MIRZA ALI KHAN, 65, & FAMILY
Media
£10m (new entry)

● Mirza Ali Khan is company secretary of Ali International, a London-based business which does not list its main activities, but has subsidiaries in the multimedia business.

In 1997, the limited accounts of Ali International showed a £1.25m profit.

Dividends of £1m were also paid out in 1997. Ali Khan and several family members own 90% of the business which is easily worth £10m taking a conservative valuation of the media/leisure sector. With dividends etc., the family are easily worth £10m.

90th=
SATISH CHATWANI, 46, & FAMILY
Hotels and wholesalers
£10m (£10m)

● Chatwani trained as an accountant but was barred from returning to Uganda by Idi Amin in 1973. He built up an accountancy practice in the UK before moving into hotels.

In 1989, he took over Copson, a quoted builders' merchant, as a shell company. But in 1991, disenchanted with the stock market, Chatwani took Copson private in a deal valuing it at £6m.

The business has since been renamed Kanta Enterprises and its activities embrace wholesaling of toiletries and household goods as well as hotels.

We value Kanta at around £8m on the back of £402,000 profit on sales of £15.4m in the year to March 1997. This is only slightly down on 1996 when it made £2.9m profit, but exceptional items were largely responsible for that. Other assets will easily keep the Chatwanis at £10m.

90th=
RATILAL, 68, & VILASGAURI DHANANI, 61
Food
£10m (new entry)

● Ratilal Dhanani is managing director of Wealmoor, a Stanmore-based fruit and vegetable importer and wholesaler. The business was incorporated in 1973 and achieved a £1.1m profit in the year to March 1997. It has a solid balance sheet with over £4m of net assets, and we value the company on the profit figure at around £10m. Dhanani and his wife, Vilasgauri, own the business.

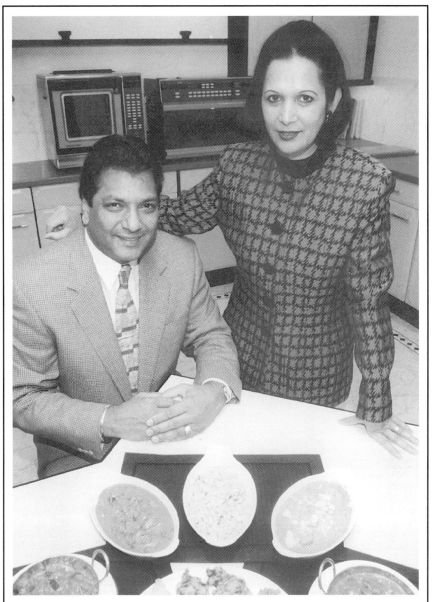

90th=
LAK, 50, & KAMALJIT BASRAN, 48
Food
£10m (£8m)

● Lak Basran reckons he is the first Indian from Mars! Not a reference to interstellar activity but his work in food sales with the Mars confectionery business. That was in 1978, after Basran had graduated from Salford University with an engineering degree. He came to Britain in the late 1950s to join his father who had come earlier to work in factories and save enough for a family home.

His wife Kamaljit had much the same upbringing and both followed their father's advice and sought an education. They were the first in their respective families to graduate from university. Kamlajit studied history and went into teaching. Their respective experiences led them to start up in business together.

In the late 1980s, they began cooking snacks at home to sell to local delicatessens. Today, their company, Stockport-based Authentic Indian Foods, is a major supplier to supermarkets, pubs and restaurants. They also own a frozen food marketing company.

Last year, their businesses made good profits on sales of around £7.5m. With other assets, the Basrans are worth perhaps £10m.

90th=
GURBAKSH BHALLA, 59, & FAMILY
Industry
£10m (new entry)

● Gurbaksh Bhalla runs a sizeable manufacturing operation in Southall. Advance Moulding Components is a plastics manufacturing operation started in 1968. Bhalla and his family own all the business through a holding company, Advance Engineering, which only made £5,374 profit on sales of £825,000 in 1997, but it has £5.2m of net assets. Advance Moulding made £529,000 profit on sales of £10.7m. In all we reckon the Bhalla assets are worth perhaps £10m conservatively.

90th=
JINDY KHERA, 48, & FAMILY
Food production
£10m (£10m)

● Jindy Khera is managing director of KTC Edibles, reputedly Britain's largest independent cooking oils and fats business.

It was started by his father, Jernail in 1973, who came to Britain from the Punjab in 1958. Jindy's brother Santokh is production director.

In 1997, Birmingham-based KTC increased profits to £216,000 on sales of £37m. We reckon it is worth about £10m, given its large sales volumes and valuable property. The family has 90% of the shares. Other assets, including Jindy's car collection, add £1m.

90th=
SHANTILAL DHAMECHA, 68, & FAMILY
Food
£10m (£8m)

● Shantilal Dhamecha has a small stake in the family-owned Dhamecha Foods, which has interests in cash and carry, property dealing and the manufacture of paper disposable products. The rest of the shares are held by the Dhamecha family. In the year to March 1998, Dhamecha Foods saw its profits rise sharply from £705,664 to just over £1m on sales up by £10m at £76.2m. On these figures, the business

would easily be worth £10m even in today's depressed climate.

90th=
DILBAG SINGH, 59, & GURMAIL KAUR, 53
Textiles
£10m (£10m)

● Dilbag Singh and Mrs Gurmail Kaur each own 50% of Dilbag Cloth House Ltd, a Bradford textile importer and distributor.

They are directors of the business which was started in 1993. In the year to September 1997, Dilbag Cloth House saw its profits rise a healthy 39.4% to £735,004. Lower values in the textiles sector though means we stick with the same £10m valuation as last year despite the impressive profits growth.

90th=
VIPEN KHANNA, 52, & FAMILY
Petrol retailer
£10m (£7.5m)

● Vipen Khanna is chairman and managing director of TSS, a family-owned

garage business based in Croydon. The company was incorporated in 1992. Khanna and his family own all the shares in the business directly or in trust. In the year to April 98, TSS made £275,314 pretax profits on sales of £28.6m, but Khanna is forecasting a healthy 1998-99 with a £35m turnover and profits of £550,000. Though values have fallen sharply in the

motors sector, the business is worth £9m. We add around £1m for other assets.

90th=
SUNIL, 36, & SANJIV KOTECHA, 33
Electronics
£10m (£20m)

● Profits have fallen sharply at Just Rams, the West London distributor of electronic components owned by Sunil and Sanjiv Kotecha. The business, incorporated in 1990, saw profits fall from £2m to £813,000 on sales of £23.4m in the year to June 1997. It is worth perhaps £10m.

90th=
ABDUL OMAR, 60, & FAMILY
Textiles
£10m (new entry)

● Abdul Omar is managing director of Paramount Knitwear, a Leicester-based knitwear and hosiery wholesaler, which was incorporated in 1974. A newly established holding company owns all the shares in the business. Omar and his family have a majority of the newly created Paramount Holdings company which made £1.6m profit on sales of £9.68m in the year to March 1997. With £8m of net assets, it is easily worth £10m. Paramount Knitwear itself actually made £2.4m profit on sales of £14.5m in the same period.

90th=
SWARN MEHTA, 60, & FAMILY
Food
£10m (£10m)

● Swarn Mehta has a 45% stake in Minor Weir & Willis Ltd, a Birmingham-based fruit and vegetable wholesaler. Other Mehta family members and family trusts own the balance of the equity in the profitable company established in 1963. We value the business at around £10m on the back of £851,000 profit and sales of £27.7m in 1996. It has a solid balance sheet with net assets of £5.6m. The 1997 accounts had not been filed as we did our research so we stick with last year's figure.

90th=
PARDEEP, 42, & ARTEE PASSI, 37
Textiles
£10m (new entry)

● Husband and wife team Pardeep and

Artee Passi run two sound and profitable fabric and yarn companies in Manchester. Golden Dollar Clothing only publishes modified accounts, but it did have £759,000 of assets in the year to March 1997. It was incorporated in 1981. But the real jewel in their crown is GD Yarns, a yarn purchaser and seller. Incorporated in 1985, it made an £872,000 profit in the year to March 1997. It is worth perhaps £9m on these figures. In all we value the Passis, who own both firms, at £10m.

90th=
KIRAN SHAH, 44
Toys
£10m (£4m)

● Chartered accountant Kiran Shah is finance director and company secretary of The Character Group, a quoted distributor of exclusive branded toys based in Kingston, Surrey. It was floated on the stock market in June 1995. The shares have risen sharply in the last year and Shah's 3.3m shares, at 301.5p each (December 1998) are worth £9.97m.

90th=
RUMI VERJEE, 41
Retailing
£10m (new entry)

● Verjee trained as a barrister before launching the UK franchise for Domino's Pizza in the 1980s. He sold the business back to the Americans and went into property development converting the Brompton Hospital in Chelsea. He is now the proprietor of Thomas Goode the London china shop, according to the Independent (11/09/98), though the company is in fact owned by a Virgin Isles company. Goode is worth £5m on the back of £266,000 profit on sales of £4.3m in year to March 1998. Other assets take him to £10m.

90th=
CHARAN, 53, & SHALINDAR SOHAL, 49
Textiles
£10m (£4m)

● The Sohals began in the clothing trade in 1971 armed with three sewing machines and they worked night and day,

gradually expanding to over 200 machinists in the late 1970s and early 1980s. Hit by a flood of cheap imports in the 1980s, they were forced to close their business. But ambition prevailed and they set up again with a smaller workforce and their Birmingham-based company, Orbit International, has gone from strength to strength. They have ridden the recession in textiles by putting work before pleasure and continually reviewing clothes ranges and the customer base. It works.

Orbit made £360,000 profit on sales of £4.9m in the year to the end of September 1998, and is forecast to make £1m profit on £7m sales in 1999. We value the company at £7m this year. Other assets and commercial property take the Sohals to £10m.

They have laid the foundations for their three sons, who work in the business, to take the company forward. "It is up to them to build the skyscraper for the next generation," says Charan Sohal.

90th=
RAJINDER LOOMBA, 55, & FAMILY
Fashionwear
£10m (£10m)

● Rajinder Loomba is chairman and managing director of Rinku of London PLC, a wholesaler of women's and infants' clothes. He has a 54% stake in the company and other family members own the balance of the shares in the company which was started in 1980. In the year to June 1997, Rinku of London pushed up profits by nearly £100,000 to £374,000 on sales up sharply to £9.6m. The increased profits and other assets help keep Loomba and his family at £10m despite lower company values in the clothes sector.

90th=
IMTIAZ SHER & FAMILY
Textiles
£10m (£15m)

● Sher is a director of Sher Brothers (Glasgow), a family-owned clothes wholesaler, and took over running the company in January 1998. Profits at the Glasgow-based company fell from £962,000 to £793,000 in 1997 on sales down some £1m at £42.9m.

Lower company values in the textiles sector and the lower profits make a £10m valuation seems appropriate.

90th=
KUSUM, 53, and NIKESH RADIA, 25
Car sales
£10m (£6m)

● Mrs Kusum Radia owns all the shares in DNR North London, a London holding company, with subsidiaries involved in car dealing and property. It operates a Toyota franchise. Radia is a director and her son Nikesh manages the business, which started in 1988. DNR made £239,498 profit on sharply higher sales of £8.7m in the year to June 1998. It is easily worth over £9m on these figures. We add £750,000 for property and other assets, taking the Radias to £10m.

90th=
MOHAMMED SARWAR, 46
Cash & carry
£10m (£10m)

● Mohammed Sarwar came to Britain from Pakistan in 1978 and settled in Glasgow. A year later he launched United Wholesale, a cash-and-carry operation

which has since grown into a huge business. Sarwar was elected as Labour MP for Glasgow Govan in May 1997 and was, last month finally acquitted of corruption charges. In 1997, profits rose 24% to £582,000 on sales up £5m to £84.6m. Despite the rise, company values have fallen and we reckon United Wholesale is worth £15m. That values Sarwar's 45%

stake at £6.75m. Other assets including United Cash & Carry take him to £10m.

114th=
ARSHAD AHMED, 39, & FAMILY
Textiles
£9m (£18m)

● Ahmed is company secretary and one of three family members on the board of Aziz Textiles, a Birmingham-based company which sells textiles and loose material. They each have a 20% stake.

Profits at Aziz Textiles grew from £1.45m to £1.61m on sales up marginally at £16.8m in the year to September 1997. With much lower company values in the textiles sector, we value the business at around £15m on these figures and the Ahmeds' stake at £9m.

114th=
MOHAMMED RAMZAN, 41
Cash & carry
£9m (£10m)

● Mohammed Ramzan is the business partner of Mohammed Sarwar, the Labour MP for Glasgow Govan. Between them, they own United Wholesale Grocers, a huge cash-and-carry company.

Ramzan is managing director of the company incorporated in 1982. In 1997, profits rose 24% to £582,000 on sales up £5m to £84.6m.

Despite the rise, food company values have fallen and we reckon United Wholesale would be lucky to command a £15m rating. That values Ramzan's 55% stake at £8.25m. Other assets take him to £9m.

114th=
SWATI PATEL, 40
Industry
£9m (£9m)

● Swati Patel trained as a pharmacy technician but is now a director of Miswa Chemicals, a private company which makes car care products and insecticides. The Northamptonshire-based company was started in 1979 by her father, Ratilal Patel, the managing director. In 1993, he transferred the bulk of his shares to Swati, and she now has an 88.3% stake.

We value the business at the same level

as last year despite a slight rise in profit to £549,414 on sales of £4.9m in the year to March 1998 as chemical company values are down.

117th=
MOHAMED ESMAIL, 54, & FAMILY
Hotels and fast food
£8m (new entry)

● Mohamed Esmail is managing director of SME Group, a holding company which has subsidiaries in the fast food and hotel business.

The Harrow-based company was incorporated in 1988, and is owned by Esmail and his family.

We value the business at around £8m on the back of £647,000 profit and sales of £9.5m in the year to March 1997.

117th=
FUKHERA KHALID, 30
Cash & carry
£8m (£12m)

● Fukhera Khalid is a director, and 99.8% shareholder, of Elbrook, a private wholesale cash-and-carry business dealing in groceries and drinks.

The business, which was incorporated in 1984, opened a new warehouse in Surrey which helped to boost trade.

In the year to July 1997, Elbrook made a £584,000 profit on sales of £63.5m.

The profits fall (from £640,000 in 1996) and lower company values leads to a reduced £8m valuation.

117th=
MUKESH KEJRIWAL, 36, & FAMILY
Textiles
£8m (£12m)

● Kejriwal is a director of Exportex, a family-owned business based in Stockport which imports textiles and wholesales wines and spirits. Two other family members are also directors and the family owns all the equity.

Exportex's pre-tax profits fell £160,000 to £500,625 on sales of £21m in the year to September 1997. We lower the value of the business and the Kejriwal family to around £8m as a result.

117th=
MANHAR AMLANI, 49
Property and electronics
£8m (£6.4m)

● Manhar Amlani was born in a small Ugandan village and arrived in Britain in 1972 with just £16 in his pocket. After working as an engineer for Smiths Industries, he founded his own business in 1977 and started developing a stream of electronic inventions. Initially he worked from his kitchen but moved into a factory in 1981 in South Wales. By 1992, his company, Fulleon had won a Queen's Award for Export. He sold up in 1992 for £3m. Amlani later went into property and sold up in 1997 for £6m. A wise investment in one of the Virgin Fast Track 100 companies has added £2m and we value him at £8m this year.

117th=
AFZAL, 43, &
AKMAL KHUSHI, 42
Textiles
£8m (£8m)

● Afzal and Akmal Khushi own all the shares in Jacobs and Turner, a Glasgow-based clothes manufacturer and wholesaler.

The business, which was incorporated in 1970, made £802,000 profit on sales of £23.7m in the year to June 1997. No new accounts had been filed when we did our research and we stick with last year's valuation, even though it was possibly a little conservative. The company made a £1,200 donation to the Labour Party during the year.

117th=
RAJAN MULCHAND, 51, & FAMILY
Consumer goods
£8m (£24m)

● Rajan Mulchand, who describes himself as a general merchant, is a director of Laltex, a private trading company incorporated in 1962. The Manchester-based company imports and exports clothing, electrical/electronic equipment and consumer goods. Laltex saw profits fall sharply from £1.4m to £768,000 on sales down £4m at £29.1m in the year to February 1998. As a result we cut the value of the business to £10m. The Mulchands have 80%.

123rd
SHANTILAL MAJITHIA, 53
Petrol retailing
£7.5m (£7.5m)

● Shantilal Majithia is chairman of MPK Garages, a privately-owned retail petrol station operator based in Leicester. He owns all the shares in the company having bought out a partner in the year to February 1997.

A sharp improvement in profits in the year to March 1998 saw MPK make £323,000 on sales of £30.7m. We stick with the same £7.5m value as last year as company values in the motor trade have fallen quite sharply in 1998.

124th
GURPAL SINGH, 64
Property
£7.2m (£7.2m)

● Gurpal Singh owns Woodblox PLC, a commercial property company incorpo-

rated in 1986. Its main asset is a Leicester Square building which was revalued in 1996. With offices, a restaurant and hotel in the building, it is worth over £7.1m in the 1997 accounts. This is the figure we still use to underpin Singh's valuation.

125th=
MANMOHAN, 59, & AJIT CHADHA, 55
Food production
£7m (£5m)

● Manmohan and Ajit Chadha used to own Chadha International Foods, an importer of noodles and beansprouts based in West London. In March 1997, they sold the business to the quoted foods group, WT Foods, in a deal that valued Chadha at £6.7m.

We estimate the after-tax proceeds for the Chadha brothers to be around £5m. The family also have other business assets including a small property company, C&S International, worth around £2m on the back of £81,850 profit in the year to July 1997. We did not include this last year and this explains our re-rating this year.

125th=
MANZOOR CHAUDHARY, 47
Food retailing
£7m (£4m)

● A good year for Manzoor Chaudhary,

who owns 88% of the shares in the London-based Pricecheck Supermarkets chain. The business, which was incorporated in 1993, saw its turnover rise sharply in the year to the end of January 1998 from £5.3m to £7.5m. With profits of £539,156 and a strong net asset base, we value Pricecheck at about £7.5m (on par with quoted food retailers).

125th=
SHEETAL KAPOOR, 35
Computing
£7m (new entry)

● Sheetal Kapoor is a director and sole owner of a small company called Hotel and Travel Reservations, which provides reservation services. The business which was incorporated in 1990, is based in London. It made £341,000 profit on sales of £2.3m in the year to March 1997. It is easily worth £5m on these figures. Other assets including the fast growing Cordex Computing business take Kapoor to perhaps £7m.

125th= CHANDRAKANT SHAH, 50, & FAMILY
Textiles
£7m (new entry)

● Chandrakant Shah is managing director of Mister Dee International, an East End-based textile wholesaler and property developer, which was started in 1976. All the shares in the business are owned by Shah and his family. In the year to June 1997, Mister Dee made a £402,288 profit on sales of just £1.4m. It has a strong balance sheet and would easily be worth £7m on these figures we reckon.

125th=
FAROUK RANDERA, 44, & FAMILY
Textiles
£7m (new entry)

● Arriving in Britain from Bombay as an eight year old in 1963, Farouk Randera grew up in London's East End. His father had died before the move to London, leaving his mother to bring up four children. In the mid-1970s, after completing his education, Randera went into the garment industry, learning the whole production process from fabric processing to dying and printing. He built up good contacts in the business but by 1981, tired of being an employee, Randera started his own company buying and selling textiles in Britain. Progress was steady through the 1980s, and his firm, Zaftex, started importing from the Far East in 1985, initially in a small way. Randera came through the recession of 1989-92 to make Zaftex one of the largest textile suppliers to the garment industry in Britain and Europe. His wife, Shahana, is active in the business, which we reckon is worth at least £5m on the back of projected profits of £575,000 and sales of £4.9m in the year to March 1999. Other assets and property add perhaps £2m.

125th=
JAYANTI CHANDARANA, 63, & FAMILY
Industry

£7m (£3m)
● Jayanti Chandarana was the first Ugandan Asian refugee to set up his own business in Britain. He started with a small haberdashery shop in Leicester and now runs two companies. He attributes his success to a "bit of hard work, honesty and luck." His two companies, Boston Dyers and West End Fabrics, together made £290,000 profit on sales of £9.8m in their latest accounts. They are worth around £5m together and we add around £2m for other assets including commercial property.

131st
PARESH DUSARA, 39
Telecommunications
£6.5m (£7.3m)

● Paresh Dusara owns around 10.8% of Dedicated Microcomputers, a manufacturer of computer systems for the security industry based in Manchester. He is a director of the fast-growing business which was started in 1982. 3i, the venture capital company, has taken a stake in the company which we value at £60m on the back of £4.495m profit on sales of £32.1m in the year to June 1997 (profits are down £1.4m in the year). That values Dusara's stake at around £6.5m.

131st
MARKHAN JOHAL, 47, & FAMILY
Cash & carry
£6.5m (£5m)

● Markhan Johal is chairman of Hyperama, a private wholesaler of groceries, wines, spirits, tobacco and household goods based in Nottingham. Family trusts and a Guernsey trust own most of the company. We assign a third to Johal. Hyperama is worth about £20m even though profits were just £573,000 profit on sales of £55m in the year to June 1997. Adding in the bulk of the directors' £1.2m pay to the bottom line easily takes the company value to £20m.

131st
KARAMJIT KHERA, 60
Cash & carry
£6.5m (new entry)

● Karamjit Khera is a director of Hyperama, a private wholesaler of groceries, wines, spirits, tobacco and household goods based in Nottingham. Most of the shares are owned by family and Guernsey trusts. We assign around a third to Khera, whom we overlooked last year. Sorry for that. Hyperama is worth about £20m even though profits were just £573,000 profit on sales of £55m in the year to June 1997. Adding in the bulk of the directors' £1.2m pay to the bottom line easily takes the company value to £20m.

131st
SURAT SANGHA, 41
Cash & carry
£6.5m (£5m)

● Sangha is a director of Hyperama, the Nottingham cash and carry operation. Most of the shares are held in Guernsey trusts and other family trusts. We assign around a third to Sangha. Hyperama is worth about £20m even though profits were just £573,000 profit on sales of £55m in the year to June

1997.

Adding in the bulk of the directors' £1.2m pay to the bottom line easily takes the company value to £20m.

135th=
NAZIR AWAN, 46, & FAMILY
Audio and video sales, property
£6m (new entry)

● In 1961, Nazir Awan's father arrived in Birmingham from Pakistan to work in a local car components company. His family followed to Birmingham, and young Nazir trained as a mechanical engineer. He was a natural trader, and after a spell working in Northern Ireland, he bought a shop in Birmingham, later branching out into electrical wholesaling.

Awan Marketing is the UK's largest audio and video tape distributor, worth £5m on the back of £500,000 profit and £5m sales. Property assets add £1m.

135th=
BHUPATRAI MEHTA, 52, & FAMILY
Electrical distributor
£6m (£10m)

● Bhupatrai Mehta is a director of Sherwood Agencies, which imports, exports and wholesales electrical and fancy goods.

The Manchester-based firm was incorporated in 1974, and one third of the shares are held by a Jersey company.

Mehta also has a 33.3% stake. With net assets of around £5.2m and profits of £181,000 on sales of £18.8m in the year to May 1997, Sherwood is worth £6m. We assume all the shares are controlled by the Mehta family. The 1998 accounts had not been filed as we did our research but with lower company values in the sector this year, we cut the value of the business and Mehta family to £6m.

135th=
ABDUL AZIZ, 62
Textiles
£6m (£12m)

● Abdul Aziz is managing director of Aziz Textiles, a private Birmingham-based company which sells textiles and loose material. He has a 40% stake in the profitable business, which was incorporated in 1977. Profits at Aziz Textiles grew from £1.45m to £1.61m on sales up marginally at £16.8m in the year to September 1997. With much lower company values in the textiles sector, we value the business at around £15m on these figures and Aziz's stake at £6m.

135th=
ALNUR, 44, & YASMIN DHANANI, 44
Hotels
£6m (new entry)

● Alnur Dhanani is managing director of Amyn Hotels, a central London hotel group. The company was started in 1972 by Dhanani and his wife Yasmin, who is also a director. Though Amyn Hotels only made a small profit, one of its subsidiaries, Tronicgold made £617,000 profit on sales of £2.5m in 1997. With net assets of £5.4m, it is safe to value the Dhananis at around £6m.

135th=
ROEHITS & RASHMI KHAGRAM
Leisure and industry
£6m (£6m)

● Khagram and his brother Rashmi came from Uganda to live in Britain. They set up business in 1981, on the back of the oil boom, and have interests in restaurants, electrical contracting and marble. According to The Mail on Sunday (8/1/95), their various businesses made profits of £400,000 on sales of £3m in 1994, valuing them at £6m.

We stick with that figure and valuation.

135th=
MAHMOUD KHAYAMI, 69, & FAMILY
Car dealer
£6m (new entry)
● Mahmoud Kayami is a director of

Sigma Holdings, a Slough-based car dealer incorporated in 1983.

With his family and trusts, he owns all the shares in the business which we value at around £6m on the back of £584,000 profit and sales of £31m in 1997.

Sigma has net assets of £4.6m and our valuation seems fair.

135th=
NARENDRA, 48, & MINAXA SHAH, 46
Food producing
£6m (new entry)

● Narendra and Minaxi Shah own all the shares in Premier Fruit & Nut Ltd, a London-based importer of edible nuts. Narendra Shah is managing director and Minaxi Shah is company secretary of the business, which was founded in 1986.

In the year to March 1997, Premier saw its profits rise sharply from £144,000 to £424,000 on sales unchanged at £21m. We value the company at £6m.

135th=
SURINDER MEHTA, 54, & FAMILY
Industry
£6m (new entry)

● Surinder Mehta and his family own Polyclear (Southampton) a manufacturer of polythene film. Mehta chairs the profitable company, which was incorporated in 1976. In the year to June 1997, it made £442,406 profit on sales of £3.7m. With a strong balance sheet, it is easily worth £6m even in today's depressed climate.

135th=
SHEIKH ABDUL RAUF
Cash and carry
£6m (new entry)

● Rauf is a shareholder in the Bestway cash-and-carry business, which was started in 1976 by Anwar Pervez. Rauf has a 3.1% stake in the West London -based company. Bestway is worth at least £200m on the back of £24m profit and sales of £670m in the year to June 1998. That values Rauf's stake at around £6m.

135th=
RESHAM LALLY, 58, & FAMILY
Property
£6m (new entry)

● Resham Lally is managing director of Bilston Properties, a West Midlands management consultancy and property developer.

The company, which was incorporated in 1984, is wholly owned by Lally and his family. We value the company at around £6m on the back of £472,764 profit and £4.3m of net assets in the year to June 1997.

135th=
KHALID SHERIFF, 38, & FAMILY
Fashionwear
£6m (new entry)

● Khalid Sheriff is managing director of KTS Group, a ladies and children's clothes wholesaler based in London's East End.

The business, which was incorporated in 1991, made £453,000 profit on sales of £12.3m in 1996. We value it at around £6m on these figures. The Sheriff family own the business.

147th=
MANICK CHORARIA, 46, & FAMILY
Electrical distribution
£5.5m (new entry)

● Manick Choraria and his family run a number of profitable electrical distributors including Freerose Limited and Alvabond. Freerose is worth around £3.5m on the back of £171,000 profit and sales of £8.8m in the year to March 1998. Alvabond made £59,184 profit on sales of £3.6m in the year to March 1997. We value it at around £1.5m. The Choraria family also own Exectravel, a small business worth perhaps £500,000. In all we value them at £5.5m.

147th=
GURU SETH, 53
Sports goods and equipment
£5.5m (new entry)

● Guru Seth is managing director of Ascot (SF) International, a Surrey-based manufacturer and wholesaler of sports clothes and equipment. It was incorporated in 1984 and made £507,000 profit on sales of £19.1m in 1997.

It is easily worth £5m. His second company, Greenace Properties only has a small turnover and profit but has around £578,000 of net assets. In all Seth, who owns all the shares in both, is easily worth £5.5m.

149th
KIRTI PATEL
Pharmaceuticals
£5.4m (new entry)

● Kenyan-born Kirti Patel is operations director of Goldshield, a pharmaceutical and healthcare company in 1991. The Croydon-based company was floated on the stock market in June 1998 valued at £57.9m. By December 1998, at 245.5p each, Kirti Patel's 2.15m shares were worth £5.27m. Share options and other assets take him to £5.4m.

150th
MUQUIM AHMED, 44
Distribution and property
£5.2m (new entry)

● Muquim Ahmed came from Bangladesh in 1974 to study engineering at South East London College. After two years studying, he started helping his father

export goods from Britain and Holland to Bangladesh. Business was good and he diversified into property, buying the Naz cinema in London's Brick Lane. He was a millionaire at 26 and went into electrical wholesaling as well as expanding his property portfolio. He suffered setbacks arising from the BCCI collapse. But he has bounced back and his property portfolio and other assets are now worth £5.2m.

151st=
ATHAR AHMAD, 60, & FAMILY
Catering equipment
£5m (£3m)

● Athar Ahmad owns 75% of the shares in General Catering Supplies, a London-based retailer of catering equipment. He is managing director of the business and other members of his family own the rest of the equity. In the year to March 1998, General Catering made £169,394 profit on sales of £5m. We reckon it is worth around £3m on these figures. But we did not include his other business, Mayfair Housing and Commercial last year, which had £2.2m of net assets in the year to April 1998. Ahmad and his family are worth £5m.

151st=
RAJIV BATRA, 37
Fashion
£5m (new entry)

● At 19, Rajiv Batra joined his family's textile business in Bombay. In 1990, using £100,000 of savings, he launched Ink (Clothing) to design and make clothes in London with his partner, Ketan Shah. The business took off in 1994 when FHM Magazine gave Ink its Best Ad award ahead of the likes of Hugo Boss. In 1997, Ink made £91,443 profit on sales of £3.359m. We assume Batra owns the 70% of the company held in a Jersey trust. The name Ink is worth £5m, and we assume other family assets take him to £5m.

151st=
ARUN & SAROJ BHUWANIA
Industry
£5m (£7m)

● There are three Bhuwanias on the

board of Delta Trade International, a chemical wholesaler based in London. The company is actually owned by Avenue Marketing, based in Douglas, Isle of Mann.

We assume that the Bhuwania family own Avenue Marketing.

The business, founded in 1990, saw profits fall in 1997 from £293,841 to £155,000 on sales also down from £17.3m to £14.8m. Its asset base also fell by £1m to £5.7m.

We value Delta Trade and the Bhuwania family at around £5m this year

151st=
ARUNA CHOPRA, 39, & FAMILY
Fashion
£5m (£5m)

● Aruna Chopra is a director of Chopra Manufacturing, a family-owned wholesaler of fashion dresses based in London's East End. The company only filed abbreviated accounts in 1996 against full accounts in 1995. These showed a slight decline in net assets from £401,000 to £386,000. We assume profits and sales were in line with 1995's figures of £217,000 and £3.1m respectively. A £5m valuation is appropriate.

151st=
PREM ANAND, 63
Textiles
£5m (£10m)

● Prem Anand owns Marvelfairs, which sells army uniforms and badges. He came to Britain from India in the early 1960s after a spell in West Africa. This gave him excellent contacts with the local military, who are now good customers. Indeed his entry in the 1997 list prompted a Rwandan delegation to call at Eastern Eye to find out where Marvelfairs is based so they could order uniforms. With profits of £212,000 on sales of £3.2m in 1995, we value the business at £5m, reflecting lower company values this year.

151st=
ZAHOOR HYDER & FAMILY
Furniture and beds
£5m (new entry)

● Zahoor Hyder's family comes from Kashmir and settled in the UK in 1965. At the age of 17, in 1984, he joined the family bed and furniture maker, Highgate Beds. He left in 1997 to start his own furniture distributor called Hyder International, which is expanding rapidly. In 1997, it made a small £105,000 profit on sales of £700,000. Hyder forecasts it will achieve £1.5m sales in 1998. It is worth around £2m on these figures.

He owns all the company. We add £3m for Highgate Beds and other family assets.

151st=
DARSHAL DOAL, 47
Fashion
£5m (£4m)

● Darshal Doal is managing director of Doal Fashions, a West Midlands manufacturer of men's suits and coats. Established in 1989, the family-owned business turned in a profit of over £300,000 on £1.6m sales in the year to 1988. On these figures we value the business at around £3.5m and add up to £1.5m for property and other assets for the Doal family.

151st=
RAZAHUSSEIN JESSA, 54, & FAMILY
Electronics
£5m (£10m)

● Razahussein Jessa is managing director of Watford Electronics, which assembles and sells computer equipment. The business was incorporated in 1982 and is based in Luton. The Jessa family own all the shares in the company.

Jessa himself has 64% of the equity. The accounts to June 1997 show a sharp fall in profits from £550,273 to £163,000 though sales rose by over £1m to £24.5m. On that basis, we cut the value of the business to perhaps £5m.

151st=
ZAMIR HYDER, 51
Retailing
£5m (new entry)

● Zamir Hyder is managing director of Jeans West Limited, a fashion retailer based in North London. The business, which started in 1975, is totally owned by Hyder and his family. In the year to March 1997, Jeans West made £259,411 profit on sales of £9.7m. We value the company and Hyder family at £5m.

151st=
ALIA KHAN, 32
Computers
£5m (£5m)

● Alia Khan owns all the equity in Saafy Enterprises, a London computer software company. She is also a director and company secretary. In the year to November 1996, Saafy made a small loss of £13,000 on a £34.99m turnover. With healthy net assets of £3.8m, we value Saafy at £5m.

135th=
LORD ALLI, 34
Media
£6m (£6.6m)

● Waheed Alli became Britain's youngest peer last July. As Lord Alli of Norbury, the 35-year-old television magnate and Labour party advisor, has also emerged as Britain's most politically-powerful Asian.

He embodies Cool Britannia. Hardly surprising given that he was one of the New Labour thinkers behind the re-branding initiative. He is a highly-regarded New Labour insider, who unofficially advises the prime minister on the youth vote and is close to several other ministers, including Chris Smith.

Alli's position in the inner sanctum of New Labour was duly recognised in a recent poll by Channel Four and the *Observer* of the 300 most powerful people in the UK. Lord Alli came in at No 48, a couple of notches ahead of the more conventionally powerful, such as Prince Charles and Lord Irvine, the Lord Chancellor.

Planet 24, the television production company that makes the Big Breakfast, has made Alli rich. He leads a flamboyant lifestyle. He throws fabulous parties at his Kent mansion where the guest list is a political who's who of the New Labour establishment. The speed and behind-the scene manner of his rise has been astonishing. He is viewed with awe.

Profits at Planet 24 were £1m on £16.6m sales in the year to March 1998. Much of this was down to asset sales. On that basis we cut the value of the company to £15m. Alli, who earned £648,000 as a director of Planet 24 in the year to March, owns one third. Our valuation has proved to be spot on. Earlier this month, Planet 24 was taken over by Carlton in a deal worth at least £15m, valuing Alli's stake at around £5m. Other asset and dividends will take him easily to £6m.

The contrarian style of Planet 24 was illustrated in the manner in which it submitted its successful application for the Channel 4 breakfast franchise: the proposal was wrapped in a cornflake packet. With Chris Evans at the helm the show became an instant hit.

Alli is the son of first-generation immigrants. His background was typically working class though with little of the obvious interface with the Asian immigrants from India and east Africa. That persists and makes him unique. He has gained political power through the party ranks rather than through the Asian community.

He got his first job, as a researcher for a small business magazine called Planned Savings in London, through an advertisement at a local job centre.. He discovered a breathtaking aptitude for figures and became an expert at breaking down complex pages of data. He became well-known for his skills in the City and soon joined Save and Prosper as head of investment research. He shifted gear into financial publishing then financial consultancy, earning £1,000 a day. He was described by one financial chief as "extraordinary, an amazing man".

In 1992 he met Charlie Parsons, a television producer who was to prove the perfect foil for Alli, the management and numbers genius. Bob Geldof, the third member of the triumvarate at Planet 24 described Parsons as "the TV wunderkind", and Lord Alli as a "a manager to the nth degree which is why the Labour Party wanted him". Planet 24, with a structure and management sophistication devised by Alli, was a

roaring success and helped establish a remarkable professional and personal relationship between Parsons and Alli.

Politics has been an enduring passion for Lord Alli, something his Conservative critics conveniently overlooked in their attempt to demonise him: Alli is Asian, young, gay, and makes what critics describe as junk television for youths.

Alli worked for Labour during last year's election campaign, with special responsibility for wooing the youth vote, and now makes Labour party political broadcasts. He also helped organise a peace concert in Northern Ireland last year after the Good Friday accord.

In the past 18 months he has emerged as a significant behind-the-scenes political force. He is on first name terms with the prime minister and his wife, a friendship that is solid and warm. He is an advisor to Chris Smith on broadcasting and to Robin Cook on selling Britain overseas (the Foreign Office's committee for cool, 'Panel 2000').

His elevation to the Lords did not surprise those who know him, both within broadcasting or politics. He is genuinely shy, prefers to stay away from the limelight and is respected for his substantial and longstanding commitment to the party.

Last year he considered standing as an MP, possibly in Bethnal Green where ethnic in-fighting was threatening to spillover. Instead he decided to concentrate his energy at Millbank Tower, the Labour party's war room.

He has become close to the other powerhouses in the Labour party - Peter Mandelson, Chris Smith, his constituency MP in Islington, and Mo Mowlam - and is thought to be keen to settle in at the Treasury. His maiden speech was not about the gay age of consent, but on an obscure point of the Finance Bill. Having quietly received the endorsement of the highest reaches of New Labour, Lord Alli will almost certainly be a minister for the Millennium.

151st=
SAEED AWAN, 47
Computers
£5m (new entry)

● Awan is the finance director of Akhter Group, the Harlow-based computer group which he joined in 1984. With family interests, he has a 4% stake in the highly profitable business which nearly came to the stock market in 1997. Akhter is valued at well over £85m on the back of £5.9m pre-tax profits and sales of £42.2m in the year to June 1997. Awan's stake is worth around £3.5m, while his personal assets take him to £5m easily.

151st=
SHALIL BHATTESSA, 31, & FAMILY
Hotels
£5m (new entry)

● Hotelier Nalinchandra Bhattessa died in September last year, and he left £3.9m in his will published in October. He was managing director of Kensington-based Orchid Hotels, where his family owned all the shares. His will left his assets to his family, and we assume that his son, Shalil, now runs the business. Though it does not provide detailed accounts, we reckon that the will and hotel assets adds up to at least £5m of wealth for the Bhattessa family.

151st=
PRADIP, 40, & MANESH DHAMECHA, 39
Food production
£5m (new entry)

Pradip Dhamecha is finance director of Kolak Snack Foods, where Manesh Dhamecha is also a director. Between them, they have 50% of the London-based business, which was incorporated in 1984. In the year to September 1997, Kolak made profits of over £500,000 and would easily be worth about £8m. Other smaller business assets take the Dhamechas to around £5m.

151st=
SURAN GOONATILAKE, 31, & FAMILY
Computers
£5m (new entry)

● Sri Lankan-born Suran Goonatilake is business development director of Searchspace, a computer software company based in central London with an impressive blue-chip client list. He was one of four students who left University College London, in 1995 to found Searchspace with their personal savings, a company name and a laptop computer.

Searchspace is now a leader in devising software solutions. In 1997, it made £304,000 profit on £693,000 sales. In 1998, sales were forecast to reach. £1.2m. It has venture capitalists queuing to take a stake and is easily worth £20m on these figures. Goonatilake and his family have 25% of the shares.

151st
SANJAY KHAN, 39
Media
£5m (£10m)

● Sanjay Khan, who describes himself as a financial consultant, is a director of a publishing company called O.D. Nominees, The Brighton-based business made £853,606 on sales of £2.72m in the year to May 1997. On these figures, the company would be worth perhaps £15m as a media group. Khan has around 34% of the shares and we value him at around £5m.

151st=
SUKHDEV KHEBBAL, 33
Computers
£5m (new entry)

● Sukhdev Khebbal is company secretary of Searchspace, a computer software company based in central London with an impressive blue-chip client list including BT, Bass and the London Stock Exchange. Khebbal was one of four students who left University College London in 1995 to found Searchspace with their personal savings, a company name and a laptop computer. Searchspace is now a world leader in solving complex problems. In 1997, it made £304,000 profit on £693,000 sales. With sales of £1.2m in 1998 and venture capitalists keen to invest, we value Searchspace at £20m. Khebbal has a 25% stake.

151st=
SURJEET KHELA 45
Retailing
£5m (£4m)

● Surjeet Khela was a director of Bon Marche, the fast-growing Huddersfield fashion retailer. He resigned from the business in 1995, selling his shares to his cousins, the Chima brothers who had founded it with him. No price was disclosed on any share sale though he did have 39.9% of the equity. There is a note in the accounts for Bon Marche reporting the group's restructuring for a total consideration of £7.6m. This may include the purchase of Khela's shares before tax, though we are not sure. We raise him to £5m this year on the basis that any investment income will have increased his wealth.

151st=
TIRTH KHEMLANI, 70, & FAMILY
Consumer goods distributor
£5m (new entry)

● Tirth Khemlani is chairman of KB Group, a Manchester-based distributor of consumer goods. It was incorporated in 1976 and is owned by five members of the Khemlani family, who each have a 20% stake. Tirth Khemlani is one of the five and represents the family here in his role as chairman. In the year to March 1997, KB made £655,000 profit on sales of £43.8m. With lowish values among distributors this year, we value the company and family at £5m.

151st=
JAYANTILAL, 72, & PANKAJ THACKER, 38
Electronic retailing
£5m (£6m)

● The Thackers run and own Panther (UK), a Wembley-based company which sells videos, computer and other electronic equipment. We cut the value of the business to around £5m as profits and sales have fallen sharply to £107,000 and £23.3m in the year to March 1997. It was incorporated in 1983. Despite the sales, the Thackers do not lack imagination in trying to drum up business. When faced by weekend crowds trying to cram into the nearby Ikea furniture store in Brent Park, they had staff dressed as Panthers moving up and down the stationery traffic with leaflets offering the latest bargains at Panther. Your correspondent saw them in action and very fetching they looked.

151st=
SAROJ KUMAR, 46, & FAMILY
Fashion
£5m (£4m)

● Mrs Saroj Kumar owns all the shares in Goldfortune, a Manchester-based holding company which made £189,335 profit on sales of £13.488m in the year to June 1996.

With assets of £709,725, we value the business at around £3m.

Mrs Kumar was previously a director of Birmingham City Football Club. Her family used to run a large fashion empire worth around £20m which was hit by the BCCI collapse. We reckon that other assets from this period takes the family wealth to around £5m.

151st=
KRISHAN LAROIYA, 62, & FAMILY
Textiles and electrical wholesaling
£5m (new entry)

● Krishan Laroiya chairs VN & Britannic Warehouses, a Birmingham-based wholesaler of drapery, clothing and electrical goods. The business, which was incorporated in 1971, is totally owned by the Laroiya family. We value the business at around £5m on the back of £233,327 profit on sales of £4.1m in 1997.

151st=
RAMESH MELWANI, 59
Industry
£5m (£5m)

● Ramesh Melwani, a Ugandan Asian refugee, went to work in Hong Kong in the early 1970s. He started work in the docks but later moved into business on his own, and is now based in London, where he has property and agricultural chemical interests. His company, Standon Chemicals, is worth around £3m on the back of £130,567 profit and sales of £3.5m in 1997. With his other interests, we reckon he is worth at least £5m and probably more.

151st=
MOHAMMED SARWAR, 66, & FAMILY
Cash & carry
£5m (£8m)

● Mohammed Sarwar (not the Labour MP) and his family own Giro Foods, a food wholesale, merchanting and cash-and-carry business based in Birmingham. Though the family would prefer not to be included in this list, we reckon they qualify and have included them. With lower company values this year we reckon Giro Foods is worth £5m, down sharply on last year as profits

fell from £251,000 to £222,000 in the year to March 1997, even though sales rose by well over £1m to £18.9m.

151st=
RANJIT MATHRANI, 55
Food
£5m (new entry)

● Ranjit Mathrani is co-owner of the fashionable Chutney Mary restaurant group. In 1997, the group took over Veeraswamy, London's oldest curry house. Group Chutney Mary does not produce full accounts but Veeraswamy had £1m of net assets in 1996. We reckon that the combined group will be worth at least £10m. As co-owner, Mathrani will be worth perhaps £5m.

151st=
NITIN SHAH, 48, & FAMILY
Fashion
£5m (new entry)

● In 1969, Nitin Shah arrived in Britain at the age of 18 to make his fortune. After working for two leading retailers, he decided to branch out on his own and started selling jeans on commission and then on a market stall. His two brothers joined him in 1973. By 1980 they were concentrating on a wholesale business for jeans and their Pepe group was floated on the stock market in 1985. An expansion overseas in the early 1990s nearly killed Pepe. In 1992, the Shahs sold most of their stake for £7m. After-tax, we reckon they will be worth around £5m.

151st=
HARVINDER, 56, & BHUPINDER KOHLI, 49
Cash & carry
£5m (£5m)

● Harvinder and Bhupinder Kohli are directors of Clyde Importers, a cash-and-carry warehouse based in Glasgow. The Kohlis and their families own all the shares in the business.

We stick with last year's valuation of £5m for the business as profits were exactly the same at £296,989 for the 11 months to the end of 1997.

151st=
GHANSHAMDAS MULCHANDANI, 70, & FAMILY
Cash & carry
£5m (£5m)

● Ghanshamdas Mulchandani is chairman of Imperial Cash and Carry Limited, a North London-based drinks wholesaler to the off license trade. The Mulchandani family own all the shares in the business, though Ghanshamdas has 25% of the shares in his own name. We still value the business, which was incorporated in 1987, at around £5m on the back of £315,000 profit on sales up sharply at £29.77m in the year to June 1997.

151st=
BHARAT RAGHU & FAMILY
Health care
£5m (new entry)
● Bharat Raghu runs East Anglia Care Homes, a Norfolk-based company which manages nursing homes. It was incorporated in 1988 and the Raghu family owns the business via family trusts.

We value the company at around £5m on the back of £327,993 profit in the year to July 1997.

151st=
SUDHIR PATEL, 44, & FAMILY
Electronic and video retailing
£5m (new entry)

● Sudhir Patel is managing director of two separate electronic and video retailers based in London's Tottenham Court Road.

Ask Electronics, incorporated in 1983, and Harp Electronics, incorporated a year later, made £226,000 profit together on sales of over £16m in 1997. We value them at around £5m. Patel and his family own all the shares in both companies.

151st=
AHMED PATEL, 56, & FAMILY
Petrol retailing
£5m (£2m)

● Ahmed, Yakub and Yunus Patel each own a third of AY & Y Patel (Dewsbury) Ltd, a West Yorkshire-based company which owns petrol stations. All three are directors, led by Ahmed Patel as managing director.

The business was started in 1987. The business saw profits sharply increase in the year to March 1997 from £41,860 to £208,499 on sales up £2m to £7.9m. We value the business at around £5m on these figures.

151st=
CHANDRAKANT PATEL, 59
Retailing
£5m (new entry)

● Chandrakant Patel came from Fiji to Britain in 1958 and started his own retail operation in 1975. He runs the Capital newsagent chain through his Vapgate holding company. He also has Maynews, another newsagency chain and interests in America and Australia.

Maynews only made a small £45,000 profit on £10.1m sales in the year to June 1997. Vapgate made a loss on £1m sales in the same period. Together they could be worth £2m. We add £3m for his assets overseas

151st=
SALMAN RUSHDIE, 51
Author
£5m (new entry)

● Salman Rushdie's fifth book, The Satanic Verses, won the 1988 Whitbread Novel Award, but it was scant reward for the Indian-born writer, one of the finest of his generation.

The Satanic Verses provoked outrage in the Muslim world and a fatwa from Ayatollah Khomeini, which has blighted Rushdie's life for the past decade. This year the fatwa appeared to be lifted and Rushdie is resuming something resembling a normal life.

Rushdie's guarded and cloistered existence over the past 10 years has not hindered his output. He just failed to win the Booker Prize in 1995 with The Moor's Last Sigh while other works such as East, West and Imaginary Homelands were well received. In 1995 he received a reported £1m advance from Jonathan Cape.

While he has helped defray some of the cost of his police protection, his massive worldwide sales (seven novels, one travel book, one collection of essays), notably Midnight's Children, the Booker Prize-winning novel, easily give him a £5m valuation.Born into a wealthy family, Rushdie was educated at Rugby school and was an advertising copy writer before turning to books. Midnight's Children, his account of the birth of a nation, remains his best selling novel, earning him significant royalties nearly 20 years after its publication. He will be much richer if his US literary agent, Andrew Wylie, known as the "Jackal" for his ability to extract massive advances for his clients (among whom are Martin Amis), manages to sell Rushdie's diaries of his life under the fatwa for the £5m asking price. We await the outcome.

151st=
CHUNILAL NATHWANI, 63, & FAMILY
Food wholesaler
£5m (£8m)
● Chunilal Nathwani is chairman of Velji Bhovan, a family-owned general grocery wholesaler based in West London. The business was incorporated in 1976. There are five Nathwanis on the board - each with a 20% stake in the company. We value the family at around £5m this year reflecting lower company values even though profits at Velji Bhovan rose from £291,000 to £305,000 in 1997 on sales down marginally

at £13.8m.

151st=
JAY PABARI, 46
Computers
£5m (£5m)

● Jay Pabari was 20 when he left Uganda as a refugee from the Amin terror. After four years working for someone else, he started his own import and shipping company. He moved into computers in 1986. He now owns OMD Technology, and told the Mail on Sunday (19/10/97) that he was expecting a £15m turnover in 1998 after recently starting a new computer distribution company. We value the business at around £5m.

151st=
NAMITA PANJABI
Food
£5m (new entry)

● Namita Panjabi is co-owner of the fashionable Chutney Mary restaurant group. In 1997, the group took over Veeraswamy, London's oldest curry house. Group Chutney Mary does not produce full accounts but Veeraswamy had £1m of net assets in 1996. We reckon that the combined group will be worth at least £10m. As co-owner, Panjabi will be worth perhaps £5m.

151st=
ASHVIN PATEL, 51, & FAMILY
Consumer electronics
£5m (new entry)
● Ashvin Patel is managing director of Spectravideo, a consumer electronics products distributor based in Wembley, West London. The business, which was incorporated in 1977, made £202,171 profit on sales of £7.5m in the year to March 1998.

We value it at around £5m. Patel and his family own virtually all the shares.

151st=
MOOSA PATEL, 59
Property
£5m (new entry)

● Moosa Patel owns 35% of the voting shares in Contessa Property & Investment

Limited, a property developer based in London's Brick Lane. It was started in 1976 and made £475,592 profit in the year to July 1997.

With low borrowings and £4m of net assets, it is easily worth £6m. We assume that Patel family trusts owns the rest of the shares. Two young Patels are directors of the business who we assume are his sons.

151st=
RAJENDRA & TUSHAR PATEL
Industry
£5m (new entry)

● The Patel brothers own Blowplast, a Buckinghamshire plastics company which makes plastic milk bottles for the likes of Tesco. In the year to March 1997, Blowplast made £256,000 profit on sales of £3.9m. It is worth around £5m on these figures.

151st=
JATINDER SEHMI, 51, & FAMILY
Pharmaceuticals
£5m (£5m)
● Jatinder Sehmi is managing director of Rochmills, a distributor of pharmaceutical products and perfumes based in Northampton. The business, which was incorporated in 1976, saw its profits fall slightly from £376,232 to £346,467 in 1997 on sales of £5.5m. Despite the profits fall, we stick with last year's valuation as the pharmaceuticals sector is much more valuable this year. The Sehmi family own all the shares in the business.

151st=
RAJNIKANT, 50, & ANILKUMAR SHAH, 45
Fashion
£5m (£4m)
● Rajnikant Shah is managing director of Second Image, a private wholesaler of men's and boy's clothing based in West London. Anilkumar Shah is the other director. The business was incorporated in 1986. and they have 95% of the shares between them. The 1996 accounts show £52,760 profit on £4.7m of sales. It also has assets of around £4.6m. We value the Shahs at slightly above the assets figure.

151st=
HARISH, 46, & AJAY SODHA, 42
Travel agency
£5m (£5m)

● Harish Sodha is managing director of Keyfeed, a London-based travel agency which was established in 1980. Ajay Sodha is also a director. They each have a 50% stake in the company. We stick with last year's £5m valuation of the business as profits rose slightly to £214,000 on sales of £14.7m in the year to the end of September 1997.

151st=
RAJESH TAILOR, 38, & FAMILY
Computers
£5m (new entry)

● Rajesh Tailor is managing director of Tai Computer Systems, a fast-growing computer component company based in North London.

He founded the business with his two cousins, Steve and Rajnikant, in 1991, and sales have soared from £1.6m in 1994 to £9.3m in 1997. Profits in the year to September 1997 were £202,000 and on this basis, we value the fast-growing business at perhaps £5m. The Tailor cousins own it all. The strong growth results from Tai's flexibility and a tight rein on costs.

151st=
KAMAL SHARMA, 30
Computers
£5m (new entry)

● Tiring of working for a large company, Sharma (pictured above) branched out on his own, setting up Nugen Media Distribution, a Maidenhead-based computer distributor in 1997 with three colleagues, Simon Young, Andy Downs and Steven O'Neill.

The business is one of the fastest growing UK companies, and achieved profits of around £500,000 on sales of £2.8m in its first year.

In the year to May 1999, Nugen will have notched up £9m of sales. Sharma, as group managing director, owns all the shares, and we value his stake at perhaps £5m. He will go a lot higher ...

151st=
MUKESH & NARESH THAKKAR
Fashion
£5m (new entry)

● Mukesh and Naresh Thakkar are the directors and owners of Mauritz (London) Ltd, a private company based in North London, which wholesales ladies' fashion-wear. It was incorporated in 1993 and made £374,227 profit on sales of £5.6m in the year to May 1997. With low borrowings, we reckon the business is worth £5m. We value the Thakkars at this figure.

151st=
NARESH SHAH, 44, & FAMILY
Pharmaceuticals
£5m (£4m)

● Naresh Shah is managing director of Jumbogate, a wholesale chemist based in Harrow, West London. We value the business - started in 1982 - at around £5m on the back of profits of £329,000 and sales of £14.3m in the year to March 1997. His wife Shweta Shah is company secretary. They own all the shares

151st=
AHMED ZAHEDIEH, 48
Media
£5m (£3m)

●Ahmed Zahedieh is company secretary of Wilmington, a London-based publisher of specialist magazines which came to the stock market in December 1995. His 2.763m shares at 186p each (December 1998) are worth £5.13m.

151st=
RAJU & SUNNY TULI
Retailing
£5m (new entry)

● In 1983, Raju Tuli borrowed £3,000 from his mother to buy some branded jeans, which he sold in markets around his Scottish home. From these beginnings, he has created The Jean Scene, one of Scotland's fastest-growing retailers, which is expanding into England and Ireland. With his brother, Sunny, he owns all the shares in The Jean Scene, which we value at around £5m on the back of its fast growth. From £1m, sales in 1994, it achieved £5.4m sales in 1998 and profits of £204,611.

151st=
RANA TALWAR, 51
Banking
£5m (new entry)
● Rana Talwar, who hails from India, was appointed group chief executive at Standard Chartered Bank in 1997, the first Indian head of a FTSE 100 company. Educated in India at St Stephens College and Delhi University, he started work as a Citicorp executive trainee in 1969 and worked his way up the company before moving to Standard Chartered. He has nearly £500,000 worth of Standard Chartered shares, around £2m in options, and with a £1m salary, and other assets will be worth around £5m.

151st=
WASIM AKHTER, 27
Retailing
£5m (new entry)

● Wasim Akhter was head boy at his grammar school, but his teachers were disappointed with his 2 O-Levels. Ten years later, they need not worry. Akhter is the latest manifestation of the Asian youth fashion culture that has spawned Shami Ahmed.

Born in Rochdale, Akhter is the eldest son of a hairdresser from Karachi who came to Britain in the 1960s. His father ran an import business but Akhter decided to branch out on his own. He established his own import business in Florence distributing Italian fashions to UK supermarkets. Last year, he invested £5m in

Barneys Department Store in Manchester, which will sell designer labels at cut prices in a stylish setting. A similar £5m venture is planned in Leeds.

No figures are available yet on Barneys' success, but as a sighting shot, we reckon Akhter makes it into this list already at £5m and will go a lot higher in future.

151st=
NAZMU VIRANI, 51, & FAMILY
Property
£5m (new entry)

● Two years ago Nazmu Virani was said to covet a slot in any list of Asian worthies, such was his desire for rehabilitation following his conviction on charges arising from the collapse of the Bank of Credit and Commerce.

This year the consummate deal-maker is back. Virani, who as chief executive of Control Securities could do no wrong during the heady 1980s, is in at No 151 with a valuation of £5m.

This time his vehicle is Cygnet Properties and Leisure, a property company which over the past 18 months has quietly built up a portfolio with a valuation nudging £20m. Barclays, which backed him more than two decades ago when he bought his first shop, is backing him this time round, too, evidence of Virani's enduring standing as an exceptional entrepreneur.

Cygnet is Ofex-quoted and capitalised at £5.3m (at December 1998). His family has a large stake and they are easily worth £5m.

Significantly, Cygnet's first major acquisition was in Leicester, a Gujarati strong-hold where Virani is revered among the commercial classes. At his heyday with Control Securities, Gujarati shareholders famously filled 17 pages of Control's share register.

The debut acquisition was made last year, when Virani, now aged 51 and rounder but still energetic, paid £1.6m for the Leicester International Hotel complex. It was the company's first acquisition since it was listed on the Ofex share market in 1997.

Virani plans to convert the hotel into a swish 220-bedroom complex complete with serviced offices and exhibition space. Since then Virani has tied up further deals totalling £5.5m.

BCCI is in the past, he says. "I was a scapegoat. I was caught between two elephants," he says: Idi Amin, who, in 1972, expelled Virani and 30,000 other Asians; and the Serious Fraud Squad, which in the early 1990s, came under intense pressure to produce convictions in the largest bank fraud in British banking history. It caught only small fry such as Virani.

His claims of being duped in the BCCI affair cut little water during the criminal hearing. He may have emerged as a scapegoat but one who knew exactly what he was doing in his dealings with his BCCI backers.

Virani was a larger than life character. He is a former Asian Businessman of the Year who in five years of deal-making converted Control Securities from a hollow shell to the country's 13th biggest property group, which at its peak was capitalised at £600m. It was an empire comprising 800 pubs, 23 hotels, a brewery and property in the UK and continental Europe.

He was an icon in the British-Gujarati community, often caricatured as "England's greatest living Gujarati". His downfall was all the more devastating for

a community with precious few leaders either in commerce or politics. He mixed easily in parliament as well as the City, two no-go areas for most Asians. He was on first name terms with political leaders.

He remains unassuming, with no obvious sign of bitterness or enmity towards the SFO or the country where he made his second fortune (the first, more vast than anything subsequent, was in east Africa) and where he is now on the way to making a third.

He talks without rancour of the indignity of prison or the injustice of a system which dealt out punishment in a seemingly selective way. His gentle outward piety disguises a sharp business mind that is thinking several steps ahead. He learned to think on his feet, first in east Africa, where his family ran a long-established trading empire. It was an empire that taught its pupils well; and taught them, too, that cutting-edge business can lead to bloody blows.

He has suffered at the hands of despots before. Perhaps that is one reason why Virani speaks with extraordinary equanimity when recalling BCCI and how so many others escaped scott-free. He says he simply wants to get on with the next deal.

Wealth index

POS	WEALTH (£m)	
1	1300	Hinduja, Sri & Gopi
2	1200	Mittal, Lakshmi
3	450	Chandra, Subhash
4	325	Paul, Lord
5	300	Grovit, Felix
6=	200	Singh, Jasminder
6=	200	Singh, Tom
8	150	Madhvani, Manubhai
9=	120	Lalvani, Gulu
9=	120	Pervez, Sir Anwar
11	113	Patel, Bhikhu & Vijay
12=	100	Chandaria, Ratilal
12=	100	Mohsan, Tahir
12=	100	Shivdasani, Sonu
12=	100	Thakrar, Rasiklal
16	90	Jatania, Mike
17	85	Puri, Nat
18	72	Mughal, Humayan
19	70	Thakrar, Rashmi
20	61	Caan, James
21=	60	Ahmed, Iqbal
21=	60	Ahmed, Shami
21=	60	Bagri, Lord & Apurv
21=	60	Chima, Gurchait
25	50	Kumar, Rajan
26=	40	Noon, Gulam
26=	40	Patel, Naresh & Mahesh
28	36	Matto, John
29=	35	Dharamshi, Shirazali
29=	35	Musry, Nissim
29=	35	Ruia, Anil
29=	35	Sandhu, Amarjit
29=	35	Suterwalla, Fakhruddin
29=	35	Warsi, Perween
35=	30	Bhatia, Gulshen
35=	30	Dhillon, Tej & Bobby
35=	30	Pathak, Kirit & Meena
35=	30	Rasul, Maq
35=	30	Sachdev, Ramesh
35=	30	Sahni, Jatti & Avneet
35=	30	Sethia, Nirmal
35=	30	Varma, Moni
43=	28	Alimahomed, Abdul
43=	28	Rana, Diljit
45=	26	Bhatti, Abdul
45=	26	Chaudhary, Adalat
45=	26	Sheikh, Mohammed
48=	25	Chandaria, Dinesh
48=	25	Shah, Anant & Vipin
50=	24	Correia, Tom & Melba
50=	24	Gulhati, Satinder
50=	24	Sehgal, Mukesh
53	23	Choudrey, Zameer
54=	22	Chadha, Gurbachan
54=	22	Mehta, Bharat
56	21	Wickremeratne, Sunil
57=	20	Matharu, Harpal
57=	20	Mittal, Pramod
57=	20	Mohidin, Mukhtar
57=	20	Passi, Rajesh
57=	20	Prabhu, Sudhakar
57=	20	Reddy, Girish
57=	20	Sarwar, Mohamed
57=	20	Sidhu, Kanwaljit
57=	20	Tayub, Rashid
57=	20	Vohra, Anoop
67=	15	Ahmad, Munir
67=	15	Binani, Gokul
67=	15	Daya, Moez
67=	15	Dewan, Ramesh
67=	15	Dhamija, Dinesh & Tani
67=	15	Gandhi, Jayantilal
67=	15	Kotecha, Madhusudan
67=	15	Lit, Avtar
67=	15	Patel, Ajit
67=	15	Patel, Anwar
67=	15	Patel, Harshadrai
67=	15	Ruia, Jitendra
67=	15	Shah, Bharat
67=	15	Shah, Mahendra
67=	15	Zafar, Mohammed
82	14	Ahmed, Ajaz
83=	13	Asaria, Liyakat & Sultan
83=	13	Wouhra, Trilok
85=	12	Bhullar, Ajmair
85=	12	Damji, Zahir & Shafin
85=	12	Kallumpram, Ashok
85=	12	Khan, Rabnawaz
85=	12	Pagarani, Kishore
90=	10	Ahluwalia, Inderjit
90=	10	Ahluwalia, Sukhpal
90=	10	Ahmed, Bashir
90=	10	Ali Khan, Mirza
90=	10	Basran, Lak & Kamal
90=	10	Bhalla, Gurbaksh
90=	10	Chanrai, Damodar
90=	10	Chatwani, Satish
90=	10	Dhamecha, Shantilal
90=	10	Dhanani, Ratilal
90=	10	Khanna, Vipen
90=	10	Khera, Jindy
90=	10	Kotecha, Sunil & Sanjiv
90=	10	Loomba, Rajinder
90=	10	Mehta, Swarn
90=	10	Omar, Abdul
90=	10	Passi, Pardeep & Artee
90=	10	Sarwar, Mohammed
90=	10	Shah, Kiran
90=	10	Sher, Imtiaz
90=	10	Singh, Dilbag
90=	10	Sohal, Charan
90=	10	Verjee, Rumi
90=	10	Radia, Kusum
114=	9	Ahmed, Arshad
114=	9	Patel, Swati
114=	9	Ramzan, Mohammed
117=	8	Amlani, Manhar
117=	8	Esmail, Mohamed
117=	8	Kejriwal, Mukesh
117=	8	Khalid, Fukhera
117=	8	Khushi, Afzal
117=	8	Mulchand, Rajan
123	7.5	Majithia, Shantilal
124	7.2	Singh, Gurpal
125=	7	Chadha, Manmohan
125=	7	Chandarana, Jayanti
125=	7	Chaudhary, Manzoor
125=	7	Randera, Farouk
125=	7	Kapoor, Sheetal
125=	7	Shah, Chandrakant
131=	6.5	Dusara, Paresh
131=	6.5	Johal, Markhan
131=	6.5	Khera, Karamjit
131=	6.5	Sangha, Surat
135=	6	Alli, Lord
135=	6	Awan, Nazir
135=	6	Aziz, Abdul
135=	6	Dhanani, Alnur
135=	6	Khagram, Roehits
135=	6	Khayami, Mahmoud
135=	6	Lally, Resham
135=	6	Mehta, Bhupatrai
135=	6	Mehta, Surinder
135=	6	Rauf, Sheikh Abdul
135=	6	Shah, Narendra
135=	6	Sharif, Khalid
147=	5.5	Choraria, Manick
147=	5.5	Seth, Guru
149	5.4	Patel, Kirti
150	5.2	Ahmed, Muquim
151=	5	Ahmad, Athar
151=	5	Akhter, Wasim
151=	5	Anand, Prem
151=	5	Awan, Saeed
151=	5	Batra, Rajiv
151=	5	Bhattessa, Shalil
151=	5	Bhuwania, Arun
151=	5	Chopra, Aruna
151=	5	Dhamecha, Pradip
151=	5	Doal, Darshan
151=	5	Goonatilake, Suran
151=	5	Hyder, Zahoor
151=	5	Hyder, Zamir
151=	5	Jessa, Razahussein
151=	5	Khan, Alia
151=	5	Khan, Sanjay
151=	5	Khebbal, Sukhdev
151=	5	Khela, Surjeet
151=	5	Khemlani, Tirth
151=	5	Kohli, Bhupinder
151=	5	Kumar, Saroj
151=	5	Laroiya, Krishan
151=	5	Mathrani, Ranjit
151=	5	Melwani, Ramesh
151=	5	Mulchandani, G.
151=	5	Nathwani, Chunilal
151=	5	Pabari, Jay
151=	5	Panjabi, Namita
151=	5	Patel, Ahmed
151=	5	Patel, Ashvin & Shila
151=	5	Patel, Chandrakant
151=	5	Patel, Moosa
151=	5	Patel, Rajendra & Tushar
151=	5	Patel, Sudhir
151=	5	Raghu, Bharat
151=	5	Rushdie, Salman
151=	5	Sarwar, M.
151=	5	Sehmi, Jatinder
151=	5	Shah, Naresh & Shweta
151=	5	Shah, Nitin
151=	5	Shah, Rajnikant
151=	5	Sharma Kamal
151=	5	Sodha, Harish
151=	5	Tailor, Rajesh
151=	5	Talwar, Rana
151=	5	Thacker, Jayantilal
151=	5	Thakkar, Mukesh
151=	5	Tuli, Raju & Sunny
151=	5	Virani, Nazmu
151=	5	Zahedieh, Ahmed

BRITAIN'S RICHEST ASIAN 200

Researched, written and compiled by
PHILIP BERESFORD, The Sunday Times Richest 1000 & KHOZEM MERCHANT, Financial Times

• Publisher *Sarwar Ahmed* • Project Manager *Nadeem Khan* • Picture Editor *Sohail Anjum* •

BLACK WHO'S WHO
A Who's Who of Black Achievers in Britain

The Black community in Britain is contributing to the wealth and development of the nation, achieving notable and exceptional success in the arts, in business and in the professions - at just about every level. The first BLACK WHO'S WHO profiles over 500 Black achievers and is essential reading for those wishing to research, study or access the Black experience in British society.

Black Who's Who entries range from the rich and famous to lesser known achievers and the community's unsung heroes. It is an informative resource that illustrates the determination and efforts required to become a Black achiever in Britain. Five hundred stories have emerged...

Entries in the Who's Who were nominated by **New Nation** and **Caribbean Times** readers. Listings include achievers in various fields and professions, those who received awards and those who have worked on behalf of the community. Nominees submitted background details and personal profiles, the result provides a rare insight into the struggles and achievements experienced in Britain's Black community.

There has been a Black presence in Britain for almost 500 years, yet no comprehensive record of their achievements exists outside the worlds of sport and music. The Black Who's Who will prove invaluable to those in the media, marketing and PR, as well as organisations seeking members, specialists, mentors, patrons and business connections. Students will find the Black Who's Who a useful reference directory, while the general reader will discover a new dimension to the Black community in Britain.

Available from Ethnic Media Group •
148 Cambridge Heath Road, London E1 5QJ •
Tel: 0171 702 8012 • Fax: 0171 702 7937   Price (UK) £30.00

WHO'S WHO OF BLACK ACHIEVERS

First Edition

BLACK WHO'S WHO

Published by

New Nation

&

Caribbean Times

Introducing ArRum

The UK's first Private Members Club for Muslims

ArRum is a unique and new Private Members Club
for Muslim professionals and entrepreneurs.

ArRum has the very best and most innovative
features that any Private Members Club can offer:

● **ArRum Social Club,** with fine dining, relaxing lounge, private function room,
internet bay and the opportunity to meet like minded people;

● **ArRum Social Events,** offering an exciting and fun filled calender of events and activities to cater for
all tastes:

● **ArRum Business Focus,** introducing entrepreneural ventures to financiers, private investors and
venture capitalists and facilitating business networking;

● **ArRum Career Compass,** a non profit making service providing advice on CV's, job applications and
offering work placements and mentorship;

Such is the popularity and demand for this concept that **ArRum** has already attracted in excess of 800
members who are typically drawn from the global corporate communities of Goldman Sachs, Morgan
Stanley, Credit Lyonnais, Linklaters and Paine, Anderson Consulting, Guy's Hospital, DJ Freeman, Oxbridge,
London School Of Economics, Harvard and Stanford Universities to name but a few.

The club, situated in fashionable Clerkenwell, was purpose built by renowned architects/interior
designers Litman Goddard Hogarth, to ensure it met the precise expectations and tastes of its members.
As members enter into the world of **ArRum**, crossing over a specially commissioned glass bridge, over-
looking an elegant water fountain, they will experience an atmosphere of tradition, fused with the contemporary.

The private dining area, with its glass roof, benefits from the expertise and culinary genius of
BEST INDIAN CHEF OF THE YEAR 1997, Henry Lobo, ex head-chef of the much revered Veeraswammy
restaurant. After you have satisfied your appetite, you can relax and sip tea or coffee in the reading
lounge with a roaring fireplace, or quench your thirst at the bar serving a colourful array of non-alcoholic
drinks. For those of you at the cutting edge of technology, you can surf the waves at the dynamic and
buzzing Internet bay. With artists exhibiting and performers showcasing their talents at **ArRum**, the club
is sure to be a hub of activity throughout the week.

For further information on ArRum,
call Reedah Nijabat on 0181 924 4417
or info@ArRum.co.uk

ArRum, 4 Addison Road, London E17 9LT

digiscan

HIGH END REPRO FACILITY

Unit 2, Bayford Industrial Centre, Bayford Street, London E8 3SE

Dainippon Screen imagesetter
Hercules imagesetter
Hewlett Packard designjet
Dainippon Screen drum scanner

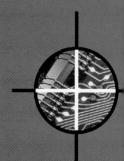

B1 film output

posters

magazines

banner advertising

point of sale

worldwide campaigns

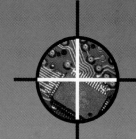

A0 posters

tel 0181 985 9988
tel 0181 986 6072
fax 0181 986 3167
isdn0181 985 7045

email: graphic@digiscan.demon.co.uk

Graphic
Digiscan
Limited

LIEUTENANT
CAPTAIN
MAJOR
COLONEL

We now have more ethnic minorities in positions of real power than ever before.
So nowadays, there's only one group of people being held back. Racists.
If you think you could be an Officer in today's Army call 0345 3000 111
quoting ref WW002 or write to the Army, Freepost, CV37 9BR.

ARMY
BE THE BEST

http://www.army.mod.uk The Army is committed to Equal Opportunities.

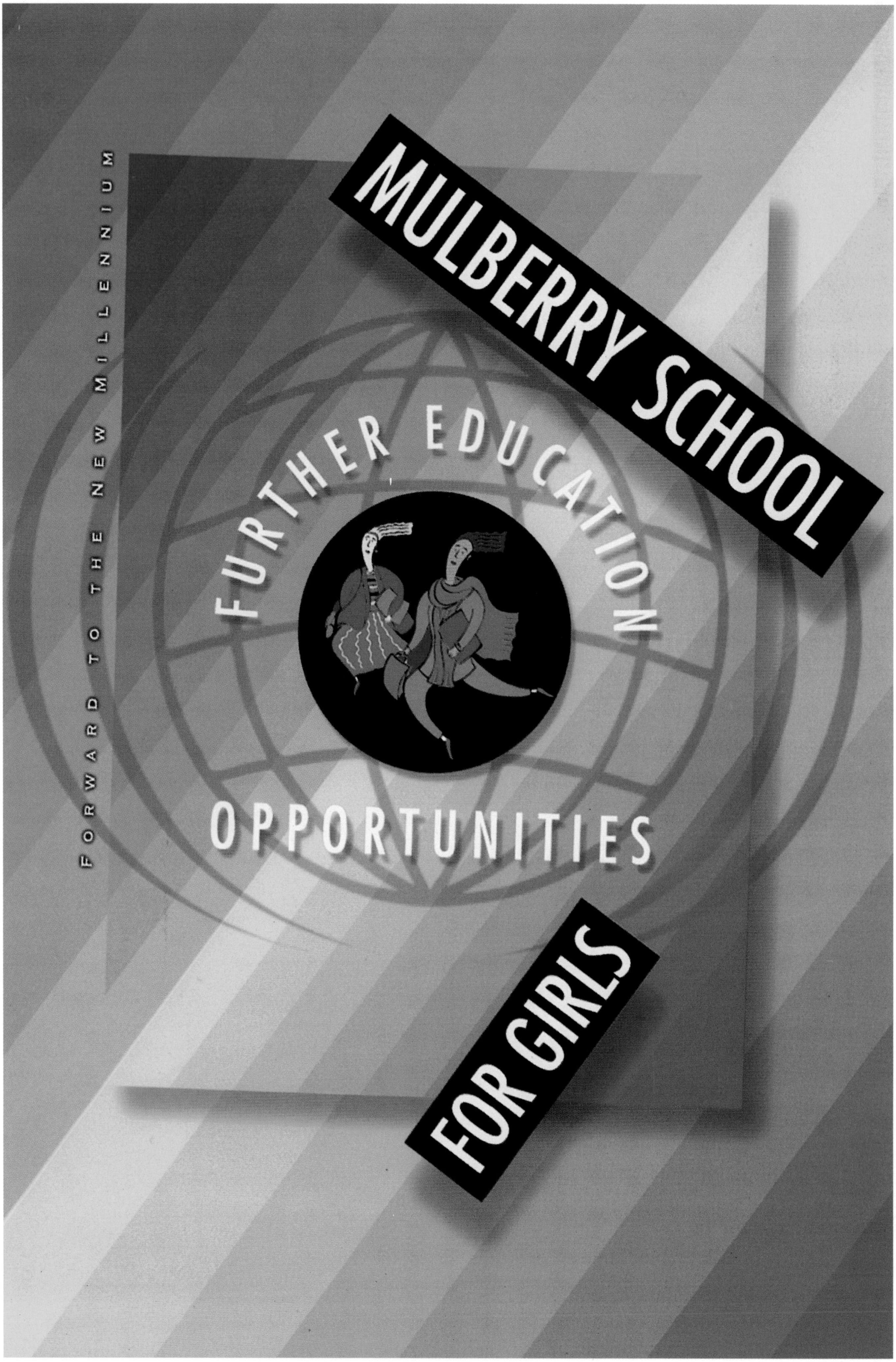

MULBERRY SCHOOL

FORWARD TO THE NEW MILLENNIUM

FURTHER EDUCATION

OPPORTUNITIES

FOR GIRLS

MULBERRY SCHOOL FOR GIRLS is a popular school and has extended its range of courses in further education.

Mulberry School is situated in its own pleasant extensive grounds close to the City and Docklands, and easily accessible by public transport. It also has an independent Further Education Building on a seperate site with excellent facilities.

MATURE STUDENTS

The school welcomes mature women from the community who may wish to return to education on either a part-time or full-time basis.

EQUAL OPPORTUNITIES

Mulberry School aims to promote equality of opportunity for all students.

ADMISSION PROCEDURE

All students wishing to further their education will be expected to complete an application form and attend a personal interview to discuss their choice of courses. Advice sessions will take place regularly on Wednesdays between 4pm-6pm.
There will be an opportunity to combine some courses with other schools in the Borough and Tower Hamlets College.

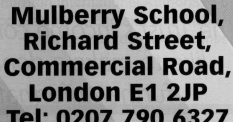

**Mulberry School,
Richard Street,
Commercial Road,
London E1 2JP
Tel: 0207 790 6327
Fax: 0207 265 9882**

NatWest

has the experience and

understands

how to help Asians make their

businesses

a success.

Talk to one of our small business advisers about how we can help.

 **NatWest**

National Westminster Bank Plc. Registered Office: 41 Lothbury, London EC2P 2BP. Registered Number: 929027 England.

MORLEY & SCOTT
Chartered Accountants

Advisers to the Asian business community

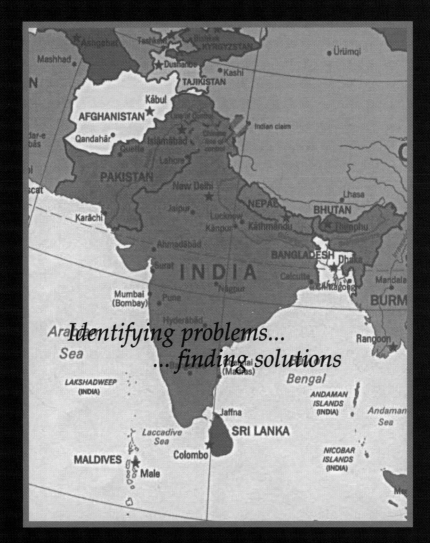

Identifying problems...
...finding solutions

Tony Sarin - Partner
London Office
Lynton House, 7-12 Tavistock Square, London WC1H 9LT
Tel: 0171 387 5868 Fax: 0171 388 3978 e-mail ms@morley-scott.co.uk

INVESTOR IN PEOPLE

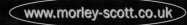

www.morley-scott.co.uk

Morley & Scott is a member firm of
GMN International, a network of
independent accountancy firms

Other offices in Slough, Winchester, Hove and Marlow. Associated Offices throughout the world

bringing you more choice
sharing our success

24 hours a day
365 days a year

digital quality sound & vision from
ZEE Digital Network includes

regional language channels,
and much, much, more to come...

0870 600 28 88

Reach out to over 1 million potential customers in the UK
& Europe, to advertise ring +44 (0) 208 839 4060

Keeping you in touch

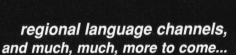

Calls may be monitored and recorded to check the quality of service being provided.

We are pleased to be associated with 'Asians in the Millennium.'

South Asian Banking, 27 Poultry, London EC2P 2BX or call 0171 260 3920.

YOUR WORLD OF FINANCIAL SERVICES

Issued by HSBC Bank plc

NOTES

NOTES

NOTES